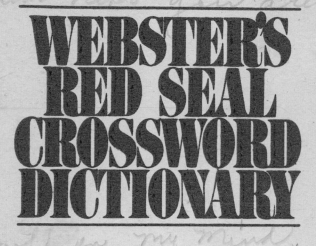

WEBSTER'S RED SEAL CROSSWORD DICTIONARY

Compiled and Edited by Norman Hill

WARNER BOOKS

A Warner Communications Company

sentimental but it is
the way I picture
each one of you as I
think of you individually

FOREWORD

During the past decade the editors of this publication have done extensive research in lexicography, have edited tens of thousands of crossword puzzles, checked and evaluated hundreds of thousands of definitions and words. Now it is with great pride and pleasure that we present this new and unique reference book—a crossword puzzle dictionary conceived, designed and painstakingly compiled to best accomplish the single purpose for which a crossword puzzle dictionary is intended: to provide efficient, simplified help for the puzzle solver.

Webster's Red Seal Crossword Dictionary contains thousands of entries which are used by leading professional crossword constructors, and which appear most frequently in crossword puzzles published in magazines, books and newspapers. The definitions have been carefully edited by a staff of some of America's most experienced, most expert editors.

We have included those definitions which will be of maximum usefulness to the puzzle solver. As a result we believe you will find *Webster's Red Seal Crossword Dictionary* to be a complete, handy, reliable guide and solving aid.

Definitions are listed alphabetically, and worded just as they appear in puzzles. Where more than one answer word might fit the definition, additional possibilities are offered.

There is no confusing clutter of so-called "special categories" —no detours and confusing road signs; no meandering listings of Indian tribes, mythological beings or foreign weights and measures. What you hold in your hand is the easiest-to-use, most efficient alphabetical dictionary of crossword puzzle definitions available anywhere. We commend it to you with our best wishes for many hours of pleasurable puzzle solving.

Norman Hill
Editor

A

aardvark **ANTEATER**
aardvark's diet **ANTS**
aardwolf **HYENA**
Aare **SWISS RIVER**
Aaron **BIBLICAL PRIEST**
Ab **HEBREW MONTH**
abaca **MANILA HEMP**
abalone **MOLLUSK, ORMER**
abandon **DESERT, STRAND,**
MAROON
abandoned (law) **DERELICT**
abase **DEGRADE, DEMEAN,**
LOWER. HUMBLE
abasement **SHAME, DISHONOR**
abash **DISCONCERT**
abate **DIMINISH, EBB,**
SLACKEN, LET UP,
DEDUCT, SUBSIDE
abatement **REDUCTION,**
DECREASE
abbey head **ABBOT, ABBESS**
abbreviate **SHORTEN,**
ABRIDGE, REDUCE
abdicate **RESIGN, RENOUNCE**
abdomen **BELLY, STOMACH**
PAUNCH
Abe Lincoln symbol
(2 wds.) **STOVEPIPE HAT**
Abel's brother **CAIN, SETH**
abet **ENCOURAGE, HELP,**
INCITE, SANCTION
abhor **HATE, LOATHE,**
DETEST, DESPISE
abject **BASE, WRETCHED**
able **CAPABLE, COMPETENT,**
QUALIFIED, SKILLED
able to be examined **TESTABLE**
able to fly **VOLANT**
abluent **CLEANER, CLEANSER**
ablution **BATH, WASHING,**
CLEANSING
ably **EFFICIENTLY, CAPABLY**
COMPETENTLY
Abner's friend **LUM**
abode **DWELLING, RESIDENCE,**
HOME, HEARTH
abolish **ANNUL**
abomasum **RUMINANT**
abominable **ODIOUS,**
HORRIBLE

abominable snowman **YETI**
abomination **DETESTATION,**
ABHORRENCE
aborigine **PRIMITIVE, NATIVE**
about **ANENT**
above **ATOP, ON, UPON,**
OVER, OVERHEAD,
SUPERIOR
aboveboard **OPEN, FRANK,**
CANDID
abrade **SAND, SCRAPE,**
RUB OFF
Abraham's father **TERAH**
abrasion **EROSION**
abroad **OVERSEAS**
abrogate **ANNUL, CANCEL**
abrupt **SUDDEN, BRUSQUE**
abscond **RUN OFF, DECAMP**
absconding soldier **DESERTER**
absence **LACK**
absence of sound **SILENCE**
absent **AWAY, LACKING**
absolute **ENTIRE, COMPLETE**
absolutely **PURELY,**
WHOLLY, REALLY
absolute ruler **DESPOT,**
DICTATOR, TYRANT
absolve **PARDON, FORGIVE**
absorb **CONSUME, SWALLOW**
absorb information **DIGEST,**
LEARN
absorb moisture **IMBIBE**
abstain from **ESCHEW**
abstain from food **FAST**
abstain from meat
(those who) **VEGETARIAN**
abstract **STEAL, DIVERT**
abstract being **ESSE**
abstruse **PROFOUND,**
SUBTLE, RECONDITE
abundantly supplied **REPLETE**
abuse **DAMAGE, INJURE**
abusive speech **TIRADE**
abyss **CHASM, PIT, GULF**
Abyssinian ruler **AMEER,**
AMIR, EMIR
accelerate **SPEED**
accelerate a motor **REV**
accent **STRESS**
accented part of a verse **ARSIS**
accept as true **BELIEVE**
accepted rule **CANON**
access **DOOR**
access to a mine **ADIT**
acclaim **ECLAT, APPLAUD,**
HAIL, WELCOME

accredited	**APPROVED**
accrue	**INCREASE**
accumulate	**AMASS, STORE**
accumulated matter	**HEAP**
	ACCRETION
accurate	**EXACT**
accuse	**BLAME**
accustom	**INURE, ENURE**
accustomed	**WONT**
ace	**CARD**
acerbity	**RANCOR**
ache	**PAIN, HURT,**
	YEARN, LONGING
accommodate	**SERVE, OBLIGE**
accompany	**ESCORT, ATTEND**
accomplice	**ALLY**
accomplish	**DO, COMPLETE,**
	PERFECT
accomplishment	**DEED, FEAT**
accord	**UNISON, HARMONIZE,**
	AGREE, GRANT, BESTOW
according to fact	**TRUE**
according to law	**LEGAL**
accost	**GREET**
account	**TAB**
accountable	**LIABLE**
account book	**LEDGER**
accounting	**BILL**
accounting term	**DEBIT, CREDIT,**
	NET, PROFIT,
	LOSS, ASSET
account juggler	**EMBEZZLER**
achieve	**DO, PERFORM**
achievement	**DEED, FEAT**
achromatic	**COLORLESS**
acid	**SOUR, TART**
aciform	**SHARP**
acknowledge	**AVOW, OWN**
acknowledge a greeting	**NOD**
acorn	**NUT**
acorn tree	**OAK**
acquaint	**INFORM, TELL**
acquiesce	**COMPLY, AGREE,**
	GAIN, GET
acquire by labor	**EARN**
acquired skill	**ART**
acquire knowledge	**LEARN**
acquisitive	**GREEDY**
acquit	**PARDON, ABSOLVE**
acrid	**BITTER, TART**
acrimony	**BITTERNESS**
acrobatic performer	**TUMBLER**
	ROPEDANCER
acrobat's bar	**TRAPEZE**
acrobat's feat	**STUNT, SPLIT**
acrobat's garment	**LEOTARD**
acrogen	**FERN, MOSS, PLANT**
acrolith	**STATUE**
acromion	**SHOULDER, SCAPULA**

across (prefix)	**TRANS**
acrostic	**PUZZLE**
act	**FEAT, DEED,**
	PERFORMANCE, BEHAVIOR,
	DO, PERFORM, BEHAVE,
	EMOTE, PRETEND, PRETENSE
Actaeon	**HUNTER, STAG**
act against	**OPPOSE**
act as a bearer	**CARRY**
act as a butler	**BUTTLE**
act as a model	**POSE**
act as chairman	**PRESIDE**
act as mediator	**INTERCEDE**
actin	**PROTEIN**
acting a role (2 wds.)	**ON STAGE**
actinia	**RAY, SEA ANEMONE**
actinolite	**ASBESTOS,**
	AMPHIBOLE
action	**DEED**
active	**VIGOROUS, AGILE,**
	LIVELY, BUSY, SPRY
active person	**DOER**
activity	**MOTION**
act of daring	**FEAT**
act of learning	**LOAN**
act of stealing	**THEFT**
act of taking for	
one's own	**ADOPTION**
actor	**THESPIAN**
actor Ameche	**DON**
actor Andrews	**DANA**
actor Arness	**JAMES**
actor Astaire	**FRED**
actor Autry	**GENE**
actor Backus	**JIM**
actor Barry	**GENE**
actor Blore	**ERIC**
actor Brand	**NEVIL**
actor Brynner	**YUL**
actor Burr	**RAYMOND**
actor Cameron	**ROD**
actor Carney	**ART**
actor Crabbe	**BUSTER**
actor Dailey	**DAN**
actor Drury	**JAMES**
actor Duryea	**DAN**
actor Ferrer	**JOSE, MEL**
actor Flynn	**ERROLL**
actor Fonda	**HENRY, PETER**
actor Ford	**GLENN**
actor Grant	**CARY**
actor Graves	**PETER**
actor Guinness	**ALEC**
actor Heflin	**VAN**
actor Holbrook	**HAL**
actor Hudson	**ROCK**
actor Hunter	**TAB**
actor Jannings	**EMIL**
actor Janssen	**DAVID**

actor Jourdan	**LOUIS**	actress Chase	**ILKA**
actor Keith	**BRIAN**	actress Christian	**LINDA**
actor Karloff	**BORIS**	actress Claire	**INA**
actor Knotts	**DON**	actress Collins	**JOAN**
actor Kruger	**OTTO, HARDY**	actress Dahl	**ARLENE**
actor Ladd	**ALAN**	actress Davis	**BETTE**
actor Lancaster	**BURT**	actress Day	**DORIS**
actor Lugosi	**BELA**	actress Dee	**SANDRA**
actor MacAuthur	**JAMES**	actress Dennis	**SANDY**
actor MacDowell	**RODDY**	actress Dickinson	**ANGIE**
actor MacMurray	**FRED**	actress Drew	**ELLEN**
actor March	**HAL, FREDRIC**	actress Duke	**PATTY**
actor Massey	**RAYMOND**	actress Dunne	**IRENE**
actor McQueen	**STEVE**	actress Farrow	**MIA**
actor Milland	**RAY**	actress Feldon	**BARBARA**
actor Mineo	**SAL**	actress Fisher	**GAIL**
actor Mitchum	**ROBERT**	actress Fleming	**RHONDA**
actor Montand	**YVES**	actress Foch	**NINA**
actor Murray	**DON, JAN, KEN**	actress Fontaine	**JOAN**
actor Newman	**PAUL**	actress Gabor	**EVA, ZSA ZSA**
actor Nielsen	**LESLIE**	actress Gam	**RITA**
actor Nimoy	**LEONARD**	actress Gardner	**AVA**
actor O'Brien	**PAT**	actress Hagen	**UTA**
actor O'Toole	**PETER**	actress Harding	**ANNE**
actor Parker	**FESS**	actress Haver	**JUNE**
actor Perkins	**TONY**	actress Havoc	**JUNE**
actor Powell	**WILLIAM**	actress Hayworth	**RITA**
actor Price	**VINCENT**	actress Hepburn	**AUDREY,**
actor Randall	**TONY**		**KATHARINE**
actor Sharif	**OMAR**	actress Hopkins	**MIRIAM**
actor Shatner	**WILLIAM**	actress Jeanmaire	**RENEE**
actor Sinatra	**FRANK**	actress Jones	**JENNIFER,**
actor Sparks	**NED**		**SHIRLEY**
actor Steiger	**ROD**	actress Lanchester	**ELSA**
actor Stewart	**JAMES**	actress Lange	**HOPE**
actor Taylor	**ROD, ROBERT**	actress Leigh	**JANET, VIVIEN**
actor Torn	**RIP**	actress Louise	**TINA, ANITA**
actor Van Dyke	**DICK**	actress Lupino	**IDA**
actor Wallach	**ELI**	actress Magnani	**ANNA**
actor Wayne	**JOHN**	actress Mayo	**VIRGINIA**
actor Weaver	**DENNIS**	actress Medford	**KAY**
actor West	**ADAM**	actress Merkel	**UNA**
actor's audition	**TRYOUT**	actress Merrill	**DINA**
actor's hint	**CUE**	actress Mills	**JULIET, HAYLEY**
actor's part	**ROLE**	actress Moore	**TERRY, MELBA**
actors in a play	**CAST**	actress Moorehead	**AGNES**
act pretentiously		actress Neal	**PATRICIA**
(2 wds.)	**SHOW OFF**	actress Novak	**KIM**
actress Albright	**LOLA**	actress Oberon	**MERLE**
actress Angeli	**PIER**	actress O'Hara	**MAUREEN**
actress Arden	**EVE**	actress Parker	**ELEANOR**
actress Balin	**INA**	actress Pitts	**ZASU**
actress Bancroft	**ANNE**	actress-playwright	
actress Baxter	**ANNE**	Gordon	**RUTH**
actress Benaderet	**BEA**	actress Rainer	**LUISE**
actress Bernhardt	**SARAH**	actress Raines	**ELLA**
actress Blake	**AMANDA**	actress Redgrave	**VANESSA,**
actress Cannon	**DYAN**		**LYNN**
actress Charisse	**CYD**	actress Ritter	**THELMA**

actress Rush	BARBARA	adjust	ALINE, ALIGN, ADAPT
actress Shearer	NORMA	adjutant bird	ARGALA,
actress Sheridan	ANNE		MARABOU, STORK
actress Sommars	JULIE	administer	MANAGE
actress Southern	ANN	administer corporal	
actress Stanwyck	BARBARA	punishment	SPANK, LASH
actress Storm	GALE		WHIP, PADDLE
actress Taylor	LIZ, ELIZABETH	admirer	BEAU, SWAIN
actress Thomas	MARLO	admiring group	
actress Tierney	GENE	(2 wds.)	FAN CLUB
actress Toren	MARTA	admissible	WORTHY, PROPER,
actress Turner	LANA		ACCEPTABLE
actress Welch	RAQUEL	admission	ENTRY
actress Weld	TUESDAY	admit	ALLOW, OWN
actress West	MAE	admit being	
actual	REAL	true	ACKNOWLEDGE
actuality	FACT	admonish	WARN
aculeus	STING, PRICKLE	admonition	REBUKE
acumen	INSIGHT	adnate	JOINED
acuminate	SHARPEN, TAPER	ado	FUSS, HUBBUB, TO-DO
acute	SHARP	adobe	BRICK, MUD
adage	PROVERB, SAYING	adolescent	TEEN
Adam and Eve's home	EDEN	adopt	ASSUME, ACCEPT
Adam's ale	WATER	adorable	CUTE
Adam's grandson	ENOS	adorably pretty (5 wds.)	AS
Adam's mate	EVE		CUTE AS A BUTTON
adapt	ADJUST	adore	IDOLIZE, LOVE,
add	TOTAL, SUM UP		WORSHIP, DOTE
addax	ANTELOPE	adorn	DECORATE, TRIM,
adder	VIPER, SNAKE, ASP		EMBELLISH
addict	USER	Adriatic port of Italy	BARI
addicted	DEVOTED,	adroit	DEXTEROUS
ATTACHED, HABITUATED		adulterate	MIX, DEBASE
addition	INCREASE	adult female	WOMAN
additional	EXTRA, MORE,	adult insect	IMAGO
	SUPPLEMENTARY	adult male	MAN
addition to a house	ELL	advance	GAIN, PROCEED, GO
addle	MUDDLE, CONFUSE,	advanced in years	AGED, OLD
	SPOIL	advancement	PROGRESS
add on	ANNEX, APPEND	advantage	EDGE, HEAD START
address	SPEAK, SPEECH	advantageous	USEFUL
address with friendliness	GREET	advantageous	
add salt	SEASON	purchase	BARGAIN
add sugar	SWEETEN	adventure	INCIDENT, EVENT,
ade	FRUIT DRINK		EXPERIENCE
adduce	CITE	adventurous deed	GEST, GESTE
adequate	SUITABLE	adversary	FOE, ENEMY
adhere	STICK, CLEAVE	adverse	HOSTILE,
adherent of a king	ROYALIST,		UNFAVORABLE
	TORY	adversity	DISASTER,
adhesive	STICKY		CALAMITY
adhesive strip	TAPE	advertisement	NOTICE
adhesive substance	PASTE,	advertising sign	POSTER,
	GLUE		BILLBOARD, BILL
adieu	FAREWELL	advice	COUNSEL
adjacent	NEAR, NEXT	advise	COUNSEL, SUGGEST
adjoin	ABUT, CONTIGUOUS	advise (arch.)	REDE
adjuration	APPEAL, COMMAND	advise of danger	WARN, ALERT
		advocate	SUPPORT

Aegean Island,
   former name **NIOS**
aerial toy **KITE**
aerie **NEST**
aery **ETHEREAL**
Aesop's island home **SAMOS**
affable **EASY, POLITE**
affair **INCIDENT**
affectation **POSE**
affected manner **AIRS**
affection **LOVE, FONDNESS**
affectionate **LOVING,**
   DEMONSTRATIVE
affirm **ASSERT, ATTEST,**
   AVOW, ACKNOWLEDGE,
   AVER
affirmative reply **YES, YEA,**
   AY, AYE
affix a signature **SIGN,**
   ENDORSE
afflatus **IMPULSE**
affliction **TROUBLE, SORROW**
affluent **WEALTHY**
afford **SPARE**
affray **MELEE, BRAWL**
affright **TERROR**
affront **INSULT**
Afghan prince **AMIR, AMEER,**
   EMIR
aflame **BURNING**
afoot **BREWING**
afoul **TANGLED**
afraid **SCARED**
African antelope **ELAND, GNU**
African-Arabian
   waters (2 wds.) **RED SEA**
African dialect **BANTU,**
   SWAHILI, BEMBA, LINGALA,
   CONGO, HAUSA, MANDINGO
African hemp **IFE**
African hunting
   expedition **SAFARI**
African land **ALGERIA,**
   BOTSWANA, BURUNDI,
   CAMEROON, CHAD, CONGO,
   DAHOMEY, EGYPT, ETHIOPIA,
   GABON, GAMBIA, GHANA,
   GUINEA, KENYA, LESOTHO,
   LIBERIA, LIBYA, MALAWI,
   MALI, MAURITANIA,
   MOROCCO, NIGER, NIGERIA,
   RHODESIA, RWANDA,
   SENEGAL, SOMALIA, SUDAN,
   TANZANIA, TOGO, TUNISIA,
   UGANDA, ZAMBIA
African land (2 wds.) **IVORY**
   COAST, SOUTH AFRICA,
   UPPER VOLTA
African lily **ALOE**

African nut tree **KOLA, COLA**
African river **CONGO, JUBA,**
   NIGER, NILE, SHIRE,
   VAAL, VOLTA, VELE
African tree **SHEA**
Afrikaans **LANGUAGE**
Afrikander **BOER**
aft **ASTERN**
after **FOLLOWING, BEHIND,**
   LATER
after-dinner candy **MINT**
aftermath **RESULT**
aftermost **LAST**
afternoon beverage **TEA**
afternoon party **TEA**
afternoon
   performance **MATINEE**
afternoon show **MATINEE**
afternoon sleep **SIESTA, NAP**
afternoon snack **TEA**
aftersong **EPODE**
afterthought (abbr.) **PS**
aftertime **FUTURE**
afterward **LATER**
again **ANEW, OVER, ENCORE**
against **ANTI, CON**
agama **LIZARD**
agapanthus **LILY**
agape **LOVE**
agar **GEL, MEDIUM**
age **ERA, EPOCH,**
   LIFETIME, EON
aged **OLD, ANCIENT,**
   RIPENED, MATURED
aged, as meat **CURED**
aged beer **LAGER**
ageless **ETERNAL**
agenda **PROGRAM**
agenesis **ABSENCE**
agent **DEPUTY,**
   REPRESENTATIVE
age-old **ANCIENT**
age on the vine **RIPEN**
agglomeration **HEAP, MASS**
agglutinant **GLUE**
aggrandize **EXALT**
aggregate **SUM, TOTAL**
aggressive **PUSHY**
agile **NIMBLE, LIVELY,**
   SPRY, ACTIVE
agitate **STIR**
Agnes Moorehead role **ENDORA**
ago **PAST**
agony **TORTURE**
agree **ACCORD, ASSENT,**
   CONCUR, CONSENT
agreeable **PLEASANT**
agreement **PACT**

agreement between
nations **TREATY**
agrestic **RURAL, RUSTIC**
agricultural home **FARM**
agricultural implement **HOE,
HARROW, PLOW,
REAPER, SICKLE**
agriculture **FARMING,
HUSBANDRY**
agrimony **FLOWER**
aguardiente **BRANDY**
ague **FEVER**
ahead **FORWARD**
ah me! **ALAS**
aid **ABET, ASSIST, HELP**
Aida role **RADAMES,
AMNERIS, AMONASRO**
aide **ASSISTANT**
aid in diagnosing **X-RAY**
aiguille **DRILL**
ail **SICKEN, TROUBLE**
ailanthus **TREE**
ailment **DISEASE**
aim **OBJECTIVE, DIRECT,
GOAL, POINT, END**
air **AURA, ATMOSPHERE,
VENTILATE, TUNE, MELODY**
airborne **ALOFT, FLYING**
air circulator **FAN**
aircraft **AIRPLANE, GLIDER,
HELICOPTER, JET**
airedale **DOG, BREED**
air hero **ACE**
airman **AVIATOR, FLIER,
PILOT**
airplane (Fr.) **AVION**
airplane enclosure **COCKPIT**
airplane space **SEAT**
airplane varnish **DOPE**
air pollution **SMOG**
airport, for short **DROME**
air rifle **BB**
airscrew **PROPELLER**
airstrip **RUNWAY**
Air Traffic Control (abbr.) **ATC**
air travel term **NONSTOP**
airy **LIGHT, LOFTY**
airy farewell **TATA**
ait **ISLET, EYOT**
aitch **"H"**
ajar **OPEN**
akin **RELATED**
Akkadian sun god **SHAMASH**
alacrity **SPEED**
alae **WINGS**
alar **WINGED, WINGLIKE**
alarm **FEAR, WARN, ALERT**
Alaskan native **ALEUT, ESKIMO**

Alaskan transportation **SLED
SKIDOO**
alate **WINGED**
alb **ROBE, CLOAK**
albacore **TUNA**
Albanian currency **LEK**
albeit **ALTHOUGH**
albite **FELDSPAR**
alcoholic beverage **GIN,
SCOTCH, BOURBON, VODKA,
RUM, MEAD, SPIRITS, WHISKEY**
alcohol lamp **ETNA**
alcove **NICHE, NOOK**
alder (var.) **OWLER**
alegar **VINEGAR**
alehouse **PUB, TAVERN,
INN, BAR**
ale mug **TOBY**
alert **ATTENTIVE, WATCHFUL
WARN, ALARM**
Aleutian island **ATTU**
Aleut's home **IGLOO**
alewife **HERRING**
alexipharmic **ANTIDOTAL**
alfalfa **GRASS, FODDER**
alga **SEAWEED**
Algerian governor **DEY**
Algerian port **ORAN**
alien **FOREIGN, STRANGE,
FOREIGNER**
alienate **ESTRANGE**
alight **DISMOUNT**
alike **SIMILAR, SAME**
aline **STRAIGHTEN**
alive **VITAL**
all **EVERYBODY, EVERYTHING**
allargando **SLOWER**
allay **SLAKE**
allege **AVER, STATE**
allegiance **LOYALTY**
allegorical work **FABLE**
allegro **FASTER**
alleviate **EASE, RELIEVE**
all excited **AGOG**
alley **LANE**
alliance **UNION**
allied **UNITED**
alligator **CROCODILE**
alligator pear **AVOCADO**
all male party **STAG**
allot **APPORTION, ASSIGN,
DISTRIBUTE, METE, DOLE**
allow **LET, PERMIT, OWN,
ADMIT**
allowable **PERMISSIBLE**
allowable under law **LEGAL,
LICIT**
allowance **SHARE, RATION**

allowance for cash payment **DISCOUNT**
allowance for waste **TRET**
allow as a discount **REBATE**
allow liquid to fall **SPILL**
allow to fall **DROP**
allow to go free **RELEASE**
alloy **COMBINE, MIX, DEBASE**
all right **OK, OKAY, ROGER**
allspice **MYRTLE, PIMIENTO**
all the time (3 wds.) **DAY AND NIGHT**
all tied up (2 wds.) **EVEN STEVEN**
allude **REFER**
allure **ATTRACT, ENTICE, VAMP**
allurement **FASCINATION**
alluring sea creature **MERMAID, SIREN**
alluring woman **SIREN**
alluvion **FLOOD**
ally **CONFEDERATE**
almandine **GARNET**
almond **NUT**
almost **NEARLY, NIGH**
almost alike **SIMILAR**
alms box **ARCA**
almshouse **POORHOUSE**
aloe **LILY**
aloft **ABOVE, UP**
aloha state **HAWAII**
aloha symbol **LEI**
alone **SOLITARY, SOLO, UNACCOMPANIED**
along in years **AGED, OLD**
aloof **REMOVED**
alphabet **LETTERS**
alphabetic character **LETTER**
Alpine cottage **CHALET**
Alpine country **FRANCE, SWITZERLAND, AUSTRIA, ITALY**
Alpine peak **MATTERHORN, JUNGFRAU**
Alpine primrose **AURICULA**
Alpine region **TIROL, TYROL**
alsike **CLOVER**
also **AND, TOO, PLUS**
also-ran **LOSER**
alter **ADAPT, CHANGE, VARY, AMEND**
alterant **DYE**
alter, as a dress (2 wds.) **MAKE OVER**
altercation **QUARREL, SCRAP**
alternate **STANDBY**
alternately (2 wds.) **BY TURNS**
alternating current (abbr.) **AC**

alternative **OPTION, CHOICE**
alternative word **OR**
althea **FLOWER, HOLLYHOCK**
alto **VIOLA**
alum **ASTRINGENT, STYPTIC**
always **EVER, FOREVER**
always (poet.) **EER**
alyssum **MUSTARD**
amadavat **SONGBIRD**
amadou **PUNK, TINDER**
amalgam **ALLOY, MIXTURE, BLEND**
amalgamation **UNION, BLEND**
amass **ACCUMULATE, GATHER**
amass and conceal **HOARD**
amateur **DILETTANTE**
amateur radio operator **HAM**
amaze **ASTONISH, STUN, AWE**
amazement **SURPRISE**
Amazon tributary **APA, ICA**
ambassador **ENVOY**
ambiguous **UNCLEAR, VAGUE**
ambition **DESIRE**
amble **STROLL, MEANDER**
ambo **PULPIT**
ambush **TRAP**
amend **CORRECT, REVISE, ALTER, CHANGE**
American Beauty **ROSE**
American bird **EAGLE**
American black snake **RACER**
American blackbird **GRACKLE**
American buffalo **BISON**
American cheese **CHEDDAR**
American dish **HOTDOG, HAMBURGER**
American eagle **BALD**
American folk singer **IVES, SEEGER, GUTHRIE**
American humorist **ADE, TWAIN**
American in Britain **YANK**
American Indian **CREE, HOPI, UTE, ERIE, NAVAJO, OTO, APACHE, POHO, SIOUX, OMAHA, CROW**
American Indian tent **TEPEE, TIPI, TIPEE**
American ivy **CREEPER**
American patriot **OTIS, HALE, HENRY**
American soldiers **GI'S**
American spotted cat **MARGAY**
American symbol **EAGLE**
American vegetable **CORN, MAIZE, SQUASH**
America's uncle **SAM**
amiable **CORDIAL, AGREEABLE**
amianthus **ASBESTOS**

amicable   FRIENDLY
amid   AMONG
amidone   METHADONE
amiss   ASTRAY, WRONG
amity   PEACE, FRIENDSHIP
ammonia compounds   AMINES
ammonite   FOSSIL
ammunition   SHOT, SHELLS
among   AMID, MID
amoretto   CUPID
amorous look   OGLE
amorphous   SHAPELESS
amort   SPIRITLESS
amortize   PRORATE
amount   SUM, TOTAL
amount carried   LOAD
ampere (abbr.)   AMP
ampersand   AND
amphibian   TOAD, FROG,
                SALAMANDER
amphitheater   ARENA
ample   PLENTIFUL, ENOUGH
amplify   ENLARGE, MAGNIFY
amplitude   BREADTH, SCOPE
amulet   CHARM
amuse   DIVERT, ENTERTAIN
amusement   GAME
amusement
  enterprise   CARNIVAL
amusing   COMICAL, FUNNY
amusing play   COMEDY
amylaceous   STARCHY
amylum   STARCH
analyze grammatically PARSE
analyze ore   ASSAY
Ananias   LIAR
anaphora   REPETITION
anarchy   DISORDER
anasarca   DROPSY
anatomical networks   RETIA
anatomical pouch   SAC
ancestor of the pharaohs RA, RE
ancestry   FAMILY, LINEAGE
anchor   MOOR, FIX, TIE
anchor chain   CABLE
ancient   OLD, OLDEN, AGED
ancient British chariot ESSED,
                        ESSEDA
ancient Chinese capital   SIAN
ancient Greek coin   OBOL
ancient Hebrew ascetic ESSENE
ancient Irish capital   TARA
ancient Italian   LATIN, ROMAN
               OSCAN, ETRUSCAN
ancient Italian family ESTE
ancient king   ARTHUR,
               DAVID, SAUL
ancient kingdom on
  Persian Gulf   ELAM

ancient Mexican MAYA, AZTEC
                TOLTEC
ancient musical
  instrument   LYRA, LYRE,
                LUTE
ancient name of Vich   AUSA
Ancient of Days   GOD
ancient Peruvian   INCA
ancient Phoenician port SIDON,
                TYRE
ancient poet BARD, PSALMIST
ancient port of Rome   OSTIA
ancient psalmist   DAVID
ancient Roman garmentsTOGAS
ancient Roman
  magistrate   AEDILE, EDILE
ancient sacred writings
  of Persia   AVESTA
ancient serf   HELOT, ESNE
ancient stringed
  instrument   LUTE, LYRA,
               LYRE, KITHARA
ancient Sudanese   NUBIANS,
                    NUBA
ancient Syria   ARAM
ancient theatres   ODEON,
                    ODEUM
ancient two-wheeled
  chariot   ESSED, ESSEDA
ancient writing   RUNE
ancon   CONSOLE
and   ALSO, NEXT, PLUS
and (Fr.)   ET
Andaman Islands'
  neighbor   NICOBAR
andante   MODERATE
Andes animal   LLAMA
Andes country PERU, BOLIVIA,
           CHILE, VENEZUELA,
           ECUADOR, ARGENTINA
andesite   FELDSPAR, GRANITE
Andes mountain   SORATA
Andes vulture   CONDOR
and not   NOR
and others (2 wds.,
  Lat. abbr.)   ET AL
Andrew Jackson's nickname
  (2 wds.)   OLD HICKORY
android   ROBOT
andromeda   STAR
and sign   AMPERSAND
and so on (2 wds.,
  Lat. abbr.)   ETC.
Andy's partner   AMOS
anecdote   TALE, YARN
anechoic   SOUNDPROOF
anele   ANOINT
anemone   BUTTERCUP
anent CONCERNING, ABOUT

anesthetic	ETHER, CHLOROFORM, GAS
anew	AFRESH, OVER
angel	CHERUB, SPIRIT
angelic	HEAVENLY, GOOD
angelic child	CHERUB
angelica	PARSLEY
angel's headdress	HALO
angel's instrument	HARP
anger	ENRAGE, IRE, WRATH, RAGE, MADDEN
angina	SPASM
angioma	TUMOR
angle	BEVEL, FISH, CORNER
angle of a leaf	AXIL
anglepod	MILKWEED
angler's bait	LURE
angleworm	BAIT
Anglo-Saxon Letter	EDH
Anglo-Saxon slave	ESNE
angry	CROSS, IRATE, MAD, ENRAGED, WRATHFUL
anguish	DISTRESS, PAIN
angular	GAUNT
angwantibo	LEMUR
anhydrous	WATERLESS
ani	CUCKOO, BLACKBIRD
anil	INDIGO
anile	INFIRM, WEAK
aniline product	DYE
animal	BRUTE, BEAST, BIPED
animal claw	TALON
animal doctor	VET
animal enclosure	CAGE, PEN
animal fat	TALLOW
animal flesh	MEAT, BEEF, PORK, HAM, VEAL, BACON, LAMB
animal food	FODDER
animal foot	PAW, PAD, HOOF
animal garden	ZOO
animal hair	FUR, MANE
animal hide	PELT
animal home	LAIR, DEN, BURROW, NEST
animal nail	CLAW
animal of South America	TAPIR, LLAMA, APARA, COATI, PACO, ALPACA
animal of the cat family	LION, CHEETAH, TIGER, PANTHER, COUGAR, JAGUAR, OCELOT, CARACAL, LEOPARD
animal park	ZOO
animal's coat	FUR, PELT, HIDE, PELAGE
animal's den	LAIR

animal skin	PELT, FUR
animal's limb	LEG
animal trainer	TAMER
animate	INSPIRE, CHEER, PROMPT
animated	ALIVE, LIVELY
animato (mus.)	ANIMATED
anime	RESIN
animosities	ENMITIES
animus	SOUL
anisette	LIQUEUR
anjou	PEAR
anklebone	TALUS
ankle coverings	SPATS
ankle mishap	SPRAIN
anklet	SOCK
annals	ARCHIVES
Anne Bancroft role (2 wds.)	MIRACLE WORKER
annex	ADD
annihilate	ANNUL, EXTINGUISH, DESTROY
announce	REVEAL, REPORT, TELL
annoy	IRK, PESTER, TEASE, RILE
annoying	TIRESOME
annoying bird	PIGEON
annoying child	BRAT
annoying feeling	ITCH
annoying insect	GNAT, MITE
annoying one	PEST, NUISANCE
annual	YEARLY
annual contest (2 wds.)	MISS AMERICA
annually	YEARLY
annuity	PAYMENT
annul	ABOLISH
annulus	CIRCLE
anomalous	ABNORMAL, DEVIANT
anon	PRESENTLY, SOON, SUBSEQUENTLY
anonymous	NAMELESS, ANON
anopheles	MOSQUITO
another name	ALIAS
another name for Candia	HERAKLION
another way around	DETOUR
answer	RESPOND, REPLY
answer the purpose	SERVE
ant	EMMET, PISMIRE, TERMITE
antagonism	ENMITY
antagonist	RIVAL
antarctic bird	PENGUIN
Antarctic explorer	BYRD
Antarctic sea	ROSS

ant cow	APHID
antecedent	ANCESTOR
Anthony's nickname	TONY
anthracite	COAL
antiaircraft fire	FLAK
antiar	UPAS, POISON
antibiotic	SULFA
antic	CAPER, DIDO, PRANK
anticipate	AWAIT, WAIT
anticipation	HOPE
antidote	REMEDY
antimacassar	DOILY
antipasto	APPETIZER, SALAD
antipathy	HATE, HATRED
antiprohibitionists	WETS
antiquated	OLD, PASSE, AGED, ANCIENT
antique	ANCIENT, QUAINT, OLD
antiquity	YORE
antiseptic liquid	IODINE
antithesis	CONTRAST, OPPOSITE
antler	HORN
antlered animal	DEER, ELK, MOOSE
antre	CAVE, CAVERN
antrum	CAVITY
anvil (ant.)	INCUS
anxiety	CARE, WORRY, FEAR
anxious	EAGER
any	SOME
apace	SWIFTLY, QUICKLY
apart from	ASIDE, SEPARATE
apartment	FLAT
apartment (abbr.)	APT
apartment building	TENEMENT
apartment occupant	TENANT
apart (prefix)	DIS
apathy	INDIFFERENCE, PASSIVITY
ape	GORILLA, CHIMPANZEE, SIMIAN, ORANGUTAN, MIMIC, IMITATE, MONKEY, MOCK, COPY
apeak	VERTICAL
aper	COPYCAT, MIMIC
apercu	INSIGHT
aperitif	LIQUEUR, WINE
aperture	GAP, OPENING, ORIFICE
apex	SUMMIT, TOP, ACME
aphid	INSECT, LOUSE
aphorism	MAXIM, ADAGE
apiary dweller	BEE
apiece	EACH
apish	SILLY
aplomb	POISE
apocryphal	SPURIOUS

apology	PLEA
apoplexy	PARALYSIS, STROKE
Apostle Paul	SAUL
apothecary's weight	DRAM
appall	DISMAY
apalling	TERRIBLE
apparel	DRESS, RAIMENT, GARB, SUIT, COAT
apparel of skins	PELT
apparent	SEEMING
apparition	GHOST, SHADE, SPECTRE
appeal	PLEAD
appear	SEEM, SPRING UP, TURN UP
appear again	RECUR
appearance	ASPECT, FACET, LOOK
appease	PACIFY
appel	DARE, CHALLENGE
appellation	TITLE, NAME
append	ADD, ATTACH, ANNEX
appendage	TAIL, LIMB
appetite	DESIRE, RELISH
applaud	CLAP, CHEER
apple (Fr.)	POMME
apple center	CORE
apple drink	CIDER
applejack	CIDER, BRANDY
apple of one's eye	PET, FAVORITE
apple-pie order	NEAT
apple seed	PIP
Appleseed	JOHNNY
appliance	DEVICE, MACHINE, TOOL
applique	DECORATE
apply	SPREAD, PLACE, REQUEST
apply lightly	DAB
apply powder	DUST
appoint	NAME, FURNISH
appointment	DATE, TRYST
apportion	DOLE, ALLOT, METE
apposite	APT
appraise	RATE
appreciate	ESTEEM, ESTIMATE, NOTICE
appreciative	GRATEFUL
apprehend	DISCERN
apprehension	FEAR, TREPIDATION
apprentice	TRAINEE, NOVICE
apprise	TEACH, INFORM
approach	NEAR, COME
approachable	RECEPTIVE
approbate	APPROVE

appropriate **ADOPT, SEEMLY, FIT, FITTING**
approve **OK, OKAY**
approved model **STANDARD**
approximal **ADJOINING**
approximately **ABOUT, AROUND**
approximation **LIKENESS, NEARNESS**
April shower **RAIN**
apron-like garment **SMOCK**
apropos **TIMELY, APT**
apt **LIKELY, APRÓPOS**
apteryx **KIWI**
aquarium **TANK**
aquarium fish **MOLLY, GUPPY, GOURAMi, PLATY**
aquatic animal **OTTER, SEAL, WHALE, SEACOW, SEALION, SEA ELEPHANT, WALRUS, HIPPOPOTAMUS**
aquatic bird **SWAN, TERN, DUCK, TEAL, DRAKE, GULL, PENGUIN, FALK**
aquatic rodent **MUSKRAT, BEAVER**
aquatic sport **SWIM, DIVE, BOAT, SAIL, FISH, SURF, WATER SKI**
aquatint **ETCHING**
aquavit **LIQUOR, APERITIF**
aqua vitae **LIQUOR, ALCOHOL**
aqueous **WATERY**
Ara **CONSTELLATION, MACAW**
Arab **BEDOUIN, SEMITE, YEMENITE**
Arab chieftain **EMIR, AMIR, AMEER**
Arab chieftain's domain **EMIRATE**
Arab country **YEMEN, OMAN, ADEN, SYRIA, LEBANON, EGYPT, JORDAN, MOROCCO, ALGERIA, TUNISIA, LIBYA, SUDAN, IRAQ, KUWAIT, MUSCAT**
Arab garment **ABA, BURNOOSE**
Arabian coffee **MOCHA**
Arabian coin **DINAR**
Arabian gazelle **ARIEL**
Arabian gulf **ADEN, AQABA**
Arabian name **SAUD**
Arabian port **ADEN**
Arabian prince **EMIR, AMIR, AMEER, EMEER**
Arabian ship **DHOW**
Arabian territory **OMAN**
arable grassland **LEA, LEY**

arachnid **SPIDER, MITE, TICK, SCORPION**
araneid **SPIDER**
arbalest **CROSSBOW**
arbiter **UMPIRE**
arbitrary **ABSOLUTE, DESPOTIC**
arbitrary assertion (colloq.) **SAY-SO**
arbor **BOWER**
arcane **HIDDEN, SECRET**
arch (Scot.) **PEND**
Archbishop of Canterbury **ANSELM, BECKET**
arched way **ARCADE, LOGGIA, PORTICO**
archer **BOWMAN**
archer's missile **ARROW**
archimage **MAGICIAN, WIZARD**
archives **ANNALS**
arch of a circle **SECTOR**
Arctic abode **IGLOO, IGLU**
Arctic bird **SKUA**
Arctic charr **TROUT**
Arctic expanse **ICE**
Arctic inhabitant **ESKIMO, ALEUT**
arctics **BOOTS, OVERSHOES**
Arctic vehicle **SLED, SLEIGH, DOGSLED**
ardent affection **LOVE**
ardor **ELAN, ZEAL**
arduous journey **TREK**
are **EXIST**
area **REGION, SURFACE**
area in a house **ROOM**
areca **PALM**
arena **AMPHITHEATER**
arenaceous **SANDY**
argala **STORK, MARIBOU**
Argentine dance **TANGO**
Argentine plains **PAMPAS**
argol **TARTAR**
argot **CANT, SLANG**
argue **DEBATE, REBUT, FIGHT, QUARREL**
argument **SPAT, QUARREL, DEBATE, FIGHT**
arid **DRY, SERE**
arid expanse **DESERT**
Aries **RAM**
Arikara **REE**
ariose **MELODIC**
arise **GET UP, COME UP, ASCEND**
arithmetic, for short **MATH**
arithmetic sign **PLUS, MINUS, EQUAL**
Arizona college town **TEMPE**

Arizona Indian **APACHE, PIMA,**
PAPAGO, HOPI, NAVAJO
Arizona lizard
(2 wds.) **GILA MONSTER**
Arizona river **GILA, SALT,**
COLORADO
ark **BOAT**
ark builder **NOAH**
arkose **SANDSTONE**
ark's landing place **ARARAT**
arm **LIMB, BRANCH,**
TENTACLE
armada **FLEET**
arm and hand joint **WRIST**
armature **DEFENSE, COVERING**
arm bone **ULNA**
arm covering **SLEEVE**
armed band **POSSE**
armed conflict **WAR, BATTLE**
Armenian cap **CALPAC,**
CALPACK, KALPAK
Armenian mountain **ARARAT,**
ARA, ARAGATIS, TAURUS
Armenian people **GOMER**
arm extremity **HAND**
armistice **TRUCE**
armorbearer **SQUIRE,**
ARMIGER
armored mammal **ARMADILLO**
arms **WEAPONS**
arms and legs **LIMBS**
army **FORCES, TROOPS**
army acronym **AWOL**
army base **CAMP**
army bed **COT**
army chaplain **PADRE**
army group **UNIT, CADRE**
army meal **MESS**
army officer **CAPTAIN,**
COLONEL, MAJOR,
GENERAL, LIEUTENANT
army shoe **BOOT**
army trader **SUTLER**
Army Transport Service
(abbr.) **A.T.S.**
army unit **CORPS, REGIMENT**
aroid **TARO**
aroma **BOUQUET, ODOR,**
FRAGRANCE, SCENT, SMELL
aromatic **REDOLENT,**
FRAGRANT
aromatic beverage **TEA**
aromatic gum resin **MYRRH**
aromatic herb **MINT, DILL,**
SPEARMINT, SAGE, CARUM
aromatic medicinal ingredient
(2 wds.) **BAY RUM**
aromatic ointment **NARD**
aromatic product **SPICE**

aromatic seed **ANISE, CUMIN**
around **ABOUT**
around (prefix) **PERI**
arouse a response
(3 wds.) **RING A BELL**
arraign **CHARGE, ACCUSE**
arrange **ASSORT**
arrange and edit **COMPILE**
arrange in folds **DRAPE**
arrange in layers **TIER,**
LAMINATE
arrange in order **SORT**
arrange in rows **ALINE, ALIGN**
arrangement **SETUP,**
DISPOSITION
Arras **TAPESTRY**
array **DRESS, DECK, ADORN**
arrears **BEHIND**
arrest **NAB, STOP, CHECK**
arrive **COME**
arrive at **REACH**
arrive by plane **LAND**
arrogance **PRIDE**
arrogant **PROUD, HAUGHTY**
arrogant manner **HAUTEUR**
arrogate **USURP, TAKE**
arrow **DART, SPEAR, SHAFT**
arrow case **QUIVER**
arrow point **BARB**
arrow poison **CURARE, INEE,**
URARI, UPAS, ANTIAR
arrow-shaped **HASTATE**
arroyo **BROOK, CREEK,**
GULCH
art **CUNNING, KNACK**
art (Lat.) **ARS**
artery **AORTA**
art gallery **SALON, MUSEUM**
article **AN, THE, ITEM**
article of apparel **SHIRT,**
BLOUSE, DRESS, ROBE,
JACKET, VEST, SKIRT,
WAIST
article of bedding **SHEET,**
SPREAD, BLANKET,
PILLOWCASE
article of cosmetics **ROUGE,**
LIPSTICK, MASCARA,
LINER, POWDER
article of faith **TENET,**
DOCTRINE, DOGMA
article of food **CORN, RICE,**
BREAD, STEAK, CHOP,
VEGETABLE, FRUIT
article of furniture **TABLE,**
CHAIR, SOFA, SETTEE,
DAVENPORT, BOOKCASE,
BED, DRESSER

article of jewelry **RING, NECKLACE, BRACELET, EARRING**
articles of merchandise **WARES**
artifice **RUSE, SUBTERFUGE**
artificer **ARTISAN, SMITH**
artificial **FALSE**
artificial butter **OLEO**
artificial coloring **DYE**
artificial front **FACADE**
artificial hairpiece **WIG, TOUPEE, FALL**
artificial ice floor **RINK**
artificial language **IDO, ESPERANTO**
artificially high voice **FALSETTO**
artificially sprouted grain **MALT**
artificial silk **RAYON**
artificial water channel **FLUME**
artificial waterway **CANAL**
artillery **CANNON**
artillery emplacement **BATTERY**
artillery fire **SALVO**
artisan **CRAFTSMAN**
artist **PAINTER, SCULPTOR**
artiste **ACTOR, PERFORMER**
artistic person **AESTHETE**
artist's cap **BERET**
artist's equipment **EASEL, PALETTE**
artist's medium **INK, OIL, TEMPERA**
artist's paint holder **PALETTE**
artist's specialty **PAINTING, LANDSCAPE, PORTRAIT, STILL LIFE, SCULPTURE, ETCHING**
artist's stand **EASEL**
artist's work **COLLAGE, PAINTING, MASTERPIECE, PORTRAIT, MINIATURE**
artist's workshop **ATELIER, STUDIO**
artless **OPEN, CANDID**
artlessness **NAIVETE**
art of discourse **RHETORIC**
art of government **POLITICS**
art of self-protection **DEFENSE**
arui **AOUDAD**
arum **CUCKOOPINT, CALLAS**
as **WHILE**
asa **PHYSICIAN, HEALER**
as a certainty **FOR SURE, SURELY**

as a close race (3 wds.) **NIP AND TUCK**
as a rule **NORMALLY**
ascend **ARISE, CLIMB, RISE**
ascenseur **ELEVATOR, LIFT**
ascertain **LEARN, PROVE**
ascertain bearing **ORIENT**
ascertain the dimensions **MEASURE**
ascertain the number **COUNT**
ascetic **HERMIT, AUSTERE**
ascot **TIE, CRAVAT, SCARF**
ascribable **DUE, ATTRIBUTABLE**
ascribe **ASSIGN**
asea **BEFUDDLED, BEWILDERED**
as far as **TO**
ash **TREE**
ash can (Brit.) **DUSTBIN**
ash-colored **GRAY**
ashen **PALE, LIVID**
Asia Minor mountain **IDA**
Asia Minor sea **AEGEAN, BLACK**
Asian country **IRAN, LAOS, VIETNAM, CHINA, THAILAND, INDIA, PAKISTAN, IRAQ, ADEN, AFGHANISTAN, CAMBODIA, JAPAN, QATAR, NEPAL, CEYLON, KOREA, KUWAIT, MACAO, MALAYSIA, PHILIPPINES**
Asian sea **ARAL, CASPIAN, DEAD**
Asian treeless tract **STEPPE**
Asian Turk **TATAR**
Asiatic fiber plant **HEMP**
Asiatic mountains **PAMIRS, ALTAI, ELBURZ, HIMALAYA, KARAKORUM, KUNLUN, TAURUS, URALS**
ask **INQUIRE, INVITE, REQUEST**
ask alms **BEG**
askew **ALOP, AWRY, OBLIQUE**
ask for **SOLICIT**
ask for a job **APPLY**
ask for charity **BEG**
ask forcibly **DEMAND**
ask for payment **DUN**
as of now (2 wds.) **TO-DATE**
aspect **APPEARANCE, PHASE, FACET, SIDE**
aspen **POPLAR**
asperity **ACRIMONY, ROUGHNESS**

asperse **DEFAME, SLANDER**
aspersion **CALUMNY**
asphalt **BITUMEN**
aspiration **HOPE**
aspiring actress **STARLET**
asp **SNAKE, ADDER, VIPER**
ass **DOLT, FOOL**
assail **BESET**
Assam worm **ERIA**
assault **ATTACK**
assemblage **CREW**
assemble **COLLECT, GATHER, MEET, MUSTER**
assembly **COMPANY, MEETING**
assent **CONSENT, AGREEMENT, COMPLY**
assert **AFFIRM, AVER, AVOW, ALLEGE, CLAIM**
assert as fact **POSIT**
assertion **DECLARATION, STATEMENT**
assertion of right **CLAIM**
assess **CHARGE, LEVY, ESTIMATE**
assess taxes **LEVY**
asset **PROPERTY, RESOURCE**
assign **ASCRIBE, DELEGATE**
assign a portion **ALLOT**
assignation **TRYST**
assigned chore **TASK, STINT, JOB**
assignment **TASK**
assimilate **ABSORB**
assist **AID, HELP, ABET**
assistance **AID, HELP, WELFARE**
assistant **AIDE, HELPER**
associate **COMRADE, COMPANION, PARTNER, COLLEAGUE**
Associated Press (abbr.) **AP**
associates **KITH**
association **CLUB, LEAGUE, ORGANIZATION**
assort **CLASSIFY**
assortment **VARIETY**
assuage **ALLAY**
assume an attitude **POSE**
assume an upright position **STAND**
assume control (2 wds.) **TAKE OVER**
assumed manner **AIRS**
assumed name **ALIAS**
assurance **APLOMB, TRUST**
asterisk **STAR**
astern **AFT**

asthmatic **WHEEZY**
astir **ACTIVE, UP**
astonish **AMAZE, ASTOUND, STUN**
astound **AMAZE**
astral **STARRY, STELLAR**
astride **ASTRADDLE**
astringent **ALUM, STYPTIC**
astronaut Cooper **LEROY**
astronaut's "all right" **AOK**
astronaut's feat (2 wds.) **SPACE WALK**
astronaut's ferry **LEM**
astronaut's garment (2 wds.) **SPACE SUIT**
astronaut's report (2 wds.) **NO GO**
astronomer's tool **TELESCOPE**
astute **SHREWD**
asunder **APART**
Aswan sight **DAM**
Aswan's river **NILE**
as well **ALSO, TOO, AND**
asylum **HAVEN**
at **NEARBY**
at a disadvantage (4 wds.) **OUT ON A LIMB**
at a distance **AFAR, OFF**
at all **EVER**
at all events (3 wds.) **IN ANY CASE**
at all times **EVER**
at bat **UP**
ate **DINED, CONSUMED, GOBBLED**
at ease **POISED, RELAXED, COMFORTABLE**
atelier **STUDIO**
ates **SWEETSOP**
at flood level **AWASH**
at full speed **ALL-OUT**
at hand **NEAR**
Athena **PALLAS**
Athenian historian **XENOPHON**
Athenian lawgiver **SOLON**
Athenian statesman **PERICLES**
Athens' rival **SPARTA**
at highest point **ZENITH, APEX, APOGEE**
athletic center **GYMNASIUM, GYM**
athletic contest **TOURNAMENT, GAME, BOUT, MATCH, MEET**
athletic star **ACE, PRO**
at home **IN**
atimon **MUSKMELON**
Atlantic fish **SALEMA**

Atlantic island	**CANARY**	at that place	**THERE**
atlas chart	**MAP**	at that time	**THEN**
at last	**FINALLY**	at the back	**AFT, ASTERN**
at liberty	**FREE**	at the front	
at long last	**FINALLY**	(3 wds.)	**TO THE FORE**
atmosphere	**AIR, AURA,**	at the middle	**CENTRAL**
	AMBIANCE	at the middle point	**MID**
atmospheric disturbance		at the peak	**ATOP**
	STATIC, STORM	at the same time	**TOGETHER**
atmospheric weight		at the summit	**ATOP**
(2 wds.)	**AIR PRESSURE**	at the tip	**APICAL**
at no cost	**FREE, GRATIS**	at this place	**HERE**
at no time	**NEVER**	at this time	**NOW**
at odds	**OUT**	attic	**GARRET**
atoll	**ISLET, REEF**	Attila's followers	**HUNS**
atom	**WHIT, PARTICLE**	attire	**DRESS, GARB,**
atomic	**MINUTE, SMALL**		**CLOTHING, ARRAY**
atomic device	**REACTOR, BOMB**	attired	
atomic number (abbr.)	**AT. NO.**		**CLAD, DRESSED,**
atomic particle	**PROTON,**		**GARBED, BEDECKED**
	NEUTRON, ELECTRON,	attitude	**AIR, SLANT**
	ION	attorney	**LAWYER, COUNSELOR**
atomize	**SPRAY**	attorney's charge	**FEE**
atone	**EXPIATE**	attract	**ALLURE, LURE,**
atonement	**AMENDS**		**ENTICE, INVITE**
atop	**ON, UPON, OVER,**	attraction	**CHARM, LURE**
	SURMOUNTING	attractive	**CUTE, MAGNETIC,**
at present	**NOW**		**INVITING**
at rest	**EASE**	attrap	**ADORN, ARRAY**
atrocious	**CRUEL, WICKED**	attribute	**PROPERTY, REFER,**
attach	**APPEND, ANNEX**		**ASSIGN, CREDIT**
attachment	**AFFINITY**	attrition	**FRICTION**
attach to	**ANNEX**	at what place	**WHERE**
attack	**SET ON, BESET,**	at what time	**WHEN**
	ASSAULT, ASSAIL	auberge	**INN**
attack by waiting	**SIEGE**	auction	**SALE**
attacker	**ASSAILANT**	auctioneer	**SELLER**
attack on all sides	**BESET**	auctioneer's word	**SOLD,**
attack repeatedly	**PELT,**		**GOING, GONE**
	ASSAIL	auction participant	**BIDDER**
attain	**REACH**	audacious	**BOLD, INSOLENT**
attainment	**ARRIVAL**	audacity	**GALL, NERVE,**
attain recognition	**ARRIVE**		**CHEEK**
attain success	**WIN**	audible respiration	**SIGH**
attempt	**TRY, ESSAY**	audibility	**ALOUD**
attend	**ESCORT, LISTEN**	audience	**EAR, ATTENTION**
attendance	**PRESENCE**	auditorium	**HALL**
attendant	**ESCORT, SERVANT**	auditory	**OTIC, AURAL**
attendant on board		auger	**TOOL, BORE**
ship	**STEWARD**	augment	**EKE, ADD, SWELL**
attending	**AT, WITH**	augury	**OMEN, FORETOKEN,**
attend to	**SEE**		**PORTENT, SIGN**
attention	**EAR, AUDIENCE**	aura	**ATMOSPHERE, AIR,**
attention-getting sound	**AHEM,**		**EMANATION**
	PST	auricle	**EAR, PINNA**
attentive	**ALERT**	auricular	**OTIC**
attestation	**TESTIMONY**	Aurora	**EOS**
atter	**POISON, VENOM, STING**	auspices	**EGIS, AEGIS**

austere	**SEVERE, HARSH**
Australian animal	**KOALA,**
	KANGAROO, PLATYPUS,
	ECHIDNA
Australian badger	**WOMBAT**
Australian beverage	**KAVA**
Australian bird	**EMU**
Australian capital	**CANBERRA,**
	PERTH
Australian cedar	**TOON**
Australian city	**ADELAIDE,**
	SYDNEY, GEELONG,
	BRISBANE
Australian dog	**DINGO**
Austrian capital	**VIENNA**
authentic	**REAL**
author Bellow	**SAUL**
authoress Ferber	**EDNA**
author Fleming	**IAN**
author Gardner	**ERLE**
author Harte	**BRET**
author Hunter	**EVAN**
authoritative	
example	**PRECEDENT**
authoritative rule	**LAW**
authoritative standard	**NORM**
authority	**POWER, SAY**
authority on governmental	
law	**PARLIAMENTARIAN**
authorize	**LICENSE**
author Levin	**IRA**
author of "The Inferno"	**DANTE**
author of "Picnic"	**INGE**
author of "Pygmalion"	**SHAW**
author of "Robinson	
Crusoe"	**DEFOE**
author of "The Raven"	**POE**
author of "The Song of	
Hiawatha"	**LONGFELLOW**
author Tolstoy	**LEO**
author Turgenev	**IVAN**
author unknown (abbr.)	**ANON**
author's alias	
(2 wds.)	**PEN NAME**
authoritative command	**FIAT,**
	DECREE
auto	**CAR**
autocracy	**MONARCHY**
autocrat	**DESPOT**
auto frame	**CHASSIS**
auto fuel	**GAS, PETROL,**
	GASOLINE
autograph	**SIGNATURE**
automation	**ROBOT**
auto part	**STARTER, CHOKE,**
	TRANSMISSION, SPARK
	PLUG, CARBURETOR,
	RADIATOR, HORN
auto power source	**BATTERY**
autumn	**FALL**
autumn pear	**BOSC**
autumnal beverage	**CIDER**
auxiliary	**HELPER, AID, ALLY**
auxiliary verb	**HAD, WAS,**
	ARE, MAY, CAN, WILL,
	HAS, MUST, IS, SHALL,
	SHOULD, COULD
available	**READY, HANDY**
available, as fresh	
fruit	**IN SEASON**
available money	**CAPITAL**
available space	**ROOM**
avalanche	**SLIDE, FALL**
avarice	**GREED**
avaricious	**MISERLY, STINGY**
avatar	**ARCHETYPE**
avaunt	**ADVANCE**
ave	**HAIL!**
avenge	**VINDICATE**
avenge a wrong (3 wds.)	
	SETTLE A SCORE
avenue	**STREET, BOULEVARD,**
	ROADWAY
aver	**AFFIRM, ASSERT,**
	DECLARE
average	**MEAN, NORM,**
	MEDIAN, SO-SO,
	PAR, ORDINARY
averse	**RELUCTANT**
aversion	**DISLIKE**
avert (2 wds.)	**WARD OFF**
aviary	**BIRDHOUSE,**
	SANCTUARY
aviation	**FLYING**
aviator	**AIRMAN, PILOT**
avid	**EAGER, ENTHUSIASTIC,**
	GREEDY
avoid	**AVERT, EVADE, SHUN,**
	STEER CLEAR OF
avoid as hurtful	**ESCHEW**
avoirdupois weight	**TON**
avow	**DECLARE, AVER,**
	CONFESS
awabi	**ABALONE**
awaft	**AFLOAT, ADRIFT**
awaiting	**PENDING**
awaken	**ROUSE, STIR**
award	**GRANT, PRIZE,**
	MEDAL, RECOGNIZE
aware of	**ONTO, COGNIZANT,**
	CONSCIOUS
away	**ABSENT, OUT**
away (prefix)	**APO, AP, DE**
away from	**ABSENT, OUT**
away from the coast	**INLAND**
away from the wind	**ALEE**

awe	DREAD, FEAR
awful	TERRIBLE, HORRIBLE, BAD, GRISLY
awkward	MALADROIT, CLUMSY, UNGAINLY, INEPT, GAUCHE
awkward person	LOUT, CLOD
awning	TILT, SHELTER
awry	AGEE, AMISS, WRONG
ax	ADZ(E), HATCHET
axiom	MAXIM, SAW, LAW
axis	LINE
axle	PIN, SPINDLE
aye	YES, YEA
azure	BLUE

B

baa	BLEAT
ba-ba	CAKE
babacoote	LEMUR
babble	PRATE, PRATTLE
baboon	APE
baby bear	CUB
baby carriage	PRAM, BUGGY
baby frog	TADPOLE
babyish	CHILDISH, PUERILE
Babylonian deity	ANU, ISHTAR, BEL, NEBO, MAROUK, BAAL
Babylonian people	ELAMITE
baby powder	TALC, TALCUM
baby rabbit	BUNNY
baby's apron	BIB
baby's bed	CRADLE, CRIB, BASSINET
baby's game	PEEKABOO
baby's good-bye	TATA
baby's hat	BONNET
baby sheep	LAMB
baby shoe	BOOTEE, BOOTIE
baby's napkin	BIB
baby's plaything	RATTLE, TOY
baby's supervisor	NURSEMAID, NANNY
baby's toy	RATTLE
baby's underclothing	DIAPER
Bacchanals' cry	EVOE
bachelor	CELIBATE
bachelor's last words (2 wds.)	I DO
bacillus	GERM, MICROBE, BACTERIA
back	SUPPORT, UPHOLD, AFT, AID, ENDORSE
backbone	SPINE

back country	HINTERLAND, STICKS, BUSH
back end	REAR
background	REAR, EXPERIENCE
background of a play	SETTING
backless chair	STOOL
backless top	HALTER
back of the foot	HEEL
back of the neck	NAPE
back out	WITHDRAW
back pain	NOTALGIA
back street	ALLEY
back talk	SASS
back up	ACCUMULATE, REVERSE
backward	REVERSE, SHY
backwater	BAYOU
backyard barrier	FENCE
bacon portion	RASHER
bacteria	GERMS
bacterial culture	AGAR
bad	EVIL, NAUGHTY
bad dream	NIGHTMARE
bade	ORDERED, COMMANDED, SUMMONED
badge	EMBLEM, TOKEN, INSIGNIA
badger	TEASE
badgerlike animal	RATEL
Badger State	WISCONSIN
badinage	BANTER, REPARTEE
badly	ILL
badness	EVIL
baffle	OUTWIT
baffling question	POSER
bag	POKE, SAC(K), POUCH, PURSE
bagatelle	TRIFLE
bag closure	DRAWSTRING
baggage	LUGGAGE, SUITCASES, CASES, GRIPS, TRUNKS, VALISES
baggage handler	PORTER, BELL HOP
baggy	LOOSE
baggy knickers (2 wds.)	PLUS FOURS
bagpipe horn	DRONE
bail	SCOOP
bait	LURE
bake	COOK, ROAST
bake eggs	SHIRR
baker's dozen	THIRTEEN
baker's shovel	PEEL
bakery item	PIE, CAKE, CREAM PUFF, BREAD, ROLL, BUN, TART, DANISH, PASTRY, COOKIE

baking dish **RAMEKIN, SHEET, CASSEROLE**
baking ingredient **SODA, YEAST, FLOUR, SALT**
baking chamber **OVEN, OAST, KILN**
baking item **PIN, ROLLER**
baking pit **IMU, UMU**
baking soda **SALERATUS**
baking tin (2 wds.) **PIE PAN, CAKE PAN, COOKIE SHEET**
baksheesh **TIP, ALMS**
Balaam's mount **ASS**
balance **POISE**
balance-sheet loss **DEFICIT**
balance unsteadily **TEETER**
bald **HAIRLESS**
balderdash **NONSENSE**
bald head **PATE**
bale **BUNDLE**
Balearic island **MAJORCA**
baleful **EVIL, SINISTER, DIRE, HARMFUL, MALIGNANT**
balk **FOIL**
ball **DANCE**
ballad **SONG**
ballast **WEIGHT**
ballerina **DANCER**
ballerina's strong points **TOES**
ballet **DANCE**
ball of medicine **PILL**
ball of paper **WAD**
ball of yarn **CLEW**
ballot **VOTE, TICKET**
ballot caster **VOTER**
ball park events (2 wds.) **HOME RUN, DOUBLE PLAY, TRIPLE PLAY, BASE HIT, DOUBLE HEADER, LADY'S DAY, SHUTOUT**
ballroom dance **FOX TROT, RUMBA, SAMBA, WALTZ, TANGO, TWO STEP, CARIOCA, POLKA**
balls of fringe **TASSELS**
ball team **NINE**
ballyhoo **PUBLICITY**
balmy **MILD, INSANE**
balsam tree **FIR**
Baltic city **DANZIG**
Baltic port **RIGA**
Baltic river **ODER, NEVA, NARVA, NEMAN, DAL, VISTULA, UME, TORNE**
Baltimore **PORT**
Baltimore bird **ORIOLE**
balustrade **RAILING**
Bambi **DEER**

bambino **BABY**
Bambi's mother **DOE**
bamboolike grass **REEDS**
bamboo medicine **TABASHEER, TABASHIR**
bamboo stem **CANE**
bamboozle **HOAX**
ban **INTERDICTION, INTERDICT, PROHIBIT, PROHIBITION, FORBID, EXCOMMUNICATE**
banal **HACKNEYED, TRITE**
banana **PLANTAIN**
banana republic **HONDURAS**
band **ORCHESTRA, GROUP**
bandage **BIND, TOURNIQUET**
bandicoot **RAT**
band instrument **DRUM, SNARE DRUM, SAX, TUBA, FIFE, BUGLE, FLUTE, HORN**
bandit **OUTLAW, ROBBER**
bandleader **CONDUCTOR**
bandleader Arnaz **DESI**
bandleader Weems **TED**
bandleader's stick **BATON**
bandleader's wand **BATON**
bandy **CART**
bane **RUIN, HARM, WOE**
baneful **HARMFUL**
bang **BEAT, SLAM**
bang a door **SLAM**
banishment **EXILE**
banister **RAIL, RAILING**
bank **RIVERSIDE, MOUNT, RIDGE**
bank employee **TELLER, GUARD**
bank payment (abbr.) **INT**
bankrupt **RUIN**
bank safe **VAULT**
bank transaction **LOAN**
banner **FLAG**
banquet **FEAST, REPAST**
bantam car **JEEP**
banter **BADINAGE**
Bantu language **ILA**
baptismal vessel **FONT**
baptismal water **LAVER**
bar **COUNTER, STRIPE, TAVERN, INN**
barb **THORN**
barbarian **GOTH**
barbarous **CRUEL**
barbecue **COOKOUT**
barber's concern **HAIR, BEARD**
barber's tool **RAZOR, CLIPPER**
barb of feather **PINNULA, PINNULE**

bard	**MINSTREL, POET**
Bard's river	**AVON**
bare	**EMPTY, NUDE,**
	UNDECORATED, UNVEIL
barefaced	**IMPUDENT,**
	SHAMELESS
barely	**HARDLY**
barely audible	**FAINT**
bargain	**DICKER**
bargain basement event	**SALE**
barge	**SCOW, BOAT**
barge-load of eoal	**KEEL**
bar item	**ALE, BEER**
bark	**SKIN, YELP**
bark at	**BAY**
bark-like	**CORTEX**
barnyard bird	**ROOSTER,**
	GOOSE, HEN, DUCK,
	GANDER, CHICKEN
barnyard sound	**MOO, OINK,**
	CLUCK, BAA, MAA,
	QUACK, WHINNY, CROW
bar of metal	**INGOT**
bar of soap	**CAKE**
barometer line	**ISOBAR**
baronet's title	**SIR**
barracks	**CASERN**
barrage	**CANNONADE**
barranca	**RAVINE**
barrel	**KEG, CASK**
barrel band	**HOOP**
barrel organ	**HURDY-GURDY**
barrel section	**STAVE**
barrel stopper	**BUNG**
barren	**ARID, FRUITLESS,**
	CHILDLESS, DEVOID
barrier	**BAR, BLOCKADE**
barrier around a yard	**FENCE**
barrister's concern	**TRIAL,**
	BRIEF, CASE
barroom	**TAP**
barter	**SWAP, TRADE**
bartizan	**TURRET**
Bartlett	**PEAR**
Bartok	**BELA**
base	**FOUNDATION, FOUND**
baseball	**NATIONAL PASTIME**
baseball catcher	**BACKSTOP**
baseball club	**BAT, TEAM,**
	NINE
baseball coup	**NO-HITTER,**
	SHUTOUT, HOME RUN,
	TRIPLE PLAY, HOMER
baseballer Aaron	**HANK**
baseballer Agee	**TOMMY**
baseballer Berra	**YOGI**
baseballer DiMaggio	**JOE, DOM**
baseballer Gehrig	**LOU**

baseballer Hodges	**GIL**
baseballer Kaline	**AL**
baseballer Koufax	**SANDY**
baseballer Mantle	**MICKEY**
baseballer Maris	**ROGER**
baseballer Musial	**STAN**
baseballer Ott	**MEL**
baseballer Robinson	**JACK,**
	FRANK, BROOKS
baseballer Ruth	**BABE**
baseballer Seaver	**TOM**
baseballer Slaughter	**ENOS**
baseballer Williams	**TED**
baseball fan	**ROOTER**
baseball field	**DIAMOND**
baseball game	
divisions	**INNINGS**
baseball glove	**MITT**
baseball goal	**HOME**
baseball hit	**HOMER, DOUBLE,**
	TRIPLE, SINGLE
baseball nickname	**BABE,**
	LEFTY
baseball nine	**TEAM**
baseball official	**UMPIRE, UMP**
baseball player	**FIELDER,**
	PITCHER, SHORTSTOP,
	INFIELDER, OUTFIELDER,
	CATCHER, BATTER,
	CENTER FIELDER, RIGHT
	FIELDER
baseball position	**PLATE,**
	BASE, OUTFIELD,
	INFIELD, SECOND
	BASE, SHORTSTOP
baseball stick	**BAT, FUNGO**
baseball stopover point	**BASE**
baseball team number	**NINE**
based on	
experience	**EMPIRICAL**
base in Greenland	**ETAH**
baseman	**INFIELDER**
basement	**CELLAR**
base of leaf	**AXIL**
bashful	**COY, SHY, TIMID,**
	MODEST
basic	**FUNDAMENTAL**
basic food	**BREAD, RICE,**
	GRAIN, WHEAT
basin	**TANK, SINK, VESSEL**
basis	**GROUNDWORK, ROOT,**
	FOUNDATION
basis of argument	**PREMISE**
bask	**LUXURIATE**
basketball group (abbr.)	**N.B.A.**
basketball misplay	**FOUL**
basketball team	**FIVE**
basket twig	**WATTLE**

basket willow	**OSIER**
Basque game	**PELOTA**
Basque headwear	**BERET**
basslike marine fish	**SNAPPER**
basswood tree	**LINDEN**
bast	**FIBER**
baste	**HEM, SEW, MOISTEN**
bat	**HIT, CLUB**
bastion	**EPAULE**
bath	**SAUNA, TUB**
bathe	**LAVE, WASH**
bath house	**CABANA**
bathing place	**TUB**
bathrobe fabric	**TERRY**
bathroom fixture	**SHOWER, TUB, SINK**
Batman or Robin	**CRIMEFIGHTER**
baton	**STICK**
batter	**RAM, HITTER**
battery plate	**GRID**
battle	**DUEL, WAR, FRAY, FIGHT, MELEE**
Battle-Born State	**NEVADA**
battle memento	**SCAR**
battle with lances	**JOUST**
bauble	**PLAYTHING**
bauxite	**ORE, ALUMINUM**
bay	**COVE, INLET, TREE**
bay bird	**SNIPE, PLOVER**
bayou	**CREEK, ESTUARY**
Bay State	**MASSACHUSETTS**
bay tree	**LAUREL**
bay window	**ORIEL**
bazaar	**FAIR**
bazaar stall	**BOOTH**
be	**EXIST**
beach	**SHORE, STRAND, SEASIDE, PLAYA**
beach feature	**DUNE, SAND**
beacon	**LIGHT**
be adjacent to	**ABUT**
beadle	**USHER**
be afraid	**FEAR**
be agitated	**SEETHE**
be agreeable to	**PLEASE**
beak	**NIB, BILL**
beaker	**CUP**
beam	**EMIT, GIRDER**
be a match for	**COPE**
be ambitious	**ASPIRE**
be a member	**BELONG**
beam of light	**RAY**
bean	**LIMA, SOY**
bear	**CARRY, GRIZZLY, SUPPORT, KOALA, POLAR TOLERATE, STAND, SUFFER, ABIDE, YIELD**
bear (Lat.)	**URSUS, URSA**
bear cat	**PANDA**
beard of grain	**AWN**
bearded titmouse	**REEDLING**
bearing	**MIEN, PRESENCE**
bearlike	**URSINE**
bearlike animal	**PANDA**
bear's home	**DEN**
bear up under	**TOLERATE**
bear witness to	**ATTEST**
beast	**ANIMAL, BRUTE**
beastly	**BRUTAL, CRUEL**
beast of burden	**ASS, CAMEL, HORSE, OX, MULE, BURRO. LLAMA, ELEPHANT**
beast's stomach	**MAW**
beat	**POUND, TEMPO, RHYTHM, WHIP, THROB, PULSE, PULSATE**
beat back	**REPULSE**
beaten way	**PATH**
beatitude	**JOY, HAPPINESS**
Beatles' drummer	**RINGO**
Beatles' movie	**HELP, HARD DAY'S NIGHT, YELLOW SUBMARINE, LET IT BE**
beatnik's abode	**PAD**
beau	**ESCORT, LOVER, ADMIRER**
beautiful	**FAIR, LOVELY, PRETTY**
beautify	**ADORN**
beauty	**GRACE**
beauty aid	**CURLER, WIG, COSMETIC**
beauty of movement	**GRACE**
beauty preparation	**COSMETIC**
beauty shop	**SALON, PARLOR**
beauty spot	**MOLE**
beaver skin	**PELT, PLEW**
Beaver State	**OREGON**
be beholden to	**OWE**
be careful of	**BEWARE**
because	**FOR, SINCE, AS**
be chief feature of	**DOMINATE, STAR**
beck	**BIDDING**
beckon	**MOTION, WAVE**
be clothed in	**WEAR**
becloud	**DARKEN, CONFUSE**
become a Benedict	**WED**
become accustomed	**INURE, ENURE**
become adept in	**MASTER**
become a nun	**TAKE THE VEIL**
become apparent	**EMERGE**
become a tenant	**RENT**

become aware of	SENSE
become bankrupt	FAIL
become better	IMPROVE
become buoyant	FLOAT, LEVITATE
become covered with fungus	MILDEW
become crooked	BEND
become curved	BEND
become depressed	DESPOND
become different	ALTER
become dirty	SOIL
become drowsy	NOD
become entangled	MAT
become faded	PALE
become firm	GEL, SET
become fond of	TAKE TO
become formed	TAKE SHAPE
become frayed	WEAR
become furious	RAGE
become ill	AIL
become indistinct	BLUR
become insipid	PALL
become insufficient	RUN SHORT
become less	ABATE
become less stern	RELENT
become lively	PERK
become manifest	EMERGE
become mature	RIPEN, AGE
become mellow	AGE, RIPEN
become more genial	THAW
become more profound	DEEPEN
become morose	SOUR
become old	AGE
become one	MERGE
become overcast	DIM
become oxidized	RUST
become reconciled	MAKE UP
become ripe	MATURE
become smaller	DWINDLE
become sound	HEAL
become sour	TART
become stale	STAGNATE
become submerged	SINK
become thin with use	WEAR
become twisted	GNARL
become unwoven	RAVEL
become very cold	FREEZE
become visible	APPEAR
become void	LAPSE
become weary	TIRE
become worn	FRAY
become zealous	ENTHUSE
becoming	FIT, PROPER
be compelled	MUST
be concerned	CARE
be contiguous	ABUT

be correct size	FIT
bed	COT, FOUR POSTER, COUCH, BUNK, BERTH, CHAISE
bed and board	HOME
bedaub	SMEAR, SOIL
bedaze	STUN
bed board	SLAT
bed cover	BLANKET, SPREAD, QUILT, COMFORTER, SHEET, COVERLET
bedding	LINEN
bedeck	ADORN
be deeply affected by	TAKE TO HEART
be defeated	LOSE
be deficient	FALL SHORT, LACK
bedevil	HARASS, CONFUSE
bedim	CLOUD
bedlam	MADHOUSE
Bedlington	TERRIER
bed of flowers	GARDEN
bed of straw	PALLET
Bedouin	ARAB
bedroom	CHAMBER
bedroom furniture	DRESSER, VANITY, BUREAU, NIGHTSTAND
bedroom shoe	SLIPPER, MULE
bedside light	LAMP
bedspread material	CHENILLE
be dull	BORE
bee	APIS
beech	TREE
beef	MEAT
beef animal	STEER
beef cattle	LONGHORN
beef fat	SUET
Beehive State	UTAH
beekeeper	APIARIST
beelzebub	DEVIL, SATAN
beep	HONK
bee product	HONEY
be enough	DO, SUFFICE
be equal	TIE
beer	LAGER, PILSNER, BREW, SUDS
beer barrel	CASK, KEG
beer cask	BUTT
beer glass	STEIN, MUG
beer ingredient	HOPS, MALT, YEAST
beerlike drink	ALE, STOUT, PORTER
beer maker	BREWER
beer mug	STEIN
bee's home	HIVE
beet	CHARD, SUGAR

beet genus	**BETA**
beetle	**DOR**
beetleheaded	**STUPID**
beetlenut palm	**ARECA**
befall	**BETIDE, HAPPEN**
be festive	**REVEL**
be finical	**FUSS**
before (Lat.)	**ANTE**
before (poet.)	**ERE**
before (prefix)	**PRE**
before all others	**FIRST**
before birth	**PRENATAL**
before deductions	**NET**
beforehand	**IN ADVANCE, AHEAD**
before long	**ANON, SOON**
before noon (abbr.)	**AM**
before this	**ERE, SINCE**
beforetime	**FORMERLY**
befoul	**SOIL**
befriend	**ASSIST, ABET**
befuddle	**CONFUSE**
befuddled	**ASEA, IN A FOG, AT SEA, CONFUSED, MUDDLED**
beg	**PLEAD, ENTREAT, IMPLORE, CADGE, SPONGE, MOOCH, BESEECH**
beget	**PRODUCE, PROCREATE**
begetter	**PARENT**
beggar	**MENDICANT, BUM, PANHANDLER, PAUPER**
beggarly	**MEAN, INDIGENT**
begin	**OPEN, START, SET OUT, FALL TO**
begin a battle	**ATTACK**
begin a day	**RISE, AWAKEN**
begin again	**RENEW, REOPEN**
begin an ocean voyage	**SAIL, EMBARK**
begin eating	**DIG IN**
beginner	**STARTER, TIRO, TYRO, NOVICE, GREENHORN, TENDERFOOT, NEOPHYTE, FRESHMAN**
beginning	**ONSET, NASCENT, EMERGING, ROOT, START**
beginning of day	**DAWN, SUNRISE**
beginning of flight	**TAKEOFF**
beginning of marriage	**HONEYMOON**
beginning of social career	**DEBUT**
beginning socialite	**DEB**

beginning worker	**APPRENTICE, TRAINEE**
begin to develop	**BUD**
begin war	**ATTACK**
begird	**SURROUND**
begone	**SHOO, SCAT, GO, LEAVE, BEAT IT, VAMOOSE**
begonia	**FLOWER**
begrime	**SOIL**
begrudge	**ENVY**
beguile	**DECEIVE, CHEAT, DELUDE**
beguiled	**AMUSED**
beguine	**DANCE**
behalf	**PART, SUPPORT**
behalf of	**FOR**
behave	**ACT**
behave badly	**MISBEHAVE**
behave childishly	**CRY**
behave foolishly	**CARRY ON**
behave menacingly	**THREATEN, FRIGHTEN**
behave theatrically	**EMOTE**
behave with dignity	**ACT ONE'S AGE**
behavior	**COMPORTMENT, DEPORTMENT, MANNER**
behest	**COMMAND**
behind	**AFTER, LATE, SLOW**
behind a ship	**ASTERN**
behind in payments	**IN ARREARS**
behind the curtain	**BACKSTAGE**
behold	**LO**
behold (Lat.)	**ECCE**
beige	**TAN, ECRU**
be ill	**AIL**
be imminent	**IMPEND**
be in a fury	**RAGE**
be in command	**LEAD**
be in contact	**TOUCH**
be in debt	**OWE**
be indignant	**RESENT**
being	**ESSENCE, EXISTENCE**
being (Fr.)	**ETRE**
being (Lat.)	**ESSE**
being broadcast	**ON THE AIR**
being in a fairy tale	**OGRE**
being from Aladdin's lamp	**GENIE**
be in harmony	**AGREE**
be in store for	**AWAIT**
be interested	**CARE**
be irritated	**FRET**
be kept waiting	**COOL ONE'S HEELS**
belabor	**ASSAIL**
beldam	**HAG**

belfry **TOWER**
Belgian capital **BRUSSELS**
Belgian port **OSTEND, ANTWERP**
belie **DENY**
belief **CREDO, CREDENCE, CREED, RELIGION, FAITH**
believe **OPINE, THINK, JUDGE**
believer (suffix) **IST**
believer in facts **REALIST**
believer in God **THEIST**
belittle **DISPARAGE**
bell **CHIME, GONG**
bellicose **WARLIKE**
belligerent **HOSTILE**
bellow **ROAR**
bell-shaped flower **TULIP**
bell-shaped hat **CLOCHE**
bell sound **BONG, TINKLE, DING, GONG, PEAL, TOLL, CHIME**
bell tower **BELFRY, CAMPANILE**
be lofty **TOWER**
belonging to him **HIS**
belonging to me **MINE**
belonging to the thing **ITS**
belonging to us **OUR, OURS**
belongings **PROPERTY**
beloved **DEAR**
beloved Disciple **JOHN**
below **BENEATH, UNDER, UNDERNEATH**
below key **FLAT**
belt **STRAP, BAND**
belt fastener **BUCKLE**
belt of calm **DOLDRUMS**
beluga **CAVIAR**
be made up of **CONSIST**
be master of **POSSESS**
be merciful **SPARE**
be mistaken **ERR**
bemoan **LAMENT**
be moodily silent **SULK**
bemuse **DAZE**
Ben Cartwright's boy **HOSS, JOE**
bench **SEAT, PEW, CHAIR**
bend **CURVE**
bend down **STOOP**
bend downward **SAG**
bender **SPREE**
bend low **CROUCH**
bend over **STOOP**
bend the head **BOW**
be near **STAND BY**
beneath **BELOW, UNDER, UNDERNEATH**

beneath the earth **UNDERGROUND**
benediction **BLESSING, PRAYER**
benefactor **HELPER, PATRON**
beneficial **USEFUL**
beneficiary of a will **HEIR**
benefit **STEAD**
benevolence **KINDNESS**
Bengal capitol **CALCUTTA**
Bengal cat **TIGER**
bent pipe **SIPHON**
bent to one side **WRY**
be obedient **BEHAVE**
be of consequence **MATTER**
be of importance **MATTER**
be of one mind **AGREE**
be of the opinion **BELIEVE**
be of use **AVAIL**
be on fire **BURN**
be on one's feet **STAND**
be overly fond **DOTE**
be present **ATTEND**
be quiet **SH**
berate **NAG, SCOLD**
Berber **ARAB**
be ready for **AWAIT**
be reluctant **BALK**
beret **CAP**
be revived **COME TO**
Berliner **GERMAN**
Berlin's divider **WALL**
Bernstein, for short **LEN**
berry **CURRANT**
beseech **BEG, ENTREAT, PLEAD, IMPLORE**
be sensitive to **FEEL**
beset **ATTACK, BESIEGE**
be sick **AIL**
beside (prefix) **PARA, PAR**
besides **ALSO, ELSE, TO BOOT, TOO**
besiege **BESET, ATTACK**
be situated **LIE, SIT, SETTLED**
besmear **SOIL**
besom **BROOM**
be sorry for **PITY**
be sparing **STINT**
bespatter **DAUB. SPLASH**
best **OUTSTRIP, BEAT, OUT-DO, GREATEST, LARGEST**
bestial **BRUTAL. CRUEL**
bestow **GRANT, AWARD, GIVE**
be successful **GO FAR**
be sufficient **AMPLE, DO**
be suitable **FIT**
bet **WAGER**

betel palm	ARECA
betray	SELL
betrayal	TREASON
be sparing	STINT
be undecided	WAVER
be unsuccessful	FAIL
be victorious	WIN
be without	LACK
be worthy of	DESERVE
be wrong	ERR
beach	SHORE, STRAND, SEASIDE, PLAYA
beach feature	DUNE, SAND
betrothed	ENGAGED
better balanced	SANER
betting factor	ODDS
betting method	PARLAY
betting odds	PRICE
between (Fr.)	ENTRE
between (prefix)	INTER
bevel	SLANT
bevel corners	SPLAY
beverage	TEA, ALE, BEER, COFFEE, MILK, SODA, WINE
beverage container	TEAPOT, GLASS, TUMBLER, BOTTLE, CARTON, CAN, FLASK, PITCHER, CUP
beverage glasses	STEMWARE, TUMBLERS
bevy	FLOCK
bewail	LAMENT, MOAN
bewildered	AT SEA, ASEA, BEFUDDLED, LOST, CONFUSED
bewitch	CHARM
beyond	YONDER, ABOVE
beyond control	OUT OF HAND
beyond the limit	OUT
bias	SLANT, PREJUDICE
bias binding	TAPE
bib	TUCKER
Biblical angel	RAPHAEL, GABRIEL, MICHAEL
Biblical boat	ARK
Biblical brother	ABEL, CAIN, JOSEPH, ESAU, JACOB, REUBEN, SIMEON, BENJAMIN. JUDAH
Biblical character	LOT, ARA, IRA, ABEL, JOAB, JOB, AMOS, MICAH, MOSES, AARON, ZADOK, ELI, BOAZ
Biblical dancer	SALOME
Biblical garden	EDEN, GETHSEMANE
Biblical hero	NOAH
Biblical king	ASA, HEROD, HIRAM, DAVID, SOLOMON, SAUL, JOSIAH, AHAB, OMRI, HEZEKIAH, JEHORAM, AHAZ, ELAH
Biblical land	OPHIR, ELAM, MOAB, CANAAN, EGYPT
Biblical liar	ANANIAS
Biblical measure	OMER
Biblical mountain	ARARAT, SINAI, CARMEL, JARMAK, EBAL, THABOR, NEBO, GARIZIM, LEBANON
Biblical name of Syria	ARAM
Biblical passage	TEXT
Biblical Patriarch	MOSES, NOAH
Biblical preposition	UNTO
Biblical pronoun	THY, THOU, THINE
Biblical plotter	HAMAN
Biblical priest	AARON, LEVI, SADOC
Biblical prophet	HOSEA, AMOS, MICAH. ISAIA, DANIEL, OSEE, JOEL, ABDIA, JONAH, NAHUM, HABACUC, ELIA
Biblical story	PARABLE
Biblical strong man	SAMSON
Biblical tower	BABEL
Biblical town	CANA, LOD, HEBRON
Biblical tribe	ANAK, LEVI, DAN
Biblical vessel	ARK
Biblical weed	TARE
Biblical witch's home	ENDOR
Biblical word	SELAH
bicker	ARGUE
bicuspid	TOOTH
bicycle for two	TANDEM
bicycle part	PEDAL
bid	OFFER, COMMAND
biddy	HEN
bide	TARRY, WAIT
big	LARGE, HUGE, IMMENSE, VAST, MAMMOTH, GIANT, GIGANTIC, COLOSSAL
big and strong	BURLY
Big Bend State	TENNESSEE
big book	TOME
big boy	MAN
big bundle	BALE
big coffee pot	URN
big deer	ELK
bigeye	FISH
big girl	WOMAN
big house	PRISON, PEN
big leaguer	PRO

big man	**TITAN, GIANT**
big monkey	**APE, GORILLA,**
	ORANGUTAN
big name in golf	**PALMER,**
SNEAD, HOGAN, CASPER,	
BEARD, NICKLAUS, WOOD	
bigoted	**NARROW**
bigotry	**PREJUDICE**
big top	**TENT**
bijou	**JEWEL, GEM**
bile	**CHOLER, ANGER**
bilk	**CHEAT, SWINDLE**
bill	**NIB, BEAK, INVOICE,**
TARIFF, CHECK, NEB	
billabong	**LAGOON**
billboard	**SIGN, POSTER**
billiard shot	**CAROM, MASSE,**
BANK, BREAK, DRAW, KISS	
billiard stick	**CUE**
billiards	**POOL**
bill of fare	**MENU**
bill of lading (abbr.)	**BL**
billow	**SURGE, WAVE**
billowy expanse	**OCEAN, SEA**
billy	**CLUB**
billy or nanny	**GOAT**
bin	**CRIB. BOX**
binary	**DOUBLE, DUAL,**
	TWOFOLD
bind	**TIE, LASH, BANDAGE**
bind closely	**ALLY, TIE**
binding custom	**LAW**
bind up	**GIRD, TRUSS**
binge	**SPREE, TOOT**
bingo	**GAME**
biographer Ludwig	**EMIL**
biography	**LIFE**
biological classification	**GENUS**
biological determinant	**GENE**
birchbark boat	**CANOE**
bird	**AUK, FINCH, ORIOLE,**
SERIN, TERN, CANARY, OWL,	
SPARROW, SWALLOW,	
SWAN, RAVEN, PARROT,	
PARAKEET, WREN, HAWK,	
CROW. EAGLE, DOVE,	
CHICKADEE, BLUEJAY,	
CARDINAL, GROSBEAK,	
REDPOL, BUZZARD,	
OSPREY, VULTURE, ERNE,	
ALBATROSS, PIGEON, LOON,	
QUAIL, GROUSE, PENGUIN,	
PETREL, BOOBIE, FALCON,	
STORK, SWIFT. GULL,	
DODO, THRUSH	
bird (Lat.)	**AVIS**
bird (prefix)	**AVI**
bird call	**NOTE, TWEET, SONG,**
	TRILL, CHIRP, TWEE
bird clapper	**SCARECROW**
bird class	**AVES**
bird claw	**TALON**
bird enclosure	**CAGE**
bird feed	**SUET, SEED**
bird home	**NEST, AVIARY**
bird keeper	**AVIARIST**
bird of Jove	**EAGLE**
bird of peace	**DOVE**
bird of prey	**EAGLE, HAWK,**
	KITE, OWL, FALCON,
	BUZZARD, VULTURE
bird's arm	**WING**
bird's beak	**BILL, NEB**
bird's crop	**CRAW**
bird's flapper	**WING**
bird's food	**SEED**
bird's home	**NEST, AERIE**
bird's perch	**ROOST**
bireme	**GALLEY, SHIP**
birth	**ORIGIN**
birthday figure	**AGE**
birthmark	**NEVUS, MOLE**
birthright	**HERITAGE**
birthstone for April	**DIAMOND**
birthstone for August	**PERIDOT**
birthstone for	
December	**TURQUOISE**
birthstone for	
February	**AMETHYST**
birthstone for January	**GARNET**
birthstone for July	**RUBY**
birthstone for June	**PEARL**
birthstone for	
March	**AQUAMARINE**
birthstone for May	**EMERALD**
birthstone for November	**TOPAZ**
birthstone for October	**OPAL**
birthstone for	
September	**SAPPHIRE**
bis	**TWICE**
biscuit	**BUN**
bisect	**HALVE**
bishop	**PRELATE**
bishopric	**SEE**
bishop's hat	**MITRE**
bishop's throne	**SEE**
bison	**BUFFALO**
bisque	**SOUP**
bistro	**BAR**
bit	**MORSEL. SCRAP**
bite	**MOUTHFUL, NIBBLE,**
	GNAW, NIP, SNAP,
	STING, TANG, CHEW
bite impatiently	**CHAMP**
bite off	**GNAW**
biting	**ACRID, CAUSTIC**

bit of floating dust	MOTE	blast	EXPLOSION
bit of news	ITEM	blast of wind	GUST
bits of fluff	LINT	blaze	FLAME, FLARE, FIRE,
bitter	ACRID		CUT, FLASH
bitter nut	KOLA	blaze brightly	FLARE
bitter vetch	ERS	blazing	AFIRE
bivalve	CLAM, MUSSEL	bleak	DESOLATE
bivouac	CAMP, ENCAMP	bleat	BAA, MAA
bizarre	OUTRE, ODD	blemish	SCAR, SPOT, FLAW,
Bizet opera	CARMEN		DEFECT
blab	TELL, TATTLE	blend	MERGE, MIX
black	EBON, EBONY	bless	HALLOW
black and blue	LIVID	blessed	BLEST, HALLOWED,
black art	MAGIC		SAINT
black-backed gull	COB(B)	blessing	BOON, GRACE,
Black Beauty	HORSE		BENEDICTION
black bird	ANI, CROW, DAW,	blessing (arch.)	BENISON
	RAVEN, GRACKLE, MERLE	blimp	BALLOON, DIRIGIBLE
blackboard	SLATE	blind fear	PANIC
black bread	RYE	blink	WINK
black buck	SASIN	blithe	MERRY, GAY
black dairy cow	KERRY	blockade	SIEGE
black death	PLAGUE	blockhead	ASS, DOLT, DOPE,
black diamond	COAL		OAF, FOOL, DUNCE
blacken	CHAR	bloke	CHAP
black eye	SHINER	blond	GOLDEN, FAIR,
black face	MINSTREL		FLAXEN
blackface music		blood-building meat	LIVER
show	MINSTREL	blood deficiency	ANEMIA
blackfin	FISH, SNAPPER	blood fluid	PLASMA
black flag	JOLLY ROGER	blood giver	DONER
black fuel	COAL	blood (prefix)	HEMO, HEMA,
black gold	OIL		HEM
blackguard	SCOUNDREL	blooper	ERROR, BLUNDER
black hole	CELL, BRIG	blossom	BLOOM, FLOWER
black lacquer	JAPAN	blot	SPOT, STAIN
black leg (Brit.)	SCAB	blot out	ERASE
black magic	WITCHCRAFT	blouse	WAIST
blackmail	EXTORT	blouse ruffle	JABOT
black mark	DEMERIT	blow	HIT, STROKE
Blackmore heroine	LORNA	blow a horn	TOOT, HONK
blacksmith shop	FORGE	blow hard	BRAGGART
black snake	RACER	blue	AZURE, INDIGO, SAD,
black tea	BOHEA		MOPEY
blackthorn fruit	SLOE	blue dye	ANIL
black-tongued dog	CHOW	blue fin	TUNA
blacktop	PAVE	blue flag	IRIS
black widow	SPIDER	Bluegrass State	KENTUCKY
black wood	EBONY	blue jeans material	DENIM
blade	SWORD, KNIFE, DIRK	Blue Law State	CONNECTICUT
blade bone	SCAPULA	blue or white	
blame	ACCUSE, CENSURE	bird	GREAT HERON
blameless	INNOCENT	blue-pencil	EDIT
blanch	ETIOLATE, WHITEN	blue pigment	BICE, SMALT
blanched	PALE, WHITE	Blue Point	OYSTER
blank	VOID, EMPTY	blue pottery	DELFT
blank book	TABLET	blueprint	PLAN
blase	BORED, JADED	blue-white star in Lyra	VEGA

bluff	GRUFF, RUDE, HOODWINK
bluish gray	SLATE
bluish-white metal	ZINC
blunder	ERR, MISTAKE, ERROR, SNAFU
blunt	DULL
blur	DIM, OBSCURE
blurt out	BLAT, BLAB
blush	REDDEN
blushing	ROSY
boa	SERPENT, SNAKE, PYTHON, SCARF
boar	PIG
board	PLANK
boarder	ROOMER
boardinghouse fare	HASH
boarhound	GREAT DANE
boast	BLOW, BRAG
boat	CANOE, SHIP, VESSEL
boat basin	MARINA
boat paddle	OAR
boat ride	SAIL
boat rope	HAWSER, LINE
boat's company	CREW
boat side	GUNWALE
boat's radio	SHIP-TO-SHORE
boat's power source	OUTBOARD MOTOR
boat trip	SAIL, CRUISE
bobble	ERR, BUNGLE, MISS, FUMBLE
bobwhite	QUAIL
bodice	WAIST
body	TORSO, TRUNK
body builders	LIFTS, WEIGHTS
body height	STATURE
body injuries	LESIONS
body limb	LEG, ARM
body of advisers	CABINET, BOARD
body of police	POSSE
body of ship	HULL
body of soldiers	REGIMENT
body of students	CLASS
body of water	BAY, LAKE, SEA, OCEAN, POND, RIVER, STREAM, CREEK
Boer	AFRIKANER
boff	JOKE
bog	MORASS, FEN, MARSH, SWAMP, MIRE
bog down	MIRE, SLOW, IMPEDE, HINDER
bogus	SHAM, ERSATZ
Bohemian	ARTY
Bohemian city	PRAGUE
Bohemian reformer	HUSS

boil	STEW, SIMMER, SEETHE
boil down	CONDENSE, REDUCE
bold	PERT, DARING, SASSY, NERVY, CHEEKY, BRAVE, VENTURESOME
boldness	COURAGE, DARING
bolero	DANCE, JACKET
Bolivian mountains	ANDES
Bolshevik	LENIN, TROTSKY
bolster	PILLOW
bombastic speech	HARANGUE
bond	TIE, BAIL
bondage	SLAVERY
bondsman	SLAVE
bone	OS
boneblack	CHARCOAL
bone-dry	ARID
boner	BLUNDER
bone structure	SKELETON
bongo	DRUM
bonito	ALBACORE
bonnet	HAT, TOQUE
boo	HISS
boob	SAP, DOPE, FOOL, DOLT
book	FOLIO, TOME
bookbinding leather	ROAN
book cover	BINDING
bookish	STODGY
bookkeeper's entry	DEBIT, CREDIT
bookkeeping term	ENTRY, POST
book (Lat.)	LIBER
book leaf	PAGE
book of a poem	CANTO
book of fiction	NOVEL
book of maps	ATLAS
book of Norse myths	EDDA
book of photographs	ALBUM
book page	FOLIO, LEAF
book part	PAGE, CHAPTER, LEAF, SPINE
boom	SPAR
boon	BLESSING, FAVOR
Boone	DANIEL, DANL
boorish	RUDE
boost	LIFT
booster	FAN
boot	KICK
bootblack's specialty	SHINE
booth	LOGE, SEAT, ETALL
booty	LOOT, SPOILS
bop	HIT, PUNCH
Bordeaux wine	CLARET, MEDOC, GRAVES, SAUTERNE
border	EDGE, RIM, HEM, MARGIN, SELVAGE

bordering tool	**EDGER**
border on	**ABUT**
border saloon	**CANTINA**
bore	**DRILL, TIRE, EAGRE**
bore into	**TAP**
bore witness	**ATTESTED**
boreal	**NORTHERN**
boredom	**ENNUI, TEDIUM**
boring	**TEDIOUS**
boring tool	**BRACE AND BIT, AUGER, DRILL**
born	**NEE**
Borneo ape	**ORANG**
borough	**BURG**
borrow dishonestly	**CADGE, PLAGERIZE**
borrow money on	**PAWN**
Bosc	**PEAR**
bosom	**BREAST**
bossy	**COW**
botch	**BUNGLE, MESS**
both	**TWO**
bother	**AIL, ANNOY, PESTER**
bottle	**FLASK**
bottle cap	**LID**
bottle cap remover	**OPENER**
bottle dweller	**GENIE**
bottle part	**NECK**
bottle sealer	**CAP, CORK**
bottle-shaped container	**FLASK**
bottle stopper	**CORK**
bottle top	**CAP**
bottom	**BASE**
bottomless	**DEEP, ENDLESS**
bottomless pit	**HELL**
bottom out	**LEVEL**
bottom surface	**BED, FLOOR**
bottom support of a column	**PEDESTAL**
bough	**BRANCH**
boulevard	**STREET, AVENUE, ROAD**
bouillon	**BROTH, STOCK**
boulder	**ROCK**
bounce	**DAP, REBOUND**
bound	**TIED, DESTINED**
boundary	**LIMIT, LINE, BORDER**
boundary line	**FENCE**
bounder	**CAD, ROUE, LOUT**
boundless	**ENDLESS, LIMITLESS**
bounteous	**AMPLE, PLENTIFUL**
bountiful	**PLENTIFUL, ABUNDANT**
bounty	**REWARD**
bouquet	**AROMA, CORSAGE, ODOR, POSY, NOSEGAY**

bourbon	**WHISKEY, CORN MASH**
bout	**PRIZEFIGHT, MATCH, SPELL**
boutonniere	**FLOWER, CARNATION**
boutonniere location	**LAPEL**
boutique	**SHOP**
bouzouki	**MANDOLIN**
bovine animal	**STEER, OX, COW, BULL**
bovine sound	**LOW, MOO**
bow	**KNOT, CURTSY, STOOP**
bowed	**BENT**
bower	**ARBOR**
bowfin	**AMIA**
bowie	**KNIFE**
bowl	**BASIN**
bowler	**HAT, DERBY**
bowlike curved line	**ARC**
bowline	**KNOT**
bowling alley	**LANE, GREEN**
bowling norm	**AVERAGE**
bowling piece	**PIN**
bowling place	**ALLEY, GREEN**
bowling term	**SPARE, STRIKE**
bowling target	**PIN, TENPIN**
bowman	**ARCHER**
bow of a ship	**PROW**
bowsprit	**BOOM, SPAR**
box	**CASE, CRATE, CARTON, FIGHT, SPAR, LOGE**
boxberry	**WINTERGREEN**
boxcars	**TWELVE**
box cautiously	**SPAR**
boxer Baer	**MAX**
boxer Clay	**CASSIUS**
boxer Palooka	**JOE**
boxer Patterson	**FLOYD**
boxer's nickname	**CHAMP**
box for alms	**ARCA**
box for coal	**BIN**
boxing blow	**JAB, HOOK, KO, KNOCKOUT, KAYO, CROSS**
boxing contest	**BOUT**
boxing coup	**KO, KAYO, KNOCKOUT**
boxing ring	**ARENA**
boxing strategy	**ONE-TWO**
box-of-evils op'ener	**PANDORA**
box supper	**SOCIAL**
box top	**LID**
box up	**CONFINE**
boy	**LAD, SON, MALE, TAD**
boycott	**BLOCK**
boyfriend	**BEAU**

boyhood **YOUTH**
boys and girls **CHILDREN**
boy's book author **ALGER**
Boy Scout **CUB, EAGLE**
Boy Scout activity **HIKE**
Boy Scout group **TROOP**
boy's plaything **TOY SOLDIER, CAP GUN, FOOTBALL, BASEBALL**
bozo **GUY, FELLOW**
BPOE member **ELK**
brace **PAIR, TWOSOME, SUPPORT, COUPLE**
bracer **TONIC**
bracing **CRISP**
bracket candlestick **SCONCE**
brackish **SALTY, BRINY**
brad **NAIL**
brag **BOAST**
Brahman **PUNDIT, AYA**
braid **PLAIT**
brain **MIND**
brainless **STUPID**
brainstorm **IDEA**
brainwash **CONDITION, CONVINCE**
brainy **SMART**
braise **COOK**
brake **STOP**
bran **CEREAL**
branch **ARM, BOUGH**
branch (biol.) **RAMUS**
branches of learning **ARTS**
branch of the armed forces **MARINES, NAVY, ARMY, AIR FORCE, COAST GUARD, NATIONAL GUARD**
branch off **FORK**
brand **MARK, TRADEMARK**
brandish **SHAKE, WAVE**
brass hat **GENERAL**
brass instrument **BUGLE, CORNET, TUBA, TRUMPET, TROMBONE**
brassy **BOLD**
brave **DARING, COURAGEOUS, INDIAN**
brave man **HERO**
bravery **COURAGE**
brawl **FIGHT, MELEE**
Brazilian dance **SAMBA**
Brazilian export **RUBBER**
Brazilian parrot **ARA**
Brazilian port **BELEM, RIO, NATAL, CEARA**
Brazilian river **AMAZON**
Brazilian rubber tree **SERINGA**
breach **CHASM, GAP**

breadbasket **STOMACH**
bread cakes **ROLLS, MUFFINS**
bread crust **RIND**
bread made of corn meal **PONE**
breadmaking ingredient **YEAST**
bread spread **OLEO, BUTTER, MARGARINE, JELLY, JAM, CURD, MUSTARD, MAYONNAISE**
breadwinner **DAD, PAPA, FATHER, POP**
breadwinning ability **EARNING POWER**
break **SMASH, SPLIT, SHATTER**
breakable **FRAGILE**
break asunder **DISRUPT**
breakdown in law and order **ANARCHY**
breakers **SURF, WAVES**
breakfast **MEAL**
breakfast bread **ROLLS, BUN, SCONE, COFFEE CAKE**
breakfast food **CEREAL, BACON, EGGS, PANCAKE, HOTCAKE, WAFFLE, HAM, OMELET, GRITS, OATMEAL**
breakfast fruit juice **ORANGE, GRAPEFRUIT**
breakfast sweet (2 wds.) **COFFEE CAKE**
break in two **SNAP**
break into many pieces **SHATTER**
break of day **DAWN, SUNRISE**
break out **ERUPT**
break ranks **DISBAND**
break rules **DISOBEY**
break short **SNAP**
break suddenly **BURST, SNAP**
break the seal **OPEN**
break up **SEPARATE, DISPERSE**
breakwater **PIER, JETTY**
breast **BOSOM**
breastbone **STERNUM**
breathe **RESPIRE, INHALE**
breathe hard **PANT, GASP, WHEEZE**
breathe one's last **DIE, EXPIRE**
breathe spasmodically **SIGH**
breathing **ALIVE**
breathing organ **LUNG**
bred **ENGENDERED, RAISED, REARED**
breeches **TROUSERS**
breed **CLASS**
breed of cat **SIAMESE, PERSIAN**

breed of dog **SETTER, POODLE, SPANIEL, PUG, SCHNAUZER, TERRIER, SCOTTIE, WHIPPET, CHOW, SAMOYED, COLLIE, SHEPHERD**

breed of horse **ARAB, BARB, THOROUGHBRED, CLYDESDALE, MORGAN, SHIRE**

breeze **WIND, ZEPHYR**
breezy **AIRY**
breezy farewell **TATA**
Breton **CELT**
brew **STEEP**
brick carrier **HOD**
bricklayer **MASON**
brick red **SARAVAN**
bridal attendant **MAID OF HONOR**
bridegroom's attendant **BEST MAN, USHER**
bride's mate **GROOM**
bride's portion **DOWERY**
bridge **SPAN**
bridge (Fr.) **PONT**
bridge expert **GOREN**
bridge play **SLAM**
bridge score **GAME**
bridge strategy **FINESSE**
bridge structure **ARCH**
bridle **HALTER, HARNESS**
bridle part **BIT, REIN, HEADSTALL**
brief **SHORT**
brief and compact **CONCISE**
brief excerpt **SCRAP**
brief in speech **CURT, TERSE**
brief look **GLIMPSE, GLANCE**
briefly brilliant star **NOVA**
brief news statement **BULLETIN**
brief outline **SKETCH**
brief preface **PROEM**
brief swim **DIP**
brier **THORN**
brig **BOAT**
brigand **PIRATE, THIEF**
bright **SHINY, BRILLIANT**
bright but cheap **TINNY**
bright color **RED, CRIMSON, SCARLET, YELLOW, GOLD, CORAL**
brighten **CLEAR UP, LIGHT UP**
brightly colored bird **ORIOLE, PEACOCK**
bright person **BRAIN, GENIUS**
bright planet **EVENING STAR, VENUS**

brilliance **ELAN, LUSTER, SHINE, GLOW**
brilliance of success **ECLAT**
brilliant **BRIGHT, VIVID**
brilliant Asian pheasant **TRAGOPAN**
brilliant fish **OPAH**
brilliant planet **VENUS**
brim **EDGE, RIM**
brimless hat **CAP**
bring **CARRY, FETCH**
bring about **CAUSE**
bring back **RESTORE, RETURN**
bring forth **EDUCE**
bring into existence **CREATE, GENERATE, CONCEIVE**
bring into line **ALINE, ALIGN**
bring into play **USE**
bring legal action **SUE**
bring out **ELICIT, EDUCE, EVOKE**
bring out into the open **AIR, REVEAL**
bring to a finish **GO THROUGH WITH, END, CLOSE, FINALIZE, CONCLUDE**
bring to an end **CLOSE**
bring to bay **TREE, CORNER, TRAP**
bring to earth **LAND**
bring to life **RENEW**
bring to light **DETECT, PUBLICIZE**
bring to completion **FINISH, END**
bring together **UNITE**
bring to memory **REMIND**
bring to mind **RECALL**
bring to ruin **UNDO**
bring to the attention **REMIND, RAISE**
bring up **REAR, RAISE**
bring upon oneself **INCUR**
brink **EDGE, RIM, VERGE**
briny **SALINE, SALTY**
briny expanse **SEA, OCEAN**
brioche **ROLL**
brisk **LIVELY**
bristle **AWN, SETA**
bristle (prefix) **SETI**
British airplane **SPITFIRE**
British beverage **TEA**
British car **ROLLS ROYCE**
British carbine **STEN**
British cavalryman **DRAGOON**
British coin **SHILLING, PENNY**
British colony **BAHAMA, BERMUDA, GIBRALTAR, HONG KONG**

British county **SHIRE**
British daisy **GOWAN**
British essayist **STEELE, ADDISON, CHESTERTON**
British flag **UNION JACK**
British flyers (abbr.) **R.A.F.**
British foreign minister **EDEN**
British gun **STEN**
British imperial color **RED**
British island **MALTA**
British isle **MAN, WIGHT**
British king **GEORGE, HENRY, EDWARD, RICHARD, CHARLES**
British man-of-war **GALATEA**
British manufacturing city **LEEDS**
British meal **TEA**
British nobleman **EARL, LORD, BARON, BARONET, PEER, DUKE**
British peeress **DAME, LADY, DUCHESS, BARONESS**
British pennies **PENCE**
British prep school **ETON, HARROW**
British prime minister **CHURCHILL, WILSON**
British princess **ANNE, MARGARET, ALEXANDRA**
British school **ETON, HARROW, OXFORD, CAMBRIDGE**
British sea hero **NELSON**
British streetcar **TRAM**
British taproom **PUB**
British weight **STONE**
Briton **CELT**
brittle **CRISP**
broad **WIDE, VAST**
broadcast **AIR**
broaden **WIDEN**
broad flat bottle **FLASK**
broad humor **FARCE**
broad minded **LIBERAL**
broad necktie **ASCOT**
broad scarf **SHAWL**
broad smile **GRIN**
broad street **BOULEVARD, AVENUE**
broadtail **KARAKUL**
broad thin piece **SHEET**
Broadway backer **ANGEL**
Broadway light **NEON**
Broadway musical **HAIR, CAMELOT, HELLO DOLLY, MAME, COMPANY, APPLAUSE, FANNY, FUNNY GIRL, TENDERLOIN, FIORELLO, ZORBA**

Broadway offering **DRAMA, COMEDY, MUSICAL, REVUE, PLAY**
Broadway patron **GOER**
brochette **SKEWER**
brochure **PAMPHLET**
brogan **SHOE**
broil **GRILL**
broiler **CHICKEN**
broil in covered kettle **BRAIZE**
broiling meat **STEAK**
broil on gridiron **GRILL**
broke **PENNILESS**
broke bread **ATE**
broken open **SPRUNG**
broken pottery **SHARD**
broker **AGENT, REPRESENTATIVE**
broker's advice **SELL, BUY**
bromide **CLICHE**
bronze **TAN**
brooch **PIN**
brood **COVEY, HATCH**
brook **RILL, STREAM, RIVULET**
broom **BESOM**
brose **OATMEAL**
broth **SOUP, BOUILLON**
brother **FRA**
brother (abbr.) **BR., BRO.**
brother (Fr.) **FRERE**
brotherly **LOYAL**
brother of Abel **CAIN**
brother of Cain **ABLE**
brother of Esau **JACOB**
brother of Moses **AARON**
brother's daughter **NIECE**
brother's son **NEPHEW**
brought about **DID**
brought into life **BORN**
brought up **BRED, REARED**
brow **FOREHEAD**
brown **TAN, COCOA, BEIGE, CHOCOLATE, SEPIA**
brown bread **GRAHAM, WHOLE WHEAT**
browned **RISSOLE**
brown ermine **STOAT**
brownie **CAKE, ELF**
brownish **RUSSET, UMBER**
brownish purple **PUCE**
brownish yellow **AMBER**
brown kiwi **MOA**
brown pigment **UMBER**
browse for bargains **SHOP**
bruin **BEAR**
bruise **BUMP, WELT**
brusque **CURT, TERSE, BLUNT**

brute	**ANIMAL, BEAST**
brutish	**COARSE, RUDE**
bryophyte	**MOSS, LIVERWORT**
bubble	**GLOBULE**
bubble up	**BOIL**
bubbling	**BOILING**
buccaneers	**PIRATES, PRIVATEER, SEA ROVER**
buckboard	**WAGON**
bucket	**PAIL, TUB**
bucket handle	**BAIL**
Buckeye State	**OHIO**
bucolic	**PASTORAL, RUSTIC**
Buddha's mother	**MAYA**
Buddhist monk	**LAMA**
Buddhist shrine	**TOPE, STUPA**
buddy	**PAL, CHUM, PARTNER, MATE, FRIEND**
budge	**STIR, MOVE**
budget	**SCHEDULE**
buff	**POLISH, TAN**
buffalo	**BISON**
buffalo of India	**ARNA**
buffet	**CUPBOARD, MEAL**
buffet about	**TOSS**
buffoon	**MERRY ANDREW, JESTER, CLOWN**
bug	**INSECT**
bugaboo	**GOBLIN, SPECTER**
bugbear	**GHOST, BOGIE, HOBGOBLIN**
buggy	**CARRIAGE, PRAM**
bugle	**HORN**
bugle call	**TAPS, REVEILLE, RETREAT**
bugle note	**MOT**
build	**CONSTRUCT, ERECT, MAKE, ESTABLISH**
build castles in the air	**DREAM**
building	**HOUSE, SKYSCRAPER, OFFICE, CHURCH, FACTORY, SETBACK, HI RISE**
building addition	**ELL, WING, ANNEX**
building beam	**GIRDER**
building block	**STONE**
building diagram	**PLAN**
building entrance	**DOOR**
building front	**FACADE**
building ground	**LOT, PLOT, SITE**
building location	**SITE**
building material	**LUMBER, STEEL, STONE, WOOD, BRICK, CONCRETE**
buildings along the Rhine	**CASTLES**
building support	**ANTA**

building wing	**ELL, ANNEX, EXTENSION**
bulb	**ROOT, GLOBE**
bulbous vegetable	**ONION**
Bulgarian city	**SOFIA**
Bulgarian river	**DANUBE**
bulge	**SWELL**
bulkhead	**WALL, FIREWALL**
bulky	**MASSIVE, HEAVY**
bull (Sp.)	**TORO**
bulldozer	**GRADER**
bullet	**PELLET, SLUG**
bullet diameter	**CALIBER**
bullfight cheer	**OLE**
bullfighter	**TORERO, MATADOR, PICADOR**
bully	**MENACE, TOUGH, HOODLUM**
bulwark	**RAMPART**
bum	**HOBO, TRAMP, BEGGAR, PANHANDLER**
bumpkin	**YOKEL, RUBE, HICK, HILLBILLY**
bun	**ROLL, BREAD, CHIGNON**
bunch	**CLUSTER**
bunch of grass	**TUFT**
bundle	**BALE, PACK, WRAP, PACKAGE**
bundle maker	**BALER**
bundle of cotton	**BALE**
bundle of grain	**SHEAF**
bundle of sticks	**FAGOT**
bungle	**BOTCH**
bungling	**CLUMSY**
bunk	**BED**
bunny	**RABBIT**
bunting	**ETAMINE**
buoy	**FLOAT**
burden	**LOAD, ONUS**
burdened	**LADEN**
burdensome	**HEAVY**
bureau	**CHEST, DRESSER, DESK, OFFICE, BUSINESS, DEPARTMENT**
burglar	**THIEF**
burglarize	**ROB**
burglary	**LARCENY, THEFT**
burgle	**ROB**
burgundy	**WINE**
burial place	**CEMETERY**
burlap fiber	**JUTE**
burlesque	**PARODY**
burly	**BULKY, STOUT**
Burmese	**LAI**
Burmese capital	**RANGOON**
Burmese tribe	**TAI**
burn	**CHAR, SINGE, SEAR, SCALD**

burning **AFIRE, AFLAME, FLAMING, TORRID, HOT, PASSIONATE**
Burning Bush **WAHOO**
burning glass **LENS**
burning mountain **VOLCANO**
burning oil **KEROSENE**
burn in hot water **SCALD**
burnish **GLAZE**
burro **ASS**
burrowing animal **MOLE, VOLE, GROUNDHOG**
burry **PRICKLY**
bursa **CAVITY**
bursar **TREASURER**
bursary **TREASURY**
burst **ERUPT, EXPLODE**
burst of activity **SPASM**
burst of thunder **CLAP**
burst open **POP, EXPLODE, ERUPT**
bury **INTER**
bus **TRANSPORT**
busby **HAT**
bush **SHRUB**
bushy clump (Brit.) **TOD**
business **TRADE, WORK**
business agreement **DEAL**
business deal **SALE**
business deficit **LOSS**
business house **FIRM**
business man **TYCOON**
business note **MEMO, MEMORANDUM**
business program **AGENDA**
business organization **CARTEL, COMPANY, CORPORATION, CONGLOMERATE**
businessman **MERCHANT, WHOLESALER**
bus station **DEPOT, TERMINAL**
bustle **TO-DO, HUBBUB, ADO**
bus token **FARE**
busybody **MEDDLER**
busy insect **ANT, BEE**
busy place **HIVE**
but **SAVE, EXCEPT**
but (Gr.) **ABER**
but (Lat.) **SED**
butcher **SLAY, SLAUGHTER**
butcher's tool **SLICER, KNIFE, CLEAVER, BLOCK. SCALE**
butch's pal **SPIKE**
butler **SERVANT**
butlery **PANTRY**
butt **RAM, TARGET**
butte **MESA**
butter maker **CHURN**

butter portion **PAT**
butter substitute **OLEO, MARGARINE**
butterfly **IO, SATYR, MONARCH**
butterfly snare **NET**
butting animal **GOAT**
buttock **RUMP**
butt of joke **IT**
button **STUD**
button-down **COLLAR**
button fastener **LOOP, HOOK**
buttress **PILE**
buy **PURCHASE**
buyer **SHOPPER**
buy off **BRIBE**
buzz **HUM, DRONE**
buzzing insect **DOR, BEE, WASP, HORNET, FLY**
by **AT, NEAR**
by and by **ANON, SOON, PRESENTLY**
by and large **MAINLY**
by birth **NEE**
bygone days **PAST, AGO**
by itself **ALONE, SOLO, SOLITARY, LONELY, LONE**
Byelorussian town **PINSK, MINSK**
by means of **PER, THROUGH**
by mouth **ORAL**
by-pass **DETOUR**
by reason **RATIONAL**
by slow stages **GRADUAL**
bystander **ONLOOKER, WITNESS**
by the side of **BESIDE**
byway **PATH, LANE**
by way of **VIA**
byword **PROVERB**
by word of mouth **PAROL**

C

ca **CALCIUM, CIRCA**
cab **TAXI**
cabal **INTRIGUE, PLOT, SCHEME**
cabalistic **OCCULT**
caballero **SENOR, CAVALIER**
cabana **BEACHHOUSE, LANAI**
cabbage broth **KALE**
cabbage dish **SLAW, SAUERKRAUT**

cabin **STATEROOM, SHED**
cabin bed **BERTH**
cabinet **CASE, CUPBOARD**
cable **WIRE, ROPE**
cad **BOUNDER, ROUE, LOUT**
cadence **LILT, BEAT, MEASURE**
Caesar's enemy **SULLA,**
POMPEY, CASSIUS
Caesar's language **LATIN**
cafe employee **WAITER,**
WAITRESS, COOK,
DISHWASHER, HOST,
HOSTESS, CASHIER
cafe patron **EATER, DINER**
DRINKER
cage for poultry **COOP**
cage of an elevator **CAR, CAB**
Cain's brother **ABEL**
Cairo's river **NILE**
caisson **WAGON**
cajole **COAX, WHEEDLE**
cake **PASTRY, HARDEN**
cake mix **BATTER**
cake of soap **BAR**
cake topping **ICING, FROSTING,**
SAUCE, FRUIT, WHIPPED
CREAM, ICE CREAM
calabash **GOURD**
calaboose **JAIL, PRISON**
calamity **DISASTER**
calculate **COMPUTE**
calculate
approximately **ESTIMATE**
calculation
instrument **ABACUS,**
ADDING MACHINE, COMPUTER
Calcutta hemp **JUTE**
caldron **VAT, KETTLE, POT**
Caledonian **SCOT**
calendar **ALMANAC**
calf meat **VEAL**
caliber **BORE**
California city **NAPA, SALINAS,**
SAN FRANCISCO, LOS
ANGELES, FRESNO,
SACRAMENTO
California fruit **KUMQUAT**
California mountain **SHASTA**
California rockfish **RENA**
California tree **REDWOOD**
California wine district **NAPA**
Caliph's name **ALI**
call **SHOUT, TELL, PAGE,**
PHONE, TELEPHONE,
SUMMON, VISIT, RING UP,
YELL, SHRIEK, HOLLER,
SCREAM
call for quiet **SH, HUSH**

call forth **EVOKE, SUMMON**
calling **TRADE, VOCATION**
call it quits **STOP, CEASE**
callous **UNFEELING**
callow **GREEN**
call the roll **MUSTER**
call to the phone **PAGE**
calm **SERENITY, TRANQUILITY,**
LULL, QUIET, PEACE,
PEACEFUL
calmative **SEDATIVE**
calm endurance **PATIENCE**
calumet **PIPE, PEACE PIPE**
calumny **SLANDER, LIBEL**
calyx leaf **SEPAL**
camel-like mammal **LLAMA**
camelopard **GIRAFFE**
Camelot's king **ARTHUR**
Camelot's magician **MERLIN**
camera adjustment **FOCUS**
camera glass **LENS**
Cameroon tribe **IBO, BETI,**
BULU
camp bed **COT**
camp shelter **TENT**
campus building **DORM, QUAD,**
HALL, LIBRARY, CHAPEL
can **TIN**
Canadian capital **OTTAWA,**
VICTORIA, EDMONTON,
REGINA, WINNIPEG,
QUEBEC, ST. JOHNS,
HALIFAX, FREDERICTON
Canadian mountain **LOGAN**
Canadian peninsula **GASPE**
Canadian province **ONTARIO,**
QUEBEC, NEW BRUNSWICK,
NOVA SCOTIA, BRITISH
COLUMBIA,
NEWFOUNDLAND,
MANITOBA,
SASKATCHEWAN,
ALBERTA
canal **WATERWAY**
canal near Egypt **SUEZ**
canal system in northern
Michigan **SOO**
Canal Zone lake **GATUN**
canape **APPETIZER**
canard **RUMOR**
canary **BIRD, WARBLER**
canary's home **CAGE**
cancel **ANNUL, VOID**
Cancer **CRAB**
candid **HONEST, FRANK, OPEN,**
ABOVEBOARD
candidate **NOMINEE**
candied fruit **SWEETMEAT**

candle	**TAPER**	caoutchouc	**RUBBER**
candle drippings	**WAX**	cap	**BERET, HAT**
candle holder	**SCONCE**	capa	**CLOAK**
candy flavor	**LEMON, ORANGE,**	capability	**CAPACITY**
	CHERRY, PEPPERMINT,	capable	**ABLE, COMPETENT**
	CARAMEL, CHOCOLATE,	capable of (2 wds.)	**UP TO**
	MINT, LICORICE, RUM	capable of cultivation	**ARABLE**
cane	**WHIP, BEAT, THRASH,**	capable of flying	**VOLANT**
	STICK, PADDLE, STEM	capable of learning	**TEACHABLE**
cane-cutting knife	**BOLO**	capacious	**LARGE, ROOMY**
cane sugar	**SUCROSE**	capacity	**VOLUME**
canine	**TOOTH, DOG, FOX,**	cape	**CLOAK, HEADLAND,**
	WOLF, EYETOOTH		**NESS, PROMONTORY**
canine cry	**YELP, YAP, YIP,**	Cape Kennedy launching	
	BARK, WOOF, ARF,	(comp. wd.)	
	BOWWOW, GROWL, GRR,		**LIFT-OFF, BLAST-OFF**
	ROWF	Cape Kennedy	
canine home	**KENNEL**	platform	**GANTRY**
canine pet	**DOG**	Cape Kennedy rocket	**AGENA,**
canine tooth	**FANG, EYETOOTH**		**APOLLO, MERCURY,**
canine with rabies			**GEMINI**
(2 wds.)	**MAD DOG**	Cape Kennedy	
canker	**ULCER, SORE**	routine	**COUNTDOWN**
can metal	**TIN**	caper	**ANTIC, TRICK, FROLIC**
cannon	**GUN**	caper about	**CAVORT**
cannon fire	**BARRAGE,**	capillus	**HAIR**
	BATTERY	Capistrano resident	**SWALLOW**
cannon handle	**ANSE**	capital	**MAIN, MAJOR**
cannon shot	**GRAPE**	capital of	
canoe	**BOAT, BIRCHBARK,**	Alabama	**MONTGOMERY**
	PROA	capital of Alaska	**JUNEAU**
canoe of Malaysia	**PROA**	capital of Albania	**TIRANA**
canon	**LAW, CODE, RULE,**	capital of Arizona	**PHOENIX**
	CRITERION	capital of Arkansas	**LITTLE**
canonized man	**SAINT, ST.**		**ROCK**
canonized woman (Fr.)	**SAINTE,**	capital of Austria	**VIENNA**
	STE.	capital of Bolivia	
canonized woman (It.)	**SANTA**	(2 wds.)	**LA PAZ**
canopy	**ROOF**	capital of	
cant	**ARGOT, JARGON, SLANG,**	California	**SACRAMENTO**
	SLANT, INCLINE, TOP	capital of Canada	**OTTAWA**
cantabile	**FLOWING**	capital of Colorado	**DENVER**
cantaloupe	**MELON,**	capital of	
	MUSKMELON	Connecticut	**HARTFORD**
cantata	**MOTET**	capital of Cuba	**HAVANA**
canteen	**FLASK**	capital of Delaware	**DOVER**
canter	**GAIT, LOPE**	capital of Egypt	**CAIRO**
canticle	**ODE, SONG, CHANT**	capital of Florida	**TALLAHASSEE**
cantina	**SALOON, BAR**	capital of France	**PARIS**
cantle	**NOOK, SLICE**	capital of Georgia	**ATLANTA**
canto	**SONG, VERSE**	capital of Germany	**BERLIN,**
cantor	**SOLOIST, PRECENTOR**		**BONN**
canvas	**DUCK**	capital of Greece	**ATHENS**
canvas bed	**COT**	capital of Guam	**AGANA**
canvas frame	**EASEL**	capital of Haiti	
canvas home	**TENT**		**PORT-AU-PRINCE**
canvass	**POLL**	capital of Hawaii	**HONOLULU**
canyon	**GORGE, CHASM**	capital of Hungary	**BUDAPEST**

capital of Idaho   **BOISE**
capital of Illinois   **SPRINGFIELD**
capital of
  Indiana   **INDIANAPOLIS**
capital of Indonesia   **DJAKARTA**
capital of Iowa   **DES MOINES**
capital of Iraq   **BAGHDAD**
capital of Italia   **ROMA**
capital of Italy   **ROME**
capital of Kansas   **TOPEKA**
capital of Kentucky **FRANKFORT**
capital of
  Louisiana   **BATON ROUGE**
capital of Lydian
  Empire   **SARDIS**
capital of Maine   **AUGUSTA**
capital of Maryland   **ANNAPOLIS**
capital of
  Massachusetts   **BOSTON**
capital of Michigan   **LANSING**
capital of Minnesota   **ST. PAUL**
capital of Mississippi   **JACKSON**
capital of Missouri   **JEFFERSON
                              CITY**
capital of Montana   **HELENA**
capital of Morocco   **RABAT**
capital of Nebraska   **LINCOLN**
capital of Nevada   **CARSON CITY**
capital of New
  Hampshire   **CONCORD**
capital of New Jersey   **TRENTON**
capital of New Mexico
                          SANTA FE
capital of New York   **ALBANY**
capital of Nicaragua   **MANAGUA**
capital of Nigeria   **LAGOS**
capital of North
  Carolina   **RALEIGH**
capital of North
  Dakota   **BISMARCK**
capital of North Vietnam **HANOI**
capital of Norway   **OSLO**
capital of Ohio   **COLUMBUS**
capital of Oklahoma
                    OKLAHOMA CITY
capital of Oregon   **SALEM**
capital of Paraguay   **ASUNCION**
capital of
  Pennsylvania   **HARRISBURG**
capital of Peru   **LIMA**
capital of Philippines
                        QUEZON CITY
capital of Phoenicia   **TYRE**
capital of Poland   **WARSAW**
capital of Rhode
  Island   **PROVIDENCE**

capital of Senegal   **DAKAR**
capital of South
  Carolina   **COLUMBIA**
capital of South Dakota   **PIERRE**
capital of Soviet
  Union   **MOSCOW**
capital of Spain   **MADRID**
capital of Tennessee **NASHVILLE**
capital of Texas   **AUSTIN**
capital of Tibet   **LHASA**
capital of Utah   **SALT LAKE CITY**
capital of Venezuela   **CARACAS**
capital of
  Vermont   **MONTPELIER**
capital of Virginia   **RICHMOND**
capital of Washington   **OLYMPIA**
capital of West Germany   **BONN**
capital of West
  Pakistan   **LAHORE**
capital of West
  Virginia   **CHARLESTON**
capital of Western Samoa   **APIA**
capital of Wisconsin   **MADISON**
capital of Wyoming   **CHEYENNE**
capital of Yemen   **SANA(A)**
capital of Yugoslavia **BELGRADE**
capsule   **PILL, PELLET,
                              TABLET**
Captain Kidd   **PIRATE,
                          BUCCANEER**
captain of a ship   **SKIPPER**
captivate   **ENTRANCE**
captor   **TAKER**
capture   **NAB, SEIZE, CATCH,
                           GRAB, TAKE**
capture again **RETAKE, REGAIN**
capuchin monkey   **SAI**
car   **AUTO, AUTOMOBILE**
carabao   **BUFFALO**
carafe   **BOTTLE, DECANTER**
caramel   **CANDY, FLAVOR**
carat   **GEM WEIGHT**
caravansary   **INN**
caravan station   **SERAI**
caraway   **SEED**
carbohydrate   **STARCH**
carbon   **COPY, SOOT**
carbonated beverage   **POP,
                               SODA**
carcass   **BODY, CORPSE**
card   **ACE, DEUCE, TREY**
card (Fr.)   **CARTE**
cardboard box   **CARTON**
card combination   **TENACE,
                           FLUSH, PAIR**

card game CANASTA, GIN,
LOON, PINOCHLE, POKER,
HEARTS, RUMMY, BEZIQUE,
CRIBBAGE, CASINO, CANFIELD,
KLONDIKE, RUSSIAN BANK,
MONTE CARLO, BRIDGE,
WHIST
cardigan SWEATER, JACKET
cardinal BIRD
cardinal point NORTH, SOUTH,
EAST, WEST
cardinal's office HAT
cardinal's symbol (2 wds.)
RED HAT
card of admission PASS
cards and letters MAIL
card suit SPADES, HEARTS,
DIAMONDS, CLUBS
card wool COMB
care ANXIETY, MIND, WORRY,
TROUBLE, HEEDFUL,
CAUTION, WISH
careen LURCH
career PROFESSION, VOCATION
career beginning DEBUT
carefree HAPPY, GAY
careful CAUTIOUS
careful management
PRUDENCE
careless LAX, LAZY
car entrance DRIVEWAY
caress FONDLE, PET, PAT,
STROKE
caretaker CUSTODIAN
car fuel GAS, PETROL,
GASOLINE
car gear REVERSE, LOW,
DRIVE, PASSING
cargo LOAD
cargo compartment HOLD
cargo ship TRAMP, TANKER,
FREIGHTER
cargo stower STEVEDORE
Caribbean island NEVIS,
GRENADA, PUERTO RICO,
ANTIGUA, CUBA, JAMAICA,
HAITI, BARBADOS, DOMINICA,
MARTINIQUE, MONSERRAT
caribou MOOSE, DEER
caricature PARODY,
BURLESQUE
car ignition device STARTER
carillon CHIME
Carl Sandburg creation POEM
carmine SCARLET
car model SEDAN, COUPE,
CONVERTIBLE, HARDTOP
carnal EARTHY

carnation PINK
carnival FESTIVAL
carnival attraction
(2 wds.) SIDE SHOW
carousel (comp. wd.)
MERRY-GO-ROUND
carp CAVIL
car part (2 wds.) TIE ROD
carpentry tool AWL, HAMMER,
SAW, AUGER, RASP, MITER
BOX, LEVEL, PLUMB LINE,
PLANE
carpet RUG, MAT
carpet nap PILE
carport GARAGE
carp's home POND
carriage STATURE
carriage dog DALMATIAN
carried away RAPT
carried on the back TOTE
carrier PORTER
carrion ROTTEN, VILE
carry BEAR, TOTE, LUG
carry across water FERRY
carry away REMOVE
carrying guns ARMED
carry into effect EXECUTE
carry on WAGE, CONTINUE,
ENSUE
carry out PERFORM, EXECUTE
carry tales TATTLE
carry the day WIN
cart WAGON
cartel POOL, TRUST
carter TEAMSTER
Carthaginian PUNIC
Carthaginian queen DIDO
cartilage GRISTLE
cartridge SHELL
carve CUT, SLICE
carved gem CAMEO
carve letters upon ENGRAVE
Casals' instrument CELLO
cascade WATERFALL
case ETUI, BOX, CRATE,
CARTON
case for small articles ETUI
cash MONEY
cash drawer TILL
cashew NUT
cashmere WOOL
cask BARREL, TUN
casket BOX, COFFIN
cask part STAVE
cask's circular strip HOOP
cask stave LAG
Caspian SEA
cassava starch food TAPIOCA

cassowary **EMU**
cast **PLAYERS, THROW, PITCH, TOSS**
cast a ballot **VOTE**
cast aside **DISCARD, REJECT**
caste **CLASS**
castle **PALACE**
castle ditch **MOAT**
castles in the air **DREAMS**
cast off **SHED, SLOUGH**
Castor or Pollux **STAR**
Castro's country **CUBA**
casual utterance **REMARK**
casualty **ACCIDENT**
cat **FELINE, TABBY, PUSSY**
cataclysm **DISASTER**
catalogue **LIST**
catamaran **FLOAT, RAFT**
catastrophe **CALAMITY, DISASTER**
catch **NAB, GRAB, SEIZE, SNATCH, TAKE**
catch on to **GLOM**
catch sight of **ESPY**
catch up with **OVERTAKE**
catching implement **HOOK**
catchword **SLOGAN**
cat command **SCAT, SHOO**
category **BRACKET, CLASS**
cater **SERVE**
catharsis **PURGE**
Catholic cleric's cap **BIRETTA**
Catholic prayer (Lat., 2 wds.) **AVE MARIA, PATER NOSTER**
Catholic service **MASS**
catkin **AMENT**
cats and dogs **PETS**
cat's foot **PAW**
cat sound **PURR, MEOW, MIAOW, MEW, MIAOU**
cat's prey **MOUSE, CANARY**
cattle (arch.) **KINE**
cattle bedding **STRAW**
cattle enclosure **CORRAL**
cattle genus **BOS**
cattleman **DROVER**
cattle thief **RUSTLER**
Caucasian **ARYAN**
Caucasian goat **TUR**
caudal appendage **TAIL**
caught in a net **ENMESHED**
cauldron **POT**
cause **GIVE RISE TO, REASON**
cause dough to rise **LEAVEN**
cause of Cleopatra's death **ASP**
cause of tension **STRESS**
cause to jump the track **DERAIL**

cause to remember **REMIND, RECALL**
cause to slant **TILT**
cause to stand out **EMBOSS**
cause to stick **MIRE**
cause to take root **RADICATE**
causeway **DIKE**
causing amusement **FUNNY**
causing feeling **EMOTIVE**
caustic **ACRID, BITTER**
caustic substance **ACID, LYE**
caustic wit **IRONIC, CUTTING, SARCASTIC**
cauterize **SEAR**
caution **WARN**
cautious **WARY**
cautiously **CAREFULLY, GINGERLY**
cavalcade **MARCH, PARADE**
Cavalier State **VIRGINIA**
cavalry **TROOP**
cavalry horse **LANCER, MOUNT**
cavalry man **TROOPER, DRAGOON**
cavalry soldiers **LANCERS**
cavalry sword **SABER, SABRE**
cavalry unit **TROOP**
cave **CAVERN**
caveat **WARNING**
cave in **COLLAPSE**
cavern **CAVE**
cavernous **DEEP, HOLLOW**
caviar **ROE**
cavil **CARP**
caviler **CRITIC**
cavity **HOLE**
cavort **PRANCE**
cay **INLET**
cayenne **PEPPER**
cease **STOP, DESIST, HALT**
cease-fire **TRUCE, ARMISTICE**
cease friendship with (2 wds.) **PART COMPANY**
ceaseless **CONTINUAL**
cebine monkey **SAI**
Cebu hemp **MANILA**
cedar **TREE, SAVINE**
cede **YIELD**
Celebes ox **ANOA**
celebrate **OBSERVE, REVEL**
celebrated **FAMOUS**
celebration **RITE, FETE, FESTIVAL**
celebrity **LION, STAR**
celerity **SPEED**
celery portion **STALK**
celestial **HEAVENLY**
celestial being **ANGEL**

celestial body	COMET, SUN, STAR, MOON, PLANET, ASTEROID	certainty	FACT
		certificate	DOCUMENT
		certify	ATTEST, VERIFY
celestial instrument	HARP	certitude	SURENESS
celestial visitor	COMET	cerulean	BLUE
celibate	SINGLE	cessation	LULL
cell	ROOM	cessation of war agreement	
cellar	BASEMENT, PANTRY	(2 wds.)	PEACE TREATY
Celt	GAUL, BRITON	cetacea	WHALES
Celtic language	ERSE, GAELIC, MANX, WELSH, BRETON	Ceylonese canoe	BALSA
		Ceylon moss	AGAR
Celtic peasant	KERN	chagrin	SHAME
Celtic priest	DRUID	chain	CATENA, BIND, FETTER, SHACKLE
Celtic sea deity	LER		
cement	PUTTY	chain cable	BOOM
cemetery	GRAVEYARD	chain of mountains	RANGE, RIDGE
censurable quality	DEMERIT		
censure	BLAME, CONDEMN	chain of rocks	REEF
cent	PENNY	chain part	LINK
Centennial State	COLORADO	chain reaction	SEQUENCE
center	CORE, MID, MIDDLE, NUCLEUS, HUB	chain sound	CLANK, CLINK
		chair	SEAT
center of activity	FOCUS	chair covers	TIDIES
center of interest	FOCUS	chair of state	THRONE
center of sail	BUNT	chair part	LEG, SPLAT, SEAT, BACK, ARM
center of target	EYE		
Central American country	NICARAGUA, HONDURAS, GUATEMALA, EL SALVADOR, COSTA RICA, PANAMA	chaise	CHAIR, CARRIAGE
		chalcedony	AGATE, SARD
		Chaldean city	UR
		chalet	CABIN, HUT
Central American Indian	CARIB, MAYA	chalice	GOBLET, CUP
		chalice cover	PALL
Central American oil tree	EBOE	chalk	CRAYON
Central American rodent	PACA	chalk remover	ERASER
central point	PIVOT	chalk up	SCORE
century plant	AGAVE, MAGUEY, ALOE	chalky	PALE, WHITE
		challenge	DARE, DEFY
ceramic earth	CLAY	chalumeau	CLARINET, REED
ceramic piece	VASE, PITCHER, POT, PLATE	chamber	ROOM
		chamber beneath the Vatican	CATACOMB
ceramic square	TILE		
ceramics	POTTERY	chamberlain	ATTENDANT, STEWARD
ceramics maker	POTTER		
cerated	WAXED	chameleon	LIZARD
cere	ANOINT, WAX	chamfer	BEVEL
cereal	GRAIN, BRAN	champ	BITE
cereal dish	BOWL	champagne	WINE
cereal grain	OAT, RICE, RYE, BARLEY, WHEAT, CORN	champagne bucket	ICER, COOLER
		champion	DEFENDER, WINNER
cereal grass	OAT, RICE, RYE, WHEAT, BARLEY	chance	FATE, LUCK
		chancel seats	SEDILIA
cereal spike	EAR	chancel table	ALTAR
ceremonial	FORMAL, RITUAL	change	ALTER, AMEND, VARY
ceremonial post	TOTEM	changeable	ERRATIC, FICKLE
ceremony	RITE	change a constitution	AMEND
cerise	RED	change a manuscript	REVISE
certain	SURE	change an alarm	RESET
certainly	OF COURSE, YES	change color	DYE, FADE
certainly not	NO		

change course **VEER, TACK**
change direction **TURN, VEER**
changed state **MUTATION**
change for the better **REFORM**
change from evil **REPENT**
change into bone **OSSIFY**
changeling (arch.) **IDIOT**
change off **TAKE TURNS**
change one's address **MOVE**
change order of **TRANSPOSE**
change position **TURN OVER, MOVE, SHIFT, REVERSE**
change the decor **REDO**
change the mind **RECONSIDER**
channel **VEIN, RIVER, STRAIT**
Channel Island **JERSEY, SARK, GUERNSEY, ALDERNEY**
channel marker **BUOY**
chant **INTONE, SINGSONG**
Chantilly product **LACE**
chaos **MESS**
chap **FELLOW**
chaparral **THICKET**
chaparral cock **ROAD RUNNER**
chapeau **HAT**
chapel **SANCTUARY**
chaperon **DUENNA**
chaplain **MINISTER, PADRE, PRIEST**
chaplet **ANADEM, BEADS, WREATH**
chapter of Koran **SURA**
char **BURN, SEAR, SCORCH, TASK**
character **PERSONALITY, NATURE**
characteristic **TRAIT, EARMARK**
characterization **ROLE**
characterize **REPRESENT**
characterized by (suffix) **MORPH**
character of a people **ETHOS**
character part **ROLE**
characters in a play **CAST**
charcoal **FUEL**
charcoal grill **BRAZIER**
charge **FEE, RATE**
charged atom **ION**
charge for use of road **TOLL**
charge with crime **ACCUSE**
charge with gas **AERATE**
chariot **CART**
charisma **GRACE, CHARM**
charitable **GENEROUS**
charity **ALMS, GIVING**
charity gift **DOLE, ALMS, DONATION**
charlatan **QUACK, FRAUD**
Charles Goren's domain (2 wds.) **CONTRACT BRIDGE**

Charles Lamb **ELIA**
charley horse **CRAMP**
Charlotte Corday's victim **MARAT**
charm **ENAMOR, ENTHRALL, FASCINATE, TALISMAN, TOKEN**
charming **WINSOME**
chart **GRAPH, MAP**
charter **HIRE, GRANT**
chary **FRUGAL, WARY, SHY**
chase **PURSUE**
chase away **ROUT**
chaste **PURE, VESTAL**
chasten **DISCIPLINE, PUNISH**
chastise **BERATE, CHASTEN, SCOLD**
chastity **PURITY, VIRTUE**
chat **GAB, CHATTER, PRATE, CHIN, CHEW THE RAG, CHEW THE FAT, GABBLE**
chatter **PRATE, PRATTLE**
cheap **INEXPENSIVE, TINNY**
cheap metal **TIN**
cheat **SWINDLE, DUPE**
check **REIN, TAB, BILL, STOP, ARREST**
check by danger **DAUNT**
checkers **DRAFTS, DRAUGHTS**
cheer **RAH, BRAVO, BRAVA, OLE, HURRAH, HURRAY, LIVEN, ELATE, GLADDEN**
cheerful **ROSY, PLEASANT**
cheerful expression **SMILE, GRIN**
cheerless **BLEAK, DRAB, DULL, DEPRESSING**
cheese dish **RAREBIT, FONDUE**
cheese variety **EDAM, GOUDA, BRIE, GRUYERE**
chef **COOK**
chef's garment **APRON**
chef's specialty **SALAD**
chelonian **TURTLE, TORTOISE**
chemical analysis **ASSAY**
chemical compound **ESTER**
chemical element **ANTIMONY, BARIUM**
chemical particle **ION**
chemical product of the body **HORMONE**
chemical salts **SALS**
chemical suffix **ANE, ASE, IDE, ITE, INE**
chemist's burner **BUNSEN, ETNA**
chemist's shop **PHARMACY**
chemist's workplace **LAB**

cherish	**LOVE, TREASURE, HOLD DEAR**
cherished	**DEAR**
cherished animal	**PET**
cherry	**OXHEART, MORELLO, BING**
cherry-colored	**CERISE**
cherry orange	**KUMQUAT**
cherry seed	**PIT**
chess move	**GAMBIT**
chess piece	**MAN, PAWN, KING, QUEEN, KNIGHT, BISHOP, CASTLE, ROOK**
chess victory	**CHECKMATE, MATE**
chest	**BOX, CASE, STRONGBOX**
chest bone	**RIB**
chestnut horse	**ROAN**
chest of drawers	**DRESSER, BUREAU, COMMODE**
chest sound	**RALE**
chew	**MASTICATE, GNAW, MUNCH, BITE**
chewing gum	**CHICLE**
chewing gum flavor	**SPEARMINT**
chew the cud	**RUMINATE**
chewy candy	**CARAMEL, TAFFY, TOFFEE, NOUGAT**
chic	**MODISH, STYLISH**
chick's mother	**HEN**
chicken	**HEN, CAPON, FOWL, FRYER**
chicken feed	**MASH**
chicken pen	**COOP**
chicory	**HERB, ENDIVE**
chide	**SCOLD, BERATE**
chief	**MAIN, HEAD**
chief character	**HERO**
chief executive	**PRESIDENT**
chief of fairies	**PUCK**
chief ore of lead	**GALENA**
chief part	**MAIN**
chief ruler	**GOVERNOR**
chiffonier	**CABINET**
chignon	**BUN, KNOT**
child	**KID, TOT, YOUNGSTER, TODDLER**
childish	**PUERILE, INFANTILE**
child of necessity	**INVENTION**
child's cry	**SNIVEL**
child's game	**JACKS, TAG, MARBLES, KICK THE CAN, RED ROVER, HIDE AND SEEK, JUMP ROPE, HOPSCOTCH**
child's hat	**BONNET, TAM, BERET, CAP**
child's marble	**AGATE, TAW**

child's play	**EASY, SIMPLE**
child's salary	**ALLOWANCE**
child's sock	**ANKLET**
child's stroller (comp. wd.)	**GO-CART**
child's toy	**YOYO**
child's vehicle	**SCOOTER, BIKE, WAGON, CARRIAGE**
Chilean coin	**CONDOR**
Chilean export	**NITER, NITRATES**
Chilean Indian	**ONA**
Chilean mountains	**ANDES**
chill	**FREEZE, ICE, COOL**
chilling tale (2 wds.)	**GHOST STORY**
chilly attitude	**STANDOFF**
chime	**PEAL, RING**
chimney dirt	**SOOT**
chimney passage	**FLUE**
chimpanzee	**APE**
chinaware	**DISHES**
Chinese	**SINIC**
Chinese drink	**TEA**
Chinese dynasty	**MING, CHING, SUNG, TANG, WEI**
Chinese fish sauce	**SOY, SOYA**
Chinese fruit	**LITCHI, LICHEE**
Chinese idol	**JOSS, GHOS**
Chinese island	**AMOY, FORMOSA**
Chinese laborer	**COOLIE**
Chinese measure	**LI, TU**
Chinese nurse	**AMAH**
Chinese pagoda	**TAA**
Chinese philosophy	**TAO**
Chinese poet (2 wds.)	**LI PO**
Chinese porcelain	**MING**
Chinese port	**AMOY**
Chinese ship	**JUNK**
Chinese society	**TONG**
Chinese staple grain	**RICE**
Chinese temple	**TAA**
Chinook State	**WASHINGTON**
chip of stone	**SPALL**
chirp	**PEEP, PIP, TWEET, TWEE, CHEEP, CHIRRUP**
chisel	**CUT, GOUGE, SHAPE**
chiseler	**MOOCHER, SPONGER**
chitchat (2 wds.)	**SMALL TALK**
chivalrous	**VALIANT, GALLANT**
chocolate tree	**CACAO**
choice	**OPTION, SELECTION**
choice cut of beef	**SIRLOIN**
choice morsel	**TIDBIT**
choice part	**ELITE**
choice seashore location	**OCEANFRONT**
choir leader	**CANTOR**

choir voice **ALTO, SOPRANO, BASS, BARITONE, TENOR**
choke **OBSTRUCT, STRANGLE**
choke back **REPRESS, STIFLE**
choke coil **REACTOR**
choke up **CLOG, SPEECHLESS**
choler **IRE, SPLEEN**
choleric **ANGRY**
Chomolungma's other name **EVEREST**
choose **ELECT, SELECT, OPT, PICK**
choose over **PREFER**
choosy **PARTICULAR, FINICKY**
chop **HEW, CUT, DICE, MINCE**
chop-chop **QUICKLY, HURRY**
chop finely **DICE, MINCE**
chop off **LOP**
chopped cabbage dish **SLAW**
chopped meat dish **HASH, MINCE, HAMBURGER**
chopping tool **AX, AXE, HATCHET, KNIFE**
choppy **ROUGH, JERKY**
chord **HARMONY**
chord composition **CANTATA**
chore **ERRAND, TASK**
chortle **CHUCKLE**
chorus **REFRAIN**
Chosen **KOREA**
chosen few **ELITE**
chosen field **CAREER**
chosen people **ISRAELITES, HEBREWS**
christen **DUB, NAME**
Christian **GENTILE**
Christian era (abbr.) **A.D.**
Christiania **OSLO**
Christmas **HOLIDAY, NOEL, YULE, YULETIDE**
Christmas carol **NOEL**
Christmas Carol character **TIM, SCROOGE**
Christmas decoration **HOLLY, IVY, TREE**
Christmas plant **HOLLY, MISTLETOE**
Christmas song **CAROL, NOEL**
Christmas trimming **TINSEL**
chromosome **GENE**
chronic **CONSTANT**
chronicle **ACCOUNT, HISTORY**
chubby **PLUMP**
chum **FRIEND, PAL, BUDDY, PARTNER**
chunk **SLAB**
chunky **LUMPY, PLUMP**
church **BASILICA, CATHEDRAL**

church bench **KNEELER, PEW**
church body **CANON, SYNOD, CONGREGATION**
church calendar **ORDO**
church canticle **VENITE**
church council **SYNOD**
church court **ROTA**
church dignitary **PRELATE**
church district **PARISH**
church fast **LENT**
church gallery **LOFT**
church hymn **ANTHEM**
church law **CANON**
church minister **PASTOR, PRIEST**
church morning service **MATINS**
Church of Latter-day Saints **MORMON**
church officer **SEXTON, WARDEN**
church official **ELDER, DEACON, CARDINAL**
Church of Rome **LATERAN, CATHOLIC**
church part **ALTAR, APSE, NAVE, CHANCEL, CHOIR LOFT, VESTRY, BAPTISTRY**
church pulpit **AMBO**
church seat **PEW**
church service **MASS**
church singing group **CHOIR**
church tower **STEEPLE, SPIRE**
church vault **CRYPT**
church vestry room **SACRISTY**
churl **BOOR**
churlish **SURLY**
chute **FLUME, SLIDE**
chutney **RELISH**
CIA employee **SPY, AGENT**
cicada **LOCUST**
cicatrix **SCAR**
cider source **APPLE**
cigar **STOGIE, PANATELA, PANATELLA**
cigar residue **ASH**
cigarette **FAG, CIG, BUTT**
cigarette end **STUB, BUTT**
cilium **EYELASH**
cinch **GIRTH, SNAP**
cinchona **QUININE**
Cincinnati ball club **REDS**
cincture **BELT**
cinder **ASH**
cinema house **THEATER, THEATRE, MOVIE**
cinnabar **ORE**
cinnamon **CASSIA**
cipher **CODE, ZERO**

circle	SET, CLIQUE	city in Brittany	NANTES
circle a planet	ORBIT	city in California	SAN MATEO,
circle of light	HALO		SANTA BARBARA, LOS
circle of persons	CORDON		ANGELES, FRESNO, SAN
circle part	ARC		FRANCISCO, PALO ALTO,
circlet	HOOP, RING		SACRAMENTO, SAN DIEGO
circlet of light	AUREOLE(A)	city in Delaware	WILMINGTON
circuit	CYCLE, LOOP	city in England	OLDHAM,
circuit-breaker	FUSE		LONDON, LIVERPOOL,
circuit rider	ITINERANT,		BIRMINGHAM, MANCHESTER
	MINISTER	city in Florida	OCALA, TAMPA,
circuitous	ROUNDABOUT		MIAMI, MIAMI BEACH,
circular	OVAL, ROUND		TALLAHASSEE, ORLANDO
circular cloak	CAPE	city in Georgia	ATLANTA
circular figure	LOOP	city in Germany	EMDEN, ESSEN,
circulate	DIFFUSE, MIX		ULM, BERLIN, BONN
circumference	PERIMETER	city in Hawaii	HONOLULU, HILO
circumscribe	ENCLOSE, LIMIT	city in Illinois	PEKIN, CHICAGO,
circumspect	DISCREET		SPRINGFIELD, PEORIA
circumstance	EVENT	city in India	AGRA, NEW DELHI,
circumvent	EVADE, AVOID		VARANASI, MADRAS,
circus	ARENA		CALCUTTA, KAPUR
circus (2 wds.)	BIG TOP	city in Indiana	SOUTH BEND,
circus animal	LION, TIGER,		GARY, INDIANAPOLIS,
ELEPHANT, APE, HORSE,		TERRE HAUTE, HAMMOND
CHIMPANZEE, GORILLA,		city in Iowa	AMES
	SEAL	city in Italia	ROMA, MILANO,
circus attraction	SIDE SHOW,		FIRENZE, PISA, NAPOLI, SIENA
	FREAK, CLOWN	city in Italy	ASTI, MILAN, ROME,
circus caller	BARKER		NAPLES, GENOA, FLORENCE,
circus ring	ARENA		PARMA, VENICE
circus shelter	TENT	city in Kansas	HUTCHINSON,
circus tent (2 wds.)	BIG TOP		TOPEKA, WICHITA
Cisalpine land	ITALY, GAUL	city in Kentucky	LOUISVILLE
Cistercian monk	TRAPPIST	city in Kwangtung	
cistern	TANK	province	MACAO, CANTON
citadel	FORT, REFUGE	city in Louisiana	NEW ORLEANS
citadel in Texas	ALAMO	city in Michigan	NILES,
citation	SUMMONS		LANSING, DETROIT, SAGINAW,
cite	QUOTE		ANN ARBOR
cite as proof	ADDUCE	city in Minnesota	ROCHESTER,
citizen	SUBJECT, NATIVE		MINNEAPOLIS
citrus drink	ADE	city in Mississippi	NATCHEZ,
citrus fruit	LEMON, LIME,		JACKSON, BILOXI,
ORANGE, GRAPEFRUIT			GULFPORT, VICKSBURG,
city	TOWN, METROPOLIS		GREENVILLE
city dirt	SOOT	city in Montana	BUTTE
city district	WARD	city in Nebraska	OMAHA,
city division	DISTRICT,		LINCOLN
	PRECINCT	city in Nevada	ELKO, RENO
city executive	MAYOR	city in New Hampshire	KEENE
city in Alabama	MOBILE,	city in New Jersey	ORANGE,
SELMA, MONTGOMERY,			NEWARK, PATERSON,
	BIRMINGHAM		TRENTON
city in Alaska	JUNEAU,	city in New	
	FAIRBANKS	Mexico	ALBUQUERQUE
city in Arizona	TUCSON,	city in New York	OLEAN,
	PHOENIX		SYRACUSE, UTICA, TROY,
city in Brazil	RIO		SCHENECTADY, WHITE PLAINS

city in Nicaragua **LEON**
city in Normandy **CAEN**
city in North Carolina **RALEIGH, DURHAM**
city in North Dakota **MINOT**
city in northern France **LILLE**
city in North Vietnam **HANOI**
city in Norway **OSLO, HAMMAR, BERGEN**
city in Ohio **DAYTON, TOLEDO**
city in Oklahoma **ADA, TULSA, ENID**
city in Oregon **SALEM, EUGENE, PORTLAND**
city in Pakistan **LAHORE**
city in Pennsylvania **ALTOONA, YORKTOWN, SCRANTON, PHILADELPHIA, PITTSBURGH, ERIE**
city in Peru **LIMA**
city in Poland **LODZ, POSEN**
city in Quebec **MONTREAL**
city in Russia **OREL, MOSCOW, LENINGRAD, MINSK, PINSK**
city in Sicily **ENNA**
city in Spain **JAEN, AVILA, CADIZ, MADRID, TOLEDO, BARCELONA**
city in Tennessee **MEMPHIS, NASHVILLE, KNOXVILLE, JACKSON**
city in Texas **DALLAS, WACO, EL PASO, HOUSTON, LUBBOCK**
city in The Netherlands **ROTTERDAM, AMSTERDAM, THE HAGUE**
city in Turkey **ISTANBUL**
city in Utah **OGDEN**
city in Washington **TACOMA, SEATTLE**
city in Wyoming **LARAMIE**
city man **DUDE, SLICKER**
city manager **MAYOR**
city official **ALDERMAN, MAYOR**
City of Light **PARIS**
city of Manasseh **ANER**
city of Paris **TROY**
city of Pied Piper legend **HAMELIN**
City of Rams **CANTON**
City of Saints **MONTREAL**
City of Wheels **DETROIT**
city on Lake Ontario **OSWEGO**
city on the Allegheny **OLEAN**
city on the Arno **PISA**
city on the Danube **ULM**
city on the Loire **NANTES**

city on the Mississippi gulf coast **BILOXI, GULFPORT, PASCAGOULA**
city on the Mohawk **UTICA**
city on the Nile **CAIRO**
city on the Oka **OREL**
city on the Po **TURIN**
city on the Rhone **ARLES**
city on the Seine **PARIS**
city on the Thames **LONDON**
city on the Truckee **RENO**
city on the Vltava **PRAGUE**
city problem **SMOG, CRIME, HOUSING, SANITATION, TRAFFIC**
city prosecutor (abbr.) **D.A.**
city slicker **DUDE, SOPHISTICATE**
city square **BLOCK, PLACE**
city thoroughfare **STREET, AVENUE, BOULEVARD, ROAD**
city train **EL, SUBWAY**
civet **CAT**
civic **URBAN**
civic corruption **GRAFT**
civil **POLITE**
civil defense item (2 wds.) **GAS MASK**
civil disorder **RIOT**
civilian clothes **MUFTI**
civilian, to gobs **LANDLUBBER**
civilities **AMENITIES**
civilized **REFINED**
Civil War general **LEE, GRANT, MEADE, SHERMAN**
civil wrong **TORT**
clad **ATTIRED**
claim **ASSERT, AVER**
claimant **PRETENDER**
claim as due **DEMAND**
clairvoyant **SEER**
clam dish **CHOWDER**
clam genus **MYA, VENUS**
clammy **DAMP, DANK**
clamor **NOISE**
clamor of pursuit (3 wds.) **HUE AND CRY**
clamorous **LOUD**
clamp **VISE**
clan **TRIBE, FAMILY**
clandestine **SECRET**
clan quarrel **FEUD**
clap **APPLAUD**
claret **WINE**
clash **CONFLICT**
clasp **EMBRACE, HUG, FASTEN**
class **SORT, KIND, RANK, GENRE, TYPE, VARIETY**

classical Chinese poet
(2 wds.) **LI PO**
classification of plants **GENUS**
classified item **AD**
classify **SORT, RATE, ASSORT**
classroom favorite
(2 wds.) **TEACHER'S PET**
classroom period **HOUR**
classroom talk **LECTURE**
clatter **RATTLE, DIN**
clause **ARTICLE, STIPULATION**
claw **TALON**
clay and sand mixture **LOAM**
clay building block **BRICK**
clayey earth **MARL**
clay worker **POTTER**
clean **WASH**
clean a floor **SCRUB, MOP,**
SWEEP, SWAB
clean and neat (comp.
wd.) **WELL-GROOMED**
clean a painting **RESTORE**
cleaning implement **DUSTER,**
MOP, DUSTPAN, VACUUM,
CLOTH
cleanse **PURIFY**
cleanse of impurities **PURGE**
cleanse of soap **RINSE**
cleanse the feathers **PREEN**
cleansing agent **SOAP,**
DETERGENT, WATER
clean up **POLICE**
clear **BRIGHT, LUCID**
clear a space
(2 wds.) **MAKE ROOM**
clear-cut **DECIDED**
clear of accusations **ABSOLVE,**
ACQUIT
clear profit **NET**
clear up **SOLVE**
cleave **REND, RIVE, SEVER,**
SPLIT, CUT
clef **BASS, TREBLE**
cleft **RIFT, CRACK, SPLIT**
clemency **LENIENCY, MERCY**
clement **MILD**
clench **CLUTCH, GRASP**
clenched hand **FIST**
Cleopatra's handmaiden **IRAS,**
CHARMIAN
Cleopatra's river **NILE**
Cleopatra's snake **ASP**
clergyman **CLERIC, PRIEST,**
VICAR, MINISTER, PASTOR,
RECTOR, PARSON, RABBI,
MONK
clergyman's residence **MANSE,**
RECTORY

clergyman's speech **SERMON**
clergyman's title **REVEREND**
cleric **CLERGYMAN**
clerical collar **RABAT**
clerical mantle **COPE**
clerical vestment **ALB**
cleric of early Irish
Church **ERENACH**
Cleveland's first name **GROVER**
Cleveland's waterfront **ERIE**
clever **CUTE, WITTY**
cleverness **WIT**
clever phrase **MOT**
cliche **PLATITUDE, BROMIDE**
click **SNAP**
cliff **BLUFF**
climate (poet.) **CLIME**
climax **PEAK, APEX**
climax of a joke
(2 wds.) **PUNCH LINE**
climb **ASCEND, SCALE**
climb down **DESCEND**
climbing device **LADDER**
climbing plant **IVY, LIANA,**
VINE
climb on all fours **CLAMBER**
climb on top of **MOUNT**
clime **CLIMATE**
clinch **SEAL, SECURE**
cling **ADHERE, STICK**
clinging crustacean **BARNACLE**
clinic **INFIRMARY, HOSPITAL**
clinical **IMPERSONAL**
Clio **MUSE**
clip **SNIP, TRIM, SHEAR**
clipped **SHORN**
clipper **LINER, SHIP**
clique **CLAN, SET, GROUP**
cloak **MANTLE, ROBE**
clock **TIMEPIECE**
clock dial **FACE**
clock face **DIAL**
clock sound **TICKTOCK, TICK,**
TOCK
clod **LUMP**
clodhopper **LOUT, DOLT**
clog **BLOCK, JAM**
cloister **ABBEY, CONVENT**
cloistered **SECLUDED**
cloistered woman **NUN**
close **NEAR, SHUT, END,**
COVER
close acquaintance **FRIEND**
close at hand **NEARBY**
close by **AT, HANDY, NEAR**
closed car **SEDAN**
close falcon eyes **SEEL**
close firmly **BAR, SEAL**

closefisted	**STINGY, MISERLY**
close friend	**CHUM, PAL, BUDDY**
closemouthed	**TACITURN**
closeness	**INTIMACY**
close noisily	**SLAM**
close relative	**NIECE, NEPHEW, AUNT, UNCLE, BROTHER, SISTER, MOTHER, FATHER, SON, DAUGHTER, PARENT, SIBLING**
close securely	**SEAL**
close tightly	**CLENCH, SEAL**
close to	**AT, BESIDE, NEAR**
close to tears	**SAD**
closet	**WARDROBE, LOCKER**
clot	**MASS, THICKEN**
cloth	**FABRIC**
cloth belt	**SASH**
cloth dealer	**DRAPER**
clothe	**DRESS, GARB**
clothe with authority	**VEST**
clothes	**APPAREL**
clothes (colloq.)	**TOGS**
cloth gaiters	**SPATS**
clothing	**GARB, ATTIRE, TOGS, DRESS**
clothing fabric	**HOPSACKING, TRICOT, COTTON, SERGE, WORSTED, TWEED, WOOL, CORDUROY, DENIM, LINEN, VELVET, FUR, VELOUR, PONGEE, CHIFFON, SATIN, NYLON, ACETATE, SUEDE, LEATHER, SILK, RAYON**
cloth made of flax	**LINEN**
cloth measurements	**YARD**
cloth of gold	**LAME**
cloth piece	**BOLT**
cloth ridge	**WALE**
cloth scrap	**RAG, REMNANT**
cloth used as wall hanging	**TAPESTRY**
cloth worn over the head	**SCARF, KERCHIEF, MANTILLA, VEIL**
clothes moth	**TINEA**
clothespress	**WARDROBE**
clothes tinter	**DYER**
clothes tree	**COATRACK**
cloud	**CUMULUS, NIMBUS, CIRRUS, STRATUS**
clouded	**OBSCURE, OVERCAST**
cloud of smoke	**FUME**
cloud region	**SKY**
cloudy	**DIM, GLOOMY**
clout	**SWAT**

clown	**BUFFOON, COMEDIAN, COMIC**
clownish	**AWKWARD**
cloy	**GLUT, SATE**
club	**BAT, CUDGEL**
club fees	**DUES**
clublike weapon	**MACE**
clue	**HINT, INKLING**
clump	**WAD**
clumsy	**ALL THUMBS, AWKWARD**
clumsy boat	**ARK, TUB**
clumsy fellow	**LOUT, OAF**
cluster	**TUFT**
cluster of flowers	**BUNCH**
cluster of shrubs	**BUSH**
clutch	**GRASP, BUNCH, NUMBER, CLUSTER**
clutch at wildly	**CLAW, GRIP**
coach	**CAR, STAGE**
coach and four	**TALLY-HO**
coach dog	**DALMATIAN**
coagulate	**CLOT, GEL, SET**
coagulum	**CLOT, CURD**
coal	**ANTHRACITE, FUEL**
coal bed	**SEAM**
coal digger	**MINER**
coalesce	**MERGE, UNITE**
coal excavation	**MINE**
coal fuel product	**COKE**
coal hod	**SCUTTLE**
coalition	**ALLIANCE**
coal mine	**PIT, COLLIERY**
coal oil	**KEROSENE**
coal pit	**MINE, STRIP-MINE**
coal product	**TAR, COKE**
coal scuttle	**HOD**
coal tar	**EOSIN**
coal tunnel entrance	**ADIT**
coal unit	**TON**
coarse	**ROUGH, CRUDE**
coarse and sticky	**TACKY**
coarse cord	**TWINE, ROPE**
coarse corn meal	**SAMP**
coarse file	**RASP**
coarse grain	**MEAL**
coarse grass	**REED**
coarse hair	**SETA**
coarse hairnet	**SNOOD**
coarse hominy	**GRITS, SAMP**
coarse part	**DREGS**
coarse tobacco	**SHAG**
coarse wool cloth	**TWEED**
coast	**SEASHORE, SHORE**
coastal projection	**CAPE, NESS**
coaster	**SLED, DISK**
Coast Guard lady	**SPAR**
coast of India	**MALABAR**

coat	COVER	coin of the realm	SPECIE
coat arm	SLEEVE	coin opening	SLOT
coat collar	LAPEL	coin's date space	EXERGUE
coat lapel	FLAP	cola purchase	SIXPACK
coat of arms	CREST	colander	SIEVE
coat of mail	ARMOR	colate	FINISH, STRAIN
coat sleeve	ARM	cold	ALGID, FRIGID, CHILLY,
coat with color	PAINT		COOL
coat with gold	GILD	cold Adriatic wind	BORA
coat with icing	GLAZE	cold and bleak	RAW
coat with metal	PLATE	cold and damp	RAW
coating on grain	BRAN	cold cubes	ICE
coating on iron	RUST	cold dish	SALAD, ASPIC, ICE
coating on teeth	ENAMEL		CREAM, SHERBET
coax	URGE, WHEEDLE, CAJOLE	cold feet	COWARDICE
cob vegetable	CORN	cold season	WINTER
cobbler's form	LAST	cold storage	DEEP FREEZE,
cobbler's tool	AWL		FREEZER
cock	ROOSTER	cold wind (Fr.)	BISE
cocktail seafood	SHRIMP,	coliseum	STADIUM
	OYSTER, CLAM, HERRING	collaborate	AID
cocktail snack	CANAPE	collapse	DEFLATE
coconut tree	PALM	collarbone	CLAVICLE
codfish dish	SCROD	collar fastener	STUD, BUTTON
coelenterate	HYDRA, POLYP,	collar of a coat	LAPEL
	CORAL	collar shape	VEE
coerce	FORCE	collate	COMPARE, ASSEMBLE
coercion	DURESS	collect	ASSEMBLE, AMASS,
coffee (sl.)	JAVA		GATHER
coffee bean	NIB	collect gradually	GLEAN
coffee container	CUP, MUG	collection set	GROUP
coffee dispenser	URN, POT,	collection of animals	ZOO,
	PERCOLATOR, CARAFE		MENAGERIE
coffee grinder	MILL	collection of facts	ANA, DATA
coffee house	CAFE	collection of papers	DOSSIER
cogent	POTENT, STRONG	collection of sayings	ANA
cogitate	THINK	collection of tents	CAMP
cognizant	AWARE, CONSCIOUS	collection of type	FONT
cognomen	NAME	collective	CO-OP
cogwheel	GEAR	collectivism	SOCIALISM
coil	WIND, SPRING	colleen	LASS
coin	MONEY, DIME, NICKEL,	college	SCHOOL
	QUARTER, MINT	college administrator	DEAN
coincide	AGREE	college building, for short	
coincide in part	OVERLAP		DORM
coin factory	MINT	college campus	QUAD
coin manufacture	MINTAGE	college cheer	RAH
coin of ancient Greece	OBOL,	college course	SEMINAR, LOGIC
	DRACHMA	college court	QUAD
coin of Bulgaria	LEV	college dance	HOP, PROM
coin of France	ECU, SOU,	college degree (abbr.)	BA, BS,
	CENTIME, FRANC		MA, MS, PHD, AB, BFA,
coin of India	RUPEE		LLD, MD, DDS
coin of Iran	RIAL	college discussion	
coin of Italy	LIRA	group	SEMINAR
coin of Japan	SEN, YEN	college examination	ORAL
coin of Mexico	PESO	college girl	COED
coin of the Bible	TALENT	college graduate	ALUMNUS

college group **DEBATING TEAM, FOOTBALL TEAM, FRATERNITY, FRAT, SORORITY**
college half-year **SEMESTER**
college head **DEAN**
college official **DEAN**
college president (sl.) **PREXY**
college song **GLEE**
college student **JUNIOR, SENIOR**
college subject **ECONOMICS, ANATOMY, BIOLOGY, CHEMISTRY, TRIGONOMETRY, CALCULUS, LITERATURE**
college term **SEMESTER, TRIMESTER**
collegian's jacket **BLAZER**
collide **CLASH**
collie (2 wds.) **SHEEP DOG**
colliery **MINE**
collision **CRASH**
colloidal substance **GAL**
colloquy **DISCOURSE, SPEECH**
Cologne (Ger.) **KOLN**
Colombia city **BOGOTA**
colonist **SETTLER**
colonize **PLANT, SETTLE**
colonnade **STOA**
colony **SETTLEMENT**
color **DYE, HUE, TINT, PAINT, SHADE, BLUSH, REDDEN, RED, YELLOW, BLUE, CERISE, SCARLET, BEIGE, BROWN, TAN, ECRU, CORAL, OLIVE, GREEN, PURPLE, VIOLET, PINK, AZURE**
color (suffix) **CHROME**
Colorado city **ASPEN, DENVER**
Colorado Indian **UTE**
Colorado mountain (2 wds.) **PIKES PEAK**
Colorado park **ESTES**
Colorado ski resort **ASPEN**
Colorado tributary **GILA**
color a picture **TINT**
color-changing lizard **AGAMA**
color graduation **SHADE, TONE, TINE, HUE**
color of moleskin **TAUPE**
color slightly **TINGE, TINT**
colorful **PICTURESQUE, VIVID**
colorful bird **BLUE JAY, BALTIMORE ORIOLE, PEACOCK**
colorful fabric **CHINTZ PRINT**
colorful lizard **AGAMA**
colorful parrot **MACAW**

colorful warm-water denizen (2 wds.) **PARROT FISH**
colorless **ASHEN, DRAB, PALE, PALLID, TRANSPARENT**
colorless alcohol **NEROLI**
colorless crystalline compound **TAURINE**
colossal **HUGE, IMMENSE**
colt **YEARLING**
coltish **FRISKY**
colt's father **SIRE**
colt's mother **DAM, MARE**
Columbus' birthplace **GENOA**
Columbus' departure port **PALOS**
Columbus' ship **NINA, PINTA, SANTA MARIA**
Columbus' sponsor **ISABELLA, SPAIN**
column **PILLAR**
column shaft **SCAPE**
columnist's entry **ITEM**
columnist Wilson **EARL**
comatose **TORPID**
comb rat **GUNDI**
combat **FIGHT, BATTLE, WAR, DUEL**
combatant **FIGHTER**
combat vehicle **TANK**
combination **UNION, MERGER**
combine **MERGE, UNITE, WED, MARRY, MELD, MIX**
combustion **FIRE, BURNING**
combustion remnant **ASH**
come **APPROACH, ARRIVE, NEAR**
come across **FIND**
come back **RETURN**
come between **MEDDLE**
come by **GET, GAIN**
come close to **NEAR, APPROACH**
comedian Abbott **BUD**
comedian Benny **JACK**
comedian Caesar **SID**
comedian Carney **ART**
comedian Conway **TIM**
comedian DeLuise **DOM**
comedian Durante **JIMMY**
comedian Hill **NORMAN**
comedian Hope **BOB**
comedian Kamen **MILT**
comedian Kaye **DANNY**
comedian King **ALAN**
comedian Knotts **DON**
comedian Lahr **BERT**
comedian Mostel **ZERO**

comedian Shriner	HERB
comedian Skelton	RED
comedian Sparks	NED
comedienne Arden	EVE
comedienne Ball	LUCILLE
comedienne Prentiss	PAULA
come forth	EMERGE, EMANATE
come in	ENTER
come in first	WIN
come in second	LOSE
come into port	LAND
come into sight	APPEAR
come into view	LOOM
comely	PRETTY
come-on	TEASER
come out	EMERGE
come to	REACH
come to an end	HALT, STOP, CEASE, TERMINATE
come to earth	ALIGHT, LIGHT, LAND
come to nothing	FIZZLE
come to rest	STOP
come to terms	AGREE
come together	MEET, MERGE, UNITE, AGREE
comet's train	TAIL
comet tail	STREAMER
come up	ARISE, VISIT
come upon	FIND
come upon (2 wds.)	MEET WITH
come upon unawares (3 wds.)	TAKE BY SURPRISE
comfort	EASE, SOLACE, SOOTHE
comfortable	PLEASANT
comfortable chair	RECLINER
comforter	QUILT, BLANKET
comic	FUNNY, DROLL
comical	AMUSING
comic section	FUNNIES
comic strip detective	DICK TRACY
comic strip sailor	POPEYE
coming into being	GENESIS
coming-out party	DEBUT
comma	CAESURA, PAUSE
command	ORDER, BID, EDICT
commander	LEADER
commander-in-chief	PRESIDENT
commandment	LAW, PRECEPT
command to a horse	GEE, WHOA, HAW, GIDDYAP
commemorate	CELEBRATE
commemoration	MEMORY
commemorative pillar	STELE
commence	BEGIN, INITIATE

commend	PRAISE, APPROVE
comment	REMARK
commentator Sevareid	ERIC
comment on	NOTE
commerce	TRADE
commercial building	MART
commercial flight (2 wds.)	AIR TRAVEL
commercial ship	STEAMER
commercial spiel (2 wds.)	SALES PITCH
commiserate	CONDOLE
commission	PERCENTAGE
commit a faux pas	ERR
commit theft	ROB
commode	CHEST
commodious	SUITABLE, COMFORTABLE
common	ORDINARY
common (prefix)	CENO
common adder	ASP
common ailment	COLD, FLU
common ancestor	ADAM, EVE
common ant	PISMIRE
common conjunction	AND
common level	PAR
common metal	IRON, TIN, NICKEL, STEEL, COPPER, BRASS
common newt	EFT
common people	DEMOS
commonplace	TRITE, BANAL, HACKNEYED
commonplace remark	PLATITUDE
common practice	USAGE
common sailor (2 wds.)	DECK HAND
common tree	ELM, OAK, MAPLE, PINE
common verb	ARE, IS, BE
common viper	ADDER
commonwealth	STATE
commotion	ADO, TO-DO, NOISE, STIR, RACKET, DISTURBANCE
communalism	SOCIALISM
commune in Belgium	NIEL
communicant	MEMBER
communicate	CONVEY
communicating instrument	TV, PHONE, TELEGRAPH, SATELLITE, TELSTAR
communication	MESSAGE, LETTER, WIRE, CALL
communion	FELLOWSHIP, SHARE
communion cloth	CORPORAL

communion plate	**PATEN**
communion table	**ALTAR**
communion vessel	**PYX**
communique	**MESSAGE**
communist	**RED**
commute	**EXCHANGE, SUBSTITUTE**
compact	**DENSE, SOLID, SNUG, SERRIED**
compact body of troops	**PHALANX**
companion	**MATE, PAL, BUDDY, FRIEND, SPOUSE, ASSOCIATE, PARTNER**
companionable	**SOCIAL**
companion for ham	**EGGS**
companion of odds	**ENDS**
company	**GUESTS**
company (Fr. abbr.)	**CIE**
company of people	**CREW, GANG**
company of troupers	**CAST**
comparable to (3 wds.)	**AS GOOD AS**
comparative	**RELATIVE**
comparative conjunction	**THAN**
compare	**CONTRAST, LIKEN**
compare critically	**EXAMINE**
comparison	**SIMILE**
compartment aboard a ship	**CABIN, GALLEY, STATEROOM, BERTH**
compass point	**ENE, NNE, SSE, SSW, ESE, WSW, WNW, NNW, NE, NW, SE, SW, NORTH, SOUTH, EAST, WEST**
compassion	**TENDERNESS, PITY**
compassionate	**TENDER**
compatible	**AGREEABLE**
compatriot	**COLLEAGUE**
compel	**FORCE**
compendium	**SUMMARY**
compensate	**PAY**
compensate for	**RECOUP**
compensation	**PAY, REWARD**
compete	**VIE**
compete in a race	**RUN**
competence	**ABILITY**
competent	**ABLE, CAPABLE**
competition	**CONTEST, RACE**
competition between retailers (2 wds.)	**PRICE WAR**
competitive game	**SPORT, TENNIS, BASEBALL, HOCKEY**
competitor	**RIVAL**
compilation	**REPORT, DIGEST**
compile	**AMASS, EDIT**

compiler of game rules	**HOYLE**
complacent	**SMUG**
complacently self-satisfied	**SMUG**
complain	**MOAN, GRIPE, BEEF**
complainant	**PLAINTIFF**
complaining	**QUERULOUS**
complain loudly (3 wds.)	**RAISE THE ROOF**
complaint	**ILLNESS, AILMENT**
complaisance	**COURTESY, AMENITY**
complaisant	**CIVIL**
complement	**ADJUNCT**
complete	**ENTIRE, WHOLE, TOTAL, UTTER, FINISH, ACCOMPLISH**
complete agreement	**UNISON**
complete collection	**SET**
completed	**DONE**
complete failure	**WASHOUT**
completely mistaken (2 wds.)	**OFF BASE**
completely waterless (comp. wd.)	**BONE-DRY**
complex	**INTRICATE, CONFUSED**
compliment	**FLATTER**
complimentary ticket	**PASS**
comply	**SUBMIT, OBEY**
comply with	**OBSERVE**
comply with commands	**OBEY**
component	**UNIT, PART**
component of atom	**PROTON, ION**
comport	**BEHAVE**
comportment	**BEHAVIOR**
compose	**WRITE**
composed	**CALM**
composer	**AUTHOR**
composer Bernstein	**LEONARD**
composer Dvorak	**ANTON(IN)**
composer Stravinsky	**IGOR**
composite picture	**MONTAGE**
composition	**ESSAY**
composition for two	**DUET**
composure	**POISE, SERENITY**
compound	**COMBINE, ESTER**
compound tincture	**ELIXIR**
comprehend	**UNDERSTAND, GRASP**
comprehensive	**EXTENSIVE, WIDE**
comprise	**INCLUDE**
compulsion	**DURESS**
compunction	**REMORSE, REGRET**
compute	**CALCULATE, COUNT**

computerized
production **AUTOMATION**
comrade **MATE, COMPANION,
FRIEND, PAL, CHUM,
COLLEAGUE**
conceal **COVER, HIDE, MASK**
conceal by false
appearance **DISGUISE**
concealed **HID, HIDDEN,
COVERT**
concede **ADMIT**
conceit **EGO, VANITY**
conceited **VAIN**
conceited person **EGOTIST**
conceive **IMAGINE, SUPPOSE**
concentrate **FOCUS**
concentration **ATTENTION**
concept **IDEA**
conception **NOTION, DESIGN**
concern **CARE, INTEREST**
concerned **ANXIOUS**
concerning **AS TO, IN RE,
ANENT, ABOUT, RE**
concerning a title **TITULAR**
concerning origin **GENETIC**
concerning the ear **OTIC**
concernment **WORRY, ANXIETY**
concert by single
performer **RECITAL**
concert grand **PIANO**
concert halls **ODEA, ODEONS**
concert instrument **OBOE,
PIANO, VIOLIN, HARP,
CELLO, FLUTE, TUBA**
concession **FAVOR**
conch **SHELL**
concierge **CUSTODIAN, SUPER**
conciliate **PACIFY, MOLLIFY**
conciliatory bribe **SOP**
concise **LACONIC, TERSE,
BRIEF**
concise summary **PRECIS**
conclave **MEETING**
conclude **CLOSE, END, FINISH**
concluding passage **CODA**
conclusion **END, FINALE,
FINIS, CLIMAX**
conclusive **DECISIVE, FINAL**
concoct **BREW**
concoction **INVENTION**
concord **AGREEMENT, UNISON**
concordat **COVENANT**
concrete **SOLID, FIRM**
concrete surface **PAVEMENT**
concretion **PEARL**
concur **AGREE**
condemn **CONVICT, DOOM**
condensation **DEW**

condense **ABRIDGE**
condensed
representation **EPITOME**
condign **DESERVED,
SUITABLE**
condiment **RELISH, SEASONING**
condition **CIRCUMSTANCE,
STATE**
conditional release from
prison **PAROLE**
conditional stipulation **PROVISO**
condition made **PREMISE**
conditions **TERMS**
condone **FORGIVE, PARDON**
conducive to peace **IRENIC**
conduct **BEHAVIOR, LEAD**
conduct oneself **BEHAVE**
conductor **DIRECTOR, LEADER**
conductor's stick **BATON**
conduit **CHANNEL, TUBE**
cone-bearing tree **FIR, PINE**
cone-shaped cap **FEZ**
confederate **ALLY**
Confederate soldier **REB**
Confederate States Army
(abbr.) **CSA**
confederation **UNION, LEAGUE**
confer **BESTOW**
conference site, 1945 **YALTA**
confess (3 wds.) **OWN UP TO**
confession of faith **CREDO,
CREED**
confide **TRUST, RELY**
confidence **TRUST**
confident **CERTAIN, SURE**
confine **COOP UP, PEN**
confine by bars **JAIL, CAGE**
confined to a locality **ENDEMIC**
confinement **DETENTION**
confirm **RATIFY**
confiscate **SEIZE**
conflagration **FIRE, BLAZE**
conflict **STRIFE, CLASH, WAR,
BATTLE, FIGHT**
conform **ADAPT**
conform to shape **FIT**
confound **AMAZE, ASTONISH**
confront **FACE, MEET**
confuse **ADDLE, MIX UP**
confused **ASEA, AT SEA**
confused fight **MELEE,
FREE-FOR-ALL**
confused mess **MISHMASH**
confused state **MESS**
confusion **DISORDER, CHAOS**
confute **DENY**
congeal **FREEZE, ICE**
congenial **FRIENDLY**

conger **EEL**
congressional office **SPEAKER, SENATORSHIP, WHIP**
congressman (abbr.) **REP**
congressman's trip **JUNKET**
coniferous tree **FIR, PINE, LARCH**
conjecture **GUESS**
conjugal **BRIDAL, MARITAL**
conjunction **AND, OR, BUT, NOR**
conjunction (Fr.) **ET**
conjunction (Ger.) **UND**
conjunction (Lat.) **ET**
conjunction (Sp.) **Y**
conjure **INVOKE**
conjuror's handiwork **SPELL**
connect **JOIN, WED, MARRY, WELD**
connected group **NEXUS**
Connecticut university **YALE**
connection **LINKAGE, RELATION**
connective **AND**
conquer **BEST, BEAT, WIN**
conscious **AWARE, AWAKE**
consecrate **BLESS**
consecrated **HOLY, BLESSED, BLEST**
consent **AGREE, ASSENT**
consequence **RESULT**
conservationist **FORESTER, ECOLOGIST**
conservative group
(2 wds.) **OLD GUARD**
consider **PONDER**
considerable **NOTABLE**
considerable amount **WAD**
considerate **KIND**
consideration **ESTEEM, ATTENTION**
considering **SINCE**
consign **SEND, DELIVER**
consistent **REGULAR**
consolation **COMFORT**
console **SOLACE, COMFORT, SOOTHE**
consolidate **UNITE, COMBINE**
consomme **SOUP**
consort **SPOUSE, PARTNER**
consort of Amon-Ra **MUT**
conspicuous **NOTICEABLE, SALIENT**
conspiracy **CABAL, INTRIGUE**
constant **TRUE, STEADY, REGULAR**
constantly **AT EVERY TURN, ALWAYS**

constellation **ARA, ORION, LEO, CENTAURUS, LYRA, BOOTES, VIRGO, AQUILA, GEMINI, SCORPIUS, CYGNUS, CRUX, CETUS, COMA, ARIES, GRUS, PAVO, VELA, DORADO, CARINA, AURIGA, TAURUS, LYNX**
consternation **DISMAY, ALARM**
constituent **COMPONENT, FACTOR**
constituent part **ELEMENT**
Constitution
State **CONNECTICUT**
constrain **CHECK, CURB**
constraint **DURESS**
constrict **CONTRACT**
construct **MAKE, ERECT, BUILD**
construct anew **REMAKE**
construction beam
(2 wds.) **I BAR, T BAR**
constructive **CREATIVE**
constructor **BUILDER**
construe **INTERPRET**
consul of old Rome **CATO**
consult **CONFER**
consultation **CONFERENCE, DISCUSSION**
consume **EAT, USE**
consummate **COMPLETE, IDEAL**
consumption **TUBERCULOSIS**
contact **TOUCH**
contact by phone **CALL**
contagious **INFECTIOUS**
contain **HOLD**
container **CAN, TIN, VAT, CRATE, CARTON**
container for face
powder **COMPACT**
container for oranges **CRATE**
containing air **PNEUMATIC**
containing fine soil **SILTY**
containing fire **IGNEOUS**
containing gold **AURIC**
containing iron **FERRIC**
containing orifices **POROUS**
contaminate **TAINT**
contemn **SCORN, RIDICULE**
contemplate **CONSIDER**
contemplative **THOUGHTFUL, SEDATE**
contemporary **MODERN**

contemporary painter **DALI, WYETH, WARHOL, TAMAYO, PICASSO, RAY O'KEEFFE, RIVERS, MIRO, MOTHERWELL, OLDENBURG, GUSTON, INDIANA, POLLOCK, KUPKA, LEVINE, DINE, EVERGOOD, CHIRICO, CHAGALL, ALBERS, ARP, BACON, BENTON, BRAQUE, DIX**
contempt **DISDAIN, SCORN**
contemptible **MEAN**
contemptibly cheap person **PIKER**
contend **COPE, VIE**
content **HAPPY, PLEASED**
contention **STRIFE**
contentment **PLEASURE**
contest **COMPETITION, RACE, GAME**
contestant **ENTRANT**
contestant for office **CANDIDATE**
contest at law **LITIGATE**
contest necessity **BOX TOP**
contiguous **TOUCHING**
continent **AFRICA, ASIA, NORTH AMERICA, EUROPE, AUSTRALIA, SOUTH AMERICA**
contingent **CAUSAL**
continual **CONSTANT**
continue **ENDURE, PERSIST**
continue a journey (2 wds.) **PUSH ON**
continuing story **SERIAL**
contract **CHARTER**
contraction **SPASM**
contract of ownership **DEED**
contradict **DENY, REBUT**
contradiction **PARADOX, DENIAL, REBUTTAL**
contrary **UNLIKE, OPPOSITE**
contrary current **EDDY**
contrast **COMPARE**
contribute **SHELL OUT, DONATE, GIVE**
contribution **DONATION, GIFT, BEQUEST**
contrivance **DEVICE, TRICK**
contrive **CONCOCT**
control **CHECK, DIAL, MASTERY, REGULATE, MANAGE**
control of emotions **RESTRAINT**
controversial **POLEMIC**

controversy **DEBATE, DISPUTE**
conundrum **RIDDLE**
convene **MEET, SIT, CALL**
convenient **HANDY**
convent **CLOISTER**
convent inmate **NUN**
convent room **CELL**
convention **MEETING**
conventional **ACCEPTED, CORRECT**
convention representative **DELEGATE**
conventions **MORES**
converge **FOCUS**
conversant **FAMILIAR, SKILLED**
conversation **CHAT, TALK**
conversational pause **ER, UH, AHEM**
converse **TALK, CHAT, GAB**
convert **CHANGE**
convert into money **CASH**
convert into ordinary language **DECODE**
convertible **CAR, COUCH, SOFA**
convex molding **OVOLO**
convey **BRING**
conviction **FAITH, BELIEF**
convince **ASSURE**
convivial **FESTIVE, GAY**
convoke **SUMMON**
cook **CHEF**
cook bacon **FRY**
cook by simmering **STEW**
cooked fruit dish **COMPOTE, APPLESAUCE**
cooked sufficiently **DONE**
cooker **STOVE, RANGE, POT**
cookery **CUISINE**
cookie **SNAP**
cook in an oven **BAKE, ROAST**
cook in fat **FRY, SAUTE**
cooking device **GRIDDLE, STOVE**
cooking fat **LARD, OIL, GREASE, BUTTER, SUET**
cooking mixture **BATTER**
cooking pot **OLLA**
cooking vessel **PAN, POT, SAUCEPAN, SKILLET**
cook in water **BOIL**
cook lightly in liquid **POACH**
cookout **BARBECUE**
cook over live coals **BROIL, GRILL**
cook quickly **FRY, SEAR**
cook's formula **RECIPE**
cook's measure **TABLESPOON, TEASPOON, CUP, PINCH, DASH**

cook slowly **STEW**
cookstove **RANGE**
cook up **CONCOCT, DEVISE**
cook with dry heat **BAKE, ROAST**
cool **CHILLY, FROSTY**
cool and reserved **ALOOF**
cooled **ICED**
cooled lava **AA**
cooler **JAIL, ICER**
coolheaded **CALM**
coolie **LABORER**
cooling beverage **ADE**
cooling device **FAN**
cool off **CHILL**
cool season **FALL**
cool to low point **FREEZE**
coonskin **CAP**
coop **CAGE, PEN**
cooperate **ASSIST, CONSPIRE**
cooperate secretly **CONNIVE**
cootie **LOUSE, BUG**
cope **CONTEND**
copious **PLENTIFUL**
copper and tin alloy **BRONZE, PEWTER**
copper coin **CENT, PENNY**
Copperfield's wife **DORA, AGNES**
copter **GIRO**
copy **APE, MIMIC, CARBON, XEROX**
copycat **APER**
coral island **ATOLL**
coral reef **KEY**
coral ridge **REEF**
corbel **BRACKET**
Corcyra **CORFU**
cord **STRING, TWINE**
cord-and-stone weapon **BOLA**
corded fabric **REP(P)**
cordial **GENIAL**
cordon **CIRCLE**
cord on an Arab headdress **AGAL**
cord ornament **TASSEL**
cordwood measure **STERE**
core **HEART, CENTER**
cornbread **PONE**
corncob **PIPE**
corner **NOOK, TREE**
cornered **ANGULAR, CAUGHT**
cornet **TRUMPET, HORN**
cornfield weed **DARNEL**
corn-heating utensil **POPPER**
Cornhusker State **NEBRASKA**
cornice **EAVE**
corn porridge **SAMP, MUSH**

corn spike **EAR, COB**
corny **TRITE, BANAL**
corny actor **HAM**
coronet **TIARA, CROWN**
corporal **BODILY**
corporation **BODY**
corpse **BODY, CADAVER**
corpulence **FAT, OBESITY**
corpulent **FAT, OBESE**
corral **PEN, RING**
correct **AMEND, EMEND, TRUE, REVISE, EDIT, RIGHT**
correct a manuscript **EDIT**
corrida cheer **OLE**
corridor **HALL**
corrode **RUST, EAT**
corrupt **LOW, BASE**
corruption **VICE**
corsage **BOUQUET**
corset string **LACE**
cortege **PARADE, RETINUE, PROCESSION**
cortex **BARK, RIND**
cos **LETTUCE**
cosmetic **ROUGE, CREAM, LIPSTICK, SHADOW, MASCARA, LINER, BASE, POWDER**
cost **PRICE, RATE**
costly **DEAR, EXPENSIVE**
costly fur **SABLE, MINK, ERMINE**
cost of membership **DUES**
cost of passage **FARE**
costume **ATTIRE, CLOTHING**
cot **BED**
cote **COOP**
coterie **CLIQUE, SET**
cote sound **COO**
cottage cheese lumps **CURDS**
cotton bundle **BALE**
cotton fabric **LISLE, PIMA, MUSLIN, PERCALE, VOILE, FLANNEL**
cotton pod **BOLL**
cottontail **HARE, RABBIT, PETER**
cottonwood **TREE**
couch **SOFA, SETTEE, DIVAN, DAVENPORT**
cougar **PUMA, CAT**
counsel **ADVICE**
count **NUMBER**
count calories **DIET, REDUCE**
countenance **FACE, VISAGE**
counter **OPPOSE, BAR**

counterfeit BOGUS, FAKE, PHONY, SHAM, IMITATION, ERSATZ
counterfeit coin SLUG
countermand ABOLISH, CANCEL
counterpane COVER
counterpart DUPLICATE, TWIN
countersign PASSWORD
counter tenor ALTO
counting of votes cast POLL
countless INFINITE
Count of music BASIE
country STATE, LAND, NATION, WOODS
country bumpkin (sl.) RUBE, HICK
country by-way LANE
country estate VILLA
country festival FAIR
country hotel INN
country place VILLA, CABIN, FARM
country road LANE
countrywide NATIONAL
county PARISH
county in England SHIRE
coup BLOW, UPSET
coupe AUTO, CAR
couple PAIR, TWO, TWOSOME, DUO, LINK
couple together BRACKET
courage HEART, METTLE, BRAVERY, NERVE
courageous BRAVE
courageous man HERO
courant GAZETTE
courier MESSENGER
course PATH, WAY, ROUTE, PATHWAY
course of instruction CLASS
court WOO
court case TRIAL, SUIT
court cry OYES, OYEZ, HEAR YE
courteous CIVIL, POLITE
court game TENNIS, SQUASH
court hearing OYER
court order FIAT, WRIT
court proceedings TRIAL
court reporter's machine STENOTYPE
courtroom panel JURY
courtroom procedure TRIAL, SUIT
court session ASSIZE
courtyard PATIO
cousin of Absalom AMASA

couth REFINED, POLISHED
couturiere MODISTE
cove BAY, INLET
covenant BOND, CONTRACT
cover CONCEAL, LID, TOP
cover a package WRAP
covered avenue ARCADE
covered porch VERANDA
covered with frost HOARY
covered with moisture DEWY
covered with velvety growth MOSSY
cover girl MODEL
covering of trees BARK
coverlet BEDSPREAD
covert HIDDEN, PRIVATE
cover the face MASK
cover the inside LINE
cover up CONCEAL
cover with a sheath GLOVE
cover with asphalt PAVE
cover with cloth DRAPE
cover with concrete PAVE
cover with gold paint GILD
cover with turf SOD
covet DESIRE
covey BEVY, FLOCK
cow DAUNT, TERRIFY
coward CRAVEN
cowardice FEAR
cowbell CAMPION
cowboy RIDER, ROPER
cowboy country WEST
cowboy event RODEO
cowboy gear STIRRUP, SADDLE, RIATA, LASSO, LARIAT, CHAPS
cowboy movie WESTERN, OATER
cowboy Rogers ROY
cowboy's breeches CHAPS
cowboy's concern HERD
cowboy's nickname TEX
cowboy's rope LARIAT, RIATA, LASSO
cowboy's shoes BOOTS
cower CRINGE
cowfish GRAMPUS
cow genus BOS
cowgirl Evans DALE
cowl HOOD
cows CATTLE, KINE
cow's chewed food RUMEN, CUD
cow's home BARN
cow's low MOO
cow's offspring CALF
cowskin HIDE

cow sound	MOO
coy	DEMUR, SHY
Coyote State	SOUTH DAKOTA
cozen	CHEAT
cozy	SNUG
cozy home	NEST
cozy room	DEN
cozy talk	CHAT
crab	CANCER
crab's pincer	CLAW
crack	BREAK, SPLIT
Cracker State	GEORGIA
crackle	SNAP, CRUNCH, POP
crackpot	NUT, LUNATIC
crack through which water escapes	LEAK
cradle	BASSINET, CRIB
cradle song	LULLABY
craft	BOAT, ART, SKILL
craft of the far north	KAYAK, ICEBREAKER
crafty	SLY, WILY, CLEVER
crag	TOR, PRECIPICE
cram	STUFF, RAM, STUDY
cramp	SPASM, ACHE
crane	DERRICK
crane arm	GIB
cranium	SKULL
crank	GROUCH, HANDLE
cranky	TESTY, CROSS
crash against	RAM
crate	CASE, CARTON
cravat	TIE
crave	DESIRE
craven	AFRAID, COWARDLY
craving	LUST, HUNGER, DESIRE
crawl	CREEP
crawling animal	REPTILE
crayon drawing	PASTEL
craze	FAD, MANIA
crazy	DAFT, NUTS, NUTTY, CRACKED, MAD
cream	ELITE
crease	FOLD
create	ORIGINATE, MAKE, BUILD
create pictures	PAINT, DRAW
creative person	ARTIST
creator of Fantasyland	DISNEY
creator of the Thesaurus	ROGET
creature	ANIMAL, BEING
credence	TRUST
credential	VOUCHER, PASS
creed	RELIGION, BELIEF
creek	INLET, STREAM, BAYOU
creep	CRAWL

creep furtively	SNEAK
creeping creature	WORM, SNAKE, REPTILE
Creole State	LOUISIANA
crescent point	CUSP
crestfallen	ASHAMED
crest of hair	TOPKNOT
crew	TEAM, GANG
crew member	MAN
cricket team	ELEVEN
crime	SIN, OFFENSE
criminal	FELON, CROOK, HOODLUM, MISCREANT
crimson	RED
cringe	COWER
crinkled fabric	CRAPE, CREPE
crinoline	PETTICOAT, SLIP
cripple	DISABLE, MAIM
crippled	LAME
crisis	EMERGENCY
crisp and fragile	BRITTLE
crisp cookie	SNAP
criterion	RULE, TEST, BASIS
critical	ACUTE
criticize	CARP, CAVIL
criticize severely (colloq.)	PAN
critic's account	REVIEW
critic's place (2 wds.)	AISLE SEAT
croak	CAW
Croatian	SERBIAN
crochet	HOOK, KNIT
crockery	CHINA
crocodile	ALLIGATOR
crone	HAG
crony	CHUM, PAL
crook	BEND, THIEF, ROBBER
crooked	ASKEW, AWRY
croon	SING
crooner Crosby	BING
crooner Vallee	RUDY
crop	HARVEST
cross	TRAVERSE
cross a river	FORD
crossbar	AXLE
crossbeam	TRAVE
crossed wood framework	LATTICE
cross in a church	ROOD
cross out	DELE
crouch	BEND, STOOP
crouch in fear	COWER
crow	ROOK
crowbar	LEVER
crowd	HORDE, PACK, MOB
crowded	DENSE
crown	DIADEM, TIARA, CORONET

crow's call	CAW	cultivate	FARM, PLOW, GROW,
crucible	POT		RAISE, REFINE
crucifix	CROSS	cultivate the soil	TILL, FARM
crude	RAW	cultivator	HOER
crude metal	ORE	culture	ART, POLISH
crude rubber	PARA	culture medium	AGAR
crude watercraft	RAFT	culvert	CONDUIT, UNDERPASS
cruel	MEAN, BRUTAL,	cummerbund	SASH, BELT
	SADISTIC	cunning	SLY, CLEVER, ART,
cruel joke	HOAX		SLYNESS
cruel person	BRUTE, MEANIE,	cup	MUG
	SADIST BULLY	cupbearer of gods	HEBE
cruet	VIAL	cupboard	CABINET, CLOSET,
cruise	SAIL		PANTRY
crumb	BIT, PIECE	Cupid	AMOR. EROS
crumble	MOLDER	Cupid's mother	VENUS
Crusader's enemy	SARACEN	Cupid's title	DAN
crush	MASH	cupidity	AVARICE, GREED
crustacean	CRAB, SHRIMP	cupola	DOME
cry	SOB, WEEP, BAWL	cup rim	LIP
cry of a lamb	BLEAT, BAA,	cuprum	COPPER
	MAA, BLAT	cup-shaped flower	TULIP
cry of an owl	HOOT	cur	MONGREL, MUTT
cry of despair	ALAS	curate	PRIEST
cry of pain	OUCH, YIPE, OW	curative	REMEDY
cry of sorrow	ALAS	curb	ARREST, CHECK
cry of surprise	OH, HO, OHO,	cure	HEAL, REMEDY
	AHA	curious	ODD
cry of triumph	AHA, EUREKA	curl	TRESS, RINGLET
cry out	SCREAM, SHOUT	curl the lip	SNEER
crypt	VAULT	curly cabbage	KALE, ENDIVE
cryptic	SECRET, OCCULT	curly-haired dog	POODLE
crystal	GLASS	curly letter	ESS
crystalline gem	IOLITE	curmudgeon	MISER
Cuban capital	HAVANA	currant	BERRY
Cuban dance	CONGA	currency	MONEY
cubicle	CELL	currency exchange	
cubic meter	STERE	premium	AGIO
cuboid	BONE	current	TIDE, PRESENT
cub's home	DEN	current events	NEWS
cuckoo	ANI	current fad	CRAZE
cuckoopoint	ARUM	current fashion	MODE
cucumber	PICKLE	current of air	DRAFT, BREEZE
cud	RUMEN	current style	FAD, TREND
cud chewer	COW	curry a horse	GROOM
cuddle	NESTLE, SNUGGLE	curse	SWEAR, HEX, OATH
cuddy	CABIN, GALLEY	cursory	HASTY, CARELESS
cudgel	CLUB, STAVE	curt	ABRUPT
cue	HINT, SIGNAL	curtail	SHORTEN
cuff	SLAP, STRIKE	curtain	DRAPE
cuff ornament	STUD, LINK,	curtain fabric	NINON, SCRIM
	BUTTON	curtain pole	ROD
culinary expert	CHEF	curtsy	BOW
cull	CHOOSE, SORT	curve	ARC, BEND, HOOK,
culmination	CLIMAX, ACME		TWIST, BOW
culpability	GUILT	curved bone	RIB
cult	SECT	curved doorway	ARCH
		curved garland	FESTOON

curved glass	LENS
curved inward	ADUNCOUS, CONCAVE
curved molding	OGEE
curved roof	DOME
curvy letter	ESS
cushion	PAD, MAT, PILLOW, SOFTEN
Cush's father	HAM
Cush's son	NIMROD, SEBA
cushy	EASY
custard	FLAN
custodian	CARETAKER, JANITOR
custody	CHARGE, TRUST
custom	HABIT, USAGE, MODE
customary	USUAL
customary method	HABIT
customer	BUYER, CLIENT, USER, PATRON
customs	MORES
cut	HEW, SEVER, SAW, SLICE
cut across	TRANSECT
cut apart	SEVER
cut at random	SLASH
cut back	PINCH, REDUCE, DECREASE
cut dead	SNUB
cut down	HEW
cut down a tree	FELL
cut down wood on land	CLEAR
cut fine	DICE, MINCE
cut for insertion in mortise	TENON
cut grass	MOW
cut hair	CLIP, BOB, STYLE, TRIM
cut in	INTERRUPT
cut in small pieces	HASH
cut in squares	DICE, CUBE
cut into cubes	DICE, MINCE
cut into pieces	CHOP
cut into slices	CARVE
cut in two	HALVE, SEVER, SPLIT, BISECT
cut it out	STOP
cut jaggedly	SNAG
cut lengthwise	SLIT
cut lumber	SAW
cut of beef	EYE ROAST, FLANK, SIRLOIN, RUMP ROAST, T-BONE, STEAK, RIB ROAST, CHUCK
cut off	LOP, SNIP
cut off the beard	SHAVE
cut off tops	CROP
cut of lamb	LEG, SHOULDER, CHOP, ROAST, CROWN

cut of meat	CHOP, STEAK, LOIN
cut one's teeth	TEETHE
cut on slant	BEVEL
cut out	OMIT, ELIMINATE
cut out for	FIT, SUITED
cut-price deal	SALE, BARGAIN
cut short	CROP, LOP
cut timber	LUMBER
cut to deep slope	SCARP
cut up	KIBITZ, CARVE
cut with scissors	SNIP
cute	ADORABLE, LOVABLE, DARLING
cuticle	PELLICLE, SKIN
cutter	SLOOP
cutting	SHARP
cutting diamond	BORT
cutting edge	BLADE
cutting implement	KNIFE, SHEARS, SCISSORS, SAW, BLADE, RAZOR, AX, AXE
cuttlefish ink	SEPIA
Cyclades island	DELOS
cylindrical	TERETE
cymbal	TAL
Cymric	WELSH, BRETON, CORNISH
cyprinoid fish	IDE
Cyprus city	NICOSIA
cyst	POUCH, SAC
czar	PETER, IVAN
czardas	DANCE

D

dabber	PAD
dad	FATHER, PAPA, DADDY, SIRE
daffy	WACKY, BATTY, NUTS
dagger	DIRK
dagger thrust	STAB
daily record	DIARY, JOURNAL
dainty	CHIC, CUTE, FASTIDIOUS
dairy animal	COW
dairy product	CHEESE, MILK, CREAM, BUTTER, EGG
dais	STAND, PLATFORM
daisy phrase (3 wds.)	HE LOVES ME
Dakota	SIOUX
dale	VALLEY, VALE, DELL
dally	LINGER
Dalmatian (2 wds.)	COACH DOG
dam	BLOCK, RESTRAIN

damage	HARM, SPOIL, MAR, RUIN
damask	LINEN, PINK
dame	WOMAN, GIRL
damp	HUMID, MOIST, WET
damp and cold	DANK
damsel	MAID
damson	PLUM, BULLACE
dance	WALTZ, POLKA, SAMBA, RHUMBA, CONGA, BALL, PROM, HOP, JIG, TANGO, FRUG, TWIST, BALLET, TAP
dance orchestra	BAND, COMBO, GROUP
dancer	HOOFER, TAPPER, BALLERINA
dancer Astaire	FRED
dancer Bolger	RAY
dancer Charisse	CYD
dancer Chase	BARRIE
dancer for Herod	SALOME
dancer Kelly	GENE
dance routine (2 wds.)	TIME STEP
dancer Rogers	GINGER
dancer Tallchief	MARIA
dancer Verdon	GWEN
dance step	CHASSE, PAS, GLISSADE
dancing mate	PARTNER
dancing shoe	PUMP, SLIPPER
dandelion	WEED
dandy	FOP
danger	PERIL
dangerous	RISKY
dangerous fish	SHARK
dangerous woman	SIREN
danger signal	ALARM, ALERT, SIREN
dangle	HANG
Danish coin	KRONE
dank	DAMP, SOGGY
danseuse	BALLERINA
Danube tributary	ENNS, ISAR
dapper	NATTY
dapple	FLECK
dappled	PIED
dare	CHALLENGE, VENTURE
daring	BOLD, HEROIC, NERVE
daring deed	FEAT
dark	DIM, DUSKY, INKY, BLACK, UNLIGHTED
dark blue	NAVY
dark brown fur	SABLE, MINK, BEAVER
darken	DIM, SHADOW
dark gray	TAUPE

dark-haired girl	BRUNETTE
dark mood	ANGER
darkness (prefix)	SCOTO
dark-skinned	DUSKY, SWARTHY
darling	MINION, PET
darn	MEND
dart	ARROW, FLIT
dash	SHATTER, TEAR, RACE
data	INFORMATION, FACTS, STATISTICS
date	APPOINTMENT
date book	CALENDAR
dated	PASSE
date tree	PALM
datum	FACT
daub	SMEAR
daughter of Cadmus	INO
daughter of Eioneus	DIA
daunt	SCARE, COW
davenport	SOFA, COUCH, DIVAN, SETTEE
David Copperfield's first wife	DORA
David Copperfield villain	HEEP
David's daughter	TAMAR, THAMAR
David's father	JESSE
David's son	AMNON, SOLOMON, ABSALOM
David's wife	MICHAL, ABITAL, ABIGAIL, BATHSHEBA
dawdle	MOPE, LINGER
dawn	SUNUP, DAYBREAK, SUNRISE
dawn (Sp.)	ALBA
dawn moisture	DEW
day (Fr.)	JOUR
day (Heb.)	YOM
day before a feast	EVE
daybreak	DAWN, SUNUP, SUNRISE
daydream	CHIMERA
day of rest	SABBATH
days long gone (2 wds.)	OLDEN TIMES, ANCIENT HISTORY
daytime performance	MATINEE
day work	LABOR
daze	STUN
dazzle	BLIND
dazzling	BRILLIANT
dead city (2 wds.)	GHOST TOWN
deaden the sound of	MUFFLE
deadfall	SNARE, TRAP
dead heat	TIE
dead language	LATIN
deadly	FATAL, LETHAL
deadly snake	ASP, VIPER
deadlock	STALEMATE

Dead Sea city	**SODOM**
dead tired	**WEARY**
deal	**PACT**
dealer	**DISTRIBUTOR,**
	SALESMAN, RETAILER
dealer in salvaged	
trash	**JUNKMAN**
deal sparingly	**DOLE**
deal with	
beforehand	**ANTICIPATE**
dear	**BELOVED**
dear one (Fr.)	**CHERI**
death	**DECEASE, DEMISE**
deathly pale	**ASHEN, ASHY**
debar	**EXCLUDE**
debase	**DEGRADE**
debatable	**MOOT, ARGUABLE**
debate	**ARGUE, DISCUSS**
debilitated	**FEEBLE, INFIRM**
debit	**CHARGE**
debonair	**URBANE, SUAVE**
debonair fellow	
(2 wds.)	**CITY SLICKER**
debris	**RUBBLE**
debt	**OBLIGATION**
debtor's note	**IOU**
Debussy opus (2 wds.)	**LA MER**
decade	**TEN**
decadence	**DECAY**
decamp	**FLEE**
decant	**POUR**
decanter	**BOTTLE**
decay	**ROT, SPOIL**
decay of timber	
(2 wds.)	**WET ROT**
deceit	**GUILE, CHICANERY**
deceitful	**TRICKY, FALSE**
deceive	**FOOL, TRICK,**
	BEGUILE, DELUDE, DUPE,
	MISLEAD
deceived easily	**GULLIBLE**
December song	**CAROL, NOEL**
December 24th	
(2 wds.)	**CHRISTMAS EVE**
December visitor	**SANTA**
decent	**PROPER**
deception	**FRAUD**
deceptive	**ILLUSORY**
decide	**SETTLE**
decimal unit	**TEN**
decimeter	**LITER**
decipher	**READ, DECODE**
decision	**RESOLUTION**
decisive	**CONCLUSIVE**
deck hand	**TAR, SALT, GOB,**
	SAILOR
deck out	**ARRAY**
declaim	**ORATE**

declaim violently	**RANT**
declamation	**ORATORY**
declaration	**AVOWAL,**
	STATEMENT
declaration of allegiance	**OATH,**
	PLEDGE
declare	**AVER, AVOW, ASSERT,**
	ALLEGE, SAY, STATE
declare invalid	**ANNUL**
declare untrue	**DENY**
declination	**REFUSAL**
decline	**DESCENT, EBB,**
	REFUSE
declining	**DECADENT**
declivity	**SCARP**
decode	**TRANSLATE**
decompose	**ROT, DECAY**
decompression sickness	**BENDS**
decorate	**ADORN, TRIM,**
	PAINT, GILD, BEDECK, DECK,
	ORNAMENT
decorated	**ORNATE**
decorate with	
woodworking	**PANEL, INLAY**
decorating metal	**NIELLO**
decoration	**DECOR, MEDAL,**
	BADGE, ORNAMENT
decorative	**ORNAMENTAL**
decorative fold	**PLEAT**
decorative hanging	**FESTOON**
decorative pellet	**BEAD**
decorative stamp	**SEAL**
decorous	**STAID**
decorum	**DIGNITY, PROPRIETY**
decoy	**LURE**
decrease	**ABATE, WANE, EBB**
decree	**EDICT, BULL**
decree beforehand	**DESTINE**
decreed	**FATED**
decrement	**LOSS, WASTE**
decrepit	**INFIRM, SENILE**
decry	**BELITTLE, BOO**
decrypt	**DECODE**
dedicate	**DEVOTE**
deduce	**DERIVE, INFER**
deduct	**SUBTRACT**
deduct from bill	**REBATE**
deduction	**REBATE**
deed	**ACT, ACTION, FEAT,**
	CONTRACT, BOND
deem	**JUDGE**
deep	**PROFOUND**
deep affection	**LOVE**
deep apprehension	**FEAR,**
	FOREBODING
deep blue pigment	**SMALT**
deep blue stone	
(2 wds.)	**LAPIS LAZULI**

deep bow	SALAAM	deform	MAIM
deep canyon	CHASM	defraud	CHEAT, MULCT
deep crimson	CARMINE	defray	MEET, SETTLE, PAY
deep dish	BOWL	deft	ADEPT
deep ditch	TRENCH	defy	OPPOSE
deepen a channel	DREDGE	degenerate	DECAY, DEPRAVE
deep gorge	RAVINE	degradation	DISHONOR,
deep hole	PIT		DISGRACE
deep in tone	LOW	degrade	ABASE, DEBASE,
deeply engrossed	RAPT		DEMEAN
deeply tinge	IMBUE	degree	STEP, STAGE
deep mud	MIRE	degree of a slope	GRADE
deep sleep	TRANCE	deign	CONDESCEND
deep space	OUTER SPACE	deity	GOD
deep valley	RAVINE	deity (name of) *See under*	
deer	HIND, DOE, STAG, ROE,	*Greek deity, Norse deity, etc.*	
	HART	dejected	SAD, MOROSE, GLUM
deer meat	VENISON	Delaware Indian	LENAPE
deer pathway	RUN	Delaware town	CHESTER
deer's horn	ANTLER	delay	RETARD, DETAIN, HOLD
deface	MAR		UP, PUT OFF
defamation	SLANDER, LIBEL	dele	ERASE
defamatory statement	LIBEL	delete's opposite	STET
defame	SMEAR, LIBEL	delegate (abbr.)	REP
default	FAILURE, NEGLECT	delete	ERASE, REMOVE
defeat	BEAT, THWART, ROUT,	deliberate	CAREFUL, CAUTIOUS
	SUBDUE	delicacy	TACT
defeat at bridge	SET	delicate	FRAIL, FRAGILE,
defeated one	LOSER		TENDER
defeat soundly	ROUT	delicate plant	MOSS
defect	FLAW, IMPERFECTION	delicate skill	FINESSE
defection	DESERTION	delicious	TASTEFUL, TASTY
defective	BAD, POOR	delicious beverage	NECTAR
defective bomb	DUD	delight	JOY, PLEASE
defective vision	ANOPIA,	delightful	NICE
	MYOPIA	delightful abode	EDEN
defend	PROTECT, SHIELD	delight in	LOVE, SAVOR
defendant's answer	PLEA	delineate	DRAW
defense	BULWARK,	delirious	RAVING
	PROTECTION	deliver	BRING, RENDER
defenseless	NAKED	deliver an address	SPEAK
defense missile	NIKE, ICBM	deliver formally	PRESENT
defense organization		dell	VALLEY, VALE, DALE
(abbr.)	NATO	delude	DUPE, FOOL
defensible	TENABLE	deluge	FLOOD, SWAMP
defensive slope	GLACIS	demand obedience	
defensive wall	PARAPET	(3 wds.)	SNAP THE WHIP
defensive work	FORT,	demand payment	DUN
	RAMPART	demean	DEBASE, ABASE,
defer	DELAY, RETARD		DEGRADE
defer temporarily	TABLE	demeanor	MANNER
deficient	DEFECTIVE, SCARCE	demented	INSANE
defile	CORRUPT, SOIL	Democrat's symbol	DONKEY
define	DESCRIBE	demolish	DESTROY
definite	FIXED, EXACT	demon	DEVIL, FIEND
definite article	THE	demon of Arabian lore	JINN(I),
definition	MEANING		DJINN, GENIE
deflect	DIVERT	demonstrate	PROVE, SHOW

demonstrative pronoun **THAT**
demoralize **DISCOURAGE**
demos **POPULACE, PEOPLE**
demur **OBJECT, BALK, HESITATE**
demure **SHY, COY**
den **LAIR**
denomination **SECT, CULT, CLASSIFICATION**
denote **SIGNIFY, MEAN**
denounce **ACCUSE, BLAME**
dense **COMPACT**
dense growth of trees **FOREST**
dense row of shrubs **HEDGE**
dent **BATTER**
dental filling **INLAY**
dentine **IVORY**
dentist's degree (abbr.) **DDS**
denude **BARE, STRIP, EXPOSE**
deny **REPUDIATE, WITHHOLD**
depart **GO, LEAVE**
departed **GONE, LEFT, WENT, DECEASED**
department **FIELD, SECTION**
department of France **EURE**
depart secretly **ABSCOND**
depart suddenly **BOLT**
depart this life **DIE**
departure **EXIT**
departure port of Columbus **PALOS**
depend **RELY**
dependable **RELIABLE**
dependent **SUBJECT**
depend upon **HINGE**
depict **PORTRAY**
deplete **DRAIN, EXHAUST**
deplorable **WRETCHED**
deplore **BEMOAN**
deploy **SPREAD, SCATTER**
deport **BANISH, EXILE**
deportment **AIR, BEHAVIOR**
deposit **LAY, PUT, PLACE**
deposit, as a ballot **CAST**
deposit of resources **FUND**
depositor's concern **INTEREST**
depot **WAREHOUSE, STATION, TERMINAL**
depraved **EVIL, BAD**
depravity **CORRUPTION, EVIL**
deprecate **DECRY, BELITTLE**
depress **SADDEN**
depressed **LOW, BLUE**
depression **GLOOM**
depression initials **NRA**
depress with fear **COW**
deprivation **LOSS**
deprive **DEBAR, DISPOSSESS**

deprived of (Fr.) **SANS**
deprived of social rights **UNDERPRIVILEGED**
deprive of sensation **NUMB**
deprived of strength **ENERVATED, DEBILITATED**
deputy **AGENT, REP, ASSISTANT**
deranged **INSANE, DEMENTED**
derby **HAT, BOWLER**
deride **RIDICULE**
derision **SCORN, CONTEMPT**
derivation **ORIGIN, CAUSE**
derive **DEDUCE, INFER, ORIGINATE**
derogatory **SNIDE**
descend (2 wds.) **GO DOWN**
descendant **SCION, HEIR**
descent **FALL**
describe grammatically **PARSE**
descriptive name **TITLE**
desert **ABANDON, STRAND, LEAVE, WASTELAND**
desert animal **CAMEL**
desert dweller **ARAB, BEDOUIN**
deserted in love **LORN, FORLORN, BEREFT**
deserter **RAT**
Desert Fox **ROMMEL**
desert green spot **OASIS**
desert hallucination **MIRAGE**
desert illusion **MIRAGE**
desert in Asia **GOBI**
desertlike **ARID**
desert nomad **ARAB**
desert plant **AGAVE, CACTUS, YUCCA**
desert region of Africa **SUDAN**
desert region of shifting sand **ERG**
desert ship **CAMEL**
desert shrub **TETEM**
desert train **CARAVAN**
desert wind **SIROCCO, SIMOON, SAMIEL**
deserve **EARN, MERIT**
deserving of reproach **BLAMABLE**
desiccated **DRY, ARID**
design **PATTERN, PLAN**
designate **NAME, APPOINT**
design of initials **MONOGRAM**
design on fabric **BATIK**
desirable **VALUABLE**
desire **COVET, WANT, ASPIRE, WISH, HOPE, YEN, YEARN**
desire a lofty object **ASPIRE**
desist **CEASE, STOP**

desk	ESCRITOIRE, SECRETARY, BUREAU
desolate	BLEAK, FORSAKEN, STARK
desolation	RUIN
despair	HOPELESSNESS
desperate	FRANTIC
despise	HATE, LOATHE, SCORN
despondent	FORLORN
despot	TSAR, TYRANT, DICTATOR
dessert pastry	PIE, CAKE, ECLAIR, TART
destination	GOAL
destine	DOOM
destined	FATED, IN THE CARDS
destiny	FATE, LOT
destitute	DEVOID, NEEDY, POOR
destitute of light	DARK
destitution	POVERTY, WANT
destroy	RUIN
destroyed	KAPUT
destroyed by fire	BURNT
destroyer	SHIP
destroy most of	DECIMATE
destroy power of	ANNUL
destruction	ERADICATION, LOSS, RUIN
destructive	HARMFUL
destructive insect	PEST
destructive prowler	VANDAL
destructive rodent	RAT
destructive storm	TORNADO, HURRICANE, GALE, SQUALL, BLIZZARD
desultory	CURSORY, RAMBLING
detach	SEPARATE, SEVER
detached	UNCONCERNED
detail	ITEM
detain	HOLD, KEEP
detect	DISCOVER
detecting device	RADAR, SONAR
detective Queen	ELLERY
detective's case (sl.)	CAPER
detective Spade	SAM
detention	DELAY
deter	WARN, DISSUADE
detergent	SOAP
deteriorate	DEGRADE, DEBASE
deterioration	DECAY, DECLINE
determination	GRIT, RESOLVE
determine	WILL
determined	FIRM, RESOLUTE
detest	ABHOR, LOATHE, HATE

detraction	DEROGATION
detriment	HARM, LOSS
Detroit baseball team	TIGERS
deuce	CARD, TWO
DeValera's land	ERIN, EIRE
devastate	RAVAGE
devastation	HAVOC
develop	UNFOLD
develop into	BECOME
deviate	DEFLECT
device	MACHINE, GADGET
device for runners (2 wds.)	STARTING BLOCK
devil	DEMON, SATAN, FIEND
devilfish	MANTA, RAY
devise	INVENT, CONTRIVE
devise unfairly (2 wds.)	TRUMP UP
devoid	LACKING
devoid of light	DARK
devotion of nine days	NOVENA
devour	EAT, CONSUME
devout	HOLY, PIOUS
dew	MOISTURE
dexterity	AGILITY
dexterous	ADROIT, DEFT
diabetic's need	INSULIN
diabolical	FIENDISH
diacritical mark	TILDE
diagonal	CATERCORNER, SLANT
diagram	GRAPH, MAP
dialect	IDIOM, LINGO, SLANG, ARGOT
dial pointer	HAND
diamond	GEM, JEWEL, STONE
diamond call (2 wds.)	BATTER UP, PLAY BALL
diamond man	PITCHER, CATCHER, BATTER
diamond ring	SOLITAIRE
diamonds (sl.)	ICE, ROCKS
Diamond State	DELAWARE
diamond surface	FACET
diaphanous	SHEER
diary	JOURNAL, LOG
dictate	COMMAND, DIRECT
diction	STYLE
dictionary	LEXICON, GLOSSARY
dido	ANTIC, TRICK, CAPER
die	EXPIRE, DECEASE
diesel engine	MOTOR
diet	REGIMEN
dieter's concern	FLAB, FAT, POUNDS, CALORIES, BULGE, PAUNCH
diet fruit	GRAPEFRUIT

differ	VARY	dinner	MEAL, BANQUET
different	ELSE, OTHER	dinner bell	GONG
differentiate	CONTRAST,	dinner course	DESSERT,
	DISTINGUISH		ENTREE, SALAD, FISH,
differently	OTHERWISE		MEAT, SOUP, APPETIZER
difficult	HARD	dinner jacket	TUXEDO
difficult journey	TREK	dinosaur	LIZARD
difficult problem	POSER	Dinsmore	ELSIE
difficult sailing		dint	FORCE
(3 wds.)	AGAINST THE WIND	diocese	SEE, BISHOPRIC
difficult		dip	IMMERSE, DUNK, SOP
situation	PREDICAMENT	dip Easter eggs	TINT, DYE
difficulty	SNAG	dip into liquid	RINSE
diffident	TIMID, SHY	diploma	CERTIFICATE,
diffuse	SPREAD, EXPAND		DEGREE
diffused with color	IRIDESCENT	diplomacy	TACT
dig	EXCAVATE	diplomat	CONSUL
dig cherrystones	CLAM	diplomatic	TACTFUL
digging implement	SPADE,	diplomat's aide	ATTACHE
	SHOVEL	dip out	BAIL
digit	FINGER, TOE, NUMBER,	dipper	LADLE
	NUMERAL	dire	DISASTROUS, DREADFUL,
dignified	SEDATE		FATAL, CRITICAL
dignify	ENNOBLE	direct	LEAD, MANAGE, AIM
dignity	DECORUM, MAJESTY	direct attention	REFER
dig ore	MINE	direction	GUIDANCE, EAST,
digress	DEVIATE		NORTH, SOUTH, WEST,
dig up	UNEARTH		EASTWARD, WESTWARD,
dike	LEVEE		NORTHWARD, SOUTHWARD,
dilate	EXPAND, WIDEN		RIGHT, LEFT
dilemma	PLIGHT, PROBLEM	direction mark	ARROW
dilettante	AMATEUR,	directive	ORDER
	DABBLER	director	LEADER, MANAGER
diligence	CARE, INDUSTRY	director Kazan	ELIA
dill	ANET, SPICE	director Penn	ARTHUR
dim	PALE	director Preminger	OTTO
dimension	LENGTH, HEIGHT,	dirge	LAMENT
	WIDTH	dirigible	BLIMP
diminish	ABATE, LESSEN,	dirk	DAGGER, SNEE
	PETER OUT, TAPER	dirndl	SKIRT
diminish gradually	TAPER	dirt	FILTH, GRIME, SOIL,
diminutive	SMALL, PETITE		SOOT
diminutive being	GNOME, ELF,	dirty	IMPURE, SOOTY,
DWARF, BROWNIE, GREMLIN			FILTHY, GRIMY, SOILED
diminutive suffix	ETTE, ULE	disability	WEAKNESS
dimwit	DUNCE, FOOL, DOLT	disable	CRIPPLE
din	CLATTER, NOISE,	disadvantage	HANDICAP
	UPROAR, RACKET	disagree	DIFFER, ARGUE
dine	EAT, SUP	disagreeable	NASTY,
dine at home (2 wds.)	EAT IN		UNPLEASANT
diner	EATERY, EATER	disagreeable child	BRAT
ding	RING	disagreeable person	CRAB,
dinghy	ROWBOAT		GROUCH
dingy	DUSKY, DRAB, WORN,	disagreeable sight	EYESORE
	SHABBY	disagreeable woman	SHREW
dining room furniture	TABLE,	disagreement	CLASH, DISPUTE
CHAIR, SERVER, CART,		disappear	VANISH
	BUFFET	disappoint	FAIL

disapproval **CENSURE**
disarray **CONFUSION, DISORDER**
disassemble (2 wds.) **TAKE APART**
disaster **CALAMITY, CATASTROPHE**
disastrous **DIRE, TRAGIC**
disavow **RETRACT**
disburse **SPEND**
disc **RECORD**
discard **SET ASIDE, THROW AWAY, TOSS OUT, SCRAP**
discern **DETECT, PERCEIVE**
discharge **DISMISS, UNLOAD, EMIT, FIRE**
discharge a debt **PAY, PAY UP**
discharge a gun **SHOOT, FIRE**
disciple **STUDENT, FOLLOWER**
discipline **CHASTEN**
disclaim **DISAVOW**
disclaimer **DENIAL**
disclaim formally **ABJURE**
disclose **BARE, REVEAL**
discomfit **THWART, FOIL, ROUT**
discompose **UNSETTLE**
disconcert **ABASH**
disconnect **SEPARATE**
disconsolate **SAD**
discontent **RESTLESS**
discontinue **STOP, HALT**
discord **CONTENTION, STRIFE**
Discordia **ERIS**
discount **REBATE, KICKBACK**
discourage **DAUNT**
discourage through fear **DETER**
discourse **LECTURE, DEBATE**
discourteous **RUDE, IMPOLITE**
discover **ESPY, FIND, DETECT**
discover by chance (2 wds.) **RUN ACROSS**
discoverer of America **COLUMBUS**
discover suddenly (2 wds.) **HIT ON**
discovery-minded traveler **EXPLORER**
discreet **CAUTIOUS, PRUDENT**
discrepancy **VARIANCE**
discretion **TACT**
discrimination **PRUDENCE**
discuss **DEBATE**
discussion basis **TOPIC**
disdain **SCORN**
disease **AILMENT, MALADY**
disembark **LAND**
disencumber **RID, RELIEVE**
disfigure **DEFACE, MAR, SCAR**

disgrace **SHAME**
disguise **MASK, CAMOUFLAGE**
disgust **DISTASTE, DISLIKE**
disgusting **NASTY**
dish **PLATE, BOWL, SAUCER, CUP**
dishes **CHINA**
dish of appetizers (2 wds.) **RELISH TRAY**
dish of cabbage **SLAW**
dish of greens **SALAD**
dish of stewed fruit **COMPOTE**
dishonest **FALSE, UNTRUE**
disinclined **AVERSE**
disinclined to work **LAZY**
dislike **HATE, LOATHE, DESPISE**
disloyal **FALSE, UNTRUE**
dismal **GLOOMY, DREARY**
dismal failure **FLOP**
dismantle **STRIP**
dismantled ship **HULK**
dismay **APPALL, COW, DAUNT**
dismiss **DISCHARGE, DROP**
dismissal (Fr.) **CONGE**
dismiss forcibly **EXILE**
dismiss from office **AMOVE, REMOVE, IMPEACH**
dismount **ALIGHT, UNSEAT**
disobedient **NAUGHTY**
disobey **DEFY, REBEL**
disorder **MESS**
disorderly **UNRULY**
disorderly crowd **MOB**
disorderly flight **ROUT**
disorganize **CONFUSE**
disown **RENOUNCE**
disparage **BELITTLE**
disparaging remark **SLUR**
disparity **ODDS, INCONGRUITY**
dispatch **SEND**
dispatch boat **AVISO**
dispel **DISPERSE, BANISH**
disperse **SCATTER**
disperse in defeat **ROUT**
display **SHOW, FLAUNT**
display cards for a score **MELD, DECLARE**
display stand **RACK**
displease **ANNOY, VEX**
displeased **OUT OF HUMOR, CROSS**
dispose **ARRANGE**
disposed **PRONE**
dispossess **DIVEST**
dispute **HAGGLE, WRANGLE, QUARREL, CONTEST, FIGHT, DEBATE**

disregard **PASS OVER, IGNORE, NEGLECT**
disreputable **LOW, BASE**
disrespectful **RUDE**
disrupt **REND, TEAR**
dissent **DISAGREE, DIFFER**
dissenting vote **NAY**
dissertation **TRACT, THESIS, TREATISE**
dissipate **DIFFUSE**
dissolve **MELT, THAW**
dissuade **DETER**
distance measure **MILE, FOOT, ROD, YARD, INCH**
distant **FAR, AFAR**
distant (prefix) **TELE**
distaste **AVERSION, DISGUST**
distasteful **BITTER**
distemper **AILMENT, VIRUS**
distend **DILATE, SWELL**
distinct **CLEAR, PLAIN**
distinct (comp. wd.) **CLEAR-CUT**
distinct part **UNIT**
distinction **HONOR, RENOWN, DIFFERENCE**
distinctive **PECULIAR**
distinctive air **AURA**
distinctive character **CACHET**
distinctive manner of writing **STYLE**
distinctive mark **STAMP**
distinctive quality **TALENT**
distinctive taste **SAVOR**
distinguish **DISCERN**
distinguished **EMINENT**
distinguishing feature **TRAIT**
distort **WARP**
distorted **AWRY**
distract **DIVERT**
distress **TROUBLE, ANGUISH**
distress call **SOS, HELP**
distribute **ALLOT, DOLE, APPORTION**
distribute cards **DEAL**
district **AREA, REGION, TERRITORY**
district attorney (abbr.) **DA**
district in Saudi Arabia **ASIR**
distrust **DOUBT**
disturb **TROUBLE, WORRY**
disturbance **UPROAR**
disturb suddenly **STARTLE, ALARM**
disturb the peace **RIOT**
disunite **SEVER, DIVORCE**
disuse **DISCARD**
ditch **TRENCH, RHINE, RINE**

ditch around a castle **MOAT**
ditty **SONG, AIR**
divan **SOFA, COUCH, SETTEE**
diva's forte **ARIA**
dive **PLUNGE, RUSH**
divers **SUNDRY**
diver's disease **BENDS**
diversion **GAME, SPORT, AMUSEMENT**
divest **DEPRIVE**
divest of office **DEPOSE**
divide **CLEFT, PART, SPLIT, SEPARATE, SUNDER**
divided into two lobes **BIFID**
divide into regular steps **GRADUATE**
divide into strata **LAYER**
divide in two parts **BISECT**
dividing wall **SEPTUM, PARTITION**
divine **HOLY, SACRED**
divine being **DEITY, GOD**
divine gift **BLESSING**
diving bird **AUK, LOON, GREBE**
diving duck **SMEE, SCOTER**
divinity **FUDGE**
division **SEGMENT, SECTION, RIFT, PART, PORTION**
division of ancient Greece **ELIS**
division of a poem **PASSUS, CANTO, VERSE, COUPLET**
division of Great Britain **WALES, SCOTLAND, ENGLAND, IRELAND**
division of the year **SEASON, MONTH**
division preposition **INTO**
divorce **SEPARATE, DISUNITE**
divorce capital **RENO**
divorced person **EX**
divot **CLOD, TURF**
divulge **TELL, INFORM**
Dixie **SOUTH**
Dixieland **JAZZ**
dizziness **VERTIGO**
dizzy **GIDDY**
do **PERFORM, ACT**
do a jackknife **DIVE**
do a risky deed (3 wds.) **BELL THE CAT**
do away with **ABOLISH**
dobbin **HORSE**
docile **GENTLE, TAME**
dock **PIER, WHARF**
docket **TICKET**
doctor **PHYSICIAN**
doctor's assistant **NURSE**

doctors' group **AMA**
doctor's helper (abbr.) **RN**
doctrine **ISM, TENET, CREDO**
doctrine adherent (suffix) **IST**
doctrine of
  inevitable **FATALISM**
doctrine of selfishness **EGOISM**
doc's penmanship **SCRAWL**
document **PAPER**
document addition **RIDER**
document file **DOSSIER**
documentary **FILM**
dodder **TREMBLE, TOTTER**
dodderer **CODGER**
doddering old age **SENILITY**
do detective work
  (2 wds.) **TRACK DOWN**
dodge **DUCK, ELUDE**
dodge an issue **SIDESTEP**
dodo **FOGY**
doe **HIND, DEER**
doer **ACTOR**
doer of odd jobs
  (2 wds.) **HANDY MAN**
do farm work **HOE, SOW, MILK,**
  REAP, PLOW, HARVEST
doff **REMOVE**
dog **PET, CANINE**
dog doctor, for short **VET**
dog-drawn vehicle **SLED**
dogged **STUBBORN**
doggerel **NONSENSE VERSE**
doggie-in-window locale
  (2 wds.) **PET SHOP**
dog house **KENNEL**
dogie **CALF**
doglike animal **WOLF, FOX**
dogma **TENET, BELIEF,**
  TEACHING
dogmatic sayings **DICTA**
dog salmon **KETA**
dog-tired (2 wds.) **ALL IN**
dog's delight **BONE**
dog's foot **PAW**
dog's growl **GNAR, ROWF,**
  GRRR
dog's lead **LEASH**
dog's name **FIDO, ROVER,**
  KING, REX, LADY, LASSIE
dog's tail movement **WAG**
dog's tooth **FANG**
dog's treats **BONES**
dog's wagger **TAIL**
dogwood **TREE**
do housework **CLEAN, DUST,**
  SWEEP, POLISH, WAX,
  WASH, MOP

doily **MAT**
do in **KILL**
do intensive research **DELVE**
do laundry **WASH**
dolce **SWEET, SMOOTH**
doldrums **CALM**
dole **ALLOTMENT, ALLOCATE,**
  DISTRIBUTE, ALLOT,
  APPORTION, METE, PORTION
doleful **SAD**
doll **TOY, PUPPET**
dollar bill **ONE, SINGLE**
dollop **LUMP, HELPING**
dolman **SLEEVE**
dolor **GRIEF, SORROW**
dolphin **PORPOISE**
dolt **BLOCKHEAD**
domain **FIELD, REALM**
dome **CUPOLA**
domestic **TAME, NATIVE**
domestic animal **CAT, DOG,**
  PET, CANARY, PARAKEET,
  COW, SHEEP, HORSE, HEN,
  ROOSTER, DUCK, BULL,
  STEER, RAM, EWE, GOAT
domestic animals **CATTLE**
domesticate **TAME**
domestic employee **SERVANT,**
  MAID, HOUSEBOY, BUTLER,
  COOK
domestic
  establishment **MENAGE**
domicile **ABODE, RESIDENCE**
dominant **CHIEF, SUPREME**
dominate **REIGN, RULE**
dominating **BOSSY**
domination **RULE**
domineer **BULLY, TYRANNIZE**
domineering **OVERBEARING**
Dominican friar **JACOBIN**
dominion **TERRITORY**
domino **MASK, TILE, ROBE**
don **TUTOR**
Don Adams program
  (2 wds.) **GET SMART**
donate **GIVE, CONTRIBUTE**
donating **GIVING**
donation **GRANT, GIFT**
done **FINISHED, OVER**
done for **DEAD**
done in **TIRED**
donjon **KEEP, TOWER**
Don Juan's mother **INEZ**
do newspaper work **EDIT,**
  REPORT, REWRITE
donkey **ASS, BURRO**
donkey's cry **BRAY**
donna **LADY, MADAM**

donor	**GIVER**	draft animals	**OXEN**
Don Quixote's steed	**ROSINANTE**	draftsman	**DRAWER**
doodad	**TRINKET, BAUBLE**	draftsman's need	
doodle	**SCRIBBLE**	(2 wds.)	**GRAPH PAPER**
doom	**FATE**	drag	**HAUL, TOW, PULL**
door	**PORTAL**	drag loosely	**TRAIL**
door (Ital.)	**PORTA**	drama	**THEATER, PLAY**
doorbell	**CHIME**	drama division	**ACT, SCENE**
door clasp	**HASP, KNOB**	dramatic part	**ROLE**
door column	**ANTA**	dramatis personae	**CAST**
door fastening	**LATCH**	draped garment	**TOGA**
door frame	**JAMB**	drastic social change	**REFORM**
door joint	**HINGE**	draught	**DOSE, PORTION**
door molding	**ASTRAGAL**	draw	**PULL, SKETCH,**
door-to-door			**DELINEATE**
salesman	**PEDDLER**	draw a mark below	**UNDERLINE**
doorway sign	**EXIT**	draw back	**RECEDE**
doorway structure	**ARCH**	draw close	**NEAR**
dope	**NARCOTIC, OPIUM**	drawer knob	**PULL**
dor	**BEETLE**	drawforth	**EDUCE, EVOKE**
dormant	**LATENT**	draw game	**STALEMATE**
dormer window	**LUCARNE**	drawing	**SKETCH**
do sums	**ADD**	drawing room	**SALON, PARLOR**
dot	**PERIOD, SPOT, SPECK**	draw letters	**PRINT**
dote on	**ADORE**	draw off	**SIPHON**
do the crawl	**SWIM**	draw out	**ELICIT**
doting	**FOND**	draw through thin paper	**TRACE**
double	**TWIN, TWOFOLD**	draw tight	**CINCH**
double chair		dread	**FEAR**
(2 wds.)	**LOVE SEAT**	dreadful	**DIRE**
double curve	**ESS**	dream	**FANTASY, REVERIE**
doubt	**DEMUR, DISTRUST**	dreamer	**VISIONARY**
dough	**PASTE, MONEY, BREAD**	dreamland	**SLEEP**
doughnut-shaped roll	**BAGEL**	dreary	**BLEAK**
do up	**PREPARE**	dreary (poet.)	**DREAR**
dour	**GLOOMY**	dredge	**SCOOP**
dove	**PIGEON**	dregs	**LEES, SEDIMENT**
doves' home	**COTE**	drench	**SOAK, SOP, SOUSE**
dove sound	**COO**	Dresden	**PORCELAIN, CHINA,**
dowdy	**SHABBY**		**MEISSENWARE**
dowdy woman	**FRUMP**	dress	**CLOTHE, FROCK,**
down	**FUZZ**		**GOWN, CLOTHING, GARB,**
down (arch.)	**ADOWN**		**APPAREL, ATTIRE**
down (prefix)	**DE**	dressage	**HORSEMANSHIP**
downcast	**BLUE, SAD**	dress border	**HEM**
downpour	**RAIN, TORRENT**	dress carefully	**PREEN, PRIMP**
downright	**CANDID**	dress down	**SCOLD**
downtown Chicago	**LOOP**	dressed	**CLAD**
downwind	**LEEWARD**	dressed pelt	**FUR**
down with (Fr., 2 wds.)	**A BAS**	dresser	**BUREAU, VALET**
downy	**SOFT**	dress feathers	**PREEN**
downy duck	**EIDER**	dress flax	**TED**
downy surface	**NAP**	dressing	**TOPPING, STUFFING,**
do wrong	**ERR**		**SAUCE**
doxology	**HYMN, FORMULA**	dressing gown	**NEGLIGEE,**
doze	**DROWSE, NAP, SLEEP**		**ROBE, WRAPPER**
drab	**COLORLESS, DULL**		
draft	**DOSE, PORTION**	dressmaker	**MODISTE**

dress material **SILK, CREPE, COTTON, SATIN, RAYON, NYLON, ARNEL**
dress style **EMPIRE, SACK, A-LINE, MOD**
dress the hair **COMB**
dress trimming **RUCHE, RUFFLE**
dress up **PRIMP**
dress warmly (2 wds.) **BUNDLE UP**
dressy **STYLISH, ELEGANT**
dribble **TRICKLE**
dried cut grass **HAY**
dried plum **PRUNE**
dried up **SERE**
drift **TENDENCY, TREND, FLOAT, PILE**
drill **BORE**
drill into again **RETAP**
drink **IMBIBE, QUAFF**
drink heavily **TOPE**
drinking cup **MUG, TOBY**
drinking salutation **PROSIT**
drinking tube **STRAW**
drinking vessel **CUP, MUG, GLASS, STEIN**
drink like a dog **LAP**
drink slowly **SIP**
drink to excess **TIPPLE**
drink to health of **TOAST**
drip **TRICKLE**
drip-dry **NO IRON**
dripping wet **SODDEN**
drive **IMPEL, PROPEL**
drive a golf ball (2 wds.) **TEE OFF**
drive at **AIM**
drive away **SHOO**
drive back **REPULSE, REPEL**
drive backward **REVERSE**
drive forward **IMPEL, PROPEL**
drive frantic **BEDEVIL**
drive-in **RESTAURANT, MOVIE**
drive insane **MADDEN**
drive obliquely **SLICE**
drive out **EXPEL**
driver **CHAUFFEUR**
driver's compartment **CAB**
driveway covering **GRAVEL**
drizzle **RAIN**
droll **FUNNY**
dromedary **CAMEL**
drone **HUM, BUZZ, BEE**
drool **SLAVER**
droop **SAG, WILT**
drooping on one side **ALOP**
drooping tree **WILLOW**

droopy **TIRED**
drop **FALL, GLOBULE**
drop down suddenly **DIP, PLUNGE**
drop from sight **VANISH**
drop heavily **PLOP**
drop in **VISIT, CALL**
droplet **BEAD**
drop off **DECLINE, DECREASE**
drop slowly **SINK**
dropsy **EDEMA**
dross **WASTE**
dross of metal **SLAG**
drove **FLOCK**
drown **INUNDATE, SUBMERGE**
drowse **DOZE, NOD**
drowsy **SLEEPY**
drudge **SLAVE**
drudgery **LABOR, GRIND**
drug **MEDICINE, OPIATE, DOPE**
drug container **CAPSULE**
druggist **APOTHECARY, PHARMACIST**
drug plant **ALOE, POPPY**
drugstore **PHARMACY**
drug-yielding crocus **SAFFRON**
drum **TAMBOR, KETTLE**
drunkard **SOT, SOUSE, TIPPLER**
dry **ARID, SEAR, SERE**
dryad **NYMPH**
dry, as wine **SEC**
dry dishes **WIPE**
dryer **BLOWER**
dry goods dealer (Brit.) **DRAPER**
drying cloth **TOWEL**
drying kiln **OAST**
dry outer part **HUSK**
dry river bed **WADI**
dry rot **FUNGUS**
dry run **REHEARSAL**
duad **PAIR, COUPLE**
dual **TWOFOLD**
dub **TAP, NAME**
dubious **DOUBTFUL**
duck **MALLARD, TEAL, SMEE, PINTAIL**
ducklike bird **COOT**
duck's call **QUACK**
duct **CANAL, TUBE**
ductile **DOCILE, FACILE**
dud **FLOP, FIZZLE**
dude **TENDERFOOT**
due **OWING**
duel **CONTEST**

duelist's aide	SECOND
duet	TWO, TWOSOME, DUO
due to motion	KINETIC
duffer's bugaboo	TRAP
duke (Fr.)	DUC
duke's wife	DUCHESS
dukedom	DUCHY
dull	DREARY, BLUNT,
	BORING, TEDIOUS, DRAB
dull blow	THUD
dull color	GRAY, GREY
dull fellow	CLOD
dull pain	ACHE
dull routine	RUT
dull thump	THUD
duly	PROPERLY
Dumas character	ARAMIS
dumb	MUTE
dumbbell	DUNCE
dumb girl	DORA
dump dweller	RAT
dun	TAN
dunce	FOOL
dunderhead	ASS
duo	PAIR, TWOSOME, DUET,
	TWO
dupe	TRICK, FOOL
duplicate	REPLICA, COPY,
	CARBON
duplicate part	SPARE
duplication	COPY, REPLICA
durable	LASTING, CONSTANT
duramen	HEARTWOOD
duration	TERM, TIME, SPAN,
	TENURE
duress	IMPRISONMENT,
	FORCE
during the time that	WHILE
dusk	GLOAM, TWILIGHT
dusky	DARK
dust cloth	RAG
dust matter	LINT
dust speck	MOTE
dustbowl victim	OKIE
Dutch cheese	EDAM, GOUDA
Dutch coin	STIVER, GUILDER
Dutch commune	EDE
Dutch embankment	DIKE
Dutch flower	TULIP
Dutch Guiana	SURINAM
Dutch landholder	PATROON
Dutch measure	AHM, AUM
Dutch pottery	DELFT
Dutch South African	BOER
Dutch uncle	EME
duty	TASK, TARIFF
dwarf	ELF, RUNT
dwell	ABIDE, RESIDE, LIVE

dweller	TENANT
dwelling place	ABODE, HOME,
	DOMICILE, RESIDENCE,
	HOUSE, APARTMENT, VILLA,
	FARM, RANCH, ESTATE,
	DUPLEX, PENTHOUSE, COOP
dwell on unduly	HARP
dwindle	TAPER, WANE
dyad	PAIR, COUPLE
dybbuk	SPIRIT
dye	COLOR, STAIN, TINT,
	ANIL, TINGE
dye compound	ANILINE,
	EOSIN
dye for butter	ACHIOTE,
	ANNATTO, ARNATO
dyed rabbit fur	LAPIN
dyeing tub	TANK, VAT
dyer	STAINER
dynamic	POTENT
dynamite explosion	BLAST
dynamo	GENERATOR
dyspeptic	GLOOMY,
	GROUCHY, MOROSE

E

each	APIECE, EVERY,
	EVERYONE, ALL
each and every	ALL
eager	AGOG, ANXIOUS,
	ARDENT, AVID,
	ENTHUSIASTIC, KEEN,
	IMPATIENT
eagerness	ALACRITY, FERVOR
eagerness for action	ELAN
eagle	ERN, ERNE
eagle's claw	TALON
eagle's nest	AERIE, EYRIE,
	EYRY, AERY
ear	AURICLE
ear (prefix)	OT, OTO
earache	OTALGIA
eared seal	OTARY
earlier	PRIOR
earliest	FIRST, SOONEST
earliest born	ELDEST, FIRST
early	PREMATURE
early Briton	PICT, CELT,
	ANGLE, JUTE
early dwelling place	CAVE
early mattress	
stuffing	STRAW
early part of day	MORN,
	MORNING
early part of night	EVENING

early stringed
  instrument **LUTE, LYRE**
early violin **REBEC**
earn **MERIT, DESERVE**
earnest **SINCERE, ZEALOUS**
earnest effort **UTMOST, BEST**
earnings **SALARY, WAGES,**
PROFIT
ear of corn **SPIKE**
ear ornament **EARRING**
ear part **LOBE**
ear shell **ABALONE**
earshot **HEARING**
earsplitting **LOUD**
earth **WORLD, LAND, SOIL,**
PLANET
earth deity **TARI, GEB, KEB**
earth deposit **SILT**
earthenware **CROCKERY**
earthenware jar **OLLA**
earthenware vessel **JAR, OLLA**
earthly **MUNDANE, PROFANE**
earth mover **BULLDOZER**
earthnut **TRUFFLE**
earthquake **TREMOR, SEISM**
earth's axis end **POLE**
earth's satellite **MOON**
earth's sister planet **VENUS**
earth's star **SUN, SOL**
earthworm **ANNELID**
earthy **SENSUAL**
earthy deposit **MARL**
earwax **CERUMEN**
ease **ALLEVIATE, RELIEVE,**
LUXURY, SOOTHE
easel **STAND**
ease off **ABATE**
ease up **RELENT**
easily broken **FRAGILE**
easily cut, as a steak **TENDER**
easily deceived **GULLIBLE**
easily fooled person **DUPE**
easily frightened **SKITTISH**
easily hurt **SENSITIVE**
easily managed **DOCILE**
east **ORIENT**
Easter flower **LILY**
eastern **ORIENTAL**
eastern caravansary **SERAI**
eastern Catholic **UNIATET**
eastern potentate **RAJAH**
eastern priest **ABBA**
eastern title **AGA**
Easter preparatory
  season **LENT**
East Indian bird **SHAMA**
East Indian cedar **DEODAR**
East Indian cereal grass **RAGI**

East Indian island **BALI**
East Indian pepper plant **BETEL**
East Indian sailor **LASCAR**
East Indian timber tree **TEAK**
East Indian tree **POON**
East Indian weight **BAHAR, SER**
East Indian wood **ENG, ALOES**
east wind god **EURUS**
easy **FACILE**
easy does it **CAREFUL**
easy gait **LOPE**
easy gallop **CANTER**
easy-going horse **PADNAG**
easy-going walker **AMBLER**
easy job **SINECURE**
easy mark (2 wds.)
SOFT TOUCH
easy task **CINCH, SNAP**
easy winner
  (comp. wd.) **SHOO-IN**
eat **CONSUME, DEVOUR, DINE,**
SUP, ERODE
eat at eight **DINE**
eat away **ERODE**
eat by regimen **DIET**
eatery **DINER**
eat grass **GRAZE**
eat greedily **GOBBLE**
eating alcove **DINETTE**
eating utensil **FORK, SPOON,**
KNIFE
eat noisily **SLURP**
eat peanuts **MUNCH**
eat sparingly **DIET**
eau de vie **BRANDY**
eavesdrop **LISTEN**
ebb **ABATE, RECEDE,**
SUBSIDE
ebb and flow **TIDE**
ebony **BLACK**
ebullient **BUBBLING**
eccentric **ODD, QUEER**
eccentric piece **CAM**
ecclesiastic **PRIEST**
echinoderm **STARFISH**
echo **REVERBERATE,**
RESOUND, REPEAT, APE,
MIMIC
eclat **ACCLAIM**
eclipse **DARKEN**
economical **FRUGAL, THRIFTY**
economize **SAVE, SCRIMP**
ecstasy **RAPTURE**
ectoskeleton **SHELL**
Ecuador capital **QUITO**
Ecuador islands **GALAPAGOS**

ecumenical **UNIVERSAL, GENERAL, WORLDWIDE, ALL**
eddy **SWIRL, WHIRLPOOL**
Eden **PARADISE**
edge **ADVANTAGE, BRINK, VERGE, BORDER, BRIM, RIM, MARGIN, LIP**
edge of a molding **ARRIS**
edge of a street **CURB, KERB**
edge of woven fabric **SELVAGE**
edging **HEM**
edgy **NERVOUS, TENSE**
edible bean **LENTIL**
edible bivalve **MUSSEL, CLAM, OYSTER**
edible bulb **ONION**
edible crustacean **LOBSTER, CRAB**
edible fish **CARP, TUNA**
edible fruit **PLUM, PEAR, APPLE, ORANGE**
edible fungus **MUSHROOM**
edible green pod **OKRA**
edible Japanese shoot **UDO**
edible marine fish **GRUNT**
edible nut **ALMOND, CASHEW, FILBERT, PECAN, WALNUT, PEANUT, HAZELNUT**
edible part of fruit **PULP**
edible root **CARROT, RADISH, POTATO, BEET, PARSNIP, TURNIP, TARO**
edibles **FOODS**
edible seaweed **DULSE**
edible seed **BEAN, PEA**
edible tuber **POTATO, OCA, YAM**
edict **DECREE**
edification **INSTRUCTION**
edifice **BUILDING**
edify **INSTRUCT, ENLIGHTEN**
edit **REVISE**
Ed Sullivan, e.g. **EMCEE**
educate **TEACH, TRAIN, SCHOOL**
education **TRAINING**
educe **ELICIT, EVOKE**
eel **LAMPREY, CONGER**
eerie **SPOOKY, WEIRD**
efface **ERASE, EXPUNGE**
effect **FINISH, FULFILL, RESULT**
effective **USEFUL, EFFICIENT**
effeminate **WOMANLY**
effervescent **VOLATILE**
efficiency **ABILITY, EFFICACY**
efficient **ABLE, CAPABLE, COMPETENT, VALID**

eft **NEWT**
egg **GOAD, INCITE**
egg (prefix) **OVI**
egg cell **OVUM**
egg center **YOLK, NUCLEUS**
egg covering **SHELL**
egg dish **OMELET, SOUFFLE**
egg drink **NOG**
egg layer **HEN**
egg on **URGE**
egg part **YOLK, WHITE**
egg-shaped **OVAL, OVATE, OVOID**
egg white **ALBUMEN**
egis **AUSPICES, PATRONAGE**
ego **SELF, CONCEIT**
egotism **CONCEIT, VANITY**
egotistic **VAIN**
egress **EXIT**
egret **HERON**
Egyptian **COPTIC, COPT**
Egyptian astral body **KA**
Egyptian beetle **SCARAB**
Egyptian boat **BARIS**
Egyptian dam site **ASWAN**
Egyptian dancing girl **ALME**
Egyptian deity **SEB, SET(H), APET, OPET, ISIS, AMON, ANUBIS, OSIRIS, BUBASTIS, MA, THOTH, RA, BES, AANI, HAPI, PTAH, SATI, HORUS, ATON, HERSHEF**
Egyptian governor **PASHA**
Egyptian king **PTOLEMY, FAROUK**
Egyptian king's crown **ATEF**
Egyptian lily **LOTUS, CALLA**
Egyptian measure **ABDAT, CUBUT**
Egyptian paper **PAPYRUS**
Egyptian peninsula **SINAI**
Egyptian queen of gods **SATI**
Egyptian reed **PAPYRUS**
Egyptian river **NILE**
Egyptian sacred bull **APIS**
Egyptian seaport **SUEZ**
Egyptian stone **ROSETTA**
Egyptian sun disk **ATEN**
Egyptian sun god **RA**
Egyptian symbol **SCARAB**
Egyptian tomb **PYRAMID**
eider **DOWN, DUCK**
eight (comb. form) **OCTO**
Eire **IRELAND, ERIN**
Eisenhower memorial museum site **ABILENE**

Eisenhower's nickname **IKE**
either **OR**
ejaculate **EXCLAIM**
eject **OUST**
eke **SUPPLEMENT**
elaborate **FANCY**
elaborate meal **FEAST**
elan **ARDOR, ENTHUSIASM, VERVE, DASH**
elapse **EXPIRE, PASS**
elastic **PLIABLE**
elate **GLADDEN**
elation **GLADNESS, JOY, HAPPINESS**
elder **OLDER, SENIOR**
elderly **AGED, OLD, ANCIENT**
elderly person (2 wds.) **SENIOR CITIZEN**
elder statesman of Japan **GENRO**
eldest of the Pleiades **MAIA**
elect **CHOOSE, SELECT**
elector **VOTER**
electrical device **RESISTOR**
electrical engineer (abbr.) **EE**
electrically charged particle **ION, PROTON**
electrical unit **AMP, FARAD, OHM, VOLT, WATT, MHO**
electric current (abbr.) **AC, DC**
electric current path **CIRCUIT**
electrician **WIRER**
electrified particle **ION**
electromotive unit **VOLT**
electronic beam **LASER**
electronic speed-check **RADAR**
elegance **GRACE, POLISH**
elegance of manners **REFINEMENT**
elegant **REFINED, POLISHED**
elegant appetizer **CAVIAR, PATÉ**
elegant attire **ARRAY**
element **INGREDIENT, FACTOR**
elementary **PRIMARY**
elementary schoolbook **PRIMER**
elephant call **TRUMPET**
elephant cry **BARR**
elephant dentin **IVORY**
elephant driver **MAHOUT**
elephant saddle **HOWDAH**
elephant's ear **TARO**
elephant's tooth **TUSK**
elephant's tusk **IVORY**
elevate **EXALT, RAISE, UPLIFT, REAR**
elevated railroad **EL**
elevation **HILL**

elevator **LIFT**
elevator direction **UP, DOWN**
elf **SPRITE, PIXIE, GNOME, BROWNIE**
elicit **EVOKE, EDUCE**
elide **OMIT, SLUR**
eligible **FIT, WORTHY**
eliminate (2 wds.) **RULE OUT**
elite **CREAM**
elk **MOOSE**
elk's horn **ANTLER**
elliptical **OVAL, OVATE**
elm **TREE**
Elmo Roper item (2 wds.) **STRAW VOTE**
elongate **LENGTHEN, STRETCH**
elope **ABSCOND**
eloquence **RHETORIC, ORATORY**
eloquent **EXPRESSIVE**
else **OTHERWISE**
elucidate **EXPLAIN, ILLUSTRATE**
elude **EVADE, AVOID**
emaciated **LEAN, SKINNY**
emanate **ISSUE, FLOW**
emanation **AURA**
emancipate **LIBERATE, FREE**
embankment **LEVEE**
embark **SAIL**
embarrass **ABASH**
embarrassment **SHAME**
embellish **ADORN, DECORATE**
ember **COAL**
embezzle **STEAL**
emblem **BADGE, TOKEN**
emblem of grief **RUE**
emblem of United States **EAGLE**
embody **EMBRACE, COMPRISE**
embolden **STIMULATE**
embrace **CLASP, HUG**
embroidery **NEEDLEWORK**
embroidery silk **FLOSS**
embroil **PERPLEX, TROUBLE**
emcee Linkletter **ART**
emcee Mack **TED**
emcee Sullivan **ED**
emend **CORRECT**
Emerald Isle **EIRE, ERIN, IRELAND**
emerge from an egg **HATCH**
emergency **CRISIS, NECESSITY**
emergency sum (2 wds.) **MAD MONEY**
emery **CORUNDUM**
emigrant **SETTLER**
emigrate **MIGRATE, MOVE**

Emily Post behavior (2 wds.) **GOOD MANNERS**
eminent **ILLUSTRIOUS, PROMINENT**
emissary **AGENT**
emit **DISCHARGE, VENT**
emit rays of light **RADIATE**
emit vapor **REEK, STEAM**
emmet **ANT**
emote **OVERACT, ACT, HAM**
emotion **SENTIMENT, FEELING**
emotionally detached **CLINICAL**
emotional shock **TRAUMA**
empathy **COMPASSION**
emperor **RULER**
emphasis **STRESS, ACCENT**
emphasize **ACCENT, STRESS, UNDERSCORE, PLAY UP**
emphatic **STRONG, FORCEFUL**
emphatic request **DEMAND**
Empire State (2 wds.) **NEW YORK**
Empire State city **OLEAN, YONKERS, UTICA, ALBANY, TROY**
Empire State of the south **GEORGIA**
employ **HIRE, TAKE ON, USE, UTILIZE**
employee **HAND, HELP**
employee's hourly record **TIME CARD**
employer **BOSS**
employment **WORK**
emporium **STORE, MART**
empower **ENABLE, ENTITLE**
empty **BARE, VOID, BLANK, INANE, UNOCCUPIED**
empty bullet **SHELL**
empty place **SPACE, BLANK, SHELL, VACANT, VOID**
emulate **IMITATE**
emulation **RIVALRY, IMITATION**
emulsion **PAP**
enable **EMPOWER, PERMIT**
enact **DECREE**
enamel **GLAZE, PAINT**
enamor **CHARM**
enchant **CHARM, BEWITCH**
enchantment **SPELL**
enchantress **SIREN**
encina **OAK**
encircle **ENCLOSE, RING**
encircled **GIRT**
encircling strap **BELT, CINCTURE**
enclose **ENVELOP, FENCE**
enclosed automobile **SEDAN**

enclosed in this **HEREWITH**
enclose in paper **WRAP**
enclosure **CAGE, PEN**
enclosure for horses **CORRAL**
encomiast **EULOGIST**
encomium **PRAISE**
encompass **INCLUDE**
encore **AGAIN, BIS**
encounter **MEET, MEET WITH**
encourage **ABET, PROD, EGG ON**
encroach **TRESPASS**
encroach on **INVADE**
encrust **CAKE**
encumber **HINDER**
encumbrance **BURDEN**
encyclopedic **COMPREHENSIVE**
end **CONCLUDE, CONCLUSION, FINISH, TERMINATE, TERMINUS, OUTCOME, RESULT, AIM, GOAL, OMEGA, PURPOSE**
end (Lat.) **FINIS**
endanger **IMPERIL**
endearment **CARESS**
endeavor **ATTEMPT, STRIVE**
endemic **NATIVE**
endless **ETERNAL**
endocrine **GLAND, GLANDULAR**
end of a pencil **STUB, ERASER**
end of a spar **YARDARM**
endowment **GIFT, BEQUEST**
endurable **BEARABLE**
endurance **PATIENCE, TOLERANCE**
endure **LAST, BEAR, TOLERATE**
enemy **FOE**
energetic **VIGOROUS**
energize **ACTIVATE**
energy **VIM, VIGOR, PEP**
energy unit **ERG**
enervate **WEAKEN, SAP**
enfeeble **WEAKEN**
enfold **WRAP, ENVELOP**
enforce **EXECUTE**
enfranchise **FREE**
engage **HIRE, WIN**
engage, as gears **MESH**
engage in a contest **COMPETE**
engage in reverie **DREAM**
engage in small talk **CHAT, GAB, JAW**
engage in sport **PLAY**
engage in winter sport **SKI, SKATE**
engagement **TROTH, DATE, BETROTHAL**

engagement ring	**SPARKLER**
engender	**BREED**
engine	**MOTOR**
engineer	**DESIGNER**
engineer's helper	**OILER**
English actor	**TREE, MILLS,**
	REDGRAVE
English admiral	**NELSON**
English air force	**R.A.F.**
English architect	**WREN**
English architecture	**TUDOR**
English bard	**SCOP**
English cathedral city	**ELY,**
	COVENTRY, ST. ALBANS
English city	**BRISTOL,**
	LIVERPOOL
English coin	**SHILLING, PENNY**
English coins	**PENCE**
English college	**OXFORD, ETON**
English composer	**ARNOLD,**
	BLIS, BRITTEN, ELGAR,
	PURCELL
English conservative	**TORY**
English count	**EARL**
English county	**SHIRE**
English derby town	**EPSOM**
English dynasty	**TUDOR,**
	STUART
English game	**CRICKET**
English heather	**LING**
English island	**WIGHT**
English manufacturing city	
	LEEDS, LIVERPOOL
English nursemaid	**NANNY**
English poet	**MILTON, BYRON,**
	SHELLEY, KEATS
English policeman	**BOBBY**
English porcelain	**SPODE**
English potter	**SPODE**
English prep school	**ETON,**
	HARROW
English princess	**ANNE,**
	MARGARET
English professor	**DON**
English pudding	**PUD**
English racetrack	**ASCOT**
English region (2 wds.)	
	LAKE DISTRICT,
	HOME COUNTIES
English resort	**BATH,**
	BRIGHTON
English river	**AVON, DEE,**
	HUMBER, THAMES
English rowboat	**PUNT**
English school	**ETON, HARROW**
English statesman	**PITT**
English streetcar	**TRAM**
English tavern	**PUB, TAPROOM**

engrave	**ETCH**
engraver's tool	**BURIN**
engross	**ABSORB**
engrossed	**ENRAPT, RAPT**
engulf	**DROWN, SWAMP**
enigma	**RIDDLE**
enjoin	**ORDER, DIRECT**
enjoy	**LIKE**
enjoy a book	**READ**
enjoy a cigar	**SMOKE**
enjoy a meal	**DINE, EAT, SUP**
enjoyment	**FUN, AMUSEMENT**
enlarge	**WIDEN, PROJECT**
enlarge a hole	**REAM**
enlighten	**INFORM, TEACH**
enlist	**ENROLL**
enlisted man	**GI**
enliven	**ANIMATE**
enmity	**MALICE**
ennui	**TEDIUM, BOREDOM**
enormity	**VASTNESS**
enormous	**HUGE, VAST,**
	LARGE, BIG
enough	**ADEQUATE, PLENTY**
enrage	**ANGER, MADDEN**
enrapture	**ENCHANT, CHARM**
enroll	**ENTER, REGISTER**
en route (3 wds.)	**ON THE WAY**
ensconce	**CONCEAL, HIDE**
ensign (abbr.)	**ENS.**
ensnare	**ENTRAP, NET**
ensue	**FOLLOW**
entangle	**SNARL**
enter	**BEGIN**
enter in writing	**SET DOWN**
enterprise	**VENTURE**
entertain	**AMUSE, TREAT,**
	REGALE
entertain at one's	
own expense	**TREAT**
entertainer	**ACTOR, STAR**
entertaining	**AMUSING**
entertain lavishly	**FETE,**
	REGALE
entertainment	**FUN, PLEASURE**
	SHOW
entertainment group (abbr.)	
	USO
enthrall	**FASCINATE**
enthralled	**RAPT**
enthusiasm	**ELAN**
enthusiast	**FAN**
enthusiastic	**AVID, EAGER**
enthusiastic applause	**OVATION**
enthusiastic review	**RAVE**
entice	**ALLURE, LURE, TEMPT**
enticement	**TEMPTATION**
enticing woman	**SIREN**

entire	ALL, TOTAL, WHOLE
entirety (2 wds., sl.)	
	WHOLE HOG
entire range	GAMUT
entirely	ALL
entity	BEING, UNITY
entourage	TRAIN
entrance	DOOR, ACCESS
entrance fee	ADMISSION
entrance hall	FOYER
entrance to a garden	GATE
entrance way	ENTRY
entrancing	RAVISHING
entrant	CONTESTANT, PARTICIPANT
entrap	CATCH, ENSNARE
entreat	BEG, BESEECH, PRAY, PLEAD
entreaty	PLEA
entrechat	LEAP
entry	ENTRANCE, ACCESS
entwine	ENLACE, LACE, TWIST
enumerate	COUNT, LIST
enunciate	UTTER, ARTICULATE
enure	HARDEN
envelop	ENCLOSE
envelop in paper	WRAP
envious	JEALOUS, COVETOUS
environment	LOCALE, SURROUNDINGS
envision	SEE
envoy	MESSENGER
envy	JEALOUSY
enzyme (suffix)	ASE
eoan	AURORAL
eon	ETERNITY, ERA, AGE
ephemeral	TRANSIENT, FLEETING
epi	FINIAL
epic	HEROIC
epic poem	EPOS, EPODE, EPOPEE
epic story	SAGA
epicurean	SENSUAL
epidemic	PLAGUE
episode	SCENE
epistle	LETTER, MISSIVE
epithet	NAME, APPELATION
epitome	SYNOPSIS, PRECIS
epoch	ERA, AGE
epoxy	ENAMEL, RESIN
equable	EVEN, STEADY
equal	EVEN, PEER
equal (Fr.)	EGAL
equality	PAR
equality (Fr.)	EGALITE
Equality State	WYOMING

equalize (2 wds.)	LEVEL OFF
equanimity	POISE
equation	FORMULA
equidistant lines	PARALLEL
equilibrium	BALANCE
equine	HORSE, ZEBRA, ASS
equine father	SIRE
equine gait	CANTER, TROT, GALLOP, LOPE
equine mother	DAM
equine sound	SNORT, WHINNY, NEIGH
equine trappings	CAPARISON
equinox	VERNAL, AUTUMNAL
equip	RIG, FIT OUT, OUTFIT
equipage (arch.)	CREW, RETINUE
equipment	GEAR
equitable	FAIR, IMPARTIAL
equitably	FAIRLY
equitation	DRESSAGE
equity	FAIRNESS
equivalent to	TANTAMOUNT
equivocal	UNCERTAIN
equivocate	LIE
equivocation	EVASION
equivoque	PUN
era	AGE, EPOCH, EON
eradicate (2 wds.)	ROOT OUT
erase	DELE, EXPUNGE, RUB OUT
Erato	MUSE
ere	BEFORE, RATHER
erect	BUILD, UPRIGHT
ere long	ANON, SOON
eremite	HERMIT, RECLUSE
eremite's hut	CELL
erenow	HERETOFORE
ergo	THUS, HENCE
ergot	FUNGUS
Erin	IRELAND, EIRE
Erinyes	FURIES
Erle Stanley Gardner stories	MYSTERIES,
ermine	STOAT
ern	OSPREY
Ernest Borgnine role	MARTY
erode	EAT, WEAR
Eros	AMOR, CUPID
erose	WORN, JAGGED
erotic	SENSUAL
err	MISDO, SIN
errand	SHORE, MISSION, TASK
errand boy	PAGE, MESSENGER
errant	ITINERANT
errantry	CHIVALRY
erratic	ECCENTRIC
erroneous	MISTAKEN

error	BLUNDER, LAPSE, MISTAKE, SLIP, FALLACY
ersatz	SYNTHETIC, ARTIFICIAL, BUTTER, OLEO
Erse	GAELIC
erst	ONCE, FORMERLY
erudite	LEARNED, WISE
erupt	BURST, EJECT
Esau's brother	JACOB
Esau's country	EDOM
Esau's wife	ADA, JUDITH, BASEMATH, MAHELETH
escape	ELUDE, EVADE, FLEE, LAM
escargot	SNAIL
eschew	AVOID, SHUN
escort	CHAPERONE, USHER
eskers	OSAR
Eskimo	AMERIND, ALEUT
Eskimo boat	UMIAK, KAYAK, OOMIAK
Eskimo house	IGLOO, IGLU
Eskimo knife	ULU
Eskimo vehicle	SLED
espouse	EMBRACE, ADOPT
esprit de corps	MORALE, SPIRIT, UNITY
espy	SEE
essay	TRY, ATTEMPT, THEME
essay	THEME, TOPIC
essence	PERFUME
essential	IMPERATIVE, NECESSARY
essential part	PITH, CORE, CRUX, GIST
establishment	SHOP
establish the truth	PROVE
estate	MANOR, PROPERTY
estate employee	GARDENER, GATEMAN
esteem	RESPECT, REVERE
esthetic judgment (2 wds.)	GOOD TASTE
estimable	WORTHY
estimate	ASSESS, GUESS, RATE
estimated worth	VALUE
estimation	ESTEEM, REGARD
estop	BAR, PROHIBIT
estrange	ALIENATE
estuary	BAY, FIRTH
etape	STOREHOUSE
etch	ENGRAVE
etching fluid	ACID
eternal	AGELESS, ENDLESS, PERPETUAL
Eternal City native	ROMAN
eternally	ALWAYS, EVER, E'ER, FOREVER
eternity	EON
ethanol	ALCOHOL
ether	ANAESTHETIC
ether compound	ESTER
ethereal	AIRY
ethereal being	SYLPH
ethereal salt	ESTER
ethical	MORAL
ethics	MORALS
Ethopian lake	TANA
Ethiopian native	GALLA
Ethiopia's neighbor	ERITREA
Etruscan deity	LAR, LARES (PL.)
Eucharistic plate	PATEN
eulogize	LAUD, GLORIFY
eulogy	ELOGE
Euphrates tributary	TIGRIS
European apple	SORB
European beetle	DOR
European blackbird	MERL
European capital	BERN, BONN, OSLO, PARIS, ROME, MADRID
European dormouse	LEROT
European farmer	PEASANT
European flatfish	TURBOT
European gull	MEW
European mountain district	TYROL
European mountains	ALPS
European river	ELBE, RUHR
European sandpiper	TEREK
European shad	ALOSE
European shark	TOPE
evade	CIRCUMVENT, ELUDE, AVOID, ESCAPE
evade, as a question	PARRY
evade, as duty	SHIRK
evaluate	RATE
evanesce	DISAPPEAR, VANISH
evanescent	FLEETING
evangelical	GOSPEL
Evangeline's home	ACADIA
evaporate (2 wds.)	DRY UP
even	LEVEL, FLAT
even (Lat.)	ENIM
even (poet.)	E'EN
even a little bit (2 wds.)	AT ALL
evening	TWILIGHT, DUSK
evening (Ger.)	ABEND
evening (poet.)	EVE
evening cloak	WRAP
evening dress	GOWN
evening in Italy	SERA
evening party	SOIREE

evening song	SERENADE, VESPER
evening star	VENUS, VESPER
even one	ANY
even score	TIE
event	OCCURRENCE
eventual	ULTIMATE, FINAL
ever	ALWAYS
ever (poet.)	E'ER
Everglade	SWAMP
evergreen shrub	JUNIPER, MYRTLE
Evergreen State	WASHINGTON
evergreen tree	CEDAR, FIR, SPRUCE, YEW, PINE
everlasting	ETERNAL
evermore	FOREVER, ALWAYS
every	ALL, ANY, EACH
everyday	COMMON, ORDINARY
everything	ALL
everything counted (2 wds.)	ALL TOLD
every 24 hours	DAILY
Eve's mate	ADAM
Eve's origin	RIB
evict	EJECT, OUST
evidence	PROOF
evident	OBVIOUS
evil	BAD, BADNESS, SIN, MALEVOLENT, WICKED
evil deed	SIN
evil giant	OGRE
evil grin	LEER, SNEER
evil omen	KNELL
evil one	DEVIL, SATAN
evil spirit	DEMON
evince	SHOW, MANIFEST
evocation	INDUCTION
evoke	SUMMON
evolution	DEVELOPMENT
evolutionary	GENETIC
ewer	PITCHER
ewe's mate	RAM
exacerbate	IRRITATE
exact	PRECISE
exacting	STRENUOUS
exactitude	PRECISION, ACCURACY
exact likeness	COPY
exactly (3 wds.)	TO A T, TO A TEE
exactness	PRECISION
exact opposite	ANTIPODE
exact satisfaction	AVENGE
exaggerate	OVERDO, OVERSTATE
exalt	ELATE, ELEVATE, HONOR
exaltation of spirit	ELATION

examination	TEST, FINAL, MIDTERM
examine	TEST
examine eggs under a light	CANDLE
examine judicially	TRY
examine minutely	SIFT
example	MODEL, SAMPLE
exanimate	DEAD, INERT
exasperate	RILE
exasperation	ANNOYANCE
exclamation of pity	ALAS
excavate	DIG
excavation	PIT, HOLE, CAVITY
excavator	SHOVEL
exceed	OUTDO, EXCEL
exceedingly	VERY
excel	EXCEED OUTDO
excellence	VIRTUE
excellent	FINE, SPLENDID
excelling others	BEST
except	SAVE, BUT
except for	SAVE
except that	ONLY
exception	DISSENT
exceptional	UNCOMMON, RARE
excerpt	EXTRACT
excess	OVERAGE
excessive	EXORBITANT, UNDUE
excessive interest	USURY
excessively	UNDULY, TOO
exchange	SWAP, TRADE, BARTER
exchange discount	AGIO
exchange for money	SELL
exchange letters	CORRESPOND
exchange place	FAIR, MARKET, MART
exchange premium	AGIO
exchequer	TREASURY
excise	TAX, DUTY
excite	PROVOKE, WORK UP, ENTHUSE
excite the attention of	INTEREST
excite to action	ROUSE
excited	AGOG
excitement	ADO, STIR
exciting	HECTIC
exclaim	CRY OUT
exclamation	AHA, OHO
exclamation of annoyance	DRAT
exclamation of approval	BRAVO
exclamation of disappointment	AW
exclamation of disbelief	BAH

exclamation of disgust **UGH, POOH**
exclamation of doubt **HUMPH**
exclamation of horror
(2 wds.) **OH NO**
exclamation of pity **ALAS**
exclamation of sorrow **ALAS**
exclamation of surprise **WOW, OH, HO**
exclamation of
triumph **AHA, AH**
exclude **BAR, RULE OUT, DEBAR**
exclusive **SELECT**
exclusive news story **SCOOP**
exclusive right **PATENT**
excoriate **CHAFE, IRRITATE**
excruciate **TORTURE**
excruciating **PAINFUL**
exculpate **ACQUIT**
excursion **JUNKET, TRIP, TREK, TOUR**
excuse **ALIBI, PLEA**
execrate **ABHOR, CURSE, CONDEMN**
execute **EFFECT, PERFORM**
executive ability **LEADERSHIP**
executive's bag **BRIEFCASE**
executor's
responsiblity **ESTATE**
exemplar **MODEL**
exemplify **ILLUSTRATE**
exempt **FREE, CLEAR**
exercise **ACTIVITY**
exercising device
(2 wds.) **LONG HORSE**
exertion **DINT**
exhale **RESPIRE, EMIT**
exhaust **DEPLETE, FAG, SPEND, BUSH, WEAR OUT**
exhausted **TIRED, SPENT**
exhaustion **FATIGUE**
exhibit **DISPLAY**
exhibition at its best **SHOWCASE**
exhilarate **ELATE**
exhort **URGE**
exhortation **PLEA, SERMON**
exhume **DISCLOSE, REVEAL**
exigency **EMERGENCY, NEED**
exigent **URGENT**
exile **DEPORT**
exist **AM, ARE, IS, BE, LIVE**
existed **BEEN, WAS, WERE**
existence **BEING, LIFE**
existence (Lat.) **ESSE**
existent **ALIVE**
exit **EGRESS**

exodus **HEGIRA**
exonerate **CLEAR**
exorbitant **EXCESSIVE**
exorbitant interest rate **USURY**
exotic **ALIEN, STRANGE**
expand **DEVELOP, DILATE, ENLARGE**
expanse **REACH, SPREAD**
expansion **INCREASE, GROWTH**
expansive **BROAD, WIDE**
expatriate **EXILE, BANISH**
expect **AWAIT**
expectation **HOPE**
expedient **POLITIC, WISE**
expedite **HASTEN**
expedition **EXCURSION, JOURNEY**
expel **OUST, EVICT, EJECT**
expend **DISBURSE, CONSUME**
expenditure **OUTLAY**
expense **COST**
expensive **DEAR, COSTLY**
expensive fur **MINK, SABLE, ERMINE**
experience anew **REENACT**
experiment **TEST**
expert **PRO, ADEPT, SKILLED, ACE**
expert bridge player **MASTER**
expert flyer **ACE**
expert golfer **ACE, PRO**
expertise **SKILL**
expiate **ATONE**
expire **DIE, RUN OUT, LAPSE**
explain **INTERPRET, DEFINE**
explain a word **DEFINE**
explanation **DESCRIPTION**
expletive **GOSH, GEE**
explicit **CLEAR**
explode **BURST, POP, DETONATE, ERUPT**
explode in muffler **BACKFIRE**
exploit **FEAT, USE, DEED**
explore **EXAMINE, SEARCH**
explorer **PIONEER**
explosion **BLAST**
explosive **TNT, NITRO**
explosive device **BOMB, GRENADE, MINE**
explosive noise **POP**
expose **BARE**
exposed **BARED, BARE, OPEN, FRANK**
expose to view **OPEN**
expound **ORATE**
express **DECLARE, TELL**
express a choice for **PREFER**

express an idea **OPINE**
express disapproval **ADMONISH**
express discontent **COMPLAIN**
express disdain **SNIFF**
express gratitude **THANK**
express impatience **TUT**
expressing love **ROMANTIC**
express in words **PHRASE, SAY, STATE**
expression of contempt **BOO**
expression of good will **VIVA**
express merriment **LAUGH**
express road **FREEWAY**
express scorn **SNEER**
express sorrow **LAMENT**
express sympathy **CONDOLE, CONSOLE**
expunge **ERASE, DELE, DELETE**
exquisite **PERFECT**
extant **BEING, EXISTENT**
extemporaneous **IMPROMPTU**
extempore (comp. wd.) **AD-LIB**
extend **OFFER, REACH**
extend across **SPAN**
extend a loan **LEND**
extend a subscription **RENEW**
extend over **COVER**
extend to **REACH**
extend upward **RISE**
extensive **LONG, VAST**
extensive plain **PRAIRIE**
extent **RANGE, SCOPE, LENGTH**
extent of influence **SCOPE**
exterior **OUTER**
exterminate **ANNIHILATE, DESTROY**
external **OUTER**
extinct **DEAD**
extinct bird **DODO, MOA**
extinct wild ox **URUS, AUROCHS**
extinguish **DOUSE, QUELL**
extol **PRAISE**
extract **EDUCE**
extraction **ORIGIN, STOCK**
extraneous **EXTERNAL, FOREIGN**
extraordinary **RARE, SINGULAR**
extra pay **BONUS**
extrasensory perception (abbr.) **ESP**
extra small pup **RUNT**
extra supplies **RESERVES**
extra tire **SPARE**
extravagance **WASTE**
extravagant **FANCY**
extreme **DIRE, RADICAL, DRASTIC**
extreme alarm **PANIC**

extreme anger **RAGE**
extreme conservative **DIEHARD**
extreme fear **HORROR, TERROR, PANIC**
extreme fondness **LOVE**
extremely **AWFULLY, VERY**
extremely poor **DESTITUTE**
extremely violent argument (comp. wd.) **KNOCK-DOWN-AND-DRAG-OUT**
extremist **RADICAL**
extremity **END, TOE, FINGER**
extricate **DISENTANGLE**
exuberant **PROLIFIC**
exudation **SECRETION**
exude **EMIT, SPEW, SEEP, OOZE**
exult **ELATE**
exultant **JUBILANT**
exultation **GLEE, JOY**
exult maliciously **GLOAT**
exuviate **MOLT**
eye **ESPY, OBSERVE, SCRUTINIZE, WATCH**
eye amorously **OGLE, LEER**
eye boldly **STARE**
eye disease **GLAUCOMA, TRACHOMA**
eye drop **TEAR**
eyeglass **LENS, MONOCLE**
eyelashes **CILIA**
eye make-up **MASCARA**
eye membrane **RETINA**
eyes (slang) **GLIMS**
eyesight **VISION**
eyetooth **CANINE**
eyre **COURT, TOUR, CIRCUIT**

F

fable **PARABLE, MYTH**
fabled bird **ROC**
fabled marine creature **MERMAID**
fabled one-horned animal **UNICORN**
fabliau **TALE, STORY**
fabric **TEXTILE, MATERIAL, CLOTH**
fabricate **MAKE**
fabrication **LIE, FIB**
fabric glaze **CIRE**
fabric junction **SEAM**
fabric woven from flax **LINEN**
fabulist **AESOP**
fabulous **WONDERFUL**
fabulous beast **DRAGON**

fabulous bird	ROC	fake	COUNTERFEIT, PHONY,
fabulous one-horned			FRAUD, SHAM, PRETEND,
animal	UNICORN		ERSATZ, FORGERY
facade	FACE, FRONT	fake coin	SLUG
face	VISAGE	fake jewelry	PASTE
face covering	VEIL, MASK	fakir	YOGI, DERVISH
face part	CHIN, NOSE, LIP,	Falasha	HAMITE
	MOUTH, CHEEK, EYE	falchion	SWORD
face with stone	REVET	falcon	KESTREL
facet	SIDE, ASPECT, PHASE	falderal	NONSENSE
facetious	SARCASTIC, WITTY	fall	AUTUMN
facile	EASY	fallacious	CRAFTY, DECEITFUL
facilitate	AID, ASSIST	fallacy	ERROR
facility	EASE, FLUENCY	fall back	RECEDE, RETREAT
facing	TOWARD	fall back into former state	
facsimile	LIKENESS		RELAPSE
fact	DATUM	fall back on	RELY, DEPEND
faction	SIDE	fall behind	LAG
factitious	ARTIFICIAL, SHAM	fall flower	ASTER, MUM
factor	AGENT, ELEMENT	fall guy	PATSY, CHUMP, MARK
factory	MILL, PLANT	fallible	HUMAN
factory fuel	COAL	fall in	MEET, COLLAPSE
factory superintendent		fall in drops	DRIP
	FOREMAN	fall in flakes	SNOW
factotum	HANDYMAN	falling sickness	EPILEPSY
facts and figures	DATA	fall month	SEPTEMBER,
factual	TRUE		OCTOBER
faculty	ABILITY	fall noisily	CRASH
fad	RAGE, CRAZE, MANIA	fall off	DECLINE
fade	PALE, DIM	fall of rain	SHOWER
fade away	EVANESCE	fall out	DISAGREE, QUARREL
faded star (comp. wd.)		fall over	TOPPLE
	HAS-BEEN	fallow	IDLE, INACTIVE
Faerie Queene	UNA	fall short	FAIL
fail	MISS, FLUNK	fall suddenly	DROP, SLUMP,
fail in duty	LAPSE		COLLAPSE
failing	FAULT	fall to	BEGIN, START
fail to follow suit	RENEGE	fall upon	ASSAIL, ATTACK
fail to hit	MISS	false	RECREANT, UNFAITHFUL,
fail to mention	OMIT		UNTRUE
fail to win	LOSE	false appearance	GUISE
failure	FLOP, DUD	false belief	DELUSION
failure at Cape Kennedy		false claim	PRETENSE
(2 wds.)	NO GO	false coin	SLUG
faint	FEEBLE	false face	MASK
fair	JUST	false front	POSE
fair grade	CEE	false god	IDOL
fairly	SOMEWHAT	false hairpiece	WIG, PERUKE,
fair to middling	PASSABLE		FALL, TOUPEE
fairy	ELF, SPRITE	falsehood	LIE, FIB
fairy stick	WAND	false jewelry	PASTE
fairy tale creature	ELF, GNOME,	false name	ALIAS
	OGRE, TROLL	false report	CANARD, RUMOR
faith	CONVICTION, TRUST	false show	TINSEL
faithful	TRUE, LOYAL	false signature	FORGERY
faithful counselor	MENTOR	false step	SLIP
faith healer Roberts	ORAL	false teeth	DENTURE
faithless	FALSE	falsify	FORGE, LIE

falter **HESITATE, STUMBLE**
faltering speech **STUTTER**
fame **HONOR, RENOWN, NAME,**
REPUTE
familiar **INTIMATE**
familiar emblem **EAGLE**
familiarity **FRIENDSHIP**
familiar with **CONVERSANT**
family **HOUSE, CLAN**
family car **AUTO, SEDAN,**
COUPE, STATION WAGON
family group **CLAN**
family imp **BRAT**
family man **FATHER**
family member **MAMA, PAPA,**
MOM, DAD, SISTER,
BROTHER, JUNIOR, SIS
family name **SURNAME**
family of kings **DYNASTY**
family of medieval
Ferrara **ESTE**
famine **HUNGER, SHORTAGE**
famish **STARVE**
famous **EMINENT, KNOWN**
famous uncle **SAM**
fan **ENTHUSIAST, SUPPORTER**
fanatic **CRANK, ZEALOT**
fanatical **RABID**
fanatic devotion **CULT**
fanciful **WHIMSICAL**
fanciful reverie **DAYDREAM**
fancy **ELABORATE**
fancy dive **GAINER**
fancy fabric **LACE**
fancy trappings **REGALIA,**
FINERY
fancy vase **URN**
fane **BANNER, PENNANT**
Fanny Farmer specialty **RECIPE**
fantastic **BIZARRE**
fantastic trick **ANTIC**
fantasy **DREAM**
far **DISTANT, REMOTE**
far (prefix) **TEL(E)**
farce **COMEDY**
farcical **ABSURD**
far down **DEEP**
fare **DIET, PASSAGE, GO**
Far East **ORIENT**
farer **TRAVELER**
farewell **ADIEU**
farewell (Sp.) **ADIOS**
farewell party (comp. wd.)
SEND-OFF
farewell to the Islands **ALOHA**

farm animal **CALF, SOW, COW,**
BULL, STEER, HORSE,
SHEEP, MARE, EWE,
RAM, GOAT
farm animals **LIVESTOCK,**
CATTLE
farm building **BARN, SILO**
farm implement **REAPER,**
GIN, TRACTOR, PLOW
farming **AGRICULTURE**
farm laborer **HAND**
farm measure **ACRE**
farm out **HIRE, LET**
farm product **CROP**
farm tenant **COTTER, COTTIER**
farmyard sound **MOO, BAA,**
BLEAT, OINK, CLUCK,
WHINNY
far-off **DISTANT**
far-reaching **VAST**
farrow **PIG**
far-sighted **SHREWD**
fascinate **CHARM**
fashion **CRAZE, FAD, MODE,**
STYLE, MODEL, FORM,
MANNER, ASPECT, SORT,
VOGUE
fashionable **CHIC**
fashionable resort **SPA**
fashionable section
of Boston **BACK BAY**
fashionably elegant **SWANK**
fashion name **DIOR, CHANEL,**
PARNIS, BROOKS,
CARDIN, PUCCI,
VALENTINO, GRES
fast **FLEET, RAPID, QUICK,**
SPEEDY
fast car **RACER**
fast driver
(2 wds.) **SPEED DEMON**
fasten **GLUE, NAIL, RIVET, TIE,**
LACE, CLASP, CLIP, PIN,
SNAP, LATCH
fastener **CLASP, PIN**
fasten firmly **ANCHOR, BIND,**
NAIL
fastens **CLASPS**
fasten shut **BAR**
fasten with stitches **SEW**
fasten with string **TIE**
fastidious **NEAT, DAINTY**
fastidious man **DUDE, FOP**
fasting period **LENT**
fast plane **JET**
fat **CORPULENT, OBESE,**
PLUMP, LARD, GREASE,
STOUT, ROTUND, CHUBBY

fatal **LETHAL**
fatality **DEATH**
fata morgana **MIRAGE**
fate **DESTINY, DOOM, KARMA, KISMET**
fateful time for Caesar **IDES**
Fates **PARCAE, ATROPOS, CLOTHO, LACHESIS**
father **DAD, SIRE, POP, DADDY, POPPA, PAPA, PA, PAW**
father (Fr.) **PERE**
father (Lat.) **PATER**
father (poetic) **SIRE**
father (Sp.) **PADRE**
fatherhood **PATERNITY**
father of Enos **SETH**
father of Horus **OSIRIS**
father of Zeus **KRONOS, CRONUS, CRONOS**
father or mother **PARENT**
father's wife **MOTHER**
fathom **DELVE**
fatigue **TIRE, WEARY, WEARINESS**
Fatima's husband **ALI, BLUEBEARD**
fat lot **LITTLE, NOTHING**
fat of swine **LARD**
fat of the land **LUXURY**
fattened, as cattle (comp. wd.) **CORN-FED**
fatty **ADIPOSE**
fatuity **STUPIDITY**
fatuous **FOOLISH**
faubourg **SUBURB, QUARTER, SECTION**
faucet **SPIGOT, TAP**
fault **FLAW, FAILING**
faultfinder **CARPER**
faultfinding **CENSORIAL**
faultless **PERFECT, PURE**
faulty **AMISS**
faun **SATYR**
faux pas **ERROR**
favor **RESPECT, INDULGENCE, PARTIALITY**
favorable **HELPFUL**
favorable to progress **LIBERAL**
favoring **FOR, PRO**
favoring neither **NEUTRAL**
favorite **PET**
favoritism **BIAS, PREJUDICE**
fawn **DEER**
fawning **SERVILE, OBSEQUIOUS**
fay **FAIRY**
faze **DISTURB, DISCONCERT**
feal **LOYAL, FAITHFUL**
fealty **LOYALTY, HOMAGE**

fear **DREAD, TERROR, FRIGHT, ALARM**
fearful **ANXIOUS, AWFUL, DREADFUL**
fearless **BOLD, BRAVE**
fearsome **AWFUL, AWESOME, TIMID**
feasible **POSSIBLE**
Feast of Booths **SUCCOTH, SUKKOTH**
Feast of Lights **CHANUKAH**
Feast of Lots **PURIM**
Feast of Nativity **CHRISTMAS**
Feast of Weeks **SHAVUOT, SHABUOTH**
feat **ACHIEVEMENT, DEED**
feather **PLUME**
feather barb **PINNULA**
feathered friend **BIRD**
feathers **PLUMAGE, DOWN**
feather scarf **BOA**
feature **QUALITY, MOTIF**
febrile **FEVERISH**
fecund **FERTILE**
federal **NATIONAL**
federate **UNITE**
federation **ALLIANCE**
fedora **HAT**
fee **CHARGE**
feeble **WEAK, PUNY**
feeble-minded person **MORON, DOLT, IDIOT, IMBECILE**
feed **NOURISH**
feed the kitty **ANTE**
feed to fill **SATE**
feel **TOUCH, SENSE**
feel affection for **LIKE**
feel contrite **REPENT**
feeler **TENTACLE, ANTENNA, BARBEL**
feel indignation **RESENT**
feel indisposed **AIL, SICK**
feeling **SENSATION, EMOTION**
feeling deeply **INTENSE**
feeling of resentment **PEEVE**
feeling of weariness **ENNUI**
feel in the dark **GROPE**
feel intuitively **SENSE**
feel melancholy **GRIEVE**
feel one's way **GROPE**
feel regret **REPENT, RUE**
feel sorrow **MOURN**
feign **SHAM, PRETEND, PUT ON, ACT**
feign illness **MALINGER**
feint **SHAM**
feisty **AGGRESSIVE**

felicitate	CONGRATULATE, GREET	feminine title	MADAM, MISS, MAM
felicity	BLISS, RAPTURE	femininity	WOMEN
feline	CAT	femme fatale	SIREN
feline sound	MEW, MIAO, MEOW	femur	THIGH
feline treat	CATNIP	fen	MARSH, SWAMP, BOG
fell	CUT, BEAT	fence	WALL, HEDGE, RAIL
fellow	CHAP	fence opening	GATE, TURNSTILE
fellowship	COMPANY, BROTHERHOOD	fence post	STAKE
felon	CRIMINAL	fencer	DUELIST
felonious	MALICIOUS	fence stake	POST
felony	CRIME	fence step	STILE
female	WOMAN, GIRL	fence straddler's domain (4 wds.)	MIDDLE OF THE ROAD
female antelope	DOE		
female bird	HEN	fence timber	RAIL
female child	GIRL	fencing hit	PUNTO, TOUCHE
female colt	FILLY	fencing position	CARTE
female deer	DOE	fencing sword	EPEE, FOIL, SABER
female deity	GODDESS		
female domestic	MAID	fend	PARRY, RESIST
female elephant	COW	fender	BUMPER
female goat	NANNY	fender mishap	DENT
female hog	SOW	fennel genus	NIGELLA
female horse	MARE	fenstra	OPENING
female host	HOSTESS	fen water	MIRE
female knight	DAME	feral	WILD, SAVAGE
female monster	GORGON, MEDUSA, STHENO, EURYALE	fermented drink	ALE, CIDER, WINE, BEER
female ovine	EWE	fermenting vat	GYLE
female parent	MOTHER	fern genus	ANEMIA
female pig	SOW	fern leaf	FROND
female relative	AUNT, MOTHER, DAUGHTER, SISTER, GRANDMA	ferocious	FIERCE, VIOLENT
		ferret	WEASEL
female religious (abbr.)	SR.	ferrous metal	IRON
female ruff	REEVE, REE	ferry	CARRY, TRANSPORT
female sailor	WAVE	fertile	FRUITFUL, FECUND
female saint (abbr.)	STE.	fertile spot in a desert	OASIS
female sandpiper	REEVE, REE	fertilizer	MARL
female servant	MAID	fervent	ARDENT
female sheep	EWE	fervent appeal	PLEA
female sibling	SISTER	fervor	ARDOR, ZEAL
female's mate	MALE, HUSBAND	festival	FETE, GALA, FAIR, FIESTA
female soldier	WAC		
female sovereign	PRINCESS, QUEEN	festival of Passover	SEDER
		festive	GALA
female spirit	BANSHEE, BANSHIE	festivity	MIRTH, REVEL
		feta	CHEESE
female student	COED	fetch	BRING
female swimmer	MERMAID	fete	GALA
female voice	ALTO, SOPRANO	fetid	RANK
female warrior	AMAZON	fetish	TOTEM, IDOL
feminine	FEMALE, WOMANLY	fetter	MANACLE, CHAIN
feminine (suffix)	ETTE	fettel	CONDITION
feminine garment	SKIP, SKIRT, DRESS, BRA	feud	DISPUTE, VENDETTA
		feudal castle	MANOR

feudal chief	**LORD, OVERLORD, BARON**	fight	**STRUGGLE, BATTLE, WAR, QUARREL**
feudal estate	**FIEF**	fight against	**RESIST**
feudal slave	**SERF, ESNE**	fighter pilot	**ACE**
feudal tenant	**VASSAL**	fighter's exercise	**LEG WORK**
fever	**HEAT, FIRE**	fighting equipment	**ARMS**
feverish	**FEBRILE, EXCITED**	figure	**NUMBER, SHAPE**
fewer	**LESS**	figure applied to fabric	
fewest	**LEAST**		**APPLIQUE**
fey	**ODD**	figure in a Millet painting	
fez ornament	**TASSEL**		**GLEANER**
fiance	**BETROTHED, INTENDED**	figure on a card	**SPADE, HEART, CLUB, DIAMOND**
fiasco	**FAILURE**		
fiat	**DECREE, EDICT**	filament	**THREAD**
fib	**LIE**	filament for cloth	**FIBER**
fiber	**STAPLE, SISAL, KAPOK**	filch	**PILFER, STEAL**
fiber cluster	**NEP**	file	**RASP**
fiber plant	**FLAX, HEMP, SISAL**	fill	**GLUT, SATE**
fibril	**HAIR**	fill again	**REPLENISH**
fibula	**BUCKLE, CLASP**	fill a gun	**LOAD**
fickle	**UNSTABLE, FAITHLESS**	fill a suitcase	**PACK**
fiction	**NOVEL**	filled with interstices	**AREOLAR**
fictional story	**TALE, YARN, NOVEL, FABLE, ROMANCE**	fill with ambition	**INSPIRE**
		fill with determination	**STEEL**
fictitious	**FALSE**	fill with ennui	**BORE**
fictitious name	**ALIAS**	fill with joy	**ELATE**
fiddling emperor	**NERO**	fill with love	**ENAMOR**
fidelity	**DEVOTION, LOYALTY**	fill with pride	**ELATE**
Fidel's capital	**HAVANA**	filly	**MARE**
fidget	**FUSS, FRET**	film	**MOVIE, CINEMA**
fidgety	**NERVOUS, RESTIVE**	film spool	**REEL**
Fido	**DOG**	filmy	**SHEER**
Fido's offspring	**PUPPY, PUP**	filter	**STRAIN**
Fido's treasure	**BONE**	filth	**DIRT**
fiduciary	**TRUSTEE**	filthy	**CRUDDY, DIRTY, SOILED**
fief	**FEE**	filthy hut	**STY**
field	**LOT, CLEARING, AREA**	finagle	**SCHEME, CONTRIVE**
field edge	**RAND**	final	**LAST, ULTIMATE**
field flower	**DAISY**	finale	**FINISH, CODA**
field mouse	**VOLE**	finalize	**COMPLETE**
field of action	**ARENA**	finally (2 wds.)	**AT LAST**
field of granular snow	**NEVE, FIRN**	finally and decisively (4 wds.)	**ONCE AND FOR ALL**
fiend	**DEMON, DEVIL**	final opportunity (2 wds.)	
fiendish	**MALICIOUS**		**LAST CHANCE**
fierce	**VIOLENT, FIERY**	final performer (2 wds.)	
fiery	**ARDENT, FIERCE, HOT**		**ANCHOR MAN**
fiery jewel	**OPAL**	financial	**FISCAL, PECUNIARY**
fiesta	**FESTIVAL, HOLIDAY**	financial center in N.Y. (2 wds.)	**WALL STREET**
fifteenth century royal family	**PLANTAGENET, YORK, TUDOR, LANCASTER**	financially solvent (3 wds.)	**IN THE BLACK**
		financial sponsor	**PATRON**
fifth tire	**SPARE**	find	**DISCOVER, LOCATE**
fifth zodiac sign	**LEO**	find a sum	**ADD**
fiftieth state	**HAWAII**	find direction	**ORIENT**
fifty percent	**HALF**	find fault	**NAG, CARP, CAVIL**

find guilty	**CONVICT**
finding	**CONCLUSION,**
	SOLUTION
find of treasure	**TROVE**
find out	**DISCOVER, DETECT**
find position of	**LOCATE**
find the answer	**SOLVE**
fine	**EXCELLENT, PENALTY,**
	TARIFF
fine bits of thread	**LINT**
fine cord	**THREAD**
fine cotton fabric	**BATISTE**
fine English china	**SPODE**
fine jet of water	**SPRAY**
fine line, in printing	**SERIF**
fine linen	**CAMBRIC**
finely	**NICELY**
fine porcelain	**SPODE, LIMOGES**
fine rock debris	**SAND**
finery	**GAUD, LUXURY**
fine sensitiveness	**DELICACY**
fine soil	**SILT**
finesse	**CUNNING, SUBTLETY**
finest	**BEST**
fine suiting	**TWEED, SERGE**
fine whetstone	**HONE**
finger	**DIGIT**
finger jewelry	**RING**
fingernail moon	**LUNULE**
fingerprint mark	**LOOP, WHORL**
finial	**EPI**
finis	**END**
finish	**END, CONCLUDE,**
	TERMINATE, COMPLETE
finished	**OVER, DONE**
finished garment edge	**HEM**
finish line	**TAPE**
finite	**LIMITED**
Finland	**SUOMI**
Finnish city	**HELSINKI, ABO**
Finnish lake	**ENARE**
Finnish steam bath	**SAUNA**
fiord	**INLET**
fire	**FLAME, BLAZE**
fire a gun	**SHOOT**
firearm	**GUN, RIFLE**
firebug's crime	**ARSON**
firecracker	**PETARD**
firedog	**ANDIRON**
fire god	**VULCAN, YAMA**
fireman	**STOKER**
fire opal	**GIRASOL**
fireplace	**GRATE, HEARTH**
fireplace facing	**MANTEL**
fireplace fuel	**LOGS, COAL,**
	PEAT
fireplace shelf	**HOB, MANTLE**
fireplug	**HYDRANT**

fire residue	**ASH, ASHES**
fire-stirring rod	**POKER**
firewater	**WHISKEY, LIQUOR**
fire whistle	**SIREN**
firewood	**FUEL**
fireworks	**ROCKETS,**
	SPARKLERS
firm	**HARD, SOLID, STRICT,**
	STERN
firmament	**SKY, HEAVEN**
firm grasp	**GRIP**
firmly established	**DEEP-SET**
firn	**NEVE**
first	**PRIMAL, LEADING**
first appearance	**DEBUT**
first beginning	**ORIGIN**
first class	**PRIME**
first day	**SUNDAY**
first drawing	**DRAFT**
first garden	**EDEN**
first Hebrew letter	**ALEPH,**
	ALEF
first king of Israel	**SAUL**
first king of Rome	**ROMULUS**
first man	**ADAM**
first performance	**DEBUT,**
	PREMIERE
first person	**I, ME**
first principle	**ELEMENT**
first-rate	**SUPER, A ONE, TOP**
	NOTCH
first reader	**PRIMER**
first-row position	
(2 wds.)	**IN FRONT,**
	UP FRONT
first state	**DELAWARE**
first water	**BEST, PUREST**
first woman	**EVE**
first word of Caesar's boast	
	VENI
first word on the wall	**MENE**
first zodiac sign	**ARIES**
firth	**ESTUARY**
fisc	**TREASURY, EXCHEQUER**
fiscal	**FINANCIAL**
fiscal department	**TREASURY**
fiscal officer	**TREASURER,**
	CONTROLLER
fish	**ANGLE, DACE, IDE, TUNA,**
	GAR, CARP, SHAD, SOLE,
	PIKE, PORGY, RAY, SHARK,
	SKATE
fish appendage	**FIN**
fish bait	**WORM**
fish basket	**CREEL**
fish bowl	**AQUARIUM**
fish-catching fence	**WEIR**
fish-eating diving bird	**LOON**

fish-eating mammal	**OTTER, WHALE, DOLPHIN, SEAL, PORPOISE**
fish eggs	**ROE**
fisherman's boot	**WADER**
fisherman's snare	**NET**
fish fin (Sp.)	**ALETA**
fish from moving boat	**TROLL**
fish gig	**SPEAR**
fish hawk	**OSPREY**
fishhook leader	**SNELL**
fishhook part	**BARB**
fishing appurtenance	**CORK, FLOAT**
fishing cork	**FLOAT**
fishing duck	**MERGANSER, SHELDRAKE**
fishing eagle	**OSPREY**
fishing float	**BOBBER**
fishing fly	**LURE**
fishing gear	**TACKLE**
fishing lure	**BAIT**
fishing net	**SEINE, TRAWL**
fishing pole	**ROD**
fishing rod	**POLE**
fishing snare	**NET**
fishing vessel	**SMACK, BOAT, TRAWLER**
fish limb	**FIN**
fish lung	**GILL**
fish lure	**BAIT**
fish nostril	**GILL**
fish of the carp family	**DACE**
fishpound	**WEIR**
fish roe	**CAVIAR, EGGS**
fish sauce	**ALEC**
fish spear	**GIG**
fish through ice	**CHUG**
fish trap	**EELPOT, WEIR**
fish with a moving line	**TROLL**
fishy	**SUSPECT**
fissile rock	**SHALE**
fission	**DIVISION**
fissure	**CLEFT**
fisticuffs	**BOXING**
fistula	**CAVITY**
fit	**SUITABLE, PROPER**
fit for farming	**ARABLE**
fitful	**RESTLESS**
fitness	**DECORUM**
fit of anger	**HUFF, RAGE**
fit of petulance	**RAGE, TANTRUM**
fit of resentment	**PIQUE**
fit of temper	**TANTRUM**
fit out	**EQUIP**
fit together closely	**DOVETAIL**
fit to one's use	**ADAPT**
fix	**REPAIR**
fix definitely	**SETTLE**
fixed	**SET**
fixed charge	**FEE, RATE**
fixed in position	**STABILE**
fixed pay	**STIPEND, SALARY**
fixed period of time	**TERM**
fixed prices	**RATES**
fixed residence	**HOME**
fixed routine	**ROTE**
fixed star	**VEGA**
fixed time period	**TERM**
fix up	**MEND**
fizz	**HISS, BUBBLE**
flabby	**WEAK, LIMP**
flaccid	**LIMP**
flag	**BANNER, IRIS, CATTAIL**
flag flower	**IRIS**
flagon	**FLASK, BOTTLE**
flagrant	**GLARING**
flagstone	**SLAB**
flail	**BEAT, FLOG**
flair	**KNACK, TALENT**
flair for gardening (2 wds.)	**GREEN THUMB**
flaky storm	**SNOW**
flam	**CHEAT, TRICK**
flamboyant	**ORNATE, GARISH**
flame	**BLAZE, FIRE**
flaming	**ARDENT**
flaming light	**TORCH**
flame-loving insect	**MOTH**
Flanders treaty city	**GHENT**
flank	**SIDE**
flare	**FLAME, FLICKER**
flash	**FLARE, BLAZE**
flash lamp	**STROBE**
flashlight (Brit.)	**TORCH**
flash of lightning	**BOLT**
flash out	**GLINT**
flashy	**GAUDY, GARISH**
flask	**AMPULE, CANTEEN**
flat	**LEVEL, EVEN, SMOOTH, TENEMENT, APARTMENT**
flat and even	**LEVEL**
flatbed	**TRUCK**
flat-bottomed boat	**BARGE, DORY, PUNT, SCOW**
flat cap	**BERET**
flat circular plate	**DISK**
flat disc-like sea urchin (2 wds.)	**SAND DOLLAR**
flatfish	**SOLE**
flat fold in cloth	**PLEAT**
flatfoot	**COP, DETECTIVE**
flat hat	**CAP**
flatland form	**MESA**
flat shallow container	**TRAY**

flat surface **PLANE**
flat tableland **MESA**
flatten **DEPRESS, EVEN**
flatter **COMPLIMENT, PRAISE**
flattery (2 wds.) **SWEET TALK**
flaunt **BRANDISH**
flavor **SAPOR, TASTE, SEASON**
flavoring plant **ANISE**
flavorsome **TASTY**
flaw **DEFECT**
flawless **PERFECT**
flaxen **WHITE, TOW**
flax fabric **LINEN**
flaxseed **LINSEED**
flay **REPROVE**
fled **RAN**
flee **LAM, RUN, SPLIT, ESCAPE**
fleecy white clouds **CIRRI**
flee in panic, as cattle **STAMPEDE**
fleet **FAST**
fleet of ships **NAVY, ARMADA**
Flemish **DUTCH**
flesh **MEAT**
flesh and blood **MORTAL**
fleshy **BEEFY, PLUMP**
fleshy berry **PEPO**
fleshy fruit **PEAR, APPLE, PEACH**
fleur de lis **LILY, IRIS**
flex **BEND, CONTRACT**
flexible **LIMP, PLIABLE**
flexible tube **HOSE**
flexor **MUSCLE**
flick **MOVIE**
flicker **WAVER**
Flickertail State **NORTH DAKOTA**
flier **AVIATOR, PILOT**
flight **FLYING, HOP**
flightless bird **EMU, MOA, RATITE**
flight of steps **STAIRS**
flighty person **RATTLEBRAIN**
flimflam **NONSENSE, SWINDLE**
flimsy **THIN, TRANSPARENT**
flinch **WINCE**
fling **TOSS, CAST, THROW**
flint **FIRESTONE, CHERT**
flip **TOSS**
flippant **GLIB**
flipper **FIN**
flippered animal **SEAL**
flirt **OGLE**
flit **DART**
float **RAFT, WAFT**
floating home **HOUSEBOAT**

floating ice mass **BERG, FLOE, ICEBERG**
float in the air **SOAR, LEVITATE**
float of logs **RAFT**
float on water **BOB**
float upward **RISE, SURFACE**
flock **BEVY, HERD**
flock member **EWE, RAM, LAMB**
flock of herons **SEDGE**
flock tender **SHEPHERD**
floe **BERG**
flog **LASH**
flood **DELUGE**
flooded stream **FRESHET**
flood gate **SLUICE**
floor **STORY**
floor covering **CARPET, RUG, MAT, TILE, LINEOLEUM, SKIN**
flooring square **TILE**
flora **PLANTS**
flora and fauna **BIOTA**
floral emblem of Wales **LEEK**
floral ornament **ROSETTE**
Florentine family **MEDICI**
Florentine iris **ORRIS**
florid **ORNATE**
Florida city **MIAMI, TAMPA, SARASOTA, OCALA**
Florida county **DADE**
Florida food fish **POMPANO**
Florida game fish **SNAPPER**
Florida Indian **SEMINOLE**
Florida islets **KEYS**
Florida key **LARGO, WEST**
Florida race track **HIALEAH**
Florida region **EVERGLADES**
flotilla **NAVY, FLEET**
flounder **FISH**
flourish **GROW, PROSPER**
flour manufacturer **MILLER**
flout **JEER, SCORN, SPURN**
flow **RUN**
flow back **EBB, RECEDE**
flower **ASTER, CANNA, LILY, DANDELION, ROSE, DAHLIA, ZINNIA, PEONY, TULIP, MUM, DAISY, POSY, PRIMROSE, LILAC, ARUM, PANSY, GERANIUM, VIOLET, PHLOX, PETUNIA, BEGONIA, PINK, CARNATION, STOCK, SEDUM, MARIGOLD, ANEMONE, POPPY, CLOVER, IRIS, FOXGLOVE, GEUM, CROCUS**
flower band **WREATH**
flower circle **WREATH**
flower holder **VASE, URN**

flowering climbing plant **SMILAX**
flower leaf **PETAL, SEPAL**
flowerless plant **MOSS, VINE,**
FERN, IVY
flower of Holland **TULIP**
flower part **PETAL, SEPAL,**
STEM, STALK
flower plot **BED**
flower stalk **STEM**
flower-to-be **BUD**
flowing **FLUENT, COPIOUS**
flowing forth **EMANATE**
flowing garment **ROBE, CAPE**
flowing oil well **GUSHER**
flub **BLUNDER**
fluctuate **WAVER**
flue **CHIMNEY**
fluent **LIQUID, SMOOTH**
fluent in speech **GLIB**
fluff **DOWN, FLOSS**
fluff from cloth **LINT**
fluffy **SOFT**
fluid **LIQUID, WATER**
fluid measure **DRAM, PINT,**
QUART, CUP
fluid rock **LAVA**
flunk **FAIL**
flurry **ADO, BUSTLE**
flush **BLUSH, REDDEN**
flush with success **ELATE**
flute **WOODWIND**
flutelike instrument **OBOE**
flutter **FLAP, WAVE, WAVER**
flutter over **HOVER**
fly **SOAR, WING, AVIATE**
fly before the wind **SCUD**
flyer **PILOT, ACE**
fly high **SOAR**
flying (3 wds.) **ON THE WING**
flying boat **SEAPLANE**
flying body **METEOR**
flying creature **BIRD**
flying equipment **WING**
flying fish **SAURY**
flying honker **GOOSE**
flying machine **PLANE**
flying mammal **BAT**
flying saucer (abbr.) **UFO**
flying toy **KITE**
fly quickly **FLIT**
fly's enemy **SPIDER**
flyspeck **ERROR, FLAW, SPOT**
foal **HORSE, COLT**
foam **SPUME, FROTH, LATHER**
foaming **SPUMOUS, SUDSY**
fob **POCKET, CHAIN**
focus **CENTER, CONVERGE**
fodder **FEED, SILAGE**

fodder storage structure **SILO**
fodder tower **SILO**
foe **ADVERSARY, ENEMY**
fog **MIST, HAZE**
fog and smoke **SMOG**
foggy **CLOUDY, DIM**
foghorn **SIREN**
foible **WEAKNESS**
foil **FRUSTRATE, SWORD**
fold **NAP, CREASE**
folder **LEAFLET**
folding bed **COT**
folding money **DOLLAR**
fold of cloth **PLEAT**
fold of skin **DEWLAP**
fold over **LAP**
foliage **LEAVES**
folio **BOOK**
folk **PEOPLE**
folk knowledge **LORE**
folklore **LEGENDS**
folklore creatures **GNOME,**
TROLL, ELF, SPRITE
folklore genie **SANDMAN**
folksinger Ives **BURL**
folksinger Guthrie **WOODY,**
ARLO
folksinger Seeger **PETE**
folk song **BLUES**
folkways **MORES**
follow **ENSUE, TAIL, CHASE**
follower **ITE, ADHERENT**
follow exactly **TRACE**
following **AFTER**
following story **SEQUEL**
follow orders **OBEY**
follow secretly **SHADOW**
follow the chase **HUNT**
folly **MADNESS**
fond **LOVING**
fondle **CARESS, PET**
fondly **TENDERLY**
fondness **AFFECTION, LOVE**
font **POOL, POND, BASIN**
food **CHOW, EATS, VICTUALS,**
GRUB, EATABLES, EDIBLES,
NOURISHMENT
food constituent **VITAMIN**
food container **CAN, TIN, JAR,**
BOX
food counter **BAR**
food dressing **SAUCE**
food fish **COD, BASS, SOLE,**
SHAD, TROUT, EEL,
HALIBUT, TUNA, SALMON
food for animals **FORAGE**
food for cattle **FODDER**
food for infants **PAP**

food from heaven	MANNA
food of the gods	AMBROSIA
food quickly prepared (2 wds.)	
	SHORT ORDER
food regimen	DIET
food sauce	CONDIMENT
food scrap	ORT
food served	MENU
food shortage	FAMINE
foodstuff	CEREAL
food topping	SAUCE, GARNISH
fool	ASS, IDIOT
fool away	FRITTER
foolhardy	BRASH, RASH
fool hen	GROUSE
foolish	INANE, SILLY
foolish act	FOLLY, BONER
foolishness	NONSENSE
foolish person	GOOSE, DOLT
foolish show	FARCE
foolproof	SIMPLE
foolscap	PAPER
fool's gold	PYRITE
fool's paradise	LIMBO
foot	PES, HOOF
foot affliction	CORN
footage	LENGTH
football cheer	RAH
football in England	RUGBY
football kick	PUNT
football pass	LATERAL
football play	DROP KICK,
TOUCHDOWN, PUNT, RUN,	
	PASS
football player	BACK, END,
CENTER, TACKLE,	
FULLBACK, HALFBACK	
football score	TOUCHDOWN
football team	ELEVEN
foot bone	TARSUS
footboy	PAGE
foot covering	SHOE, BOOT,
	SOCK
foot digit	TOE
footed vase	URN
footing	POSITION
foot it	SCUD
footless	APOD
foot lever	PEDAL
footlike part	PES
footlocker	TRUNK
footloose	FREE
footnote	ADDITION, P.S.
foot part	TOE, HEEL, INSTEP,
ARCH, SOLE, BALL	
footpath	TRAIL
footprint	STEP, TRACK
footrace	DASH

footrest	OTTOMAN, HASSOCK
foot trail	PATH
footwear	SHOES
foozle	BUNGLE
fop	DANDY
for	PRO
for (Sp.)	POR
forage	BROWSE
forage acre	PASTURE
forage grass	REDTOP
forage plant	CLOVER
foray	RAID
forbear	ABSTAIN
forbearance	MERCY
forbid	BAN
forbidden	TABOO
Forbidden City	LHASA, LASA
forbidding	GRIM
force	COMPEL, OBLIGE, DINT,
	POWER, STRENGTH
force (Lat.)	VIS
forced	COMPELLED,
	COMPULSORY
forced laborer	SLAVE
forceful blow	BASH
force into less space	COMPRESS
force onward	URGE
force to go	DRIVE OUT
force unit	DYNE
for credit	ON THE CUFF
ford a stream	WADE
for each	PER
for each person	APIECE
forearm bone	ULNA
forebear	ANCESTOR
forebode	AUGUR
foreboding	OMEN,
	PREMONITION
forebrain	PROSENCEPHALON
forecast	PRESAGE
forecaster	SEER
foreclose	DEBAR, PREVENT
forefather	ANCESTOR
forefinger	INDEX
forego	PRECEDE
foregoing	FORMER
forehead	BROW
foreign	STRANGE, ALIEN
foreign agent	SPY
foreigner	ALIEN
foreign service residence	
	CONSULATE
foreknow	PRECONCEIVE
foreknowledge	PRESCIENCE
forlock	BANGS
foreman	BOSS, MANAGER
foremost	LEADING, FIRST

forenoon (abbr.)	A.M.
forensic	RHETORICAL
foreordain	DESTINE
forepiece of a cap	VISOR
forest	WOODS
forestall	AVERT
forest animal	DEER, BEAR
forest clearing	GLADE
forest god	PAN
forest home	CABIN
forest open space	GLADE
forest ox	ANOA
forest warden	RANGER
foretell	BODE
foretoken	OMEN
forever	ALWAYS, AYE
foreword	PREFACE
for example (abbr.)	E.G.
for fear that	LEST
forfeit	LOSE, PENALTY
forge	SMITHY
forget	OMIT
forgive	CONDONE, PARDON
forgo	QUIT, WAIVE
for instance	AS
fork over	PAY
fork prong	TINE
forlorn	FORSAKEN, DESOLATE
form	MOLD, SHAPE
form a jelly	GEL
formal	STIFF
formal argument	DEBATE
formal attitude	POSE
formal dance	BALL
formal dress	GOWN
formal letter	EPISTLE
formalities	ETIQUETTE
formality	CEREMONY
formal meeting	CONFERENCE
formal objection	PROTEST
formal procession	PARADE
formal speech	ORATION, ADDRESS
formal structure	FORMATION
form a spider web	SPIN
format	PLAN
formed at the base of mountains	PIEDMONT
formed by the sea	MARINE
formed like a needle	ACERATE
formed like lips	LABIAL
for men only	STAG
former	ONE TIME, ONCE
former boy	MAN
former candidate Stevenson	ADLAI
former college man	ALUMNUS
former European coin	DUCAT
former French premier	DE GAULLE
former German coin	TALER, KRONA
former Japanese statesman	ITO
former labor group (abbr.)	IWW
formerly	ERST, ONCE
formerly Persia	IRAN
former Moslem edict	IRADE
former New York governor	DEWEY
former Russian ruler	TZAR, CZAR
former screen star (2 wds.)	GRETA GARBO, PEARL WHITE, THEDA BARA
former Soviet leader	LENIN, STALIN, KHRUSHCHEV
former state in Germany	PRUSSIA
former time	PAST
former Turkish president	INONU
former President's nickname	IKE
formicary	ANTHILL
formidable	ALARMING, APPALLING
forming container	MOLD
form of architecture	DORIC, IONIC
form of hoisting crane	DAVIT
form of polite address	MADAM
Formosa	TAIWAN
Formosa city	TAIPEI
formula	RECIPE
for nothing	GRATIS
forsake	LEAVE, DEPART, GO, DESERT, ABANDON, STRAND
forsaken	DESOLATE
forswear	REJECT, RENOUNCE
fort	STRONGHOLD
forth	FORWARD
forthcoming	DUE
for the most part	IN GENERAL, MAINLY
forthwith	AT ONCE
fortification	REDAN
fortify	ARM
fortitude	STRENGTH
fortress	TOWER
fortuitous	ACCIDENTAL
fortuity	CHANCE
fortunate	LUCKY
fortune	LOT, LUCK, FATE

forty winks	**NAP**
forward	**ON**
forward part	**FRONT**
forward part of a ship	**PROW, BOW**
for what reason	**WHY**
foss	**DITCH, MOAT**
fossil	**BONE**
foster	**PROMOTE**
foul	**FILTHY, NASTY**
foulard	**SCARF, TIE**
found	**BASE, ESTABLISH**
foundation	**BASE, BASIS**
founded on experience	**EMPIRICAL**
founder	**STUMBLE, FAIL**
founder of Carthage	**DIDO**
foundling	**WAIF, ORPHAN**
fountain	**WELLHEAD**
fountain drink	**COLA, SODA, SHAKE, MALTED, FLOAT, COOLER**
fountain man (2 wds.)	**SODA JERK**
fountain nymph	**NAIAD**
four	**TETRAD**
four (Ger.)	**VIER**
four (prefix)	**TETRA, TETR**
four-door car	**SEDAN**
four-flush	**BLUFF**
four-in-hand	**TIE, CRAVAT**
fourpenny	**NAIL**
four-poster	**BED**
fourth estate	**PRESS**
fourth month	**APRIL**
fowl	**BIRD**
fowl product	**EGG**
fox's foot	**PAD**
foxy	**SLY, CRAFTY**
foyer	**LOBBY**
fracas	**SET-TO**
fraction	**PART, DIVISION**
fractious	**CROSS, FRETFUL**
fracture	**BREAK**
fragile	**DELICATE, BREAKABLE, FRAIL**
fragment	**CHIP, PIECE, SCRAP, SHRED, WISP, SHARD**
fragment left at meal	**ORT**
fragment of earthern vessel	**SHARD**
fragrance	**AROMA, ODOR, SCENT, BOUQUET, PERFUME**
fragrant	**OLENT, REDOLENT**
fragrant ointment	**BALM, NARD**
fragrant plant	**MINT**

fragrant root in perfume	**ORRIS**
fragrant wood	**CEDAR**
frail	**WEAK, DELICATE, FRAGILE**
frailty	**WEAKNESS**
frambesia	**YAWS**
frame	**FORM, CONSTRUCT, OUTLINE**
frame for stretching	**TENTER**
frame of mind	**MOOD**
framework	**LATTICE**
France	**GAUL**
franchise	**RIGHT, LICENSE**
franchised	**PATENTED**
Franciscan	**FRIAR, MONK**
Franco's land	**SPAIN**
frangible	**FRAGILE**
frank	**OPEN, CANDID**
Frankish	**GALIC**
Franklin	**BEN**
frankness	**CANDOR**
frantic	**FRENZIED**
frantic cry	**HELP**
frappe	**ICED**
fraternal	**BROTHERLY**
fraternal member	**ELK**
fraternize	**ASSOCIATE**
fraud	**FAKER, FAKERY, PHONY**
fraud (2 wds.)	**MARE'S NEST**
fraudulent	**FAKE, CUNNING**
fraught	**LADEN**
fray	**RAVEL, BATTLE**
frazzle	**WEAR, FRAY**
freak	**MONSTER, QUIRK**
freakish	**ODD, QUEER**
freckle	**SPOT**
Fred Astaire's sister	**ADELE**
free	**LOOSE, UNFETTERED, RELEASE, RID, LIBERATE, GRATIS**
free access (2 wds.)	**OPEN DOOR**
free and easy	**INFORMAL**
free commercial	**PLUG**
freedom	**LIBERTY, LICENSE**
freedom from activity	**REST, RESPITE**
freedom from narrow restrictions	**LATITUDE**
freedom from strife	**PEACE**
freedom from worry (3 wds.)	**PEACE OF MIND**
freedom of access	**ENTREE**
freedom of action	**LEEWAY**
free entertainment	**TREAT**
free food or money	**HANDOUT**
free-for-all	**FRACAS**

free from bacteria **ASEPTIC**
free from coarseness **REFINED**
free from danger **RESCUE,
SAFE, SECURE**
free from guilt (3 wds.)
IN THE CLEAR
free from liability **EXEMPT**
free from suspicion **ABSOLVE,
CLEAR**
freely **WILLINGLY**
free ticket **PASS**
free time **LEISURE**
freeway **PIKE**
freeze **CHILL, ICE**
freezing rain **SLEET**
freight **CARGO**
freighted **LADEN**
freighter **SHIP**
French annual income **RENTE**
French article **LE, LA, LES,
UN, UNE**
French author **DUMAS, HUGO**
French capital **PARIS**
French cheese **BRIE**
French chemist **PASTEUR**
French city **BREST, PARIS,
NICE, NIMES,
METZ, LILLE**
French cleric **ABBE, PERE**
French coin **SOU, ECU, FRANC**
French composer **BIZET,
RAVEL**
French conjunction **ET**
French dance **CANCAN**
French dog **POODLE**
French dramatist **RACINE,
ANOUILH**
French duke **DUC**
French edict **ARRET**
French father **PERE**
French friend **AMI**
French impressionist **MANET,
MONET**
French island **ILE**
French cream **CREME**
Frenchman **GAUL**
French negative **NON**
French noble **DUC**
French painter **DEGAS, MANET,
MONET, RENOIR, DAVID**
French pirate in America
LAFITTE
French police **SURETE**
French resort **NICE, NIMES,
CANNES**
French revolutionary leader
MARAT

French river **ISERE, LOIRE,
OISE, SEINE**
French school **ECOLE, LYCEE**
French sculptor **RODIN**
French service cap **KEPI**
French shooting contest **TIR**
French short story **CONTE**
French singer **CHANTEUSE**
French stock exchange **BOURSE**
French street **RUE**
French subway **METRO**
frenzied **FRANTIC, MAD**
frenzy **FUROR, RAGE**
frequent **FAMILIAR, USUAL**
frequent a place **HAUNT**
frequently **OFTEN**
frequently (poet.) **OFT**
fresh **NEW, STRONG**
freshen **PERK**
freshet **STREAM**
freshwater duck **TEAL**
freshwater fish **CARP, IDE,
DACE, PIKE**
freshwater porpoise **INIA**
fret **WORRY, STEW**
fretful **CROSS**
friar **MONK**
friar's title **FRA**
friend **CHUM, PAL, BUDDY,
MATE**
friend (Fr.) **AMI**
friend (Sp.) **AMIGO**
friendly correspondent
(2 wds.) **PEN PAL**
Friendly Islands **TONGA**
friendly talk **CHAT**
friend of Peter Pan **WENDY**
friendship **AMITY**
frieze **BORDER**
frigate **SHIP**
fright **PANIC, FEAR**
frighten **SCARE, TERRIFY**
frighten away **SHOO**
frightful **AWFUL, HORRIBLE**
frigid **COLD, ICY, FROZEN**
frill **RUCHE, LACE**
frilly trimming **LACE, RUFFLE**
fringe **EDGE**
fringed ornament **TASSEL**
frisk **FROLIC, CAVORT**
frisky **PLAYFUL**
frisson **CHILL, SHIVER**
frivolous **PETTY, TRIVIAL**
frock **DRESS**
froglike amphibian **TOAD**
frog's sound **CROAK**
frolic **CAPER, REVEL, ROMP,
SPREE**

from OF
from a distance AFAR
from head to foot
(comp. wd.) CAP-A-PIE
from now on HENCEFORTH
from one side to the other
ACROSS
from the heart SINCERE
from the time of SINCE
from this place NATIVE
frond LEAF
front FORE, VAN
frontage FACADE, EXPOSURE
frontier merchant TRADER
frontiersman BOONE,
CROCKETT
frontier transportation STAGE
front lawn YARD
front part of a coat LAPEL
frontrunner LEADER
frost a cake ICE
frosting ICE, ICING
frosty ICY, HAUGHTY
frothy FOAMY, SPUMOUS
frothy brew ALE
frothy dessert MOUSSE
froufrou SWISH, RUSTLE
frown SCOWL
frowsy UNKEMPT, MESSY
frozen dessert FRAPPE, ICE,
ICE CREAM, GLACE
frozen pendant ICICLE
frozen rain SLEET, HAIL
frozen water ICE
fructuous FRUITFUL
frugal SAVING, THRIFTY
frugality ECONOMY
fruit LEMON, LIME, ORANGE,
APPLE, PEAR, MELON,
PEACH
fruit center CORE
fruit covering PERICARP
fruit decay BLET
fruit drink ADE, CIDER,
NECTAR, JUICE
fruitful FERTILE
fruit in bunches BANANA,
GRAPE
fruition FULFILLMENT
fruit jar rubber ring LUTE
fruitless VAIN, IDLE
fruit of a palm DATE, FIG
fruit of Jove PERSIMMON
fruit of paradise POMELO
fruit of pine CONE
fruit or vegetable dish SALAD
fruit pastry PIE, TART
fruit preserve COMPOTE

fruit seed PIP, PIT
fruit skin PEEL, RIND
fruit spread JELLY, JAM,
PRESERVE, MARMALADE
fruit stone PIT
fruit sugar FRUCTOSE
frump DOWDY
frustrate FOIL
frustrator of plan MARPLOT
fry YOUNG, BROOD
fryer CHICKEN
frying pan SPIDER, GRIDDLE,
SKILLET
fry quickly SAUTE
fuchsia PURPLE
fucus PAINT, DYE
fudge CANDY
fuel COAL, WOOD, GAS, PEAT,
OIL
fuel-carrying ship COALER,
OILER, TANKER
fuel-conveying tube.
(2 wds.) GAS PIPE
fugitive REFUGEE, RUNAWAY
Fujiyama, e.g. VOLCANO
fulcrum SUPPORT, PROP
fulfill FINISH, COMPLETE
fulfill a command OBEY
fulfill the demands of SATISFY
full REPLETE, SATED
full-length UNABRIDGED,
UNCUT
fulness PLENUM
full of (suffix) OSE
full of ecstatic joy RAPTUROUS
full of happenings EVENTFUL
full of holes, as a roof LEAKY
full of life ANIMATE
full of meaning PITHY
full of ringlets CURLY
full of small openings POROUS
full of vigor PEPPY
full of zest RACY
fully WHOLLY, UTTERLY
fully grown ADULT, MATURE
fully sufficient ADEQUATE
fulsome INSINCERE
Fulton's folly CLERMONT
fume REEK, SMOKE
fun AMUSEMENT, SPORT
function ROLE
fund STOCK, STORE
fundamental BASAL, BASIC
funeral bell TOLL, KNELL
funeral hymn DIRGE
fungus MILDEW, MOLD
funny COMIC, AMUSING

fur-bearing animal **MARTEN, OTTER, SEAL, MINK, RABBIT, SABLE**
fur-cloak **PELISSE**
furious **IRATE, MAD, ANGRY**
furlough **LEAVE**
furnace **OVEN, OAST, KILN**
furnish **PROVIDE, DECORATE**
furnished with shoes **SHOD**
furnish food **CATER**
furnish with weapons **ARM**
furnishings **FURNITURE**
furniture item **BED, COUCH, CHAIR, TABLE, SOFA, DAVENPORT**
furniture polish **WAX**
furniture set **DINETTE, SUITE**
furniture wheel **CASTER**
furor **HOOPLA**
furrow **SEAM**
furs **PELTRY**
further **ADVANCE**
further direction **REFERRAL**
furthermore **MOREOVER**
furtive **SNEAKY, STEALTHY**
furtive glimpse **PEEP, PEEK**
fur wrap **STOLE**
fury **RAGE**
furze genus **ULEX**
fuse **CIRCUIT**
fused by heat **MOLTEN**
fuse together **WELD**
fuss **ADO, TO-DO, POTHER, BOTHER, STIR, STEW**
fusty **MUSTY, MOLDY**
futile **USELESS, VAIN**
fuzz **LINT, FLUFF**
fylfot **SWASTIKA**

G

gab **CHAT, CHATTER, GABBLE**
gabble **BABBLE, CHATTER, JABBER**
gaberdine **COAT**
Gabriel, for one **ANGEL**
gad **ROVE, ROAM**
Gaelic **ERSE**
gag **JOKE**
gage **SECURITY**
gaiety **MIRTH**
gain **ACQUIRE, PROFIT**
gain a victory **WIN, TRIUMPH**
gain as clear profit **NET**
gain by labor **EARN**
gain command of **MASTER**
gain control (2 wds.) **SEW UP**

gain courage (2 wds.) **TAKE HEART**
gainer **DIVE**
gainful **PROFITABLE**
gain knowledge **LEARN**
gain on **NEAR**
gain over expense **NET, PROFIT**
gainsay **DENY**
gain victory **OVERCOME, WIN, TRIUMPH**
gait **CANTER, PACE, TROT**
gaited horse **PACER**
gaiters **SPATS**
gala **FESTIVAL, FETE, BALL, FESTIVE, FIESTA**
Galatea's lover **ACIS**
gale **STORM**
gall **NERVE**
gallant **NOBLE, HEROIC**
gallery hanging **OIL**
galley sweep **OAR**
Gallic affirmative **OUI**
gallop **GAIT**
gamble **BET, WAGER**
gambler **BETTOR**
gambler's capital **STAKE**
gambling cubes **DICE**
gambling game **FARO, POKER, BLACKJACK**
gambol **CAPER, FRISK**
gambrel **ROOF**
game **SPORT**
game animal **DEER, ELK, MOOSE**
game at cards **FARO, LOO**
game at marbles **TAW, MIB**
gamecock spur **GAFF**
game collection **BAG**
game fish **BASS, CERO, TARPON, TROUT, PIKE**
game like bowling **TENPINS**
game of checkers **DRAUGHTS**
game of strategy **CHESS, GO**
game played on horseback **POLO**
game played with clubs **GOLF**
game result **SCORE**
game stealer **POACHER**
gamester **GAMBLER**
gamin **URCHIN, WAIF**
gaming cubes **DICE**
gammon **BACON**
gamut **RANGE, SCOPE**
gamy **SPOILED**
gander **GOOSE**
gang **CREW**
gangling **LANKY**
gangster **HOODLUM, THUG**

gangster Capone **AL**
gangster's girl friend **MOLL**
gang up on **ATTACK, OPPOSE**
gaol **PRISON**
gap **OPENING, HOLE, LACUNA,**
HIATUS
gape **YAWN, STARE**
gar **NEEDLEFISH**
garb **ATTIRE, CLOTHE,**
CLOTHING
garbage **TRASH**
garbage barge **SCOW**
garbanzo **BEAN, CHICKPEA**
garble **DISTORT**
garcon **WAITER**
garden amphibian **TOAD, FROG**
garden flower **PETUNIA, ROSE,**
PEONY, ASTER,
ZINNIA, DAHLIA,
PANSY,
garden for animals **ZOO**
garden implement **HOE, RAKE,**
TROWEL
garden moisture **DEW**
garden party **FETE**
garden pest **APHID, WEED,**
BEETLE
garden plant **RADISH, TOMATO,**
BEAN, CARROT, POTATO,
ASPARAGUS, BEET,
TURNIP, PEA
garden plot **BED**
garden portulaca
(2 wds.) **ROSE MOSS**
Garden State **NEW JERSEY**
garden tool **HOE, RAKE,**
TROWEL
garden walk **PATH**
gargantuan **HUGE, GIGANTIC**
gargle **RINSE**
gargling liquid **MOUTHWASH**
gargoyle **SPOUT**
garish **GAUDY, LOUD**
garland **WREATH, LEI, ANADEM**
garlic-like herb **SHALLOT**
garlic part **CLOVE**
garment **WRAP**
garment edge **HEM**
garment maker **TAILOR**
garment of old Rome **TOGA**
garment piece **SLEEVE, YOKE,**
COLLAR, LAPEL
garment protector **APRON, BIB,**
SMOCK
garner **GATHER, COLLECT**
garnish **ADORN, EMBELLISH**
garret **ATTIC**
garrison **POST, FORT**

garrote **STRANGLE**
garrulous **TALKY, TALKATIVE**
garter **SUPPORT**
gas **FUEL, PETROL, VAPOR,**
FUME
gas burner **JET**
gaseous compound **ETHANE**
gaseous element **ARGON, NEON**
gaseous hydrocarbon **ETHANE**
gash **CUT, SLASH**
gasoline container **TANK**
gasoline in Britain **PETROL**
gasoline rating **OCTANE**
gasp **PANT**
gastronome **EPICURE,**
GOURMET
gastropod **ABALONE, SNAIL**
gastropod genus **OLIVA**
gat **CHANNEL**
gate **DOOR, PORTAL**
gatefold **FOLD-OUT, INSERT**
gatekeeper **WARDEN**
gateway **ENTRY, PORTICO**
gather **AMASS, ASSEMBLE,**
REAP, ACCUMULATE,
COLLECT, GLEAN
gathering of people **MEETING,**
ASSEMBLY
gather in sails **FURL**
gather into folds **PLEAT, SHIRR**
gauche **AWKWARD, CLUMSY**
gaucho **COWBOY**
gaucho's weapon **BOLA(S)**
gaudy **GARISH, LOUD**
gaudy trifle **GEWGAW**
gauge **METER, MEASURE**
Gaul **FRENCHMAN**
gaunt **BONY, SKINNY**
gauntlet **GLOVE**
gay **CHEERY, JOYOUS, MERRY**
gay city **PAREE, PARIS**
gay time **LARK, SPREE**
gaze **PEER, STARE**
gazelle **ARIEL, GOA**
gaze with greed **GLOAT**
gear **EQUIPMENT**
gear tooth **COG**
gee **GOLLY**
gekko **LIZARD**
gelatinous substance **AGAR,**
AGAR-AGAR
gem **JEWEL, STONE**
gem carved in relief **CAMEO**
gem face **FACET**
gem of the mountains **IDAHO**
Gem State **IDAHO**
gem surface **FACET**
gem weight **CARAT**

gender	SEX
Gene Tierney role	LAURA
genealogical record	TREE
genealogy	LINEAGE, PEDIGREE
general	COMMON, UNIVERSAL
general course	TREND
general Eisenhower	IKE
generally	USUALLY
general's aides	STAFF
general's assistant	
	AIDE-DE-CAMP, AIDE
generate	PRODUCE
generation	AGE, ERA
generic	TYPICAL
generous	OPEN-HANDED,
	CHARITABLE
genesis	BIRTH, ORIGIN
genial	CORDIAL, WARM
genius	TALENT
genteel	POLITE, POLISHED
gentle	MILD, TAME, KIND,
	SOFT
gentle blow	TAP
gentle creature	LAMB
gentlefolk	NOBILITY
gentleman	SIR
gentleman (Sp.)	SENOR
gentleman's gentleman	VALET
gentlemen's agreement	
	HANDSHAKE
gentle reproof	ADMONITION
gentle tap	PAT
genuflect	KNEEL
genuine	REAL, BONA FIDE,
	PURE, TRUE
genus	CLASS
genus of African tree	COLA
genus of ants	ECITON
genus of apes	SIMIA
genus of apple trees	MALUS
genus of bees	APIS
genus of beetles	SITOPHILUS
genus of cattle	BOS
genus of chickpeas	CICER
genus of currants	RIBES
genus of frogs	RANA
genus of maples	ACER
genus of olive trees	OLEA
genus of palms	ARECA
genus of rodents	MUS
genus of sheep	OVIS
genus of snakes	OPHIDIA
geographical dictionary	
	GAZETTEER
geographical division	ZONE
geological period	ERA

geometrical figure	CONE,
	CUBE, POLYGON,
	SQUARE, OCTAGON
geometrical line	RADIUS,
	DIAMETER
George Gershwin's brother	IRA
George Sand classic	LELIA
Georgia city	AUGUSTA,
	MACON, ATLANTA
germ	SEED
German	TEUTON
German article	DAS, DER, DIE
German city	BADEN, ESSEN,
	EMDEN, BONN, BERLIN,
	FRANKFURT, HAMBURG
German coin	TALER
German composer	LEHAR,
	STRAUS, BRAHMS, WAGNER
German dive bomber	STUKA
German fascist	NAZI
German folk dance	ALLEMANDE
German goblin	KOBOLD
German-made pistol	LUGER
German measles	RUBELLA
German negative	NEIN
German philosopher	KANT,
	HEGEL
German river	ELBE, ISAR,
	ODER, RHINE
German submarine	
(comp. wd.)	U-BOAT
German title	HERR, FRAU
germ culture	AGAR
gesture	ACT, MOTION
get	RECEIVE, OBTAIN,
	PROCURE, GAIN
get along	MANAGE
get a scolding	
(2 wds., colloq.)	CATCH IT
get as deserved	EARN, MERIT
get away	ESCAPE, FLEE
get back	REDEEM
get better of	BEST
get bigger	GROW, INCREASE
get by force	EXTORT, PRY
get by reasoning	DERIVE
get lost	STRAY
get on	BOARD
get on a horse	MOUNT
get out (sl.)	SCRAM
get ready	PREPARE
get rid of (2 wds.)	CLEAR OFF
get the advantage of	BEST
get the best of	MASTER
get the point	UNDERSTAND,
	SEE
get up	ARISE, STAND
get-up	OUTFIT

get well **RECOVER, HEAL, MEND**
gewgaw **TRINKET**
Ghandi's country **INDIA**
ghastly **HIDEOUS**
ghat **PASS, STAIRS**
gherkin **CUCUMBER, PICKLE**
ghost **SPIRIT, SPOOK, SHADE**
ghostly **EERIE, EERY**
giant **TITAN**
giant beggar of Ithaca **IRUS**
giant of fairy tales **OGRE**
gibberish **CHATTER, JARGON**
gibbon **APE**
gift **PRESENT**
gibe **SNEER, SCOFF**
giddy **DIZZY**
gift bearer **GREEK, DONOR**
gift recipient **DONEE**
gifted speaker **ORATOR**
gift to the needy **ALMS**
gigantic **HUGE, IMMENSE**
giggle **LAUGH, TITTER, SNICKER**
giggling sound **TEHEE**
gilding **GILT**
gill **SMALL LIQUID MEASURE**
gimcrack **GEWGAW, TRINKET**
gimpy **LAME**
gin-and-tonic garnish **LIME**
ginger **PEP**
ginger cookie **SNAP**
gingerly **CAREFULLY**
gingili **SESAME**
gin mixer **TONIC**
giraffe-like animal **OKAPI**
gird **BIND, BELT**
girl **GAL, LASS, MAID, MAIDEN**
girl of song **MARIE, LOLA, DAISY, MARY, JEANNIE, LAURA, MARTA, WENDY**
girl of the Twenties **FLAPPER**
girl servant **MAID**
girth **HOOP, BAND**
GI's ID (2 wds., colloq.) **DOG TAG**
gist **POINT, MEAT**
give **DONATE**
give an account of **RELATE, REPORT, TELL**
give and take **BANDY**
give a new title to **RENAME**
give another title to **RENAME**
give assent **AGREE**
give away **BESTOW, GRANT**
give back **REPAY, RETURN, RESTORE**
give claim to **ENTITLE**

give consent **ACCEDE**
give due credit **PRAISE**
give ear **HEED, LISTEN**
give evidence **TESTIFY**
give forth **EMIT**
give in **RELENT**
give information **REPORT**
give legal force to **VALIDATE**
give light **SHINE, GLOW**
give meaning to **DEFINE**
give name to **DUB, TITLE**
give notice **WARN**
given to loose chatter **GOSSIPY**
give off fumes **REEK**
give one's word **PROMISE**
give outlet to **VENT**
give out sparingly **DOLE, METE**
give silent assent **NOD**
give temporarily **LEND**
give the alarm **WARN, ALERT**
give the meaning of **DEFINE**
give up **CEDE, YIELD**
giving **GENEROUS**
glacial epoch (2 wds.) **ICE AGE**
glacial ice **SERAC**
glacial ridge **ESKER**
glacial sand **NEVE**
glacial term **STOSS**
glad **HAPPY, JOYFUL**
gladden **ELATE**
glade **VALE**
glamour **CHARM, ALLURE**
glance **LOOK, PEEK**
glare **SHINE, GLEAM**
glaring **OBVIOUS**
Glasgow resident **SCOT**
glass bottle **CARAFE**
glass container **JAR, BOTTLE**
glass-enclosed room **SOLARIUM, SUNROOM**
glasses part **LENS, FRAME**
glass to reflect image **MIRROR**
glassy **SMOOTH**
gleam **GLINT, SHINE**
glee **EXULTATION, JOY, BLISS, ELATION**
glib **FLIP, SMOOTH**
glide aloft **SOAR**
glide on snow **SKI**
glide over ice **SKATE**
glider **SWING**
glimpse **ESPY, NOTICE**
glisten **GLITTER, SHINE**
glisten brightly **SPARKLE**
glitter **GLARE, SHINE**
globe **SPHERE, ORB, WORLD, PLANET, BULB**
globule **DROP**

gloom	DARKNESS
gloomy	GLUM, BLUE, SAD
glorify	PRAISE
glorious	SPLENDID, NOBLE
glory	GRANDEUR, HONOR
gloss	LUSTER, POLISH, SHEEN, SHINE
glossa	TONGUE
glossy	SHINY
glossy black bird	RAVEN
glossy fabric	SATEEN, SATIN
glossy paint	ENAMEL
glossy shoe material (2 wds.)	PATENT LEATHER
glove	GAUNTLET, MITTEN
glove leather	CALF, KID
glow	SHINE
glowing coal	EMBER
glucose	SUGAR
glue	PASTE
glue shut	SEAL
glum	SULLEN, SAD
glut	SATE, SATIATE
glutton (colloq.)	HOG, PIG
gluttony	GREED
glyph	CARVING
gnarl	KNOT, SNARL
gnash	GRIND
gnat	MIDGE
gnaw	CHEW
gnome	ELF, GREMLIN, TROLL, BROWNIE
gnu	WILDEBEEST
go	DEPART, LEAVE
go (poet.)	WEND
go aboard, at depot	ENTRAIN
goad	INCITE, PROD, SPUR, URGE, EGG ON
go ahead	CONTINUE, PROCEED
goal	AIM, OBJECTIVE, END, TARGET
go along with	AGREE
go around	DETOUR
go astray	ERR, SIN
goat	KID
go at	ATTACK
goatee	BEARD
go away	SCRAM, SHOO, DEPART, LEAVE, SCAT
gob	TAR, SAILOR
go back	RETURN
go back on a promise	RENEGE
go back to	REVERT, RETURN
go bad	SPOIL, ROT
gobble	EAT
gobbler	TURKEY
go before the wind	SCUD
go-between	AGENT

go beyond	OVERREACH
goblet	GLASS
goblet part	STEM
goblin	SPRITE, GHOST, HAUNT
go by	ELAPSE, PASS
go by car	RIDE
go by ship	SAIL
god	IDOL, DIETY
god-fearing	DEVOUT, PIOUS
godforsaken	DESOLATE, FORLORN
god, goddess (name of)—(See under Greek deity, Norse deity, etc.)	
godliness	PIETY
godly	DIVINE
god of the east	ALLAH
go easily	AMBLE
go forward	ADVANCE, PROGRESS
go from store to store	SHOP
go furtively	SNEAK, STEAL
goggle	STARE, GAPE
goggles	GLASSES
go in	ENTER, PENETRATE
gold	WEALTH, MONEY
gold (Sp.)	ORO
gold cloth	LAME
Gold Coast	GHANA
gold coin	EAGLE
gold color	YELLOW
gold in heraldry	OR
gold in mass	BULLION
gold leaf	GILT
gold plated statuette	OSCAR
golden	GILT
golden bird	ORIOLE
golden bronze	ORMOLU
golden calf	IDOL
golden fish	CARP
golden fleece seeker	JASON
golden horde	MONGOLS
Golden State	CALIFORNIA
golf club	WOOD, PUTTER, IRON, DRIVER
golf club face	LOFT
golf course	LINKS
golf course item	HOLE
golfer Hogan	BEN
golfer Lema	TONY
golfer Palmer	ARNOLD
golfer Sarazen	GENE
golfer Snead	SAM
golf expert	PRO
golf gadget	TEE
golf hazard	BUNKER, TRAP
golf hole	CUP, BYE
golf mound	TEE

golf norm	**PAR**
golf score	**BIRDIE, PAR, EAGLE, BOGEY**
golf shout	**FORE**
golf term	**BIRDIE, FORE**
Golgotha	**CALVARY**
goliard	**MINSTREL, JESTER**
Goliath	**GIANT**
Goliath's slayer	**DAVID**
golly	**GEE, GOSH**
gondola	**BOAT**
gone	**LEFT, AGO**
gone by	**PAST, AGO**
gone from home	**AWAY, OUT**
goober	**PEANUT**
good	**HONEST**
good (Fr.)	**BON**
good (Scot.)	**GUDE**
good-by	**FAREWELL, TA-TA**
good-by, in Madrid	**ADIOS**
good-by, in Tokyo	**SAYONARA**
good-for-nothing	**IDLER**
good fortune on first venture	**BEGINNER'S LUCK**
good judgment	**PRUDENCE**
good luck symbol	**MASCOT, TALISMAN**
good name	**CREDIT, HONOR**
goodness	**VIRTUE**
good news	**EVANGEL**
goods	**MATERIAL, WARES**
goods for sale	**WARES**
good turn	**FAVOR**
gooey	**STICKY**
gooey mud	**SLIME**
goof	**BLUNDER**
go off	**EXPLODE**
go on	**CONTINUE**
go on a cruise (2 wds.)	**SET SAIL**
go one better	**OUT DO**
go on foot	**WALK, MARCH**
goose egg	**O, ZERO**
goose genus	**ANSER**
go over	**EXAMINE**
go over a bridge	**CROSS**
go over and change	**REVISE**
gore	**PIERCE**
gorge	**CANYON**
gorgeous	**MAGNIFICENT, SPLENDID**
gorgon	**MEDUSA**
gorilla	**APE**
gorse	**FURZE**
gosh	**GEE, GOLLY**
go softly	**TIPTOE**
gospel	**TRUTH**
gossamer	**FILMY, THIN**
gossip	**TALK, TATTLER, DIRT**

go swiftly	**FLIT, RACE, RUN, HIE, HASTEN, SCUD**
go swimming	**BATHE**
Gothic arch	**OGIVE**
Gothic window	**ORIEL**
go through	**EXPERIENCE**
go through with	**COMPLETE**
go to bed	**RETIRE, TURN IN**
go together	**MATCH**
go too far	**OVERSTEP**
go to the bottom	**SINK**
goulash	**STEW**
go under	**FAIL**
Gounod's opera	**FAUST**
go up	**RISE, ASCEND, CLIMB**
gourd	**PEPO, MELON**
gourmand	**EPICURE, GOURMET**
govern	**RULE**
governess	**NANNY**
governing board member	**REGENT**
government agent (comp. wd.)	**T-MAN, G-MAN**
government assistance (2 wds.)	**FEDERAL AID**
government by a few	**OLIGARCHY**
government levy	**TAX**
governor	**REGENT**
Gower Champion's wife	**MARGE**
gown	**DRESS**
go wrong	**ERR, SIN**
grace	**CHARM**
graceful	**ELEGANT**
graceful animal	**DEER**
graceful bird	**SWAN**
graceful horse	**ARAB**
graceful loser (2 wds.)	**GOOD SPORT**
gracious	**BENIGN, KIND**
gradation	**STEP**
grade	**RANK**
gradual	**SLOW**
graduate	**ALUMNUS**
graduate of Annapolis (abbr.)	**ENS**
graduate's memento (2 wds.)	**CLASS RING**
grafted (Her.)	**ENTE**
grafting twig	**SCION, CION**
grain	**OAT, RICE, WHEAT, BARLEY, SEED**
grain for beer	**BARLEY**
grain for bread	**WHEAT**
grain for grinding	**GRIST**
grain for weddings	**RICE**
grain for whiskey	**RYE**
grain grinding place	**MILL**

grain mildew	**RUST**	grazing land	**PASTURE, LEA**
grain of corn	**KERNEL**	grease	**OIL, FAT, LARD**
grain warehouse	**ELEVATOR**	great **LARGE, VAST, BIG, HUGE**
grainy	**GRANULAR**	Great Britain principality
grammarian's concern	**SYNTAX**		**WALES, SCOTLAND**
grammatical mark	**TILDE**	greater in number	**MORE**
grampus	**ORC**	greatest **EXTREME, UTMOST**
grand	**GREAT, EPIC**	great folly	**MADNESS**
Grand Canyon State	**ARIZONA**	great-hearted	**BRAVE,**
grandee	**NOBLEMAN**		**GENEROUS**
grandeur	**MAJESTY**	great in size **VAST, GIGANTIC**
grange	**FARM**	great knowledge	**LORE**
Granite State **NEW HAMPSHIRE**	Great Lake	**ERIE, HURON,**
grant	**CEDE**		**MICHIGAN, ONTARIO,**
granting that	**IF**		**SUPERIOR**
grant temporarily	**LEND**	great lie (colloq)	**WHOPPER**
granular	**GRAINY**	greatly	**MUCH**
granular snow	**NEVE**	greatly excited	**ENTHUSED,**
grape plant	**VINE**		**AGOG**
graph	**CHART**	greatly happy	**BLISSFUL,**
graphic **VIVID, LUCID, CLEAR**		**JOYFUL, ELATED**
graphic layout	**MAP**	great misfortune	**DISASTER**
grapple	**WRESTLE**	great Mogul emperor	**AKBAR**
grasp **CLUTCH, HOLD, TAKE**	great number	**MULTITUDE**
grasp firmly	**CLENCH**	great operatic tenor	**CARUSO**
grasp grimly	**GRIP**	great part	**BULK**
grasping **AVID, GREEDY**	great personage	**MOGUL**
grasping device	**TONGS**	great pleasure	**DELIGHT**
grasp roughly	**GRAB**	great plenty	**ABUNDANCE**
grass	**LAWN, CEREAL**	great realm	**EMPIRE**
grass cloth	**JUTE, HEMP**	great respect	**AWE**
grass cutter	**MOWER**	great success	**HIT**
grass dried for fodder	**HAY**	Great White Way	**BROADWAY**
grassland	**LEA, PASTURE**	great world	**SOCIETY**
grass leaf	**BLADE**	greedy	**AVID**
grasshopper's cousin	**CICADA,**	greedy person	**MISER**
	LOCUST, MANTIS	Greek assembly	**AGORA**
grass roots	**BASICS**	Greek biographer	**PLUTARCH**
grassy area **LAWN, PASTURE,**	Greek capital	**ATHENS**
	LEA, SAVANNA	Greek city	**SPARTA**
grassy field (poet.)	**MEAD**	Greek coin	**OBOL**
grate **RASP, SCRAPE**	Greek colonnade	**STOA**
grateful **APPRECIATIVE, GLAD**	Greek colony	**IONIA**
gratify	**PLEASE**	Greek column	**CARYATID**
gratify one's vanity	**FLATTER**	Greek commune	**DEME**
grating	**GRID**	Greek cupid	**EROS**
gratis	**FREE**	Greek cynic	**TIMON**
gratitude	**THANKS**	Greek dialect **DORIC, AEOLIC,**
gratuitous	**BASELESS**		**EOLIC**
gratuity	**TIP**	Greek deity	**AMPHITRITE,**
grave **SERIOUS, SOBER**	**APHRODITE, APOLLO, ARES,**
grave robber	**GHOUL**	**POSEIDON, ZEUS, HERMES,**
gravy	**SAUCE**	**HERA, HECATE, ARTEMIS,**
gravy server	**BOAT**	**HEBE, ERIS, ATHENA, EROS,**
gray **DISMAL, NEUTRAL**	**EOS, DEMETER, DIONYSUS,**
grayish blue	**SLATE**	**NIKE, PAN, PLUTO, TRITON,**
grayish red (2 wds.) **ASH ROSE**	**MOIRA, CYBELE, NEMESIS,**
gray with age	**HOARY**	**BACCHUS**

Greek district	**DEME**	Greek portico	**STOA**
Greek dog	**GREYHOUND**	Greek ruler	**EPARCH**
Greek epic poem	**ILIAD,**	Greek sea	**AEGEAN, IONIAN**
	ODYSSEY	Greek slave	**HELOT**
Greek epic poet	**HOMER**	Greek sorceress	**MEDEA**
Greek games city	**NEMEA**	Greek sun god	**APOLLO**
Greek god—(See Greek deity)		Greek sylvan deity	**SATYR**
Greek goddess of agriculture		Greek temple	**NAOS**
	DEMETER	Greek theater	**ODEUM, ODEA**
Greek goddess of discord	**ERIS**	green	**UNRIPE, ENVIOUS**
Greek goddess of peace	**IRENE**	greenback	**DOLLAR, BILL**
Greek goddess of the dawn	**EOS**	Green Bay football team	
Greek goddess of the moon			**PACKERS**
	ARTEMIS	green citrus fruit	**LIME**
Greek goddess of victory	**NIKE**	green-eyed	**JEALOUS**
Greek goddess of youth	**HEBE**	green (Fr.)	**VERT**
Greek god of love	**EROS**	green gem	**JADE, EMERALD**
Greek goddess—(See Greek deity)		green herbage	**GRASS**
		Greenland's colonizer	**ERIC**
Greek hero	**THESEUS, AJAX**	Greenland settlement	**ETAH**
Greek island	**CRETE, SAMOS,**	green light	**GO-AHEAD, GO**
	CORFU	Green Mountain State	**VERMONT**
Greek Juno	**HERA**	green onion	**SCALLION**
Greek lawgiver	**SOLON**	green plum	**GAGE**
Greek letter	**BETA, ALPHA,**	green quartz	**PRASE**
THETA, KAPPA, PI, PSI, RHO,		green rock-growth	**MOSS**
OMEGA, CHI, ETA, DELTA,		green rust	**PATINA**
PHI, TAU, MU, EPSILON,		green spot	**OASIS**
GAMMA, ZETA, ETA, IOTA,		green stone	**EMERALD, JADE**
LAMBDA, NU, XI, OMICRON,		greensward	**LAWN, SOD**
SIGMA, UPSILON		greet	**ACCOST, HAIL, SALUTE**
Greek malignant spirit	**KER**	greeting	**HULLO, HELLO, HI**
Greek marker	**STELE**	greeting message	**CARD**
Greek mathematician and inventor	**ARCHIMEDES**	gregarious	**SOCIAL**
Greek measure	**DAKTYLOS,**	gremlin	**GNOME, BROWNIE,**
	BEMA		**ELF, SPRITE**
Greek money	**DRACHMA**	Gretna Green figure	**ELOPER**
Greek monster	**GORGON**	grief	**SORROW**
Greek mountain	**OSSA, PELION**	grieve	**LAMENT**
Greek muse	**ERATO, CLIO,**	grieve bitterly (4 wds.)	**EAT**
CALLIOPE, EUTERPE,			**ONE'S HEART OUT**
MELPOMENE, POLYMNIA,		grievous	**LAMENTABLE**
TERPSICHORE, THALIA,		grill	**BROIL**
URANIA		grim	**AUSTERE**
Greek mythological youth		grimace	**MOUE, SNEER**
	ADONIS	grime	**DIRT, SOOT, DUST**
Greek nymph	**OREAD**	grin	**SMILE**
Greek paradise	**ELYSIUM**	grind	**CRUSH**
Greek people	**DEMOS**	grinding machine	**MILL**
Greek philosophers	**PLATO,**	grinding stone	**EMERY**
	SOCRATES	grinding tooth	**MOLAR**
Greek philosophy school	**STOIC**	grind with the teeth	**CHEW,**
Greek physician	**GALEN**		**MASH, GNASH**
Greek platform	**BEMA**	grip	**GRASP, VALISE**
Greek poet	**HOMER, ARION**	grisly	**GHASTLY, GRIM**
Greek poetess	**SAPPHO**	gristle	**CARTILAGE**
Greek port	**CORFU, PIRAEUS**	grit	**SAND**

grizzly **BEAR**
groan **MOAN**
grooming aid **COMB, BRUSH,**
TALC, TONIC, RAZOR
groom's attendant
(2 wds.) **BEST MAN**
groove **RUT**
grotesque **BIZARRE**
grotto **CAVE, CAVERN**
grotto (poet.) **GROT**
grouchy person **CRAB, CRANK**
ground **LAND, SOIL**
ground-breaking tool **SPADE**
ground grain **MEAL**
groundless **UNFOUNDED**
ground plot **LOT**
grounds **BASIS**
ground squirrel **GOPHER**
group **LOT**
grouper **MERO**
group of actors **CAST, TROUPE**
group of animals **HERD**
group of criminals **GANG**
group of customers **CLIENTELE**
group of eight **OCTET**
group of facts **DATA**
group of families **TRIBE, CLAN**
group of five **QUINTET, PENTAD**
group of Indians **TRIBE**
group of lions **PRIDE**
group of musicians **BAND,**
ORCHESTRA, COMBO,
DANCE BAND
group of nine **ENNEAD**
group of persons **TEAM, CROWD**
group of pictures **SET**
group of points **LOCI**
group of related species **GENUS**
group of rooms **SUITE**
group of seamen **CREW**
group of seven **HEPTAD**
group of ships **FLEET, ARMADA**
group of singers **CHOIR**
group of six **SEXTET**
group of states **EMPIRE**
group of students **CLASS**
group of ten **DECADE, DECAD**
group of three **TRIAD, TRIO**
group of two **DYAD, DUET, DUO,**
PAIR, BRACE
group of Western allies **NATO**
group spirit **MORALE**
group transportation
(2 wds.) **CHARTERED BUS**
grove of trees **COPSE, FOREST**
grovel **FAWN, CRINGE**
grow **EXPAND, RAISE**
grow dim **FADE, WANE**

grow drowsy **NOD**
growing in pairs **BINATE**
grow in length **ELONGATE**
growl **SNARL**
grow molars **TEETHE**
grow more intense **DEEPEN**
grown boy **MAN**
grown up ugly duckling **SWAN**
grow old **AGE**
grow out of **DEVELOP**
grow quickly **SPROUT**
growth **RISE, INCREASE**
grow thin **EMACIATE**
grow tiresome **BORE**
grow weary **TIRE**
grow worse **DETERIORATE**
grub **FOOD, VICTUALS**
grubby **MESSY, UNTIDY**
grudge **SPITE, ENVY**
gruesome **LURID, MACABRE**
gruff **ABRUPT, BRUSQUE**
grumble **COMPLAIN**
Guam capital **AGANA**
Guam seaport **APRA**
guanaco **LLAMA**
guarantee **ASSURE**
guaranty **PLEDGE, WARRANTY**
guard **SENTINEL**
guardhouse **BRIG**
guardian **PATRON,**
CUSTODIAN
guard spirit of old Rome **LAR**
Guatemalan **MAYAN**
Gudrun's husband **ATLI**
guess **SUPPOSE, ESTIMATE**
guessing game **CHARADE**
guest **LODGER, VISITOR**
guide **LEAD**
guide a car **STEER,**
DRIVE
guide a plane **PILOT**
guide to solution of
a mystery **CLUE**
guidon **PENNANT, BANNER**
Guido's high note **ELA**
guile **CRAFT, CUNNING**
guileless **NAIVE**
guillotine **BEHEAD**
guilty **CULPABLE,**
BLAMABLE
guilty person **CULPRIT**
guilty regret **REMORSE**
guinea pig **CAVY**
guise **ASPECT, SEMBLANCE**
gulch **RAVINE**
gulf **ABYSS**
gulf between Africa
and Arabia **ADEN**

gulf of Australia **CARPENTARIA**
gullet **MAW, THROAT**
gullible fellow **DUPE**
gull-like bird **TERN**
gully **GUTTER**
gum **RESIN**
gumbo **OKRA, SOUP**
gumption **NERVE**
gums **ULA**
gum tree **SAPODILLA**
gun **FIREARM, MUSKET, RIFLE, PISTOL**
gun an engine **REV**
gun barrel cleaner **RAMROD**
gun cavity **BORE**
gun dog **SETTER**
gunny bag **SACK**
gunpowder ingredient **NITRE**
gun tube **BARREL**
guru **TEACHER**
gush **POUR, SPURT**
gush forth **SPEW**
gusto **ZEST, ELAN**
guy **CHAP, FELLOW**
gymnasium pad **MAT**
gyp **CHEAT, SWINDLE**
gypsy man **ROM**
gyrate **WHIRL, ROTATE**

H

habiliment **CLOTHING, DRESS, ATTIRE**
habit **CUSTOM, WONT, OUTFIT, ATTIRE**
habitat **LOCALITY**
habitation **ABODE**
habitual **USUAL, CUSTOMARY**
habitual drunkard **SOT**
habituate **INURE**
hack **TAXI**
hackamore **HALTER, BRIDLE**
hackle **BRISTLE**
hackneyed **BANAL, TRITE, STALE**
hack up **CHOP**
hades **HELL, INFERNO**
hag **CRONE**
haggard **GAUNT, WEARY**
Haggard novel **SHE**
haggle **BARGAIN, DICKER**
hail **AVE, GREET, SLEET**
hair **TRESSES, MANE**
hair curler **ROLLER**
hair-do **AFRO, SET, STYLE**
hair-do holder **NET**
hair dye **HENNA**

hair grooming aid **COMB, BRUSH**
hairless **BALD**
hair ointment **POMADE**
hair on horse's foot **FETLOCK**
hair on lion's neck **MANE**
hair pad **RAT**
hair piece **SWITCH, FALL, WIG, TOUPEE**
hair ribbon **SNOOD**
hair ringlet **TRESS, CURL**
hair roll **CHIGNON**
hair style **UPDO, SHINGLE**
hair tint **RINSE**
hairy man **ESAU**
Haitian city **PORT-AU-PRINCE**
Haitian magic **OBEAH, OBI**
halcyon **TRANQUIL, CALM**
hale **HEALTHY, ROBUST**
half **PART, PARTIAL**
half (prefix) **SEMI, DEMI, HEMI**
half a quart **PINT**
half a score **TEN**
half-diameter **RADIUS**
half gainer **DIVE**
half hitch **KNOT**
half man and half bull **CENTAUR**
half mask **DOMINO**
half moon **CRESCENT**
half-suppressed laugh **SNICKER**
halfway **MID**
halfwit **FOOL, DOLT**
hall **PASSAGE, CORRIDOR**
Halley's constellation **APUS**
hallow **DEDICATE, BLESS**
hallowed place **SHRINE**
Halloween alternative **TRICK, TREAT**
Halloween beverage **CIDER**
hall rug **RUNNER**
hallucination **DELUSION**
hallux **BIG TOE**
halo **AURA, NIMBUS**
halt **CEASE, STOP, DESIST, ESTOP**
halter **LEAD**
halve **BISECT**
hambletonian **TROTTER, RACE**
hamburger garnish **ONION, PICKLE, MUSTARD, CATSUP, RELISH**
hame **HARNESS**
Hamilton bill **TEN**
Hamite **SOMALI**
hamlet **TOWN, VILLAGE, DORP**
Hamlet's home **ELSINORE, DENMARK**

Hamlet's sweetheart	**OPHELIA**
hammer	**SLEDGE**
hammer part	**PEEN, CLAW,**
	HEAD
hammerhead	**SHARK**
hammerlike tool	**MALLET**
hammock cord (comp. wd.)	
	TIE-TIE
hamper	**BASKET, IMPEDE**
Ham's son	**CUSH**
hamstring	**DISABLE**
hand	**WORKER**
handbag	**PURSE**
handball point	**ACE**
hand blow	**SLAP**
handcuff	**MANACLE**
Handel masterwork	**MESSIAH**
hand down	**BEQUEATH**
handicap	**BURDEN, PENALTY**
hand implement	**SHOVEL,**
	PICK, HOE
handkerchief	**BANDANA,**
	HANKY
handle	**LEVER, TREAT**
handle of a knife	**HAFT**
handle of a sword	**HILT**
handle of a whip	**CROP**
handle roughly	**MAUL**
handle rudely	**PAW**
handle well	**COPE**
handling	**TREATMENT,**
	CONTROL
handsome man	**ADONIS**
hand-to-hand fight	**MELEE**
handy carryall (2 wds.)	
	SHOPPING BAG
hang	**PEND, SUSPEND**
hang above	**HOVER**
hang around	**LOITER**
hanger on	**PARASITE**
hang in folds	**DRAPE**
hanging tuft of threads	**TASSEL**
hang loosely	**LOLL, SAG, DROOP**
hangman's knot	**NOOSE**
hang on	**PERSEVERE**
hang on to	**HOLD, KEEP,**
	RETAIN
hang overhead	**HOVER**
hank	**SKEIN**
hanker	**ITCH, YEN, DESIRE**
hank of twine	**RAN**
haphazard (3 wds.)	**HIT OR MISS**
haphazardly (2 wds.)	
	AT RANDOM
happen	**BETIDE, OCCUR,**
	TAKE PLACE
happen again	**RECUR**
hapless	**UNLUCKY**

happening	**EVENT**
happen to	**BEFALL**
happily	**LUCKILY**
happiness	**GLADNESS, JOY,**
	ELATION, BLISS
happy	**GLAD, JOYFUL,**
	BLISSFUL
happy bird	**LARK**
happy cat sound	**PURR**
happy expressions	**SMILE, GRIN**
harangue	**ORATE**
harass	**ANNOY, PLAGUE**
harbinger	**HERALD**
harbor	**HAVEN, PORT**
harbor boat	**TUG**
harbor city	**PORT**
harbor craft	**FERRYBOAT,**
	TUGBOAT
harbor guide	**PILOT**
harbor sight	**SHIP**
hard	**DIFFICULT, SOLID**
hard and fast	**STRICT**
hard ball	**BASEBALL**
hard-bitten	**STUBBORN, TOUGH**
hard-boiled	**TOUGH, CALLOUS**
hard candy	**LEMON DROP**
hard cash	**MONEY**
hard coal	**ANTHRACITE**
hard core	**ABSOLUTE**
hard cover	**BOUND**
hard drawn	**TENSE**
hard drinker	**TOPER, SOT,**
	SOUSE
harden	**SET, STEEL, GEL, INURE**
hardened	**CALLOUS, FROZEN**
hard finish	**ENAMEL**
hard-fisted	**STINGY, MISERLY**
hard handed defense	**KARATE**
hard hearted	**CRUEL, MEAN**
hard lump of earth	**CLOD**
hardly	**BARELY**
hardly ever	**RARELY**
hard metal	**IRON, STEEL**
hardness	**RIGOR**
hard-nosed	**SHREWD**
hard of hearing	**DEAF**
hard question	**POSER**
hard resin	**COPAL**
hard rock	**SLATE**
hard-shelled fruit	**NUT**
hardship	**PRIVATION, RIGOR**
hard to describe	**NONDESCRIPT**
hard up	**NEEDY, LACKING**
hardware	**TOOLS**
hardwood	**TEAK**
hardwood tree	**MAPLE, OAK**
hard work	**LABOR, TOIL**
hard worker	**DEMON**

hardy	**BOLD, DARING**
hardy cabbage	**KALE**
hardy person	**SPARTAN**
Hardy's heroine	**TESS**
harebrained	**RECKLESS, RASH**
harem apartment	**ODA**
hark	**LISTEN**
harm	**DAMAGE, MAR, HURT**
harmless	**GENTLE, DOCILE**
harmonious	**AGREEABLE**
harmonize	**AGREE, BLEND**
harmony	**UNISON, ACCORD**
harmony in pitch	**TUNE**
harness attachment	**REIN**
harry	**HARASS, ANNOY**
harsh	**SEVERE**
harshest	**SEVEREST**
harsh speech	**TIRADE**
hart	**DEER, STAG**
Harvard's rival	**YALE**
harvest	**CROP, REAP**
harvest fly	**CICADA**
hash	**MINCE**
hash over	**DISCUSS**
hassle	**CONTENTION**
hassock	**FOOTSTOOL**
haste	**SPEED, SWIFTNESS**
hasten	**HIE, RUN, SPEED**
hasty	**HURRIED, FLEET**
hasty meal	**SNACK**
hat	**BONNET, CAP, BERET, CHAPEAU**
hat accessory	**VEIL, RIBBON**
hatch	**PLOT, PLAN**
hatchet	**AX, AXE**
hat crown	**POLL**
hate	**ABHOR, DETEST, LOATHE**
hateful	**ODIOUS**
hat material	**FELT, STRAW**
hatred	**ODIUM, DISLIKE**
haughtiness	**ARROGANCE, PRIDE**
haughty	**PROUD, ALOOF**
haughty one	**SNOB**
haul	**DRAG, TOW, TUG**
haul down flag	**STRIKE**
hauling charge	**CARTAGE**
hauling wagon	**DRAY**
haulm	**STRAW**
haul up	**REST, STOP**
haunch	**HIP**
haunt	**DEN, HABIT**
hausen	**BELUGA**
hautboy	**OBOE**
have	**OWN, POSSESS, HOLD**
have affection for	**LIKE, LOVE**
have ambitions	**ASPIRE**
have a meal	**EAT, DINE, SUP**

have another opinion	**DIFFER**
have a quarrel (2 wds.)	**FALL OUT**
have at	**ATTACK, STRIKE**
have being	**ARE**
have benefit	**ENJOY**
have courage (2 wds.)	**BEAR UP**
have debts	**OWE**
have done	**FINISH**
have effect	**ENURE, INURE**
have faith	**TRUST**
have high regard for	**ADMIRE**
have interest in	**CARE**
have life	**LIVE, EXIST**
have need of	**LACK**
have reference to	**PERTAIN**
have the ability	**CAN**
have the courage	**DARE TO**
have to	**MUST**
have to do with	**DEAL**
haven	**HARBOR, PORT, ASYLUM**
having a backbone	**VERTEBRATE**
having a beak	**ROSTRATE**
having a good memory	**RETENTIVE**
having antlers	**HORNED**
having a tail	**CAUDATE**
having auricles	**EARED**
having boots	**SHOD**
having equality of measure	**ISOMETRICAL**
having feet	**PEDATE**
having fine scenery	**SCENIC**
having knowledge	**AWARE**
having leaves	**FOLIAR**
having left a will	**TESTATE**
having less hair	**BALDER**
having liberty	**FREE**
having limits	**FINITE**
having little warmth	**COLD**
having made a will	**TESTATE**
having offensive odor	**OLID**
having one foot	**UNIPED**
having onionlike forms	**BULBED**
having pile	**NAPPY**
having ringlets	**CURLY**
having wealth position, etc.	**SUCCESSFUL**
having wings	**ALAR, ALATE**
Hawaiian city	**HILO, HONOLULU**
Hawaiian Dance	**HULA**
Hawaiian export	**COPRA, PINEAPPLE**
Hawaiian food fish	**LANIA, ULUA**
Hawaiian food staple	**TARO**
Hawaiian garland	**LEI**
Hawaiian goddess	**PELE**
Hawaiian greeting	**ALOHA**

Hawaiian guitar **UKULELE, UKE**
Hawaiian hawk **IO**
Hawaiian island **OAHU**
Hawaiian lava **AA**
Hawaiian mahogany **KOA**
Hawaiian pepper **AVA**
Hawaiian porch **LANAI**
Hawaiian root **TARO**
Hawaiian salutation **ALOHA**
Hawaiian town **HILO**
hawker **PEDDLER**
Hawkeye State **IOWA**
hawk-like bird **KITE**
hawk's claws **TALON**
hawkshaw's **SLEUTH**
hawk's victims **PREY**
Hawthorne heroine **HESTER**
hay fever **POLLEN**
hay field **MEADOW**
hayseed **RUBE, HICK**
haystack **STADDLE**
haywire **CRAZY, WACKY**
hazard **RISK**
hazardous **UNSAFE, RISKY**
haze **MIST, FOG**
hazelnut **FILBERT**
hazy **CLOUDY, MURKY**
he (Fr.) **IL**
head **PATE, CHIEF, NOODLE,**
NOGGIN, BEAN
headache **MIGRAINE**
headache remedy **ASPIRIN**
headcloth **SCARF**
head cook **CHEF**
head covering **CAP, HAT, HOOD,**
SCARF, BERET, VEIL
headdress **FEATHER**
headed pin **RIVET**
heading **TITLE, BEARING,**
DIRECTION
headland **CAPE, NESS, RAS**
headless (Fr.) **ETETE**
headline **CAPTION**
headliner **STAR**
headlong **RECKLESS, HASTY**
headman **CHIEF**
head money **BOUNTY**
head of a monastery **ABBOT**
head of a nunnery **ABBESS**
head skin **SCALP**
headstrong **RASH**
heal **CURE, MEND**
heal, as bone **KNIT**
healer **BALM**
healing **CURATIVE**
healing profession **MEDICINE**
health resort **SPA**
healthy **HALE, ROBUST**

healthy (Lat.) **SANA**
heap **MOUND, PILE, STACK**
heap of stone **CAIRN**
hear **HEED, LISTEN**
hear about **LEARN**
hearing organ **EAR**
hearken **HEED, LISTEN**
hearsay **RUMOR, GOSSIP**
heart **CORE**
heartbeat **PULSE**
heartbreak **GRIEF, SORROW**
hear tell **LEARN**
hearten **CHEER**
hearth **FIRESIDE**
heartless **COLD, HARD, CRUEL**
heart of the matter **GIST**
hearty **WARM**
hearty enjoyment **ZEST**
hearty laugh (comp. wd.) **HA-HA**
hearty meat dish **STEW**
hearty relish **GUSTO**
heat **WARMTH, PRESSURE**
heat content **ENTHALPY**
heater **STOVE, OVEN**
heath (Brit.) **MOOR**
heathen (arch.) **PAYNIM**
heathen deity **IDOL**
heather **LING, ERICA**
heath plant **ERICA**
heath tree **BRIER, BRIAR**
heating apparatus **ETNA,**
OVEN, OAST, KILN,
BOILER, BRAZIER,
STOVE
heating chambers **OVEN**
OAST, KILN
heating material **FUEL, OIL,**
GAS, WOOD
heave **HOIST, LIFT**
heave to **STOP**
heaven **PARADISE**
heavenly **DIVINE, SUBLIME,**
CELESTIAL
heavenly altar **ARA**
heavenly being **ANGEL**
heavenly body **COMET, STAR,**
PLANET, SUN,
MOON, METEOR
heavenly city **ZION, VALHALLA**
heavenly instrument **HARP**
heavens **SKY**
heavenward **UP**
heavily built **STOCKY**
heavily loaded **LADEN**
heavy **WEIGHTY, LEADEN**
heavy affliction **WOE**
heavy board **PLANK**
heavy blow **CLOUT**

heavy book	TOME	height	STATURE
heavy burden	LOAD	heighten	ENHANCE
heavy cord	ROPE	heinous	HIDEOUS,
heavy curtain	DRAPE		OUTRAGEOUS
heavy element	LEAD	heir	SON, SCION
heavy-footed	SLOW, DULL	held in readiness (2 wds.) ON ICE	
heavy grouping of reeds CLUMP		hell	HADES, INFERNO
heavy-handed CLUMSY, HARSH		hello	HI, GREETING
heavy-hearted	SAD	helmsman	PILOT
heavy hydrogen	DEUTERIUM	help	ABET, AID, ASSIST
heavy impact	SLAM	helper ALLY, AIDE, ASSISTANT	
heavy metal	LEAD	helpful	USEFUL
heavy nail	SPIKE	help in crime	ABET
heavy rainfall	STORM	helping	PORTION
heavy-set	STOUT, STOCKY	help in solving a mystery	CLUE
heavy shoe	BOOT, BROGAN,	helpless	POWERLESS
	CLOG	helpmate	WIFE
heavy sleepers	SNORERS,	Helsinki native	FINLANDER
	BUNTING	helter-skelter	RUSHED,
heavy spar	BARITE		DISORDERLY
heavy string	CORD, TWINE,	hem	BORDER, EDGE
	ROPE	hemi	HALF
heavy twilled cotton	DENIM	hem in	ENCLOSE
heavy volume	TOME	hemorrhage	BLEEDING
heavy weight	TON	hemp	FENNEL, SISAL
heavy with moisture	SODDEN	hemp cord	ROPE
Hebrew	SEMITE, SEMITIC	hen	CHICKEN, PULLET
Hebrew abode of dead	SHEOL	henchman	MINION
Hebrew ascetic	ESSENE	hen fruit	EGG
Hebrew lawgiver	MOSES	hens	POULTRY
Hebrew letter	ALEF, BETH,	herald	MESSENGER
GIMEL, DALETH, MEM,		heraldic bearing	ORLE
TETH, PE, YOD, HE,		heraldic cross	PETTEE,
VAU, ZAYIN, CHETH,		POMMEE, MOLINE, TAU,	
VODH, CAPH, LAMEDH,		MALTESE, FOURCHEE,	
NUN, SAMEKH, AYIN,		BOTONEE, CROSSLET	
SADHE, KOPH, RESH,		Hera's husband	ZEUS
SIN, SHIN. TAV		Hera's son ARES, HEPHAETOS	
Hebrew lyre	ASTOR	herb	SAGE, ANISE, BASIL
Hebrew marriage custom		herb of the teasel family	
	LEVIRATE		SCABIOSA
Hebrew measure	OMER	Hercules' captive	IOLE
Hebrew month TISHRI, ADAR,		herd	DROVE, FLOCK
ELUL, AB, KISLEV		here (Fr.)	ICI
Hebrew patriarch	ABRAHAM,	hereditary INHERENT, INNATE	
ISAAC, JACOB		hereditary factor	GENE
Hebrew prophet	MOSES,	heretic DISSENTER, TRAITOR	
DANIEL, AMOS,		heritage LEGACY, BIRTHRIGHT	
HOSEA, MICAH		hermit EREMITE, RECLUSE	
Hebrew prophetess	DEBORAH	hermit's hut	CELL
Hebrew Sabbath	SATURDAY,	hernia support	TRUSS
	SHABBAT	hero of comics	SUPERMAN,
Hebrew school	CHEDER	BATMAN, DICK TRACY	
Hebrew teacher	RABBI	heroic	EPIC
heckle	BADGER, PESTER	heroic tale	SAGA
hectic	FEVERISH	heroine of A Doll's House	NORA
hedge shrub	PRIVET	heroine of The Rose Tattoo	
heed	HEAR		ROSA

heroism	**VALOR, BRAVERY**
heron	**EGRET**
hero's award	**MEDAL**
herring	**CISCO, SPRAT**
herring alec	**PICKLE**
herring family fish	**ALEWIFE**
he-she dispute (2 wds.)	
	LOVERS' QUARREL
hesitate	**DEMUR, FALTER,**
	PAUSE, STUMBLE, WAVER
hesitation of speech	**STUTTER**
heterogeneous	**VARIANT, MIXED,**
	DISSIMILAR
hew	**CUT, CHOP**
hew out	**CARVE**
hex	**JINX**
Heyerdahl's raft (2 wds.)	
	KON TIKI
Hialeah event (2 wds.)	
	HORSE RACE
hiatus	**GAP, PAUSE**
Hiawatha's nurse	**NOKOMIS**
Hibernian	**ERSE**
hickory nut	**PECAN**
hidden	**INNER, LATENT,**
	COVERT
hidden obstacle	**SNAG**
hidden supply	**CACHE**
hide	**CONCEAL, COVER,**
	MASK, PELT, SKIN
hideous	**GHASTLY, HORRIBLE**
hideous giant	**OGRE**
hiding place	**CACHE, LAIR**
hie	**HASTEN, HURRY,**
	SPEED, RUN
hiemal	**WINTRY**
hieratic	**SACERDOTAL**
hieroglyphic	**SYMBOL**
hierology	**LORE, FABLE**
hi-fi	**STEREO**
high	**TALL, LOFTY**
highbinder	**SWINDLER**
highborn	**NOBLE**
highboy	**BUREAU, CHEST**
highbrow	**INTELLECTUAL**
high card	**ACE**
high-class	**SUPERIOR**
high craggy hill	**TOR**
high day	**FESTIVAL, HOLIDAY**
higher than	**ABOVE**
highest note	**ELA**
highest point	**ACME, APEX,**
	SUMMIT
high-flying bird	**LARK, EAGLE**
high-hatter	**SNOB**
high honkers (2 wds.)	
	WILD GEESE
high in pitch	**ALT**

high intensity light beam	**LASER**
high in value	**DEAR**
high keyed	**TENSE**
highlander	**SCOT**
highlander's cap	**TAM**
highly	**EXTREMELY**
highly seasoned dish	**OLLA,**
	PODRIDA
highly sensible	**PRUDENT**
high male singing voice	**TENOR**
high-minded	**NOBLE**
high mountain	**ALP**
high note	**ELA, ALT**
high-pitched	**SHRILL**
high plateau	**MESA**
high pointed hill	**TOR**
high priced	**COSTLY**
high priest of Israel	**ELI**
high rank	**EMINENCE**
high regard	**ESTEEM, RESPECT,**
	HONOR
high rubber boot	**WADER**
high school dance	**HOP, PROM**
high school student	
(comp. wd.)	**TEENAGER**
high sea	**MAIN**
high shoe	**BOOT**
high spirits	**ELATION, GLEE**
high structure	**TOWER**
high strung	**TENSE, NERVOUS**
high temperature	**HEAT**
high time	**SPREE**
high up	**ALOFT**
highway	**ROAD, ROUTE, PIKE**
highway charge	**TOLL**
highway curve	**ESS**
highway division	**LANE**
highway exit	**RAMP**
highway Inn	**MOTEL**
highwayman (2 wds.)	
	ROAD AGENT
highway sight	**BILLBOARD**
highway to the far north	**ALCAN**
high winds	**GALE, SQUALL,**
	STORM, HURRICANE,
	TORNADO, CYCLONE
high wire	**TIGHTROPE**
hijack	**STEAL, CAPTURE**
hike	**MARCH, TRAMP**
hilarious	**FUNNY, MERRY**
hilarious comedy	**FARCE**
hilarity	**GLEE, MIRTH**
hill	**HEAP, MOUND**
hill (Sp.)	**MORRO**
hill dweller	**ANT**
hillock	**KNOLL**
hill of beans	**TRIFLE**
hillside (Scot.)	**BRAE**

hilly	**RUGGED, STEEP**
Hilo garland	**LEIS**
hilt	**HANDLE**
Himalayan animal	**PANDA**
Himalayan monkshood	**ATIS**
Himalayan mountain	**EVEREST**
Himalayan ox	**YAK**
hind	**DOE, DEER**
hinder	**DETER, STOP, SET BACK**
hinder (law)	**ESTOP, ESTOPPEL**
Hindi dialect	**URDU**
hindrance	**OBSTACLE, BURDEN, IMPEDIMENT**
Hindu ascetic	**SADHU, SADDHU, YOGI**
Hindu ascetic practice	**YOGA**
Hindu chief	**SIRDAR**
Hindu coin	**ANAA**
Hindu cymbals	**TAL**
Hindu deity	**DEVI, VAC, UMA, KALI, MATRIS, AGNI, SIVA, DEVA, KAMA, RAMA, YAMA, VISHNU, KRISHNA, INDRA, USAS, SURYA, VARUNA, SHAKTI, GANESA**
Hindu doctrine	**KARMA**
Hindu garment	**SARI**
Hindu guitar	**SITAR**
Hindu incarnation	**AVATAR**
Hindu king	**RAJAH**
Hindu literature	**VEDA**
Hindu noble	**RAJAH**
Hindu queen	**RANEE, RANI**
Hindu religious teacher	**SWAMI**
Hindu sacred city	**BENARES, BANARAS**
Hindu social class	**CASTE**
hinged tabletop folding to wall	**DROP TABLE**
hint	**CLUE, CUE, SUGGESTION**
hint (Brit.)	**CLEW**
hinterland	**BACKWOODS**
hip (sl.)	**AWARE, COOL**
hipbone	**ILIUM, ILIA (pl.)**
hippie's home	**PAD**
hippocampus (2 wds.)	**SEA HORSE**
Hippocrates	**PHYSICIAN**
hippodrome	**ARENA**
hippopotamus (2 wds.)	**RIVER HORSE**
hire	**EMPLOY, ENGAGE, RENT, LEASE, LET, CHARTER**
hired help	**HAND**
hireling	**SERF, MERCENARY**
hirsute	**HAIRY**
hirundine	**SWALLOW**
hiss	**SIBILANCE**
hissing sound	**SISS**
historian	**CHRONICLER**
historical records	**ANNALS**
historic island of the Philippines	**LEYTE**
historic period	**ERA, EPOCH**
history	**ACCOUNT, RECORD**
histrionics	**THEATRICS**
hit	**STRIKE, BAT**
hitch	**CATCH, TWIST**
hitchhike	**THUMB**
hit hard	**SWAT, SMOTE, SMITE, SLAP**
hither	**HERE**
hithermost	**NEAREST**
Hitler follower	**NAZI**
hit lightly	**TAP**
hit or miss	**CARELESS**
hit out at	**ATTACK, CRITICIZE**
hit-show sign (abbr.)	**S.R.O.**
hit the road	**SCRAM**
hit with the open hand	**SLAP**
hive dweller	**BEE, WASP, HORNET**
hive product	**HONEY**
hoard	**SAVE**
hoarder	**MISER**
hoarfrost	**RIME**
hoarse	**HARSH, GRATING**
hoax	**FOOLER**
hobble along	**LIMP**
hobbling	**LAME**
hobby	**AVOCATION, PURSUIT**
hobgoblin	**IMP, SPRITE**
hobo	**BUM, TRAMP, VAGRANT**
hock	**PAWN**
hockey game	**BANDY**
hockey player	**SKATER**
hodgepodge	**MESS, MIXTURE, HOTCHPOTCH**
hoe	**WEED, DIG**
hog	**PIG, SWINE**
hog food	**SLOP**
hog meat	**HAM, PORK, BACON**
hogshead	**CASK**
hoi polloi	**RABBLE**
hoist	**HEAVE, LIFT**
hoisting device	**CRANE**
hold	**GRASP, KEEP, CLASP**
hold an opinion	**DEEM**
hold back	**DELAY, DETAIN, PREVENT, RESTRAIN, RETARD**
hold dear	**CHERISH**
hold fast	**CLING, ADHERE**
hold firmly	**CLASP, GRASP, GRIP**

hold in check	**CURB, REIN**
holding device	**CLAMP, VISE**
holding of property	**TENURE**
hold in greater favor	**PREFER**
hold out	**ENDURE, LAST**
hold session	**SIT, MEET**
hold spellbound	**ENTHRALL,**
	MESMERIZE, HYPNOTIZE
hold sway	**RULE**
hold up	**ROB, ROBBERY**
hold up well	**WEAR**
hold within fixed limits	**CONTAIN**
hole	**CAVITY, PIT,**
	EXCAVATION, CAVE, CAVERN
hole enlarger	**REAMER**
hole in a mold	**SPRUE**
hole in a pan	**LEAK**
hole-in-one	**ACE**
hole-making tool	**AWL**
holey cheese	**SWISS**
holiday	**FESTIVAL**
holiness	**SANCTITY, PIETY**
holler	**ROAR, YELL**
hollow	**EMPTY**
hollow grass	**REED, BAMBOO**
holly tree	**ILEX**
Hollywood event	**ACADEMY**
	AWARDS, PREMIERE,
	SCREENING, SHOWING
Hollywood hopeful	**STARLET**
Hollywood luminary	**STAR**
Hollywood's elephant boy	**SABU**
holm	**AIT**
holm oak	**ILEX**
holocaust	**DESTRUCTION**
holy (Fr.)	**SACRE**
holy city of Islam	**MECCA**
holy Image	**ICON**
Holy Land	**PALESTINE**
holy person	**SAINT**
Holy Roman Empire (abbr.)	
	H.R.E.
holy souvenir	**RELIC**
holy water receptacle	**FONT**
homage	**HONOR**
homard	**LOBSTER**
homburg	**HAT**
home	**ABODE, DWELLING,**
	HOUSE, APARTMENT,
	FIRESIDE, HEARTH,
	RESIDENCE
home base	**PLATE**
home-grown	**DOMESTIC**
home in Madrid	**CASA**
homeless child	**WAIF**
homelike	**HOMEY**
homely	**UGLY, PLAIN**

homemade	**DOMESTIC**
home of Abraham	**UR**
home of Adam and Eve	**EDEN**
home of Irish kings	**TARA**
home of Scarlett O'Hara	**TARA**
home party (2 wds.)	**OPEN**
	HOUSE
Homeric epic	**ILIAD, ODYSSEY**
Homeric poem	**EPIC, ILIAD,**
	ODYSSEY
Homeric wise man	**NESTOR**
homesickness	**NOSTALGIA**
homesite	**LOT**
homesteader	**SETTLER**
homicide	**MURDER**
homily	**ADAGE, SERMON**
hominy	**SAMP, GRITS**
homogeneous	**UNIFORM, ALIKE**
homo sapiens	**MAN**
Honduras Indian	**LENCA**
hone	**SHARPEN, WHET**
honest	**TRUTHFUL, JUST,**
	FRANK, OPEN, CANDID, FAIR
honesty	**SINCERITY,**
	FRANKNESS, CANDOR
honey (pharm.)	**MEL**
honey badger	**RATEL**
honey bee genus	**APIS**
honeycomb cell	**ALVEOLUS**
honeycomb product	**BEESWAX**
honey maker	**BEE**
honk	**TOOT, BEEP**
honor	**EXALT**
honorable	**HONEST, EXALTED,**
	ESTEEMED
honorary disc	**MEDAL**
honorary title for retired VIP's	**EMERITUS**
Honshu bay	**ISE**
hood	**COWL**
hooded cape	**AMICE, DOMINO**
hooded vestment	**COPE**
hoodwink	**DUPE**
hoofbeat sound	**CLOP, CLIP**
hoofer	**DANCER**
hook	**GAFF**
Hoosier State	**INDIANA**
hoot	**JEER, HISS**
hop	**LEAP, JUMP**
hope	**ASPIRATION, WISH**
hopeful time	**TOMORROW**
hopeless	**DESPERATE**
hop kiln	**OAST**
hopping insect	**FLEA**
hop stem	**BINE**
horde	**CROWD, MULTITUDE,**
	HOST, MOB
horizon	**SKYLINE**

horizontal **PLANE, LEVEL**
horn **CORNET, BUGLE, ANTLER, CORNUCOPIA**
horn blare **FANFARE, TANTARA**
horned animal **STAG, ELK, MOOSE**
horned cud-chewer **GOAT, COW**
horned viper **ASP**
horn of plenty **CORNUCOPIA**
horns **BRASS**
horn sound **TOOT, HONK**
horrible **HATEFUL, REPULSIVE**
horror **DISGUST, AVERSION**
hors d'oeuvre mixture **DIP**
horse **FOAL, ROAN, MARE, NAG, PLUG STALLION, STEED, RIG**
horse and buggy **RIG**
horseback game **POLO**
horse bet **PARLAY, WAGER**
horse color **ROAN**
horse command **GEE, HAW, WHOA**
horsedoctor, for short **VET**
horsefeathers **NONSENSE, BUNK**
horse food **HAY, OATS, FODDER**
horsehair **CRINOLINE**
horselaugh **GUFFAW**
horselike mammal **MULE, DONKEY, BURRO, ZEBRA**
horseman **EQUESTRIAN, RIDER, JOCKEY**
horseman's goad **SPUR**
horse measure **HAND**
horse opera **WESTERN**
horse race **DERBY**
horse racing (4 wds.) **THE SPORT OF KINGS**
horse rope **HALTER, HACKAMORE**
horse's ankle **HOCK**
horse's foot **HOOF**
horse's gait **LOPE, TROT, CANTER, GALLOP**
horse's gear **HARNESS, REIN, SADDLE, BRIDLE, BLINDER**
horse's long neck-hair **MANE**
horse soldiers **CAVALRY**
horse's shoe spur **CALK**
horse-training rope **LONGE**
horticulturist **FLORIST, GARDENER**
hose **STOCKINGS**
hospitable **FRIENDLY, CORDIAL**
hospital **INFIRMARY, CLINIC**
hospital assistant (2 wds.) **NURSE'S AIDE**

hospital doctor **INTERN, RESIDENT**
hospitalization **INSURANCE**
hospital section **WARD**
host **ARMY, MULTITUDE**
hostelry **INN, TAVERN, HOTEL, MOTEL**
hostile **CONTRARY, OPPOSED**
hostile criticism **CENSURE**
hostile feeling **ANGER**
hostile force **ENEMY, FOE**
hostile incursion **RAID**
hostility **WAR, BATTLE, FIGHT**
hostler **GROOM**
hot **TORRID**
hot and humid **STICKY, TROPIC, TORRID**
hot chocolate **COCOA**
hotel **INN, HOSTEL**
hotel guest **PATRON**
hotheaded **RASH, HASTY**
hothouse **GREENHOUSE**
hot Mexican specialty **TAMALE**
hot spring **GEYSER, SPA**
hot vapor **STEAM**
hot water tank **BOILER**
hound **DOG**
hound's quarry **HARE, FOX**
hour and minute **TIME**
hourglass **TIMER**
hourglass contents **SAND**
hourly **HORAL, HORARY**
house **RESIDENCE, DWELLING**
house (Sp.) **CASA**
house addition **ELL, WING**
house and grounds **PREMISES**
House and Senate **CONGRESS**
houseboat **BARGE**
house-breaker **BURGLAR**
housebroken **TRAINED**
house broker **REALTOR**
housecoat **ROBE**
house fuel **GAS, OIL, COAL, WOOD**
household **MENAGE**
household animal **PET, DOG, CAT**
household appliance **WASHER, DRIER, STOVE, IRON, TOASTER, BLENDER, MIXER, REFRIGERATOR**
household gods **LARES, PENATES, LARS**
household linen **NAPERY**
housekeeper **MATRON**
house member **LEGISLATOR, REP**
housemother **CHAPERONE**

house of healing	HOSPITAL
house of logs	CABIN
house pet	DOG, CAT, FISH, CANARY, PARAKEET
house plant	FERN, IVY
house projection	DORMER
housetop	ROOF
housetop feature	GABLE, EAVE
housewifely	DOMESTIC
housewife's title (abbr.)	MRS.
house wing	ELL, ADDITION
housing	LODGING, SHELTER
Houston ballplayer	ASTRO
hovel	HUT
hover	LINGER, SUSPEND
however	YET
howl	BAY, WAIL
hoyden	TOMBOY
hub	CENTER
hubbub	ADO, TO-DO, STIR
hub of a wheel	NAVE
Huckleberry Finn character	JIM
Huckleberry Finn's craft	RAFT
huckster	HAWKER, PEDDLER
huddle	CONFER
hue	COLOR, TINT, SHADE
huffy	TESTY, TOUCHY
hug	CLASP, CARESS, FONDLE, HOLD
huge	BIG, ENORMOUS, LARGE, VAST
huge animal	ELEPHANT, HIPPO, RHINO
huge continent	ASIA
huge stone	BOULDER
Huguenot	PROTESTANT
huitre	OYSTER
hulky	HEAVY
hull	HUSK
hullabaloo	HUBBUB
hulled corn	SAMP
hum	DRONE, BUZZ
human being	ADAMITE, MAN, MORTAL, PERSON, WOMAN
human bondage	SLAVERY
humane	KIND, MERCIFUL
humanity	MANKIND
human trunk	TORSO
humble	ABASE, MEEK, MODEST
humbug	ROT, BAH
humdrum	MONOTONOUS, TRITE, BANAL
humid	DANK, MOIST, DAMP
humiliate	SHAME, DISGRACE
humility	MODESTY
hummock	KNOLL
humor	WIT
humorist	COMIC, WIT, WAG, COMEDIAN, SATIRIST
humorous	COMIC, FUNNY
humorous play	FARCE, COMEDY
humor to excess	PAMPER
hump	BULGE, LUMP
hump-backed animal	CAMEL, DROMEDARY
Hun	VANDAL
hunch	INTUITION
hunchback	QUASIMODO
hundredth anniversary	CENTENNIAL
Hungarian	MAGYAR
Hungarian wine	TOKAY
hunger pain	PANG
hungery	STARVING, UNFED
hungry rodent	SHREW
Hung Wu dynasty	MING
hunt	CHASE, SEARCH, SEEK
hunt for bargains	SHOP
hunter	NIMROD, CHASER, SEEKER
hunter's shelter	LODGE, CAMP, TENT
hunter's shoe	BOOT
hunting dog	BASSET, SETTER, POINTER, BEAGLE, HOUND
hunting expedition	SAFARI
hurdle	JUMP, BARRIER
hurl	THROW, FLING, SLING, TOSS
hurly-burly	TUMULT
hurrah, for short	RAH
hurricane	GALE, TEMPEST, STORM
hurricane center	EYE
hurry	RACE, DASH, HASTEN, SPEED, RUN, HIE, SHAKE A LEG, GET A MOVE ON
hurt	ACHE, PAIN, WOUND
husband	MAN, SPOUSE
husbandman	FARMER
husband of Bathsheba	URIAH
husband of Isis	OSIRIS
husband of Minnehaha	HIAWATHA
husbandry	FARMING
hush	QUIET, CALM
hush-hush business process (2 wds.)	TRADE SECRET
husk	HULL
husk of wheat grain	BRAN
hustle	RUSH, DRIVE
hustler	PROMOTER
hut	HOVEL, SHANTY

hutch	**CHEST**
hygiene	**SANITATION**
hymn of joy	**PEAN, PAEAN**
hymn of thanksgiving	**TE DEUM**
hymn's finale	**AMEN**
hypersensitivity	**ALLERGY**
hyphen	**DASH**
hypnotic spell	**TRANCE**
hypocrisy	**SHAM**
hypocrite	**DECEIVER**
hypocritical	**FALSE, INSINCERE**
hypocritical sorrow (2 wds.)	
	CROCODILE TEARS
hypothesis	**THEORY**
hyssop	**MINT, FIGWORT**

I (Ger.)	**ICH**
Iago's wife	**EMILIA**
iatric	**MEDICAL**
Iberian lady	**DONA**
ibex	**GOAT**
Ibsen character	**ASE, NORA,**
PEER GYNT, HEDDA GABLER,	
LONA, HELMER	
ice	**COOL, FROST, CHILL**
ice carrier	**TONGS**
ice cream drink	**SODA, SHAKE,**
MALTED, FROSTED, FLOAT	
ice cream holder	**CONE**
iced	**GLACE**
ice fishing gear	**GIG**
Icelandic epic	**EDDA**
Icelandic giant	**ATLI**
Icelandic legend	**SAGA**
Icelandic literary work	**EDDA**
ice mass	**BERG, FLOE**
ice runner	**SKATE**
ice tower	**SERAC**
ichneumon	**MONGOOSE**
icicle	**STALACTITE**
icing	**GLAZE**
icon	**IMAGE**
icy	**FRIGID, FROSTY, COLD**
icy precipitation	**SLEET, HAIL**
Idaho city	**BOISE**
ide	**FISH**
idea	**BRAINSTORM, THOUGHT,**
CONCEPTION, INSPIRATION,	
OPINION, CONCEPT, NOTION	
idea (prefix)	**IDEO**
ideal	**PERFECT**
identical	**TWIN, SAME, ALIKE,**
	SIMILAR
identical sibling	**TWIN**
identify	**RECOGNIZE, NAME**

idiocy	**FOLLY**
idiom	**PHRASE**
idiomatic	**COLLOQUIAL**
idiot	**FOOL, IMBECILE**
idiotic	**INANE, FOOLISH**
idle	**INACTIVE, LAZY**
	LOITER
idle away time	**LOAF**
idle rumor	**GOSSIP**
idle talk	**PATTER, PRATE**
idler	**LOAFER**
idol	**HERO, GOD, IMAGE,**
	DEITY, WORSHIP
idolize	**ADORE, DEIFY,**
	WORSHIP
idyll	**POEM**
if	**PROVIDED, PROVISO**
if not	**ELSE**
igloo builder	**ESKIMO, ALEUT**
igneous rock	**BASALT**
ignite	**LIGHT, FIRE**
ignoble	**MEAN, BASE**
ignominious	**VILE**
ignominy	**SHAME, INFAMY**
ignorant	**UNTAUGHT, DENSE**
ignore	**ELIDE, NEGLECT**
I have found it	**EUREKA**
ilk	**KIND, TYPE**
ill	**SICK, AILING, TROUBLE,**
	WOE, BAD
ill-boding	**DIRE**
ill-bred person	**CAD**
illegal business	**RACKET**
illegal eavesdropping device	
	WIRETAP
Illinois city	**PEORIA, CHICAGO**
illiterate signature	**EX**
ill-tempered person	**CRAB**
ill-tempered woman	**SHREW**
illusion	**CHIMERA**
illustration	**EXAMPLE, DRAWING**
illustration placed within	
another	**INSET**
illustrator	**ARTIST**
illustrious	**EMINENT, GRAND**
ill will	**RANCOR**
illuminate	**LIGHT**
I love (Lat.)	**AMO**
image	**ICON, IDOL, LIKENESS,**
	PICTURE
imaginary	**FANCIFUL,**
	ILLUSORY
imaginary marine creature	
	MERMAID
imagination	**FANCY**
imagine	**DREAM, CONCEIVE**
imbecile	**DOLT, MORON**
imbed firmly (2 wds.)	**SET IN**

imbibe	**DRINK**	imposing	**IMPRESSIVE,**
imbue	**COLOR, SUFFUSE**		**STRIKING**
imbue thoroughly	**STEEP,**	imposing series	**ARRAY**
	SATURATE	imposture	**RUSE, PRETENSE**
imitate	**MIMIC, APE, COPY**	impotent	**BARREN, STERILE**
imitate Sam Spade	**TAIL**	impoverished	**NEEDY, POOR**
imitation	**COPY, ERSATZ,**	impregnable	**INVINCIBLE,**
	MIMICRY		**SECURE**
immaculate	**PURE**	impression	**DENT, IDEA,**
immature	**INFANTILE, YOUNG**		**STAMP**
immediately	**ANON, SOON,**	impressive	**AWESOME**
	AT ONCE	imprison	**IMMURE**
immediately following	**NEXT**	imprisonment	**DURESS**
immense	**VAST, HUGE, LARGE,**	impromptu (2 wds.)	**AD LIB**
	ENORMOUS	improve	**BETTER**
immerse	**DIP, DUNK**	improvident	**PRODIGAL**
imminent	**IMPENDING,**	improvise (2 wds.)	**AD LIB**
	THREATENING	imprudent	**RASH, HASTY**
immoral	**CORRUPT, EVIL**	impudence	**BRASS, SASS**
immortal	**ETERNAL**	impudent	**BRASSY, FRESH,**
immortal spirit	**ANGEL**		**SASSY, PERT**
immunity	**EXEMPTION**	impugn	**ATTACK, CHALLENGE,**
imp	**PIXIE**		**REFUTE**
impair	**MAR, WEAR, INJURE**	impulse	**URGE, WHIM**
impalpable	**VAGUE, INTANGIBLE**	impulsive	**RASH, HASTY**
impart	**CONVEY, BESTOW**	impure	**UNCLEAN, CORRUPT**
impartial	**FAIR, EQUITABLE**	impute	**ASCRIBE, ATTRIBUTE**
impart knowledge to	**EDUCATE,**	inability	**IMPOTENCE**
	TEACH	in abundance	**GALORE**
impassive	**STOICAL, STOLID,**	inaccuracy	**ERROR, MISTAKE**
	APATHETIC	inaccurate	**FAULTY**
impatient	**EAGER**	inactive	**IDLE, INERT**
impeach	**CENSURE, DENOUNCE**	inactivity	**INERTIA**
impeccable	**SPOTLESS,**	in addition	**ALSO, TOO, AND,**
	PERFECT		**YET**
impede	**HINDER**	inadequate	**WANTING**
impediment	**OBSTACLE, SNAG**	in a difficult position	**TREED**
impel	**URGE, PROD, EGG ON,**	in a direct line (4 wds.)	
	SPUR, PROPEL		**AS THE CROW FLIES**
impend	**LOOM**	in agreement (2 wds., Fr.)	
impersonate	**MAKE LIKE, MIMIC**		**EN RAPPORT**
impervious to rain	**LEAKPROOF**	in a line	**ALONG, AROW**
impetuous	**RASH, BRASH,**	in all places	**EVERYWHERE**
	HASTY	in ancient times	**EARLY**
impetuous person	**HOTHEAD**	inane	**POINTLESS, TRITE,**
implement	**TOOL**		**FOOLISH**
implement of warfare	**WEAPON**	inanimate	**INERT, LIFELESS**
impolite	**RUDE**	in another direction	**AWAY**
importance	**MOMENT, VALUE**	in another place	**ELSEWHERE**
important	**VITAL**	in any case	**ANYWAY**
important bridge card	**TRUMP**	in any manner	**SOMEWAY**
important occurrence	**EVENT**	in any way (2 wds.)	**AT ALL**
important part	**PITH, LEAD**	in a pile	**AHEAP**
importune	**URGE, COAX, BEG,**	inappropriate	**INEPT, UNFIT**
	PLEAD	in a row	**ALINED, AROW**
impose a tax	**ASSESS, LEVY**	in a sheltered place	**ALEE**
impose restrictions (2 wds.)		in a short time	**SOON, ANON**
	CLAMP DOWN	inaugurate	**START**

in bad temper	CROSS
in behalf of	FOR
in between	MID
inborn	INNATE, NATURAL
inbred	INNATE
Inca country	PERU
incandescence	GLOW
incapable of being obliterated	
	INDELIBLE
incapacity of	QUA
incarnate	EMBODIED,
	PERSONIFIED
incarnation of Vishnu	RAMA
in case that	IF, LEST
incense	ENRAGE, INFURIATE
incense burner	CENSER,
	THURIBLE
incentive	MOTIVE
inception	START, INITIATION
incessant	UNENDING
inch along	EDGE, CREEP
incident	EVENT
incidental information	
	SIDELIGHT, TRIVIA
incite	GOAD, SPUR, URGE
incivility	DISRESPECT
inclement	SEVERE, STORMY
inclination	SLOPE, TREND,
	TENDENCY
incline	SLANT, SLOPE, TILT
inclined walkway	RAMP
incline the head	BOW, NOD
include	CONTAIN, INVOLVE
incoherent	GARBLED
income	REVENUE, SALARY,
	WAGES
income from housing	RENTAL
in common	ALIKE
in company of	WITH
incomparable	UNRIVALED,
	PEERLESS, SUPREME
incompatible	CONTRARY
incompetence	INABILITY
incompetent	INEPT
incomplete	UNFINISHED
in conflict (2 wds.)	AT WAR
incongruous expression	
(2 wds.)	IRISH BULL
inconsistent	VARYING
inconstant	CHANGING,
	UNSTABLE
in controversy (2 wds.)	AT ISSUE
incorrect (prefix)	MIS-
increase	INCREMENT, GROWTH
increased by	PLUS
increase in size	GROW, SWELL
increase in wages (2 wds.)	
	PAY RAISE

increment	INCREASE
incrustation	SCAB
inculcate	INSTILL, IMBUE
incumbent	BINDING, REQUIRED
in current style	MODISH
incursion	RAID, INROAD
incus	ANVIL
in debt	OWING
indeed	AYE, YES, REALLY,
	OF COURSE
indefatigable	TIRELESS,
	UNTIRING
indefinite	UNCERTAIN, VAGUE
indefinite amount	SOME, ANY
indefinite article	AN, A
indefinite number	MANY,
	SEVERAL, SOME, ANY
indelible	FIXED
indemnify	GUARANTEE
independent	FREE,
	UNENCUMBERED,
	AUTONOMOUS
independent thing	ENTITY
index	FILE, LIST
India, class of	CASTE
India rubber	CAOUT CHOUC
Indian	CREE, ERIE, OSAGE,
	PAWNEE, UTE, SIOUX,
	APACHE, PIMA, NAVAHO
Indiana city	GARY, SOUTH
	BEND, TERRE HAUTE,
	FORT WAYNE,
	INDIANAPOLIS
Indianapolis competitor	RACER,
	DRIVER
Indianapolis 500	RACE
Indian boat	CANOE
Indian buffalo	ARNA, ARNEE
Indian coin	ANNA
Indian drum	TOMTOM
Indian garment	SARI
Indian group	TRIBE
Indian maize	CORN
Indian mercenary	SEPOY
Indian of Peru	INCA
Indian of Yucatan	MAYA
Indian pony	CAYUSE
Indian rainy season	MONSOON
Indian ruler	RAJAH
Indian state	NEPAL
Indian tent	TEPEE, WIGWAM,
	TIPEE, TIPI
Indian territory	OKLAHOMA
Indian tribe	ERIE, SIOUX
Indian trophy	SCALP, COUP
Indian unit of weight	SER
Indian warrior	BRAVE
Indian woman	SQUAW

indicate assent **NOD**
indicate beforehand **PORTEND, PRESAGE**
indication **CLUE, SIGN, HINT**
indifference **APATHY**
indifferent **ALOOF, BLASE, DISINTERESTED, SO-SO**
indigence **WANT, POVERTY, NEED**
indigenous **NATIVE, INNATE**
indignation **ANGER, IRE**
indignity **INSULT, AFFRONT**
indigo dye **ANIL**
indirect **DEVIOUS**
indirect allusion **HINT, CLUE**
indiscreet **RASH**
in disorder **ASKEW, MESSY, UNTIDY**
indispensable **ESSENTIAL, NECESSARY**
indistinct **DIM, VAGUE, FAINT**
individual **ONE, PERSON, UNIT**
Indo-European **ARYAN**
indolent **OTIOSE, LAZY**
Indonesian capital **DJAKARTA**
Indonesian island **BALI, JAVA, SUMATRA**
indorse **RATIFY, CONFIRM**
induce **EVOKE, LEAD**
indulge **PAMPER, FAVOR**
indulger in fantasy **DREAMER**
industrial fuel **COKE**
industrious **BUSY, DILIGENT**
industrious creature **ANT, BEE**
industry **ACTIVITY**
inebriated **DRUNK**
in effect **OPERATIVE**
ineffective **USELESS**
inept serviceman (2 wds.) **SAD SACK**
in equal degree **AS**
in error **WRONG, MISTAKEN**
inert **IDLE, INACTIVE, PASSIVE**
inert gas **ARGON, NEON**
inevitable outcome **DOOM, FATE, DESTINY**
in excess **OVER, TOO**
in existence **ALIVE**
inexpensive **CHEAP**
inexpensive cigar **STOGIE**
inexperienced **RAW, YOUNG, GREEN, NEOPHYTE, NOVICE, TYRO**
infallible **UNERRING**
infamous **CONTEMPTIBLE, BASE**
infamous Roman emperor **NERO**
infamy **DISHONOR, DISGRACE**

infant **BABY**
infant cupid **AMOR**
infant enclosure **CRIB, PLAYPEN**
infant food **PAP, PABLUM, FORMULA, MILK**
infant garment **DIAPER, SACQUE, BUNTING**
infant's bed **CRIB, CRADLE, BASSINET**
in favor of **PRO, FOR**
infect **POISON, POLLUTE**
infer **DEDUCE**
inference **CONCLUSION**
inferior **BENEATH, POOR**
inferior in size **PUNY, RUNTY**
inferior race horse **PLATER**
inferior ship accommodations **STEERAGE**
infernal **SATANIC, DEMONIC, HELLISH, DAMNABLE**
infielder **BASEMAN**
infiltrate **PENETRATE**
infinite **UNLIMITED, BOUNDLESS**
infinity of time **EON**
infirm **WEAK, FEEBLE**
inflame **IRRITATE, CHAFE**
inflame with love **ENAMOR**
inflate **EXPAND**
inflexible **STIFF, FIRM**
inflict **IMPOSE**
in flight (3 wds.) **ON THE WING**
influence **IMPRESS, PRESTIGE**
influence with flattery **WHEEDLE, PANDER**
infold **WRAP**
informal chat at meal (2 wds.) **TABLE TALK**
informal letter **NOTE**
informal talk **CHAT, GAB**
information **DATA, DOPE, INFO, FACTS**
informed **AWARE, HEP, HIP**
infrequent **RARE**
infrequently **SELDOM, RARELY**
infringe **TRESPASS, VIOLATE**
in front **AHEAD**
infuriate **ENRAGE**
infuse **INSTILL, IMBUE**
in general favor **POPULAR**
ingenious **CLEVER**
ingenuous **NAIVE**
in good condition **SOUND, FIT, HEALTHY**
in good order **NEAT**
ingratiate **CHARM, FLATTER**
ingredient **ELEMENT**
inhabitant **DENIZEN, RESIDENT**
inhabitant of (suffix) **ITE**

inhabited by a ghost **HAUNTED**	inquire curiously **PRY**
inherent character **NATURE**	inquiry **QUESTION, RESEARCH**
inheritor **HEIR**	inquiry for lost goods **TRACER**
in high spirits **MERRY**	inquisition **PURGE, INQUEST**
iniquity **EVIL**	inquisitive **PRYING, CURIOUS**
initiate **START, BEGIN**	inquisitive (sl.) **NOSY**
in itself (2 wds.) **PER SE**	in rags **TATTERED**
injure **DAMAGE, HARM,**	in recent times **LATELY**
WOUND, MAR, HURT	in regard to (Scot.) **ANENT**
injure seriously **MAIM, CRIPPLE**	inroad **RAID, INCURSION**
injure with a knife **STAB**	insane **CRAZY, MAD**
injure with horns **GORE**	insane person **LUNATIC,**
injurious **DELETERIOUS**	**MADMAN**
injury **WOUND, HURT, DAMAGE**	insanity **MANIA, LUNACY**
injury mark **CICATRIX, SCAR,**	insatiable **GREEDY**
SCAB	inscribe **ENGRAVE, WRITE, STELE**
injustice **WRONG, INEQUITY**	inscribed tablet **STELE**
ink **DRAW, WRITE**	inscription **EPIGRAPH, LEGEND**
inkling **CLUE, HINT, IDEA**	inscrutable **MYSTERIOUS**
ink stain **BLOT**	insect **ANT, BEE, BEETLE,**
ink writing instrument **PEN,**	**ROACH, BUG, KATYDID,**
QUILL, PRESS	**MANTIS, APHID, LOCUST,**
inky **BLACK**	**FLY, WASP, TICK, FLEA,**
inland sea **LAKE**	**MOTH, TERMITE**
inlay **FILLING**	insect antenna **FEELER**
inlay work **MOSAIC**	insect at a picnic **ANT**
inlet **BAY, RIA**	insect bite **STING**
in line **AROW**	insect egg **NIT**
in lower position **DOWN, BELOW**	insect feeler **PALP**
in manner of (Fr.) **A LA**	insect pupa **CHRYSALIS**
in motion **ASTIR**	insect stage **PUPA, LARVA,**
inn **HOTEL, TAVERN, MOTEL,**	**EGG, ADULT**
HOSTEL	insect trap **WEB**
innate **INHERENT**	insecticide **PARIS GREEN, DDT**
innate skill **TALENT, ABILITY,**	insidious **DECEITFUL**
FLAIR	insight **INTUITION**
in neat layers **STACKED**	insignificant **PETTY, SLIGHT**
inner **INSIDE, INTERIOR**	insignificant matter **TRIVIALITY**
Inner Hebrides island **IONA**	insinuate **INTIMATE, HINT**
inner self **EGO**	insipid **TASTELESS, WATERY**
inner surface of the hand **PALM**	in so far as (Lat.) **QUA**
innocent **NAIVE, PURE**	insolence (2 wds.) **BACK TALK**
innocuous **HARMLESS**	insolent **OFFENSIVE, RUDE**
in no manner **NOT**	insolvent **BANKRUPT**
in no way **NOWISE**	in some other place **ELSEWHERE**
inordinate **EXCESSIVE, UNDUE**	in sour spirits **CROSS**
inordinate self-esteem **EGO,**	inspiration **IDEA**
CONCEIT	inspire **AWE**
inorganic substance **METAL,**	in spite of **DESPITE**
PLASTIC	instant **MOMENT, SECOND,**
in other words (4 wds.)	**WINK, MINUTE, TRICE**
THAT IS TO SAY	instead **LIEU**
in place of **INSTEAD**	instigate (2 wds.) **STIR UP,**
in present conditions (2 wds.)	**SPUR ON, ROUSE UP,**
AS IS	**URGE ON**
in progress **AFOOT**	instruct **EDUCATE, TEACH,**
in proper manner **DULY**	**COACH, TUTOR**
in pursuit of **AFTER**	instructor, for short **PROF**
inquire **ASK, REQUEST**	instrument board **PANEL**

insubordination **DEFIANCE, REVOLT**
in such a manner **SO, THIS**
insult **AFFRONT, INDIGNITY**
in support of **FOR, BEHIND**
insurance payment **PREMIUM**
insurgent **REBEL**
intact **WHOLE, COMPLETE**
integer **NUMERAL, UNIT, ENTITY**
integrity **HONESTY**
intellect **MIND**
intellectual **EGGHEAD**
intelligence **SENSE, WIT**
intelligent **SMART, BRAINY, BRIGHT**
intelligible **CLEAR, LUCID**
intemperance **EXCESS**
intend **AIM, MEAN, PLAN**
intensify **ENHANCE**
intensity **ENERGY, FORCE**
intent **RAPT**
intent look **STARE**
intention **AIM, GOAL, END**
intentional **DELIBERATE**
intentionally (2 wds.) **ON PURPOSE**
inter **BURY**
interdict **CUT, DEBAR, BAN**
interdiction **BAN**
interest **PROFIT, CONCERN**
interest-bearing certificate **BOND**
interfere **MEDDLE, INTRUDE, TAMPER**
interfering **MEDDLESOME**
interim **MEANTIME**
interim ruler **REGENT**
interior **INNER, INSIDE**
interjection **ALAS, OH**
interlace **ENTWINE, WEAVE**
interlaced design **FRET, LACE**
interlock **KNIT, UNITE**
interloper **INTRUDER**
intermediate (law) **MESNE**
intermediate (prefix) **MES**
interminable **ENDLESS, INFINITE**
intermittent **BROKEN, PERIODIC**
intermittently (3 wds.) **OFF AND ON**
internal **INNER**
internal revenue supporter **TAXPAYER**
international monopoly **CARTEL**
international tennis cup **DAVIS**
international treaty **PACT**

international understanding **ENTENTE**
interpose **INTERCEDE**
interpret **EXPLAIN, TRANSLATE**
interpretation **EXPLANATION**
interrupt (2 wds.) **CUT IN, BUTT IN**
intersect **CROSS, CUT**
intersection of lines **ANGLE**
intersection sign **STOP, YIELD**
interstice **PORE, CHINK, CREVICE, INTERVAL**
intertwine **LACE**
interurban railroad **EL**
interval of relief **RESPITE**
intervene (2 wds.) **STEP IN, MEDDLE IN**
intervening (law) **MESNE**
interweave **MAT**
in that case **THEN**
in that place **THERE**
in the center **AMID**
in the direction of **TOWARD, TO**
in the future **LATER**
in the interim **MEANWHILE**
in the know **AWARE, HEP, HIP**
in the last month **ULTIMO**
in the middle of **AMID**
in the offing **NEAR, SOON**
in the past **AGO**
in the place **AT**
in the same place (abbr.) **IBID.**
in the time of **DURING**
in this manner **SO, THUS**
in this place **HERE**
intimate **CLOSE, FAMILIAR**
intimation **HINT, CLUE**
intimidate **DAUNT, DISMAY**
intolerable **UNBEARABLE**
intone **CHANT**
intoxicating liquor **SPIRITS**
intrepid **BRAVE, BOLD**
intricate **COMPLEX**
intrigue **CABAL, PLOT**
intrinsic **GENUINE**
introduction **PREFACE, PRELUDE**
introductory discourse **PROEM, PREFACE**
introductory performance **PRELUDE, OVERTURE**
in truth **INDEED, VERILY**
intuitive feeling **HUNCH**
inundation **FLOOD**
invading throng **HORDE, MOB**
invent **DEVISE, CREATE**
invention protection **PATENT**
inventor Whitney **ELI**

invigorating medicine	TONIC	irrational	FOOLISH, ABSURD
invisible	UNSEEN	irregularly notched	EROSE
invisible emanation	AURA	irrelevant	EXTRANEOUS
invitation	BID	irreligious	IMPIOUS
invite	ASK, ATTRACT, LURE	irresolute	UNDECIDED
invocation	PRAYER, SERMON	irresponsible	UNRELIABLE
invoice	BILL	irrigate	WATER
invoke	ELICIT	irrigation dike	LEVEE
involve	ENTAIL, INCLUDE	irritable	FRETFUL, TESTY
inward	INNER, INTERN	irritate	IRK, RILE, NETTLE,
in what place	WHERE		TEASE
in what way	HOW	irritated	SORE
in what way (Lat.)	QUO MODO	irritation	PIQUE
iota	JOT	is	EXISTS
IOU endorser	OWER	is (Sp.)	ES, ESTA
Iowa college town	AMES	Isaac's mother	SARAH
Iran	PERSIA	Isaac's son	DSAU, JACOB
Iran's neighbor	IRAQ, IRAK	is able to	CAN
Irani ruler	SHAH	is angered at	RESENTS
irate	ANGRY, MAD, WRATHFUL,	is appropriate	SUITS
	FURIOUS	is aware of	KNOWS
ire	ANGER, CHOLER	is compelled	MUST
Ireland	ERIN, EIRE,	is concerned	CARES
	EMERALD ISLE	is curious	WONDERS
irenic	SERENE, PEACEFUL	is disposed kindly toward	
iridescent	OPALINE	(2 wds.)	TAKES TO
iridescent gem	OPAL	is excessively fond of	DOTES
iris	IXIA, FLAG, RAINBOW	Ishmael's mother	HAGAR
iris with fragrant roots	ORRIS	is human	ERRS
Irish	CELTIC, ERSE	is inclined	LEANS
Irish cattle	KERRY	is indebted to	OWES
Irish chemist	BOYLE	isinglass	MICA
Irish city	BELFAST, CORK	is in store for	AWAITS
Irish clan	SEPT	Isis' husband	OSIRIS
Irish county	MAYO, CORK	Islamic holy city	MECCA,
Irish dagger	SKEAN		MEDINA
Irish dance	REEL	Islamic name	ALI
Irish dish	STEW	island (Fr.)	ILE
Irish emblem	SHAMROCK	island (Ital.)	ISOLA
Irish expletive	ARRAH, GO-ON	island in the Mediterranean	
Irish fairy	BANSHEE	ELBA, MALTA, CYPRUS,	
Irish Free State	EIRE	CORSICA, SICILY	
Irish fuel	PEAT	island in the West Indies	CUBA,
Irish-Gaelic	ERSE		JAMAICA
Irish island group	ARAN	island nation	HAITI, IRELAND,
Irish king's home	TARA		JAPAN, FORMOSA
Irish lass	COLLEEN	island near Athens	SALAMIS
Irish moss	CARRAGEEN	island near Corsica	ELBA,
Irish poet	WILDE, YEATS		SARDINIA
Irish republic	EIRE	island near Greece	CRETE
Irish sea god	LER	island near Italy	MALTA
Irish seaport	COBH	island of exile	ELBA,
irk	ANNOY		ST. HELENA
iron bar	ROD	island off China	NATSU HAINAN
iron clothes	PRESS	island off Mozambique	IBO
iron coating	RUST	island off Scotland	IONA
iron compound	FERRITE, STEEL	island of saints	ERIN
iron rod	BAR		

island of the Aegean **LEROS, IOS, DELOS, MELOS, NAXOS**
island of the Bahamas **BIMINI**
island of the Cyclades **DELOS, ANDROS, TENOS, NAXOS, MELOS**
island of the Philippines **SAMAR**
island republic **EIRE, IRELAND, PHILIPPINES**
islands between North and South America (2 wds.) **WEST INDIES**
islands near Florida **BAHAMAS, KEYS**
island south of Australia **TASMANIA**
island south of Sicily **MALTA**
isle in a river **AIT**
isle in the Bay of Naples **CAPRI**
isle off coast of Ireland **ARAN**
islet **AIT**
ism **DOCTRINE**
is no more **GONE**
is not (arch.) **NIS**
is not well **AILS**
is obliged to **MUST**
isolate **SEPARATE, SECLUDE**
isolation **SOLITUDE**
isometrics **EXERCISES**
is on fire **BURNS**
is overfond **DOTES, SPOILS**
is possible **MAY**
is present at **ATTENDS**
Israel, formerly **PALESTINE**
Israeli coins **MILS**
Israeli folk dance **HORA**
Israeli port **HAIFA, ELATH**
Israeli round dance **HORA**
is situated **LIES**
is successful **WINS, TRIUMPHS**
issue **EMIT, FLOW**
issue forth **EMANATE**
is suitable to **BECOMES**
isthmus **NECK**
is unable to (contr.) **CAN'T**
is unsuccessful **FAILS**
is worthy of **DESERVES**
Italian actress **LOREN, MAGNANI**
Italian affirmative **SI**
Italian art center **SIENA, ROME, VENICE, FLORENCE**
Italian capital **ROME**
Italian city **GENOA, TURIN**
Italian coin **LIRA**
Italian commune **ASOLA**

Italian delicacy **RAVIOLI, SPAGHETTI, PASTA, ANTIPASTO**
Italian epic poet **TASSO**
Italian family **ESTE, BORGIA**
Italian family of violin makers **AMATI**
Italian house **CASA, VILLA**
Italian housewife's title **SIGNORA**
Italian innkeeper **PADRONE**
Italian island **LIDO, SICILY**
Italian lady **DONNA**
Italian lake **ALBANO, COMO**
Italian monetary unit **LIRA**
Italian monk **FRA**
Italian poet **DANTE**
Italian port **GENOA, NAPLES, BARI**
Italian resort **LIDO, CAPRI**
Italian river **ARNO, PO, TIBER**
Itch **HANKER, URGE**
item **DETAIL, PARAGRAPH**
itemize **DETAIL**
item of clothing **TOG**
item of gossip **RUMOR**
item often tossed **SALAD, COIN, BALL**
item of value **ASSET**
itinerant **ARRANT, ERRANT, NOMAD**
itinerary **ROUTE**
it is (contr.) **'TIS, IT'S**
itty-bitty **TINY**
Ivan the Terrible **TSAR**
ivory **DENTINE**
ivy **VINE**
Ivy League member **YALE, HARVARD, PRINCETON, DARTMOUTH, COLUMBIA**
ixia **IRIS**

J

jab **POKE, THRUST, BLOW, PUNCH**
jabber **CHATTER, PRATE, PRATTLE**
jabberwocky **NONSENSE, GIBBERISH**
jabot material **LACE**
jack at cards **KNAVE**
jacket **COAT**
jack-in-the-pulpit **ARUM**
jackrabbit **HARE**
jacks or better **OPENERS**

Jack Sprat's meat	**LEAN**	jerky	**CHOPPY, MEAT**
Jack Tar's drink	**GROG**	jest	**JOKE, JAPE, QUIP**
Jacob's brother	**ESAU**	jesting talk	**JAPERY**
Jacob's father	**ISAAC**	jet	**FLY, BLACK, PLANE**
Jacob's father-in-law	**LABAN**	jet black	**RAVEN**
Jacob's first wife	**LEAH, LEI**	jet pilot	**FLYER**
Jacob's son **JOSEPH, LEVI, DAN,**		jetty	**WHARF, PIER**
RUBEN, AS(H)ER, BENJAMIN,		Jew	**SEMITE, HEBREW**
SIMEON, JUDA, ISSACHAR,		jewel	**GEM**
ZABULON, GAD, NEPHTHALI		jeweled coronet	**TIARA**
Jacob's wife	**LEAH, RACHEL**	jeweler's weight	**CARAT**
jacquard	**LOOM**	Jewish ascetic	**ESSENE**
jade	**TIRE**	Jewish bible	**TORAH**
jagged	**ROUGH**	Jewish Day of Atonement	
jai alai	**PELOTA**		**YOM KIPPUR**
jail (Brit.)	**GAOL**	Jewish feast **PASSOVER, SEDER,**	
jail breaker	**ESCAPEE**		**PESACH**
jail room	**CELL**	Jewish leader	**RABBI**
jalousie	**BLIND, SHUTTER**	Jewish month	**HESHVAN,**
Jamaican witchcraft	**OBEAH**	**KISLEV, TEBET, SHEBAT,**	
Jane Austen title	**EMMA**	**ADAR, VEADAR, NISAN,**	
Jane Eyre author	**BRONTE**	**IYAR, SILVAN, TAMMUZ,**	
Japan	**NIPPON**	**TISHRI, AB, ELUL**	
Japanese aborigine **AINO, AINU**		Jewish nation	**ISRAEL**
Japanese-American	**NISEI,**	Jewish prayer book	**SIDDUR**
SANSEI, ISSEI, KIBEI		Jewish quarter	**GHETTO**
Japanese beverage	**SAKE, TEA**	Jewish school	**(C)HEDER**
Japanese coin	**SEN, YEN**	Jewish scripture	**TORAH**
Japanese drama	**NO, NOH**	Jewish spiritual leader	**RABBI**
Japanese metropolis	**KYOTO,**	Jewish teacher	**RABBI**
	TOKYO	jib	**BOOM, CRANE**
Japanese musical instrument		jibe	**TAUNT**
	KOTO	jiffy	**INSTANT**
Japanese outlaw	**RONIN**	jiggle	**VIBRATE**
Japanese pagoda	**TAA**	jingle	**TINKLE, VERSE**
Japanese plant	**UDO**	jinx	**HEX**
Japanese port **KOBE, OSAKA**		job	**CHORE, TASK**
Japanese robe	**KIMONO**	job for Perry Mason	**CASE**
Japanese sash	**OBI**	Job's home	**UZ**
Japanese statesman	**ITO**	jocose	**JOKING, PLAYFUL**
Japanese zither	**KOTO**	jocular	**COMICAL**
jar	**JOLT, SHAKE**	jocund	**CHEERFUL**
jar cover	**LID, TOP**	jog	**TROT**
jardiniere	**URN, VASE, POT**	joggle	**DOWEL**
jargon	**CANT, ARGOT**	johnnycake	**PONE**
Jason's ship	**ARGO**	Johnson's vice president	
jaunt	**TRIP**		**HUMPHREY**
jaunty	**PERKY**	join	**ADD, CONNECT, UNITE,**
java	**COFFEE**	**WED, MARRY, TIE, WELD,**	
Javanese tree	**UPAS**	**MELD, SOLDER, YOKE**	
Jayhawk State	**KANSAS**	join forces	**UNITE**
jazz music	**BEBOP**	join securely	**TENON**
jealous	**ENVIOUS**	join strands	**SPLICE**
jealousy	**ENVY**	joint	**ELBOW, KNEE, ANKLE**
jeer	**MOCK, JIBE**	join the army	**ENLIST**
jeer at	**TAUNT**	join the colors	**ENLIST**
jelly	**ASPIC, GELATIN**	join the race	**RUN**
jerk (colloq.)	**YANK**		

joint on which a door swings	**HINGE**
joke	**GAG, JEST**
joke anthology	**ANA**
jokester	**WAG, WIT**
jollity	**MIRTH**
jolly	**JOCULAR, MERRY**
jolly boat	**SKIFF, YAWL**
jolt	**JAR**
Jonah	**JINX**
josh	**TEASE**
Joshua's partner to Canaan	**CALEB**
Joshua tree	**YUCCA**
jostle	**SHOVE, PUSH**
jot	**IOTA**
jounce	**JOLT, BOUNCE**
journal	**NEWSPAPER, PAPER, DIARY, RECORD, LOG**
journalist	**REPORTER**
journalist Sevareid	**ERIC**
journey	**TOUR, TRAVEL, TRIP, TREK**
journey for another	**ERRAND**
journey's interruption	**STOPOVER**
joust	**TILT**
jovial	**JOLLY**
jowl	**CHOP, JAWBONE**
joy	**GLEE, ELATION, HAPPINESS, BLISS**
Joyce Kilmer poem	**TREES**
joyful	**ELATED, GLAD, GAY MIRTHFUL, JUBILANT**
joyous	**HAPPY, GLAD**
Jubal	**MUSICIAN**
jubilant	**ELATED, JOYFUL**
jubilation	**REJOICING**
Judas tree	**CERCIS, REDBUD**
Judean king	**ASA, HEROD**
judge	**DEEM, OPINE**
judge in a dispute	**ARBITER**
judge's aide (2 wds.)	**COURT CLERK**
judge's bench	**BANC**
judge's chambers	**CAMERAS**
judge's command (4 wds.)	**ORDER IN THE COURT**
judge's concern	**CASE**
judge's gown	**TOGA, ROBE**
judge's hammer	**GAVEL**
judgeship	**CHAIR**
judgment	**DECISION**
judicial order	**WRIT**
judiciary	**BENCH**
judicious	**WISE, PRUDENT**

Judy Garland movie	**WIZARD OF OZ, A STAR IS BORN, THE PIRATE, EASTER PARADE**
jug	**EWER, PITCHER**
juice drink	**ADE**
juicer	**REAMER**
juicy	**SUCCULENT**
juicy fruit	**ORANGE, LEMON, GRAPEFRUIT, PEAR, PLUM, PEACH, LIME**
Juliet's lover	**ROMEO**
Julliard specialty	**MUSIC**
jumbled medley	**OLIO**
jumbled type	**PI**
jump	**LEAP, HOP**
jumping insect	**FLEA**
jumping stick	**POGO**
jump on	**SCOLD**
jump suit	**OVERALLS**
junction	**MEETING, UNION**
juncture	**SEAM, JOINT**
June bug	**DOR**
jungle cat	**TIGER, PANTHER, LION**
jungle drum	**TOM-TOM**
jungle snake	**BOA**
junior	**NAMESAKE**
Junior League event (2 wds.)	**DEBUTANTE BALL**
junior or senior (2 wds.)	**COLLEGE STUDENT**
junior's father	**SENIOR**
juniper bush	**SAVIN**
juniper tree	**CEDAR**
junket	**TOUR, TRIP**
jupe	**SKIRT**
Jupiter	**JOVE**
jurisdiction	**AUTHORITY**
jury	**PANEL**
just	**ONLY, FAIR**
just gone by	**PAST**
justice	**FAIRNESS**
justify	**WARRANT**
just perfect	**IDEAL**
just right (3 wds., sl.)	**ON THE BEAM**
Jute leader	**HORSA, HENGIST**
Jutland native	**DANE**
juvenile	**YOUNG, YOUTHFUL, CHILDISH, CHILD**

K

Kaddish	**PRAYER**

karate blow **CHOP**
karma **FATE**
kasha **MUSH, GROATS**
katydid **INSECT, GRASSHOPPER**
kayak **CANOE**
keen **SHARP**
keen enjoyment **ZEST**
keen insight **ACUMEN**
keen intuitive power (2 wds.) **SIXTH SENSE**
keenly desirous **EAGER, AVID**
keenly eager **AVID**
keenly honed **SHARP**
keenness **ACUMEN**
keen relish **GUSTO**
keep **RETAIN, HOLD, RESERVE, MAINTAIN**
keep afloat **BUOY**
keep clear of **EVADE, SHUN**
keeper **GUARD, WARDEN**
keeper of an elephant **MAHOUT**
keep going **SUSTAIN**
keep in check **RESTRAIN**
keeping **CUSTODY, CHARGE**
keepsake **TOKEN, MOMENTO**
keepsake box **CHEST**
keep within one's means (4 wds.) **MAKE BOTH ENDS MEET**
keg **BARREL, CASK**
kelp **ALGA**
ken **UNDERSTANDING**
kennel dwellers **CANINE, DOG**
kennel sound **YAP, YELP, YIP, WOOF, BOWWOW, ROWF, GRRR**
Kentucky blue grass **POA**
Kentucky college **BEREA**
Kentucky Derby entry **HORSE**
kernel **CORN, SEED, GERM**
kerosene **OIL**
kerosene lantern **LAMP**
ketch **SAIC**
ketone **ACETONE**
kettle **POT**
kettle drum **TYMPANUM**
key **OPENER, SOLUTION**
keyboard instrument **ORGAN, PIANO, SPINET**
keyhole **SLOT**
Keystone State **PENNSYLVANIA**
kick **BOOT**
kick a football **PUNT**
kid **CHILD, GOAT**
kill **SLAY, MURDER**
kill a fly **SWAT**
killed **SLEW, SLAIN**

killer whale **ORC**
killick **ANCHOR**
Kilmer poem **TREES**
kiln **OAST, OVEN**
kiloliter **STERE**
kilt **PLEAT, SKIRT**
kimono **ROBE**
kimono sash **OBI**
kin **FAMILY, RELATIVES**
kind **ILK, SORT, TYPE, CLASS, GENTLE, NICE, GENRE**
kindle **LIGHT, FIRE**
kindly **NICE**
kindness **COMPASSION**
kind of **SOMEWHAT, RATHER**
kind of art **POP, OP, MODERN**
kind of automobile **STATION WAGON, SEDAN, COUPE, ROADSTER, HOT ROD**
kind of bark **CANELLA**
kind of beaver **EAGER**
kind of beer **LAGER, BITTER, PILSNER**
kind of bread **RYE, WHITE, WHEAT, CORN**
kind of cheese **EDAM, BRIE, GOUDA, SWISS, CHEDDAR, STILTON**
kind of clock **ALARM**
kind of cloth **COTTON, SILK, SATIN, RAYON, NYLON, LINEN**
kind of corn bread **PONE**
kind of couch **DIVAN, SETTEE, LOVE SEAT**
kind of dog **PUG, POM, PEKE, MUTT, CUR, SPANIEL, HOUND**
kind of fabric **CORD, SCRIM**
kind of feed **BRAN**
kind of firecracker **DEVIL**
kind of fuel **GAS, OIL, PEAT, COAL, WOOD**
kind of grain **WHEAT, OATS**
kind of hammer **PEEN, GAVEL**
kind of income **RENT**
kind of lettuce **COS, BIB, BOSTON, ICEBERG, ROMAINE**
kind of marble **AGATE, TAW**
kind of meat **PORK, HAM, BEEF, VEAL, STEAK, LAMB**
kind of moth **LUNA, MILLER**
kind of music **OPERA, POP, ROCK, BLUES, COUNTRY, JAZZ**
kind of nut **PECAN, ALMOND, WALNUT**
kind of onion **LEEK**
kind of overshoe **GAITER**

kind of paper	RICE
kind of pastry	PIE, CAKE,
	TART, COOKIE
kind of pie	MINCE, APPLE,
	PUMPKIN
kind of power	ATOMIC,
	ELECTRIC
kind of race	RELAY
kind of rocket	RETRO
kind of salesmen (comp. wd.)	
	DOOR-TO-DOOR,
	HOUSE-TO-HOUSE,
	TRAVELING
kind of sea food	SHRIMP, CLAM,
	CRAB, LOBSTER
kind of signal	DANGER, ALARM,
	STOP, GO
kind of singing club	GLEE
kind of slipper	MULE
kind of soil	LOAM
kind of stew	POTTAGE
kind of test	ORAL
kind of trowel	PLANE
kind of velvet	PANNE
kind of violin (sl.)	STRAD
kind of weapon	BAZOOKA,
	GUN, RIFLE,
	ARROW, CANNON
kind or class	SORT
king	RULER, MONARCH
king (Fr.)	ROI
king (Lat.)	REX
King Arthur's capital	CAMELOT
King David's grandfather	OBED
kingdom	REALM
kingfish	OPAH
King James' translation	BIBLE
kingly	REGAL, ROYAL
King Minos' daughter	ARIADNE
King Mongkut's land	SIAM
King Mongkut's tutor	ANNA
king of beasts	LION
king of birds	EAGLE
king of fairies	OBERON
king of gods	JUPITER
king of Israel	AHAB, DAVID,
	SAUL
king of Judah	ASA
king of Judea	HEROD
king of Norway	OLAF
king of Persia	DARIUS
king of the golden touch	MIDAS
king of the Huns	ATLI, ATTILA
king of the Lapithae	IXION
king of the Visigoths	ALARIC
king of Troy	PRIAM
king's baton	SCEPTER
king's blue	COBALT

king's chair	THRONE
king's hat	CROWN
king's representative	VICEROY
king (Sp.)	REY
king's son	PRINCE
king's yellow	ORPIMENT
kinship	AFFINITY
kinsman	RELATIVE
Kirghiz mountain range	ALAI
kiss	SMOOCH, BUSS
kit	OUTFIT, GEAR
kitchen appliance	TOASTER,
	OPENER, STOVE,
	REFRIGERATOR, GRILL
kitchen gadget	CORER, DICER,
	RICER, PRESS, CUTTER, HILL
kitchen garment	APRON
kitchen implement	SPATULA,
	KNIFE, SPOON, SCRAPER,
	SIEVE
kitchen rug	MAT
kitchen stove	RANGE
kitchen vessel	KETTLE, POT,
	PAN, SAUCEPAN
kite	ELANET
kite part	TAIL
kith	FRIENDS
kitsch	SHALLOW, POP
kitten's cry	MEW, MEOW
Kiwanis member	MAN
kiwi	BIRD
klatch (klatsch)	GATHERING,
	HEN PARTY, BREAK
knack	ART, TALENT, FLAIR
knapsack	BAG
knave	RASCAL, JACK
knead	MASSAGE
knee	PATELLA, JOINT
kneehole and rolltop	DESKS
knickknack	NOTION, WHATNOT
knife edge	BLADE
knife for dissecting	SCALPEL
knife maker	CUTLER
knife swinger	SLASHER
knight	CAVALIER, SIR
knight errant	PALADIN
knightly champion	PALADIN
knightly quest	GRAIL
knight's assistant	PAGE
knight's clothing	ARMOR
knight's lance banner	
	GONFALON
knight's title	SIR
knit	WEAVE
knitting stitch	LOOP, PURL,
	CABLE, KNIT
knitting wool	YARN
knives	CUTLERY

knob	**NODE**	labyrinth	**MAZE**
knock	**RAP, TAP**	lac	**RESIN**
knock about	**WANDER**	lace	**DASH, FRILL, SHOESTRING**
knock against	**BUMP**	lace collar	**RUFF**
knock down	**FLOOR, KO, KAYO**	lacelike fabric	**NET**
knock it off	**STOP**	lacerate	**RIP, TEAR,**
knock off	**QUIT, KILL**		**SCRATCH, CUT**
knockout	**KO, KAYO**	lachrymal drop	**TEAR**
knoll	**HILL**	lack	**ABSENCE, NEED, WANT**
knot	**NODE, BOW, NOOSE**	lackadaisical	**LISTLESS**
knot in cotton fiber	**NEPS**	lackey	**TOADY, FOOTMAN**
knot in wood	**GNARL, KNAR**	lacking	**SHY, SHORT**
knot in wool	**NOIL**	lacking boldness	**TIMID**
knot of hair	**BUN**	lacking good taste	
knotty	**INTRICATE**		**INDECOROUS,**
knout	**FLOG**		**UNSEEMLY**
know	**WIST, REALIZE**	lacking hair	**BALD**
knowhow	**SKILL**	lacking heat	**COLD**
knowing	**ALERT, SCIENT,**	lacking money	**POOR, NEEDY,**
	AWARE		**INDIGENT**
knowledge	**KEN, LORE**	lacking strength	**WEAK**
knuckle under	**YIELD**	lackluster	**DULL**
knurl	**NODULE, KNOT**	lack of energy	**ATONY**
kobold	**GNOME, GOBLIN**	lack of interest	**APATHY**
kohlrabi	**CABBAGE**	laconic	**TERSE, CONCISE**
Konrad Adenauer's nickname		lacquer	**ENAMEL**
	DER ALTE	lacquered metalware	**TOLE**
kooky	**SILLY, CRAZY**	lacuna	**GAP, HIATUS**
Korea	**CHOSEN**	lacy	**DELICATE, FILMY**
Korean Border river	**YALU**	lacy frill	**RUCHE, ROUCHE**
Korean city	**SEOUL**	lacy plant	**FERN**
Korean seaport	**PUSAN**	lad	**BOY, STRIPLING**
kosher	**CLEAN, RIGHT,**	ladder round	**RUNG, STEP,**
	PROPER		**RUNDLE**
Krupp works site	**ESSEN**	lade	**LOAD**
		laden	**FREIGHTED**
		ladies' man	**ROMEO,**
L			**CASANOVA, DON JUAN**
		lading	**CARGO, LOAD**
laager	**CAMP**	ladle	**DIPPER, SCOOP**
Laban's daughter	**RACHEL,**	ladrone	**BANDIT, THIEF**
	LEAH	lady	**DAME, WOMAN, MADAM,**
lab burner	**ETNA, BUNSEN**		**DONNA**
lab substance	**AGAR**	lady (Sp.)	**SENORA**
label	**STICKER, TAB, TAG,**	ladylike	**FEMININE**
	TRADEMARK	lady's gown	**DRESS, FROCK**
labial	**LIP**	lag	**DELAY, LINGER**
labor	**TOIL, WORK**	lag behind	**LOITER, TARRY**
laboratory tube	**PIPETTE**	lager	**BEER**
laborer	**COOLIE, TOILER,**	laggard	**SLUGGISH, STRAGGLER**
	WORKER, HAND	lagniappe	**GRATUITY**
labor group	**UNION, ILO, CIO,**	lagoon	**POND**
	AFL, GUILD	laic	**SECULAR, LAITY**
laborious	**ARDUOUS,**	lair	**DEN**
	DIFFICULT	laity	**LAYMEN**
labor stoppage	**STRIKE**	lake	**POOL**
Labrador dog	**RETRIEVER**	lam	**FLEE, ESCAPE**
	NEWFOUNDLAND	Lama land	**TIBET**

lambaste **THRASH, SCOLD**
lambent **GLOWING, LUMINOUS**
lamblike **GENTLE, MEEK**
lamb's father **RAM**
lamb's mother **EWE**
Lamb's pen name **ELIA**
lambskin leather **SUEDE**
lame **CRIPPLED, GIMPY**
lamebrain **NUMBSKULL**
lament **BEMOAN, MOAN, RUE, SIGH, WAIL**
lamentation **GRIEF**
lamia **VAMPIRE**
lamp **LIGHT, TORCH**
lampblack **SOOT**
lampoon **SATIRE**
lamprey **EEL**
lampshade **GLOBE**
lanai **VERANDA**
lanate **WOOLLY**
lance **SPEAR**
lance contest **JOUST**
lancer **SOLDIER**
land **DISEMBARK, ALIGHT, SOIL, TERRAIN, COUNTRY CARRIAGE, WAGON**
land broker **REALTOR**
land contract **DEED**
land drawing **MAP**
land measure **ACRE, AREA, PLOT, LOT**
land parcel **LOT**
land title **DEED**
landed property **ESTATE, REAL ESTATE**
landing boat **LST**
landing pier **WHARF**
landing place **AIRPORT, RUNWAY, AIRSTRIP, STOLPORT**
Land of Alley Oop **MOO**
Land of Enchantment **NEW MEXICO**
Land of Opportunity **ARKANSAS**
Land of Rising Sun **JAPAN**
Land of Ten Thousand Lakes **MINNESOTA**
Land of the Midnight Sun **ALASKA**
Land of the Sheiks **ARABIA**
land on **CRITICIZE, SCOLD**
landscape **SCENERY, VIEW**
landscape feature **SCENERY**
landslide **AVALANCHE**
lane **ALLEY**
language **TONGUE**

language of ancient Rome **LATIN**
language of North Africa **ARABIC**
language peculiarity **IDIOM**
language spoken in Brazil **PORTUGUESE**
languid **WEAK, SLOW**
languish **AIL, PINE, YEARN, ACHE**
languor **ENNUI**
lanky **GAUNT, THIN**
lap **FOLD, LIP**
Lapp **SCANDINAVIAN**
lap robe **BLANKET, RUG**
lapse **ERROR, MISTAKE**
larceny **THEFT, ROBBERY**
lard **FAT, SHORTENING, GREASE**
larder **PANTRY**
large **BIG, HUGE, VAST, ENORMOUS**
large amount **SCADS**
large antelope **GNU, ELAND**
large ape **GORILLA, ORANGUTAN**
large armadillo **PELUDO**
large artery **AORTA**
large Australian shark **MAKO**
large bag **SACK**
large barb of a feather **HERL, HARL**
large basin **TANK**
large bell **GONG**
large bird **EMU, MOA, OSTRICH, STORK**
large board **PLANK, SLAT**
large book **TOME**
large bundle **BALE**
large burrowing mammal **AARDVARK**
large candlestick **FLAMBEAU**
large canine **MASTIFF**
large canoe **BUNGO**
large cask **TUN**
large cat **LION, TIGER, PANTHER**
large Central American snake **BUSHMASTER**
large Central American tree **SAPODILLA**
large chest **TRUNK**
large cistern **TANK**
large conduit **MAIN**
large container **VAT, TUN**
large continent **ASIA**
large country house **CHATEAU, ESTATE, MANOR**

large crude boat	ARK	large wading bird	CRANE, IBIS
large cup	MUG	large warship (2 wds.)	
large cupola	DOME		AIRCRAFT CARRIER
large cut	SLAB	large wasp	HORNET
large deer	ELK	large web-footed bird	PELICAN
large dog (2 wds.)		large white bear	POLAR
	SAINT BERNARD	large wicker basket	HAMPER
large drinking vessel	FLAGON	large wooden cask	BARREL
large East Indian tree	NEEM	largo	SLOW
large fish	OPAH, TUNA	lariat	LASSO, REATA,
large fruit	MELON		RIATA, ROPE
large gateway	PYLON	laridae	GULLS
large gray wolf	LOBO	lark	FROLIC, SPREE
large heavy hammer	SLEDGE	larkspur	DELPHINIUM
large in scope	GENERAL	larrigan	MOCCASIN
large kettle	CALDRON	larva	GRUB
large knife	SNEE, BOLO	larval stage	PUPA
large ladle	SCOOP	lascivious	LEWD
large-leaved beet	CHARD	laser	BEAM
large lizard	ALLIGATOR,	lash	WHIP, FLOG
	CROCODILE	lash out	STRIKE
large mass of people	HORDE,	lass	GIRL, MAID, MAIDEN
	MOB, CROWD, HOST,	lassitude	TORPOR, LANGUOR
	MULTITUDE	lasso	LARIAT, REATA,
large mouthed pot	OLLA		RIATA, REATA,
large number	MYRIAD		RIATA, ROPE, NOOSE
large of body	BURLY	lasso expert	ROPER, COWBOY
large parrot	MACAW	last	ENDURE, FINAL, PERSIST,
large porch	VERANDA		OMEGA
large pulpit	AMBO	last dinner course	DESSERT
large quantity	MUCH, RAFT	last frontier	ALASKA
large rock	BOULDER	last Greek letter	OMEGA
large rodent	PACA, RAT	lasting	PERMANENT
larger than life	HEROIC	lasting a brief time	EPHEMERAL
large scissors	SHEARS	last inning	NINTH
large sea duck	EIDER	last in the race	LOSER
large seagoing vessel	LINER	last letter	ZED, ZEE, OMEGA
large seal (2 wds.)	SEA LION	lastly	FINALLY
large snake	BOA	last named	LATTER
large sofa	DIVAN	last offer	ULTIMATUM
large South African antelope		last part	END
	SASSABY	last queen of Spain	ENA
large spoon	LADLE	last-resort device (2 wds.)	
largess	BOUNTY, GENEROSITY		PANIC BUTTON
largest amount	MOST	last word	AUTHORITY
largest continent	ASIA	latch	LEVER, LOCK
large stewpot	OLLA	late	OVERDUE, TARDY,
largest ocean	PACIFIC		RECENT
largest of the Kuriles	ETOROFU	lateen	SAIL
large stout cord	ROPE	lately	RECENTLY
largest planet	JUPITER	latent	HIDDEN, COVERT,
large stream	RIVER		POTENTIAL, DORMANT
large tooth	TUSK	later	AFTERWARD
large town	CITY	lateral	SIDE, SIDEWARD
large truck	VAN	lateral part	SIDE
large tub	VAT	latest	NEWEST
large vase	URN	latest happenings	NEWS
large volume	TOME	latex	RUBBER
		lath	SLAT

lathe operator	TURNER
lather	FOAM, SUDS
Latin	ROMAN
Latin conjunction	ET
Latin god	DEUS
Latin poet	OVID, VIRGIL
Latvia's capital	RIGA
laud	PRAISE
laudable	WORTHY
laudanum	OPIATE
laugh	GIGGLE
laughable	COMIC, FUNNY
laugh boisterously	ROAR, SNORT
laugh brokenly	CACKLE
laugh contemptuously	SNORT
laughing	RIANT
laughing bird	LOON
laughingstock	BUTT
laugh loudly	ROAR
laugh raucously	CACKLE
laugh syllable/ HA, HO, TEE, HEE	
laughter	MIRTH
laugh to scorn	DERIDE
launch	DISCHARGE, START
launching site	PAD
launder	WASH, LAVE
launderable	TUB-FAST, WASHABLE, COLORFAST
laundering finale	RINSE
laundry appliance	WRINGER, DRYER, WASHER
laureate	DISTINGUISHED, HONORED
laurel	BAY
lava	LATITE, SCORIA
lavaliere	PENDANT
lavatory	BASIN, WASH
lave	
lavender	PURPLE
lavish	PROFUSE
lavish party	FETE
law	ACT, RULE, STATUTE, CANON, DECREE, EDICT, ORDINANCE
law (Lat.)	LEX, LEGES (PL.)
law charges	COSTS
law degree (abbr.)	LLB
lawful	LEGAL, LICIT
lawless	ILLEGAL, UNRULY
lawless crowd	MOB, GANG
lawmaker	SENATOR, LEGISLATOR
lawman	SHERIFF, MARSHAL
lawn	GREENSWARD
lawn covering	GRASS, TURF
lawn mower's path	SWATH

lawn party	FETE, BARBECUE
lawn wrecker	MOLE
law of Moses	TORAH
law officers	POLICE
law precedent (2 wds.)	RES JUDICATA
lawsuit	CASE
lawyer	ATTORNEY, BARRISTER, COUNSELOR, COUNSEL, SOLICITOR, ADVOCATE
lawyer's charge	FEE, RETAINER
lawyer's customer	CLIENT
lawyer's fee	RETAINER
lawyer's patron saint	IVES
lax	NEGLIGENT
laxative	PURGATIVE, CATHARTIC
laxity	LOOSENESS
lay	PUT, PLACE, DEPOSIT
lay in plaits	FOLD
layer	PLY, TIER, STRATUM
layer of cloth	PLY
layer of floors	TILER, CARPENTER
layer of eye	UVEA
layer of paint	COAT
layer of skin	DERMA
lay out	EXPEND, SPEND
layover	STOP
lay up	DISABLE
lay waste	RAVAGE
laze	LOAF
laziness	LETHARGY
lazy	INDOLENT, IDLE
lazy animal	SLOTH
lazybones	SHIRKER, IDLER
lazy way to fish	TROTLINE, SETLINE, TRAWL
LBJ's state	TEXAS
lea	MEADOW
leachy	POROUS
lead	DIRECT, GUIDE
leaden	HEAVY
leader	CHIEF, HEAD
lead-in	INTRODUCTION
leading	AHEAD
leading actor	STAR
leading man	HERO, STAR
lead into error	DELUDE
lead on	LURE
leaf	PAGE, SEPAL
leaf cutter	ANT
leaf fat	LARD
leafless plant	FERN
leaflet	PAMPHLET
leaf of a book	PAGE
leaf of a calyx	SEPAL

leafstalk **PETIOLE**
leafstalk used for sauce **RHUBARB**
leafy-headed vegetable **CABBAGE, LETTUCE**
league **CLUB**
League of Nations city **GENEVA**
Leah's sister **RACHEL**
leak **ESCAPE, FLAW, CRACK, DRIP**
leak out **SEEP, OOZE**
lean **RARE, SPARE, THIN, LANK, GAUNT, TILT**
lean, as a ship **CAREEN, HEEL**
leaned over **CANTED**
leaning **ALOP, TREND, TENDENCY**
lean-to **SHED**
leap **JUMP, SKIP, HOP, SPRING**
leaping creature **TOAD, FROG**
leaping insect **CRICKET, FLEA**
leaps and bounds **RAPIDLY**
learn **ASCERTAIN, MASTER**
learned **VERSED**
learned man in India **PANDIT**
learned person **SCHOLAR**
learning **LORE, KNOWLEDGE**
lease **LET, RENT**
lease payment **RENT**
leash **CURB, RESTRAIN**
least **MEREST**
least appropriate (3 wds.) **OF ALL THINGS**
least bit **IOTA**
leather **HIDE**
leatherback **TURTLE**
leather belt **STRAP**
leather bottle **MATARA**
leather fastener **STRAP, THONG**
leather gaiter **PUTTEE, SPAT**
leatherneck **MARINE**
leather punch **AWL**
leather ribbon **STRAP**
leather source **STEERHIDE**
leather splitting tool **SKIVER**
leather strap **THONG, BELT**
leather strip **STRAP**
leather whip **KNOUT**
leathery **TOUGH**
leave **DEPART, GO**
leave empty **VACATE**
leave isolated **MAROON, STRAND, ABANDON, DESERT**
leavening agent **YEAST**
leave of absence **FURLOUGH, SABBATICAL**
leave off **CEASE**

leave out **OMIT, SKIP, REMOVE, CUT, DELETE**
leave port **SAIL, EMBARK**
leaves **FOLIAGE**
leave suddenly (2 wds.) **MAKE OFF**
leaving **RESIDUE**
leaving a will **TESTATE**
lectern **DESK, STAND**
lecture **DISCOURSE, SERMON**
lecture platform **DAIS**
ledge **SHELF**
ledger entry **CREDIT, DEBIT**
lee **SHELTER**
leech **PARASITE**
leek **ONION**
leer **OGLE**
leery **WARY**
leeward **DOWNWIND**
leeway **ROOM, PLAY**
left **GONE, LIBERAL**
Left Bank location **PARIS**
leftist **RADICAL, RED**
leftover **SCRAP**
leg **CALF, GAM**
legacy **BEQUEST**
legal **LAWFUL, LICIT**
legal claim **LIEN**
legal conveyance **DEED**
legal critic **CENSOR**
legal decree **EDICT**
legal defense **ALIBI**
legal document **DEED, WRIT**
legal holiday **LABOR DAY, MEMORIAL DAY, LINCOLN'S BIRTHDAY, WASHINGTON'S BIRTHDAY, COLUMBUS DAY, ARMISTICE DAY**
legally authorized **LICENSED**
legal matter **RES**
legal order **WRIT**
legal paper **WRIT**
legal plea **ALIBI**
legal profession **BAR**
legal warning **CAVEAT**
legal writ to insure payment **ELEGIT**
leg armor **GREAVE**
legate **ENVOY**
legatee **HEIR**
legation **MISSION**
leg bone **SHIN, TIBIA**
legend **MYTH, SAGA**
legendary **MYTHICAL**
legendary bird **ROC**
legendary British king **LUD, ARTHUR**

legendary enchantress **CIRCE**
legendary hero **PALADIN**
legendary magician **MERLIN**
legendary sea creature
MERMAID
legerdemain **MAGIC, TRICKERY**
leghorn **CHICKEN**
legible **READABLE**
legion **ARMY, MULTITUDE**
legislate **ENACT**
legislative body **SENATE,**
CONGRESS, HOUSE,
PARLIAMENT
legislative enactment **LAW**
legislator **SENATOR,**
CONGRESSMAN,
REPRESENTATIVE, MP,
ASSEMBLYMAN
legislature **ASSEMBLY,**
CONGRESS
legitimate **LAWFUL, LICIT**
leg joint **HIP, KNEE**
legume **PEA, BEAN,**
VEGETABLE
lei **GARLAND, WREATH**
leisure **REST, EASE**
leisure activity **HOBBY**
leisure time **EASE**
leitmotif **THEME**
lemming **RODENT**
lemon **DEFECTIVE, CITRUS**
lemon drink **ADE**
lemonlike fruit **CITRON, LIME**
lemur **TARSIER**
lemur of Java **LORIS**
Lenape **DELAWARE**
lend **LOAN**
lend a hand **AID, HELP,**
ASSIST
lend dignity to **ENNOBLE**
lene **NONASPIRATE**
length **EXTENT**
lengthen **EXTEND**
length of office **TERM**
length of railroad **TRACK**
length of service status
SENIORITY
length of 3/4 of an inch **DIGIT**
length unit **ROD, YARD, FOOT,**
INCH, MILE
lengthwise **ALONG**
lengthy **LONG**
leniency **MERCY**
lenient **TOLERANT**
Lenin's country **RUSSIA**
Lenten observers goal
(comp. wd.) **SELF-DENIAL**

lentigo **FRECKLE**
lento **SLOW**
leonine hair **MANE**
leonine sound **ROAR**
leopard **PANTHER, CHEETAH**
leotard **TIGHTS**
Leo's home **LAIR**
Leo's son **LIONET**
lepidopteran **BUTTERFLY**
leporid **HARE**
leprechauns (2 wds.)
LITTLE PEOPLE
lesion **INJURY, WOUND**
Leslie Caron role **LILI**
less **FEWER**
less adulterated **PURER**
less bad **BETTER**
less common **RARER**
less difficult **EASIER**
lessee **RENTER, TENANT**
lessen **ABATE, WANE, EASE**
lessen the strength of
ENERVATE, DEBILITATE
lessen the tension of **RELAX**
lesser **MINOR, INFERIOR**
less expensive **CHEAPER**
less fancy **BARER**
less good **WORSE**
lesson **EXERCISE, UNIT**
lessor **LANDLORD**
less refined **COARSER**
less risky **SAFER**
less stale **FRESHER**
less than **UNDER**
less than 100 shares stock
(2 wds.) **ODD LOT**
less wild **TAMER**
let **ALLOW, HIRE, RENT,**
PERMIT
let down **LOWER, DISAPPOINT**
let fall **DROP**
let go **RELEASE, RELAX**
lethal **FATAL, DEADLY**
lethargic **SLEEPY, DULL**
lethargy **STUPOR, LANGUOR,**
TORPOR
let in **ADMIT**
let it stand **STET**
let off **EXCUSE**
let run out **SPILL**
letter **NOTE, PRINT, MISSIVE,**
EPISTLE, CHARACTER
letter carrier **POSTMAN,**
MAILMAN
letter cutter **OPENER**
lettered **LITERATE**
letterhead **STATIONERY**

letter of agreement	CARTEL
lettuce	ICEBERG, BOSTON, ROMAINE, BIBB, HEAD, COS
lettuce dish	SALAD
let up	RESPITE
Levant	EAST, ORIENT
Levantine ketch	SAIC
levee	DIKE, PIER
level	EVEN, FLAT, RAZE, RASE
leveler	PLANE
levelheaded	SENSIBLE
level of command	ECHELON
level of equality	PAR
lever	PRY, CROWBAR
leveret	HARE
leviathan	MONSTER
levis	JEANS
levitate	RISE, FLOAT
levity	GAIETY, FRIVOLITY
levy a fine	AMERCE
lewd	OBSCENE
Lewis Carroll character	ALICE
lexicon	DICTIONARY
liability	DEBT
liable	APT, PRONE, LIKELY, SUBJECT
liaison	INTIMACY
liana	VINE
liar	PERJURER, PREVARICATOR, FIBBER
lias	LIMESTONE
libation	DRINK, POTION
Liberace's instrument	PIANO
liberal	FREE
liberate	FREE, RELEASE
Liberian natives	VAI, VEI
liberty	FREEDOM, PRIVILEGE
libidinous	LEWD, WANTON
library (2 wds.)	READING ROOM
library piece	BOOKCASE
library's study enclosure	CARREL(L)
library treasure	BOOK
Libyan city	TRIPOLI, BENGASI
license	PERMIT, SANCTION
license plate	TAG
license tag	PLATE
licentious	WANTON, LIBERTINE
lichen	MOSS
lichen dye	LITMUS
lick an envelope	SEAL
lick up	LAP
licorice herb	ANISE

lid	COVER
lid clasp	HASP
Lido	RESORT, BEACH
lid remover	OPENER
lie	EQUIVOCATE, FIB, FALSEHOOD, STORY, RECLINE, FABRICATE
lie in ambush	LURK
lie in warmth	BASK
Liebfraumilch	WINE
Liederkranz	CHEESE
lief	WILLINGLY, GLADLY
lieu	STEAD, PLACE
lieutenant	SHAVETAIL, OFFICER
life	BIOGRAPHY, EXISTENCE
life and death	DIRE
lifeboat	RAFT
life jacket	MAE WEST
lifeless	INERT, DEAD
lifetime	AGE
lift	RAISE, BOOST, ELEVATOR
lifting device	LEVER, CRANE
lifting machine	CRANE
lift the hat	DOFF
lift up	BOOST, ELEVATE, RAISE
lift with effort	HEAVE, STRAIN
light	IGNITE, LAMP, CANDLE, BLITHE, TRIVIAL, AIRY, FAIR, ASPECT
light anchor	KEDGE
light and airy	ETHEREAL
light anew	REKINDLE
light beam	RAY
light beer	LAGER
light boat	CANOE, SUNFISH, SAILFISH, SKIFF
light breeze	AIR, ZEPHYR
light brown	ECRU, TAN, BEIGE
light coating	FILM
light crimson	PINK
lighted	LIT, ILLUMINATED
lighten	EASE
light-footed	NIMBLE
light four-wheeled carriage	PHAETON
light globe	BULB
light-headed	GIDDY, DIZZY
lighthouse	BEACON, PHAROS
lighting device	LAMP, TORCH, CANDLE, BEACON
light meal	LUNCHEON, SNACK, TEA
lightning bug	FIREFLY
light open wagon	CART

light portable sunshade	**PARASOL**
light red	**PINK**
light refractor	**PRISM**
light sarcasm	**IRONY**
light shoe	**SLIPPER, SANDAL**
light soup	**BROTH**
lights out	**TAPS**
light tan	**ECRU, BEIGE, KHAKI**
light touch	**DAB**
light up	**ILLUMINE, BRIGHTEN**
light weight	**DRAM**
light wood	**BALSA**
lignite	**COAL**
likable	**NICE, PLEASING, ATTRACTIVE**
like	**SIMILAR, ENJOY**
like a leopard	**SPOTTED**
like a modern refrigerator (comp. wd.)	**SELF-DEFROSTING**
like an old maid	**SPINSTERISH, FINICKY, FUSSY**
like a routine police case (3 wds.)	**OPEN AND SHUT**
like a warm spring day	**BALMY**
like a wing	**ALAR**
like better	**PREFER**
like expensive beef (comp. wd.)	**TOP-GRADE**
like metal	**STEELY**
likely	**APT, LIABLE, PRONE**
likely to turn out well	**PROMISING**
liken	**COMPARE**
likeness	**IMAGE**
like peanut brittle	**CRUNCHY**
like seawater	**SALTY**
like some diets (comp. wd.)	**SALT-FREE**
like sweater weather	**COOL**
like unfilleted fish	**BONY**
likewise	**ALSO, DITTO, TOO**
liking	**TASTE**
lilac color	**MAUVE**
lilliputian	**TINY**
lilt	**CADENCE, AIR, TUNE, MELODY**
lily	**ALOE, CALLA**
Lily Maid	**ELAINE**
lily of the sea	**CRINOID**
lily palm	**TI**
lily plant	**ALOE**
Lily Pons, for one	**DIVA**
lily-white	**PURE, BLAMELESS**
lima	**BEAN**

limb	**BRANCH, RAMAGE, LEG, ARM**
limber	**AGILE, SPRY, NIMBLE**
limbo	**HELL**
limbless reptile	**SNAKE**
Limburger	**CHEESE**
lime	**CITRUS, CEMENT**
limestone pit	**QUARRY**
lime twig	**SNARE**
limit	**END, BOUNDARY, EXTENT, RESTRICT, CONFINE, BOUND**
limited	**FINITE, NARROW**
limiting	**RESTRICTIVE**
limitless	**VAST, INFINITE**
limp	**FLACCID, FLABBY**
limpid	**BRIGHT, LUCID**
Lincoln Center offering	**OPERA, CONCERT, PLAY, BALLET**
Lindbergh book	**WE**
line	**ROPE, ROW, QUEUE, BOUNDARY**
lineage	**PEDIGREE**
line delivered to the audience	**ASIDE**
linen	**NAPERY**
line of cliffs	**PALISADES**
line of guards	**CORDON**
line of travel	**ROUTE**
line ornamenting type	**SERIF**
liner	**STEAMSHIP, PLANE**
liner's roster (2 wds.)	**PASSENGER LIST**
lineup	**ROSTER**
line with panels	**WAINSCOT**
ling	**HAKE, BURBOT**
linger	**TARRY, WAIT**
linger close by	**HOVER**
linger idly	**LOITER**
linger over a triumph	**GLOAT**
lingo	**LANGUAGE, JARGON, CANT**
linguine	**PASTA**
linguist	**POLYGLOT**
link	**CONNECTION**
linn	**POOL, RAVINE, WATERFALL**
linoleum	**FLOORING**
lint	**FLUFF**
lion	**CAT**
lioness in *Born Free*	**ELSA**
lion's cry	**ROAR**
lion's den	**LAIR**
lion's lair	**DEN**
lion's neck hair	**MANE**
lion's share	**ALL**
lip	**LABIUM, RIM**

liquefy **THAW, MELT, DEFROST, CONDENSE**
liqueur **CORDIAL**
liqueur flavoring **ANISE, MINT, COFFEE, ORANGE, CHERRY**
liquid **FLUID, WATER**
liquidate **SETTLE**
liquid dressing **SAUCE**
liquid food **SOUP, BROTH**
liquid measure **LITRE, PINT, CUP, QUART, GALLON**
liquor **SPIRITS, WHISKEY**
liquor vessel **DECANTER**
lisle **CLOTH, THREAD**
lissome **AGILE, SUPPLE**
list **CATALOGUE, REGISTER**
listel **FILLET, MOLDING**
listen **HARK, HEED, HEAR**
listen furtively **EAVESDROP**
listening **ATTENTIVE**
list individually **ITEMIZE**
listless **BORED**
list of candidates **SLATE**
list of foods **MENU**
list of investments **PORTFOLIO**
list of names **ROLL**
list of performers **CAST**
list of persons **ROTA**
litany **PRAYER, RECITAL**
literal **TRUE, EXACT**
literalism **REALISM**
literally **REALLY, ACTUALLY**
literary appendix **ADDENDUM**
literary composition **ESSAY**
literary drudge **HACK**
literary irony **SATIRE**
literary man **AUTHOR, WRITER**
literary miscellany **ANA**
literary parody **TRAVESTY**
literature **LORE, WRITINGS**
lithe **LIMBER, SUPPLE**
litigant **SUITOR**
litigate **CONTEST**
little **SMALL, TINY, WEE**
little (mus.) **POCO**
little arrow **DART**
little bone **OSSICLE**
little branch **TWIG**
little brook **RILL**
little by little **GRADUALLY**
little child **TOT, TAD**
Little Corporal **NAPOLEON**
little devil **IMP**
little fellow **SHAVER**
little piece **MORSEL**
Little Rhody **RHODE ISLAND**
little whirlpool **EDDY**
liturgy **RITE, RITUAL**

live **EXIST, RESIDE, DWELL**
live coal **EMBER**
liveliness **ANIMATION**
lively **NIMBLE, AGILE, PEPPY, ACTIVE, PERT, SPRY**
lively celebration **GALA**
lively dance **GALOP, JIG, POLKA, REEL, FANDANGO**
lively frolic **SPREE, CAPER**
lively song **LILT**
liver fluid **BILE**
liverwort **HEPATICA**
livestock **CATTLE**
livid **PALE, ASHEN**
living **ALIVE, VITAL**
living being **ANIMAL, CREATURE**
living room **PARLOR**
living room piece **DIVAN, SOFA, COUCH, END TABLE, COFFEE TABLE, LAMP, RUG**
living thing **CREATURE, ANIMAL**
lizard **ANOLE**
lizardlike amphibian **SALAMANDER**
llama **ALPACA**
llano **PLAIN**
lo **BEHOLD**
load **BURDEN, LADE, CARGO, PACK**
loaf about **LOITER, LOLL, IDLE**
loafer **SHOE, MOCASSIN**
loam **SOIL**
loam deposit **LOESS, SILT**
loan **LEND**
loan shark **USURER**
loath **UNWILLING, RELUCTANT**
loathe **DESPISE, HATE, DETEST, ABHOR**
loathing **AVERSION**
loathsome **DETESTABLE**
lobby **FOYER, HALL**
lobe **EARLAP**
lobo **TIMBERWOLF**
lobster claw **CHELA, PINCER**
local **REGIONAL, AREAL**
local businessman (2 wds.) **RETAIL MERCHANT**
local citizen (2 wds.) **NATIVE SON**
local dialect **IDIOM**
locale **AREA, SITE, ENVIRONMENT**
local geography **TERRAIN**
localism **CUSTOM**
locality **PLACE, SPOT, SITE**
locate **FIND, SITUATE**

location **PLACE, SITE, SPOT**
loch in Scotland **NESS, LEVEN, TAY, KATRINE**
lock **GATE, BOLT**
lock away **STORE, SAVE**
lockjaw **TETANUS**
lock of hair **TRESS**
lock opener **KEY**
locomotive **ENGINE**
locomotive and cars **TRAIN**
locomotive cowcatcher **PILOT**
locomotive track **RAIL**
locule **CAVITY**
locus **PLACE, SITE**
locust **CICADA**
locust tree **ACACIA, CAROB**
lode **VEIN**
lodestone **MAGNET**
lodge **CABIN**
lodge member **ELK**
lodger **ROOMER**
lodging **ROOM, QUARTERS**
lodging house **HOTEL, INN, HOSTEL**
loess **LOAM, SILT**
loft **ATTIC**
lofty **HIGH, TALL, ALPINE, GRAND, NOBLE**
lofty goal **IDEAL**
lofty mountain **EVEREST**
lofty place **PEAK, PINNACLE**
log **DIARY, RECORD**
log dwelling **CABIN**
loge **BOX, MEZZANINE**
log float **RAFT**
logger's boot **PAC**
loggia **GALLERY**
logical **SOUND, VALID**
logrolling **BIRLING**
logrolling contest **ROLEO**
logy **DULL, SLUGGISH**
Lohengrin's bride **ELSA**
loiter **DALLY, LAG, LINGER, TARRY, IDLE, LOLL**
loll **LOUNGE, LAZE, LINGER**
London district **CHELSEA, SOHO, MAYFAIR**
Londoner **COCKNEY**
London literature **ADELPHIAN**
London's cafe district **SOHO**
London trolley **TRAM**
lone **SOLE, SOLITARY**
loneliness **ISOLATION, SOLITUDE**
lonely **LONESOME, SOLITARY**
lone performance **SOLO**
loner **SINGLETON**
Lone Star State **TEXAS**

long **EXTENSIVE, LENGTHY, YEARN, PINE**
long ago **YORE**
long and slender **REEDY, LANK**
long and tiresome **TEDIOUS, BORING**
long cape **CLOAK**
long creeping reptile **SNAKE**
long curl of hair **RINGLET, TRESS**
long discourse **TIRADE**
long distance (2 wds.) **COUNTRY MILE**
long distance runner **MILER**
long dry period **DROUGHT**
longe **ROPE, RING**
long essay **TREATISE**
Longfellow hero **ALDEN**
long fish **EEL, GAR**
long for **COVET, PINE, YEARN, CRAVE**
long green **MONEY**
longhair **INTELLECTUAL**
longhand **WRITTEN**
long-handled brush **BROOM**
long heroic poem **EPOS**
longing **ACHE, YEN, DESIRE**
longing for friends **LONELY, HOMESICK**
long inlet **RIA**
long journey **ODYSSEY, TREK**
long-legged bird **STORK, STILT**
long life **LONGEVITY**
long live (Fr.) **VIVE**
long narrative **SAGA**
long narrow pennant **STREAMER**
long narrow piece **STRIP**
long-necked bird **SWAN, GOOSE**
long nose **SNOUT**
long-nosed fish **GAR**
long period of time **EON, AGE, CENTURY**
long piece of timber **BEAM**
long piece of wood **POLE**
long poem's division **CANTO**
long rolling wave **SWELL**
long seat **BENCH**
longshoreman **STEVEDORE**
long spear **LANCE**
long staff **POLE**
long step **STRIDE**
long-suffering **PATIENT**
long tale **SAGA**
long time **EON, AGE**
long tooth **TUSK, FANG**
long tube **PIPE**
long vocal solo **ARIA**

long weapon	SWORD	lorgnette	EYEGLASSES
look	SEE, VIEW	loris	LEMUR
look after	TEND, MIND	lorry	TRUCK
look-alike	TWIN, DOUBLE	lory	PARROT
look askance	LEER, OGLE	Los Angeles area	WATTS
look at	ESPY, EYE, SEE, WATCH, REGARD	Los Angeles ball club	ANGELS, DODGERS
look at flirtatiously	OGLE, LEER	Los Angeles quarterback	RAM
look back	RECALL	Los Angeles specialty	SMOG
look closely	PEER, PRY, EXAMINE	Los Angeles suburb (2 wds.)	SANTA MONICA
look for	SEEK, HUNT, SEARCH	lose	MISLAY, MISPLACE
look for game	HUNT	lose balance	TRIP
look for ore	PROSPECT	lose by neglect	FORFEIT
look forward to	ANTICIPATE	lose color	FADE, PALE
looking for trouble (4 wds.)	UP TO NO GOOD	lose courage	DESPAIR
looking glass	MIRROR	lose feathers	MOLT
look in on	VISIT, CHECK	lose force	WANE
look on	OBSERVE, REGARD	lose freshness	FADE
lookout	SENTRY	lose hair	SHED
look over	SCAN, PORE	lose luster	DIM, FADE
look slyly	PEEP, PEEK	lose out	FAIL
look steadily	GAZE, STARE	lose patience	TIRE
look sullen	POUT	lose weight	REDUCE
look to	RELY	loser's alibi (2 wds.)	SOUR GRAPES
look to be	SEEM	loss	DEPRIVATION
look up to	RESPECT	loss of memory	AMNESIA
loom	IMPEND, SHAFT	loss of reason	AMENTIA
loom bar	EASER	loss of speech	APHASIA
loom frame	LATHE	lost	GONE, MISSING
loom harness	LEAF	lot	GROUP, PLOT, FATE, LUCK
loon	DIVER	Lothario	RAKE
loop	CURL	lottery	RAFFLE
loop for lifting	TAB	loud	NOISY
loop in a rope	NOOSE	loud clamor	RACKET, DIN
loop on lace	PICOT	loud guffaw	ROAR
loose	BAGGY, SLACK	loud noise	BANG, DIN
loose garment	ROBE, SIMAR, CAPE, CLOAK	loud rushing noise	WHOOSH
loose-jointed	LIMBER	loud-voiced person	STENTOR
loosen	UNPIN, UNTIE, UNDO	Louisiana bird	PELICAN
loosen up	RELAX	Louisiana county	PARISH
looseness	SLACK	Louisiana patois	CREOLE
loose rock particles	SAND	lounge	LOLL, LOAF, LAZE
loose soil	DIRT	lout	OAF, BOOR, CAD
loot	BOOTY, PLUNDER	lovable	AMIABLE, ENDEARING
lop	CUT	love	FONDNESS
lop off	BOB	love affair	AMOUR
lope	STRIDE	love apple	TOMATO
lopsided	ALIST, ATILT, AWRY	love deity	CUPID
loquacious	TALKATIVE	love in Rome	AMORE
lord	NOBLEMAN	loveliness	PULCHRITUDE
lordly beast	LION	lovelock	TRESS
Lord's Day	SUNDAY	lovely	BEAUTIFUL, HANDSOME, COMELY
lord's wife	LADY	love of travel	WANDERLUST
lore	KNOWLEDGE	lover	ROMEO, SWEETHEART, PARAMOUR
Lorelei	SIREN		

lover of Heloise	**ABELARD**
lover's heartbeat (comp. wd.)	
	PIT-A-PAT
lovers' meeting place	**TRYST**
lovers' quarrel	**SPAT**
lover's song	**SERENADE**
love seat	**DIVAN**
love story	**ROMANCE**
love to excess	**ADORE, DOTE**
love token	**AMORET**
loving	**FOND**
loving cup	**TROPHY**
low	**BASE, DEEP**
lowbred	**VULGAR, COARSE**
low chirping note	**TWEET**
low-cost dwelling	**TENEMENT**
lower	**ABASE**
lower limb	**LEG**
lower world	**HADES, ORCUS**
lowest	**LEAST**
lowest class of animal	**AMOEBA**
lowest deck	**ORLOP**
lowest form of wit	**PUN**
lowest point	**NADIR**
lowest singing voice	**BASS**
low female voice	**ALTO**
low green shrub	**ERICA**
lowland	**BOTTOM**
low male voice	**BASS**
low spirits	**BLUES**
low step-in shoe	**LOAFER**
low tide	**NEAP, EBB**
low tufted plant	**MOSS**
low waters (2 wds.)	**EBB TIDE**
loyal	**TRUE, CONSTANT,**
	FAITHFUL
loyalist	**PATRIOT, TORY**
loyal supporter	**FAN**
loyalty	**DEVOTION, FEALTY**
Loyolite	**JESUIT**
lozenge	**PASTILLE**
luau food	**POI**
lubricant, for short	**LUBE**
lubricate	**OIL, GREASE**
lucid	**BRIGHT, CLEAR**
Lucifer	**FALLEN ANGEL,**
	SATAN, DEVIL
Lucifer's state	**PERDITION**
luck	**CHANCE**
lucky	**FORTUNATE**
lucky event	**HIT**
lucky number	**SEVEN**
lucky token	**AMULET**
lucrative	**GAINFUL**
ludicrous	**COMICAL**
luggage item	**TRUNK,**
	SUITCASE, BAG,
	GRIP, ETUI, VALISE

lukewarm	**TEPID**
lull	**HUSH, CALM**
lumber	**WOOD, TIMBER**
lumberman's boot	**PAC**
lumberman's tool	**AXE, AX, SAW**
luminary	**SUN, STAR**
luminous	**RADIANT, SHINY**
luminous heavenly	
body	**COMET, STAR,**
	MOON, PLANET
lump	**BLOB, MASS**
lump of butter	**PAT**
lump of cottage cheese	**CURD**
lump of earth	**CLOD**
lump of earth on the	
fairway	**DIVOT**
lump of tobacco	**WAD**
lunar flight control	
center	**HOUSTON**
lunacy	**MADNESS, INSANITY**
lunatic	**MANIAC**
lunchroom	**TEA SHOP, SNACK**
	BAR, COFFEE SHOP, CAFE,
	CAFETERIA, RESTAURANT
lunchtime	**NOON**
lune	**MOON, CRESCENT**
lunge	**LEAP, SPRING**
lurch	**CAREEN**
lure	**BAIT, ENTICE, TEMPT**
lure by artifice	**DECOY**
lurid	**SENSATIONAL**
lurk	**SKULK, SNEAK**
lurk about	**SNEAK**
luscious	**TASTY, SWEET**
lush	**JUICY, PROFUSE**
lust	**PASSION**
luster	**GLOSS, POLISH, SHEEN,**
	SHINE
lusterless	**DEAD, MAT**
lustrous cloth	**PANNE**
lustrous resin	**COPAL**
luxuriate	**BASK**
luxurious	**SYBARITIC**
luxurious fabric	**SILK, SATIN,**
	VELVET
luxurious fur	**SABLE, MINK,**
	ERMINE
luxury	**EASE**
Luzon headhunter	**IGOROT**
lying	**DISHONEST, PRONE**
lying across	**TRANSVERSE**
lying flat	**PRONE**
lying on the back	**SUPINE**
lynx	**CAT, WILDCAT**
lyric	**POETIC**
lyricist Gershwin	**IRA**
lyric poem	**ODE, EPODE**
lysergic acid diethylamide	**LSD**

M

macabre **WEIRD, EERIE, EERY,**
GRIM, GHASTLY, GRUESOME
macaco **LEMUR, MONKEY**
macadamia **NUT**
Macao coin **AVO**
macaroni **PASTA**
macaw **ARA, PARROT**
Macbeth's title **THANE**
maccaboy **SNUFF**
mace **SPICE**
macedoine **MEDLEY**
macerate **SOFTEN, TORMENT**
machination **SCHEME, PLOT**
machine **ENGINE, MOTOR,**
GADGET
machine part **CAM, GEAR,**
TAPPET, PAWL
machine tool **BAND-SAW, FILE,**
LATHE
machismo **VIRILITY**
mackerel's relative **BONITO,**
CERO
mackinaw **BLANKET, COAT**
mackintosh **RAINCOAT**
mackle **BLUR**
macrocosm **UNIVERSE**
macroscopic **VISIBLE**
macruran **LOBSTER, SHRIMP**
maculate **DEFILE**
mad **ANGRY, INSANE, RABID**
Madagascar mammal **LEMUR**
mad, as a dog **RABID**
madcap **RECKLESS**
madden **ENRAGE, CRAZE**
madder **DYE, CRIMSON**
made of (suffix) **INE**
made of a hard wood **OAKEN**
made of cereal **OATEN**
made of fired clay **EARTHEN,**
CERAMIC
made of flax **LINEN**
made of grain **CEREAL**
made of iron **METALLIC**
made of silver **ARGENT**
made on a loom **WOVEN**
madhouse **BEDLAM**
Madison Avenue technique
(2 wds.) **HARD SELL,**
SOFT SELL
madman **LUNATIC, MANIAC**
madness **LUNACY, INSANITY**
Madras hemp **SUNN**
Madrid boulevard **PRADO**
madrigal **LYRIC, POEM**

maelstrom **WHIRLPOOL**
Mae West role **LOU, LIL**
magazine official **EDITOR**
magic **LEGERDEMAIN,**
SORCERY, VOODOO,
ALCHEMY, NECROMANCY
magic charm **AMULET**
magician's rod **WAND**
magic lamp owner **ALADDIN**
magic stick **WAND**
magistrate **JUDGE**
magistrate's staff **MACE**
magnanimous **GENEROUS**
magnetic metal **IRON**
magnetic recording strip **TAPE**
magnificent **GRAND**
magnify **ENLARGE**
magnitude **SIZE**
magnolia **TREE**
Magnolia State **MISSISSIPPI**
mahatma (2 wds.) **HOLY MAN**
mah-jongg piece **TILE**
maid **GIRL, LASS, SERVANT**
mail **POST, SEND**
mail container **SACK**
mail room employee
(2 wds.) **OFFICE BOY**
mailbag **POUCH**
maim **CRIPPLE, DISFIGURE**
main **CHIEF, PRIME**
main artery **AORTA,**
BOULEVARD
main course **ENTREE**
Maine capital **AUGUSTA**
Maine city **BANGOR**
Maine lake **SEBAGO**
main idea **GIST**
main impact **BRUNT**
mainland **CONTINENT**
main meal **DINNER**
main movie **FEATURE**
main part **BULK**
maintain **KEEP**
maintain one's dignity
(2 wds.) **SAVE FACE**
maize **CORN**
majestic **REGAL, ROYAL,**
STATELY, GRAND
major appliance **RANGE,**
STOVE, REFRIGERATOR,
WASHER, DRYER, OVEN
majority **PLURALITY**
make **CONSTRUCT, CREATE,**
ERECT, MANUFACTURE
make a beginning **START,**
BEGIN, COMMENCE
make a brief visit **CALL**
make a cake **BAKE**

make a choice	OPT, ELECT, SELECT
make a contented sound	PURR
make active	ENERGIZE
make a decision	DECIDE
make a difference	MATTER
make a garment	SEW
make airtight	SEAL
make allusion to	MENTION
make a loan	LEND
make amends	REDRESS, ATONE
make a mess of	PI(E)
make a mistake	ERR
make an address	SPEAK, ORATE
make an edging	TAT, BIND
make angry	RILE, MADDEN, IRE
make an offer	BID
make a picture	DRAW, PAINT, ILLUSTRATE, SKETCH
make a promise	PLEDGE, VOW
make a proposal	OFFER
make a rasping sound	GRATE
make a recording	TAPE
make a speech	ORATE
make a vow	SWEAR
make bare	DENUDE
make beer	BREW
make believe	PRETEND
make beloved	ENDEAR
make better	AMEND, REFORM, RENOVATE, REPAIR, RENEW, RESTORE, REHABILITATE
make bigger	ENLARGE, MAGNIFY
make brief note	JOT
make broader	WIDEN
make brown	TAN
make butter	CHURN
make calm	ALLAY, COMPOSE
make certain	ENSURE
make cheerful	ENLIVEN
make choice	OPT, SELECT
make cloth	WEAVE
make cloudy	BLUR
make content	SATISFY
make corrections	AMEND
make designs on metal	ETCH
make different	CHANGE
make even	LEVEL
make eyes at	OGLE
make float in air	LEVITATE, FLY
make free	RID, LIBERATE
make fresh again	RENEW
make full	FILL
make fun of	RIDICULE
make gay	LIVEN, ELATE
make gentle	TAME
make happen	CAUSE
make happy	ELATE
make hard	FREEZE, STEEL
make headway	ADVANCE, PROGRESS
make holy	HALLOW, SANCTIFY, BLESS, CANONIZE
make impossible	PRECLUDE
make improvements	REVISE
make inquiry	ASK
make into coin	MINT
make into law	ENACT, LEGISLATE
make into leather	TAN
make keen, as the appetite	WHET
make known	DISCLOSE, AIR, PUBLISH, ADVERTISE, REVEAL
make lace	TAT
make less dense	RAREFY
make level	TRUE
make lively	ANIMATE
make love	WOO
make lusterless	FLATTEN
make merry	REVEL
make money	EARN, COIN, MINT
make muddy	ROIL
make multiform	DIVERSIFY
make neat	GROOM, TIDY
make objection	DEMUR, REMONSTRATE, PROTEST
make out clearly	DISCERN
make over	REDO
make pale	CHALK
make payment	PAY, REMIT
make perplexed	BAFFLE
make possible	ENABLE
make precious	ENDEAR
make preparations (2 wds.)	GET READY
make progress	ADVANCE, GAIN
make proud	ELATE
make purchases	SHOP, BUY
make quiet	HUSH, SILENCE
maker	CREATOR, MANUFACTURER
make ready	PREPARE
make report	TELL
maker of earthenware	POTTER, CERAMIST
maker of laws	LEGISLATOR
maker of pottery	CERAMIST
make slow	RETARD
make smaller	DECREASE, SHRINK

make small talk	CHAT
make soundproof	DEAFEN,
	INSULATE
make sport of	DERIDE
make tardy	DELAY, RETARD
make thread	SPIN
make unfriendly	ALIENATE
make untidy	MUSS, MESS-UP
makeup	COSMETICS
make up for	ATONE
make use of	AVAIL, EMPLOY
make void	ANNUL
make watertight	SEAL, CALK
make weary	BORE, TIRE
make well	CURE
make white	BLANCH
make wine	VINTAGE
make worse	AGGRAVATE,
	IRRITATE
making a profit (3 wds.)	
	IN THE BLACK
maladroit	INEPT
malady	ILLNESS, AILMENT
malagma	POULTICE
Malamud novel (2 wds.)	
	THE FIXER
malarial fever	AGUE
Malay ape	LAR
Malay archipelago garment	
	SARONG
Malay buffalo	CARIBOU
Malay island	JAVA
Malaysian state	PERAK
male	MASCULINE
male adult	MAN
male ancestor	SIRE
male bee	DRONE
male bird	ROOSTER
male bovine	BULL, STEER, OX
male cat	TOM
male chicken	ROOSTER
male child	SON, BOY
male deer	HART, STAG
male deity	GOD
male descendant	SON
malediction	CURSE
male elephant	BULL
malefactor	VILLAIN
male falcon	TERCEL, TIERCEL
male garment	SHIRT, TIE,
	TRUNKS, ASCOT, TUXEDO,
	OVERCOAT, JACKET
male horse	STALLION, STUD
Malemute	HUSKY
male or female	SEX
male parent	DAD, SIRE,
	FATHER, POP, DADDY,
	POPPA, PAPA, PA, PAW

male pig	BOAR
male sheep	RAM
male sibling	BROTHER
male singer	TENOR, BASS,
	BARITONE, CROONER
male swan	COB
male swine	BOAR
male title	MR., SIR
male turkey	TOM
male witch	WARLOCK, WIZARD
malevolent	EVIL
malice	SPITE
malicious	SPITEFUL
malicious burning	ARSON
malicious look	LEER
malign	SLANDER, DEFAME
malignant	POISONOUS
mall	PROMENADE
mallard	DUCK
mallet	GAVEL, HAMMER,
	SLEDGE
malodorous	RANK, FOUL
malt beverage	ALE, BEER
malt froth	BARM
malt infusion	WORT
malt liquor	BREW
maltreat	INJURE, ABUSE
maltworm	TOPER
mama	MOTHER, MOM,
	MOMMY, MA
mama hog	SOW
mama's husband	PAPA
mamba	COBRA, SNAKE
Mamie's man	IKE
mammoth	COLOSSAL,
	IMMENSE
man	MALE, MASCULINE
man about town	SOPHISTICATE
manacle	HANDCUFF
manage	RUN, ADMINISTER,
	DIRECT, OPERATE
manageable	DOCILE
management	DIRECTION,
	CONTROL
manage well (2 wds.)	GET ALONG
manager	BOSS, LEADER
manatee (2 wds.)	SEA COW
man child	BOY, SON
Manchurian border river	AMUR
Mandan	SIOUAN, SIOUX
mandrill	BABOON
mane	HAIR
man-eater	CANNIBAL, SHARK
maneuver	TACTIC
man from Amsterdam	
	NETHERLANDER, DUTCHMAN
man from Bangkok	THAI
man from Edinburgh	SCOT

man from Glasgow **SCOT**
man from Stockholm **SWEDE**
man from Tel Aviv **ISRAELI**
mangle **IRON**
mangy **SORDID, SQUALID,**
SHABBY, SEEDY
maniac **LUNATIC, MADMAN**
manicuring tool **SCISSORS,**
BRUSH, CLIPPER,
FILE, BUFFER
manifest **CLEAR, REVEAL**
manifold **DIVERSE, SUNDRY**
manioc **CASSAVA**
man in charge **BOSS, FOREMAN**
man in the street **PEDESTRIAN**
manipulate **JUGGLE, WIELD,**
RIG, HANDLE
manlike device **ROBOT**
manlike robot **ANDROID**
manly **BOLD, BRAVE,**
MASCULINE
man-made **SYNTHETIC,**
ARTIFICIAL
manner **AIR, MIEN**
manner of walking **GAIT**
man next door **NEIGHBOR**
man of action **DOER**
man of God **SAINT, PRIEST,**
RABBI, MINISTER
man of great valor **HERO**
man of great wealth **MIDAS**
man of influence **VIP**
man of law **ATTORNEY**
man of learning **SCHOLAR**
man of letters **AUTHOR**
Man of Sorrows **MESSIAH,**
CHRIST
man of the hour **HERO**
man-of-war **FRIGATE, WARSHIP,**
JELLYFISH
man on the bench **JUDGE**
manor house **MANSION**
Mansard's extension **EAVES**
man's best friend **DOG**
manservant **VALET, BUTLER,**
CHAUFFEUR, HOUSEBOY,
GARDENER, CHEF
man's garment **SUIT,**
SHIRT, PANTS, POLO SHIRT,
SPORTS JACKET, TUXEDO,
OVERCOAT, TIE
man's mate **WOMAN**
man's opera headgear **TOP HAT**
man's purchase (2 wds.) **RAZOR**
BLADE, SHAVE CREAM
man's title **SIR, MR.**
manta **DEVILFISH, RAY**

mantle **CLOAK, CAPE,**
CONCEAL
manual **HANDBOOK**
manual art **CRAFT**
manual digit **THUMB**
manufacture **MAKE, PRODUCE**
manufactured products **WARE**
manuscript (abbr.) **MS,**
MSS (pl.)
manuscript part **PAGE, FOLIO**
many **NUMEROUS**
many times **OFTEN,**
FREQUENTLY
Maori tribe **ATI**
map **PLAN, CHART, ARRANGE**
map abbreviation **ALT, LAT,**
LONG
map book **ATLAS**
maple **TREE**
maple genus **ACER**
map within a map **INSET**
maquillage **MAKEUP,**
COSMETICS
mar **DAMAGE, IMPAIR, INJURE,**
SPOIL
marabou **STORK**
marauder **BRIGAND**
marble **AGATE, TAW, MIB**
Marc Antony's wife **OCTAVIA**
Marcel Marceau's
routine **MIME,**
PANTOMIME
march **DRILL, HIKE, WALK,**
PARADE
marching order (2 wds.) **ABOUT**
FACE, RIGHT FACE,
LEFT FACE, DOUBLE TIME
march into **ENTER**
March King **SOUSA**
Margaret Mitchell hero
(2 wds.) **RHETT BUTLER**
Margaret Mitchell heroine
(2 wds.) **SCARLETT O'HARA**
margarine **OLEO**
margin **EDGE, BORDER, RIM**
marijuana (sl.) **POT, REEFER,**
MARY JANE, JOINT,
GRASS, TEA
marina **BASIN, DOCK**
marina sight **YACHT, BOAT,**
SAILS
marine **NAVAL**
marine crustacean **CRAB,**
CRAYFISH, CRAWDAD
marine fish **HAKE, OPAH, BLUE,**
TUNA
marine growth **SEAWEED**
mariner **SAILOR, SEAMAN**

marionette	DOLL, PUPPET	martini garnish	OLIVE, TWIST
marital	CONJUGAL	martini ingredient	OLIVE, GIN,
maritime	NAVAL, NAUTICAL		VERMOUTH, TWIST,
mark	TRAIT, SCAR, STAIN		ICE, VODKA
markdown	DISCOUNT, SALE	Martinique volcano	PELEE
marked aversion	DISGUST	marvel	MIRACLE, WONDER
marked by denial	NEGATIVE	marvelous	WONDERFUL
market	MART, STORE, SHOP,	mascara wearer	EYELASH
	SELL, VEND	masculine	MALE
market again	RESELL	mash	PULVERIZE, CRUSH
market place	AGORA	masher	WOLF
mark of a wound	SCAR	mask	HIDE, CONCEAL,
mark of disgrace	STIGMA		SCREEN, DOMINO
mark of omission	CARET	masked animal, for	
mark of respect	HONOR	short	COON
mark with spots	MOTTLE	ma's mate	PA
marksman	SHOT	masonry fence	WALL
marksman's goal	TARGET	mass	BULK, WAD
marl	FERTILIZER	Massachusetts cape	ANN, COD
marmalade	JELLY	Massachusetts city	SALEM,
maroon	STRAND, ABANDON,		BOSTON, CAMBRIDGE
	DESERT	Massachusetts island	
marriage	WEDDING, WEDLOCK		NANTUCKET
marriage announcement		massacre	SLAUGHTER
	BANNS	massage	RUB
marriage ceremony	WEDDING,	massive	HUGE, HEAVY
	NUPTIALS	mass of bread	LOAF
marriage notice	BANNS	mass of trees	FOREST
marriage termination	DIVORCE	mass vestment	AMICE
marriage vow (2 wds.)	I DO	mast	POLE, SPAR
married	WED, WEDDED	master	CHIEF, LORD
married woman	WIFE	master in India	SAHIB
married woman's title (Fr.)		master in music	MAESTRO
	MADAME	master of ceremonies	EMCEE
marron	CHESTNUT	master plan	STRATEGY
marrow	MEDULLA, PITH	Master Sawyer	TOM
marrowbone	KNEE	master stroke	COUP
marry	WED	mastery (2 wds.)	UPPER HAND
marry again	REWED	masticate	CHEW
marry a woman	WIVE	mat	RUG
marry in haste	ELOPE	matador's opponent	TORO,
Mars (2 wds.)	RED PLANET		BULL
marsh	BOG, FEN, SWAMP,	match	MATE
	MIRE, MORASS	matched group	SET
marshal's badge	STAR	matched group of china	
Marshal Dillon's nickname		(2 wds.)	TEA SET
	MATT	matched pair	MATES
marsh bird	RAIL, SNIPE, STILT	matchless	PEERLESS
marsh crocodile	GOA	mate	COMRADE, SPOUSE,
marsh elder	IVA		HUSBAND, WIFE,
marsh gas	METHANE		COMPANION
marshy	BOGGY, WET	material for making molds	
marshy hollow part	SWALE	(3 wds.)	PLASTER OF PARIS
marsupial	KOALA, KANGAROO	maternity bird	STORK
mart	MARKET, EMPORIUM	mate's kin	IN-LAW
marten	WEASEL	mathematics	ARITHMETIC
martenlike mammal	SABLE	math exercise	PROBLEM
martial	MILITARY	math term	SINE, COSINE

matriculate **ENROLL**
matrimonial **CONJUGAL, MARITAL**
matter **SUBSTANCE**
mature **AGE, RIPE, RIPEN**
mature person **ADULT**
maturing agent **AGER**
maudlin **EMOTIONAL, MUSHY**
mausoleum **TOMB, CRYPT**
mauve **LILAC, PURPLE**
maw **CRAW, CROP**
maw's husband **PAW**
maxilla and mandible **JAWS**
maxim **ADAGE, MOTTO, SAYING, SAW**
maximum **MOST, LIMIT**
maybe **PERHAPS, POSSIBLY, PERCHANCE**
Mayday signal **SOS**
mayhem **DESTRUCTION, VIOLENCE**
May 30th **MEMORIAL DAY,**
(2 wds.) **DECORATION DAY**
maze **TANGLE, CONFUSION**
maze of the Minotaur **LABYRINTH**
mazzard **CHERRY**
McGuffey opus **READER**
McIntosh **APPLE**
McLuhan's field **TV, MEDIA**
McNally's partner **RAND**
m.c. Mack **TED**
m.c. Sullivan **ED**
mead **DRINK, BREW**
meadow **LEA**
meadow mouse **VOLE**
meadow saffron **COLCHIUM**
meager **POOR, SCANT, SCANTY**
meal **DINNER, LUNCH, SNACK, SUPPER, TEA, REPAST, BREAKFAST**
meal fragment **ORT**
mealtime prayer **GRACE**
mealy **FRIABLE**
mean **INTEND, CRUEL, NASTY, AVERAGE**
meander **ROAM, WANDER**
mean dog **BITER**
meaning **IMPORT, SENSE, INTENT**
meaningful **SIGNIFICANT**
meaningless **EMPTY**
meaningless ritual
(2 wds.) **MUMBO JUMBO**
meanness **SPITE**
mean proportion **AVERAGE**
means **RESOURCE, WEALTH**

means of entry **ACCESS, DOOR, GATE, ENTRY**
means of escape **LOOPHOLE**
meantime **INTERIM**
measles **RUBELLA**
measly **SKIMPY**
measure **METE**
measured **UNIFORM**
measured duration **TIME**
measure of distance **MILE**
measure of heat **CALORIE, THERM**
measure of land **ACRE, ARE, LOT, PLOT**
measure of length **FOOT, ROD, METER, YARD, INCH, MILE**
measure of paper **REAM**
measure of time **HOUR, MINUTE, SECOND, DAY, WEEK, MONTH, YEAR**
measure of type **EN, EM, POINT**
measure of weight **POUND, OUNCE**
measure of wood **CORD**
measure out **ALLOT**
measure swords **DUEL**
measurer **RULER, GAUGE, SURVEYOR**
measuring strip **TAPE**
meat **FLESH, PORK, BEEF, HAM, LAMB**
meat cut **RASHER, LOIN**
meat dish **HASH, STEW**
meat jelly **ASPIC**
meat pastry **RISSOLE**
meat sauce **GRAVY**
meaty **SUBSTANTIAL**
mechanical **AUTOMATIC, REFLEX**
mechanical man **ROBOT**
mechanics of
motion **DYNAMICS**
mechanism **APPARATUS, TOOL**
medal **BADGE, PLAQUE**
meddler **BUSYBODY**
meddle (with) **TAMPER**
Mede **ARYAN**
mediate **INTERCEDE**
medical fluid **SERUM**
medical patient **CASE**
medical picture **X RAY**
medical suffix **IATRIC, OMA**
medicated lozenge **PASTILLE**
medicinal plant **ALOE, HERB, SENNA**
medicinal remedy **ANTIDOTE**
medicinal root **IPECAC**

medicinal unit	DOSE	meloid	BEETLE
medicine	DRUG	melon	CANTALOUPE, PEPO,
medicine bottle	VIAL		HONEYDEW
medicine man	SHAMAN	melon-like fruit	GOURD
medicine pellet	PILL	melon pear	PEPINO
medicine portion	DOSE	melt	DISSOLVE, THAW,
medico	PHYSICIAN, SURGEON		DEFROST
medieval dance refrain	RONDO	melt away	DWINDLE
medieval instrument	LUTE	melt down, as lard	RENDER
medieval Jewish automaton		melted rock	LAVA
	GOLEM	melting pot	CRUCIBLE
medieval poem	LAI, LAY,	melt ore	SMELT
	BALLAD, ROMANCE	melt together	FUSE
medieval slave	SERF, ESNE	member	LIMB, ELEMENT
medieval story	SAGA, ROMANCE	member of an Indian sect	
medieval viol	REBEC		PARSI, PARSEE
mediocre	SO-SO	member of boys' group	SCOUT
meditate	PONDER, BROOD,	member of crew	HAND
	THINK	member of Parliament	
Mediterranean	SEA		LORD, MP
Mediterranean area	RIVIERA	member of state	CITIZEN
Mediterranean island	CRETE,	member of the clergy	CLERIC,
	CYPRUS, MALTA		MINISTER, PRIEST, RABBI
Mediterranean sailing vessel		member of the firm	PARTNER
	SETTEE	member of a work crew	MAN
Mediterranean tree	CAROB	members of the fourth	
Mediterranean wind	SOLANO,	estate	PRESS, REPORTER
	MISTRAL	membership charge	DUES
medium	MIDDLE, HALF	membrane	TELA
medium (pl.)	MEDIA	membranous pouch	CYST
medium of exchange		memento	RELIC, REMINDER,
	CURRENCY		SOUVENIR
medley	OLIO	memento case	LOCKET,
medulla	MARROW		RELIQUARY
meek	HUMBLE	memo	NOTE
meerschaum	PIPE	memoir	RECORD, REPORT
meet	ENCOUNTER, SIT,	memorable	NOTABLE
	CONVENE, ASSEMBLE,	memorial mound	CAIRN
	CONFRONT	memory	RECOLLECTION
meet by chance (2 wds.)	COME	memory aid	MNEMONIC
	ACROSS, RUN INTO	menace	THREATEN
meeting	SESSION	menage	HOUSEHOLD
meeting program	AGENDA	menagerie	ZOO
mel	HONEY	mend	REPAIR, DARN, FIX,
melancholy	LOW, SAD, BLUE,		KNIT, HEAL
	SOMBER	mendacity	LYING, DECEIT
Melanesian native	FIJI	mender of pots	TINKER
melange	MEDLEY, MIXTURE	mendicant	BEGGAR
melee	RIOT	menial	SERVILE
mellow	RIPE, AGE, RIPEN	men in blue	POLICE
melodic	ARIOSE	Mennonite sect	AMISH
melodic sounds	MUSIC,	men's party	STAG, SMOKER
	HARMONY	mental	RATIONAL
melodious	MUSICAL,	mental acumen	WIT
	AGREEABLE	mental anguish	DOLOR
melodist	COMPOSER	mental disposition	TEMPER,
melody	ARIA, SONG, TUNE,		MOOD
	AIR, REFRAIN	mentality	ACUMEN

mentally sound **SANE**
mental position (3 wds.) **POINT OF VIEW**
mental slip **LAPSE**
mental strain **TENSION**
mention **CITE, NAME**
mentor **TEACHER**
menu (3 wds.) **BILL OF FARE**
menu item **PRIME RIBS, STEAK, CHOPS, SALAD, VEGETABLE, DESSERT, ROAST BEEF, ENTREE**
Mephistopheles **SATAN, DEVIL**
mephitic **POISONOUS, FOUL**
mercantile **COMMERCIAL**
mercenary **HIRELING**
merchandise **GOODS, WARES**
merchant **DEALER, TRADER, SELLER, VENDOR**
merciful **CLEMENT**
merciless **STONY**
Mercury's winged cap **PETASOS**
mercy **LENIENCY, PITY**
mere **ONLY, SIMPLE**
mere handful **WISP**
merely **JUST, ONLY**
merest bit **IOTA**
mere taste **SIP, BIT**
meretricious **VULGAR, GAUDY, TAWDRY**
merganser **SMEW, SHELDRAKE**
merge **BLEND, MELD, COALESCE, COMBINE**
meridian **MIDDAY, NOON**
merino **SHEEP, WOOL**
merit **DESERVE, EARN, WORTH, VALUE**
meritorious **WORTHY**
mermaid **SIREN**
mero **GROUPER, GUASA**
merriment **GAIETY, GLEE**
merry **GAY, HILARIOUS**
merry adventure **LARK, SPREE**
merry andrew **CLOWN, ZANY, BUFFOON**
merry-go-round **CAROUSEL**
merrymaking **REVEL**
merry prank **CAPER**
merry tune **LILT**
mesa **TABLELAND, PLATEAU**
mescal cactus of Mexico **PEYOTE**
mesh **NET, NETWORK**
mess **HODGEPODGE**
message **COMMUNICATION, TELEGRAM, NOTE**
message boy **PAGE**
messenger **ENVOY, HERALD**

messenger of the gods **HERMES**
messiah **SAVIOR**
messy **UNTIDY**
Met solo **ARIA**
metal **LEAD, TIN, ZINC, STEEL, IRON**
metal bar **INGOT**
metal-bearing lode **VEIN**
metal bolt **RIVET**
metal cement **SOLDER**
metal container **CAN, TIN**
metal cord **WIRE**
metal deposit **LODE**
metal disc **PATEN, MEDAL**
metal dross **SLAG**
metal fastener **NAIL, PIN, RIVET, SNAP, BOLT, SCREW**
metal globe **POME**
metallic paper **FOIL**
metallic fabric **LAME**
metallic sound **CLING, CLANK, PING, BANG**
metallic vein **LODE**
metal tag on shoelace **AGLET**
metal thread **WIRE**
metal tube **PIPE**
metal worker **TINNER, TINKER**
metal workshop **SMITHY, FORGE**
metamorphosis **CHANGE**
metaphor **TROPE**
metaphysical entity **ENTIUM, (pl.) ENTIA**
metatarsus **FOOT**
mete **ALLOT, APPORTION, DOLE, DISTRIBUTE**
meteorological device **SONDE**
meter **RHYTHM**
methane hydrocarbon **PARAFFIN**
method **MODE, SYSTEM, WAY**
method of payment (2 wds.) **INSTALLMENT PLAN**
methyl alcohol (2 wds.) **WOOD SPIRIT**
meticulous **FASTIDIOUS, PRECISE**
metier **LINE, JOB**
metrical **RHYTHMIC**
metrical stress **ICTUS**
metric foot **IAMB**
metric land measure **ARE**
metric measure **STERE**
metric quart **LITER**
metric unit **GRAM, STERE, LITER, DECARE, KILO, METER, ARE**
metric weight **KILO, GRAM**

mettle	**SPIRIT, STAMINA**	mild	**GENTLE, TAME, TENDER,**
Mexican blanket	**SERAPE**		**KIND, PLEASANT, NICE,**
Mexican coin	**PESO**		**FAIR, CLÉMENT**
Mexican corn cake	**TORTILLA**	mild cheese	**GOUDA, BRIE**
Mexican cottonwood	**ALAMO**	mildew	**MOLD**
Mexican dance	**HAT**	mild expletive	**DANG, DRAT,**
Mexican dish	**TAMALE**		**HECK, GAD, EGAD,**
Mexican dollar	**PESO**		**PFUI, DARN,**
Mexican garment	**SERAPE,**	mild oath	**EGAD**
	PONCHO	mild oath in Britain	**GOR, GAD**
Mexican gentleman	**SENOR**	mild pinch	**TWEAK**
Mexican Indian	**AZTEC, YAQUI**	militant	**HOSTILE**
Mexican laborer	**PEON**	military	**MARTIAL**
Mexican lake	**CHAPALA**	military acronym	**AWOL**
Mexican peninsula	**YUCATAN**	military aircraft	**CHOPPER,**
Mexican rubber tree	**ULE**		**PURSUIT PLANE, BOMBER,**
Mexican sandwich	**TACO**		**FIGHTER PLANE**
Mexican's hat	**SOMBRERO**	military assistant	**AIDE**
Mexican shrub	**CHIA**	military automobile	**JEEP**
Michaelmas daisy	**ASTER**	military award	**MEDAL**
Michelangelo masterpiece		military base	**FORT, POST,**
	PIETA,		**CAMP**
	DAVID, MOSES	military cap	**KEPI**
Michigan metropolis	**DETROIT,**	military depot	**BASE**
	LANSING, ANN ARBOR	military device	**SONAR, RADAR**
Mickey Mouse inventor	**DISNEY**	military ditch	**TRENCH**
microcosm	**UNIVERSE**	military division	**PLATOON,**
microorganism	**BACTERIUM,**		**SQUAD**
	GERM, VIRUS	military dress hat	**SHAKO**
microscopic	**MINUTE, TINY**	military exercise	**DRILL,**
microscopic organism	**AMOEBA**		**PARADE, BIVOUAC**
microwave amplifier	**MASER**	military expedition to Holy	
mid	**CENTRAL**	Land	**CRUSADE**
midday	**NOON**	military force	**LEGION, TROOP**
midday nap	**SIESTA**	military fugitive	**AWOL**
midday refreshment	**LUNCH**	military greeting	**SALUTE**
middle	**CENTER, MID**	military guard	**SENTRY**
Middle Eastern nation	**ISRAEL,**	military horsemen	**CAVALRY**
	SYRIA, JORDAN,	military inspection	**REVIEW,**
	EGYPT, LEBANON		**PARADE**
middle (law)	**MESNE**	military instrument	**BUGLE**
Midianite king	**REBA**	military offense	**DESERTION**
midshipman	**CADET**	military officer	**CAPTAIN,**
midst	**AMONG**		**COLONEL, SERGEANT,**
midway attraction	**RIDE, SHOW,**		**CORPORAL, LIEUTENANT,**
	SIDESHOW		**MAJOR, GENERAL**
midwestern college	**ANTIOCH,**	military operation	**SIEGE, RAID**
	OBERLIN, KENT, WAYNE,	military orchestra	**BAND**
	NOTRE DAME	military review	**PARADE**
mien	**BEARING**	military salute	**SALVO**
miff	**OFFEND**	military storehouse	**ETAPE**
might	**POWER, MAY**	military student	**CADET**
mighty	**POTENT, STRONG**	military supplies and	
mighty cataract	**NIAGARA**	weapons	**ORDNANCE**
mighty mite	**ATOM**	military truck	**CAMION**
mignon	**DELICATE**	military unit	**REGIMENT, TROOP**
migraine	**HEADACHE**	milk	**DRAIN**
migration	**TREK**	milk and egg dish	**CUSTARD**

milk cattle farm	**DAIRY**	Minotaur's owner	**MINOS**
milk giver	**COW**	minstrel	**BARD**
milk glass	**OPALINE**	minstrel's instrument	**LUTE**
milkman's daily course	**ROUTE**	minstrel's song	**LAY, LAMENT**
milky gem	**OPAL**	mint	**COIN, CANDY, PLANT,**
milquetoast	**SISSY, CASPER**		**HERB, GARNISH**
Milwaukee brew	**BEER**	mint camphor	**MENTHOL**
mime	**CLOWN, COPY, APE**	minuet	**DANCE**
mimeo master	**STENCIL**	minus	**LESS**
mimic	**APE, COPY, IMITATE**	minuscule	**PETTY, TINY**
minaret	**TOWER**	minute	**SMALL, TINY**
mince	**CHOP, DICE**	minute difference	**SHADE**
minced dish	**HASH**	minute groove	**STRIA**
minced oath	**EGAD**	minute insect	**GNAT**
mincing	**DAINTY**	minute opening	**PORE**
mind	**CARE, TEND, INTELLECT,**	minute particle	**ATOM, IOTA**
	OBEY, BRAIN	minutes	**RECORD, PROCEEDING**
mindful	**AWARE**	minutes of court	**REGISTER,**
mind's eye	**IMAGINATION**		**RECORD, ACTA**
mine	**PIT, DIG**	minutia	**DETAIL**
mine car	**TRAM**	minyan	**QUORUM, TEN**
mined fuel	**COKE**	miracle	**MARVEL, WONDER**
mine entrance	**ADIT**	mirage	**CHIMERA**
mine explosion hole	**CRATER**	mire	**MUD**
mine level	**STOPE**	mirror	**GLASS, REFLECT**
mine passage	**DRIFT, ADIT,**	mirth	**GAIETY, GLEE**
	SHAFT	mirthful	**MERRY**
mine product	**ORE, COAL,**	misanthrope	**CYNIC**
	STONES, MINERAL	misbehave (2 wds.)	**ACT UP,**
mineral	**ORE**		**CUT UP**
mineral deposit	**LODE**	misbehaving (3 wds.)	
mineral jelly	**PETROLATUM**		**OUT OF LINE**
mineral pitch	**ASPHALT**	miscalculate	**ERR**
mineral spring	**SPA**	miscellaneous	**VARIOUS**
mineral tar	**MALTHA**	miscellaneous items	**SUNDRIES**
mine shaft	**ADIT, INCLINE,**	miscellany	**OLLA, MIXTURE,**
	TUNNEL		**OLIO**
mingle	**MIX**	mischievous	**NAUGHTY**
miniature	**TINY**	mischievous child	**IMP**
minim	**SMALLEST**	mischievous person	**RASCAL**
minimal	**LEAST**	mischievous sprite	**ELF**
minimize	**BELITTLE**	miscreant	**VILLAIN, WRETCH**
minimum	**LEAST**	misdeed	**CRIME**
minister	**HELP, ATTEND**	misdemeanor	**CRIME**
minister's assistant	**DEACON**	misdo	**ERR, BLUNDER**
minister's home	**MANSE,**	miser	**SCROOGE**
	RECTORY, PARSONAGE	miserable	**UNHAPPY**
minister's speech	**SERMON,**	miserly	**STINGY**
	HOMILY	misery	**SORROW**
ministration	**SERVICE**	misfortune	**ILL, EVIL, WOE**
ministry	**CLERGY**	mishandle	**ABUSE**
minium	**VERMILION**	mishap	**ACCIDENT**
mink	**FUR**	misinterpret	**MISREAD**
minklike animal	**WEASEL,**	mislay	**LOSE, MISPLACE**
	STOAT	mislead	**DECEIVE, DELUDE**
minor	**LESSER, INFERIOR**	misplace	**LOSE, MISLAY**
minority	**FACTION**	misrepresent	**DISTORT, BELIE**
minor river	**BAYOU**		

miss GIRL, LASS, MAID, MAIDEN
misshapen DEFORMED
missile DART, ARROW, ICBM, NIKE
missing LOST
missing link APEMAN, PITHECANTHROPUS, JAVA-MAN
mission ERRAND, DELEGATION, CHURCH
Mississippi resort BILOXI
Mississippi River sight LEVEE
missive LETTER, EPISTLE
Miss Kett of the comics ETTA
Miss O'Hara SCARLETT
Miss Oyl OLIVE
misstep ERROR, TRIP
mist FOG, HAZE
mistake ERR, ERROR, BLUNDER, BONER, GOOF
mistaken WRONG
mistake in printing ERRATUM
mister (Sp.) SENOR
mistreat ABUSE
mistress DAME
mistrust DOUBT
misty FOGGY, DIM
misuse ABUSE
Mitch Miller's instrument OBOE
Mitchell novel (4 wds.) GONE WITH THE WIND
mite TICK
mitigate LESSEN
mix BLEND, STIR, MINGLE
mixed breed MONGREL
mixed greens SALAD
mixed type PI
mixed with AMONG
mix playing cards SHUFFLE
mixture MEDLEY, OLIO, HODGEPODGE, POTPOURRI, BLEND
mixture of snow and rain SLEET
mizzen MAST
moa BIRD, OSTRICH
moa genus APTERYX
moan GROAN
moat TRENCH, DITCH
mob CROWD, RABBLE, HORDE, GANG
mobile MOVABLE
mobile home TRAILER, CAMPER
mocassin PAC, SHOE
mock DERIDE, RIDICULE, APE, MIMIC
mocker nut HICKORY
mockery FARCE

mock sun PARHELION
mock-up MODEL, LAYOUT
mode CUSTOM, MANNER, FASHION, STYLE
model PATTERN, SAMPLE, EXAMPLE
model of perfection PARAGON
model of solar system ORRERY
mode of speech PARLANCE
mode of standing POSTURE
moderate LIMITED, FAIR
moderately cold COOL
moderation RESTRAINT
moderator ARBITER
modern NEW
modern appliance WASHER, DRYER
modern epiclike narrative SAGA
modern fabric NYLON, RAYON, ARNEL, ORLON, DACRON
modernize RENOVATE
modern painter DALI, STELLA, WARHOL, PICASSO, MIRO
modern philosophy EXISTENTIALISM
modern phonograph STEREO
modest SHY
modesty HUMILITY
mod fashion MINISKIRT, MIDISKIRT, MAXICOAT
modify AMEND, ALTER, CHANGE, DEFINE
modish CHIC, STYLISH
modiste DRESSMAKER, COUTURIERE
mod paintings (2 wds.) POP ART
modulation TONE
Mohammedan prince AMIR, EMIR, AMEER
Mohammedan religion ISLAM
Mohammed's birthplace MECCA
Mohammed's daughter FATIMA
Mohammed's flight HEGIRA
Mohammed's son ALI
moist DAMP, WET
molar TOOTH
molasses SIRUP, SYRUP
molasses (Brit.) TREACLE
mold FORM, SHAPE
moldy MUSTY
moleskin color TAUPE
molest INJURE, DISTURB
mollify ASSUAGE
mollusk CLAM, OYSTER
molt SHED
molten rock LAVA

moment	IMPORT, MINUTE, TRICE, SECOND
mom or dad	PARENT
mom's mate	DAD
monastery	PRIORY, CONVENT, ABBEY
monastery head	ABBOT
monastery occupant	MONK, FRA
monastery room	CELL
monastic	ASCETIC
monastic officer	PRIOR, ABBOT
monastic title	DOM
monetary	FINANCIAL
monetary penalty	FINE
monetary unit	DOLLAR
monetary unit of Japan	YEN, SEN
money	CURRENCY
money factory	MINT
money handler	CASHIER
money holder	WALLET, BANK, PURSE
money in India	RUPEE
money in Rome	LIRA
money on hand	CASH
money opening	SLOT
money saving campaign (2 wds.)	ECONOMY DRIVE
money (sl.)	GREEN, MOOLAH, GELT, BREAD
money vault	SAFE
Mongol conqueror	TAMERLANE
Mongolian monk	LAMA
mongrel dog	CUR, MUTT
monk	FRIAR
monkey	APE
monkey's treat	BANANA
monk's hood	ATIS, COWL
monk's title	FRA
monocle	EYEGLASS, LENS
monogram	INITIAL, CIPHER
monolith	MENHIR, PILLAR
monomania	LUNACY, DELIRIUM
monopoly	GAME
monotonous	HUMDRUM, TEDIOUS
monotonous song	CHANT
monotony	TEDIUM
monster	GIANT, OGRE, TROLL
monstrous	ATROCIOUS, VAST
Montana city	BUTTE, MISSOULA
Montana river	TETON
month	JANUARY, FEBRUARY, MARCH, APRIL, MAY, JUNE, JULY, AUGUST, SEPTEMBER OCTOBER, NOVEMBER, DECEMBER
month (Fr.)	JANVIER, FEVRIER, MARS, AVRIL, MAI, JUIN, JUILLET, AOUT, SEPTEMBRE, OCTOBRE, NOVEMBRE, DECEMBRE
month (Sp.)	ENERO, FEBRERO, MARZO, ABRIL, MAYO, JUNIO, JULIO, AGOSTO, SEPTIEMBRE, OCTUBRE, NOVIEMBRE, DICIEMBRE
monument	TOMBSTONE
moo	LOW
mood	TEMPER
moody	CAPRICIOUS
moody person	MOPER
moon goddess	LUNA, DIANA, ARTEMIS
moor	ANCHOR, HEATH
mooring post	BITT
mop	SWAB
mope	SULK, BROOD
moppet	BABY, DOLL
moral	ETHICAL
morale	SPIRIT
morale-raising speech (2 wds.)	PEP TALK
moralist	PRIG
morals	ETHICS
moral transgression	SIN
morass	SWAMP, BOG, FEN, MIRE
moray	EEL
morbid	UNHEALTHY
morbid sound	RALE
mordant	CAUSTIC
more	ADDITIONAL, GREATER
more agreeable	NICER
more ancient	OLDER
more arid	DRIER
more austere	STERNER
more banal	TRITER
more cautious	WARIER
more cerulean	BLUER
more clever	SMARTER
more competent	ABLER
more crafty	FOXIER, SLYER
more cunning	SLYER
more delicate	FINER
more difficult	HARDER
more disabled	LAMER
more distant	FARTHER, REMOTER
more distended	FULLER
more docile	TAMER
more domesticated	TAMER
more elegant	FINER, SMARTER
more expensive	DEARER
more famous	GREATER

more fastidious	NEATER, TIDIER, DAINTIER, NICER	more up-to-date	NEWER
		more wary	CAGIER
		more willingly	RATHER
more foxy	SLYER, SLIER	moribund	DYING
more frigid	ICIER, COOLER, COLDER	morion	HELMET
		Mormon of secret sect	DANITE
more gentle	TAMER	Mormon State	UTAH
more inclement	RAWER, ROUGHER	morning	DAWN
		morning (poetic)	MORN
more infrequent	RARER	morning after	HANGOVER
more insolent	BRASHER, SASSIER	morning coat	CUTAWAY
		morning glory genus	IPOMOEA
more intelligent	SMARTER, BRIGHTER	morning moisture	DEW
		morning performance	MATINEE
more learned	WISER	morning prayer	MATINS
more likely	APTER	morning reception	LEVEE
morello	CHERRY	morning's light	DAWN
more mature	OLDER, RIPER	morning song	ALBA
more meager	SCANTIER	morning star	MARS, VENUS
more mellow	RIPER	Moroccan capital	RABAT
more miserly	MEANER	Moroccan native	BERBER
more modern	NEWER	Moroccan ruler	SULTAN
more optimistic	ROSIER, BRIGHTER	Moroccan soldier	ASKAR
		moro chief	DATO
more or less	SOME	morón	IMBECILE
more orderly	NEATER, TIDIER	morose	GLUM
moreover	AND, BESIDES	morphine derivative	HEROIN
more painful	SORER	morro	HILL
more pallid	PALER	morsel	BIT, BITE, ORT
more precious	DEARER	morsel left at meal	ORT
more precipitous	STEEPER	mortal	HUMAN, PERSON, FATAL
more profound	DEEPER		
more rapid	FASTER	mortar	BOWL, PUTTY
more rational	SANER	mortar mixer	RAB
more recent	LATTER	mortar tray	HOD
more refined	NICER	mortgage	LIEN, LOAN
mores	CUSTOMS	mortification	CHAGRIN
more sagacious	WISER	mosaic piece	INSET, TILE
more scarce	RARER	moselle (2 wds.)	WHITE WINE
more secure	SAFER	Moses' brother	AARON
more seedy	SHABBIER	Moslem bible	KORAN
more severe	STERNER	Moslem commander	AGA
more slippery	ICIER, SLICKER	Moslem countries	ISLAM
more so	YEA	Moslem deity	ALLAH
more sour	TARTER	Moslem headgear	FEZ, TURBAN
more spacious	ROOMIER, LARGER	Moslem judge	CADI
		Moslem lawyer	MUFTI
more strange	ODDER	Moslem nymph	HOURI
more suitable	BETTER	Moslem officer	AGA
more tardy	LATER	Moslem priest	IMAM
more tender	SORER	Moslem prince	AMIR, EMIR, AMEER
more than	ABOVE, OVER		
more than enough	AMPLE	Moslem title	AGA
more than one	MANY, PLURAL	mosquito-eating bird	MARTIN
more tidy	NEATER	mosquito genus	AEDES
more uncanny	EERIER	mosquito larva	WIGGLER
more uncivil	RUDER	most attractive	PRETTIEST, CUTEST
more uncommon	RARER		

most beloved	**DEAREST**
most brazen (sl.)	**NERVIEST**
most courageous	**GAMEST,**
	BRAVEST
most desirable	**BEST**
most difficult	**HARDEST**
most distant planet	**PLUTO**
most distant point in	
an orbit	**APOGEE**
most excellent	**BEST**
most ill-boding	**DIREST**
most independent	**FREEST**
most intelligent	**SMARTEST**
mostly	**CHIEFLY, USUALLY**
most modern	**NEWEST**
most outstanding	**BEST**
most pallid	**PALEST**
most peculiar	**ODDEST**
most pleasant	**NICEST**
most precious	**DEAREST**
most precipitous	**STEEPEST**
most profound	**DEEPEST**
most rapid	**FASTEST**
most recent	**LATEST**
most ridiculous	**SILLIEST**
most sagacious	**WISEST**
most savory	**TASTIEST**
most sensible	**SANEST**
most sensitive	**SOREST**
most spirited	**LIVELIEST**
most tardy	**LATEST**
most terrible	**DIREST**
most unique	**ODDEST**
most untouched	**PUREST**
most unusual	**ODDEST, RAREST**
most wonderful	**BEST**
mot	**RETORT, SAYING**
mote	**PARTICLE**
motel feature	**POOL**
motet	**ANTHEM**
moth-eaten	**OLD, WORN**
mother	**MA, MOM, MAW, MAMA,**
	MOMMY, MOMMA, DAM,
	MADONNA
mother (Lat.)	**MATER**
mother (Sp.)	**MADRE**
mother and father	**PARENTS**
Mother Carey's chicken	**PETREL**
Mother Carey's goose	**FULMAR**
Mother Goose author	**PERRAULT**
Mother Hubbard	**GOWN**
mother of Castor and Pollux	
	LEDA
mother of Hiawatha	**NOKOMIS**
mother of mankind	**EVE**
mother-of-pearl	**NACRE**
mother of Peer Gynt	**ASE**
mother of Perseus	**DANAE**

mother of Romulus	
and Remus	**ILIA**
mother or father	**PARENT**
mother sheep	**EWE**
mother's sister	**AUNT**
mother turned to stone	**NIOBE**
motherly	**MATERNAL**
moth larva	**CATERPILLAR**
motif	**THEME**
motion	**GESTURE**
motionless	**INERT, STILL**
motion picture	**FILM**
motion picture light	**KLIEG**
motion picture machine	
	PROJECTOR
motivate	**INSPIRE**
motive	**REASON**
motive force	**POWER**
motley	**DIVERSE, MIXED**
motor	**ENGINE, TURBINE**
motorcar	**AUTOMOBILE**
motor coach	**BUS**
motor control	**STARTER**
motor court	**MOTEL**
motorist	**DRIVER**
motorist's nightmare (2 wds.)	
	TRAFFIC JAM
motorist's problem (2 wds.)	
	PARKING SPACE
motorist's tool	**JACK, WRENCH**
motorless airplane	**GLIDER**
motorman	**CONDUCTOR**
mottled horse	**PINTO**
mottled marking	**DAPPLE**
mottled soap	**CASTILE**
motto	**ADAGE, MAXIM, SAW**
mould	**MATRIX**
mound	**HEAP, TEE**
mount	**ASCEND, CLIMB**
mountain at earth's center	
	MERU
mountain cat	**BOBCAT,**
	COUGAR, PUMA
mountain crest	**ARETE, RIDGE**
mountain home	**CHALET**
mountain in Thessaly	**OSSA**
mountain lake	**TARN**
mountain lion	**PUMA**
mountain near ancient	
Troy	**IDA**
mountain nymph	**OREAD**
mountain pass	**COL, GAP**
mountain pass in India	**GHAT,**
	GHAUT
mountain peak	**TOR**
mountain pheasant	**GROUSE**
mountain pool	**TARN**
mountain ridge	**ARETE, CREST**

Mountain State **WEST VIRGINIA**
mountain system in Europe **ALPS**
mountain system in South America **ANDES**
mountaintop **PEAK**
mourn **LAMENT, GRIEVE**
mournful **DOLEFUL**
mournful cry **ALAS, ALACK, WOE IS ME**
mournful poem **ELEGY, LAMENT**
mournful song **DIRGE**
mournful sound **KNELL, MOAN, KEEN**
mourning **SORROW, GRIEF**
mouse family **RODENT**
mouser **CAT**
mouth **SPEAK, SAY**
mouthful **BITE, MORSEL, SIP**
mouth organ **HARMONICA**
mouth part **LIP, PALATE, TONGUE, GUM, TOOTH**
movable **MOBILE**
movable cover **LID, AWNING**
movable door part **HINGE**
move **STIR, BUDGE**
move along **MOSEY**
move apart **SEPARATE**
move, as Fido's tail **WAG**
move aside (2 wds.) **MAKE WAY**
move aside suddenly **DODGE**
move, as the wind **BLOW**
move back **RECEDE, RETREAT**
move back and forth **SHUTTLE**
move before the wind **SCUD, SAIL**
move forward **ADVANCE**
move furtively **LURK, SLINK, SNEAK, TIPTOE, CREEP, STEAL, SIDLE**
move in water **SWIM, FLOAT**
move like a crab **SIDLE**
move lazily **LOLL**
movement **MOTION**
movement of the hands **GESTURE**
move out **VACATE**
move over water **SAIL, FLOAT**
move quickly **RUN, SCUD, HIE, SPEED, HASTEN, BUSTLE, HUSTLE, RACE**
mover's truck **VAN**
move rhythmically **DANCE**
move sideways **SIDLE**
move slightly **BUDGE, STIR**
move slowly **EDGE, INCH**
move smoothly **SLIDE, GLIDE**
move spasmodically **TWITCH**

move stealthily **SLINK**
move suddenly **DART**
move swiftly **SCUD, DART**
move with an easy gait **LOPE, AMBLE, STROLL**
move with difficulty **WADE**
movie house **THEATRE, CINEMA**
movie queen **STAR**
movie version of a novel **ADAPTATION**
movie V.I.P. **DIRECTOR, STAR, ACTOR, PRODUCER, WRITER**
moving **ASTIR, ACTIVE**
moving air **WIND**
moving force **AGENT**
moving mechanical part **ROTOR**
moving stairway **ESCALATOR**
Mr. Bumpstead **DAGWOOD**
Mr. Claus **SANTA**
Mr. Heep **URIAH**
Mr. Kettle **PA**
Mr. Spade **SAM**
Mr. Van Winkle **RIP**
Mrs. Charles Chaplin **OONA**
Mrs. Dick Tracy **TESS**
Mrs. Eddie Cantor **IDA**
Mrs. Eisenhower **MAMIE**
mrs. in Madrid **SRA.**
Mrs. Kettle **MA**
Mrs. Nixon **PAT**
Mrs. Roosevelt **ELEANOR**
Mrs. Roy Rogers (2 wds.) **DALE EVANS**
Mrs. Truman **BESS**
Mrs. Washington **MARTHA**
much **LOTS**
much larger **HUGER**
much loved **DEAR**
much the same **ALIKE**
mucilage **GLUE, ADHESIVE**
muck **MIRE, MUD**
mud **MIRE**
muddle **MESS**
muddy **MURKY, OBSCURE**
mudguard **FENDER**
mud pie **PATTY**
mud puppy **SALAMANDER**
mud volcano **SALSE**
muffin **CRUMPET, POPOVER, SCONE**
muffle **DAMPEN, MUTE, DEADEN**
muffler **SCARF**
mug **CUP**
mugger **HAM**
muggy **HUMID, DAMP**
muir **MOOR**

mukluk	**BOOT**
mulberry cloth	**TAPA**
mulch	**SAWDUST**
mulct	**FINE, AMERCE**
mule	**SLIPPER**
muley	**COW, HORNLESS**
mulish	**STUBBORN**
mull	**PONDER**
muller	**PESTLE**
mullet hawk	**OSPREY**
mulligan	**STEW**
mulligatawny	**SOUP**
multicolored	**ROAN, PIED**
multifold	**MANY**
multiform	**DIVERSE**
multiplication word	**TIMES**
multitude	**HORDE, HOST, MOB**
munch, comic strip style	**CHOMP**
mundane	**WORLDLY**
municipal corporation	**CITY, BOROUGH**
municipality	**CITY**
municipal official	**MAYOR**
munificent	**GENEROUS**
mural painting	**FRESCO**
murder	**KILL, SLAY**
murder mystery character	**SUSPECT**
murky	**OBSCURE, DARK**
murmur	**WHISPER**
murmuring, as a brook	**BABBLING**
murmuring sound	**HUM**
muscle	**TENDON**
muscle cramp	**CRICK**
muscular	**HUSKY**
muscular tone	**TONUS**
muse	**MEDITATE, PONDER**
muse	**CALLIOPE, CLIO, ERATO, EUTERPE, MELPOMENE, POLYHYMNIA, TERPSICHORE, THALIA, URANIA**
musette	**BAGPIPE**
museum keeper	**CURATOR**
museum pieces	**ART, COLLECTION**
mush	**ATOLE**
music	**HARMONY, TUNE**
musical	**TUNEFUL, MELODIC, SHOW**
musical adaptation	**ARRANGEMENT**
musical author	**COMPOSER**
musical bells	**CHIME**
musical character	**CLEF, NOTE**
musical chord	**TRIAD**

musical composition	**ETUDE, CONCERTO, SONATA, SYMPHONY, RONDO**
musical direction	**PIANO, LARGO**
musical disk	**RECORD**
musical drama	**OPERA**
musical ending	**CODA**
musical exercise	**ETUDE, SCALE**
musical feature	**MOTIF**
musical group	**OCTET, TRIO, QUARTET, QUINTET, BAND, ORCHESTRA, COMBO**
musical group of nine	**NONET**
musical half-tone	**MINIM**
musical instrument	**FLUTE, PIPE ORGAN, BASS DRUM, FIFE, TUBA, PIANO, ORGAN, DRUM, KETTLE DRUM, TRIANGLE, LUTE, OBOE, VIOLA, VIOLIN, WOODWIND, CORNET, TRUMPET, HORN, TROMBONE, HARP, LYRE, PICCOLO, BASSOON, CELLO, GUITAR, BANJO, CLARINET, SAXOPHONE, TIMPANI, BASS**
musical interval	**SEMITONE, REST**
musical measured beat	**PULSE**
musical medley	**OLIO**
musical movement	**RONDO**
musical nocturne	**SERENADE**
musical note	**BREVE**
musical organization	**BAND, ORCHESTRA**
musical pair	**DUO, DUET**
musical pause	**REST**
musical performance	**CONCERT**
musical phrase	**LEITMOTIF**
musical pipe	**REED**
musical pitch	**TONE**
musical play	**OPERA**
musical show	**OPERETTA, REVUE**
musical sign	**REST, CLEF, NOTE, STAFF, SHARP, FLAT**
musical sound	**NOTE, TONE**
musical staff	**BAR**
musical study	**ETUDE**
musical syllable	**DO, RE, MI, FA, SO, SOL, LA, TI, TRA**
musical term	**TACET**
musical time marker	**METRONOME**

musical tone	CHORD
musical work	OPUS, OPERA, OPERETTA, SYMPHONY, CONCERTO, SONG
music buff's purchase	STEREO, ALBUM, LP, HIFI, RECORD, SPEAKER
music by two	DUET
music hall	ODEUM
musician	PLAYER
music played under lady's window	SERENADE
music syllable	DO, RE, MI, FA, SO, LA, TI
musk cat	CIVET
musket	GUN
muskmelon	CASABA
Muslim judge	CADI
Muslim mendicant	FAKIR
musty	MOLDY, FUSTY
mute	SILENT, SPEECHLESS, MUFFLE, SILENCE, QUIET
mutilate	MAIM, CRIPPLE, DISABLE
mutineer	REBEL
mutinous	RESTIVE, REBELLIOUS
mutiny	REVOLT
mutter	MUMBLE, GRUMBLE
muttonchop	SIDEBURN, WHISKERS
muzzle	GAG, RESTRAIN
my (Lat.)	MEA
myopic	NEARSIGHTED
myself	ME
mysterious	EERY, SECRET, STRANGE, WEIRD, PUZZLING
mystery	SECRET, ENIGMA
mystery tale	STORY
mystery writers' award	EDGAR
mystic	OBSCURE, OCCULT
mystic art	CABALA, CABBALA, CABBALAH
mystify	BAFFLE
myth	FABLE, LEGEND, TALE, BELIEF
mythical	FABULOUS, LEGENDARY
mythical aviator	ICARUS
mythical bird	ROC
mythical Greek bowman	EROS
mythical hunter	ORION
mythical king of Pylos	NESTOR
mythical one-horned animal	UNICORN

N

nab	GRAB, SEIZE, SNATCH
nabob	VIP, CELEBRITY, BIG WHEEL, BIG SHOT
nag	HORSE, SCOLD, FIND FAULT, CAVIL, CARP, WHINE
nagging pain	ACHE
nail container	KEG
naive	UNSOPHISTICATED, ARTLESS
naked	BARE, NUDE
name	TITLE
name for a cat	TABBY, PUSS, PUFF, KITTY
name for a dog	SPOT, FIDO, ROVER, LASSIE, REX, LADY, KING
nameless	INDEFINABLE, ANONYMOUS, OBSCURE
namely (2 wds.)	TO WIT
name of a thing	NOUN
name the letters of a word	SPELL
name to office	APPOINT
nanny	NURSE
nap	DOZE, SLEEP, SNOOZE, FORTY WINKS
nape	SCRUFF
napery	LINEN
Naples island	CAPRI
nappy leather	SUEDE
narcotic	OPIATE, DRUG
narrate	RELATE, TELL
narration	ACCOUNT
narrative	TALE, YARN, STORY
narrative poem	BALLAD, EPIC
narrator	RACONTEUR
narrow	SLENDER, THIN
narrow aperture	SLOT, SLIT
narrow band	STRIPE, TAPE, RIBBON
narrow board	SLAT, LATH
narrow boat	CANOE
narrow channel	STRAIT
narrow country road	LANE
narrow gauge	RAILROAD
narrow inlet	RIA
narrow-minded	BIGOTED, PREJUDICED
narrow opening	SLIT, SLOT
narrow path	LANE
narrow ravine	GORGE
narrow shelf	LEDGE
narrow squeak (2 wds.)	CLOSE SHAVE

narrow strip of cloth **TAPE, RIBBON**
narrow strip of leather **THONG**
narrow strip of wood **SLAT**
narrow thoroughfare **ALLEY, LANE**
narrow valley (Brit.) **COMBE**
narrow waterway **STRAIT**
narthex **VESTIBULE**
nary **NO, NOT ANY**
nary a soul (2 wds.) **NO ONE**
nasal intonation **TWANG**
NASA's capsule booster **ROCKET**
NASA's realm **SPACE**
nascent **BEGINNING**
nasty **DIRTY, SOILED, UNPLEASANT**
natal **NATIVE**
natator **SWIMMER**
nation **COUNTRY, LAND**
national **COUNTRYWIDE**
national bird **EAGLE**
national monogram **USA**
native **SON**
native-born **INDIGENOUS**
Native Dancer **HORSE**
native lump of gold **NUGGET**
native metal **ORE**
native name for Norway **NORGE**
native of (suffix) **ITE**
native of Attu **ALEUT**
native of Copenhagen **DANE**
native of Dundee **SCOT**
native of Edinburgh **SCOT**
native of Glasgow **SCOT**
native of Istanbul **TURK**
native of Madagascar **HOVA**
native of Muscat **OMANI**
native of Ontario **CANADIAN**
native of Stockholm **SWEDE**
native of Tel Aviv **ISRAELI**
native of the United States **AMERICAN**
native South African village **STAD**
nativity **CHRISTMAS, CRECHE**
natty **NEAT, SPRUCE**
natural **INNATE, INBORN, NATIVE**
natural ability **TALENT, GIFT**
natural color **ECRU, FLESH**
natural condition **NORM**
natural incline **SLOPE**
naturalism **REALISM**
naturalize **ACCUSTOM**
nature **DISPOSITION, ESSENCE**
nature's mythical maiden **NYMPH**

nature spirit **GENIE**
naught **ZERO, NOTHING**
naughty **BAD**
naughty look **LEER**
nausea **QUALM**
nauseate **SICKEN**
nauseous **DISGUSTING**
nautical **MARITIME**
nautical assent **AYE**
nautical command **AVAST, BELAY**
nautical cry **AHOY, AVAST**
nautical line **MARLINE, RATLINE**
nautical measure **KNOT, FATHOM**
nautical mop **SWAB**
nautical pole **SPAR, MAST**
nautical rope **TYE, LINE, SHEET**
nautical speed unit **KNOT**
nautical term **ALEE**
Nautilus **SUBMARINE**
Navaho hut **HOGAN**
naval **MARINE, NAUTICAL**
naval commander in
 ancient Sparta **LYSANDER**
naval force **FLEET**
naval meal **MESS**
naval officer **REAR ADMIRAL, ENSIGN, CAPTAIN**
naval strength (2 wds.) **SEA POWER**
nave **HUB**
navel **ORANGE**
navigate **GUIDE, SAIL**
navigate in air **AVIATE**
navigating instrument **COMPASS**
navigation device **LORAN, SONAR**
navy **BLUE**
navy force **FLEET**
navy line officer **MUSTANG**
navy recruit (sl.) **BOOT**
naysay **DENIAL**
near **APPROACH, AT, CLOSE**
nearest **NEXT**
nearly **ALMOST**
nearly all **MOST**
nearly corresponding **SIMILAR**
near-sighted **MYOPIC**
near-sighted cartoon
 character **MAGOO**
near the beginning **EARLY**
near the horizon **LOW**
neat **TIDY, TRIM**
neatly smart in dress **NATTY**
neb **BILL, BEAK**
Nebraska city **OMAHA**

Nebraska county **OTOE**
Nebraska Indian **PAWNEE**
necessary **ESSENTIAL**
necessitate **COMPEL, OBLIGE**
necessity **MUST**
neck and neck **EVEN, CLOSE**
neck artery **CAROTID**
neckerchief **SCARF**
neck frill **RUFF**
neck hair **MANE**
necklace bauble **BEAD**
neck of water **STRAIT**
neckpiece **SCARF, TIE, CRAVAT, ASCOT, COLLAR**
necktie **CRAVAT, ASCOT**
nectar of the gods **AMBROSIA**
nee **BORN**
need **LACK, REQUIRE, WANT**
neediness **POVERTY**
needing support **DEPENDENT**
needle case **ETUI**
needle (comb. form) **ACU**
needlefish **GAR**
needle hole **EYE**
needle-like body **SPICULE**
needle puncture **PRICK**
needlework **SEWING, DARNING, CREWEL, EMBROIDERY**
needy **IMPOVERISHED, POOR**
nefarious **EVIL, BAD**
negate **DENY**
negation **NOT**
negative **MINUS, NO**
negative answer **NAY, NO**
negative conjunction **NOR**
negative electrode **CATHODE**
negative ion **ANION**
negative particle **NOT**
negative prefix **NON, UN**
negative sign **MINUS**
neglect **OMIT, OVERLOOK, FORGET, SLIGHT, SHIRK**
negligence **CARELESSNESS**
negligent **LAX, REMISS, CARELESS**
negligible **NOMINAL**
negotiate **TREAT**
Negrito of Philippines **ATA, ITA**
neigh **WHINNY**
neighborhood **VICINITY**
neighborhood playing area **SANDLOT, PLAYGROUND**
neighboring **ADJACENT**
neighborly **FRIENDLY, SOCIABLE**
neither masculine nor feminine **NEUTER**
nemesis **FATE**

neophyte **NOVICE, TYRO**
Nepal capital **KATMANDU**
nephew of Daedalus **TALUS**
nepotism **PATRONAGE**
Neptune's scepter **TRIDENT**
Nero's successor **GALBA**
nerve **DARING, CHEEK, COURAGE**
nerve part **AXON**
nervous **EDGY, JITTERY, TENSE**
nervous twitch **TIC**
ness **HEADLAND**
nest **AERIE, EYRIE**
nestle **CUDDLE**
nestling pigeon **SQUAB**
nest of pheasants **NIDE**
net **MESH, SEINE, SNARE, PROFIT**
nether **LOWER, UNDER**
Netherlander **DUTCH**
Netherlands city **HAGUE, UTRECHT**
Netherlands commune **EDE, TIEL**
nethermost **LOWEST**
nether world **HELL**
netlike fabric **LACE**
netlike hat **SNOOD**
nettle **IRK, IRRITATE**
network **MESH, RETE, RESEAU, WEB**
neuter pronoun **IT**
neutral **IMPARTIAL**
Nevada city **RENO, CARSON**
Nevada lake **TAHOE**
neve **FIRN, GLACIER**
never (contr.) **NE'ER**
nevertheless **ALL THE SAME, JUST THE SAME, YET, STILL**
new **MODERN, RECENT, UNUSED**
new (prefix) **NEO**
newborn infant **BABE, BABY**
newborn threesome **TRIPLETS**
newcomer **STRANGER**
New England cape **COD, ANN**
New England native **YANKEE**
New England university **YALE, DARTMOUTH, HARVARD, BOSTON**
newel **STAIRPOST**
New Guinea export **COPRA**
New Hampshire city **DOVER, KEENE**
New Hampshire resort **SUNAPEE**
New Haven tree **ELM**
New Jersey city **NEWARK, TRENTON, ORANGE**

New Jersey river **RARITAN**
New Mexico art colony **TAOS**
New Mexico river **GILA, PECOS**
newly married woman **BRIDE**
news **TIDINGS**
news article **ITEM**
news gatherer **REPORTER**
newspaper **GAZETTE, JOURNAL**
newspaper article **ITEM**
newspaper columnist (2 wds.)
ROVING REPORTER
newspaper edition **DAILY,**
WEEKLY, ISSUE, MORNING,
FIRST, LATE
newspaper executive (abbr.) **ED.**
newspaper files **MORGUE**
newspaper notice (abbr.) **OBIT,**
AD
newspaperman **REPORTER,**
EDITOR, COLUMNIST,
JOURNALIST
news sheet **PAPER, JOURNAL**
newsstand fiction of 1930's
(2 wds.) **DIME NOVEL**
news story beginning **DATELINE**
news story title **HEADLINE**
new star **NOVA**
new suit (2 wds.) **SUNDAY BEST**
newt **EFT**
New Testament book **ACTS,**
COLOSSIANS, CORINTHIANS,
EPHESIANS, GALATIANS,
HEBREWS, JAMES, JOHN,
JUDE, LUKE, MARK,
MATTHEW, PETER, PHILEMON,
PHILIPPIANS, REVELATION,
ROMANS, THESSALONIANS,
TIMOTHY, TITUS
newton ingredient **FIG**
New Year's, Christmas, etc.
HOLIDAYS
New York ball club **METS, JETS,**
YANKEES, GIANTS, KNICKS
New York City stadium **SHEA,**
YANKEE
New York ghetto **HARLEM**
New York Indian **ONEIDA,**
MOHAWK
New York lake **SARANAC**
New York newspaper **TIMES,**
NEWS, POST
New York river **HUDSON, EAST,**
HARLEM
New York State city **ELMIRA,**
OLEAN, UTICA, ALBANY,
BUFFALO, ITHACA
New Zealand aborigine **MAORI**
New Zealand bird **MOA**

New Zealand clan **ATI**
New Zealand parrot **KEA**
New Zealand tree **AKE,**
MAKOMAKO
next **NEAREST, AFTER**
nice **PLEASANT, FINE**
niche **ALCOVE, NOOK**
nick **DENT**
nickel **COIN**
nickname for a
good dancer **TWINKLETOES**
nickname for a Scot **MAC**
nicotinic acid **NIACIN**
Nigerian city **EDE, LAGOS**
Nigerian tribesman **EBOE, IBO**
niggardly **STINGY**
nigh **NEAR, CLOSE**
night before a holiday **EVE**
night bird **OWL**
night clothes **PAJAMAS**
nightclub **CAFÉ**
nightclub solo (2 wds.)
TORCH SONG
nightcrawler **WORM, BAIT**
nightfall **DARK, TWILIGHT, DUSK**
night letter **TELEGRAM**
nightmare **INCUBUS**
nightshade **MOREL**
night twinkler **STAR**
nihil **NOTHING**
nil **NOTHING**
Nile bird **IBIS**
Nile queen, for short **CLEO**
Nile River dam **ASWAN**
Nile River falls **RIPON**
nilgai **ANTELOPE**
nimble **AGILE, SPRY**
nimbus **AURA, HALO**
nine days' devotion **NOVENA**
nine-headed monster **HYDRA**
ninny **FOOL, GOOSE**
nip **BITE, PINCH**
nippy **BITING, BRISK**
niter **SALTPETER**
nitrate **ESTER, SALT**
nitric acid **AQUAFORTIS**
Nixon **REPUBLICAN,**
PRESIDENT, DICK
Nixon's V.P. **AGNEW**
no (colloq.) **NIX**
Noah's boat **ARK**
Noah's son **SHEM, HAM**
nob **HEAD**
nobility **RANK, PEERAGE**
noble **GRAND, HIGH**
nobleman **BARON, EARL, LORD,**
PEER, THANE, COUNT, DUKE

noblewoman **DAME, LADY, DUCHESS, COUNTESS**
nobody **NONE, NONENTITY**
no charge **GRATIS, FREE**
nocturnal bird **OWL, BULLBAT, NIGHTINGALE**
nocturnal mammal **LEMUR**
nocturne **LULLABY, SERENADE**
Noel **CHRISTMAS, YULE**
noise **DIN, CLATTER, RACKET, SOUND**
noiseless **SILENT, STILL**
noisome **NOXIOUS, ROTTEN**
noisy dispute **FRACAS, ROW, BRAWL**
noisy impact **SLAM**
noisy swallow **SLURP**
no kidding **REALLY**
no longer active **RETIRED**
no longer are **WERE**
no longer chic **PASSE**
nomad **MIGRANT, VAGRANT**
no matter which **ANY**
nom de plume (2 wds.) **PEN NAME**
nominal **FORMAL, MERE**
nominate **NAME**
no more than **MERE, ONLY**
no one **NONE**
nonchalant **INDIFFERENT, CASUAL**
non-citizen **ALIEN**
nonconforming belief **HERESY**
none (Scot.) **NANE**
non-iron fabric (2 wds.) **DRIP DRY, PERMANENT PRESS**
nonmetallic element **BORON, IODINE**
nonpareil **PEERLESS**
nonplus **PERPLEX, STUMP**
non-productive **STERILE**
non-professional **AMATEUR, LAYMAN**
nonsense **INANITY, ROT**
nonsense poem **LIMERICK**
non-union laborer **SCAB**
nonworker **DRONE**
nook **ALCOVE**
noon **MIDDAY, TWELVE**
noonday rest **SIESTA**
noon meal **LUNCH**
noose **LOOP**
norm **STANDARD, PAR**
normal **PAR**
Norse **SCANDINAVIAN**

Norse deity **BALDUR, ODIN, FRIGGA, LOKI, HELA, BRAGI, THOR, FREY, FREYA, FRIGG, TYR, URDUR, VERDANDI, SKULD, IDUNA, HEIMDALL, FENRIS, HERMOD**
Norse god **(see Norse deity)**
Norse legend **SAGA, EDDA**
Norse letter **RUNE**
Norseman **VIKING**
Norse navigator **ERIC**
Norse night **NATT, NOTT**
Norse patron saint **OLAF**
Norse poets **SKALDS**
Norse tale **SAGA, EDDA**
Norse toast **SKOAL**
North African capital **TUNIS**
North African colony **IFNI**
North African fruit **DATE**
northeaster **STORM, GALE**
northern Britisher **SCOT**
northern constellation **LYRA**
northern European **FINN, DANE, SWEDE, LAPP**
northern horned mammal **REINDEER**
North Pole discoverer **PEARY**
North Star State **MINNESOTA**
North Vietnamese capital **HANOI**
Norwegian **NORSE**
Norwegian dramatist **IBSEN**
Norwegian sea inlet **FJORD, FIORD**
nose **PROBOSCIS, SNOUT, SNOOT**
nosegay **POSY**
nostalgic **WISTFUL, HOMESICK**
nostrils **NARES**
nosy **SNOOPY, PRYING**
notable **KNOWN, FAMOUS**
not aboveboard **EVASIVE**
not alike **UNEQUAL, DIFFERENT**
not alive **DEAD**
not all **SOME**
notandum **ENTRY, MEMO**
not any **NO, NONE**
not appropriate **INAPT**
notarize **SEAL**
not artificial **NATURAL**
not as advanced **SLOWER**
not as common **RARER**
not as early **LATER**
not as high **LOWER**
not as large **SMALLER**
not asleep **AWAKE**
not as much **LESS**
not a soul (2 wds.) **NO ONE**

not as strong	**WEAKER**
not as taut	**LOOSER**
not at all	**NEVER, NOHOW, NOWISE**
not at home	**AWAY, OUT**
notation	**MEMO, ENTRY, RECORD**
not at leisure	**BUSY, WORKING**
not a winner	**LOSER**
not bad	**GOOD**
not better	**WORSE**
not boastful	**MODEST, SHY**
not brave	**TIMID**
not brief	**LONG**
not bright	**PALE, STUPID, DUMB**
not busy	**IDLE**
notch	**NICK**
notched bar	**RATCH**
not clearly defined	**INDISTINCT**
not closed	**OPEN**
not C.O.D.	**POSTPAID, CHARGED**
not cold	**HOT, WARM**
not cooked	**RAW**
not covered	**BARE**
not dead	**ALIVE**
not definite	**TENTATIVE**
not difficult	**EASY**
not docile	**WILD**
not down	**UP**
not dry	**WET**
note	**MESSAGE, MEMO**
note contents of	**LABEL**
noted	**FAMOUS, FAMED, RENOWNED, SEEN**
note duration of	**CLOCK, TIME**
not efficient	**LAME**
not either	**NEITHER**
note (Lat.)	**NOTA**
not employed	**IDLE**
note of Guido's scale	**UT, DO, RE, MI, FA, SOL, LA**
note of the scale	**DO, RE, MI, FA, SO, LA, TI**
noteworthy	**SPECIAL**
noteworthy act	**FEAT**
not even a soul (2 wds.)	**NO ONE**
not false	**TRUE**
not fast	**SLOW**
not fastened	**LOOSE**
not fat	**LEAN, SLIM, THIN**
not feral	**TAME**
not figurative	**LITERAL**
not firm	**LOOSE**
not flexible	**RIGID**
not for publication (3 wds.)	**OFF THE RECORD**
not forward	**MODEST, SHY**
not fresh	**STALE**
not general	**LOCAL**
not genuine	**ERSATZ, FAKE, COUNTERFEIT**
not good	**BAD**
not hard	**EASY, SOFT**
not having made a will	**INTESTATE**
not heavy	**LIGHT**
not high	**LOW**
nothing	**NIL, ZERO, NAUGHT**
nothing but	**ONLY, MERE**
nothing doing	**NIX**
nothing (Fr.)	**RIEN**
nothing less than	**SAME**
nothing more than	**MERE**
not hollow	**SOLID, FILLED**
notice	**SEE, ESPY, OBSERVE**
noticeable	**SIGNIFICANT**
notify	**ANNOUNCE, INFORM**
not illuminated	**DARK**
not imaginary	**REAL**
not in	**OUT**
not in motion	**STABLE, FIXED**
not interested	**BORED**
notion	**IDEA, THOUGHT, OPINION**
not joking	**EARNEST, SERIOUS**
not living	**DEAD**
not long	**SHORT**
not long ago	**RECENTLY**
not many	**FEW**
not minor	**MAJOR**
not moist	**DRY**
not new	**OLD, USED**
not now	**LATER**
not odd	**EVEN**
not of the clergy	**LAIC, LAY**
not one	**NONE**
not open	**CLOSED, SHUT**
notoriety	**ECLAT, PUBLICITY**
notorious	**INFAMOUS**
not out	**IN, HOME, AVAILABLE**
not plump	**LEAN, SLIM, THIN**
not pretty	**UGLY, PLAIN**
not professional	**AMATEUR, LAIC**
not qualified	**UNFIT, INEXPERIENCED**
not quite	**NEARLY**
not ready	**UNPREPARED**
not regular	**UNSTEADY, SPORADIC**
not rich	**POOR**
not rigid	**LIMP, SOFT**
not ripe	**GREEN**
not separable	**INDIVISIBLE**
not shaky	**STEADY, SOLID**
not sharp	**DULL**
not short	**LONG**

not shortened, as a book **UNABRIDGED**
not shut **OPEN**
not skinny **FAT, PLUMP, STOUT**
not slow **FAST**
not smooth **ROUGH**
not so, in law **SECUS**
not soft **HARD**
not so much **LESS**
not sound **LAME**
not speaking **MUTE, SILENT**
not straight **CROOKED**
not straightforward **EVASIVE**
not suitable **INAPT, UNFIT**
not sweet **SOUR**
not talking **SILENT**
not tame **WILD**
not taut **SLACK**
not these **THOSE**
not thick **THIN**
not those **THESE**
not tight **LOOSE**
not to be considered (4 wds.) **OUT OF THE QUESTION**
not to be pacified **IMPLACABLE**
not together **APART, SPLIT**
not tough **TENDER**
not true **FALSE**
not up **ABED, DOWN, SLEEPING**
not warm **COOL, COLD**
not waterproof **POROUS, LEAKY**
not well **BADLY, ILL**
not well planned (comp. wd.) **HALF-BAKED**
not wide **NARROW**
not wild **TAME**
notwithstanding **DESPITE, YET, HOWEVER**
not working **IDLE**
not yet settled **MOOT**
not young **OLD**
nougat **CANDY, TAFFY**
nought **BAD, WORTHLESS**
noun **WORD, NAME**
noun suffix **ENT, ESE, IER, IST, ITE**
nourish **FEED**
nourishment **FOOD, NUTRIENT**
Nova Scotia **ACADIA**
Nova Scotia mountain ash **DOGBERRY**
Nova Scotian **BLUENOSE**
Nova Scotian resort **DIGBY**
novel **STORY, BOOK, UNUSUAL, NEW**
novelist Bagnold **ENID**
novelist Ferber **EDNA**

novelist Glasgow **ELLEN**
novelist Hunter **EVAN**
novelist Jackson **SHIRLEY**
novelist Kazan **ELIA**
novelist on the Orient (2 wds.) **PEARL BUCK**
novelist Uris **LEON**
novelist Zola **EMILE**
novelty **NEWNESS**
November event **ELECTION**
novice **TYRO, TIRO**
novice athlete **ROOKIE**
novocain **PROCAINE**
now **PRESENT**
now and then **SOMETIMES**
noxious **HARMFUL, POISONOUS**
nozzle **SPOUT, NOSE**
nuance **SHADE**
nub **POINT**
nubble **LUMP, KNOB**
nubby fabric **TWEED**
nucleus **CORE, HEART**
nude **BARE, NAKED**
nudge **POKE, PROD, JAB**
nugget **LUMP**
nuisance **PEST, ANNOYANCE**
null **INVALID**
nullah **GULLY, RAVINE**
nullify **CANCEL, ANNUL**
numb **TORPID, FROZEN**
number **DIGIT, NUMERAL**
number again **RENUMERATE**
numbered chart **TABLE**
number one **FIRST, BEST**
number's third power **CUBE**
numeral style **ARABIC, ROMAN**
numerous **MANY**
nun **SISTER**
nuncio **DELEGATE**
nunnery **CLOISTER, CONVENT**
nun's dress **HABIT**
nun's headdress **WIMPLE**
nun's room **CELL**
nuptial **BRIDAL**
nuptials **WEDDING**
Nureyev's milieu **BALLET**
Nureyev specialty **LEAP**
nurse **TEND, FEED**
nursemaid **NANNY**
nursery bed **CRIB**
nurse's assistant **AIDE**
nurture **FEED**
nut **ACORN, PECAN, WALNUT, HAZELNUT, FILBERT, PEANUT, ALMOND**
nutant **NODDING, DROOPING**
nutation **NOD**
nut-bearing tree **BEECH**

nutmeg spice	MACE
Nutmeg State	CONNECTICUT
nut of the oak	ACORN
nut pine of the Southwest	PINON
nutramin	VITAMIN
nutriment	FOOD, ALIMENT
nutritious	HEALTHY
nutty	CRAZY
nuzzle	NESTLE, SNUGGLE
nyala	ANTELOPE
nylon	STOCKING, FABRIC
nymph	SYLPH, SIREN

O

oaf	BLOCKHEAD, LOUT, CLOD
oak	TREE
oak-to-be	ACORN
oakum	HEMP
oar	PADDLE, ROW
oar blade	PEEL
oarlock	THOLE
oarsman	ROWER
oasis	WADI, REFUGE
oasis feature (2 wds.)	WATER HOLE
oast	KILN, OVEN
oat	GRAIN
oath	CURSE, VOW
oatmeal	PORRIDGE
obdurate	STUBBORN
obeah	WITCHERY, VOODOO
obedience	SUBMISSION
obedient	DUTIFUL, LOYAL
obeisance	HOMAGE
obelisk	NEEDLE, PILLAR, MONOLITH
obelus	DAGGER
obese	FAT, STOUT, PLUMP, OVERWEIGHT
obey	HEED, MIND, LISTEN
obfuscate	BEWILDER, CONFUSE, DIM
obi	SASH
object	AIM, END, INTENT, THING
objection	QUARREL, PROTEST
objective	END, INTENTION, AIM, GOAL
object of art	CURIO
object of dread	BOGEY
object of worship	IDOL, GOD
object to	DEMUR, PROTEST
objurgate	ABUSE, CHIDE, SCOLD, REBUKE

objurgation	REBUKE, REPROOF
obligate	BIND
obligation	DEBT, DUTY
obligatory	REQUIRED
oblige	GRATIFY, PLEASE
obliging	AGREEABLE
oblique	INDIRECT, ASKEW
obliterate	ERASE
oblivious	UNAWARE, FORGETFUL
obloquy	REPROACH, DISGRACE
obnoxious	HATEFUL
oboe	HAUTBOY, REED, HAUTBOIS
obscene	LEWD, DIRTY
obscuration	ECLIPSE
obscure	DIM, MURKY, BLUR, DARK, DARKEN
obscure corner	NOOK
obscurity	DIMNESS
obsequious	SERVILE, FAWNING
observance	CEREMONY, RITE
observant	ATTENTIVE, WATCHFUL
observe	NOTE, NOTICE, SEE, EYE
observe Lent	FAST, ABSTAIN
observer	WITNESS, SPECTATOR
obsess	PREOCCUPY
obsession	MANIA, PASSION
obsolete	PASSE
obstacle	IMPEDIMENT, SNAG
obstinate	STUBBORN, MULISH
obstreporous	TURBULENT, UNRULY
obstruct	BAR
obstruction	BARRIER, SNAG
obtain	GET, FIND, PROCURE
obtain as profit	GAIN
obtain by reasoning	DERIVE
obtain by searching	FIND
obtain by threat	EXTORT
obtain information	LEARN
obtest	BEG, PLEAD, ENTREAT
obtrusive	MEDDLING, PUSHY
obtuse	BLUNT, DULL
obverse	FRONT
obviate	AVOID, PREVENT
obvious	EVIDENT, PATENT
ocarina	FLUTE
occasion	TIME, EVENT
occasional	IRREGULAR, CASUAL
occasionally (2 wds.)	AT TIMES
occident	WEST
occlusion	BITE, BLOCK
occult	SECRET, DARK
occultism	CABALA
occult power	MAGIC

occupant **TENANT**
occupation **VOCATION, CAREER, JOB**
occupied **BUSY, ENGAGED**
occupy **FILL**
occupy a chair **SIT**
occur **HAPPEN, TAKE PLACE, COME TO PASS**
occurrence **EVENT**
occurring after death **POSTHUMOUS**
occurring frequently **COMMON**
occurring occasionally **SPORADIC**
occurring often **FREQUENT**
ocean **SEA, ATLANTIC, PACIFIC, INDIAN, ARCTIC, ANTARCTIC, MAIN**
oceanic **PELAGIC, VAST, HUGE**
ocean liner (abbr.) **SS**
ocean mammal **WHALE**
ocean movement **TIDE**
ocean route **LANE**
ocean ship **LINER**
ocean shore **SEACOAST, STRAND, BEACH**
oceans of the world (2 wds.) **SEVEN SEAS**
ocellus **EYESPOT**
ocelot **CAT**
ocher **PIGMENT, YELLOW**
octave **EIGHT**
octopus **POLYP**
octopus arm **TENTACLE**
ocular **OPTIC**
odalisque **SLAVE, CONCUBINE**
odd **PECULIAR, STRANGE**
odd-jobs doer (2 wds.) **HANDY MAN**
oddly amusing **DROLL**
oddment **SCRAP, REMNANT**
odds **ADVANTAGE**
odds (Scot.) **ORRA**
odds and ends **SCRAPS**
ode **POEM, CANTICLE**
odeon **GALLERY, HALL**
odious **HATEFUL**
odium **HATRED**
odontalgia **TOOTHACHE**
odor **AROMA, BOUQUET, SCENT, FRAGRANCE, SMELL, PERFUME**
odorous **REDOLENT**
Oedipus' father **LAIUS**
Oedipus' mother **JOCASTA**
oeillade **GLANCE, OGLE**
of **FROM**
of (Fr.) **DE**

of a branch **RAMOUS**
of a chamber **CAMERAL**
of a few words **TERSE**
of age (Lat., abbr.) **AETAT, AET**
of aircraft **AREO**
of a musical group **ORCHESTRAL**
of an artery **AORTAL**
of an era **EPOCHAL**
of an opposite color **CONTRASTING**
of a part of the brain **CORTICAL**
of a wife **UXORIAL**
of basic alteration **MUTANT**
of better quality **FINER**
of cities **URBAN**
of course **YES**
of course not **NO**
of course (sl.) **NATCH**
of different kinds **MOTLEY**
of equal score **EVEN, PAR, TIED**
off base illegally (Army sl.) **AWOL**
offend **DISPLEASE**
offend God **SIN, BLASPHEME**
offense **AFFRONT**
offensive **ABOMINABLE**
offensively obtrusive **BLATANT**
offer **BID, TENDER**
offering **GIFT, SACRIFICE**
offer marriage **PROPOSE**
offhand **IMPROMPTU**
office **CHARGE, FUNCTION**
office cabinet **FILE**
office expense account (2 wds.) **PETTY CASH**
office holder **IN**
office item (2 wds.) **RUBBER BAND, PAPER CLIP, CARBON PAPER**
office machine **ADDER, TYPEWRITER**
office record **FILE**
office routine (2 wds.) **DESK WORK, PAPER WORK**
officer's assistant **AIDE**
officer's insignia **STRIPE**
office table **DESK**
office worker **STENO, CLERK, TYPIST**
official **AUTHENTIC, REAL**
official decree **FIAT**
official grade **RANK**
official proclamation **UKASE, EDICT**
official records **ACTA, REGISTER**
official seal **STAMP**

officious **OBTRUSIVE**
offshore coral growth **REEF**
offshore radar platform
(2 wds.) **TEXAS TOWER**
offspring **SON, DAUGHTER,
CHILD, CHILDREN,
PROGENY, DESCENDANT**
off the rack (comp. wd.)
READY-TO-WEAR
off the track **ASTRAY**
off-white **GRAY, GREY, ECRU,
CREAM, IVORY**
of government **POLITICAL**
of great depth **PROFOUND,
DEEP**
of great importance
MOMENTOUS
of great size **HUGE**
of great weight **PONDEROUS,
HEAVY**
of healing (abbr.) **MED**
of highest quality **BEST**
of little importance **TRIVIAL**
of low birth **IGNOBLE, COMMON**
of marriage **MARITAL, NUPTIAL**
of medicine **MEDICAL**
of milk **LACTIC**
of mothers and fathers
PARENTAL
of musical quality **TONAL**
of no avail **FUTILE**
of no value **USELESS**
of ocean movement **TIDAL**
of one's country **NATIONAL**
of planet's path **ORBITAL**
of punishment **PENAL**
of secondary importance
INCIDENTAL
of sound **TONAL**
of speech **PHONETIC**
of superior quality **BETTER**
often **FREQUENTLY**
often-dented item **FENDER**
often-pickled vegetable **BEET,
CUCUMBER, MELON,
CAULIFLOWER, BEAN,
ARTICHOKE, MUSHROOM**
often-read item **PALM**
of that kind **SUCH**
of the backbone **SPINAL**
of the cheek **MALAR**
of the city **URBAN**
of the country **RURAL**
of the ear **OTIC**
of the hour **HORAL, TIMELY,
CURRENT**
of the mouth **ORAL**
of the nose **NASAL**

of the Orient **EASTERN**
of the pope **PAPAL**
of the same kind **AKIN**
of the sea **MARINE, MARITIME**
of the side **LATERAL**
of the skull **CRANIAL**
of the spring **VERNAL**
of the sun **SOLAR**
of the teeth **DENTAL**
of the USN **NAVAL**
ogee **ARCH**
ogle **EYE, LEER, FLIRT,
MAKE EYES**
ogre **MONSTER, GIANT**
Ohio city **TOLEDO, AKRON**
oil **LUBRICATE, OLEO, FAT,
GREASE, LUBRICANT**
oil (suffix) **OL, OLE**
oilbird **GUACHARO**
oil of rose petals **ATTAR**
oil plant **SESAME**
oil source **OLIVE, PEANUT**
oily **UNCTUOUS, GREASY**
oily fruit **OLIVE**
oily tissue **FAT, ADIPOSE**
ointment **SALVE, NARD**
okay **ALL RIGHT, YES,
SATISFACTORY**
Oklahoma city **ADA, TULSA**
Oklahoma Indian **OSAGE,
PAWNEE**
Oklahoma mountain **OZARK**
Oklahoma river **RED**
old **ANCIENT, ELDERLY,
AGED**
old boat **TUB**
old car **CRATE, JALOPY**
old card game **LOO, WHIST**
Old Colony State
MASSACHUSETTS
old Dominion **VIRGINIA**
old English bard **SCOP**
old English coin **GROAT, RYAL,
NOBLE**
old English pronoun **YE**
older **ELDER, SENIOR**
old expletive **EGAD**
Old Faithful **GEYSER**
old-fashioned **DATED, PASSE,
QUAINT**
old-fashioned heating unit
(2 wds.) **FRANKLIN STOVE**
old-fashioned photo **TINTYPE**
Old Franklin State **TENNESSEE**
old French coin **ECU, SOU, SOL,
LOUIS**
old French dance **GAVOTTE**

old frontier region of US
(2 wds.) **WILD WEST**
Old Glory **FLAG**
old Greek music hall **ODEON**
old Greek township **DEME**
old horse **NAG**
Old Line State **MARYLAND**
old maid **SPINSTER**
old movie **RERUN**
old musical instrument **LUTE**
old musical note **ELA, UT**
Old North State
　　NORTH CAROLINA
old pal **CRONY**
old picture card **TAROT**
old poet **BARD, SCOP**
old Roman official **AEDILE,**
　　EDILE, MAGISTRATE
old sailor **SALT**
old salt **TAR, GOB**
old saying **ADAGE, SAW**
old Scottish chief **THANE**
old slave **ESNE, SERF**
old sledge **SEVEN-UP**
old sol **SUN**
old squaw **DUCK**
old stringed instrument **LUTE,**
　　LYRE
Old Testament Apocrypha book
　　TOBIT, JUDITH, WISDOM OF
SOLOMON, ECCLESIASTICUS,
　　MACCABEES
Old Testament book **AMOS,**
　　CHRONICLES, DANIEL,
DEUTERONOMY, ESTHER,
　　ECCLESIASTES, EXODUS,
EZEKIEL, EZRA, GENESIS,
HABAKKUK, HAGGAI, HOSEA,
ISAIAH, JEREMIAH, JOB, JOEL,
　　JONAH, JOSHUA, JUDGES,
KINGS, LAMENTATIONS,
LEVITICUS, MALACHI, MICAH,
　　NAHUM, NEHEMIAH,
NUMBERS, OBADIAH,
PROVERBS, PSALMS, RUTH,
SAMUEL, SONG OF SOLOMON
(SONG OF SONGS), ZECHARIAH,
　　ZEPHANIAH
old time **YORE**
old violin **AMATI, STRADIVARI**
old wagon train route
　　OREGON TRAIL
old weapon **MACE, LANCE**
old witch **CRONE**
old woman **CRONE, HAG**
old-womanish **ANILE**
oleaginous **OILY, UNCTUOUS**
oleo **MARGARINE**

oleoresin **ELEMI**
olfactory organ **NOSE**
olid **FETID**
olio **HODGEPODGE, MEDLEY,**
　　MIXTURE
olive genus **OLEA**
oliver **HAMMER**
olla **JUG, POT**
oloroso **SHERRY**
Olympic event **SHOT-PUT,**
　　DASH, RELAY, GAME,
　　MARATHON, RACE
ombre **SHADED**
omega **END, LAST**
omen **AUGURY, FOREBODING,**
　　FORETOKEN, PORTENT,
　　PRESAGE, SIGN
ominous **FATEFUL, SINISTER**
omit **EXCLUDE, OVERLOOK**
omit a vowel in pronunciation
　　ELIDE
omit, in printing **DELE**
on **ATOP, UPON**
on (prefix) **EPI**
on a cruise **ASEA**
on a large scale **GIANT**
on all sides **AROUND, ABOUT**
on and on **TEDIOUSLY**
on behalf of **FOR**
once **FORMERLY**
once and again **TWICE**
once and future king **ARTHUR**
once around a track **LAP**
once famous person
　　(comp. wd.) **HAS-BEEN**
once, formerly **ERST**
once in a while **OCCASIONALLY**
once more **AGAIN, ANEW**
once upon a time **FORMERLY**
on condition that **IF**
one **AN, UNIT, UNITED,**
　　UNITY, SINGLETON
one (Fr.) **UN, UNE**
one (Ger.) **EINE, EIN**
one (Sp.) **UNO, UNA**
one against **ANTI**
one and all **EVERY**
one and only **SOLE**
one at a time (2 wds.) **SINGLE**
　　FILE
one-celled animal **AMOEBA**
one devoted to religious work
　　OBLATE
on edge **TENSE, WARY,**
　　NERVOUS
one having special talents
　　GENIUS

one horse carriage **CARIOLE, GIG**
one hundred cents **DOLLAR**
one hundred per cent **ALL, ENTIRETY, WHOLE, ENTIRE**
one in authority **MANAGER, FOREMAN, CHAIRMAN BOSS,**
one in favor of **FOR, PRO**
one in opposition **ANTI**
one issue of a newspaper **EDITION**
one kind of secretary **DESK, EXECUTIVE**
one lacking courage **COWARD**
one-man performance **SOLO**
one missing **ABSENTEE**
one of a deck **CARD**
one of an ancient race **MEDE**
one of Atilla's followers **HUN**
one of Columbus' ships **NINA, PINTA, SANTA MARIA**
one of Hamlet's alternatives **TO BE, NOT TO BE**
one of the Barrymores **ETHEL, JOHN, LIONEL**
one of the Bears **URSA**
one of the Evangelists **MARK, MATTHEW, LUKE, JOHN**
one of the Gershwins **IRA, GEORGE**
one of the Kettles **PA, MA**
one of the Muses **ERATO, CLIO, CALLIOPE, EUTERPE, MELPOMENE, POLYHYMNIA, TERPSICHORE, THALIA, URANIA**
one of the reindeer **DASHER, DANCER, PRANCER, VIXEN, COMET, CUPID, DONNER, DONDER, BLITZEN, RUDOLPH**
one of the senses **SIGHT, TOUCH, HEARING, TASTE, SMELL**
one of the Twelve **MATTHEW, JOHN, PETER, JUDAS, THOMAS, ANDREW, JAMES, PHILIP, BARTHOLOMEW, JUDE, SIMON, MATTHIAS**
one of two equal parts **HALF**
one or the other **EITHER**
one racing circuit **LAP**
onerous **HEAVY, DIFFICULT**
one seeking political asylum **REFUGEE**
one-sided **BIASED, SLANTED, PARTIAL**

one-spot **ACE**
one's self **EGO**
one's strong point **FORTE**
one time **QUONDAM**
one time only **ONCE**
one undergoing change **MUTANT**
one way up **STAIR**
one who abandons **DESERTER**
one who avoids the company of others **LONER**
one who consumes food **EATER**
one who dies for a cause **MARTYR**
one who digs for coal **MINER**
one who entertains **HOST**
one who excels **ACE**
one who fails to win **LOSER**
one who feels superior **SNOB**
one who fights for noble cause **CRUSADER**
one who forwards goods **CONSIGNOR**
one who fustrates a plan **MARPLOT**
one who goes by **PASSER**
one who governs **RULER**
one who lubricates **OILER**
one who makes forays **RAIDER**
one who roams about furtively **PROWLER**
one who stitches **SEAMSTRESS, TAILOR**
one who tells **RELATER, NARRATOR, SNITCH**
one without courage **COWARD**
on grand scale **EPIC**
on guard **ALERT**
onion **BULB**
onion genus **ALLIUM**
onion-like herb **CHIVE**
onion-like vegetable **LEEK, SCALLION**
on its way **GONE**
onlooker **WITNESS**
only **MERE, SOLE**
only fair (comp. wd.) **SO-SO**
onset **BEGINNING, START, OPENING**
onslaught **ATTACK**
Ontario capital **TORONTO**
on the affirmative side **PRO**
on the bottom **SUNK**
on the briny **ASEA, AT SEA**
on the contrary **BUT**
on the decline **DECADENT**
on the fritz **OUT OF WHACK, BROKEN**

on the go **ACTIVE**
on the left side
  (nautical) **APORT**
on the move **ASTIR**
on the ocean **ASEA**
on the peak **ATOP**
on the roof of **ATOP**
on the sheltered side **ALEE**
on the summit **ATOP**
on this **HEREON**
onus **BURDEN**
onward **FORWARD**
oodles **LOTS**
Oolong **TEA**
oomph **ENERGY**
Oopak **TEA**
ooze **SEEP, EXUDE**
opah **FISH**
opal **GIRASOL**
opaque **DARK, OBSCURE**
open **AJAR, FRANK, CANDID,**
  UNFOLD, UNWRAP, UNLOCK
open a package **UNDO, UNTIE**
open declaration **AVOWAL**
open for discussion **MOOT**
open-handed blow **SLAP**
opening **GAP, HOLE, MOUTH,**
  VENT
opening for coins **SLOT**
openings **ORA**
open-mouthed **AGAPE**
open out **SPREAD**
open place in forest **GLADE**
open shoe **SANDAL**
open to view **OVERT**
open wide, as the mouth **YAWN**
openwork fabric **LACE**
opera by Bizet **CARMEN**
opera by Massenet **MANON**
opera by Verdi **AIDA**
opera division **ACT**
opera glass **LORGNETTE**
opera hat **TOPPER**
opera highlight **ARIA**
opera prince **IGOR**
opera singer (2 wds.)
  PRIMA DONNA
opera star **DIVA**
operate **MANAGE, RUN**
operate a car **DRIVE**
operation **WORK, PROCEDURE**
operational **READY**
operative **AGENT**
ophidian **REPTILE, SERPENT**
opthalmic **OCULAR**
opthamologist **OCULIST**
opiate **NARCOTIC**
opine **THINK**

opinion **IDEA, THOUGHT**
opinionated **BIASED**
opinionated faction **SECT**
opinion opposed to doctrine
  HERESY
opinion register **POLL**
opium **DRUG, DOPE**
opium drug **CODEINE,**
  MORPHINE
opponent **ENEMY, RIVAL, FOE,**
  COMPETITOR
opportune (comp. wd.)
  HEAVEN-SENT
opportunity **CHANCE, OPENING**
oppose **RESIST, COMBAT**
opposed **ANTI**
opposite **ANTITHESIS,**
  ANTONYM
opposite side **REVERSE**
oppress **AFFLICT, PERSECUTE**
oprobrious **INFAMOUS**
opt **CHOOSE**
optic **EYE**
optical glass **LENS**
optical illusion **MIRAGE**
optical membrane **RETINA**
optical organ **EYE**
optimist **HOPER**
optimistic **ROSY**
option **CHOICE**
optional **VOLUNTARY**
oracular **WISE**
oral **SPOKEN, VOCAL, VERBAL**
oral cavity **MOUTH**
orange and black bird **ORIOLE**
orange genus **CITRUS**
orange oil **NEROLI**
orange pekoe **TEA**
orange-red **CORAL**
orange seed **PIP**
orange skin **RIND, PEEL**
orangutan **APE**
orate **DECLAIM, HARANGUE,**
  TALK, SPEAK
oration **SPEECH**
orator **SPEAKER**
oratory **ELOCUTION**
orb **EYE**
orbit **CIRCUIT**
orbital point **APSIS**
orc **GRAMPUS**
orchestra **BAND**
orchestra leader **CONDUCTOR**
orchestra leader's stick **BATON**
orchestra section **REEDS,**
  BRASS, STRINGS, TYMPANY
orchestra's location **PIT,**
  BANDSTAND

orchestrate	**ARRANGE**
ordain	**ENACT**
ordeal	**TEST, TRIAL**
order	**COMMAND, DIRECT, DIRECTIVE, NEATNESS, BID**
order for girl Friday (3 wds.)	**TAKE A LETTER**
order for writ	**PRECIPE, PRAECIPE**
order of frogs and toads	**ANURA**
order of whales	**CETE**
orderly	**NEAT**
ordinal	**REGULAR**
ordinance	**STATUTE, LAW**
ordinary	**MERE, COMMON**
ordinary writing	**PROSE**
ordnance	**ARMOR, ARMS**
ore deposit	**MINE, LODE, VEIN**
ore digger	**MINER**
ore vein	**LODE**
Oregon city	**SALEM, PORTLAND**
Oregon mountain	**HOOD**
Orel's river	**OKA**
organ	**MEDIUM, VEHICLE**
organic compound	**ESTER**
organic substance	**RESIN**
organization	**SETUP, ASSOCIATION**
organize	**ARRANGE, FORM**
organized athletics	**GAMES, SPORTS**
organized criminal society	**MAFIA, COSA NOSTRA, SYNDICATE**
organized march	**PARADE**
organized migration	**TREK, EXODUS**
organ of hearing	**EAR**
organ of sight	**EYE**
organ of speech	**TONGUE, LIP**
organ part	**REED, STOP**
organ pipe	**FLUE, REED**
organ stop	**OBOE, ORAGE**
organ tube	**PIPE**
Orient	**ASIA, EAST**
Oriental caravansary	**SERAI**
Oriental chief	**KHAN**
Oriental coin	**DINAR**
Oriental cymbal	**TAL**
Oriental destiny	**KISMET**
Oriental flower	**LOTUS**
Oriental grain	**RICE**
Oriental guitar	**SITAR**
Oriental headdress	**TURBAN**
Oriental marketplace	**BAZAAR**
Oriental nation	**JAPAN, CHINA, KOREA, VIETNAM**
Oriental nurse	**AMAH**
Oriental pagoda	**TAA**
Oriental periodic wind	**MONSOON**
Oriental potentate	**AMIR, EMIR, AMEER, EMEER**
Oriental river boat	**SAMPAN**
Oriental ruler	**CALIPH, SULTAN**
Oriental salute	**SALAAM**
Oriental sash	**OBI**
Oriental sauke	**SOY**
Oriental staple grain	**RICE**
Oriental title	**PASHA, AGA**
Oriental women's quarters	**ODA, HAREM**
origin	**GERM, ROOT, SEED**
original	**FIRST, PRIMARY**
originate	**ARISE, CREATE, DERIVE**
Orion	**CONSTELLATION, HUNTER**
orison	**PRAYER**
ormer	**ABALONE**
ornament	**BANGLE**
ornamental	**DECORATIVE**
ornamental ball	**BEAD**
ornamental bottle	**DECANTER**
ornamental button	**STUD**
ornamental fabric	**LACE**
ornamental flower holder	**URN, JARDINIERE**
ornamental knob	**STUD**
ornamental knot	**BOW**
ornamental setting	**DECOR**
ornamental stamp	**SEAL**
ornamental tuft	**TASSEL**
ornamental vase	**URN**
ornate	**OPULENT, FLORID**
orthodontist's concern	**BITE**
osar	**ESKER**
Oscar	**AWARD**
oscillate	**WAVER, VACILLATE**
osier	**WILLOW**
Osiris' wife	**ISIS**
osprey	**ERN**
ostentation	**DISPLAY, BRAVADO**
ostentatious	**POMPOUS, PRETENTIOUS**
ostentatiously fashionable (sl.)	**SWANK**
ostiole	**APERTURE, STOMA**
ostracize	**BLACKBALL, OUST**
ostrichlike bird	**EMU**
Othello villain	**IAGO**
other	**ELSE**
others (Lat.)	**ALIA**
otherwise	**ELSE, OR**
otiose	**VAIN, FUTILE**

ottoman	SOFA, STOOL, FOOTREST
Ottoman Empire	TURKEY
Ottoman governor	PASHA
oubliette	DUNGEON
ought to	SHOULD
ouija	PLANCHETTE
our (Fr.)	NOTRE
our country (abbr.)	USA
our planet	EARTH
oust	EJECT, EVICT
out	ABSENT, AWAY
out-and-out	ARRANT
outback	BUSH
outbreak	RASH
outbuilding	SHED, LEAN-TO, WC
outcast	VAGRANT, CASTAWAY
out class	EXCEL, SURPASS
outcome	END, RESULT
outcry	HUE
outdo	EXCEED, BEAT
outdoor activity	SPORT
outdoor blaze	CAMPFIRE, BONFIRE
outer	ECTAL
outer (prefix)	ECTO
outer garment	COAT, JACKET
outer layer	SKIN
outer skin	EPIDERMIS
outfit	KIT, RIG
outgrowth	EMERGENCE
outing	EXCURSION, JAUNT
out in the open	OVERT
outlandish	UNUSUAL
outlaw	CRIMINAL, FUGITIVE
outlet	VENT
outline	DRAFT, SKETCH
out-migrant	EMIGRE
outmoded	PASSE, DATED
out of	FROM
out of bed	ARISEN, RISEN
out of danger	SAFE
out of date	PASSE, DATED, OLD-FASHIONED
out of place	INEPT, INAPPROPRIATE
out of style	PASSE, DATED, OLD-FASHIONED
out of the way	ASIDE
out of town	AWAY
outrage	INSULT, FURY
outrageous	WANTON, FLAGRANT
outside portion	RIM
outspoken	CANDID, FRANK
outstanding	PROMINENT
outstrip	BEST

outward	EXTERNAL
outwit	FOIL, THWART
ova	EGGS
oval	ELLIPTICAL
oven	KILN, OAST
oven device	TIMER
over	ABOVE, ATOP, ACROSS, DONE, FINISHED
over (Ger.)	UBER
over (poetic)	O'ER
over (prefix)	SUR
overabundance	EXCESS, SURPLUS
overact	EMOTE
over-adorned	ORNATE
over again	ANEW, ENCORE
overalls material	DENIM
over and above	TOO
over and over	REPEATEDLY
overbearing	ARROGANT, HAUGHTY
overburden	OPPRESS
overcast	CLOUDY
overcome	SUBDUE, CONQUER
overcome with fear	DAUNT
overdue	LATE
overflow	SPILL
over fond of	DOTE
over-friendly politician	HANDSHAKER
overhang	JUT, PROJECT
overhasty	RASH
overhaul	RENOVATE
overhead	ABOVE
overhead railroad	EL
overjoy	ELATE
overlapping part	FLAP
overlook	CONDONE, NEGLECT, FORGET, MISS, OMIT
overpass approach	RAMP
overpower	CRUSH, MASTER
overrun	RAVAGE, BESET
oversee	SUPERINTEND
overseer of morals	CENSOR
overshadow	ECLIPSE
oversight	OMISSION, SLIP
oversized	BIG
overt	PUBLIC
overtake	PASS
over there	YONDER
overthrow	DEFEAT, ABOLISH
overture	PRELUDE
overturn	UPEND, UPSET, CAPSIZE
overweight	OBESE, FAT, PLUMP
overwhelm	AWE, CRUSH

overwrought   **SPENT, DISTURBED**
overzealous   **FANATIC**
ovine creature   **EWE, RAM, LAMB, SHEEP**
ovine mama   **EWE**
ovine papa   **RAM**
ovolo   **ELLIPSE**
ovule   **EGG, SEED**
ovum   **EGG**
owed   **DUE**
owl-like   **STRIGINE**
owl parrot   **KAKAPO**
owl's cry   **HOOT**
own   **ACKNOWLEDGE, HAVE, POSSESS**
own (Scot.)   **AIN**
owner   **PROPRIETOR**
own up   **CONFESS, ADMIT**
oxalis plant   **OCA**
oxen harness   **YOKE**
oxeye   **DUNLIN**
oxford   **SHOE**
ox-headed antelope   **GNU**
oxidation   **RUST**
oxide of iron   **RUST**
oxygen   **ELEMENT, AIR**
oxygen compound   **OXIDE**
oyster   **BIVALVE**
oyster eggs   **SPAWN**
oyster gem   **PEARL**
Ozark State   **MISSOURI**
ozone   **GAS, AIR**

P

pac   **MOCCASIN**
paca   **RODENT**
pace   **STEP, WALK, STRIDE, GAIT, MEASURE**
pace the field   **LEAD**
pachyderm   **ELEPHANT, RHINO, HIPPO**
pacific   **CALM, SERENE**
Pacific island   **BALI, SAMOA, WAKE, GUAM, TAHITI**
Pacific shark   **MAKO**
pacify   **ASSUAGE, PLACATE**
pack   **STUFF, BIND, BUNDLE, HEAP, GROUP, SET, GANG, BAND, RIG**
package   **PARCEL, ENCASE, BUNDLE, WRAP**
package of pepper   **ROBBIN**
package of wool (Australian)   **FADGE**
pack animal   **BURRO, LLAMA**

pack animal of Tibet   **YAK**
pack away   **STOW**
pack down   **TAMP**
packet   **BUNDLE, PARCEL**
pack in   **CRAM, WEDGE**
packing box   **CASE, CRATE, CARTON**
packing plant   **CANNERY**
pack it in   **GIVE UP, ADJOURN, QUIT**
pack off   **DISCHARGE, FIRE, DISMISS**
pack of hounds   **KENNEL**
pack of playing cards   **DECK**
pack the jury   **RIG**
packthread   **TWINE**
pack together   **COMPRESS**
pact   **AGREEMENT, ENTENTE, TREATY**
pad   **CUSHION**
paddle   **OAR, ROW, SPANK, TODDLE**
paddock   **FIELD, ENCLOSURE**
pad for hair   **RAT**
pad for horse's saddle   **HOUSING, TRAPPINGS**
padre   **CHAPLAIN, PRIEST**
padrone   **MASTER, PROPRIETOR**
paean   **HYMN, PRAISE**
pagan   **HEATHEN**
pagan image   **IDOL**
page   **FOLIO, LEAF**
pageantry   **POMP, SPECTACLE**
pagoda   **TA, TAA**
pagoda finial   **TEE**
paid escort   **GIGOLO**
paid golfer   **PRO**
paid notice   **AD**
pail   **BUCKET**
paillette   **SPANGLE**
pain   **HURT, ACHE**
painful   **SORE, ACHING**
painkiller   **ANALGESIC**
painstaking   **DILIGENT**
paint   **COLOR, ENAMEL**
painter   **ARTIST**
painter's stand   **EASEL**
painting and sculpture   **ART**
painting medium   **TEMPERA, OIL, ACRYLIC, PASTEL**
paint layer   **COAT**
paint splash   **BLOB**
paint the town   **CAROUSE**
pair   **COUPLE, DUO, DUET, TWO, TWOSOME, BRACE**
pair-oar   **SHELL, BOAT**
pair of horses   **TEAM, SPAN**
paisley   **SHAWL, DESIGN**

pal	BUDDY, CHUM, FRIEND, COMRADE, MATE
palace	CASTLE, RESIDENCE
palace officer	PALATINE
paladin	KNIGHT, HERO
palatable	SAPID, TASTY, SAVORY, FLAVORFUL
palate	TASTE
palate part	UVULA
palatial	ORNATE
palaver	CONFER, CHATTER
pale	ASHEN, ASHY, DIM, FADE, PALLID, WAN
pale bluish-green	BERYL
pale bluish-purple	MAUVE
pale color	PASTEL
pale red	PINK
Palestine	HOLY LAND, ISRAEL
paletot	OVERCOAT
pale yellow	FLAXEN, MAIZE
paling	FENCE
palisade	CLIFF
pall	CLOY, SICKEN
pallet	BED, QUILT
palliate	CONCEAL
pallid	PALE, WAN, ASHY, ASHEN
palm	ARECA
Palmetto State	SOUTH CAROLINA
palm fiber	TAL
palm fruit	DATE
palmyra palm fiber	TA
palpable	PLAIN, OBVIOUS
palpitation	PITAPAT
paltry	PETTY, VILE, TRASH
pamper	CODDLE, FONDLE, SPOIL
pan	SKILLET, BASIN
panacea	CURE, REMEDY
Panama city	COLON
Panama passage	CANAL
pandemonium	RIOT, RACKET, HUBBUB
pander	CATER
pane (2 wds.)	WINDOW GLASS
panel	JURY
pang	THROE, SPASM
panhandler	BEGGAR, BUM
panic	ALARM, TERROR
pant	GASP
pantomime	MIME
pantry	LARDER
papa	DADDY, FATHER, DAD
Papal court	CURIA
Papal envoy	LEGATE
Papal letter	BULL
Papal ring	FISHERMAN'S

Papal scarf	ORALE
Papal seal	BULLA
Papal throne	PETER'S
papa's wife	MAMA
paper	BOND, TISSUE, DOCUMENT, JOURNAL
paper container	POKE, BAG, SACK
paper of indebtedness	IOU
paper quantity	REAM
paper size	LEGAL, CROWN, NOTE
par	NORMAL, EQUAL
parade feature	FLOAT, BAND
paradise	HEAVEN, EDEN
paradise dweller	ADAM, EVE
"Paradise Lost" author	MILTON
paradox	ENIGMA, PUZZLE
paragon	MODEL, IDEAL
paragraph	ITEM
Paraguay tea	MATE
parallel	CONCENTRIC
parallelogram	RHOMBUS, RHOMBOID
paramount	SUPREME, EMINENT
parapet	RAMPART, WALL
paraphernalia	APPARATUS, GEAR, TRAPPINGS, EQUIPMENT
parasite	SYCOPHANT
parasitic insect	TICK, LOUSE, FLEA
parcel	PACKAGE
parcel of land	ACRE, LOT
parcel out	METE
parch	SCORCH, SEAR
parched	SERE, ARID
parchment	VELLUM, FORREL
parchment roll	SCROLL
pardon	FORGIVE
pare	PEEL
parent	MOTHER, FATHER
pariah	OUTCAST
parley	CONFER
Paris airport	ORLY
Paris art exhibition	SALON
Paris subway	METRO
park for wild animals	ZOO
park in Copenhagen	TIVOLI
parking area	LOT, GARAGE
parking payment container	METER
paroxysm	FIT, ATTACK, OUTBURST, SPASM
parrot	LORY, MACAW
parsimonious	STINGY
parsonage	MANSE, RECTORY

part	SEPARATE, SPLIT, PORTION, SHARE, ROLE, PIECE, DIVORCE	part of a printing press	PLATEN
		part of Arabia	ASIR
		part of a ship	KEEL, BRIDGE, DECK
partake	SHARE	part of a ship's bottom	BILGE
parterre	GARDEN	part of a shoe	SOLE, UPPER, LACE, TONGUE, TOE, HEEL
partial	BIASED, UNFAIR		
partiality	FAVOR		
partial refund	REBATE		
participant	ENTRANT	part of a sonnet	SESTET
participant on a discussion show	PANELIST	part of a stair	RISER, TREAD
		part of a theater	LOGE, STAGE, GALLERY, BALCONY, PARTERRE, LOBBY, MEZZANINE, BOX
participate	SHARE		
participate in an auction	BID		
participle ending	ING		
particle	ATOM, IOTA	part of a typewriter	PLATEN, ROLLER, KEY, RIBBON
particle, as of dust	MOTE		
parti-colored	PIEBALD, PIED	part of a yard	FOOT
particular	EXACT, DISTINCT, FASTIDIOUS	part of chow mein	NOODLES
		part of infinitive	TO
particular instance	CASE	part of speech	NOUN, VERB, ADVERB, ADJECTIVE, CONJUNCTION, PREPOSITION, PRONOUN
particular place	SPOT		
particular taste	SAVOR		
particularly	ESPECIALLY		
particularly miserable	WRETCHED	part of telephone number (2 wds.)	AREA CODE
partisan	FOLLOWER	part of the day	MORN, NOON, MORNING, EVENING, AFTERNOON, NIGHT
partition	SCREEN, WALL		
partly fermented grape juice	STUM, MUST		
		part of the ear	LOBE, DRUM
partly fused	FRIT	part of the eye	IRIS, LENS, UVEA, CORNEA, RETINA
partly open	AJAR		
partner	PARD, MATE, PAL		
part of a bird's wing	ALULA	part of the hand	FINGER, NAIL, KNUCKLE, PALM, THUMB
part of a book	LEAF, PAGE, CHAPTER		
part of a bottle	NECK	part of the leg	CALF, SHIN, KNEE, THIGH, ANKLE
part of a bridle	BIT		
part of a chain	LINK	part of the mouth	LIP, PALATE, TONGUE
part of a church	NAVE, APSE, CHANCEL		
		part of the psyche	EGO, ID, SUPEREGO
part of a circle	ARC		
part of a day	HOUR	part of to be	AM, IS, ARE, WAS, WERE
part of a desk set	PEN, PENCIL		
part of a dogma	TENET	part of Viet Nam	ANNAM
part of a door lock	BOLT	part of Yugoslavia	CROATIA
part of a dovetail	TENON, MORTISE	part played	ROLE
		partridge flock	COVEY
part of a flower	SEPAL, PETAL	part worked with feet	PEDAL, TREADLE
part of a fortress	REDAN		
part of a goblet	STEM	party	COMPANY, FACTION
part of a leaf	STIPEL	party for a bride	SHOWER
part of a list	ITEM	party for men	STAG
part of an old auto	CRANK	party giver	HOST, HOSTESS
part of a plant	SEPAL, ROOT, PETAL, LEAF, STEM, STALK	pascal	CELERY
		pa's mate	MA
		pass	OVERTAKE
part of a poem	STANZA, VERSE, CANTO	passable	SOSO, NOT BAD, NOT SO BAD

passage	CORRIDOR	patience	FORTITUDE,
passageway	AISLE		ENDURANCE
passageway of shops	ARCADE	patient	COOL, CALM,
pass a law	ENACT		CONSTANT, TOLERANT
pass, as time	ELAPSE	patio	COURTYARD, TERRACE
passe	DATED	patio stove	GRILL, BARBECUE
passenger	FARE, RIDER	Patrick Dennis creation	MAME
passenger vehicle	BUS, CAB,	patrimony	HERITAGE, LEGACY
	TRAIN	patriotic monogram	USA
passenger vessel	LINER	patron	CLIENT, CUSTOMER,
passing fashion	FAD, CRAZE		BENEFACTOR
passion	ARDOR, ZEAL	patron of shepherds	PAN
passionate	ARDENT, FERVENT	patron saint of	
passive	INERT	England	GEORGE
pass lightly over	SKIM, SLUR	patron saint of sailors	ELMO
pass on	RELAY	patronymic	SURNAME
Passover feast	SEDER	pattern	MODEL, MOLD
pass over smoothly	GLIDE	pause	HESITATE, RESPITE,
passport	CONGE		LETUP, BREATHER, REST
passport endorsement	VISA	pave	BLACKTOP
pass slowly	DRAG	paving liquid	TAR
pass through a sieve	SIFT	paving stone	SETT
past	AGO	paw	PATTE
pasta	SPAGHETTI, MACARONI,	pawn	HOCK, CHESSMAN
FETTUCINE, PASTINA, PASTE		Pawnee	INDIAN
paste	GLUE	pay	REMIT, SETTLE
pastel	CRAYON, HUE, PALE	pay a bill	REMIT
past events	HISTORY	payable	DUE
pastime	SPORT, HOBBY	pay a call	VISIT
pastoral	RURAL	pay attention	HEED, LISTEN
pastoral cantata	SERENATA	pay court to	WOO
pastoral deity	FAUN	pay dirt	ORE
pastoral home	FARM	pay heavily	SMART
pastoral pipe	REED	payment back	REBATE
pastoral poem	BUCOLIC, IDYL	payment for recovered item	
pastry	PIE, TART		REWARD
pastry chef	BAKER	payment owing	DUE
past time	YORE	payoff	BRIBE
pasturage	GRASS	payola	GRAFT
pasture grass	GRAMA	pay one's share	ANTE
pasture ground	FIELD,	pay out	SPEND, EXPEND
	PASTURAGE	pea	LEGUME, VEGETABLE
pasture land	LEA	peace	AMITY, SERENITY,
pasture sound	MOO, MAA, BAA		TRANQUILITY
pat	TAP, CARESS, PET,	peace agreement	TREATY
	FONDLE, STROKE	peace disturbance	RIOT
patch	COVER, MEND	peaceful	IRENIC
patch of ground	PLOT	peace pipe	CALUMET
patchwork	QUILT	peace symbol	DOVE
pate	HEAD	peach	FREESTONE, PEEN-TO
patella	KNEE	peach-like fruit	APRICOT,
paten	PLATE		NECTARINE
patent	PLAIN, GRANT,	peach seed	PIT
	OBVIOUS	Peach State	GEORGIA
pat gently	DAB	peacock genus	PAVO
path	LANE, ROUTE, TRAIL	peacock ore	BORNITE
pathetic	SAD, PITIFUL	peacock wing marking	EYESPOT
		peage	WAMPUM

pea holder	**POD**	pelt	**SKIN, FUR**
peak	**SUMMIT, APEX**	pelvic bones	**ILIA**
peal	**RING**	pen	**BALLPOINT, WRITE,**
peal of thunder	**CLAP**		**CONFINE, STY, PIGSTY**
peanut	**GOOBER**	penalize	**PUNISH, FINE**
pear	**BOSC, ANJOU**	penalty	**FINE, PUNISHMENT,**
pearl	**GEM, ORIENT**		**HANDICAP**
pear-like fruit	**AVOCADO**	penance	**CONTRITION**
peasant	**BOOR, RUSTIC, RUBE**	penchant	**BENT**
peasant's shoe	**SABOT**	pencil	**DRAW, SKETCH**
pea's home	**POD**	pencil point	**LEAD**
peat	**FUEL, MOSS**	pencil rubber	**ERASER**
pebble	**STONE**	pend	**AWAIT**
pecan	**NUT**	pendant	**AIGLET, AGLET**
pecan covering	**SHELL**	pending	**DUE**
peccadillo	**FAULT**	penetrate	**ENTER**
peck	**PRICK, JERK**	penetrating	**SHARP, ACUTE**
peculate	**EMBEZZLE, DEFRAUD**	penetrating ointment	**LINIMENT**
peculiar	**ODD, STRANGE,**	penetration	**ENTRANCE**
	OUTLANDISH	penetration in perception	
peculiarity	**QUIRK, ODDITY**		**ACUMEN**
pedal digit	**TOE**	pen fluid	**INK**
pedant	**PRIG, TEACHER**	penicillin	**MIRACLE DRUG**
pedant's specialty	**LESSON**	penitence	**REMORSE, REGRET**
peddle	**HAWK, SELL**	penitential period	**LENT**
peddler	**VENDOR, HAWKER,**	penitentiary inmate	**PRISONER**
	MONGER	penman	**SCRIBE**
pedestal part	**DADO**	pen name (Fr., 3 wds.)	
pedestal rest	**PLINTH**		**NOM DE PLUME**
pedestrian	**WALKER**	pen name of Charles Lamb	
pedicel	**STEM, STALK**		**ELIA**
peel	**PARE, RIND, SKIN**	pennant	**FLAG, BANNER**
peen	**HAMMER**	penniless	**BROKE, POOR**
peep	**PEEK, SPY**	pennon	**BANNER, PENNANT,**
peep out	**PEER**		**FLAG**
peer	**GAZE, LOOK, STARE,**	Pennsylvania city	**ALTOONA,**
	DUKE, EARL, BARON		**READING**
peerage	**RANK, LINEAGE**	Pennsylvania port	**ERIE**
peeress' coronet	**TIARA**	penny	**CENT**
Peer Gynt's mother	**ASE, AASE**	pennypincher	**MISER**
peerless	**MATCHLESS**	pen point	**NEB, NIB**
peer of the realm	**LORD**	pension	**SUBSIDY, INN**
peer's cognomen	**TITLE**	pensive	**THOUGHTFUL**
peeve	**ANNOY, PROVOKE**	Pentateuch	**TORAH**
peevish	**PETULANT**	penury	**PRIVATION, LACK,**
peg	**STAKE, PIN**		**DEARTH, DESTITUTION**
peignoir	**NEGLIGEE,**	peon	**SLAVE**
	DRESSING GOWN	people	**PERSONS, RACE**
pekoe	**TEA**	people in church	**LAYMEN**
pelage	**HAIR, FUR, WOOL**	people in general	**FOLK**
pelagic	**MARINE, OCEANIC**	people of action	**DOERS**
pelerine	**CAPE**	people of ancient Iran	**MEDES**
pelf	**BOOTY, SPOIL**	people of Belgrade	**SERBS**
Pelican State	**LOUISIANA**	people of County Cork	**IRISH**
pellet	**BULLET**	people on the town	
pellucid	**LIMPID, CLEAR,**	(2 wds.)	**CAFE SOCIETY**
	TRANSPARENT	people waiting for	
pelota	**JAI ALAI**	relief	**BREADLINE**

pep	ENERGY, ZEST, VIM, VIGOR
peplum	FLOUNCE
pepo	FRUIT
pepper	SPICE
pepper beverage	KAVA
peppermint stick (2 wds.)	CANDY CANE
pepper pot	STEW, SOUP
peppery	FIERY
peppy	ENERGETIC
Pepys' signoff (4 wds.)	AND SO TO BED
per	THROUGH
perambulator	PRAM, CARRIAGE
perceive	SEE, NOTICE, ESPY
perception	SENSE
perch	ROOST, FISH, SIT
percheron	HORSE
percolate slowly	SEEP
percussion instrument	DRUM, CYMBAL
peremptory	ARBITRARY
peremptory request	DEMAND
perennial	PERPETUAL, CONSTANT
perfect	IDEAL
perfect model	IDEAL
perfecto	CIGAR
perfect serve in tennis	ACE
perfidious	DISLOYAL, FALSE
perfidious fellow	SNEAK
perfidy	TREACHERY, TREASON
perforate	PUNCH, BORE, PIERCE
perforation	BORE, HOLE
perform	ACT, DO
performance	ACT, EXPLOIT, PRESENTATION, DEED, FEAT
performer	ACTOR
perform in a play	ACT
perform surgery	OPERATE
perfume	AROMA, SCENT, ESSENCE, ATTAR
perfume bottle	VIAL, ATOMIZER, FLACON
perfume ingredient	ATTAR, AMBERGRIS
perfume quantity	OUNCE, DRAM
perfumery root	ORRIS
perfume with spice	INCENSE
perfunctory	INDIFFERENT
perhaps	MAYBE
peril	DANGER
perimeter	BOUNDARY
period	AGE, DOT, ERA, TIME

periodical	REGULAR, RECURRENT, PUBLICATION, MAGAZINE
period in history	ERA, EPOCH, AGE
period of dryness	DROUGHT
period of holding	TENURE
period of time	SPELL, YEAR, MONTH, WEEK
period of work	SHIFT
period without war	PEACE
periphery	PERIMETER
perish	DIE
perjurer	LIAR
perk up	LIVEN
perky	JAUNTY, LIVELY
permanent	LASTING
permanent acting group	REPERTORY
permeate	IMBUE, PENETRATE
permission	CONSENT, LICENSE
permission granted	LEAVE
permit	ALLOW, LET, LICENSE
perpetual	ETERNAL
perplex	PUZZLE, BEWILDER
perplexing point	PROBLEM
perplexity	DOUBT
perquisite	PRIVILEGE, RIGHT
persecute	HARASS, OPPRESS
perseverance	TENACITY
persevere	PLOD, CARRY ON
Persia	IRAN
Persian cat	ANGORA
Persian coin	RIAL, RIYAL
Persian fairy	PERI
Persian hat	FEZ, TURBAN
Persian king	SHAH
Persian lynx	CARACAL
Persian money	DINAR
Persian nymph	PERI, HOURI
Persian or Siamese	CAT
Persian poet	OMAR
Persian priest	MAGUS
Persian product	RUG
Persian ruler	KHAN
person	INDIVIDUAL, ONE
person against	ANTI
personal	PRIVATE
personal affair (2 wds.)	PRIVATE MATTER
personal belongings	EFFECTS
personal conviction	OPINION
personality	SELF, EGO
person held prisoner	CAPTIVE
person loved to excess	IDOL, HERO
personnel	STAFF
person of power	TITAN

person of prominence
BIG SHOT NABOB
person regarded as the finest
(4 wds.) **SALT OF THE EARTH**
persons **PEOPLE**
person's manner **MIEN, STYLE**
persons over here **THESE**
person under age **MINOR**
person with very loud voice
STENTOR
perspicacity **ACUMEN**
perspire **SWEAT, SWELTER**
persuade **ACTUATE, URGE, PROD, COAX**
pert **LIVELY, SASSY, SAUCY, SPRIGHTLY, PEPPY**
pertain **RELATE**
pertaining to (suffix) **AR**
pertaining to a city **URBAN**
pertaining to a kidney **RENAL**
pertaining to an age **ERAL**
pertaining to bees **APIAN, APIARIAN**
pertaining to birds **AVIAN, ORNITHIC**
pertaining to dawn **EOAN**
pertaining to dogs **CANINE**
pertaining to form **MODAL**
pertaining to Middle Ages
MEDIEVAL
pertaining to Norway **NORSE**
pertaining to poles **POLAR**
pertaining to sheep **OVINE**
pertaining to ships **NAVAL**
pertaining to the moon **LUNAR**
pertaining to the pope **PAPAL**
pertaining to touch **TACTUAL**
pert girl **MINX**
pertinent **RELEVANT**
perturbation **WORRY**
Peru's capital **LIMA**
Peruvian beast of burden
LLAMA
Peruvian coin **SOL**
Peruvian Indian **INCA**
Peruvian plant **OCA**
perverse **CONTRARY, STUBBORN**
pessimistic **GLOOMY, CYNICAL**
pest **NUISANCE**
pester **ANNOY, TEASE**
pet **FAVORITE, DOG, CAT, FONDLE, CARESS, STROKE**
petard **BOMB**
pet bird's home **CAGE**
petiole **STALK, STEM**
petite **SMALL, TINY, LITTLE**

petition **SUE, PLEAD**
petitioner **PLEADER**
petits fours **CAKES**
pet mammal **CAT, DOG, HORSE**
peto **WAHOO**
petrified body **FOSSIL**
petrol **GAS**
petroleum **OIL**
petroleum processor **REFINER**
petroleum product **NAPHTHA**
petroleum source (2 wds.)
OIL WELL
petticoat **SLIP**
pettish **PEEVISH, CROSS**
petty **SMALL, TRIVIAL, SPITEFUL, MEAN**
petty malice **SPITE**
petty objection **CAVIL**
petty prince **SATRAP**
petty quarrel **SPAT, TIFF**
petulant **FRETFUL, TOUCHY**
Pfc's bed **COT**
phantom **GHOST, SHADE, SPOOK, HAUNT, JET**
Pharaoh's ancestor **RA**
pharos **BEACON, LIGHTHOUSE**
phase **ASPECT, STAGE, FACET**
pheasant duck **MERGANSER**
philatelist **COLLECTOR**
Philippine island **LEYTE, SAMAR, BOHOL**
Philippine knife **BOLO**
Philippine native **MORO**
Philippine plant **ABACA**
phlegmatic **DULL, SLUGGISH**
phone greeting **HELLO**
phonograph disc **RECORD**
phonograph machine **HI-FI, JUKE BOX, STEREO**
phonograph machine part **ARM, TURNTABLE, CHANGER, SPEAKER, TUNER**
phonograph record **DISC**
phosphate **SODA**
photograph **SHOT, SNAP**
photographer's flash tube
STROBE
photographer's request **SMILE**
photographic bath **TONER**
photographic device **CAMERA**
phrase **SLOGAN, SENTENCE**
phrase of apology (2 wds.)
PARDON ME
phrase of dismay
(2 wds.) **OH NO**
phrase of understanding
(2 wds.) **I SEE**

phrase with two meanings
(2 wds.) **DOUBLE ENTENDRE**
Phrygian god of vegetation
ATTIS
Phyllis Diller's husband **FANG**
physical **CORPORAL,**
TANGIBLE, CHECK-UP
physician **DOCTOR**
physician's association (abbr.)
AMA
physiognomy **FACE,**
EXPRESSION
physique **BUILD**
pianist Brubeck **DAVE**
pianist Cliburn **VAN**
piano adjuster **TUNER**
piano key **IVORY**
piano piece **SONATA, ÉTUDE**
piano student's exercise **SCALE**
piazza **SQUARE**
picayune **PETTY, TRIVIAL**
pick **CULL, PLUCK**
pick carefully **CULL**
picket **FENCE, FORTIFY,**
STRIKER, STAKE
pickle **MARINATE**
pickle bottle **JAR**
pickled fruit **OLIVE**
pickling spice **DILL**
pick out **CHOOSE, SELECT**
pick up the check **TREAT**
picnic **OUTING**
picnic dishes (2 wds.)
PAPER PLATES
picnic pest **ANT**
picture **IMAGE**
picture exhibit room **GALLERY**
picture house **CINEMA**
picture mounting **FRAME**
picture puzzle **REBUS**
picturesque **SCENIC, CHARMING**
picture stand **EASEL**
picture taker **CAMERA,**
PHOTOGRAPHER
pie **CHAOS, JUMBLE, MESS**
piebald horse **PINTO**
piece **PART, PORTION**
piece of a tree trunk **LOG**
piece of baked clay **TILE**
piece of candy **KISS**
piece of china **PLATE, SAUCER,**
CUP, BOWL, TEACUP
piece of coal **LUMP**
piece of corn **EAR**
piece of cutlery **FORK, KNIFE,**
SPOON
piece of evidence **FACT**
piece of garlic **CLOVE**

piece of ice **FLOE, BERG,**
CUBE, BLOCK
piece of information **DATUM**
piece of jewelry **CLIP, RING,**
EARRING, HATPIN,
BRACELET, NECKLACE,
EARDROP, BROOCH
piece of land **FARM, LOT,**
ACRE
piece of luggage **GRIP, TRUNK,**
BAG, ETUI, VALISE
piece of lumber **BOARD**
piece of mail **LETTER**
piece of merchandise **WARE**
piece of money **COIN**
piece of open ground **FIELD**
piece of pasteboard **CARD**
piece of postage **STAMP**
piece of property **ASSET**
piece of rock **STONE**
piece of sculpture **BUST**
piece of stage scenery **PROP,**
FLAT
piece of sugar **LUMP**
piece of work **TASK, CHORE**
piece out **EKE**
pie covering **CRUST**
pied **DAPPLED**
pied animal **PINTO**
pied diver (Brit.) **SMEW**
pie fruit **APPLE, PEACH,**
LEMON, BERRY
pieplant **RHUBARB**
pie plate **TIN**
pier **WHARF**
pierce **GORE, STAB**
piercing **SHRILL, ACUTE**
piercing tool **AWL, NEEDLE**
pierce with the horns **GORE**
pier glass **MIRROR**
pie shell **CRUST**
piety **DEVOTION, HOLINESS**
piffle **NONSENSE, TWADDLE**
pig **HOG, PORKER, SWINE**
pigeon **DOVE**
pigeonhole **CLASSIFY**
pigeon pea **DAL**
pigeon shelter **COTE**
piggery **PEN, STY**
piggin **PAIL, DIPPER**
piggish **GREEDY, SELFISH**
pigheaded **STUBBORN**
pig meat **HAM, PORK, BACON,**
CHITLINS, TENDERLOIN
pigment **COLOR, PAINT**
pigmy **DWARF**
pigpen **STY, HOVEL**
pigpen sound **GRUNT, OINK**

pigskin	**FOOTBALL**
pigsty	**HOVEL, PEN**
pigtail	**QUEUE**
pike	**FREEWAY, HIGHWAY, ROAD**
piker	**SHIRKER**
pilaster	**COLUMN**
pile	**HEAP**
pile driver head	**TUP**
pile of hay	**MOW, STACK**
pile up a fortune	**AMASS**
pilfer	**FILCH, STEAL, SWIPE**
pilgrim	**TRAVELER**
pilgrimage	**JOURNEY**
Pilgrim settler	**PURITAN**
Pilgrims' ship	**MAYFLOWER**
pill	**PELLET, TABLET**
pillage	**PLUNDER, SACK, LOOT, ROB, BOOTY**
pillar	**COLUMN, POST**
pillar of air course	**PYLON**
pillar of a staircase	**NEWEL**
pillar projecting from wall	**PILASTER**
pillbox	**HAT, FORT**
pillory	**STOCKS**
pillow	**CUSHION, PAD**
pillow covering	**SHAM, TICK**
pillow material	**FOAM RUBBER, HAIR, DOWN**
pilot	**AVIATOR, FLYER, AIRMAN, GUIDE, STEER**
pilot biscuit	**HARDTACK**
pilsener	**BEER**
pima	**COTTON**
pimento	**ALLSPICE**
pin	**BROOCH, PEG, FASTEN**
pinafore	**APRON**
pince-nez	**LORGNETTE**
pincer	**CLAW**
pincers	**FORCEPS, PLIERS**
pinch	**NIP, SQUEEZE**
Pindar opus	**ODE**
pine	**FIR, TREE, EVERGREEN**
pineapple	**PINA**
pine fruit	**CONE, NUT**
pine gum	**SANDARAC**
pine leaf	**NEEDLE**
pine tar hydrocarbon	**RETENE**
pine tree	**LARCH, SPRUCE**
pine tree exudation	**RESIN**
Pine Tree State	**MAINE**
pinion	**FEATHER**
pink	**CARNATION**
pinnacle	**PEAK, APEX**
pin one's ears back	**DEFEAT, SCOLD**
pintail	**SMEE**

pioneer	**SETTLER, EARLIEST, FIRST**
pious	**DEVOUT**
pipe	**TUBE, MEERSCHAUM, CORNCOB**
pipe fitting	**TEE**
pipe of peace	**CALUMET**
pipette	**DROPPER**
piquant	**SHARP, ZESTY, SPICY**
pique	**IRE, ANGER**
pirate	**SEA ROVER, BUCCANEER, PRIVATEER**
pirate flag (2 wds.)	**JOLLY ROGER**
pismire	**ANT**
pistol attachment	**SILENCER**
pistol (sl.)	**PIECE, ROSCOE, GAT**
pit	**HOLE, CAVITY**
pitch	**TAR, THROW, TOSS**
pitcher	**EWER**
pitcher ear	**HANDLE**
pitcher handle	**EAR**
pitcher's motions	**WINDUP**
piteous	**PATHETIC**
pitfall	**TRAP**
pith	**GIST, ESSENCE**
pith helmet	**TOPEE**
pithy statement	**APHORISM**
pitiful	**WOEFUL, SAD**
Pius	**POPE**
pivot	**SLUE, TURN, SWING**
pivotal	**FOCAL**
pixie	**ELF, IMP, SPRITE, BROWNIE, FAIRY**
placard	**POSTER**
place	**PUT, LAY, LOCATION, LOCALE, LIEU, STEAD, SET**
place (prefix)	**TOPO**
place a bet	**WAGER**
place a phone call	**DIAL**
place at intervals	**SPACE**
place between	**INSERT**
place confidence in	**RELY, TRUST**
place end for end	**REVERSE**
place for a drama critic	**AISLE**
place for animals	**ZOO, MENAGERIE**
place for art exhibit	**MUSEUM, GALLERY**
place for coal	**BIN**
place for exercise	**GYM, GYMNASIUM, HEALTH CLUB**
place for fish	**AQUARIUM**
place for money	**BANK**

place for sheets, towels, etc.
(2 wds.) **LINEN CLOSET**
place for skating **RINK**
place for the press **BOX**
place for unclaimed
mail (abbr.) **DLO**
place in proximity **APPOSE,
NEAR**
place of business **OFFICE,
STORE, SHOP,
MARKET**
place of entrance **ENTRY,
FOYER, LOBBY**
place of recreation **PARK,
RESORT**
place of retreat **HIDEAWAY,
DEN**
place of shelter **HAVEN,
REFUGE**
place of worship **ALTAR,
CHURCH, CHAPEL
TEMPLE**
places **LOCI**
place to live **HOUSE, FLAT,
APARTMENT**
place to sit **CHAIR, BENCH,
SEAT**
place to ski **SLOPE**
place to sleep **BED, COT,
BEDROOM**
placid **SERENE**
plagiarize **CRIB, PURLOIN**
plague **HARASS, FEVER**
plague carrier **RAT**
plaid **TARTAN**
plain **HOMELY, EVIDENT**
Plains Indian **OTOE, SIOUX,
CROW**
plain song **CHANT**
plaintiff **SUER, PETITIONER,
COMPLAINANT**
plaintive **WISTFUL, PATHETIC**
plait **FOLD, BRAID**
plan **SCHEME, PLOT,
BLUEPRINT, MAP**
plane **EVEN, LEVEL**
planet **MARS, PLUTO, VENUS,
NEPTUNE, MERCURY,
EARTH, URANUS, SATURN,
SPHERE, JUPITER**
planet nearest sun **MERCURY**
planet nearest us **VENUS**
planet's orbit **ELLIPSE**
plan frustrater **MARPLOT**
plank **BOARD**
plant **SEED, SOW, FACTORY,
MILL**
plantain **BANANA**

plant beginning **SEED**
plant by strewing **SOW**
plant disease **ERGOT, SMUT**
plant embryo **SEED**
plant exudation **SAP, RESIN**
plant firmly **IMBED**
plant fluid **SAP**
plant hemp **JUTE**
plant louse **APHID**
plant opening **STOMA**
plant part **ROOT, STEM,
STALK, LEAF, PETAL,
CORM, SEPAL**
plant protection **MULCH**
plant root **RADIX**
plants, collectively **FLORA,
VEGETATION**
plant seed **SOW**
plant stalk **STEM**
plant superintendent **FOREMAN**
plant with prickly leaves
THISTLE
plasterer **MASON**
Plaster of Paris **GESSO**
plastic **DUCTILE, PLIANT**
plate **DISH, PATEN, PLATTER,
REPRODUCTION, METALWARE**
platform **STAGE, ELEVATION,
POLICIES**
plating metal **TIN**
platitude **CLICHE**
platoon **UNIT**
platter **PLATE, RECORD, DISC**
plaudit **APPLAUSE, PRAISE**
plausible **LIKELY, PROBABLE**
play **DRAMA, SPORT**
play a banjo **STRUM**
play area **YARD, PARK**
play a role **ACT**
play at courtship **FLIRT**
play at tenpins **BOWL**
play boisterously **ROMP**
play busybody **NOSE, SNOOP,
PRY**
play characters **CAST**
play division **ACT, SCENE**
player **ACTOR, GAMBLER**
player's morale (2 wds.)
TEAM SPIRIT
player's part **ROLE**
play for time **STALL**
playful talk **BADINAGE,
BANTER**
playful water mammal **OTTER**
playing card **ACE, DEUCE,
TREY, TEN, KING, QUEEN,
JACK, KNAVE
DIAMOND,**
playing field **GRIDIRON, COURT**

playing marble	AGATE, TAW, MIB	plot	PLAN, SCHEME
playing the wrong role	MISCAST	plot of land	LOT, PLAT
playlet	SKIT	plowed land (Sp.)	ARADA
play on words	PUN	pluck	COURAGE, GRIT, PICK
play outline	SCENARIO	pluck a guitar	STRUM
play setting	SCENE	plug	PEG
play the first card	LEAD	plug up	STOP
plaything	TOY	plume	FEATHER
play unfairly	CHEAT	plump	FAT, OBESE, PUDGY, ROLY-POLY
play up	PLUG, ADVERTISE	plunder	LOOT, SACK, RANSACK, BOOTY, SPOILS
play up to	FLATTER	plunge	DIVE
play without dialogue	MIME, PANTOMIME	plunge in boiling liquid	POACH
playwright	DRAMATIST	plunge in liquid	DIP
playwright Albee	EDWARD	plunk	STRUM, TWANG
playwright Anouilh	JEAN	plurality	MAJORITY
playwright Coward	NOEL	plus	AND, ALSO
playwright Jones	LE ROI	plus fours	KNICKERS
playwright Rattigan	TERENCE	plush	RICH, ELEGANT
plaza	SQUARE, MALL	Plutarch work	LIVES, BIOGRAPHY
plaza cheer	OLE	ply	FOLD, LAYER, STRAND, WIELD, SUPPLY, SAIL, WORK, STEER
plea	APOLOGY, ENTREATY, PRAYER		
pleach	PLAIT, PLASH	PM beverage	TEA
plead	BEG, ENTREAT, PRAY, PETITION	poach	TRESPASS
		pocketbook	BAG, PURSE, HANDBAG, BILLFOLD
pleader	ADVOCATE, SUER	pocosin	SWAMP
pleasant	AGREEABLE, NICE	pod	COCOON, HERD
pleasant expression	SMILE	podagra	GOUT
pleasant manners	AMENITIES	podium	DAIS
please	SUIT	pod vegetable	PEA
pleased	GLAD, HAPPY	poem	ODE, VERSE, SONG, SONNET
please greatly	DELIGHT		
pleasing odor	AROMA, PERFUME, BOUQUET, FRAGRANCE	poem part	REFRAIN, EPODE
		Poe's bird	RAVEN
		poesy	VERSE
pleasure	JOY, PREFERENCE	poet	BARD
pleasure boat	BARGE, YACHT	poetess Lowell	AMY
pleasure ground	PARK	poetic	LYRIC
pleasure seeker	EPICURE	poetic contraction	E'EN, E'ER, 'TIS
pleasure ship	YACHT		
pleasure trip	JAUNT, JUNKET, CRUISE, VACATION	poetic fiction	MYTH
		poetic foot	IAMB, IAMBUS
pleat	FOLD	poetic possessive	THINE, THY
plebeian	COMMON, VULGAR	poetic preposition	ERE
plebiscite	DECREE, VOTE	poetic unit	VERSE, LINE
pledge	PROMISE, OATH, TOAST	poet Pound	EZRA
		poetry	POESY, VERSE
pledged faith	TROTH	poet Sandburg	CARL
plenary	COMPLETE, FULL	poet-singer McKuen	ROD
plentiful	AMPLE	pogonip	FOG
plenty	ENOUGH	pogrom	SLAUGHTER, PERSECUTION
plethora	EXCESS		
pliant	SUPPLE	poignant	PIERCING, BITTER, MOVING
plight	DILEMMA		
plod	TRUDGE		

point | MEANING, NUB, PROMONTORY
point a gun | AIM
point at stake | ISSUE
point-blank | BLUNT, DIRECT
pointed (Heb.) | URDE
pointed arch | OGIVE
pointed tool | AWL
pointed weapon | DAGGER, SPEAR, SWORD, ARROW, DART, LANCE
pointer | SETTER
pointing signal | ARROW
pointless | INANE, SILLY
point of departure | ZERO
point of difference | CONTRAST
point of land | SPIT
point of orbit, in astronomy | APSIS
point of view | ANGLE, SLANT
point opposite zenith | NADIR
point out | INDICATE
points in a game | SCORE
point the way | DIRECT
poise | BALANCE, CALM
poison | VENIN, ARSENIC, VENOM
poison ash | SUMAC
poison from a snake | VENOM
poisonous | NOXIOUS, TOXIC
poisonous shrub | SUMAC
poisonous snake | ASP, COBRA, VIPER, ADDER, RATTLER
poke | JAB, PROD, NUDGE, SACK, BAG
poke around | ROOT
poke fun at | RIDICULE, DERIDE
poker game | STUD, DRAW
poker holding | PAIR, STRAIGHT, FULL HOUSE, FLUSH
poker kitty | ANTE
poker money | CHIP
poker player | GAMBLER
poker stake | ANTE
Polar exploration base | ETAH
polar explorer | BYRD, PEARY
polar lights | AURORA BOREALIS
polar region | NORTH, ARCTIC, ANTARCTICA
pole | ROD, SHAFT
polecat | SKUNK
polemic | CONTROVERSIAL
police (colloq.) | COPS, FUZZ
police action | RAID
policeman (sl.) | FLATFOOT
policeman's shield | BADGE
policy | PRINCIPLE, PLAN

polish | BUFF, GLOSS, LUSTER, SHINE, SHEEN, RUB
Polish city | CRACOW, WARSAW
polished | ELEGANT, REFINED
polishing stone | EMERY
polite | CIVIL, REFINED
polite society (2 wds.) | BON TON
politic | PRUDENT
political group | BLOC, PARTY, CLUB, LOBBY
political meeting | RALLY
political party | REPUBLICAN, DEMOCRATIC, LIBERAL, COMMUNIST, CONSERVATIVE, SOCIALIST
politician | STATESMAN, CANDIDATE
pollack fish | SEY, COD
pollen bearer | BEE
polliwog | TADPOLE
pollute | CONTAMINATE, TAINT, DEFILE
polo stick | MALLET
Polynesian | HAWAIIAN, SAMOAN, TAHITIAN, MAORI, TONGAN
Polynesian dance | HULA
Polynesian fabric | TAPA
Polynesian god | ATEO, TIKI
Polynesian occupation (2 wds.) | PEARL DIVER
pompous | HAUGHTY, ARROGANT
pompous show | PARADE
poncho | SARAPE, SERAPE
pond | POOL, LAGOON
pond duck | MALLARD
ponder | MULL, MUSE, THINK
ponderous | HEAVY, INERT, DULL, MASSIVE
pone | CORNBREAD
pongee | SILK, SHANTUNG, TUSSAH
Pons specialty | ARIA
pontiff | BISHOP
pontoon | BOAT, BRIDGE
pooch | DOG
pool | LINN, RESERVOIR
poolside dressing room | CABANA
poop | STERN, DECK, DATA
poor | MEAGER, NEEDY
poor area | SLUM, GHETTO
poor person (comp. wd.) | HAVE-NOT

pop   SODA, BURST, FATHER, DADDY
pope's headdress   MITRE
pope's scarf   FANON, ORALE
pop into the oven   BAKE
poplar   ASPEN, TREE
popover   MUFFIN
poppycock   NONSENSE
pop's wife   MOM
pop the question   PROPOSE
populace   DEMOS
popular   LIKED
popular dessert   PIE, CAKE, ICE CREAM
popular flower   ROSE, DAISY, MUM
popular girl   BELLE
popularly supposed   REPUTED
popular Mother's Day gift (2 wds.)   POTTED PLANT
popular snack   BURGER, CHIPS, WIENER, FRANK, DANISH
popular success   HIT
popular TV program   WESTERN, SOAP OPERA, COMEDY
populate   PEOPLE
population center   CITY, MEGALOPOLIS
porcelain clay   KAOLIN
porcelain ware   CHINA
porch   PORTICO, VERANDA, STOA
porch swing   GLIDER
porcine animal   PIG, HOG
porcine home   PIGSTY, STY, PEN
porcine mother   SOW
porcupine   HEDGEHOG
porcupine quill   SPINE
pore   STUDY, STOMA
pork fat   LARD
pork pie   HAT
porpoise   DOLPHIN
porridge   CEREAL, MEAL
porringer   BOWL
port   WINE, HARBOR, HAVEN
portable   MOVABLE, MOBILE
portable home   TRAILER
portable light   LANTERN, FLASHLIGHT
portable lodge   TENT, CAMPER
portable steps   LADDER
portable sunshade   PARASOL
portal   GATE, DOOR
portcullis   GATE, SHUT, BAR, GRATING
portend   BODE, FORETOKEN
portent   OMEN, SIGN, EVENT

porter   ALE, DOORMAN
portico   STOA, PORCH, COLONNADE
portion   PART, SHARE
portion of bacon   RASHER
portion of land   LOT, PARCEL, ACRE
portion of medicine   DOSE
portion out   ALLOT, DOLE, METE
portly   OBESE, PLUMP, FAT
portmanteau   BAG, CASE
port of Rome   OSTIA
port of the South Seas   APIA
port on the Weser River   BREMEN
portrait   PHOTO, PICTURE
portrait by Da Vinci (2 wds.)   MONA LISA
portrait on fifty dollar bill   GRANT
portrait on five dollar bill   LINCOLN
portrait on one dollar bill   WASHINGTON
portrait on one hundred dollar bill   FRANKLIN
Portugal and Spain   IBERIA
Portuguese coin   REI
Portuguese islands   AZORES
Portuguese lady   DONA
Portuguese title   DOM
pose   SIT
posh   ELEGANT
position   PLACE, POST, SITE, STANCE, ARRANGE, JOB
position halfway between   MIDPOINT, CENTER
position in education   DEAN, TEACHERAGE, CHAIR, PROFESSORSHIP, CHAIRMAN, PRESIDENT, PRINCIPAL
positive   CERTAIN, SURE
positive electrode   ANODE
positive pole   ION
positive quantity   PLUS
possess   HAVE, OWN, HOLD
possessed   MAD, BEWITCHED
possession   ASSET
possessive pronoun   HER, HERS, HIS, MY, YOUR, OUR, THEIR, MINE, THEIRS, OURS
possible   FEASIBLE, LIKELY
possibly   MAYBE
post   PILLAR, COLUMN, MAIL
postage stamp paper   PELURE
post a letter   MAIL, SEND

post and wire barrier **FENCE**
post boat **PACKET**
postcard message (4 wds.)
WISH YOU WERE HERE
poster **BILL, PLACARD**
postpone **DEFER, DELAY,**
TABLE
postpone indefinitely **SHELVE**
postponement **RESPITE, RAIN**
CHECK, DELAY,
DEFERMENT
post service **MAIL**
postulate **CLAIM, STIPULATE**
posture **ATTITUDE, STANCE**
posy **NOSEGAY, FLOWER,**
BOUQUET
pot **PAN, KETTLE, SAUCEPAN**
potash **NITER, SALIN**
potassium carbonate **POTASH**
potassium compound **ALUM**
potation **DRAFT, DRINK**
potato **SPUD, TUBER**
potato bud **EYE**
potato masher **RICER**
potato squasher **MASHER**
pot cover **LID**
potent **POWERFUL, STRONG**
potentate **RULER**
potential **LATENT, POSSIBLE**
potential prune **PLUM**
potential steel **IRON**
potential trouble source
TINDERBOX
pother **ADO, FUSS, ROW**
potiche **VASE**
potion **DRAFT, DOSE**
potpourri **OLIO, COMBINATION,**
MIXTURE
potsy **HOPSCOTCH**
pottage **SOUP, STEW**
potter's clay **ARGIL**
pottery **CERAMICS**
pottery clay **KAOLIN**
pottery fragment **SHARD,**
SHERD,
potto **LEMUR, KINKAJOU**
pouch **BAG, SAC**
poultry **CHICKENS, HENS**
poultry product **EGG, CHICKEN,**
DUCK
pounce **SPRING, LEAP**
pound **BEAT**
pound (abbr.) **LB.**
pound down **TAMP**
pounder **PESTLE**
pour **TEEM**
pourboire **TIP**
pour down **RAIN**

pour forth **GUSH, SPOUT**
pout **SULK, MOPE**
poverty **LACK, INDIGENCE**
poverty-stricken **NEEDY,**
POOR, DESOLATE
powder base **TALC**
powdery dirt **DUST**
power **ENERGY, STRENGTH,**
LEVERAGE
powerful **HEFTY, POTENT,**
STRONG
powerful businessman
TYCOON,
MAGNATE
powerful explosive **TNT**
powerful light beam **LASER**
powwow **CONFERENCE**
practical **PRAGMATIC,**
WORKABLE
practical joke **HOAX, CAPER,**
TRICK
practice **CUSTOM, DRILL**
practice a performance
REHEARSE
pragmatic **PRACTICAL,**
DOGMATIC
prairie **PLAIN, STEPPE**
Prairie State **ILLINOIS**
praise **COMPLIMENT, LAUD,**
EXALT
praise insincerely **FLATTER**
prance **CAPER, CAVORT,**
CURVET
prank **DIDO, TRICK, CAPER,**
ANTIC
prate **CHATTER, PRATTLE,**
TWADDLE
prattle **PRATE, CHATTER**
prawn **SHRIMP**
pray **ASK, PLEAD**
prayer **PLEA, ENTREATY,**
AVE, THANKS
prayer beads **ROSARY**
prayer book **MISSAL**
prayer ending **AMEN**
prayer shawl **TALLIS, TALLITH**
praying insect **MANTIS**
praying figure **ORANT**
preach **ORATE, SERMONIZE**
preacher **PARSON, MINISTER**
pre-adult insect **PUPA**
Preakness **RACE**
preamble **PREFACE**
precarious **INSECURE,**
DUBIOUS
precarious situation (3 wds.)
TOUCH AND GO
precedence **PRIORITY**

preceding **PRIOR, PREVIOUS**
precept **LAW, RULE**
precious **DEAR**
precious jewel **GEM, PEARL, DIAMOND, RUBY, EMERALD, OPAL, GARNET**
precious metal **GOLD, SILVER, PLATINUM**
precious stone **GEM, AGATE**
precipice **CRAG**
precipitate **HASTY, RASH, RUSH, HURRY**
precipitation **RAIN, SNOW, SLEET, HAIL**
precipitous **STEEP**
precis **SUMMARY, EPITOME**
precise **ACCURATE, CORRECT**
preclude **BAR, AVERT**
predatory **PREYING, DESTRUCTIVE**
predecessor of the bus **HORSECAR, TROLLEY**
predetermine **DESTINE, ORDAIN**
predicament **SCRAPE**
predicate (abbr.) **PRED**
predict **AUGUR, BODE**
prediction **PROPHECY, FORECAST**
predominant **UPPERMOST**
preen **PRIMP**
preface **FOREWORD, PROLOGUE**
prefer **FAVOR, SELECT**
preferably **RATHER**
preference **TASTE, CHOICE**
prehistoric dwelling **CAVE**
prehistoric era (2 wds.) **STONE AGE**
prehistoric man (2 wds.) **CAVE DWELLER, APE MAN**
preholiday period **EVE**
prejudice **BIAS**
preliminary draft **SKETCH, OUTLINE**
prelude **PREFACE, PROEM**
premeditated **INTENTIONAL**
premier **CHIEF, FIRST**
preoccupied **ENRAPT**
prep school in England **ETON, HARROW**
prepare **ARRANGE**
prepare a salad **TOSS**
prepare, as beer **BREW**
prepare copy **EDIT**
prepared **READY, READIED**

prepare food by canning **PRESERVE**
prepare for war **ARM**
prepare the way for **PAVE**
prepare to fire **AIM**
prepare to testify (3 wds.) **TAKE THE STAND, TAKE AN OATH**
preposition **INTO, OF, ON, IN, OFF, FROM, BY, FOR, ONTO**
preposterous **ABSURD, SILLY**
prerecord a broadcast **TAPE**
prerogative **PRIORITY, RIGHT**
presage **OMEN, PORTEND**
presbyter **MINISTER, ELDER**
prescribe **LIMIT, ORDER**
prescribed amount **DOSE**
presence **AIR, MIEN**
present **HERE, GIVE, GIFT**
present as a gift **BESTOW, DONATE**
present for acceptance **OFFER**
presentiment **PREMONITION**
presently **ANON, SOON**
present time **NOW, TODAY**
preserve **SAVE**
preserve vegetables **CAN, FREEZE, PICKLE**
president **GEORGE WASHINGTON, JOHN ADAMS, THOMAS JEFFERSON, JAMES MADISON, JAMES MONROE, JOHN QUINCY ADAMS, ANDREW JACKSON, MARTIN VAN BUREN, WILLIAM HENRY HARRISON, JOHN TYLER, JAMES KNOX POLK, ZACHARY TAYLOR, MILLARD FILLMORE, FRANKLIN PIERCE, JAMES BUCHANAN, ABRAHAM (ABE, HONEST ABE) LINCOLN, ANDREW JOHNSON, ULYSSES SIMPSON (HIRAM ULYSSES) GRANT, RUTHERFORD B. HAYES, JAMES ABRAM GARFIELD, CHESTER ALAN ARTHUR, GROVER CLEVELAND, BENJAMIN HARRISON, WILLIAM McKINLEY, THEODORE ROOSEVELT, WILLIAM HOWARD TAFT, WOODROW WILSON, WARREN G. HARDING, JOHN CALVIN (CAL, SILENT CAL) COOLIDGE, HERBERT CLARK HOOVER, FRANKLIN DELANO**

ROOSEVELT, HARRY S.
TRUMAN, DWIGHT DAVID
(IKE) EISENHOWER, JOHN
FITZGERALD KENNEDY,
LYNDON BAINES JOHNSON,
RICHARD MILHOUS NIXON
president (abbr.) **PRES.**
presidential advisers **CABINET**
president of the Confederacy **DAVIS**
president of Yugoslavia **TITO**
president's no **VETO**
presiding officer **CHAIRMAN**
presiding officer of the House **SPEAKER**
presiding officer's mallet **GAVEL**
press **FORCE, URGE**
press agent's concern **PUBLICITY**
press clothes **IRON, STEAM**
press down **RAM, TAMP**
press for payment **DUN**
pressure **STRESS**
prestidigitator **MAGICIAN, CONJURER, JUGGLER**
prestige **INFLUENCE**
presume **ASSUME**
presumption **AUDACITY**
presumptuous **INSOLENT, ARROGANT**
presuppose **POSIT**
pretend **SHAM, LET ON, SUPPOSE, ACT, FAKE, FEIGN, POSE, SEEM**
pretender **CLAIMANT**
pretense **ACT, POSE, SHAM**
pretentious **AFFECTED**
pretext **EXCUSE**
pretty **BONNY, CUTE, BEAUTIFUL**
prevail **REIGN**
prevail upon **PERSUADE**
prevalent **RIFE**
prevaricate **LIE, FIB**
prevent **AVERT, DETER, WARD OFF, ESTOP, BAR, DEBAR**
previous **PRIOR, FORMER**
prey **QUARRY**
prey upon **HUNT, PLUNDER**
price **RATE, COST, FARE, FEE**
price label **TAG, TAB**
price of passage **FARE**
price per unit **RATE**
prick **PIERCE**
prickle **THORN, NETTLE**
prickly fin **ACANTHA**
prickly heat **MILIARA**

prickly plant **THISTLE**
prickly seed **BUR, BURR**
prickly sensation **TINGLE**
prickly shrub **BRIAR**
prick painfully **STING**
pride **VANITY, CONCEIT**
priest **PASTOR, CLERIC, FATHER, PADRE**
priest's assistant **ACOLYTE**
priest's mantle **COPE**
priest's vestment **STOLE, ALB, EPHOD, AMICE**
prig **PRUDE, PEDANT**
priggish **PRIM**
prim **SEDATE, PRISSY**
prima donna **DIVA**
primary **PRINCIPAL, CHIEF**
primary color **BLUE, RED, YELLOW**
primate **APE-MAN, APE, HUMANOID**
prime **FIRST, ORIGINAL**
prime minister **PREMIER**
primeval **ANCIENT, PRIMITIVE**
primitive **CRUDE, SIMPLE**
primitive chisel **CELT**
primitive wind instrument **PANPIPE**
primitive word **ETYMON**
primp **PREEN**
primrose **YELLOW**
Prince Albert **COAT**
prince in India **RAJA, RAJAH**
princely **REGAL, AUGUST**
Prince of Darkness **DEVIL, SATAN**
Prince of Denmark **HAMLET**
prince of evil **DEVIL, SATAN, LUCIFER, MEPHISTOPHELES**
Prince of the Church **CARDINAL**
Princeton's mascot **TIGER**
principal **MAIN, CHIEF**
principal actor **STAR**
principal commodity **STAPLE**
principle **TENET**
print **PUBLISH, LETTER**
printed defamation **LIBEL**
printed fabric **PERCALE, CHINTZ**
printer's aid **DEVIL**
printer's commodity **INK, TYPE, PLATE**
printer's direction **STET, DELE**
printer's mark **CARET**
printer's measure **EN, EM**
printing error **ERRATUM**
printing for the blind **BRAILLE**
printing machine **PRESS**

printing necessity **INK**
printing process **OFFSET**
prior to **ERE, BEFORE**
priority **PRECEDENCE**
priory **CLOISTER**
prison **JAIL, CAGE, GAOL, PEN**
prison dweller **INMATE**
prisoner **CAPTIVE, INMATE**
prison official **WARDEN**
prison room **CELL**
pristine **PURE, UNTOUCHED**
private **PERSONAL, SOLDIER**
private entrance **POSTERN**
privateer **RAIDER, PIRATE, BUCCANEER**
private eye **SHAMUS**
private high school (colloq.) **PREP**
private pupil **TUTEE**
private road **DRIVEWAY**
private room **DEN**
private teacher **TUTOR**
privation **NEED, WANT**
privilege **RIGHT**
prize **AWARD, TROPHY, CUP**
prize bestowed **AWARD**
prizefight **BOUT**
prize money **PURSE**
prize ring **ARENA**
pro **FOR**
proa **OUTRIGGER**
probable **LIKELY**
probe **EXAMINE, SEARCH**
problematic **UNCERTAIN, UNSETTLED**
proboscis **NOSE, SNOUT, TRUNK**
procedure **ORDER, SYSTEM**
proceed **GO, GET ON**
proceeding **ACTION, PROCESS**
proceeds **PROFIT, INCOME**
process **METHOD**
process crude oil **REFINE**
procession **PARADE**
process leather **TAN**
proclaim **DECLARE**
proclamation **EDICT**
proclivity **BENT, LEANING**
procrastinate **DELAY, PUT OFF**
proctor **AGENT**
procurator of Judea **PILATE**
procure **ACQUIRE, SECURE**
prod **GOAD, NUDGE, POKE, URGE**
prodigy **MARVEL**
produce **GENERATE, YIELD, BEAR**

produce offspring **BREED, PROCREATE**
producer-director Preminger **OTTO**
productive **FERTILE, CREATIVE**
product of milk coagulation **CURD**
product of Pittsburgh **STEEL**
product of worms **SILK**
proem **PRELUDE, PREAMBLE**
profane **IMPURE, SECULAR**
profess **AVOW, STATE, SAY**
profession **CAREER, JOB, VOCATION, DECLARATION**
professional **EXPERT, PAID**
professional charge **FEE**
professional poet **BARD**
professional tramp **HOBO**
professor **TEACHER**
proffer **TENDER, OFFER**
proficient **ABLE, CAPABLE**
profile **CONTOUR, OUTLINE**
profit **GAIN, NET**
profit by **CAPITALIZE**
profligate **CORRUPT, VICIOUS**
profound **DEEP**
profound sleep **SOPOR, COMA, STUPOR**
profuse **LAVISH, COPIOUS**
profusion **ABUNDANCE**
progenitor **SIRE, FATHER**
progeny **SONS, OFFSPRING, CHILDREN, DESCENDANTS**
prognosis **FORECAST**
program **AGENDA, SCHEDULE**
programmer's direction (2 wds.) **READ OUT**
progress **GROWTH, ADVANCE**
progressive **LIBERAL**
prohibit **BAN, TABU, TABOO, DEBAR, ESTOP, FORBID**
prohibition **DRY**
prohibition on commerce **EMBARGO**
project **JUT, PLAN, SCHEME**
projectile **MISSILE**
projecting work, in fortification **REDAN**
prolix **WORDY, VERBOSE**
prolonged and wordy **PROLIX**
prominent **IMPORTANT**
promise **PLEDGE, WORD**
promise solemnly **VOW**
promontory **CAPE, NESS, HEADLAND, POINT**
promote **ADVANCE, ADVERTISE**

promulgate	**PUBLISH, DECLARE**
prone	**LIKELY**
prone to change	**MUTABLE**
prong	**TINE**
pronged instrument	**FORK**
pronoun	**HER, HIM, IT, ME, YOU, US, WE, HE, SHE, THEY, THEM, THIS, THOSE**
pronounce	**ARTICULATE**
pronounce indistinctly	**SLUR, GARBLE**
pronouncement	**DICTUM, DICTA (pl.)**
pronto	**QUICK**
proof	**EVIDENCE**
proof of ownership	**DEED**
proof of payment	**RECEIPT**
proofreader's mark	**CARET**
pro or con	**VOTE**
prop	**LEG, SUPPORT, BRACE**
propel	**DRIVE**
propel with oars	**ROW**
propensity	**INCLINATION**
proper	**DUE, MEET**
property	**ASSET, ESTATE, LAND, REAL ESTATE**
property manager	**TRUSTEE**
property right	**LIEN**
prophecy	**ORACLE**
prophesy	**AUGUR, PREDICT**
prophet	**SEER, AMOS, HOSEA, MICAH, ISAIAH, JOEL, OBADIAH, JONAH, NAHUM, HABAKKUK, ZEPHANIAH, HAGGAI, ZECHARIAH, MALACHI**
prophetic	**FATEFUL**
prophetic sign	**OMEN**
propinquity	**NEARNESS**
propitiate	**CONCILIATE, APPEASE**
propitious	**FAVORABLE**
proportion	**RATIO**
proposal	**OFFER, DESIGN**
propose	**OFFER, BID**
proprietor	**OWNER**
propriety	**DECORUM**
prosaic	**DRAB, INSIPID**
proscribe	**FORBID, OUTLAW**
prosecute	**SUE**
proselyte	**CONVERT**
prospect	**VISTA, VIEW**
prospector's find	**ORE**
prosper	**SUCCEED, THRIVE**
prosperity	**WEAL, WELFARE**
Prospero's helper	**ARIEL**

prosperous (2 wds.)	**WELL OFF**
prostrate	**POWERLESS, OVERCOME**
protagonist	**HERO**
protean	**VARIABLE**
protect	**DEFEND, PRESERVE**
protect an invention	**PATENT**
protect from the sun	**SHADE**
protection	**EGIS**
protective barrier	**SCREEN, GATE**
protective case for a light	**LANTERN**
protective covering	**ARMOR**
protective ditch	**MOAT**
protective garment	**APRON, COAT, SMOCK, OVERALLS**
protective layer	**COAT**
protective slope	**GLACIS**
protege	**WARD**
proteinase	**PEPSIN, TRYPSIN**
protozoan	**AMEBA**
protract	**EXTEND**
protracted	**LONG**
protracted speech	**TIRADE**
protrude	**JUT**
protuberance	**BULGE, NODE**
protuberance on a camel	**HUMP**
proud	**ARROGANT, VAIN**
prove	**VERIFY, TEST**
provender	**FODDER**
provenience	**ORIGIN, SOURCE**
proverb	**ADAGE, MAXIM, SAW**
proverbial back-breaker (2 wds.)	**LAST STRAW**
prove satisfactory (3 wds.)	**RING THE BELL**
prove to be false	**BELIE, REFUTE**
provide	**FURNISH**
provide food and service	**CATER**
provide free food	**TREAT**
provident	**FARSIGHTED, FRUGAL**
provide schooling for	**EDUCATE**
provide weapons	**ARM**
provide (with qualities)	**ENDUE, IMBUE**
province in Canada	**ONTARIO, ALBERTA, BRITISH COLUMBIA, MANITOBA, NEW BRUNSWICK, NOVA SCOTIA, QUEBEC, SASKATCHEWAN, NEWFOUNDLAND**
provincial	**RURAL**

provincial bishop	**PRIMATE**
provision	**FOOD**
proviso	**IF, CLAUSE**
provoke	**EXCITE, STIR**
prow	**STEM**
prowess	**ABILITY, VALOR**
prowl	**SNOOP, PRY, SNEAK**
proximal	**NEXT**
proximity	**NEARNESS**
proxy	**AGENT, PROCURATOR**
prudent	**DISCREET, WISE**
prudish one (colloq.)	
	BLUENOSE
prune	**TRIM**
pry	**WRENCH, LEVER, SNOOP**
pry bar	**LEVER**
prying	**CURIOUS**
psalm	**HYMN**
psalmist	**DAVID**
pseudonym	**ALIAS, NOM DE**
	PLUME, PEN NAME
psyche	**MIND**
psychotic	**INSANE**
pub	**TAVERN, BAR, SALOON**
pub beverage	**ALE, STOUT,**
	BEER
public	**OPEN, OVERT**
public discussion	**DEBATE**
public disturbance	**RIOT**
public garden	**PARK**
public house	**INN, TAVERN,**
	PUB
publicity	**BALLYHOO**
public notice	**AD**
public official	**NOTARY**
public park	**COMMONS**
public procession	**PARADE**
public road	**STREET, AVENUE,**
	BOULEVARD, PIKE
public service	**UTILITY**
public speaker	**LECTURER,**
	ORATOR
public storehouse	**ETAPE**
public vehicle	**BUS, CAB,**
	TAXI, TRAIN
public walk	**MALL**
publish	**ISSUE, PRINT**
puck	**SPRITE, ELF, DISC**
puddle	**POOL**
pudgy	**DUMPY**
Pueblo Indian	**HOPI, ZUNI**
puerile	**CHILDISH, JUVENILE**
Puerto Rican resort	**PONCE**
puff	**PANT, GASP**
Puff's friend	**SPOT**
pugilist	**BOXER**
pugnacious	**MILITANT**

puissance	**STRENGTH,**
	MIGHT, FORCE,
	POWER
pulchritude	**BEAUTY,**
	COMELINESS
pull	**HAUL, TOW, TUG, LUG,**
	DRAG, YANK, DRAW
pull down	**DEMOLISH**
pullet	**HEN**
pull into a fold	**TUCK**
pullman	**SLEEPER**
pull one's leg	**HOAX**
pull out	**EXTRACT**
pullover	**SWEATER**
pull to pieces	**TEAR, RIP, REND**
pulpit	**ROSTRUM**
pulpy substance	**POMACE**
pulsate	**THROB, BEAT**
pulse	**THROB**
pulverize	**GRIND, MASH**
pulverizing machine	
(2 wds.)	**ROD MILL**
puma	**COUGAR**
pummel	**BATTER, BEAT**
pump	**SHOE**
punch	**CUFF, SOCK**
Punch and Judy	**PUPPETS**
punching tool	**AWL**
punch server	**LADLE, BOWL**
punctilious	**FORMAL, PRECISE**
punctual	**PROMPT**
punctuation mark	**COLON,**
	PERIOD, COMMA
pungent	**ACRID, SPICY,**
	TANGY, ZESTY
pungent bulb	**ONION**
pungent flavoring	**GARLIC**
pungent refrigerant	**AMMONIA**
pungent shrub	**SAGE**
punish	**DISCIPLINE,**
	CHASTISE, FINE
punish a child	**SPANK**
punishing	**PENAL**
puny	**FEEBLE, LITTLE**
pupil	**STUDENT**
pupil (Fr.)	**ELEVE**
pupil's assignment	**LESSON,**
	HOMEWORK
pupil's record (2 wds.)	
	REPORT CARD
puppet	**DOLL**
puppeteer Lewis	**SHARI**
puppy sound	**YIP, YAP, YELP**
purchase	**BUY**
purchase back	**REDEEM**
purdah	**VEIL**
pure	**CHASTE,**
	UNADULTERATED

pure air	OZONE
purified wool fat	LANOLIN
purify	REFINE
purl	LOOP
purloin	STEAL, FILCH
purple	AMETHYST, VIOLET
purple flower	VIOLET, IRIS
purple fruit	PLUM, GRAPE
purple plum	DAMSON
purport	OBJECT, SENSE
purpose	AIM, INTENT, END, DESIGN, MEANING
purse	BAG, HANDBAG, POCKETBOOK
pursue	CHASE, GO AFTER, TAIL, FOLLOW
purvey	CATER, PROVIDE, FURNISH
push	SHOVE
push aside	SHUNT
pushcart	BARROW
push gently	NUDGE
push up	BOOST
push with the head	BUTT
pussy cat	TABBY, KITTY
put	DEPOSIT, PLACE, SET
put away for later (2 wds.)	SET ASIDE
put back	RESTORE, REPLACE
put down	LAY
put forth	EXERT
put in	INSERT
put in glass container	BOTTLE
put in opposition	PIT
put in order	ARRANGE
put in place	SET
put in scabbard	SHEATHE
put in shape	TRIM
put in tins	CAN
put into a secret language	CODE, ENCODE
put into cipher	ENCODE
put into office	ELECT
put into practice	USE
put into words	STATE, EXPRESS, VERBALIZE
put in writing	REDACT
put it there	SHAKE
put off	DELAY, POSTPONE
put on	DON
put on guard	WARN
put on the payroll	HIRE, EMPLOY
put out	ANGER, OUST
put out a tenant	EVICT
put out money	SPEND
put out of sight	HIDE, HID, CONCEAL, CONCEALED

put to proof	TEST
put to use	APPLY
put upon	IMPOSE
put up stake	ANTE
put up with	ABIDE, TOLERATE
puttee	GAITER
putty	CEMENT, SOFT, PLIABLE
puzzle	ENIGMA, POSER, CROSSWORD, RIDDLE
puzzler's friend	DICTIONARY
pyramid	TOMB
pyxis	VASE, CASE

Q

quadrille	DANCE, SQUARE
quaff	DRINK
quagmire	MARSH, BOG
quahog	CLAM
quail	COWER, QUAKE, BIRD
quaint	CURIOUS, ODD
quake	TREMBLE
qualified	ABLE, CAPABLE, COMPETENT
quality	ESSENCE, CHARACTER
quality of sound	TONE
qualm	TWINGE, PANG
quandary	DILEMMA
quantity of coal	TON
quantity of cookies	BATCH
quantity of medicine	DOSE
quantity of one baking	BATCH
quantity of paper	REAM
quantity of yarn	HANK
quarrel	ROW, SPAT, FEUD, FALL OUT, TIFF
quarry	PREY
quart	FOURTH
quarter-acre	ROOD
quarterly item due I.R.S. (2 wds.)	ESTIMATED TAX
quarter-round molding	OVOLO
quartet	FOUR, FOURSOME
quartet member	TENOR, BARITONE, BASS
quartz	AGATE, SILICA
quaver	TREMBLE, FALTER
quay	LEVEE, EMBANKMENT
queasy	DELICATE
queenly	REGAL
queen of Carthage	DIDO
queen of India	RANEE, RANI
queen of Olympian deities	HERA
queen of the fairies	MAB
queer	ODD, STRANGE, EERIE, EERY, WEIRD

queer (Scot.)	**ORRA**
quell	**SUBDUE, ALLAY**
quench the thirst	**SLAKE**
querulous	**FRETFUL, PEEVISH**
query	**QUESTION, ASK**
quest	**SEARCH**
question	**INTERROGATE, QUERY**
questionable	**IFFY, FISHY**
queue	**LINE**
quibble	**EVADE**
quick	**FAST, SPEEDY, HASTY, RAPID**
quick look	**PEEK, GLIMPSE**
quick lunch place	**DINER, EATERY**
quick plunge	**DIP**
quicksilver	**MERCURY**
quick sound	**POP**
quick to learn	**APT, CLEVER, BRIGHT**
quidnunc	**GOSSIP**
quiescent	**STILL, SERENE**
quiet	**STILL, SILENT, PEACEFUL**
quill	**PEN, FEATHER**
quilt part	**PATCH**
quilting party	**BEE**
quintessential	**PUREST**
quintet	**FIVE, FIVESOME**
quip	**SALLY, RETORT**
quit	**STOP, GIVE UP, LEAVE**
quite a few	**MANY**
quiver	**SHAKE, QUAKE, TREMBLE**
quivering motion	**TREMOR**
quixotic	**IDEALISTIC**
quiz	**EXAM, TEST, QUESTION**
quondam	**FORMER**
Quonset	**HUT**
quota	**PORTION, RATION**
quote as an authority	**CITE**
quote by Poe's raven	**NEVERMORE**
quote from memory	**RECITE**
quotidian	**DAILY, COMMON**

R

rabbet	**GROOVE, JOINT**
rabbit	**BUNNY, HARE**
rabbit snare	**NOOSE**
rabbit tail	**SCUT**
rabble	**MOB, RIFFRAFF**
rabid	**MAD, FRANTIC**
raccoon-like animal	**PANDA, COATI**

race	**CONTEST, RUN, SPEED**
race between teams	**RELAY**
racecourse	**TRACK, OVAL**
racehorse	**PACER, TROTTER**
racetrack character	**TOUT**
racetrack shape	**OVAL**
racetrack surface	**TURF**
racetrack term	**ODDS**
Rachel's father	**LABAN**
Rachel's sister	**LEAH**
racing program	**CARD**
racket	**NOISE, CLATTER, DIN**
racket string material	**GUT, CATGUT**
radar screen image	**BLIP**
radiance	**BRILLIANCE**
radiate	**SHINE, GLOW**
radical	**EXTREME**
radio detecting device	**RADAR**
radio interference	**STATIC**
radio or television system	**NETWORK**
radio waves' medium	**ETHER**
radium discoverer	**CURIE**
radium emanation	**RADON**
radius	**SCOPE**
radix	**ROOT**
rag	**TATTER**
rage	**RAVE, STORM**
ragged edge	**JAG**
raging woman	**MENAD, MAENAD**
raglan	**COAT, SLEEVE**
ragout	**STEW**
rah	**CHEER**
raid	**FORAY**
raider	**PRIVATEER, PIRATE**
rail at	**SCOLD**
rail bird	**SORA**
railroad bridge	**TRESTLE**
railroad car	**COACH, DINER, SLEEPER, PULLMAN**
railroad car connecting rod	**DRAWBAR**
railroad locomotive	**ENGINE, DIESEL**
railroad signal	**SEMAPHORE**
railroad sleeper	**TIE**
railroad station	**DEPOT, TERMINAL**
railroad track layer (2 wds., sl.)	**GANDY DANCER**
railroad vehicle	**CAR**
rail-splitter	**LINCOLN**
railway car	**TRAM**
railway mail service (abbr.)	**R.M.S.**
raiment	**APPAREL**

rain	**DOWNPOUR, POUR, SHOWER**	rapid	**FAST, SWIFT, QUICK, SPEEDY**
rain and snow	**SLEET**	rapidity	**HASTE**
rainbow	**IRIS**	rapidly	**APACE**
rainbow fish	**GUPPY**	rapier	**SWORD**
raincoat	**SLICKER**	rap on the knuckles	
rain hard	**POUR**		**REPRIMAND**
rain sound	**PATTER**	rapport	**ACCORD**
rain unit	**INCH**	rapture	**BLISS**
rainy	**WET**	rapturous feeling	**EXALTATION**
rainy season in India		rare	**INFREQUENT, SCARCE,**
	MONSOON		**UNCOMMON, UNUSUAL**
raise	**ELEVATE, REAR, ERECT,**	rare art object	**CURIO**
	GROW, LIFT, BREED,	rarefy	**DILUTE**
	UP, HOIST, BOOST	rarely	**SELDOM**
raise crops	**FARM**	rare thing	**ODDITY**
raised border	**RIM**	rascal	**ROGUE, SCAMP**
raised platform	**DAIS, STAGE**	rash	**HEEDLESS, IMPRUDENT,**
raised stripe	**RIDGE**		**OUTBREAK**
raise high	**EXALT**	rasher	**SLICE**
raise nap	**TEASE**	rasp	**FILE, GRATE**
raise to the third power	**CUBE**	rat	**RODENT**
rajah's wife	**RANEE, RANI**	ratchet	**BOBBIN, WHEEL**
rake	**ROUE, BOUNDER**	rate	**APPRAISE, PRICE, RANK,**
rakish	**DASHING, JAUNTY**		**CLASSIFY, CLASS**
rally	**SUMMON, STIR**	rate of movement	**PACE,**
ram	**TUP, SHEEP**		**SPEED**
ramadan	**FAST**	rather	**SOMEWHAT**
Rama's spouse	**SITA**	rather than	**INSTEAD**
ramble	**ROVE, WANDER,**	rather than (poetic)	**ERE**
	STROLL, STRAY	ratification	**AMEN**
rambunctious	**UNRULY, WILD**	ratify	**CONFIRM**
ramification	**OFFSHOOT,**	ration	**PORTION, SHARE**
	BRANCH	rational	**SANE**
ram in the zodiac	**ARIES**	rationale	**REASON**
ram into	**CRASH**	ratite	**OSTRICH**
ramp	**GRADING**	rat-like rodent	**VOLE**
rampant	**VIOLENT, RIFE**	ratline	**RIGGING**
rampart	**PARAPET, REDAN**	rattan	**CANE**
ram's horn	**SHOFAR**	rattle	**AGITATE, CLATTER**
ram's mate	**EWE**	rattler's sound	**HISS**
ranch animal	**EWE, RAM, COW,**	rattling sound	**CLATTER**
	SHEEP, HORSE, MARE,	raucous	**HOARSE**
	BULL, STEER	ravage	**DESTROY, DESPOIL**
rancher	**COWBOY**	rave	**RAGE, RANT**
rancid	**FOUL, ROTTEN**	ravel	**FRAY**
rancor	**SPITE, BITTERNESS**	ravelings	**LINT**
random	**CASUAL, AIMLESS**	raven	**BLACK**
range	**COOKSTOVE, STOVE**	raven-haired girl	**BRUNETTE**
range of sight	**KEN, SCOPE**	ravenous	**STARVING**
range of stables	**MEWS**	ravine	**ARROYO, GULCH**
rank	**CLASS, DEGREE,**	ravish	**ENRAPTURE**
	GRADE, RATE	raw	**INEXPERIENCED,**
rankle	**FESTER**		**UNCOOKED, GREEN**
ransack	**PILLAGE, PLUNDER**	rawboned	**LEAN**
ransom	**REDEEM**	raw herb dish	**SALAD**
rant	**RAVE**	rawhide	**PELT**
rap	**KNOCK, TAP**	rawhide whip	**QUIRT**
rapacious	**GREEDY**	raw metal	**ORE**

raw steel	**IRON**
ray	**BEAM, SKATE**
raze	**TEAR DOWN, LEVEL**
razorback	**HOG**
razor clam	**SOLEN**
razor sharpener	**STROP**
razz	**HECKLE**
re	**CONCERNING, REGARDING**
reach	**EXTEND**
reach across	**SPAN**
reach a destination	**COME, ARRIVE**
reach in time	**CATCH**
reach maturity	**RIPEN**
reach out	**STRETCH**
react	**RESPOND**
reaction	**RESPONSE**
reactionary	**TORY**
reactivation	**RENEWAL**
read	**SCAN, PORE, PERUSE**
readable	**LEGIBLE**
reader	**PRIMER, LECTOR**
readily	**WILLINGLY**
reading desk	**LECTERN**
reading room	**DEN, STUDY, LIBRARY**
reading table	**DESK**
read rapidly	**SKIM**
read up on	**STUDY**
ready	**PREPARED, RIPE**
ready (arch.)	**YARE**
ready answers	**REPARTEE**
ready cash	**MONEY**
ready for action (2 wds.)	**IN SHAPE, ON TAP**
ready for harvest	**RIPE**
ready money	**CASH**
ready to act (3 wds.)	**ON THE ALERT**
ready to receive visitors (2 wds.)	**AT HOME**
reaffirm	**REASSERT**
Reagan's state	**CALIFORNIA**
real	**GENUINE, TRUE, ACTUAL**
real estate map	**PLAT**
real event	**FACT**
realistic	**VIVID**
reality	**FACT**
realize	**KNOW**
realm	**DOMAIN**
realm of fancy (2 wds.)	**DREAM WORLD**
reamer	**JUICER**
reap	**HARVEST**
rear	**RAISE, FOSTER**
reason	**CAUSE, MOTIVE**
reasonable	**LOGICAL, SENSIBLE**

reata	**LARIAT, LASSO**
rebate	**DISCOUNT**
rebel	**RISE, REVOLT**
rebellion	**REVOLT, MUTINY**
rebellious demonstration	**RIOT**
rebound	**BOUNCE**
rebuff	**REJECT, SLAP, REPULSE, SNUB**
rebuild	**RENEW**
rebuke	**REPROACH, CHIDE**
rebus	**PUZZLE**
rebut	**DISPROVE**
recalcitrant	**STUBBORN, REBELLIOUS**
recall	**REMEMBER, RECOLLECT**
recant	**RETRACT**
recap	**TIRE**
recapitulate	**SUMMARIZE**
recede	**EBB**
receive	**GET, GAIN, ACCEPT**
receive advantage	**BENEFIT**
receive a scolding (2 wds.)	**GET IT**
receive information	**HEAR**
receiver of property	**ALIENEE**
receiver of stolen property	**FENCE**
receiving set	**RADIO**
recent	**NEW**
recently	**OF LATE, LATELY**
recently acquired	**NEW**
recent (prefix)	**NEO**
receptacle	**CASE**
receptacle for carrying things	**TRAY**
reception	**LEVEE, TEA**
reception room	**HALL, ENTRY, PARLOR, FOYER**
recess	**NOOK**
recession	**WITHDRAWAL**
recipe	**FORMULA**
recipient of a bequest	**LEGATEE**
recipient of a gift	**DONEE**
recipient of a gratuity	**TIPPEE**
recite	**READ, RELATE**
recite musically	**CHANT, INTONE**
reckless	**HASTY, RASH, IMPRUDENT**
reckon	**CONSIDER, SUPPOSE**
reclaim	**RECOVER, REDEEM**
recline	**LIE**
recline indolently	**LOLL**
recluse	**EREMITE, HERMIT**
recognize	**KNOW**
recoil	**SHY**
recollect	**RECALL, REMEMBER**

recollection	**MEMORY**
recommence	**RESUME**
recompense	**REWARD, WAGE, PAY**
recondite	**ERUDITE, LEARNED**
reconnoiter	**SCOUT, SURVEY**
record	**DISC, ENTER**
record for TV	**TAPE**
record holder	**FILE**
record keeper	**REGISTRAR**
record of a patient	**CHART, MEDICAL HISTORY**
record of events	**ANNAL**
record of the past	**HISTORY**
record player, for short	**STEREO, PHONO**
record speed	**TIME, RPM**
recount	**REPORT**
recover	**REGAIN, MEND**
recreation	**SPORT**
recreation area	**CAMP, PARK**
rectify	**CORRECT, REVISE**
recurring pattern	**CYCLE**
red	**CERISE, CRIMSON, SCARLET, COMMUNIST**
red (prefix)	**RHOD**
redact	**EDIT**
redan	**FORTIFICATION**
red-breasted bird	**ROBIN**
red chalcedony	**SARD**
redden	**BLUSH**
reddish	**RUDDY**
reddish brown	**RUST, AUBURN, MAROON**
reddish horse	**ROAN**
reddish liqueur (2 wds.)	**SLOE GIN**
reddish yellow	**AMBER, CORAL**
redeem	**SAVE, RESCUE**
redeem from captivity	**RANSOM**
red gem	**GARNET, RUBY**
red herring	**DISTRACTION**
red-letter day	**HOLIDAY**
red light	**DANGER**
red man	**INDIAN**
red meat	**STEAK, BEEF**
redness of skin	**RUBOR, BLUSH**
redolent	**FRAGRANT**
redolent wood	**CEDAR**
red planet	**MARS**
redress	**REPAIR**
red root vegetable	**BEET, RADISH**
red round vegetable	**TOMATO**
Red Sea gulf	**AQABA**
Red Square name	**LENIN**

reduce	**BATE, CUT, LESSEN**
reduced price offers	**TWOFERS**
reduce gradually	**TAPER**
reduce in rank	**DEMOTE**
reduce in value	**LOWER**
reduce light	**DIM**
reduce speed	**SLOW**
reduce to a lower grade	**DEMOTE, DEGRADE**
reduce to a mean	**AVERAGE**
reduce to ashes	**CREMATE**
reduce to fine spray	**ATOMIZE**
reduce to powder	**GRIND**
reducing program	**DIET**
reduction	**DISCOUNT, REBATE**
redundant	**EXCESS, WORDY**
red wine	**CLARET, PORT**
redwood	**TREE**
ree	**SANDPIPER, ARIKARA**
reed instrument	**OBOE**
reef material	**CORAL**
reek	**FUME**
reel	**STAGGER**
reel's companion	**ROD**
refer	**ALLUDE, MENTION**
referee	**UMPIRE**
reference book	**ATLAS, DICTIONARY**
reference mark	**ASTERISK**
reference table	**INDEX**
refer to (Lat. abbr.)	**VID.**
refinement	**POLISH**
refine metal	**SMELT**
reflect	**CONSIDER**
reflection	**IMAGE**
reform	**IMPROVE, BETTER**
refrain	**CHORUS, FORBEAR, MELODY**
refrain from noticing	**IGNORE**
refresh	**REVIVE, BRACE**
refreshing beverage	**ICED TEA, ICED COFFEE, ADE, SODA, POP**
refrigerate	**ICE, CHILL, COOL**
refuge	**HAVEN, OASIS, SHELTER**
refugee	**EMIGRE**
refund money	**REPAY**
refuse	**DECLINE, PASS UP, BALK, DENY, DROSS, TRASH**
refuse from mills	**SLAG**
refuse from sugar making	**BAGASSE**
refuse to accept	**REJECT**
refuse to give up	**PERSIST, PERSEVERE**
refute	**DENY, DISPROVE**

regal	**GRAND, KINGLY, ROYAL, STATELY**
regal attendant	**COURTIER**
regal chair	**THRONE**
regale	**TREAT, FETE**
regal fur	**ERMINE**
regal residence	**PALACE, CASTLE**
Regan's father	**LEAR**
regard	**RESPECT, ESTEEM, LOOK, WATCH**
regard highly	**ADMIRE, ADORE, ESTEEM, RESPECT**
regarding	**RE, IN RE**
regardless	**DESPITE**
regatta	**RACE**
regent	**RULER**
regimen	**DIET**
regimental commander	**COLONEL**
regimented trip	**TOUR**
regina	**QUEEN**
region	**AREA, ZONE**
regional	**LOCAL**
region of the patella	**KNEE**
register	**LIST, ENROLL**
registering of votes	**POLL**
register opposition	**PROTEST**
regret	**REPENT, RUE**
regretful	**PENITENT, SORRY, RUEFUL**
regular	**CUSTOMARY, ORDINARY**
regular method	**SYSTEM**
regulate	**ADJUST**
regulate food intake	**DIET**
regulate pitch	**KEY**
regulation	**RULE**
rehearsal	**DRILL**
rehearse	**PRACTICE, REPEAT**
reign	**RULE**
reigning beauty	**BELLE**
reimburse	**REPAY, REFUND**
rein	**CHECK, CONTROL**
reindeer	**CARIBOU**
reinforce	**BOLSTER**
reiterate	**REPEAT**
reject	**REBUFF, SPURN, TURN DOWN, VETO**
rejoice	**CELEBRATE**
rejoice in triumph	**EXULT**
rejoinder	**RETORT**
relapse	**BACKSLIDE**
relate	**PERTAIN, TELL, REPORT**
related	**AKIN, KINDRED**
related group	**CLAN**
relating to branches	**RAMAL**

relating to ebb and flow	**TIDAL**
relating to grandparents	**AVAL**
relating to Hindu literature	**VEDIC**
relating to measurement	**METRICAL**
relating to Paul VI	**PAPAL**
relating to the eye	**OPTIC**
relating to the moon	**LUNAR**
relating to time	**ERAL**
relative	**KIN**
relative of bingo	**KENO**
relatives	**KIN**
relax	**REST, SLACKEN**
relaxation	**EASE, REST**
relay	**RACE**
release	**FREE, UNTIE**
release from an obligation	**EXEMPT**
release from restraint	**FREE**
release on condition	**PAROLE**
relegate	**ASSIGN, REFER**
relent	**YIELD, DEFER**
relentless	**IMPLACABLE**
relevant	**PERTINENT**
reliable	**CERTAIN, SURE, DEPENDABLE**
reliance	**HOPE, DEPENDENCE**
relic	**SOUVENIR**
relief	**SUCCOR, COMFORT**
relief-carved gem	**CAMEO**
relief organization	**CARE**
relieve	**ALLAY, EASE**
religion	**BELIEF, CREED**
religious	**DEVOUT**
religious assembly	**CONGREGATION**
religious belief	**CREED**
religious ceremony	**RITE, RITUAL, MASS**
religious denomination	**SECT**
religious discourse	**SERMON**
religious holiday	**EASTER, CHRISTMAS, PASSOVER**
religious observance	**FAST**
religious poem	**PSALM**
religious recluse	**EREMITE**
religious service	**MASS, RITE, RITUAL**
religious sister	**NUN**
relinquish	**WAIVE, CEDE, YIELD**
relinquish throne	**ABDICATE**
reliquary	**SHRINE**
relish	**GUSTO, SAVOR**
reluctant	**AVERSE**
rely	**DEPEND**
remain	**STAY**

remainder	**REST**
remaining	**LEFT, OVER**
remain on the feet	**STAND**
remains	**ASHES, CORPSE, STAYS**
remain suspended above	**HOVER**
remain undecided	**PEND**
remark	**NOTICE**
remarkable	**NOTEWORTHY**
remarkable person (sl.)	**ONER, CORKER, LULU**
remedy	**CURE, ANTIDOTE**
remember	**RECALL, RECOLLECT**
remembrance	**MEMENTO, SOUVENIR**
remind	**REMEMBER**
reminder	**MEMO**
remiss	**NEGLIGENT, LAX**
remit	**PAY**
remnant	**LEFTOVER**
remodel (2 wds.)	**MAKE OVER**
remonstrate	**PROTEST**
remorse	**COMPUNCTION, REGRET**
remorseful	**SORRY**
remote	**FAR, DISTANT, ALOOF**
remount a gem	**RESET**
remove	**DISPLACE, SUBTRACT**
remove by cleaning	**SCOUR, SCRUB**
remove by clipping	**TRIM**
remove cover	**UNCAP**
removed	**DISTANT, REMOTE**
remove from office	**OUST, DISPLACE**
remove from print	**DELETE, DELE, ERASE**
remove moisture	**WRING, DRY**
remove rind	**PARE, SKIN**
remove the beard	**SHAVE**
remove the clothes	**STRIP**
remunerate	**PAY**
Remus' brother	**ROMULUS**
renaissance	**REBIRTH**
rend	**SPLIT, TEAR, RIP, DELIVER**
render	**GIVE, DEPICT**
rendezvous	**TRYST**
rendition	**VERSION, DELIVERY**
renegade	**TRAITOR**
renege (colloq., var.)	**RENIG**
renege (3 wds.)	**GO BACK ON**
renew	**REBUILD, RESTORE, REACTIVATE, REDO, RENOVATE**
Reno's river	**TRUCKEE**

renounce (2 wds.)	**SWEAR OFF**
renovate	**REDO, RENEW, REMODEL**
renown	**ECLAT, FAME, NOTE, ACCLAIM**
rent	**HIRE, LET, LEASE**
rental contract	**LEASE**
rental sign (2 wds.)	**TO LET**
renter	**TENANT**
renunciation	**DISCLAIMER**
rep	**CORD, RIBBING**
repair	**MEND, FIX**
repair shoes	**SOLE**
reparation	**ATONEMENT**
repartee	**RETORT, RIPOSTE**
repast	**MEAL**
repayment	**REBATE**
repeal	**CANCEL, RECALL**
repeat	**ECHO, RECUR, ITERATE**
repeatedly (3 wds.)	**OVER AND OVER**
repeat from memory	**RECITE**
repeating from memory	**ROTE**
repeat mechanically	**PARROT**
repeat performance	**ENCORE**
repeat showing	**RERUN**
repel	**REPULSE, DISGUST**
repent	**RUE**
repentance	**REMORSE**
repercussion	**EFFECT**
repertory	**THEATER**
repetition	**ROTE, ECHO**
repetition, in psychology	**ECHOLALIA**
repetition of a note	**TREMOLO**
repetitive	**REDUNDANT**
repine	**COMPLAIN, FRET**
replace	**RESET, RESTORE**
replenish	**RENEW**
replete	**SATED, FULL**
replica	**COPY, DUPLICATE**
reply	**ANSWER, RESPOND**
report	**RUMOR**
reporter	**JOURNALIST**
repose	**REST, SLEEP**
repository	**VAULT**
reprehension	**GUILT, BLAME**
represent (2 wds.)	**STAND FOR**
representation	**PORTRAYAL**
representative	**AGENT, ENVOY, DELEGATE**
representative part	**SAMPLE**
reprimand	**ADMONISH, CENSURE**
reproach	**SLUR**
reproach insultingly	**TAUNT**
reprobate	**IMMORAL, SINNER**

reproduction	**REPLICA**	resident of Helsinki	**FINN**
reprove	**TAKE TO TASK,**	resident of Mecca	**ARAB**
	CHASTISE, REPRIMAND	resident of Ocala	**FLORIDIAN**
reptile	**SNAKE, LIZARD**	resident of Perth	**AUSTRALIAN**
reptilian	**SAURIAN**	resident of Rangoon	**BURMESE**
Republican party,		resident of Rotterdam	**DUTCH**
familiarly	**GOP**	resident of Selma	**ALABAMAN**
Republican symbol	**ELEPHANT**	resident of Sitka	**ALASKAN**
Republic of Ireland	**EIRE**	resident of Sophia	**BULGARIAN**
repudiate	**DENY**	resident of Stockholm	**SWEDE**
repugnant	**ADVERSE, INIMICAL**	resident of Tirana	**ALBANIAN**
repulse	**REPEL**	resident of Vienna	**AUSTRIAN**
repulsive	**OFFENSIVE**	resident of Warsaw	**POLE**
reputation	**FAME, RENOWN**	resident of Yuma	**ARIZONAN**
repute	**CREDIT, REGARD**	residue	**ASH, SIFTINGS,**
request	**ASK, PRAYER**		**DREGS, LEES**
requiem	**DIRGE**	resign	**BOW OUT, QUIT,**
require	**DEMAND, NEED**		**ABDICATE**
requisition	**ORDER**	resilient	**ELASTIC, SUPPLE**
rescind	**REVOKE, CANCEL**	resin	**LAC**
rescue	**SAVE, REDEEM**	resinous	**PINY**
research	**STUDY**	resinous wood	**TEAK**
research room	**LAB**	resist	**OPPOSE**
reseau	**NETWORK**	resist authority	**REBEL**
resemblance	**LIKENESS,**	resist change (2 wds.)	
	SIMILARITY		**STAND PAT**
resembling	**LIKE**	resister	**OPPOSER, REBEL**
resembling bone	**OSSEOUS**	resolute	**DETERMINED**
resembling man	**ANDROID**	resolve	**DECIDE**
resembling sheep	**OVINE**	resonance	**SONORITY**
resembling wool	**LANATE**	resonant	**SONOROUS,**
resentment	**ANGER, IRE**		**VIBRATING**
reserve	**HOLD**	resort	**SPA**
reserved	**TAKEN**	resort city in Florida	**MIAMI,**
reserved in manner	**ALOOF**		**MIAMI BEACH**
reserve fund (2 wds.)		resort hotel feature	**CABANA,**
	NEST EGG		**POOL**
reservoir	**STORE**	resort near Venice	**LIDO**
reside	**DWELL, LIVE, ABIDE**	resort of New Mexico	**TAOS**
residence	**ABODE, DWELLING,**	resound	**ECHO, PEAL,**
	DOMICILE, HOME		**REVERBERATE**
residency	**TENURE**	resound vibrantly	**TRILL**
resident of (suffix)	**ITE**	resource	**ASSET**
resident of Ankara	**TURK**	resourceful	**SHARP**
resident of Avila	**SPANIARD**	resources	**MEANS**
resident of Bagdad	**IRAQI**	respect	**ESTEEM, HONOR,**
resident of Bahia	**BRAZILIAN**		**REGARD**
resident of Bali	**INDONESIAN**	respectable	**DECENT**
resident of Berlin	**GERMAN**	respectful title	**SIR**
resident of Boise	**IDAHOAN**	respective	**INDIVIDUAL**
resident of Buda	**HUNGARIAN**	respiratory organ	**LUNG**
resident of Cebu	**PHILIPPINE,**	respire	**BREATHE**
	FILIPINO	respite	**LETUP, REST, LULL,**
resident of Copenhagen	**DANE**		**POSTPONEMENT**
resident of Edinburgh	**SCOT**	resplendent	**RADIANT,**
resident of Ghent	**BELGIAN**		**SPLENDID**
resident of Glasgow	**SCOT**	respond	**REACT, ANSWER**
resident of Havana	**CUBAN**	response	**REPLY**

responsibility	**ONUS**
responsible	**RELIABLE, LIABLE**
rest	**PAUSE, RELAX, REPOSE,**
	REMAINDER
restaurant	**CAFE, DINER**
restaurant bill	**CHECK, TAB**
restaurant employee	**WAITER,**
	WAITRESS, COOK,
	BUSBOY, HEADWAITER
restful	**SERENE, SOOTHING**
resting	**ABED, DORMANT**
restitution	**REPARATION**
restive	**FIDGETY, UNEASY,**
	IMPATIENT, EDGY
restless	**NERVOUS, ANXIOUS**
rest on the knees	**KNEEL**
restore	**RENEW, RENOVATE**
restore confidence to	
	REASSURE
restore to health	**HEAL, CURE**
restrain	**LEASH, REIN, HOLD**
	BACK, CHECK, REPRESS
restraint	**CONTROL**
restrained in actions	
	RESERVED
restrict	**LIMIT**
restyle	**REDO, REMODEL**
result of rainy weather	**MUD**
result of supply and	
demand	**PRICE**
resumé	**SUMMARY**
resurface	**RETOP**
resurface a building	**FACE**
resuscitate	**REVIVE**
ret	**SOAK**
retail shop	**STORE, BOUTIQUE**
retain	**KEEP, HOLD**
retainer	**FEE**
retaining wall	**REVETMENT**
retaliate	**AVENGE, REVENGE,**
	PAY BACK
retard	**SLACKEN, SLOW**
rete	**NETWORK**
retention	**MEMORY**
reticent	**TACITURN**
retinue	**ENTOURAGE**
retired	**ABED**
retirement allotment	**PENSION**
retiring	**SHY, MODEST, TIMID**
retort	**RIPOSTE, REPARTEE**
retract	**RECANT, TAKE BACK**
retreaded tire	**RECAP**
retreat	**DEN, LAIR**
retrieve	**RECOVER**
retriever	**DOG**
retribution	**REPRISAL,**
	REVENGE
return	**REVERT, COME BACK**

return a loan	**REPAY**
return an argument	**RETORT**
return like for like	**RETALIATE**
reveal	**DIVULGE, DISCLOSE**
reveler	**MERRYMAKER**
reveler's cry	**EVOE**
revelry	**RIOT**
revenant	**GHOST, PHANTOM**
revenge	**RETALIATE**
revengeful	**VINDICTIVE**
revenue	**INCOME**
revenue (Fr.)	**RENTE**
reverberant	**RESONANT**
reverberate	**ECHO, RESOUND**
revere	**VENERATE, WORSHIP**
reverence	**AWE, RESPECT**
reverent fear	**AWE**
reverential regard	**HOMAGE**
reverie	**FANTASY, DREAM**
reversal	**HINDRANCE, SNAG**
reverse	**CONTRARY, OPPOSITE**
revert	**RETURN, REGRESS**
review	**GO OVER, RECAP**
revise	**EDIT, EMEND, CHANGE**
revive	**WAKE, FRESHEN**
revoke a law	**REPEAL**
revoke at cards	**RENEGE**
revolt	**ARISE, REBEL, RISE UP**
revolting	**OFFENSIVE**
revolution	**ROTATION,**
	REBELLION, UPRISING
revolutionary	**RED, REBEL**
revolutions per minute	
(abbr.)	**RPM**
revolve	**ROTATE, TURN, SPIN**
revolver	**PISTOL, GUN**
revolving	**ROTARY**
revolving machine part	**CAM**
revolving storm	**TORNADO,**
	CYCLONE
revulsion	**AVERSION**
reward	**BONUS, RECOMPENSE**
rewarding	**BENEFICIAL**
rhea	**EMU**
Rhine nymph	**LORELEI**
Rhine tributary	**RUHR**
Rhine wine	**MOSELLE**
Rhone tributary	**YSER**
rhumba country	**CUBA**
rhythm	**BEAT, TEMPO,**
	METER, CADENCE
rhythmic	**POETIC**
rhythmical beating	**PULSE**
rhythmic movement	**LILT**
rhythm instrument	**DRUM**
ria	**INLET**
Rialto	**BROADWAY**
Rialto sign	**S.R.O.**

riata	LARIAT, LASSO	rile	ANNOY, IRRITATE, ANGER
rib	BONE, TEASE	rill	STREAM, BROOK, RIVULET
ribbed fabric	REP	rim	BORDER, EDGE, LIP
ribbon	BOW, FILLET	rime	HOAR, HOARFROST, ICE
ribbonlike flag	STREAMER	rimose	CRACKED
ricebird	BOBOLINK	rind	PEEL, PEELING, SKIN
rice field	PADDY	ring	HOOP, CIRCLET, PEAL,
rich	WEALTHY, OPULENT		TOLL
rich cake	TORTE	ring a bell	REMIND
rich in ideas	MEATY	ringed boa	ABOMA
richly ornate	PLUSHY	ringed planet	SATURN
rich milk	CREAM	ringed worm	ANNELID
rich soil	LOAM	ringing device	BELL
rich tapestry	ARRAS	ringing sound	PLINK, TINKLE,
rickety car or truck	JALOPY,		DING, DONG
	RATTLETRAP	ringlet	CURL, TENDRIL, TRESS
ricochet	CAROM, REBOUND	ring of light	HALO, NIMBUS
rid	DISENCUMBER, FREE	ring slowly	TOLL
riddle	ENIGMA	rinky-dink	CHEAP, SHODDY
ride a bike	PEDAL	rinse	WASH
rider	PASSENGER, TRAVELER	rinsing	DREGS
Rider Haggard novel	SHE	Rio's beach	COPACABANA
ride shank's mare	WALK	riot	MELEE, PANDEMONIUM,
ride-sharing plan (2 wds.)			TUMULT
	CAR POOL	rip	TEAR, REND
ride to hounds	HUNT	ripe	MATURE, MELLOW
ridge	CREST	ripen	AGE, MATURE
ridge of rock near water	REEF	riposte	REPARTEE, RETORT
ridge of sand	DUNE	ripped	TORE, TORN
ridicule	DERIDE, MOCK,	ripple	WAVE
	TAUNT, TWIT	rise	ASCEND, CLIMB, STAND,
ridiculous	LUDICROUS,		SOAR, ELEVATE
	ABSURD	rise and fall	HEAVE, TIDE
ridiculous failure	FIASCO	rise up	REBEL
riding costume	HABIT	risible	FUNNY
riding crop	WHIP	risky	CHANCY, PERILOUS
riding exhibition	RODEO	risque	BLUE, NAUGHTY
riding horse	STEED	rissole	MEATBALL
riding shoe	BOOT	rite	CEREMONY, RITUAL
riding stick	CROP	ritual	RITE, LITURGY
riding whip	CROP, QUIRT	ritzy	SWANK
rife	PREVALENT	rivage	BANK, SHORE
rifle	GUN, SHOTGUN	rival	COMPETE, COMPETITOR
rifle noise	SHOT	rive	SPLIT
rift	SPLIT	river	STREAM
rig	OUTFIT	river (Sp.)	RIO
right	FAIR, JUST, CORRECT	river arm	ESTUARY
righteous	VIRTUOUS, PURE	river bank	RIPA
righteously angry	INDIGNANT	river barrier	DAM
rightfully	DULY	river bed	CHANNEL
right-hand page	RECTO	river boat	BARGE, FERRY
right of legal ownership	TITLE	river bottom	BED
right or left part of the		river bottom land	HOLM
body	SIDE	river crossed by Caesar	
right to choose	OPTION		RUBICON
rigid	TENSE, UNYIELDING	river crossing	FORD
rigor	HARDSHIP	river deposit	DELTA
rigorous	SEVERE, STRICT	river dragon	CROCODILE

river duck **TEAL**
river embankment **LEVEE**
river fish **SHAD, TROUT, SALMON**
river freighter **SCOW**
river in Africa **CONGO, NIGER, NILE, VELE**
river in Alaska **YUKON**
river in Arizona **GILA**
river in Australia **SWAN**
river in Austria **ENNS**
river in Bavaria **ISAR, NAAB**
river in Belgium **LYS**
river in Bohemia **ELBE**
river in China **TARIM, YALU**
river in Egypt **NILE**
river in England **AVON, TRENT, THAMES, TEES**
river in Ethiopia **ABBAI**
river in Europe **DANUBE, SAAR, ODER, YSER, RHINE, RHONE, AAR**
river in Flanders **YSER**
river in France **SEINE, ORNE, EURE, LOIRE**
river in Germany **ELBE, RHINE, RUHR, ODER, WESER**
river in Greece **ARTA**
river in Hades **STYX**
river in Hungary **RAAB**
river in India **INDUS, GANGES**
river in Ireland **ERNE, BANN**
river in Italy **ARNO, TIBER, PO**
river in Kansas **OSAGE**
river inlet **RIA**
river in Nebraska **PLATTE**
river in Nigeria **BENIN**
river in Normandy **ORNE**
river in Norway **TANA**
river in Oregon **KLAMATH**
river in Poland **WARTA, NAREV(W)**
river in Romania **SIRET**
river in Rome **TIBER**
river in Russia **URAL, OKA, NEVA**
river in Scotland **DEE, AYR**
river in South Africa **VAAL**
river in South America **APA, AMAZON, PLATA**
river in South Carolina **EDISTO, SANTEE**
river in Spain **EBRO**
river in Sweden **UME, LULE**
river in Switzerland **AAR**
river in Texas **NUECES, RED, PECOS**
river in the Congo **UELE**

river in the Netherlands **LEX, AMSTEL**
river in the Southwest **PECOS**
river into the Bay of Biscay **LOIRE**
river in Turkey **ARAS**
river in Tuscany **ARNO**
river in Wales and England **WYE**
river in Yorkshire **LEEDS, AIRE**
river island **AIT**
river mouth formation **DELTA**
river nymph **NAIS**
river passage **FORD**
river rat **THIEF**
river sediment **SILT**
riverside **BANK**
river siren **LORELEI**
river through Burgundy **SAONE**
rivet **BOLT, PIN**
riviere **NECKLACE**
rivulet **BROOK, STREAM**
road **PIKE, ROUTE, HIGHWAY, AVENUE, STREET, BOULEVARD, LANE**
road closed at one end (2 wds.) **BLIND ALLEY, DEAD END**
roadhouse **TAVERN, INN**
roadrunner **CUCKOO**
roadside eatery **DINER**
roadside hotel **MOTEL**
roadster **CAR**
road-surfacing material **BLACKTOP**
roam **ROVE, WANDER**
roam about idly **GAD**
roan **HORSE**
roar **BELLOW, HOLLER**
roast **BAKE**
roasting chamber **OVEN**
roasting ear **CORN**
roasting stick **SPIT**
roast on a spit **BARBECUE**
roast over a fire **PARCH**
rob **PILLAGE, STEAL, THIEVE**
robalo **SNOOK**
robber **STEALER, BURGLAR, THIEF, FELON**
robe **HOUSECOAT, DUSTER, WRAPPER, TOGA**
robin **BIRD**
Robin Goodfellow **PUCK**
Robinson Crusoe's man **FRIDAY**
roble **OAK**
robot **AUTOMATON**
robust **HALE, LUSTY**

rocambole	**ONION, LEEK**	Roman emperor	**NERO**
rock	**STONE, PEBBLE,**	Roman entrance hall	**ATRIUM**
	BOULDER	Roman fates	**PARCAE**
rocket fuel	**LOX**	Roman galley	**TRIREME**
rock growth	**MOSS**	Roman goddess of plenty	**OPS**
rock hawk	**FALCON**	Roman hearth goddess	**VESTA**
rocking bed	**CRADLE**	Roman highway	**ITER**
rock lobster	**CRAYFISH**	Roman historian	**LIVY**
rock moss	**LICHEN**	Roman household gods	**LARES,**
rock salt	**HALITE**		**PENATES**
rocky crag	**TOR**	Roman judge	**(A)EDILE**
Rocky Mountain park	**ESTES**	Roman matron's wear	**STOLA**
Rocky Mountain range	**TETON**	Roman orator	**CICERO**
Rocky Mountain sheep		Roman patriot	**CATO**
	BIGHORN	Roman philosopher	**SENECA**
rococo	**FLORID, ORNATE**	Roman poet	**OVID, VIRGIL**
rod	**FISHING POLE, FERULE**	Roman prelate	**POPE**
rodent	**RAT, RABBIT, MOUSE,**	Roman river	**TIBER**
	VOLE	Roman road	**ITER**
rodeo	**ROUNDUP**	Roman robe	**TOGA**
roe	**CAVIAR**	Roman shoe	**SANDAL**
Roger Moore role	**SAINT**	Roman statesman	**CATO**
rogue	**RASCAL, SCAMP**	romantic exploit	**GEST**
roil	**ANNOY, DISTURB**	romantic flower	**ROSE**
role	**PART, FUNCTION**	Roman tyrant	**NERO**
roll	**BUN, TURNOVER,**	Roman underworld god	**PLUTO**
	LIST, ROSTER	Romany	**GYPSY**
rollaway	**BED**	Romeo	**LOVER**
roll call answer	**HERE,**	romp	**PLAY, GAMBOL, CAVORT**
	PRESENT	Romulus' brother	**REMUS**
roller	**WAVE, CURLER**	rood	**CROSS**
rollick	**ROMP**	roof	**GABLE**
roll of butter	**PAT**	roof beam	**RAFTER**
roll of cloth	**BOLT**	roof edge	**EAVE**
roll of hair	**RAT, CHIGNON**	roofing liquid	**TAR**
roll of meat	**RISSOLE**	roofing material	**TILE, SLATE,**
roll of parchment	**SCROLL**		**SHINGLE, ASBESTOS**
roll of postage stamps	**COIL**	roof of the mouth	**PALATE**
roll of tobacco	**CIGAR**	roof overhang	**EAVE**
roll tightly	**FURL**	rook	**CASTLE, CROW**
roll up a flag	**FURL**	rookie	**TYRO, NOVICE**
roly-poly	**CHUBBY, PLUMP**	rook's cry	**CAW**
romaine	**COS**	room	**CHAMBER, SPACE**
Roman	**ITALIAN, LATIN**	room entrance	**DOOR**
Roman bishop	**POPE**	roomer	**LODGER**
Roman bronze	**AES**	room in a tower	**BELFRY**
romance	**NOVEL, FICTION**	room of the Last Supper	
Roman comedy writer			**CENACLE**
	TERENCE	room shape	**ELL**
Roman date	**IDES**	room side	**WALL**
Roman deity	**VENUS, MARS,**	room to move	**LEEWAY**
	DIANA, MINERVA, JOVE,	roomy	**SPACIOUS**
	AURORA, BACCHUS,	roost	**PERCH**
	CERES, CUPID, FAUN,	rooster	**COCK**
	APOLLO, JUNO, JUPITER,	rooster's mate	**HEN**
	MERCURY, JANUS,	rooster's pride	**COMB**
	NEPTUNE, VULCAN, DIS,	root	**RADIX, TUBER**
	LUNA, AMOR, NONA	rootstock	**TARO**

root vegetable **BEET, RADISH, CARROT, POTATO, TURNIP, PARSNIP**
rope **LASSO, LINE, RIATA, REATA, CORD**
rope connection **KNOT**
rope fiber **HEMP**
rope loop **NOOSE, BIGHT**
rope of flowers **GARLAND, LEI**
rope of onions **REEVE**
rope to limit animal's range **TETHER**
Rorschach **INKBLOT**
rosary bead **AVE**
roselike flower **CAMELLIA**
rose noble **RYAL**
rose oil **ATTAR**
roster **LIST, ROTA, ROLL**
rosy **BLUSHING, RED, CRIMSON**
rot **DECAY, SPOIL**
rota **COURT, ROSTER**
rotary motor **TURBINE**
rotate **SPIN, TWIRL, REVOLVE, TURN, WHIRL**
rotating machine **DYNAMO**
rotating machine part **ROTOR**
rotating piece **CAM**
rote **REPETITION, ROUTINE**
rotisserie skewer **SPIT**
rotund **ROUND, STOUT**
roue **RAKE**
rough **UNEVEN**
rough drawing **SKETCH**
rough hair **SHAG**
rough tire surface **TREAD**
round **CIRCULAR**
roundabout course **DETOUR**
rounded lump **NODULE, NODE**
rounded roof **DOME, CUPOLA**
round of applause **HAND**
round platter **DISC**
Round Table knight **GALAHAD, LANCELOT**
roundup **RODEO**
roundworm **NEMATODE**
rouse from sleep **AWAKE, WAKE, AWAKEN, WAKEN**
rouse to action **BESTIR**
rout **SCATTER, CONQUER**
route **HIGHWAY, ROAD, WAY**
route used by planes (2 wds.) **AIR LANE**
routine **ROTE**
routine job **CHORE**
rove **ROAM, WANDER**
rover's friend **FIDO, MAN**

row **LINE, TIER, LAYER, OAR, PADDLE**
rowboat pin **THOLE**
rowdy **HOODLUM**
rowel **SPUR**
rowing blade **OAR, PADDLE**
royal **REGAL, KINGLY, PRINCELY**
royal headdress **TIARA, CORONET, CROWN**
royal mace **SCEPTRE**
royal order **EDICT, DECREE**
royal purple **CRIMSON**
royal residence **PALACE, CASTLE**
Royal Scottish Academy (abbr.) **R.S.A.**
rozzer **POLICEMAN, COP**
rub **MASSAGE, STROKE**
rubber **ERASER**
rubber band **ELASTIC**
ruber city **AKRON**
rubber hoop **TIRE**
rubber overshoe **ARCTIC**
rubber rug **MAT**
rubber-soled shoe **SNEAKER**
rubber tree **ULE**
rubber tubing **HOSE**
rubbish **LITTER, TRASH, GARBAGE**
rubble **DEBRIS**
rubdown artist **MASSEUR**
rube **HICK, RUSTIC**
rubella **MEASLES**
rubicund **ROSY**
rub out **ERASE**
rubric **HEADING, TITLE**
rub the wrong way **IRRITATE**
rub together **GRATE**
ruby type **AGATE**
ruche **LACE**
ruckus **TO-DO**
ruddy **RED, REDDISH**
rude **DISCOURTEOUS, IMPOLITE, CURT**
rude cabin **HOVEL, HUT, SHACK**
rude person **BOOR**
rudimental **ELEMENTARY, INITIAL**
rue **REGRET**
rueful **DISMAL, SAD**
ruffed grouse **PARTRIDGE, PHEASANT**
ruffian **THUG, RASCAL**
ruffle **FRILL**
rug **MAT, CARPET**
Rugby's river **AVON**

rug fuzz	**LINT**
rugged	**ROBUST, ROUGH**
rugged guy (comp. wd.)	**HE-MAN**
rugged rock	**TOR**
rug surface	**NAP**
ruin	**DESTROY, SPOIL**
ruinous	**FATAL**
rule	**GOVERN, REIGN, LAW, REGULATION**
rule out	**EXCLUDE**
ruler	**SOVEREIGN, GOVERNOR, KING**
Rumanian city	**BUCHAREST**
rumble	**THUNDER**
rumen	**CUD**
ruminant mammal	**DEER, COW**
ruminate	**REFLECT, PONDER**
rumor	**REPORT**
rumple	**WRINKLE, CRINKLE**
run	**LOPE, GALLOP, TROT, FLOW, HIE, HASTEN, HURRY, SCURRY**
run after	**CHASE, PURSUE**
run aground	**FOUNDER**
run along	**LEAVE, DEPART**
run away	**FLEE, DECAMP, ESCAPE**
run away to marry	**ELOPE**
run before the wind	**SCUD**
run-down	**SUMMARY**
rune	**MYSTERY, SECRET**
run-in	**QUARREL, FIGHT**
run in haste	**SCUTTLE**
run into	**MEET**
run machinery	**OPERATE**
runner	**RACER**
runnered vehicle	**SLED**
runner-up	**LOSER**
run off the track	**DERAIL**
run out	**ELAPSE, EXHAUST**
run out on	**ABANDON, DESERT**
run swiftly, as water	**FLOW**
runt	**DWARF**
runway	**RAMP**
rupture	**BURST, BREAK**
rural	**PASTORAL**
rural backcountry (sl.)	**BOONDOCKS**
rural restaurant	**INN**
ruse	**STRATAGEM, TRICK**
rush	**SURGE**
rush hour	**PEAK**
rush hour at the diner	**NOON**
rusk of wheat grains	**BRAN**
russet	**APPLE**
Russian beer	**KVASS**

Russian beet dish	**BORSCH, BORSCHT**
Russian citadel	**KREMLIN**
Russian city	**OREL, MOSCOW**
Russian community	**MIR**
Russian co-op	**ARTEL**
Russian desert	**TUNDRA**
Russian edict	**UKASE**
Russian emperor	**TSAR, CZAR, TZAR**
Russian fighter plane	**MIG**
Russian hemp	**RINE**
Russian inland sea	**ARAL**
Russian lake	**ARAL, ONEGA**
Russian log hut	**ISBA**
Russian monetary unit	**RUBLE**
Russian monk	**RASPUTIN**
Russian mountains	**URALS**
Russian news agency	**TASS**
Russian novelist Turgenev	**IVAN**
Russian peninsula	**CRIMEA**
Russian plain	**STEPPES**
Russian river	**NEVA, URAL**
Russian ruler	**TSAR, TZAR, CZAR**
Russian satellite	**SPUTNIK**
Russian sea	**ARAL**
Russian secret police	**N.K.V.D., O.G.P.U.**
Russian tea urn	**SAMOVAR**
Russian trade union	**ARTEL**
Russian turnip	**RUTABAGA**
Russian veto word	**NIET, NYET**
Russian village	**MIR**
Russian wolfhound	**BORZOI**
rustable metal	**IRON**
rustic	**PEASANT, RURAL**
rustic retreat	**BOWER**
rustic step	**STILE**
rustic vehicle	**CART**
rustle	**SWISH**
rut	**FURROW, GROOVE**
rutabaga	**TURNIP**
ruthenium (chem. symbol)	**RU**
ruthless	**BRUTAL, CRUEL**
Ruth's husband	**BOAZ**
ruttish	**LUSTFUL**
rye fungus	**ERGOT**

S

sabbath	**SATURDAY, SUNDAY**
sabbatical	**REST, LEAVE**
saber	**SWORD**
sable	**FUR**
sabot	**SHOE**

sabotage **DESTROY**
sabra **ISRAELI, CACTUS**
sac **BURSA, POUCH**
saccharine **SWEET**
sachet **POUCH**
sack **BAG, POKE, PILLAGE, LOOT**
sack material **GUNNY**
sacrament **RITE**
sacred **HOLY, HALLOW**
sacred bird of the Nile **IBIS**
sacred book **BIBLE, KORAN, TALMUD, TORAH**
sacred Egyptian beetle **SCARAB**
sacred Egyptian bull **APIS**
sacred flower of India **LOTUS**
sacred fruit **LOTUS**
sacred hymn **CHORALE**
sacred image **ICON**
sacred memento **RELIC**
sacred song **MOTET, HYMN, CANTATA**
sacrifice **OFFERING**
sacrilegious **IMPIOUS, PROFANE**
sacristy **VESTRY**
sad **DOWNCAST, SORROWFUL, UNHAPPY, BLUE**
saddleback **HILL, RIDGE**
saddlebag **PANNIER**
saddle for an elephant **HOWDAH**
sad-faced hound **BASSET**
safari **HUNT, TREK, JOURNEY**
safe **SECURE, VAULT**
safecracker **YEGG**
safe from harm **SECURE**
safe harbor **HAVEN**
safekeeping **STORAGE**
safety **SECURITY, REFUGE**
saffron **YELLOW, ORANGE**
saffron plant **CROCUS**
sag **DROOP, WILT**
saga **TALE, EPIC, EDDA, STORY**
sagacious **WISE**
sage **HERB, WISE**
Sagebrush State **NEVADA**
sage hen **GROUSE**
sago **STARCH**
saguaro **CACTUS**
Sahara **DESERT**
said further **ADDED**
said positively **DECLARED**
sail **NAVIGATE, JIB, MAIN**
sail against the wind **TACK**
sailcloth **CANVAS**

sail fast **SCUD**
sailing **ASEA**
sailing vessel **BARK, BOAT, SHIP, SLOOP, SCHOONER, YACHT, YAWL**
sailor **TAR, GOB, SEA DOG, SEAMAN, SALT**
sailor's command **AVAST**
sailor's holiday (2 wds.) **SHORE LEAVE**
sailor's jacket **REEFER, PEA**
sailor's mop **SWAB**
sailor's patron saint **ELMO**
sailor's song **CHANTY**
sailplane **GLIDER**
sail rope **SHEET**
sails, to sailors **SHEETS**
sail upward **SOAR**
sainte (abbr.) **STE.**
saint's tomb **SHRINE**
Saint Vitus' dance **CHOREA**
salacious **LEWD**
salad fish **TUNA, SALMON, SHRIMP, HERRING, LOBSTER**
salad green **CRESS, LETTUCE, ENDIVE, ESCAROLE, CHICORY WATERCRESS**
salad ingredient **RADISH, TOMATO, LETTUCE, CUCUMBER, AVOCADO, ONION, SCALLION, WATERCRESS, CABBAGE**
salamander **EFT, NEWT**
salary **PAY, WAGE**
salary increase **RAISE**
sale **AUCTION**
sales figure, before deductions **GROSS**
sales representative **AGENT**
salient **PROMINENT**
salient point **FEATURE**
saline **SALTY**
saline drop **TEAR**
saline solution **BRINE**
sally of troops **SORTIE**
saloon **BAR, TAVERN, PUB**
salt **SEASONING, SAILOR**
salt away **SAVE**
saltine **CRACKER**
salt lake **SALINE**
salt marsh **SALINE**
saltpeter **NITER**
salt water **BRINE**
salty **SALINE**
salud **TOAST**
salutary **HEALTHFUL**

salutation	AVE, GREETING, HELLO
salvage	SAVE
salve	ANOINT, BALM
salver	TRAY
salvo	BURST
Samantha or Endora	WITCH
same	IDENTICAL, LIKE
same (Fr.)	MEME
same thing	ILK
Samoan bird	IAO
Samoan city	APIA
Samoan seaport	APIA
samovar	URN
Samoyed	SIBERIAN, HUSKY
samp	PORRIDGE, MUSH
samphire	GLASSWORT
sample	TASTE, TRY
Samuel's teacher	ELI
sanctify	BLESS
sanction	ABET, ENDORSE
sanctuary	HAVEN, REFUGE
sanctum	RETREAT
sand	GRIT
sandal	SHOE
Sandalwood island	SUMBA
sandarac tree	ARAR
sand hill	DUNE, DENE
sand lizard	ADDA
sandpiper	REE, RUFF, TEREK
sand trap	HAZARD
Sandwich Islands	HAWAII
sandwich meat	HAM, PORK, BOLOGNA, BEEF, SPAM, SALAMI, CHICKEN
sandy region	DESERT, SHORE, BEACH
sane	RATIONAL, SENSIBLE, SOUND
sanguine	CONFIDENT
sanitary	HYGENIC
sanity	REASON
Sanskrit dialect	PALI
Santa's sound	HO
sap	DRAIN, EXHAUST
sapajou	CAPUCHIN
sapid	PALATABLE
sapient	WISE
sapling	TREE
sapor	TASTE
Saracen	ARAB, MOSLEM
Sarah's original name	SARAI
Saratoga	SPA
Sarazen	GENE
sarcasm	IRONY
sarcastic	IRONIC, FACETIOUS
sarcastic grin	SNEER
sarcastic remark	TAUNT
sardonic	DERISIVE, BITTER
sash	BELT, OBI, WAISTBAND, CUMMERBUND
sassy	IMPUDENT
Satan	DEVIL
satanic	EVIL, VILE
Satan's domain	HELL, INFERNO
satchel	VALISE
sate	GLUT, FILL
satellite	MOON
satellite of Uranus	ARIEL
satiate	CLOY, FILL, SATE
satire	RIDICULE, BURLESQUE
satisfaction	CONTENTMENT
satisfactory	OK
satisfy	SATE, SATIATE, GLUT
Saturn	PLANET
Saturn's wife	OPS
satyr	FAUN
sauce	ALEC, GRAVY
saucepan	POT
saucer of a kind	COASTER
saucer-shaped bell	GONG
saucer's mate	CUP
saucy	PERT
saucy girl	MINX
sauerkraut	CABBAGE
Saul of Tarsus	PAUL
sauna	BATH
saunter	AMBLE
saurian	LIZARD
saute	FRY, BROWN
savage	FERAL
savage island	NIUE
savannah	PLAIN
savant	SCHOLAR
save	RESCUE, ECONOMIZE, SALVAGE, SALT AWAY
savine	JUNIPER
savior	REDEEMER
savoir-faire	TACT, POISE
savor	TASTE
savory	PIQUANT
savory dish	RELISH
savvy	SKILL
saw	ADAGE, MAXIM
sawbones	DOCTOR, SURGEON
sawbuck	TEN
sawfish's snout	SERRA
sawing frame	HORSE
saw lengthwise	RIP
saw-toothed	SERRATE
saxhorn	TUBA
Saxon serf	ESNE
say	SPEAK, DECLARE
say again	REPEAT, REITERATE
say casually	REMARK

say further	**ADD**	scenic	**PICTURESQUE**
saying	**BYWORD, QUOTE**	scenic river	**RHINE**
scab	**STRIKEBREAKER**	scenic view	**SCAPE**
scabbard	**HOLSTER, SHEATH**	scent	**AROMA, ODOR, SMELL,**
scalawag	**RASCAL, SCAMP**		**PERFUME, BOUQUET,**
scale	**CLIMB**		**SPOOR**
scale note	**DO, RE, MI, FA,**	scented bag	**SACHET**
	SO, LA, TI, SOL	scepter	**STAFF, BATON**
scallion	**SHALLOT, LEEK**	schedule	**SCROLL, TIME,**
scallop	**BIVALVE, MOLLUSK**		**LIST, AGENDA**
scalpel	**KNIFE**	scheme	**PLAN, PLOT**
scaly anteater	**PANGOLIN**	schism	**SPLIT**
scamp	**RASCAL, SCALAWAG,**	schnitzel	**CUTLET**
	ROGUE, IMP	scholar	**SAVANT, STUDENT**
scampi	**PRAWNS, SHRIMP**	scholarly	**ACADEMIC, ERUDITE**
scan	**READ, SCRUTINIZE**	school	**EDUCATE, TEACH,**
scandal	**DISGRACE, SLANDER**		**COLLEGE**
scandalize	**SHOCK**	school assignment	**LESSON,**
Scandinavian	**LAPP, NORSE,**		**HOMEWORK**
	FINN, SWEDE, DANE	school book	**PRIMER, READER,**
Scandinavian capital	**OSLO,**		**SPELLER, TEXT**
COPENHAGEN, HELSINKI,		school cafeteria (2 wds.)	
	STOCKHOLM		**LUNCH ROOM**
Scandinavian god	**ODIN, THOR,**	school composition	**ESSAY,**
WODEN, BALDER, FRIGGA,			**THEME**
LOKI, BRAGI, HEL, FREYA		school (Fr.)	**ECOLE, LYCEE**
Scandinavian literature	**SAGAS**	school group	**CLASS**
scanty	**MEAGER**	school intermission	**RECESS**
scapegoat (2 wds.)	**FALL GUY**	school mark	**GRADE**
scar	**CICATRIX**	schoolmaster	**DOMINIE**
scarab	**BEETLE**	school of modern art	**DADA**
scarce	**RARE**	school of seals	**POD**
scarcely	**HARDLY**	school organization (abbr.)	
scare	**FRIGHTEN, ALARM**		**P.T.A.**
scared	**AFRAID, FRIGHTENED**	schoolroom item	**CHALK,**
scarf	**NECKERCHIEF**		**ERASER, SLATE**
scarfskin	**EPIDERMIS, CUTICLE**	school semester	**TERM**
scarlet	**RED**	school sport	**TRACK,**
scarlet songbird	**TANAGER**		**FOOTBALL, SWIMMING**
Scarlett O'Hara's home	**TARA**	school task	**LESSON**
scarp	**CLIFF**	school term	**SEMESTER**
scary	**EERIE**	schooner	**SHIP, GLASS**
scary word	**BOO**	science	**ART**
scat	**BEGONE, SHOO**	science-fiction	
scathing	**CAUSTIC,**	creature	**ROBOT,**
	SCORCHING		**MUTANT, MONSTER,**
scatter	**STREW**		**ANDROID**
scatter hay	**TED**	science-fiction topic	**TIME,**
scatter seeds	**SOW**		**FUTURE**
scatter trash	**LITTER**	science of government	
scatter water	**SPLASH**		**POLITICS**
scaup	**DUCK**	science of law	
scene	**VISTA, VIEW**		**JURISPRUDENCE**
scene of action	**ARENA**	science of life	**BIOLOGY**
scene of great disorder		science of reasoning	**LOGIC**
	SHAMBLES	scientific study of	
scene of the crime	**VENUE**	lawbreaking	**CRIMINOLOGY**
scenery	**VIEW**	scintillate	**SPARKLE**

scion	**SON, HEIR, DESCENDANT**	scow	**BARGE**
		scowl	**GLOWER**
scissors	**SHEARS**	scrabble piece	**TILE**
scoff	**SNEER, JEER, DERIDE, GIBE**	scramble	**JUMBLE, RUSH**
		scrambled eggs	**OMELET**
scold	**JAW, NAG, CHIDE, UPBRAID, BERATE, FLAY, RANT, RAIL**	scrap	**FRAGMENT, ORT, SHRED**
		scrape	**PREDICAMENT, SCRATCH**
scolding woman	**SHREW**		
sconce	**BRACKET**	scraper	**STRIGIL**
scone	**CAKE**	scratch	**MAR, SCORE, SCRAPE, ABRADE**
scoop	**LADLE, SHOVEL**		
scoop of ice cream	**DIP**	scratch out	**ERASE**
scoop out water	**BAIL**	scratch with nails	**CLAW**
scope	**RANGE**	scrawl	**SCRIBBLE**
scorch	**CHAR, SEAR, SINGE**	scrawny	**LANKY, SKINNY**
score	**TALLY, TWENTY**	scream	**SHRIEK, YELL**
score a victory	**WIN**	screech	**SHRIEK**
scoring play in football	**TOUCHDOWN**	screen	**MASK**
		screen from light	**SHADE**
scoring point	**ACE, GOAL**	screen off	**SECLUDE**
scorn	**DESPISE**	scribble	**SCRAWL**
Scot	**GAEL**	scribble aimlessly	**DOODLE**
Scotch accent	**BIRR, BURR**	scribe	**PENMAN**
Scotch beret	**TAM**	scrimp	**ECONOMIZE, SAVE**
Scotch cake	**SCONE**	scrimshaw	**CARVE**
Scotch child	**BAIRN**	scriptural canticle	**ODE**
scotch cocktail (2 wds.)	**ROB ROY**	scroll	**LIST, ROLL**
		Scrooge	**MISER**
Scotch cup	**TASS**	scrounge	**PILFER**
Scotch Gaelic	**ERSE**	scrub	**SCOUR**
Scotch hill	**BRAE**	scruff	**NAPE**
Scotch lake	**LOCH**	scruff hair	**MANE**
Scotch musical instrument	**BAGPIPE**	scrumptious	**DELICIOUS**
		scruple	**QUALM**
Scotch plaid	**TARTAN**	scrutinize	**SCAN, EYE**
Scotch poet	**BURNS**	scuba man	**DIVER**
Scotch river	**DEE**	scud	**SKIM**
Scotch uncle	**EME**	scuffle	**TUSSLE, MELEE**
Scot's tiny	**WEE**	scull	**OAR**
Scottish biscuit	**SCONE**	sculpting plaster	**GESSO**
Scottish cap	**TAM**	sculptured piece	**BUST**
Scottish fabric	**TWEED**	scurry	**FLURRY, SCAMPER**
Scottish family	**CLAN**	sea	**OCEAN, CASPIAN, MEDITERRANEAN, RED, BLACK, DEAD**
Scottish Gaelic	**ERSE**		
Scottish girl	**LASS**		
Scottish heath	**MOOR**	sea (Fr.)	**MER**
Scottish highlander	**GAEL**	sea (Ger.)	**MEER**
Scottish hillside	**BRAE**	sea anemone	**POLYP**
Scottish island	**ARRAN**	sea bird	**ERN, ERNE, TERN, GULL, OSPREY**
Scottish landowner	**LAIRD**		
Scottish skirt	**KILT**	sea biscuit	**HARDTACK**
scoundrel	**RASCAL, ROGUE**	sea bottom	**BED**
scour	**SCRUB**	sea calf	**SEAL**
scourge	**BANE**	seacoast	**SHORE**
scouring rush	**HORSETAIL**	sea cow	**DUGONG, MANATEE**
scout	**SPY**	sea dog	**SALT, TAR, GOB, SAILOR**
scouting group	**PATROL**		

sea duck	EIDER
sea eagle	ERN, ERNE
sea eel	CONGER
seafaring man	MARINER, SAILOR
sea food	SHRIMP, LOBSTER, CLAM, CRAB, CRAYFISH, CRAWDAD, OYSTER
sea god	NEPTUNE
seagoing vessel	LINER, SHIP
sea gull	COB, MEW
sea in Central Asia	ARAL
seal	CLOSE, STAMP, SYMBOL
sealant	WAX
sea lettuce	ALGA, ULVA
seal's limb	FLIPPER
seam	SUTURE, LINE
sea mammal	MANATEE, WHALE, DOLPHIN, SEAL, PORPOISE, GRAMPUS, ORC
seaman	MARINE, TAR, GOB, SAILOR
seaman's chapel	BETHEL
sea mile	NAUT
sea monster	SERPENT
seamstress	DRESSMAKER
seamy	SQUALID, SORDID
seance sound	RAP
sea nymph	NEREID
sea onion	SQUILL
seaport in Alaska	NOME
seaport in Algeria	ORAN
seaport in Arabia	ADEN
seaport in Australia	BRISBANE
seaport in Bombay	SURAT
seaport in Brazil	RECIFE
seaport in Chile	ARICA
seaport in Italy	GENOA, NAPLES
seaport in Oregon	ASTORIA
seaport in Samoa	APIA
seaport in West Africa	DAKAR
seaport of the Philippines	ILOILO
sear	SCORCH, SINGE, CHAR
search	HUNT, SEEK, PROBE
searchlight	BEAM
search out	FERRET
sea robber	PIRATE, BUCCANEER
sea's ebb and flow	TIDE
sea shell	CONCH
seashore	COAST, BEACH
seashore attraction	BEACH, SURF
seashore bird	GULL
seashore feature	SAND

seaside	SHORE, COAST
sea soldier	MARINE
season	SALT
seasonable	TIMELY
seasonal song	NOEL, CAROL
seasoned egg dish (2 wds.)	SPANISH OMELET
seasoning	CONDIMENT, SALT, PEPPER, SPICE, HERB, MACE, SAGE, OREGANO, THYME, ROSEMARY, CHERVIL, TARRAGON, MUSTARD, NUTMEG, DILL, GARLIC, CAYENNE, PAPRIKA, CLOVE, BASIL, BAY LEAF
season of fasting	LENT
season of the year	WINTER, SUMMER, SPRING, AUTUMN, FALL
sea spray	SPINDRIFT
sea squirt	ASCIDIAN
sea swallow	TERN
sea swell	SURF
seat	BENCH, CHAIR
sea term	AHOY, BELAY
seat of justice	BANC
sea unicorn	NARWHAL
sea vessel	STEAMER, TANKER
sea wall	LEVEE
sea wave	BREAKER
seaweed	ALGA, ALGAE, KELP
seaweed product	IODINE
seaweed substance	AGAR
sea wolf	PIRATE
seaworthy	STURDY
seckel	PEAR
seclude	SCREEN
secluded	ALOOF, APART
secluded valley	GLEN, VALE, DALE
seclusion	PRIVACY
second	INSTANT, MOMENT, MIN
secondary school	PREP, HIGH
secondhand	USED
second lieutenant (sl.)	SHAVETAIL
second-mentioned	LATTER
second of a series	BETA
second of two	OTHER
second order of angels	CHERUB
second person	YOU
second-placer (comp. wd.)	RUNNER-UP
second selling	RESALE
secrecy	PRIVACY

secret	MYSTERY
secret agent	SPY
secretaire	DESK
secretary	AMANUENSIS, STENO
secretary's note	MEMO
secret Chinese society	TONG
secrete	HIDE
secreting organ	GLAND
secretive	SILENT
secret language	CODE
secret scheme	PLOT, CABAL
secret store	CACHE
sect	DENOMINATION
sectarian	PAROCHIAL
section	AREA, PART
sector	DISTRICT, SEGMENT
secular	LAIC
secure	SAFE
secure in place	ANCHOR
securing device	CLEVIS, VISE
securing pin	TOGGLE
security	GAGE, BOND
sedan	CAR, AUTO
sedate	DIGNIFIED, SOBER, STAID
sedative	SECONAL, SOOTHING
sedentary	FIXED, SEATED
seder	FEAST, ORDER
sediment	LEES, SILT
sedition	TREASON
seditious	INSURGENT, DISLOYAL
seduce	ENTICE, ABDUCT
seducer	SIREN
sedulous	BUSY
see	BISHOPRIC, ENVISION, OBSERVE, DISCERN, VISUALIZE, WITNESS, PERCEIVE, UNDERSTAND, ESPY
seecatch	SEAL
seed	GERM, GRAIN, OVULE, SOW
seed appendage	ARIL
seed container	POD
seed covering	ARIL, HULL, POD
seedless raisin	SULTANA
seedlet	SPORE
seedling	PLANT
seed of a mighty tree	ACORN
seed oysters	SPAT
seed planter	SOWER
seedpod	CARPEL, PISTIL
seed shrimp	OSTRACOD
seedsman	SOWER
seedy	SHABBY

seek	HUNT, SEARCH
seek ambitiously	ASPIRE
seeker of Moby Dick	AHAB
seek for by entreaty	SOLICIT
seel	CLOSE, BLIND
seem	APPEAR
seeming	APPARENT
seemingly	QUASI
seemly	PROPER, FAIR
seep	OOZE
seer	PROPHET
seeress	SIBYL
seesaw	TEETER
seethe	BOIL
segment	PART
segment of a curve	ARC
sego	LILY, BULB
segregate	ISOLATE, SEPARATE
seine	NET
seize	GRAB, NAB, GRIP, TAKE, GRASP
selze forcibly	USURP
seizure	ATTACK
seldom	RARELY
select	PICK OUT, CHOOSE, ELECT, OPT
select group	ELITE
selection	CHOICE
selective service	DRAFT
self	EGO
self-acting	AUTOMATIC
self-centered	EGOCENTRIC
self-confidence	POISE, APLOMB
self-esteem	PRIDE, EGO
self-evident	CLEAR
selfish individual	EGOIST
selfless	ALTRUISTIC
self-possession	POISE
self-reproach	REMORSE
self-righteous person	PRIG
selfsame	IDENTICAL
self-satisfied	SMUG
self-sufficient	INDEPENDENT
sell	VEND, RETAIL
sell direct to consumer	RETAIL
selling place	MARKET
sell out	BETRAY
semblance	LIKENESS
semester	TERM
semi-diameter	RADIUS
Seminole chief	OSCEOLA
semiprecious gem	OPAL, AGATE, GARNET
Semite	ARAB, JEW
Semitic deity	BAAL
Semitic language	ARAMAIC, HEBREW, ARABIC

semolina	**MEAL, FLOUR**
semper	**ALWAYS**
senate	**ASSEMBLY, COUNCIL**
senate attendant	**PAGE**
send	**TRANSMIT, DISPATCH, MAIL**
send a letter	**MAIL**
send away	**DISPATCH**
send back	**REMAND**
send flying	**ROUT**
send forth	**EMIT**
send into exile	**DEPORT**
send off	**MAIL, DISMISS**
send payment	**REMIT**
senile	**OLD, INFIRM**
senility	**DOTAGE**
senior	**ELDER, OLDER**
senorita's aunt	**TIA**
sensation	**SENSE, FEELING**
sensational	**LURID**
sense	**FEEL**
senseless	**INANE**
sense of sight	**VISION**
sense of taste	**PALATE**
sensible	**SANE**
sensitive	**TENDER**
sentence	**DECREE, JUDGMENT**
sententious	**CONCISE, TERSE**
sentimental person (colloq.)	**SOFTY**
sentinel	**GUARD**
separate	**PART, RIFT, APART, DIVIDE, DETACH**
separate article	**ITEM**
separate from	**ALOOF**
separate from others	**ISOLATE**
separate metal from ore	**SMELT**
sepia	**DUN, PIGMENT**
sept	**CLAN**
sequence of rulers	**DYNASTY**
sequestered	**SOLITARY**
sequoia	**TREE, REDWOOD**
seraglio	**HAREM**
Serb	**EUROPEAN, SLAV**
sere	**WITHERED**
serene	**CALM, PLACID, TRANQUIL**
serenity	**COMPOSURE**
serf	**ESNE, PEON**
serf of Sparta	**HELOT**
series	**SEQUENCE**
series of boat races	**REGATTA**
series of contests	**TOURNEY, TOURNAMENT**
series of happenings (3 wds.)	**CHAIN OF EVENTS**
series of heroic events	**EPOS**

series of names	**LIST, ROLL, ROSTER, ROTA**
series of propositions in logic	**SORTIES**
series of rooms	**SUITE**
series of steps	**STAIRS**
series of tones	**SCALE**
serin	**BIRD**
serious	**SOBER, SOLEMN**
seriousness	**GRAVITY**
sermon	**PREACH, DISCOURSE**
sermon giver	**PREACHER**
sermon topic	**TEXT**
serpent	**SNAKE, ASP**
serpentine	**SNAKY**
serpent's tooth	**FANG**
serrate	**NOTCHED**
serve as a lesson	**TEACH**
serve food	**CATER**
server	**TRAY**
serve tea	**POUR**
service charge	**FEE**
service station	**GARAGE**
servile	**MENIAL**
serving bowl	**TUREEN**
serving dish	**PLATTER**
serving spoon	**LADLE**
serving vessel	**TEAPOT, TRAY**
sesame plant	**TIL**
set	**CLIQUE, GEL, JELL, HARDEN, KIT**
seta	**BRISTLE**
set afloat	**LAUNCH**
set aside	**TABLE**
set at liberty	**FREE**
set back	**HINDER**
set fire to	**IGNITE, KINDLE**
set free	**RELEASE, BAIL OUT**
Seth's father	**ADAM**
Seth's son	**ENOS(H)**
set into motion	**ACTUATE**
set of actors	**CAST**
set of garments	**SUIT**
set of inquiries	**QUESTIONNAIRE**
set of matched furniture	**SUIT, SUITE**
set of organ pipes	**STOP**
set of principles	**CODE**
set of three	**TRIO**
set of tools	**KIT**
set of two	**DUAD, PAIR, DUO, COUPLE, DUET, BRACE**
set on fire	**IGNITE**
set out	**START**
setting	**LOCALE**
settle	**DECIDE, DETERMINE**
settle a bill	**PAY**

settle a question **DECIDE**
settle by intercession **MEDIATE**
settled **SEDATE**
settlement **COLONY**
settlement in Greenland **ETAH, THULE**
settler **PIONEER**
settlings **DREGS, SEDIMENT**
set-to **FIGHT**
set up **ESTABLISH**
setup **ARRANGEMENT**
set upon **ATTACK**
seven days **WEEK**
seventh day **SABBATH**
sever **CUT, SPLIT, DISUNITE**
several **VARIOUS, DIVERSE**
severe **STERN, HARSH**
severe experience **ORDEAL**
severely **SHARPLY**
severe snowstorm **BLIZZARD**
sew **BASTE, STITCH**
sewage **WASTE**
sewing implement **NEEDLE, DARNER**
sewing machine inventor **HOWE**
sew lightly **BASTE**
sex **GENDER**
sgt. **NCO**
shabby **SEEDY**
shabby clothing **RAGS**
shack **CABIN, HUT, HOVEL**
shackle **FETTER, CHAIN**
shade **COLOR, HUE, TINT, SHADOW, GHOST, GOBLIN, SPOOK**
shaded walk **ARBOR, MALL**
shade of difference **NUANCE**
shade of green **KELLY, OLIVE, LEAF, PEA**
shade of red **CORAL, CERISE, CRIMSON, SCARLET**
shade of tan **ECRU, BEIGE, KHAKI**
shade tree **ASH, ELM, OAK, ELDER**
shadow **SHADE**
shadowbox **SPAR**
shady **DISHONEST, DEVIOUS**
shaft **POLE**
shag **NAP, PILE**
shaganappi **RAWHIDE**
shaggy **FURRY, UNKEMPT**
shah country **IRAN**
shake **QUIVER, TREMBLE, SHIVER, QUAKE**
shakedown **EXTORTION**
Shakespearean hero **ROMEO, OTHELLO**

Shakespearean king **LEAR, HENRY, RICHARD, JOHN**
Shakespearean poem **ODE, SONNET**
Shakespearean sprite **ARIEL**
Shakespearean villain **IAGO**
Shakespeare's river **AVON**
Shakespeare's wife **ANNE**
shake the tail **WAG**
shake up **JAR, SHOCK**
shaky **WOBBLY**
shale **ROCK**
shallow **SUPERFICIAL**
shallow area **SHOAL**
shallow dish **PLATE**
shallow river crossing **FORD**
shalom **GREETING, PEACE**
sham **PRETEND, TRICK, FAKE, COUNTERFEIT, BOGUS**
shamas **SEXTON**
shame **FIE, DISHONOR, DISGRACE**
shameless **BRAZEN**
shamrock **CLOVER**
Shandy's creator **STERNE**
Shangri-La **UTOPIA**
shanty **HUT**
shape **FIGURE, FORM**
shaped like an egg **OVATE, OVAL**
shaped with an ax **HEWN**
shapeless **AMORPHIC**
shaping form **MOLD**
shard **FRAGMENT**
share **PARTICIPATE, PORTION, PART**
shark **GATA**
sharp **KEEN, ACUTE**
sharp bark **YIP, YAP, YELP**
sharp bite **NIP**
sharp blow **SLAP**
sharp disc on a plow **COLTER**
sharpen **HONE, WHET**
sharp end **POINT**
sharpener **EDGER, STROP**
sharp flavor **TANG**
sharp mountain ridge **ARETE**
sharpness **EDGE**
sharp of mind **KEEN**
sharp pain **STING**
sharp pointed **ACUTE**
sharp projection **BARB, JAG, SNAG**
sharp rebuke **SLAP**
sharpshooter **MARKSMAN**
sharp-sighted **ASTUTE**
sharp sound **PING**
sharp spear **LANCE**

sharp tap	**RAP**	sheltered side	**LEE**
sharp taste	**TANG, NIP**	shelter for bees	**HIVE**
shasta	**DAISY**	shepherd	**PASTOR**
shatter	**DASH, SMASH**	shepherd's pipe	**REED**
shave	**PARE**	sherbet	**ICE**
shavetail	**LIEUTENANT**	sheriff's badge	**STAR**
shaving tool	**RAZOR**	sheriff's band	**POSSE**
shawl	**WRAP, STOLE, SCARF**	sherry	**WINE**
Shawnee Indian chief		shield	**PROTECT, COVER**
	TECUMSEH	shield boss	**UMBO**
shay	**CARRIAGE**	shield from harm	**PROTECT**
she (Fr.)	**ELLE**	shift responsibility (3 wds.)	
sheaf	**BUNDLE, CLUSTER**		**PASS THE BUCK**
shear	**CLIP**	shimmer	**GLEAM, GLINT**
sheath	**SCABBARD, GLOVE**	shin	**SHANK**
sheave	**PULLEY**	shinbone	**TIBIA**
she-bear (Lat.)	**URSA**	shine	**GLEAM, GLOW, GLOSS,**
shed	**HUT, LEAN-TO**		**RADIATE, GLISTEN**
shed feathers	**MOLT, MOULT**	Shinto temple	**SHA**
shed light	**SHINE**	shiny fabric	**SATIN**
shed tears	**SOB, WEEP, CRY**	ship	**BOAT**
sheen	**LUSTER**	ship biscuit	**HARDTACK**
sheep	**EWE, RAM, LAMB**	ship boarding platform	
sheep enclosure	**FOLD**		**GANGPLANK**
sheeplike	**OVINE**	ship bow	**PROW**
sheep's bleat	**BAA, MAA**	shipbuilding wood	**TEAK**
sheep's child	**LAMB**	ship canvas	**SAIL**
sheep's coat	**FLEECE**	ship deck	**POOP, ORLOP**
sheep's hair	**WOOL**	ship deserter	**RAT**
sheep shelter	**COTE**	shipmates	**HEARTIES**
sheepskin	**PELT, DIPLOMA**	ship-model housing	**BOTTLE**
sheepskin shoe	**PAC**	ship mop	**SWAB**
sheer	**STEEP**	ship of Noah	**ARK**
sheer curtain	**SCRIM**	ship of the Argonauts	**ARGO**
sheer fabric	**TOILE, TULLE,**	ship of the desert	**CAMEL**
	VOILE	ship part	**KEEL, RUDDER**
sheerlegs	**SHEARS**	shipping box	**CRATE**
sheet	**ROPE, SHROUD**	shipping unit	**TON**
sheeting fabric	**PERCALE,**	ship prison	**BRIG**
	LINEN, MUSLIN	ship record	**LOG**
sheet of glass	**PANE**	ship's backbone	**KEEL**
sheets and tablecloths	**LINEN**	ship's bed	**BUNK**
sheik's ladies	**HAREM**	ship's boat	**DINGHY**
sheik's land	**ARABIA**	ship's body	**HULL**
sheldrake	**MERGANSER**	ship's cargo space	**HOLD**
shelf	**LEDGE**	ship's clerk	**PURSER**
shell	**ECTOSKELETON**	ship's commanding officer	
shellac	**LAC**		**CAPTAIN**
Shelley	**POET**	ship's complement	**CREW**
Shelley work	**ODE**	ship's contour (naut.)	**HANCE**
shellfish	**ABALONE, CLAM,**	ship's diary	**LOG**
	CRAB, SHRIMP	ship section	**BILGE, HOLD,**
shell out	**PAY**		**GALLEY**
shelter	**HAVEN, LEE**	ship's floor	**DECK**
shelter (Fr.)	**ABRI**	ship-shaped clock	**NEF**
sheltered from wind	**ALEE**	ship's kitchen	**GALLEY**
sheltered glen	**DELL, DALE**	ship's longboat	**GIG**
sheltered nook	**COVE**	ship's lowest deck	**ORLOP**

ship's master **CAPTAIN**
ship's officer **MATE, PURSER**
ship's parking place **MOORING, BERTH**
ship's petty officer **BOSUN**
ship's pole **MAST, SPAR**
ship's rope **HALYARD, HAWSER**
ship's station **BERTH**
ship's tiller **HELM**
ship's track **WAKE**
ships under unified control **FLEET**
shirk **EVADE**
shirtwaist **BLOUSE**
shiver **SHAKE, TREMBLE**
shoal **BANK, REEF**
shoat **PIGLET**
shock **STARTLE, IMPACT**
shoe **FOOTGEAR, SLIPPER, BROGAN, FOOTWEAR, OXFORD, PUMP, GILLIE, SANDAL, LOAFER, SNEAKER, SPECTATOR, CLOG, MULE**
shoe bottom **SOLE**
shoe fastener **LACING, LACES, BUTTONS, BUCKLES**
shoe form **LAST, TREE**
shoe grip **CLEAT**
shoemaker **COBBLER**
shoe material **LEATHER**
shoe part **HEEL, TOE, SOLE, UPPER, TONGUE**
shoestring **LACE, POTATO**
shoe tie **LACING**
shoji **PANEL, SCREEN**
shoo **SCAT**
shoofly **PIE**
shoot **TWIG**
shoot from ambush **SNIPE**
shoot game **POT**
shooting capacity **FIREPOWER**
shooting iron **GUN, PISTOL**
shooting marble **TAW**
shooting match (Fr.) **TIR**
shooting star **METEOR**
shoot out **DART**
shop **STORE, MART, MARKET**
shopper's convenience (2 wds.) **CHARGE ACCOUNT**
shopping center **MALL**
shopping reminder **LIST**
shore **COAST, SEASIDE, BEACH, STRAND**
shore bird **AVOCET, HERON, RAIL, TERN**
shore recess **COVE, INLET**

short **BRIEF, SMALL**
shortage **DEFICIT**
short and pointed **TERSE**
short and pudgy (comp. wd.) **ROLY-POLY**
short article **ITEM**
short blunt end **STUB**
short boot **SHOE**
short business trip **ERRAND**
shortcoming **FAULT**
short dagger **DIRK**
short dash **HYPHEN**
shorten **ABRIDGE**
shortening **LARD**
short explosive sound **POP**
short firearm **PISTOL**
short for gentleman **GENT**
short for hurrah **RAH**
short gaiter **SPAT**
short haircut **BOB, PIXIE, BUTCH, CREW**
shorthand **STENO**
short intermission **RECESS**
short jacket **ETON, BOLERO**
short lance **DART, DAGGER**
short-legged hound **BASSET**
short letter **NOTE, MEMO**
short-lived style **FAD**
shortly **ANON, SOON**
short note **LINE**
short pencil **STUB**
short period of calm **LULL**
short pin **PEG**
short playlet **SKIT**
short poem **SONNET**
short race **DASH, SPRINT**
shortsighted **MYOPIC**
short skirt **MINI**
short sleep **NAP, SNOOZE, CAT NAP, FORTY WINKS, DOZE**
short sock **ANKLET**
short song **DITTY**
short-spoken **LACONIC**
short story **CONTE**
short swim **DIP**
short sword **ESTOC**
short-tailed rodent **HAMSTER**
short telegraphic click **DOT**
short-tempered **EDGY, TESTY**
short thick piece **CHUNK**
short tree shoot **SPUR**
short visit **CALL**
shortwave **RADIO**
Shoshonean Indian **UTE**
shotgun **RIFLE**
shoulder band **STRAP**
shoulder blade **SCAPULA**

shoulder of a road	**BERM**	shroud	**SHEET, VEIL**
shoulder ornament	**EPAULET**	Shrove Tuesday	**MARDI GRAS**
shoulder scarf	**SHAWL, STOLE**	shrub	**BUSH, PLANT**
shout **SCREAM, YELL, HOLLER**		shrub of the southwest	
shout of applause	**CHEER,**		**MESQUITE**
	BRAVO	shrug off	**DISMISS**
shout of contempt	**HOOT**	shuck	**SHELL, HUSK**
shout of good will (Ital.)	**VIVA**	shudder	**SHAKE, TREMBLE**
shout to	**HAIL**	shuffle along	**MOSEY**
shout with joy	**SING**	shun	**AVOID**
shove	**PUSH**	shush	**HUSH, QUIET**
shovel	**SPADE**	shut	**CLOSE**
show **DEMONSTRATE, EXHIBIT**		shutdown	**LAYOFF**
show a decline	**DROP**	shut noisily	**SLAM**
show appreciation	**APPLAUD,**	shut out	**DEBAR**
	CLAP	shutter	**BLIND, JALOUSIE**
showcase	**EXHIBIT**	shuttlecock	**BIRD**
show disapproval	**HISS,**	shut up	**SILENCE**
	SNEER, SNORT	shy **COY, TIMID, MODEST,**	
show displeasure	**POUT**		**BASHFUL**
shower	**RAIN**	shylock	**USURER**
shower down	**CASCADE**	Siam	**THAILAND**
showery	**RAINY**	Siamese	**TAI**
showery month	**APRIL**	Siamese capital	**BANGKOK**
show favorable reaction		Siamese coin	**ATT**
	RESPOND	Siamese language	**THAI, TAI**
showing courage	**SPIRITED**	Siamese river	**ME NAM**
showing good judgment	**SANE,**	sib	**RELATIVE**
	SENSIBLE, LOGICAL	Siberian city	**IRKUTSK**
Show-Me State	**MISSOURI**	Siberian gulf	**OB**
show of affection	**KISS**	Siberian mongoloid	**TARTAR**
show of hands	**VOTE**	Siberian treeless tract	**STEPPE**
show ostentatiously	**FLAUNT**	sibilant sound	**HISS**
show plainly	**EVINCE**	sibling **BROTHER, SISTER**	
show to a seat	**USHER**	sibyl	**SEERESS**
show up	**SURPASS**	sic	**THUS**
showy	**SPORTY**	Sicilian harbor	**PALERMO**
showy clothes	**FINERY**	Sicilian resort	**ENNA**
showy covering	**VENEER**	Sicilian volcano	**ETNA**
showy feather	**PLUME**	sick	**ILL**
showy flower **PEONY, ROSE,**		sick bay	**INFIRMARY,**
	MUM		**DISPENSARY**
showy red flower	**POINSETTIA**	sicken	**AIL**
shred **FRAGMENT, STRIP,**		sickly **FEEBLE, INFIRM**	
RAG, TATTER, TEAR		Siddhartha	**BUDDHA**
shrew	**VIXEN**	side	**FLANK**
shrewd	**ASTUTE, WILY,**	side bone	**RIB**
CLEVER, WISE, SLY		side by side	**TOGETHER**
shriek **SCREAM, SCREECH**		side dish of greens	**SALAD**
shrill	**SHARP, KEEN**	sidekick	**COMPANION,**
shrill and piping tone	**REEDY**		**PARTNER**
shrill cry	**SCREECH**	side of a room	**WALL**
shrimp	**PRAWN**	side post of a doorway	**JAMB**
shrine	**TOMB, ALTAR**	sidereal hour angle	
shriner's hat	**FEZ**	(abbr.)	**SHA**
shrink	**SHRIVEL**	sidestep	**AVOID, ELUDE,**
shrink in fear	**COWER**	**EVADE, SLIDE, GLIDE**	
shrivel	**PARCH, SHRINK**	sidetrack	**DIVERT, DIGRESS**

sideways	ASKANCE	silt remover	DREDGE
sidewinder	SNAKE, RATTLER	silver (chem. abbr.)	AG.
sidewise	LATERAL	Silver State	NEVADA
sidle along	EDGE	silvery fish	SMELT
siesta	NAP	s'il vous plait	PLEASE
sieve	SIFT, STRAINER	simian	APE
sift	DREDGE, SIEVE	similar	AKIN, ALIKE
sigh	EXHALE, SOB	similar in kind	SUCH, LIKE,
sight	VISION, SCENE		AKIN
sight for travelers	RUINS	similarity	ANALOGY, LIKENESS
sight organ	EYE	similarly defined word	
sight-seeing trip	TOUR		SYNONYM
sigil	SEAL, SIGNET	similar to	LIKE
sign	BILLBOARD, BILL, NEON	simile	LIKE, AS
signal	CUE	simmer	STEW
signal fire	FLARE	simpatico	CONGENIAL
sign at a sellout	S.R.O.	simper	SMIRK
signature	MARK	simple	STUPID, EASY,
signet	SEAL, STAMP		MERE, PLAIN
significant	IMPORTANT	simple song	LAY
signify	MEAN, DENOTE,	simple story	PARABLE
	CONNOTE	simple substance	ELEMENT
sign of approaching		simple sugar	KETOSE
cold	SNEEZE, SNIFFLE	simpleton	NEDDY, OAF,
sign of assent	NOD		DOLT, DUNCE
sign of disapproval	BOO	simulate	FAKE
sign of fire	SMOKE	sin	ERR, TRANSGRESSION
sign of full house	S.R.O.	Sindbad's bird	ROC
sign of life	PULSE	since	AS, BECAUSE
sign of sorrow	SOB	sincere	HONEST
sign of the future	OMEN	sinew	TENDON, THEW
sign of the times	TREND	sinewy	ROPY, WIRY
sign of the zodiac	ARIES, LEO,	sinful	EVIL, IMMORAL
	PISCES, AQUARIUS,	sing	CROON, VOCALIZE,
	GEMINI, CANCER,		WARBLE, CHANT
	SCORPIO, TAURUS,		
	LIBRA, VIRGO,	singer Ames	ED
	SAGITTARIUS,	singer Bennett	TONY
	CAPRICORN	singer Boone	PAT
sign up	ENROLL, ENLIST	singer Collins	JUDY
silence	HUSH, STILLNESS	singer Como	PERRY
silent	MUM, QUIET,	singer Crosby	BING
	MUTE, TACIT	singer Fitzgerald	ELLA
silhouette	SHADOW	singer Garland	JUDY
silicate	MICA	singer Horne	LENA
silk cotton	KAPOK	singer Ives	BURL
silken	SMOOTH	singer Jolson	AL
silk fabric	CREPE, GROS	singer Martin	DEAN, TONY
silk net	TULLE	singer Peerce	JAN
silk voile	NINON	singer Presley	ELVIS
silkworm	ERI, ERIA	singer Sinatra	FRANK
sill	LEDGE	singer's list	REPERTOIRE
silly	APISH, FOOLISH,	singer Stevens	RISE
	INANE, GOOFY	singer Streisand	BARBRA
silly action	FOLLY	singer Torme	MEL
silly bird	GOOSE	singer Williams	ANDY
silly talk	DRIVEL, PRATTLE	singing bird	LARK
silt	SEDIMENT	singing syllable	TRA, LA

singing voice	ALTO, BASS, SOPRANO, TENOR, BARITONE, CONTRALTO	situation	POSITION, PREDICAMENT
single	ONE, SOLE	Siva's consort	DEVI
single-handed	UNAIDED	six-sided figure	CUBE
single-hearted	SINCERE	sixth sense (abbr.)	ESP
single-masted vessel	SLOOP	sixty-five usually (2 wds.)	RETIREMENT AGE
singleness	UNITY	sixty minutes	HOUR
single step	STAIR	size	DIMENSION
singlestick	FENCING	size of paper	DEMY
single thing	ONE, UNIT, ITEM	size of type	ELITE, PICA
single time	ONCE	sizzle	STEAM
singleton	LONER, ONE	skate	STINGRAY, RAY
sing like Bing	CROON	skate blade	RUNNER
singly (4 wds.)	ONE AT A TIME	skating arena	RINK
sing Swiss style	YODEL	skean	DAGGER, DIRK
singular	UNIQUE	skein of yarn	HANK
sing under the breath	HUM	skeleton part	BONE, SKULL, RIB, AITCHBONE, TIBIA, ULNA
sinister	EVIL		
sinister look	LEER	skeptic	AGNOSTIC
sinitic	CHINESE	sketch	PLAN, DRAW, INK
sink	BASIN, SUBMERGE	sketcher of comic pictures	CARTOONIST
sink down	SAG, DROOP		
sink plug	STOPPER	sketch through thin paper	TRACE
sinuous	SNAKY		
sinus cavity	ANTRUM,	sketchy	ROUGH
Siouan Indian	OTOE	skewer	PIN, ROD
Siouan language	TETON, DAKOTA	skid	SLIDE
		skiff	BOAT
Sioux Indian	CROW, OTOE, TETON	skilful	ADEPT, ADROIT
		skill	ART, CRAFT, TALENT
Sioux State	NORTH DAKOTA	skilled	ABLE, ADEPT, DEFT
sip	TASTE	skillet	PAN, FRYPAN
siphon	TUBE, SUCTION	skim	GLANCE, GLIDE
sire	FATHER, PROGENITOR	skimpy	SCANTY
siren	CHARMER, ALARM	skin	PELT, HIDE, RIND, PEEL, DERMIS
sire's mate	DAM		
sir (Sp.)	SENOR	skin ailment	ACNE
sir, in India	SAHIB	skin decoration	TATTOO
sir, in Malaya	TUAN	skin diver's attire (2 wds.)	WET SUIT
sirloin	STEAK		
sisal	HEMP	skinflint	MISER
sismo	SEXTO	skink	LIZARD
sisterhood	SORORITY	skin layer	DERMA
sister of Orestes	ELECTRA	skinned (dial.)	SKUN
sister's daughter	NIECE	skinny	THIN, LEAN
sit	REST, ROOST	skin opening	PORE
sit back	RELAX	skin problem	ACNE
sit-down	STRIKE	skin tone	TAN
site	LOCATION	skip	LEAP, OMIT
site of 1898 Alsakan gold rush	NOME	skip on water	DAP
		skip over	ELIDE
site of witch trials	SALEM	skipper	CAPTAIN
sit for a portrait	POSE	skipper butterfly	HESPERID
sitsang	TIBET	skipper of the Pequod	AHAB
sitting room	PARLOR	ski race	SLALOM
situate	LOCATE	skirl	PIPE

skirmish	MELEE	sleep	NAP, DOZE, REST,
skirt	MIDI, MINI, KILT,		SLUMBER
	DIRNDL, BROOMSTICK,	sleeper	PULLMAN
	GORE	sleep image	DREAM
skirt edge	HEM	sleep inducer	SEDATIVE
skirt feature	SLIT, PLEAT,	sleeping	DORMANT
	WAISTBAND	sleeping place	BED, BEDROOM
skit	SKETCH	sleepless	ALERT, AWAKE
skittish	JITTERY, JUMPY	sleep lightly	DOZE
skittish horse	SHIER	sleep noisily	SNORE
skoal	TOAST	sleepwalker	SOMNAMBULIST
skulk	LURK	sleepwear	PAJAMAS,
skull	CRANIUM		NIGHTGOWN, NIGHTIE,
skunk	POLECAT		NIGHTSHIRT
skunk-like animal	CIVET	sleepy	DROWSY
sky	HEAVEN	sleeve	ARM
sky-blue	AZURE	sleeveless garment	CAPE,
skye	TERRIER		CLOAK, VEST
sky twinkler	STAR	sleeve part	CUFF
skyward	UP, ALOFT	sleigh	SLED, PUNG
slack	LOOSE	sleight of hand	MAGIC,
slacken	ABATE, RELENT,		HOCUS-POCUS
	RETARD, EASE, LET UP,	slender	SKINNY, SVELTE,
	LOOSEN		LEAN, SLIM,
slackening bar on a loom			TENUOUS, THIN
	EASER	slender candle	TAPER
slacks	PANTS	slenderize	REDUCE
slag	DROSS, SCORIA	slender pinnacle	EPI
slake	ALLAY, QUENCH	slender pipe	TUBE
slam	BANG	sleuth	DETECTIVE
slander	ASPERSE, DEFAME	slice	CARVE, CUT
slanderous gossip	DIRT	slice a roast	CARVE
slang	CANT, ARGOT	slice of meat	CUTLET, STEAK,
slangy affirmative	YEP, YEAH,		CHOP
	OKAY	slice of toasted bread	RUSK
slangy denial	NOPE	slick	SLIPPERY, SMOOTH
slant	BIAS, INCLINE, TILT,	slicker	RAINCOAT
	SLOPE, ATTITUDE	slide	SLIP, SKID, GLIDE,
slanting	SLOPING, OBLIQUE		SLITHER
slap	CUFF, REBUFF, SMACK	slight	SMALL, SLIM
slap-happy	GIDDY	slight coloring	TINT
slash	CUT, LASH	slight depression	DENT
slate	BLACKBOARD, TILE	slightest	LEAST
slattern	CARELESS	slighting remark	SLUR
slaughter	CARNAGE, BUTCHER	slight intentionally	SNUB
slaughterhouse	ABATTOIR	slightly open	AJAR
Slav	CROAT, SERB	slightly tapering	TERETE
slave	SERF, ESNE, PEON,	slightly wet	DAMP, MOIST
	BONDSMAN, DRUDGE	slight quarrel	TIFF, SPAT
slave owner	MASTER	slight sound	PEEP
slaver	SLOBBER, DROOL	slight taste	SIP
slavery	BONDAGE	slim	SLENDER, THIN,
Slavic language	CROAT		LEAN, SVELTE
slay	KILL	slime	MUD, OOZE
slayer of Goliath	DAVID	sling	CAST, FLING
sled	COASTER, TOBOGGAN	slink	LURK
sleek	LUSTROUS	slinky	STEALTHY, FURTIVE
sleek black animal	PANTHER	slip	SLIDE

slip backwards	**RELAPSE, REGRESS**
slip by	**ELAPSE**
slipknot	**NOOSE**
slip-on garment	**TUNIC**
slipper	**MULE, SHOE, SCUFF**
slippery	**EELY, ICY**
slipshod	**SLOVENLY**
slip sideways	**SKID**
slipsole	**INSOLE**
slip the memory	**FORGET**
slip-up	**ERROR, MISHAP**
slit	**CRACK, SPLIT**
slither	**SLIDE**
sliver of wood	**SPLINTER**
slivovitz	**BRANDY**
slobber	**DROOL**
sloe	**PLUM**
slog	**PLOD, TOIL**
slogan	**CRY, CATCHWORD, MOTTO**
slop	**SPLASH**
sloping roadway	**RAMP**
slop over	**SPILL**
sloppy person	**SLOB**
slosh	**SPLASH, SLUSH**
sloth	**AI, UNAU**
slothful	**INDOLENT, LAZY**
slot machine success	**JACKPOT**
slouch	**DROOP, SAG**
slovenly	**UNTIDY, MESSY**
slow	**SLUGGISH**
slow but flowing (mus.)	**ANDANTE**
slow down (2 wds.)	**LET UP**
slow-moving mollusk	**SNAIL**
slow (mus.)	**LENTO, ADAGIO, LARGO**
slowpoke	**LAGGARD, SNAIL**
slow train	**LOCAL**
slow-witted	**DULL, STUPID**
sludge	**MUD, MIRE**
slug	**SNAIL**
slugger's special	**HOMER, KAYO**
sluggish	**LOGY, SLOW**
sluggishness	**TORPOR**
sluice	**GATE, CHANNEL**
sluice gate	**CLOW**
slumber	**SLEEP**
slum dwelling	**TENEMENT**
slumgullion	**STEW, HASH**
slump	**DROP, FALL**
slur	**INSULT**
slur over	**ELIDE**
slurp	**SUCK, GULP**
slush	**MIRE**
sly	**CUNNING, WILY, FOXY**

sly fellow	**FOX**
sly glance	**LEER**
slyly spiteful	**CATTY**
sly trick	**WILE**
smack	**SLAP**
small	**LITTLE, PETITE, TINY, TEENY, WEE**
small African antelope	**ORIBI**
small amount	**BIT, DAB, DRAM, IOTA, MITE, MORSEL**
small anchor	**KEDGE**
small and trim	**PETITE**
small and unimportant	**DINKY, TRIVIAL**
small antelope	**GAZELLE**
small anvil	**TEEST**
small aperture	**VENT**
small arms	**PISTOLS**
small arrow	**DART**
small articles case	**ETUI**
small automobile	**RUNABOUT**
small bag	**SATCHEL**
small barn	**SHED**
small barrel	**KEG**
small bay	**COVE**
small bed	**COT**
small beetle	**WEEVIL**
small bill	**DOLLAR**
small bird	**WREN, TIT**
small bit	**NIP**
small bit of food	**MORSEL**
small body of water	**POND**
small bottle	**VIAL**
small boy	**TAD**
small branch	**TWIG**
small brook	**RILL**
small brown bird	**WREN**
small bunch	**WISP**
small cabin	**HUT**
small candle	**TAPER**
small carrying bag	**SATCHEL, GRIP, ETUI**
small cask	**KEG**
small change	**SILVER**
small chicken	**BANTAM**
small child	**TAD, TOT, TODDLER**
small chunk	**WAD**
small city	**TOWN**
small coin	**CENT, PENNY, DIME, NICKEL**
small compact heap	**WAD**
small cord	**STRING**
small cube	**DIE**
small cuckoo bird	**ANI**
small cushion	**PAD**
small deer	**ROE**
small depression	**DENT**

small distance	**INCH**
small dog	**TERRIER, PUPPY, CHIHUAHUA**
small donkey	**BURRO**
small drum	**TABOR**
small duck	**SMEW, TEAL**
small engine	**MOTOR**
smallest	**LEAST**
smallest bit	**IOTA, WHIT**
smallest of the litter	**RUNT**
smallest part	**WHIT, MINIM**
small European fish	**DACE**
small explosion	**POP**
small falcon	**KESTREL**
small field	**CROFT**
small finch	**SERIN, SISKIN**
small fish	**SARDINE, SMELT, MINNOW, GUPPY**
small flap	**TAB**
small fly	**GNAT**
small forest ox	**ANOA**
small fragment	**CHIP, SHRED**
small fresh-water duck	**TEAL**
small fried cake	**FRITTER**
small garden spade	**TROWEL**
small glass of brandy	**PONY**
small green finch	**SERIN**
small group of secret plotters	**CABAL**
small gull	**TERN**
small harpsichord	**SPINET**
small heavenly body	**PLANETOID, ASTEROID, SATELLITE**
small herring	**SPRAT**
small hooter	**OWLET**
small horse	**PONY, COLT**
small hotel	**INN**
small hound	**BEAGLE**
small house	**CABIN, COTTAGE, HUT**
small in amount	**SLIGHT**
small in figure	**PETITE**
small inlet	**COVE, CREEK, RIA**
small insect	**GNAT**
small island	**AIT, CAY, ISLE, KEY, ISLET**
small jazz group	**COMBO**
small job	**CHORE**
small juicy fruit	**BERRY**
small lace mat	**DOILY**
small lake	**MERE, POND**
small leafy branch	**SPRIG**
small liquid measure	**GILL, PINT**
small lizard	**EFT, NEWT**
small mallet	**GAVEL**
small mass	**WAD**

small measure	**OUNCE**
small-minded	**NARROW, PETTY**
small monkey	**TITI**
small mound	**HILL**
small mountain lake	**TARN**
smallmouth	**BASS**
small nail	**BRAD, TACK**
small narrow valley	**RAVINE**
small nocturnal mammal	**LEMUR**
small opening	**FORAMEN, PORE**
small orange fruit	**KUMQUAT**
small part	**BIT**
small particle	**ATOM, MOTE**
small photo	**SNAPSHOT**
small piano	**SPINET**
small pie	**TART**
small piece	**BIT, FRAGMENT, MORSEL, SNIP**
small piece of food	**MORSEL**
small piece of ground	**PLAT**
small pigeon	**DOVE**
small pillow	**PAD**
small pincers	**PLIER**
small plateau	**MESA**
small pond	**POOL**
small porch	**STOOP**
small potatoes	**UNIMPORTANT**
small pouch	**SAC**
small quantity	**BIT, DAB, DROP, IOTA**
small quarrel	**SPAT, TIFF**
small restaurant	**CAFE, DINER**
small river	**STREAM, CREEK, BROOK**
small river duck	**TEAL**
small rock	**PEBBLE**
small rodent	**LEROT, MOUSE, VOLE**
small roll	**BUN**
small room	**CLOSET**
small rug	**MAT**
small sailing vessel	**LUGGER**
small salamander	**NEWT**
small sample of cloth	**SNIP**
small satellite	**MOONLET**
small-scale	**LIMITED**
small seed	**PIP**
small shelter	**SHED, LEAN-TO**
small ship	**BOAT, TUG**
small shoot	**TWIG**
small shrub	**ELDER**
small sofa	**LOVE SEAT, DIVAN**
small songbird	**WREN, CANARY**
small souvenir	**KNICKKNACK**
small spar	**SPRIT**

small spear	DART	smoked meat	HAM
small spot	SPECK, DOT	smoked pork	BACON
small steep waterfall	CASCADE	smoke flue	STACK, CHIMNEY
small stone	PEBBLE	smoker	STAG
small store	SHOP	smoker's item	CIGARET, PIPE,
small stream	CREEK, RILL,		CIGARETTE, CIGAR
	BROOK	smokestack	CHIMNEY
small sturgeon	STERLET	Smokey	BEAR
small Sumatra deer	NAPU	smoking tube	PIPE
smallsword	EPEE	smoky	HAZY
small table	STAND, TABORET	smoky quartz	CAIRNGORM
small talk	CHAT	smolder	SMOTHER, SMUDGE
small task	CHORE	smooch	KISS, BUSS, NECK
small taste	SIP, BITE	smooth	EVEN, LEVEL, FLAT,
small-time	MINOR, PETTY		GLIB, EASY
small tower	TURRET	smoothbore	GUN
small-town	PROVINCIAL	smooth cotton cloth	PERCALE
small tree branch	TWIG	smooth-faced	SHAVEN
small tropical cuckoo bird	ANI	smooth feathers	PREEN
small twig	SPRIG	smoothing tool	FILE, PLANE
small typewriter type	ELITE	smoothly courteous	URBANE
small valley	DALE, DELL,	smooth-spoken	GLIB
	GLEN, VALE	smorgasbord	BUFFET
small vegetable	PEA, BEAN	smother	STIFLE
small wagon	CART	smudge	SMEAR, SPOT,
small weight	GRAM, OUNCE		STAIN, BLUR,
small wheeled vehicle	CART		DIRTY, SOIL
small whirlpool	EDDY	smug	COMPLACENT
small wild ox	ANOA	smuggler	RUNNER
smalt	GLASS, BLUE	smug person	PRIG
smart	INTELLIGENT, BRIGHT,	smut	SOOT, DIRT
	STING, BURN	Smyrna	IZMIR
smart in appearance	CHIC,	Smyrna figs	ELEMI
	NATTY	snack	BITE
smart-looking	TRIG	snaffle	BIT
smash	SHATTER, BREAK	snag	OBSTACLE
smashup	WRECK, COLLISION	snail	SLUG
smear	SMUDGE, DEFAME,	snail genus	MITRA, TRITON
	DAUB	snail-paced	SLOW
smell	ODOR, REEK, SCENT	snake	SERPENT, VIPER,
smelly vegetable	ONION		ADDER, ASP
smelting by-product	SLAG	snake eyes	TWO, DEUCE
smelting chamber	OVEN	snake-killing mammal	
smelt ore	REFINE		MONGOOSE
smew	MERGANSER	snakeless land	EIRE
smile	GRIN, BEAM	snakelike fish	EEL
smile in a silly manner	SIMPER	snakemouth	POGONIA
smile scornfully	SNEER	snake's sound	HISS, RATTLE
smiling	RIANT	snakeweed	BISTORT
smirch	TAINT, STAIN, SULLY	snaky	SINUOUS
smirk	LEER, SIMPER	snaky letter	ESS
smite	STRIKE	snap	CLICK
smithy	FORGE	snap back	RECOVER
smock	CHEMISE, SHIFT	snappish bark	YAP
smog	MIST	snappy	SPICY, LIVELY
smoke	REEK, FUME	snappy comeback	RETORT
smoke a cigarette	PUFF	snapshot	PHOTO
smoke and fog	SMOG	snapshot, for short	PIC

snare	NET, TRAP	soap	LATHER
snarl	TANGLE	soapbark	SAPONIN
snarling dog	CUR	soap flake	CHIP
snarly	CROSS	soap foam	SUDS
snatch	GRAB, NAB	soap-frame bar	SESS
snazzy	FLASHY	soap ingredient	LYE
sneak	LURK, STEAL	soap opera	SERIAL
sneaker	SHOE	soap plant	AMOLE
sneaky	STEALTHY	soapstone	TALC
snee	DIRK	soapweed	YUCCA
sneer	GIBE, SCOFF	soar	FLY, RISE
sneeze	ACHOO	sob	CRY, WEEP
snicker	TITTER	so be it	AMEN
snide	MEAN, LOW	sober	SERIOUS, SOLEMN
sniff	SMELL, NOSE	sobriquet	EPITHET,
sniffles	COLD		NICKNAME
snifter	GOBLET	sociable	COMPANIONABLE
snip	CLIP	social	POLITE
snitch	PILFER, INFORM	social appointment	DATE
snivel	WHINE	social bud	DEB
snobbish	SNOOTY	social class	CASTE
snood	NET	social division	TRIBE
snoop	PRY	social event	PARTY, BALL,
Snoopy's adversary			RECEPTION, TEA
(2 wds.)	RED BARON	social gathering	BEE
snooty person	SNOB	social gathering for men	STAG,
snooze	DOZE, NAP		SMOKER
snoozing	ASLEEP	social grace	POISE
snout	NOSE	social group	CLAN, TRIBE
snout beetle	WEEVIL	social insect	ANT, BEE
snowbell	STYRAX	social outcast	PARIAH
snow coaster	SLED,	social rank	CASTE, CLASS
	TOBOGGAN	social set	COTERIE, CLIQUE
snow field	NEVE	social studies	CIVICS
snowflake	CRYSTAL	society	UNION, PARTNERSHIP
snow particle	FLAKE	society bud	DEBUTANTE
snow removal implement		society game	POLO, CROQUET
	SHOVEL, PLOW	society in Chinatown	TONG
snow runner	SKI	Society of Friends	QUAKERS
snow shoe	PAC	sock	ANKLET, PUNCH
snowslide	AVALANCHE	socked in	FOGGY
snow slider	SLED	sockeye	SALMON
snow vehicle	SLED, SLEIGH,	sod	GREENSWARD, TURF
	TOBOGGAN	soda	POP
snowy	WHITE	soda sipper	STRAW
snub	IGNORE	soda water	SELTZER
snuffle	SNIFF, PANT	sodden	WET
snug and warm	COZY	sodium chloride	SAL, SALT
snuggle	NESTLE	sofa	DAVENPORT, DIVAN,
snug retreat	NEST		COUCH, SETTEE
so	THUS	sofa bed	CONVERTIBLE
soak	DRENCH, SATURATE,	so far	YET
	SOP	soft	GENTLE, PLIANT
soaked	WET	soft alkali metallic element	
soak flax	RET		SODIUM
soak thoroughly	SATURATE	soft and pliable	WAXEN
soak through	OOZE	soft breeze	ZEPHYR
soak up	ABSORB	soft cap	BERET

soft chancre	CHANCROID	soldier's water flask	CANTEEN
soft cheese	BRIE	sole	L'ONE, ONLY, SOLITARY
soft coal	BITUMINOUS	solecism	BARBARISM
soft drink	COLA, POP, SODA,	solemn	SOBER
	ADE, PUNCH	solemnity	GRAVITY
soft-drink nut	COLA	solemnize	CELEBRATE
soften	ALLAY, ASSUAGE	solemn pledge	VOW, OATH,
softening device	MUTE		PROMISE
soften in temper	RELENT	solemn wonder	AWE
soft feathers	DOWN	solenocyte	FLAGELLUM
soft felt hat	FEDORA	solicit	ASK, REQUEST
soft food	PAP	solicit individually	CANVASS
softgoods	TEXTILES	solicitor	LAWYER
soft hair	FUR	solicitude	CARE
soft hat	CAP	solid	FIRM, HARD
soft in texture	SUPPLE	solid figure	CUBE, CONE
soft leather	CORDOVAN,	solidify	SET, GEL
	SUEDE	soliloquy	MONOLOGUE
softly	LOW, PIANO	solitaire	DIAMOND
soft mass	PULP	solitary	ALONE, LONE, SOLE
soft metal	MERCURY, LEAD,	solitary person	LONER
	TIN	solitude	SECLUSION,
soft metal alloy	SOLDER		LONELINESS
soft mineral	TALC	solo	ALONE
soft mud	SLIME, OOZE	Solomon	SAGE
soft palate	VELUM	so long	TA-TA
soft part of fruit	PULP	solo performance (2 wds.)	
soft pedal	DAMPER		ONE-MAN SHOW
soft plug	WAD	solution	KEY, ANSWER
soft round cap	BERET	solvent	ABOVE WATER
soft-shell	CRAB	soma	BODY
soft-shoe	TAPDANCE	somber	MELANCHOLY
soft-soaper	FLATTERER	sombrero	HAT
soft-spoken	QUIET, SUAVE	some	ANY
software	PROGRAM, DATA	somersault	TUMBLE, FLIP
soggy	WET, MOIST, DAMP	something dependable	
soigne	NEAT, TIDY	(comp. wd.)	STAND-BY
soil	DIRT, EARTH	something easy to	
soil deposit	SILT	accomplish (sl.)	PUSHOVER
soil mixture	LOAM	something extra	ACCESSORY
soil with dirt	BEGRIME	something inferior	PUNK
soiree	PARTY	something landlubbers	
sojourn	ABIDE	lack (2 wds.)	SEA LEGS
sol	SUN	something learned	LESSON
solace	CONSOLE, SOOTHE	something oppressive	BURDEN
solan	GANNET	something remarkable	LULU,
solar disc	ATEN		ONER
solar system model	ORRERY	something similar	ANALOGUE
soldering flux	ROSIN	something small	ATOM, IOTA
soldering piece	LUG	something that entertains	
soldier	PRIVATE, GI		AMUSEMENT, DIVERSION
soldier on guard	SENTRY	something to smoke	CIGAR,
soldier's address (abbr.)	APO		CIGARET, CIGARETTE,
soldiers' meal	MESS		PIPE, TOBACCO
soldier's overcoat	CAPOTE	something unexplained	
soldier's quarters	BARRACKS		MYSTERY
soldier's vacation	LEAVE,	something unique	ONER
	FURLOUGH	something worthless	TRIPE

sometime	**ONCE**	son of Isaac	**JACOB, ESAU**
sometime salt ingredient		son of Jacob	**LEVI, DAN,**
	IODINE		**JOSEPH, GIDEON,**
sometimes wild card	**DEUCE**		**ASHER, GAD, JUDAH**
somewhat	**TO A DEGREE,**	son of Judah	**ER**
	RATHER	son of Lancelot	**GALAHAD**
somewhat alike	**SIMILAR**	son of Noah	**SHEM, HAM**
somewhat colorless	**PALISH**	son of Obed	**JESSE**
somewhat youthful	**YOUNGISH**	son of Odin	**THOR**
sommelier	**STEWARD**	son of Ruth	**OBED**
somnambulist	**SLEEPWALKER**	son of Saul	**JONATHAN**
somniferous	**SOPORIFIC**	son of Seth	**ENOS**
somniloquy	**SLEEP-TALK**	sonorous	**RESONANT**
somnolent	**SLEEPY**	soon	**ANON, PRESENTLY**
son	**BOY, HEIR, SCION**	Sooner State	**OKALAHOMA**
sonance	**TONE**	sooner than	**ERE**
song	**BALLAD, LAY, TUNE,**	soot	**LAMPBLACK, SMUT, GRIT**
	ARIA, MELODY	sooth	**TRUTH, FACT**
songbird	**LARK, SKYLARK,**	soothe	**EASE, COMFORT**
	CANARY, TANAGER,	soothing ointment	**BALM,**
	WREN		**SALVE**
song for a diva	**ARIA**	soothing substance	**BALSAM**
song for a sailor	**CHANTEY**	soothing word	**THERE**
song for one	**SOLO**	soothsayer	**AUGUR**
song for two	**DUET**	sop	**DRENCH, SOAK**
songlike	**ARIOSO, LYRIC**	sophism	**FALLACY**
song of joy	**PAEN**	sophisticated	**WORLDLY**
songstress Adams	**EDIE**		**BLASE**
songstress Bailey	**PEARL**	soporific	**SEDATIVE, NARCOTIC**
songstress Brewer	**TERESA**	soprano Lehmann	**LOTTE**
songstress Cantrell	**LANA**	sora	**RAIL**
songstress Della	**REESE**	sorcerer	**WIZARD**
songstress Diahann	**CARROLL**	sorceress of myth	**CIRCE**
songstress Fitzgerald	**ELLA**	sordid	**FOUL, FILTHY**
songstress Horne	**LENA**	sore	**PAINFUL**
songstress Judy	**GARLAND**	sorely	**URGENTLY**
songstress Lanie	**KAZAN**	sorghum	**SYRUP**
songstress Lee	**BRENDA,**	sorrel	**OCA, OXALIS**
	PEGGY	sorrow	**GRIEF, WOE, DOLOR**
songstress Logan	**ELLA**	sorrowful	**SAD**
songstress Martin	**MARY**	sorry	**RUEFUL**
songstress Minnelli	**LIZA**	sorry horse	**NAG**
songstress Page	**PATTI**	sort	**TYPE, ILK, CLASS,**
songstress Piaf	**EDITH**		**CLASSIFY, KIND**
songstress Reese	**DELLA**	sortie	**FORAY, RAID**
songstress Shirley	**BASSEY**	sot	**TOPER, TOSSPOT, DRUNK**
songstress Smith	**KATE**	sotto voce	**WHISPER**
songstress Starr	**KAY**	souchong	**TEA**
songstress Stevens	**CONNIE**	souk	**MARKET**
songstress Streisand	**BARBRA**	soul	**SPIRIT, PSYCHE**
song thrush	**MAVIS**	soul (Fr.)	**AME**
songwriter	**COMPOSER**	soul seller	**FAUST**
sonnet	**POEM, VERSE**	sound	**NOISE, TONE, VALID**
son of Adam	**SETH, ABEL,**	sound a horn	**TOOT**
	CAIN	sound, as a bell	**RING, PEAL,**
son of Agamemnon	**ORESTES**		**TOLL**
son of Aphrodite	**EROS**	sound detector	**SONAR**
son of Hagar	**ISHMAEL**	sound equipment of TV	**AUDIO**

sounder	**PLUMB**
sound from a kennel	**YELP,**
YIP, YAP, WOOF, ROWF,	
BARK, BOWWOW	
sound harshly	**GRATE**
sound in harmony	**CHIME**
sound loudly	**BLARE**
sound made by sheep	**BAA,**
	MAA
soundness of mind	**SANITY**
sound of a bell	**DONG, DING**
sound of a blow	**WHAM**
sound of a cat	**MEW, MEOW,**
	MIAW
sound of a clock	**TICK, TOCK,**
ALARM, TICKING	
sound of a cow	**MOO**
sound of a dove	**COO**
sound of a rifle shot	**CRACK**
sound of a snake	**HISS,**
	RATTLE
sound of contempt	**BOO, BAH**
sound of disapproval	**BOO,**
HISS, CATCALL,	
RASPBERRY	
sound of dismissal	**SCAT,**
	SHOO
sound of hesitation	**ER, UM,**
AH, AHEM	
sound of relief	**SIGH**
sound of rustling skirts	**SWISH**
sound of surf	**ROAR**
sound of today's music	**ROCK**
sound quality	**TONE**
sound reasoning	**LOGIC**
sounds having melody	**MUSIC**
sound system	**STEREO**
sound the alarm	**ALERT**
sound track	**AUDIO**
soup	**BROTH, BISQUE,**
	CHOWDER
soupcon	**SUSPICION, HINT**
soup dish	**BOWL, TUREEN**
soupfin shark	**TOPE**
soup green	**OKRA**
soup ingredient	**ONION, LEEK,**
SPLIT PEA, CHICKEN,	
RICE, BARLEY, NOODLE	
sour	**ACID, TART**
source	**ORIGIN, BEGINNING,**
ROOT, SPRING	
source of honor	**CREDIT**
source of income	**REVENUE**
source of iodine	**KELP**
source of light	**SUN**
source of metal	**ORE**
source of ore	**MINE**
source of poi	**TARO**

source of power	**ATOM, STEAM**
source of revenue	**TAX**
source of the mighty oak	
	ACORN
source of wood	**TREE**
sourdine	**MUTE**
sourdough	**BREAD**
sour fruit	**LEMON**
sour-leaved plant	**SORREL**
sour mash	**WHISKEY**
sousaphone	**TUBA**
souse	**PICKLE, BRINE**
soused	**DRUNK**
soutane	**CASSOCK**
South	**DIXIE**
south (Fr.)	**SUD**
South African	**BOER**
South African antelope	**ELAND,**
	GNU
South African city	**DURBAN**
South African grassland	**VELDT**
South African native	**BANTU**
South African plant	**ALOE**
South African republic	
	TRANSVAAL
South African tribe	**BANTU,**
	ZULU
South African village	**KRAAL**
South American aborigine	
	ARAWAK
South American animal	**LLAMA,**
	TAPIR
South American beast of	
burden	**LLAMA**
South American country	**PERU,**
BRAZIL, CHILE,	
URUGUAY, PARAGUAY,	
ARGENTINA, VENEZUELA,	
COLUMBIA	
South American drink	**ASSAI**
South American Indian	**CARIB,**
	INCA
South American Indian	
group	**INCA**
South American knife	
	MACHETE
South American liberator	
	BOLIVAR, MARTIN
South American monkey	**SAI**
South American mountains	
	ANDES
South American ostrich	**RHEA**
South American parrot	**MACAW**
South American plains	
	LLANOS, PAMPAS
South American river	**PLATA,**
	AMAZON
South American rodent	**PACA**

South American rubber tree **PARA**
South American tree **CACAO**
South American vulture **CONDOR**
South American weapon **BOLAS**
South Dakota city **PIERRE**
southdown **SHEEP**
southeast wind **EURUS**
southern beauty **BELLE**
southern bread **PONE**
southern constellation **ARA, ARGO, LIBRA, CENTAURUS**
southern crop **COTTON, SOYBEANS, PEANUTS, TOBACCO**
southern drink **JULEP, COMFORT**
Southern France **MIDI**
southern general **LEE**
South Pacific island group **SAMOA, HAWAII, FIJI, MICRONESIA**
southpaw **LEFTY**
South Pole bird **PENGUIN**
South Pole region **ANTARCTICA**
South Seas canoe **PROA, PRAU**
South Seas paradise **TAHITI**
South Seas plant **TARO**
Southwestern river **GILA, RED**
Southwestern saloon **CANTINA**
souvenir **RELIC, MEMENTO**
sovereign **RULER**
sovereign authority **DOMINION**
sovereign of Iran **SHAH**
sovereign power **THRONE**
sovereign's domain **EMPIRE**
sovereign's residence **PALACE**
soviet **COUNCIL**
Soviet city **OREL, MOSCOW, LENINGRAD**
Soviet commune **MIR**
Soviet news agency **TASS**
Soviet plane **MIG**
Soviet police **OGPU**
Soviet refusal **NYET, NIET**
Soviet river **URAL, VOLGA, LENA**
sow **SEED, PLANT**
sowbelly **SALT PORK**
space **ROOM**
space beside one **SIDE**
space between two points **DISTANCE**
space for laying up goods **STORAGE, ETAPE**
spaceman **ASTRONAUT**

space of time **INTERVAL**
space vehicle **APOLLO**
space-vehicle booster **SATURN**
spacious **ROOMY, AMPLE**
spade **SHOVEL**
spaghetti **PASTA**
Spain and Portugal **IBERIA**
span **BRIDGE**
spangle **SPARKLE, GLITTER**
Spanish-American laborer **PEON**
Spanish-American priest **PADRE**
Spanish-American shawl **SERAPE**
Spanish article **EL, LA, UNO, LOS**
Spanish aunt **TIA**
Spanish bayonet **YUCCA**
Spanish chaperone **DUENNA**
Spanish cheer **OLE**
Spanish city **CADIZ, TOLEDO, MADRID**
Spanish conqueror **CORTEZ, PIZARRO**
Spanish dance **TANGO, FLAMENCO, BOLERO**
Spanish fleet **ARMADA**
Spanish gambling game **MONTE**
Spanish gentleman **SENOR, CABALLERO**
Spanish gold **ORO**
Spanish hero **CID, EL CID**
Spanish holiday **FIESTA**
Spanish house **CASA**
Spanish jar **OLLA**
Spanish legislature **CORTES**
Spanish mackerel **PINTADO**
Spanish matron **DONA, SENORA**
Spanish nobleman **GRANDEE**
Spanish painter **DALI, GOYA, EL GRECO**
Spanish peninsula **IBERIA**
Spanish river **EBRO, RIO**
Spanish room **SALA**
Spanish sherry **JEREZ**
Spanish title **DON, SENOR**
spanker **SAIL**
spanking **LICKING**
spar **MAST, SHADOWBOX**
spare **EXTRA**
sparing **FRUGAL, CHARY**
spark **FLASH**
sparkle **SHINE, TWINKLE, GLISTEN**
sparrowgrass **ASPARAGUS**

sparse	SCANT
spartan	SEVERE
Spartan king	MENELAUS
Spartan slave	HELOT
spasm	TIC
spasmodic	FITFUL
spat	QUARREL
spate	FRESHET
spatter	SPLASH, SPRINKLE
spatula	SCRAPER
spawn	ROE
speak	MOUTH, SAY, TALK, UTTER
speak conceitedly	BOAST, BRAG
speak eloquently	ORATE
speaker	ORATOR
speaker's platform	ROSTRUM
speak from memory	RECITE
speak imperfectly	LISP
speak in undertone	MURMUR
speak slightingly of	DEBASE
speak slowly	DRAWL
speak tearfully	SNIVEL
speak wildly	RAVE
spear	LANCE
special	NOTEWORTHY
special ability	TALENT
special approach	ANGLE
special edition	EXTRA
special event	OCCASION
specialist	EXPERT
specialist in crime	SAFECRACKER, PICKPOCKET
species	KIND, SORT
species of deer	ROE
species of moth	EGGER
species of pheasant	RINGNECK
species of water lily	LOTUS
specific	EXACT, PRECISE
specimen	SAMPLE
specious	PLAUSIBLE, LIKELY
speck	DOT, MOTE
speck of dust	MOTE
speck of moisture from the eyes	TEARDROP
spectacle	PAGEANT
spectacles	GLASSES
spectator	WITNESS
spectator's roofed area	GRANDSTAND
spectre	SHADE, GHOST, HAUNT
spectrum	RANGE
speculate	WONDER
speech	ADDRESS, TALK
speech impediment	LISP

speechless	MUTE, SILENT
speech to the audience	ASIDE
speed	RUN, SWIFTNESS, HASTEN, RACE, HIE
speed contest	RACE
speedily	APACE, QUICKLY
speed rate	TEMPO
speed up	ACCELERATE
speed upward, like a plane	ZOOM
speedy	FAST, QUICK, RAPID, HASTY, SWIFT
speedy horse	ARAB
spell	CHARM
spellbound	RAPT
spelling contest	BEE
spell of cold weather	SNAP
spelt	EMMER
spelunker's specialty	CAVE
spencer	TRYSAIL
spend	EXHAUST, DISBURSE
spend foolishly	SQUANDER
spend money	BUY
spend the summer	VACATION, (A)ESTIVATE
spendthrift	PRODIGAL
spent	EXHAUSTED, PUT OUT MONEY, EXPENDED
sphere	ORB, GLOBE
sphere of action	ARENA
sphere of operation	THEATER
spherical	ROUND
spherical body	BALL, GLOBE
sphinx land	EGYPT
spice	SEASON, PEPPER
spicy	RACY
spicy bud	CLOVE
spicy perfume	INCENSE
spicy quality	TANG, ZEST
spider	ARACHNID, TARANTULA
spider monkey genus	ATELES
spider's handiwork	WEB
spider trap	WEB
spieler	BARKER
spigot	TAP, FAUCET
spike	EAR, NAIL
spike of corn	EAR
spile	TAP, SPIGOT
spillikin	JACKSTRAW
spill over	SLOP
spin	TWIRL, WHIRL, REEL, REVOLVE, ROTATE, TURN
spindle	AXLE, AXIS
spindrift	SPRAY
spine	BACKBONE, SETA
spine bone	SACRUM

spinet	PIANO	spoor	TRACK
spinnaker	SAIL	sporadic	INFREQUENT
spinner of webs	SPIDER	sport	GAME, PASTIME,
spinning toy	TOP		BASEBALL, FOOTBALL,
spinster (2 wds.)	OLD MAID		SQUASH, HOCKEY
spiny anteater	ECHIDNA	sporting a Van Dyke	BEARDED
spiny dogfish	SHARK	sportive	PLAYFUL
spiny-finned fish	COD	sport of kings	RACING
spire	STEEPLE, TOWER	sport of shooting clay	
spire finial	EPI	pigeons	SKEET
spire ornament	FINIAL, EPI	sports enthusiast	FAN
spirit	ELAN, SOUL	sports field	ARENA
sprited	SPUNKY, BRISK	sports group	TEAM
spirited horse	STEED	sports palace	COLISEUM
spirit lamp	ETNA	sportswear	SLACKS, JERSEY,
spiritless	VAPID		SWEATER, SHORTS
spiritual being	ANGEL	sporty	FLASHY
spiritualist	MEDIUM	spot	BLOT, STAIN,
spiritus frumenti	WHISKEY		FLECK, DOT
spirochete	BACTERIA	spot card	PIP
spit	SKEWER, ROD	spotless	CLEAN
spite	MEANNESS	spot of color	BLOB
spiteful	VINDICTIVE, MALIGN	spotted	DAPPLED
spiteful woman	CAT	spotted dog	BRINDLE
Spithead	SOLENT	spotted feline	LEOPARD
spittoon	CUSPIDOR	spotted horse	PINTO
splash	SPLATTER, SPATTER	spotted wildcat	OCELOT
splash through mud	SLOSH	spotty	UNEVEN
splendid	SUPERB	spouse	MATE, WIFE,
splendor	POMP		HUSBAND
splicing machine	EDITOR	spout	GUSH, SPURT
splinter	SLIVER	spout for drawing sap	SPILE
split	CUT, CLEAVE, REND,	spray	ATOMIZE
	RIVE, DIVIDE	spread	WIDEN, DISPERSE
split into thin layers	LAMINATE	spread abroad	STREW
split second	MOMENT, WINK	spread between supports	SPAN
splotch	STAIN, SPOT	spread by rumor	NOISE
Spode	CHINA	spread defamation	LIBEL
spoil	MAR, ROT	spread for bread	BUTTER,
spoiled child	BRAT		JAM, JELLY
spoiler of plans	MARPLOT	spread for drying	TED
spoiler on a plane	FLAP	spread on thick	SLATHER
spoils	BOOTY, LOOT,	spread out	OPEN
	PLUNDER	spread out battle line	DEPLOY
spoke	RUNG, BRACE	spread outward	FLARE
spoken	ORAL, VERBAL	spread over	COVER
spoken exam	ORAL	spree	BINGE, BENDER, TOOT
sponge	CADGE	sprig	SHOOT, TWIG
sponger	MOOCHER, CADGER	sprightly	PERT
sponsor	BACKER	sprightly tune	LILT, AIR
spontaneous	IMPULSIVE	spring	SOURCE, FONT, LEAP,
spoof	PARODY, SATIRE		HOP, JUMP, COIL
spook	GHOST, HAUNT,	spring back	REBOUND
	GOBLIN, SHADE	spring bloomer	IRIS, TULIP,
spooky	EERIE		CROCUS, VIOLET, LILAC,
spool	REEL, BOBBIN		HYACINTH, LILY
spoon	NECK, SMOOCH, LADLE	spring festival	EASTER,
spoonbill	SHOVELER		PASSOVER

spring-like	**VERNAL**	stage hint	**CUE**
spring month	**MARCH, APRIL,**	stage in development	**PHASE**
	MAY, JUNE	stage of a journey	**LEG, LAP**
spring on one foot	**HOP**	stage of civilization	**CULTURE**
spring suddenly	**BOUNCE**	stage of history	**ERA, EPOCH**
spring up	**ARISE**	stage of insect growth	**LARVA**
springy	**ELASTIC**	stage of travel (obs.)	**GEST**
sprinkle	**SPATTER**	stage parentheses	**ASIDE**
sprinkle a lawn	**WATER**	stage presentation	**REVUE,**
sprinkle with flour	**DREDGE**		**PLAY, DRAMA, REVIEW**
sprinkle with powder	**DUST**	stage setting	**SCENE**
sprint	**RACE, RUN**	stage whisper	**ASIDE**
sprite	**ELF, FAIRY, GOBLIN**	stagger	**REEL**
sprite in *The Tempest*	**ARIEL**	stagnant	**FOUL, INERT**
sprout	**SHOOT, SPRIG**	stagnate	**ROT**
sprout artificially	**MALT**	stag's mate	**DOE**
spruce	**NATTY, TRIM,**	staid	**SEDATE, SOBER**
	TIDY, NEATEN	stain	**BLOT, BLEMISH,**
spry	**AGILE, NIMBLE**		**FLAW, SPOT, DYE**
spud	**POTATO**	stair	**STEP**
spun	**WOVE, WOVEN**	stair part	**RISER, TREAD**
spur	**GOAD, ROWEL,**	stair post	**NEWEL**
	IMPEL, STIMULUS	stairwell	**SHAFT**
spurious	**FALSE**	stake	**PEG, WAGER, ANTE**
spurious imitation	**SHAM**	stalactite	**ICICLE**
spurn	**DISDAIN, SCORN**	stale	**OLD, TRITE**
spy	**AGENT**	stalemate	**DRAW**
spy employed by police	**NARK**	stalk	**HUNT, STEM**
spy group (abbr.)	**CIA**	stalk game	**HUNT**
squabble	**QUARREL, BICKER**	stalk of grain	**STRAW**
squalid	**SORDID**	stalk vegetable	**CELERY**
squander	**SPEND, WASTE**	stall	**BOOTH**
square	**CORNY**	stallion	**STUD, HORSE**
square of butter	**PAT**	stalwart	**STRONG, STURDY**
square of three	**NINE**	stamina	**ENDURANCE**
squaring tool	**EDGER**	stammer	**STUTTER**
squash	**GOURD**	stamp	**POSTAGE, SEAL,**
squat	**STUBBY**		**TRAMP, STOMP**
squatter	**NESTER**	stampede	**DEBACLE**
squeal	**TATTLE**	stamping device	**DIE**
squeamish	**DELICATE**	stamp out	**CRUSH**
squeeze	**WRING, PINCH**	stance	**POSE**
squint	**PEER**	stanch	**STOP, STEM**
s-shaped molding	**OGEE**	stand	**RISE, REAR**
stab	**PIERCE**	stand against	**RESIST**
stable	**FIXED, STEADY**	standard	**NORM**
stable compartment	**STALL**	standard of perfection	**IDEAL**
stack role	**NESS**	standard quantity	**UNIT**
stadium cheer	**RAH**	stand by	**AID**
staff	**PERSONNEL, POLE**	standby	**ALTERNATE**
staff officer	**AIDE**	stand for	**REPRESENT**
staff of life	**BREAD**	stand for office	**RUN**
staff of office	**MACE, SCEPTER**	stand in	**SUBSTITUTE**
stag	**DEER, HART**	standing	**STATUS**
stage	**PLATFORM**	stand off	**EVADE**
stage comedy	**FARCE**	stand on edge	**UPEND**
stage direction	**ENTER,**	stannum	**TIN**
	EXEUNT	stanza	**VERSE**

stanza of eight lines	**TRIOLET**
staple grain	**RICE, WHEAT**
star	**TWINKLER, SUN, ASTERISK**
starch	**SAGO**
starchy edible root	**TARO**
star cluster	**NEBULA**
stare	**GAPE, OGLE, GAZE, GAWK**
stare open-mouthed	**GAPE**
stare sullenly	**GLOWER**
stark	**BARE**
star (prefix)	**ASTRO**
star-shaped	**ASTRAL, STELLATE**
start	**LEAD, BEGIN, ONSET, BEGINNING, INITIATE**
start again	**REOPEN, RESUME**
start a Model T	**CRANK**
start aside	**DODGE**
startle	**SURPRISE**
start of college cheer	**HIP**
start off	**LEAD**
start of the fiscal year (2 wds.)	**JANUARY FIRST**
start of the weekend	**SATURDAY**
start on a cruise	**EMBARK**
start out	**EMBARK**
start up again	**RENEW**
starve	**FAMISH**
stash	**HIDE**
state	**DECLARE, AVER, SAY, CONDITION, STATUS**
state (Fr.)	**ETAT**
state as a fact	**POSIT**
state further	**ADD**
state in India	**ASSAM, SIKKIM**
stately	**REGAL, TALL**
stately residence	**MANOR**
state meaning of	**DEFINE**
statement	**ASSERTION**
statement of belief	**CREDO**
state of anxiety	**SUSPENSE**
state of disorder	**MESS**
state-of-emergency crime	**LOOTING**
state of extreme happiness (2 wds.)	**SEVENTH HEAVEN**
state of feeling	**MOOD**
state of health	**CONDITION**
state of mind	**MOOD, TEMPER**
state of perfection (comp. wd.)	**FARE-THEE-WELL**
state of unconsciousness	**COMA**
state policeman	**TROOPER**
state positively	**ASSERT, AVER**
state's leader	**GOVERNOR**
state without proof	**ALLEGE**
station	**TERMINAL, DEPOT**
stationary	**FIXED, SET**
stationer's item	**INK, PAPER**
station in life	**RANK**
station wagon	**CAR**
statistics	**DATA**
statue	**BUST**
statue base	**PLINTH**
statue support	**PEDESTAL**
statue trunk	**TORSO**
stature	**HEIGHT**
status	**RANK, GRADE**
statute	**LAW**
staunch	**LOYAL, FAITHFUL**
stave	**CUDGEL**
stay	**ABIDE, REMAIN**
stay for	**WAIT**
stead	**LIEU**
steadfoot	**STAUNCH, FIRM**
steadiness	**STABILITY**
steady	**STABLE, SOLID**
steady pain	**ACHE**
steak	**MEAT**
steal	**SNEAK, ROB, THIEVE**
steal cattle	**RUSTLE**
steal furtively	**SLINK**
stealthy	**SNEAKY**
steam	**VAPOR**
steam bath	**SAUNA**
steamer	**CLAM**
steamship	**LINER**
steamship company	**LINE**
steatite	**TALC**
steed	**HORSE, MOUNT**
steel	**HARDEN, INURE**
steel beam	**GIRDER**
steelhead	**TROUT**
steep	**PRECIPITOUS**
steeple	**SPIRE**
steeplechase	**RACE**
steep slope	**SCARP, BLUFF, CLIFF**
steer	**GUIDE, PILOT, DRIVE**
steer clear of	**AVOID**
steer enclosure	**CORRAL, KRAAL**
steering apparatus	**RUDDER**
steer meat	**BEEF**
steersman	**PILOT, HELMSMAN**
steeve	**LADE, STORE**
stein	**MUG**
steinbok	**ANTELOPE**
stem	**STALK**
stem-like part	**STIPE**
stench	**ODOR, STINK**

step	**PACE, STAIR, TREAD, WALK**	stock	**STORE**
step and hop	**SKIP**	stockade (Fr.)	**ETAPE**
step of a ladder	**RUNG**	stock exchange	**BOURSE**
steppe	**PLAIN**	stock farm	**RANCH**
steps over a fence	**STILE**	stockholder's unit	**SHARE**
stereo attachment		stocking disaster	**RUN**
(2 wds.)	**TAPE RECORDER, TAPE DECK**	stocking line	**SEAM**
		stocking mishap	**SNAG**
stereotype	**PATTERN**	stocking run (Brit.)	**LADDER**
sterile	**BARREN**	stockings	**HOSE, HOSIERY, NYLONS**
stern	**GRIM, SEVERE, REAR, AFT**		
		stockings (Fr.)	**BAS**
stern-faced	**GRIM**	stock of goods	**LINE**
sternward	**ABAFT, AFT**	stock of wealth	**CAPITAL**
stevedore union (abbr.)	**ILO**	stock-quoting machine	**TICKER**
stew	**RAGOUT, SIMMER, OLLA**	stogie	**CIGAR**
stewed fruit	**COMPOTE**	stoic	**UNEMOTIONAL, STAID, STERN**
stick	**ADHERE, CANE**		
sticker	**LABEL**	stoicism	**PATIENCE**
stick out	**JUT**	stoke	**FEED**
stick together	**COHERE**	stoker	**FIREMAN**
sticky stuff	**GOO, PASTE, GLUE, OOZE, SAP**	stole	**ROBBED, SHAWL, VESTMENT, WRAP**
		stolen property	**PELF, LOOT, BOOTY**
stiff	**TENSE, RIGID**		
stiff-legged bird	**STORK**	stone	**ROCK, PEBBLE, GEM, JEWEL**
stiff-necked	**STUBBORN**		
stifle	**CHOKE, SMOTHER**	stonecrop	**SEDUM**
stigma	**BLOT, STAIN**	stonecutter	**MASON**
still	**MOTIONLESS, QUIET, YET, SILENT**	stone monument	**STELA(E)**
		stoneware (Fr.)	**GRES**
still picture	**SLIDE, SNAP, PHOTOGRAPH, SNAPSHOT**	stone worker	**MASON**
		stony	**HARD, ROCKY, COLD**
		stooge	**FOOL**
stimulant	**TONIC**	stool	**SEAT**
stimulate	**STIR, ROUSE**	stool pigeon	**INFORMANT**
stimulus to creative		stoop	**BEND, PORCH**
thought	**INSPIRATION**	stop	**CEASE, HALT, DESIST, QUIT, PAUSE**
sting	**BITE, NIP**		
stinging insect	**BEE, WASP, HORNET**	stop (naut.)	**AVAST**
		stopgap	**RESOURCE**
stinging plant	**NETTLE, SMARTWEED**	stop gradually (2 wds.)	**TAPER OFF**
stingray	**SKATE, MANTA**	stopper	**CORK, PLUG**
stingy	**MISERLY, MEAN**	stop talking (2 wds.)	**PIPE DOWN, SHUT UP**
stink	**STENCH, SMELL**		
stint	**DUTY**	stop up	**CLOG, PLUG**
stipend	**ALLOWANCE**	stopwatch	**TIMER**
stipulation	**PROVISO**	storage battery plate	**GRID**
stir	**BUDGE, AROUSE, AGITATE, ROUSE, MIX, MOVE, BUSTLE**	storage bin	**GRANARY, MOW**
		storage box	**BIN**
		storage building	**SHED, ETAPE**
stir the fire	**STOKE**	storage place	**ATTIC**
stitch	**SEW**	storage place for weapons	**ARMORY**
stitched line	**SEAM**		
St. Louis ball club	**CARDINALS**	storax	**BALSAM, RESIN**
stoa	**PORTICO**	store	**ACCUMULATE, SHOP, MARKET, MART**
stoat	**ERMINE, WEASEL**		

store correspondence	FILE	strawberry-colored horse	ROAN
stored fodder	ENSILAGE	straw hat	PANAMA
store employee	CLERK	straw man	SCARECROW
store event	SALE	straw rug	MAT
store-fodder	ENSILE	straw vote	POLL
store for future use	STASH, SAVE	stray	ROAM, ROVE, ERR, RAMBLE, WANDER
storehouse (Fr.)	ETAPE	stray dog	CUR
storekeeper	RETAILER, MERCHANT	stray from course	STRAGGLE
store label (2 wds.)	PRICE TAG	streak	STRIPE
store up	AMASS	streak in marble	VEIN
storm	GALE, RAGE, RAVE, FURY, TEMPEST, CYCLONE, TORNADO, HURRICANE	stream	BROOK, RILL, RIVER, RIVULET, CREEK
		stream along	FLOW
storm center	EYE	streamer	RIBBON
stormy	WINDY	streamlet	RILL, RUNLET
story	TALE, YARN, FLOOR	streamline	ORGANIZE
story fabricator	LIAR	street	BOULEVARD, ROAD, AVENUE
storyteller	RACONTEUR	street (Fr.)	RUE
stout	ALE, FAT, OBESE	street Arab	GAMIN, URCHIN
stouthearted	BRAVE	streetcar	TRAM
stout stick	BAT	street drain	SEWER
stout string	CORD, TWINE	street peddler	VENDOR
stove	COOKER, RANGE, OVEN	street sign	SLOW, STOP, YIELD
stove compartment	OVEN	street urchin	GAMIN
stove fuel	GAS	strength	FORCE, POWER, SINEW, THEW
stow	PACK, STORE	strengthen	BRACE, TOUGHEN
stow cargo	STEEVE	strengthen a levee	REVET
straggle	STRAY, WANDER	strengthening medicine	TONIC
straight	DIRECT, UNBENT	strenuous	SEVERE, ARDUOUS
straight course	BEELINE	stress	EMPHASIZE, STRAIN, ACCENT
straight edge	RULER		
straighten	ALINE, ALIGN	stretch	DISTEND, EXPAND
straightforward	CANDID, FRANK	stretched tight	TAUT
		stretcher	LITTER
strain	STRESS	stretch injuriously	SPRAIN
strained	TENSE, TAUT	stretch of land	TRACT, FIELD
strainer	SIEVE	stretch out	EKE
strait	NECK, NARROW	stretch the neck	CRANE
strand	ABANDON, MAROON, DESERT	stretchy	ELASTIC
		strew	SCATTER
strange	FOREIGN, ALIEN, ODD, QUEER, UNUSUAL	stria	GROOVE, CHANNEL
		striate	STRIPE, FURROW
strange (prefix)	XENO	strict	STERN, SEVERE
strangle	CHOKE, STIFLE	strictness	RIGOR
strap	BELT, STROP	stricture	CENSURE, RESISTANCE
strap on a falcon's leg	JESS		
strapping	TALL, ROBUST	stride	STEP
strass	PASTE	strident	SHRILL
stratagem	RUSE, WILE	strife	WAR, TROUBLE
Stratford's river	AVON	strigil	SCRAPER
strath	VALLEY	strike	POKE, PUNCH, HIT, SMITE, SWAT
stratum	LAYER		
stratum of ore	VEIN, SEAM	strikebreaker	SCAB
straw	HAY, SIPPER	strike lightly	PAT, TAP, RAP
strawberry bass	CRAPPIE	strike out	DELE, DELETE

strike repeatedly **BEAT**
strike with the hand **SLAP,**
SMACK
strike with the head **BUTT**
strike with violence **SLAM**
striking **REMARKABLE**
striking effect **ECLAT**
string **CORD, LACE**
stringed instrument **FIDDLE,**
HARP, VIOL, VIOLA,
VIOLIN, LUTE, LYRE,
UKULELE, BANJO,
GUITAR, CELLO,
MANDOLIN, PIANO
stringent **RIGID, SEVERE**
stringy **ROPY**
strip **SHRED, DENUDE**
stripe **BAR, STREAK**
striped horse **ZEBRA**
strip of cloth **TAPE**
strip off skin **FLAY**
strip of leather **STRAP, THONG**
strip of wood **SLAT**
stripling **LAD**
strive **AIM, CONTEND**
strive for (2 wds.) **SHOOT AT**
strive mightily **STRAIN**
strive with **VIE**
strobe **FLASH, LIGHT**
stroke **PAT, CARESS, PET**
stroke of luck (sl.) **FLUKE**
stroll **AMBLE, SAUNTER**
strong **STURDY, POWERFUL,**
POTENT
strong affection **LOVE**
strong and healthy **ROBUST**
strong and resolute **STALWART**
strong and tough **RUGGED**
strongbox **CHEST**
strong breeze **WIND**
strong cart **DRAY**
strong cloth **SCRIM**
strong cord **ROPE**
strong cotton **PIMA**
strong herb **GARLIC**
stronghold **FORT**
strong man of myth **ATLAS,**
HERCULES, TITAN
strong-minded **DETERMINED**
strong point **FORTE**
strong request **DEMAND**
strong taste **TANG**
strong upward movement
SURGE
strong wind **GALE**
strong yearning **ITCHING,**
ACHE
strop **STRAP**

strop a razor **HONE, SHARPEN**
strophe **STANZA**
structure **BUILDING, FRAME**
structure on a roof **CUPOLA**
struggle **VIE, CONTEND**
strum **THRUM**
strut **SWAGGER, PRANCE**
stub **STUMP**
stubble **BEARD**
stubborn **BALKY, DOGGED**
stubborn animal **MULE,**
DONKEY, BURRO
stubby **SHORT**
stuck-up person **SNOB**
stud **BUTTON, SCREW**
student **PUPIL**
student monitor **PREFECT**
student of an English
school **ETONIAN**
student pilot **CADET**
student's p.m. assignment
HOMEWORK
stud for shoe sole **HOBNAIL**
studio **ATELIER**
stud with ornaments **BESET,**
BEJEWEL
study **CON, READ, PERUSE,**
PORE
study closely **EXAMINE**
study course **SEMINAR**
stuff **CRAM**
stuffed shirt **PRIG**
stuffing **FILLING**
stuffy **PRIM, STODGY**
stumble **TRIP, FALL**
stumbling block **OBSTACLE**
stun **AMAZE, DAZE**
stunt **FEAT, TRICK**
stunted animal **RUNT**
stupe **COMPRESS**
stupefy **DAZE**
stupid **SIMPLE, IDIOTIC,**
ASININE
stupid fellow **SIMPLETON,**
ASS, OAF, DUNCE
stupidity **DULLNESS**
stupor **LETHARGY, TORPOR**
sturdy **STRONG, STOUT**
sturdy fabric **DENIM**
sturdy tree **OAK, MAPLE**
sturgeon roe **CAVIAR**
stutter **STAMMER**
sty **PEN, PIGPEN**
Stygian **INFERNAL**
style **FASHION, MODE**
style of singing (2 wds.)
BEL CANTO

style of type	ELITE, ROMAN, ITALIC
stylet	STILETTO
stylish	CHIC, CLASSY
stylish Britisher	TOFF
stylus	NEEDLE
styptic	ALUM
suave	SOFT, SMOOTH
subcontinent of Asia	INDIA, ASIA MINOR
subdivision	SECTION
subdue	TAME, CALM
subject	TEXT, THEME
subject of discussion	TOPIC
subject of verb	NOUN
subject to argument	MOOT
sublime	GRAND
submarine missile	POLARIS
submarine sandwich	HERO
submerge	SINK
submissive	MEEK, TAME, DOCILE
submit	DEFER, BEND
submit evidence	PROVE
subordinate	INFERIOR
subordinate ruler	SATRAP
subpoena	SUMMONS
subscription department's delight	RENEWAL
subsequently	AFTER, LATER, THEN, LATER ON
subside	EBB, SETTLE, ABATE
subsidiary	AUXILIARY
subsidy	GRANT, SUPPORT
subsist	LIVE
substance	GIST
substance for violin strings	ROSIN
substantial	MEATY
substantiate	CONFIRM
substantive	NOUN, PRONOUN
substitute	PROXY, SURROGATE
substitute in office	DEPUTY
substitute squad (2 wds.)	SCRUB TEAM, SECOND STRING
substructure	FOUNDATION
subterfuge	ARTIFICE, EXCUSE
subtle	SLY
subtle air	AURA
subtle sarcasm	IRONY
subtract	DEDUCT
suburban builder	DEVELOPER
suburban residence	VILLA, SPLIT-LEVEL, BUNGALOW, RANCH
suburban restaurant	INN
suburban shopping area	MALL, CENTER
subvert	SUPPRESS, DEMOLISH
succeed	ENSUE, ARRIVE, MAKE GOOD, WIN
succeeding	NEXT
success	PROSPERITY, HIT
succession	SERIES
successful move	COUP
succinct	TERSE, CONCISE
succotash ingredient	CORN
succulent	TASTY
succulent plant	ALOE
succumb	SUBMIT, YIELD
such and no more	MERE
suck	DRAW, INHALE
sucker	DUPE, LOLLIPOP
suckerfish	REMORA
suckle	NURSE
suction	INTAKE
sudden	ABRUPT
sudden attack	RAID, SORTIE, SWOOP
sudden blast of wind	GUST
sudden blaze	FLARE
sudden bump	JOLT
sudden burst of energy	SPURT
sudden death	OVERTIME
sudden decline	LAPSE, SLUMP
sudden downpour	CLOUDBURST, STORM, SHOWER
sudden fear	ALARM, PANIC
sudden gush	SPURT
sudden inspiration	BRAINSTORM
sudden loud noise	BANG
suddenly, like magic	PRESTO
sudden muscular contraction	TIC, SPASM
sudden pain	PANG, TWINGE
sudden shock	JOLT
sudden start	JERK
sudden stroke	COUP
sudden thrust	STAB
suds	FROTH
suds maker	SOAP, DETERGENT, SHAMPOO
sue	PLEAD
suet	FAT
suffer	ENDURE, BEAR
sufferer	VICTIM
suffer from heat	SWELTER
suffer remorse	RUE
suffering	PAIN
suffice	SERVE
sufficient	AMPLE

suffocate	CHOKE, SMOTHER	summon	CALL, CITE
suffrage	FRANCHISE,	summon by name	PAGE
	VOTE	summon forth	EVOKE
sugar	SUCROSE, GLUCOSE	summon together	MUSTER
sugar ladle	SCOOP	summon up	RALLY
sugar portion	CUBE,	sump	PIT
	TEASPOON	sumptuous	LAVISH
Sugar State	LOUISIANA	sumptuous meal	REPAST,
sugar tree	MAPLE		FEAST
sugary	SWEET	sun	STAR, SOL
suggest indirectly	HINT,	sunbeam	RAY
	ALLUDE	sunburn	TAN
suggestion	ADVICE, OPINION	sunburn preventative (2 wds.)	
sui generis	UNIQUE		TANNING LOTION
suit	BEFIT, BECOME	sundae topping	NUTS, SYRUP,
suitable	APT, FIT		CHOCOLATE, CHERRY
suitable for farming	ARABLE	sunday cut of meat	ROAST
suitable place	NICHE	sunday lecture	SERMON
suit at cards	SPADES,	sunday speech (abbr.)	SER
	DIAMONDS,	sunder	TEAR, RIP, SHRED
	HEARTS, CLUBS	sundial arm	GNOMON
suit at law	CASE	sundog	PARHELION
suitcase	GRIP, VALISE,	sundown	EVE, DUSK
	ETUI	sundry	VARIOUS, DIVERS
suitmaker	TAILOR	sunfish	BREAM
suit material	SERGE	Sunflower State	KANSAS
suit of mail	ARMOR	sunken fence	HAHA
suite of rooms	FLAT	sunless spot	SHADE
suitor	SWAIN, BEAU	sunny	BRIGHT, CHEERFUL
sulk	MOPE, POUT, BROOD	sun parlor	SOLARIUM
sulky	SULLEN	sun ring	CORONA
sullen	DOUR, GLUM,	sunrise	SUNUP, DAWN
	MOROSE	sunrise direction	EAST
sully	SMEAR, DEFILE	sun satellite	PLANET
sulphur	BRIMSTONE	sunshade	PARASOL
sultan's wives	HAREM	Sunshine State	FLORIDA,
sultry	HOT, TORRID		NEW MEXICO,
sulu	SARONG		SOUTH DAKOTA
sum	TOTAL, ADD	sunup	DAWN, SUNRISE
sum of money	FUND	Suomi	FINLAND
sum total	ENTIRETY	sup	DINE, EAT
sum up	TOT	super	GREATER, BETTER
summarize	TOT UP,	superannuate	RETIRE
	RECAP	superannuated	OBSOLETE
summary	PRECIS, BRIEF	superb	SPLENDID
summer (Fr.)	ETE	supercilious	SNOBBISH
summer drink	ICED COFFEE,	superego	CONSCIENCE
	ICED TEA, ADE	superficial	CURSORY,
summer flounder	FLUKE		SHALLOW
summer hat	PANAMA,	superfluous	EXCESSIVE,
	BOATER		PROFUSE
summer house	COTTAGE	superior	ABOVE
summer resort area	SHORE,	superlative	MOST
	BEACH, MOUNTAINS	superlative suffix	EST
summer skin tone	TAN	Superman's girl	LOIS
summer tendency	LETHARGY	supermarket	STORE
summit	ACME, APEX,	supernatural	MIRACULOUS
	CREST, PEAK, TOP	supersede	REPLACE

supervise	**OVERSEE**	surgical probe	**STYLET**
supervisor	**BOSS,**	surgical saw	**TREPAN**
	OVERSEER, DIRECTOR,	surgical stylet	**TROCAR**
	CONDUCTOR	surgical thread	**SETON**
supine	**INDOLENT,**	surly	**MOROSE, SULLEN**
	LISTLESS	surmise	**GUESS**
supper	**MEAL, DINNER**	surmount	**CONQUER,**
supplant	**REPLACE, UPROOT**		**SUBDUE**
supple	**PLIANT, ELASTIC,**	surmounting	**ATOP**
	FLEXIBLE	surname	**COGNOMEN**
supplement	**EKE**	surpass	**EXCEL, OUTDO,**
supplementary	**ADDITIONAL**		**BEST**
supplicate	**PRAY, PLEAD**	surplus	**EXCESS**
supplication	**PLEA**	surprise	**STARTLE**
supply	**PROVIDE**	surprise attack	**RAID**
supply food	**CATER,**	surrender	**CEDE, YIELD**
	NOURISH	surrender rights	**WAIVE**
supply of money	**FUNDS**	surround	**BESET**
supply provisions	**PURVEY**	surrounded by	**AMID**
supply station	**DEPOT**	surrounding (prefix)	**PERI**
supply with fuel	**STOKE**	surroundings	**DECOR,**
supply with funds	**ENDOW**		**ENVIRONMENT**
supply with weapons	**ARM**	surveyor	**LINEMAN**
support	**BEAR, LEG, PROP,**	suspend	**HANG**
	BRACE, MAINTAIN,	suspense	**ANXIETY,**
	BOOST		**UNCERTAINTY**
support a motion	**SECOND**	suspension	**DELAY**
support for a glass	**COASTER**		**FAILURE**
suppose	**GUESS, OPINE,**	suspicion	**DISTRUST**
	DEEM, THINK	suspicious	**LEERY**
supposing (2 wds.)	**AS IF**	sustain	**SUPPORT, ENDURE**
supposition	**HYPOTHESIS,**	sustenance	**FOOD**
	THEORY	Sutherland specialty	**ARIA**
suppress	**ELIDE, STIFLE,**	suture	**SEAM**
	SIT ON, STOP,	swab	**MOP**
	ESTOP	swagger	**STRUT**
supremacy	**MASTERY**	swaggering pretense of	
supreme	**UTMOST**	courage	**BRAVADO**
Supreme Court group	**NINE**	swain	**SUITOR, ADMIRER**
supreme Egyptian deity	**AMON**	swallow	**BIRD, GULP**
surcease	**RESPITE**	swallow up	**EAT, ENGULF,**
sure	**IN THE BAG,**		**DEVOUR**
	CERTAIN	swami	**PUNDIT**
sure-footed	**NIMBLE**	swamp	**BOG, FEN, MARSH,**
surf	**BREAKERS**		**MORASS**
surface	**AREA, TOP**	swamp grass	**REED**
surface a street	**PAVE**	swampish	**MIRY**
surface coating	**SCUM**	swampland tract	
surface depression	**DENT**		**EVERGLADES**
surface drain	**SEWER**	swan	**CYGNUS, COB**
surface of a gem	**FACET**	swanky dwelling place	
surfeit	**SATE, GLUT**	(2 wds.)	
surf roar	**ROTE**		**DUPLEX APARTMENT**
surge	**TIDE**	swansdown	**FLANNEL**
surge of emotion	**THRILL**	swap	**BARTER, TRADE**
surgeon's instrument	**SCALPEL**	sward	**SOD, TURF**
surgical compress	**STUPE**	swarm	**TEEM, HIVE**
surgical knife	**SCALPEL**	swarming	**ALIVE**

swarthy — **DARK, DUSKY**
swat — **STRIKE, SMACK**
sway — **SWING**
sway in the breeze — **WAVE**
swearword — **OATH, CURSE**
Swedish beer — **OL**
Swedish canton — **LAN**
Swedish city — **STOCKHOLM, UPSALA**
Swedish clover — **ALSIKE**
Swedish Nightingale — **JENNY LIND**
sweet — **SUGARY**
sweet confection — **CANDY**
sweeten — **CANDY, SUGAR**
sweetened drink — **JULEP**
sweetheart — **DREAMBOAT, LOVER, PARAMOUR, DARLING**
sweet liqueur — **CREME**
sweetmeat — **BONBON**
sweet potato — **YAM**
sweet roll — **BUN**
sweet-scented plant — **JASMINE**
sweet-smelling — **REDOLENT**
sweet song — **BALLAD**
sweet substance — **HONEY, SUGAR, SYRUP**
sweet wine — **PORT**
swell — **EXPAND, DISTEND**
swelling — **EDEMA**
swell out — **BULGE**
swerve — **SKEW, VEER, CAREEN, DIVERGE**
swift — **FAST, RAPID, QUICK**
swiftly — **APACE, FAST, QUICKLY**
swiftness — **HASTE, SPEED**
swig — **DRAFT**
swill — **SLOP, GARBAGE**
swim — **FLOAT, FLOOD**
swim fin — **FLIPPER**
swimming — **NATANT**
swimming mammal — **OTTER, SEAL, WHALE, BEAVER, PORPOISE, DOLPHIN, WALRUS**
swimming place — **POOL**
swimming pool — **TANK, NATATORIUM**
swindle — **DUPE, GYP, BILK, CON**
swindling scheme — **BUNCO**
swine — **HOG, PIG, BOAR**
swine-like — **PORCINE**
swing — **SWAY**

swing around — **SLUE**
swinging bed — **HAMMOCK**
swing music — **JIVE**
swipe — **STEAL, SWEEP**
swirl — **TWIST, EDDY**
Swiss cabin — **CHALET**
Swiss canton — **URI, ZUG**
Swiss capital — **BERN**
Swiss city — **BASEL, ZURICH, GENEVA**
Swiss cottage — **CHALET**
Swiss district — **CANTON**
Swiss lake — **ZUG**
Swiss mountain — **ALP**
Swiss mountaineer's song — **YODEL**
Swiss river — **AAR**
switch — **CHANGE, DIVERT**
sword — **RAPIER, SABER**
swordfish's snout — **SERRA**
sword handle — **HILT**
sycophant — **PARASITE, TOADY**
sylvan demigod — **SATYR**
symbol — **EMBLEM**
symbol for tellurium — **TE**
symbol for tin — **SN**
symbol of bondage — **YOKE**
symbol of peace — **DOVE**
symbol of ruthenium — **RU**
symbol of victory — **PALM, VEE**
symmetry — **BALANCE, HARMONY**
sympathize — **CARE, PITY**
sympathy — **COMPASSION**
syncopated rhythm — **RAGTIME**
synonomous — **SAME, SIMILAR**
synthetic fabric — **ORLON, RAYON, NYLON, ARNEL, DACRON**
synthetic material — **PLASTIC, FIBERGLAS, FORMICA**
syrup tree — **MAPLE**
system — **METHOD**
systematic — **REGULAR, PRECISE**
system of belief — **CREED, DOGMA**
system of moral principles — **ETHICS**
system of signals — **CODE**
system of weights — **AVOIRDUPOIS**
syzygy — **PAIR**

T

taa	PAGODA
tab	LABEL, TAG, BILL
tabanid	HORSEFLY
tabby	CAT
table	BOARD
tableau	SCENE, SKIT
tablecloth linen	DAMASK
table dish	TUREEN
table extension	LEAF
tableland	MESA
table linen	DAMASK, NAPKIN
tablemount	GUYOT
table of contents	INDEX
table protector	TRIVET
table scrap	ORT
table support	LEG
tablet	PAD, SLATE
table tennis	PING PONG
tabloid	NEWSPAPER
taboo	FORBID, BAN
tacit	SILENT, UNSPOKEN
taciturn	SILENT
tack	NAIL
tackle	HARNESS, GEAR
tact	DIPLOMACY
tad	BOY
tadpole	POLLIWOG
tag	LABEL, TAB
tag of lace	AGLET
Tahiti capital	PAPEETE
tailboard	ENDGATE
tailed amphibians	SALAMANDER, NEWT
tailless amphibian	TOAD, FROG
tailor	SEW
taint	CONTAMINATE, ADULTERATE
Taiwan	FORMOSA
Taj Mahal site	AGRA
take	GRASP, SEIZE
take a bite	TASTE
take a break	REST
take a chair	SIT
take a chance	RISK, DARE
take a dip	SWIM
take a direction	STEER
take advantage of	USE
take advice	HEED
take after	FOLLOW, PURSUE
take along	BRING, CARRY
take a meal	EAT
take another spouse	REWED

take an upright position	STAND
take a shower	BATHE
take as one's own	ADOPT
take a stroll	WALK
take a trip	TRAVEL, TREK
take away	REMOVE
take away by force	WREST
take back	RECANT, RETRACT
take by surprise (2 wds.)	BOWL OVER
take care	BEWARE
take care of	TREAT, LOOK AFTER, SEE TO, TEND
take cognizance of	NOTICE
take cover	HIDE
take evening meal	DINE, SUP
take first prize	WIN
take five	REST, BREAK
take food	EAT
take for granted	ASSUME, PRESUME
take from	DEPRIVE, SUBTRACT
take in oxygen	BREATHE, INHALE
take in sail	REEF
take into custody	ARREST
take it easy	RELAX, REST
take long steps	STRIDE
take meals for pay	BOARD
take notice	HEED, ESPY, WATCH
take off	DOFF
take offense at	RESENT
take on cargo	LADE
take out	DELE
take-out order (2 wds.)	TO GO
take part (2 wds.)	SIT IN
take pleasure in	ENJOY
take prisoner	ARREST, CAPTURE
take the bus	RIDE
take the car	DRIVE
take the sun	TAN
take to court	SUE
take to jail	ARREST
take to the air	FLY AWAY, SOAR, FLY
take turns	ROTATE, ALTERNATE, SPELL
take umbrage at	RESENT
take up again	RESUME
take up weapons	ARM
take up with	BEFRIEND
taking everything into account	OVERALL

tal **CYMBALS**
talc **STEATITE**
tale bearer **TATTLER, GOSSIP**
talent **SKILL, GIFT**
tale of adventure **GEST**
tale of daring **SAGA**
talipes **CLUBFOOT**
talisman **OMEN, CHARM, AMULET**
talk **JAW, GAB, CHAT, SPEAK, DISCUSS, CONVERSE, CHATTER, PRATE**
talkative **GARRULOUS, CHATTY**
talk back **SASS**
talk foolishly **PRATE**
talk idly **GAB, PRATE**
talk imperfectly **LISP, STUTTER, STAMMER**
talk indistinctly **SPUTTER, MUMBLE**
talking bird **MINA, MYNA, PARROT**
talk slowly **DRAWL**
talk up **PROMOTE**
talk wildly **RANT, RAVE**
tall **LOFTY, HIGH**
tall and thin **LANKY**
tall grass stalk **REED**
tallow **SUET**
tall spar **MAST**
tall structure **TOWER, SKYSCRAPER**
tall tale **YARN, FIB**
tall wading bird **CRANE**
tally **SCORE**
Talmud commentary **GEMARA**
Talmud text **MISHNA**
talon **CLAW**
talus **ANKLE**
tamarisk salt tree **ATLE**
tambour **DRUM**
tame **DOMESTICATE, GENTLE, SUBDUE, DOCILE, HARMLESS**
tame animal **PET**
Tamil **DRAVIDIAN**
tamp **PACK**
tamper **MEDDLE**
tan **BROWN, SUNBURN, ECRU, KHAKI**
tandem **TEAM, BICYCLE**
tangle **KNOT, SNARL, RAVEL, MAT**
tangled mass **MOP**
tangy herb **MINT**

tank **VAT, CISTERN**
tankard **STEIN**
tank farming **HYDROPONICS**
tanned hide **LEATHER**
tansy **WEED**
tantalize **TEASE**
Tantalus' daughter **NIOBE**
tantamount **EQUAL**
tantara **FANFARE**
tantrum **TEMPER**
tap **FAUCET, SPIGOT**
tap down **TAMP**
tape **RECORD, BIND**
taper **CANDLE**
tapering object **WEDGE**
tapering solid **CONE**
tapestry **ARRAS**
tapioca **CASSAVA**
tapioca-like food **SALEP**
taproom **BAR, SALOON, PUB**
tar **PITCH, SAILOR**
tarantula **SPIDER**
tarboosh **FEZ**
tardy **LATE, SLOW**
tare **VETCH, WEED**
target **MARK, OBJECT**
target center **EYE, BULLSEYE**
Tar Heel State **NORTH CAROLINA**
tariff **DUTY**
Tarkington hero **PENROD**
tarnish **SMUDGE, DISCOLOR**
taro paste **POI**
taro root **EDDO**
tarry **BIDE, LINGER, STAY**
tarsier **LEMUR**
tarsus **ANKLE**
tart **ACID, SOUR**
tartan fabric **PLAID**
tartar **CALCULUS**
task **CHORE, JOB, ERRAND, DUTY**
tassel **FRINGE**
taste **FLAVOR, SAVOR, SAMPLE, SIP**
taste a lollipop **LICK**
taste center **PALATE**
tasteful luxury **ELEGANCE**
tasteless **INSIPID, VAPID**
taste with pleasure **SAVOR**
tasty **SAVORY**
ta-ta **GOODBYE**
Tatar lancer **UHLAN**
tatter **RAG, SHRED**
tatting **LACE**

tattle	SQUEAL, RAT ON, TELL, SNITCH	technicality	DETAIL
		technique	METHOD
taunt	TEASE, TWIT, GIBE	tedious	LONG, BORING
taupe	MOLESKIN	tedium	ENNUI
taut	TENSE	tee-hee	TITTER, SNICKER
tavern	PUB, BAR, INN, SALOON	teel	SESAME
		teem	ABOUND
tavern beverage	ALE, BEER	teeming	FULL, REPLETE
tavern employee	BARMAID, BOUNCER	teeny	WEE
		teeter-totter	SEESAW
taw	MARBLE	teetotum	TOP
tawdry	CHEAP, GAUDY	tegula	TILE
tawny	TANNED, DUSKY	Teheran native	IRANI
tax	TOLL, LEVY, TARIFF	tela	TISSUE
taxi	CAB, HACK	telegram	WIRE, MESSAGE
taxi chauffeur	CAB DRIVER, CABBIE	telegraphy inventor	MARCONI
		telephone	CALL
taxi rider	PASSENGER, FARE	telephone book	DIRECTORY
		telephone rod	POLE
taxi ticker	METER	telephone wire	LINE
tax official	ASSESSOR	telescope	GLASS
taxus	YEW	television award	EMMY
T-bone	STEAK	television cabinet	CONSOLE
tea	CHA, OOLONG, PEKOE	television porpoise	FLIPPER
		television sound	AUDIO
teaberry	WINTERGREEN	tell	NARRATE, RELATE
tea cake	SCONE	teller of tall stories	LIAR, FIBBER
teach	EDUCATE, TRAIN, TUTOR		
		telling	VALID
teacher	PROFESSOR	tell secrets	TATTLE
teacher's concern	CLASS, STUDENT, PUPIL, LESSON	tell tales	BLAB, LIE, FIB
		temblor	EARTHQUAKE
		temerity	BOLDNESS, AUDACITY
teaching staff	FACULTY		
tea container	CANISTER	temper	DANDER, MOOD
teak	WOOD	tempera	PAINT
teal	DUCK	temperament	DISPOSITION, MOOD
team race	RELAY		
teamster	CARTER		
team's turn at bat	INNING	temperance	MODERATION
tear	RIP, REND, RIVE, SPLIT	temperate	MILD
		temper display	RAGE, TANTRUM
tear down	RAZE, DEMOLISH		
tearful	SAD	tempered iron	STEEL
tear into	ATTACK	tempest	STORM, GALE
tear into shreds	TATTER	tempestuous	INCLEMENT
tear out	UPROOT	tempo	PACE, TIME
tear producer	ONION	temporal	SECULAR, EARTHLY
tear roughly	LACERATE		
tear salad greens	SHRED		
teary	CRYING	temporary	TRANSIENT
tease	IRRITATE, TANTALIZE, TAUNT, WORRY, RAZZ, TORMENT, ANNOY, PESTER, BADGER	temporary breather	LULL
		temporary fashion	FAD, CRAZE
		tempt	ENTICE, LURE
tease wool	TUM	temptress	SIREN
teatime	FOUR	ten	DECAD, DECADE
tea urn	SAMOVAR	tenacious	PERSISTENT

tenant	ROOMER, LODGER, BOARDER, LESSEE, RENTER	term	PERIOD, COURSE
		termagant	SHREW
		terminal	STATION, DEPOT
ten cents	DIME	terminal pole	ANODE, ELECTRODE
tend	LEAN, LEAD		
tendency	DRIFT, TREND	terminate	END, FINISH
tender	SORE	term in logic	SORITES
tenderfoot	DUDE	term in office	TENURE
tending to arouse feelings	EMOTIVE	terminology	NOMENCLATURE
		termite	ANT
tending to be silent	UNCOMMUNICATIVE, TACITURN	term of address	SIR
		term of imprisonment	SENTENCE
tending to check	REPRESSIVE	term of royal address	SIRE, MAJESTY, HIGHNESS
tending to drive away	REPELLENT		
		terms	CONDITIONS
tending to wear away	EROSIVE	tern genus	STERNA
ten dollars (sl.)	SAWBUCK	terra alba	MAGNESIA
tendon	MUSCLE, THEW, SINEW	terrace	PATIO, VERANDA
		terra cotta	POTTERY
tendril	SPRIG	terra firma dweller	EARTHMAN
tend to	MIND, NURSE	terrain	LAND
tenebrous	DARK, GLOOMY	terrapin	TURTLE
tenement	FLAT, APARTMENT, SLUM	terrene	EARTHLY, WORLDLY
		terret	RING
tenement pest	RAT, ROACH	terrible	AWFUL, DREADFUL
tenet	DOGMA, DOCTRINE	terrible tsar	IVAN
tennis barrier	NET	terrier	SKYE, FOX
tennis instructor	PRO	terrific	EXCITING
tennis point	ACE	terrify	ALARM, FRIGHTEN, SCARE
tennis pro	ACE		
tennis score	LOVE	territory	AREA
tennis shoe	SNEAKER	terror	PANIC
tennis stroke	LOB	terse	CONCISE, PITHY
tennis term	LOVE, SERVE, FAULT	test	EXAM, EXAMINE, EXAMINATION, TRIAL, TRY
tennis trophy	CUP		
Tennyson hero	ENOCH	test for fit (2 wds.)	TRY ON
tenpenny	NAIL	testify	DEPONE, DEPOSE
tenpins	BOWLING	testimony	ATTESTATION
tense	EDGY, TAUT, TIME	testimony weighers in court (2 wds.)	PETIT JURY
tension	STRESS, STRAIN		
tensor	MUSCLE	test ore	ASSAY
tent	TEPEE, WIGWAM	testy	CRANKY
tentacle	FEELER, PALP	Teuton	GERMAN
tentative	PROVISIONAL, TEMPORARY	Texas bronco	MUSTANG
		Texas city	WACO, EL PASO, DALLAS, HOUSTON
tent city	CAMP		
tent-dwelling nomad	ARAB	Texas evergreen shrub	BARETTA
tent show	CIRCUS		
tenth of a decade	YEAR	Texas longhorn	STEER
tenure	TERM	Texas shrine	ALAMO
tenuous	DELICATE, THIN	textiles	MERCERY
ten years	DECADE	text of an opera	LIBRETTO
tepee	TENT, WIGWAM	text of a play	SCRIPT
tepid	LUKEWARM	texture	WALE, GRAIN
teredo	SHIPWORM		
tergal	DORSAL		

Thackeray's Miss Sharp	**BECKY**
Thailand	**SIAM**
Thailand's neighbor	**LAOS**
thalium (chemical symbol)	**TL**
thankful	**GRATEFUL**
thankless person	**INGRATE**
thanks (Fr.)	**MERCI**
that boy	**HE, HIM**
that certain air	**AURA**
thatch palm	**NIPA**
that girl	**HER, SHE**
that is (Lat., 2 wds.)	**ID EST**
that is to say	**NAMELY**
that place	**THERE**
that thing	**IT**
that which follows	**SEQUEL**
that which gives relief	**BALM**
that which must be done	**DUTY**
that which one does best	**FORTE**
that which unlocks	**KEY**
thaumaturgy	**MAGIC**
thaw	**MELT**
the (Fr.)	**LE, LA, LES**
the (Ger.)	**DAS, DER**
the (Sp.)	**LA, EL, LOS, LAS**
theater	**ARENA, STAGE**
theater attendant	**USHER**
theater award	**TONY**
theater box	**LOGE**
theater lobby	**FOYER**
theater passageway	**AISLE**
theater platform	**STAGE**
theater play	**DRAMA**
theater sign	**SRO, EXIT**
theatrical	**DRAMATIC**
theatrical company	**TROUPE**
theatrical couple	**LUNTS**
theatrical performer	**ACTOR**
theatrics	**DRAMATICS**
Theban prince	**OEDIPUS**
the best within record (comp. wd.)	**ALL-TIME**
the bounding main	**OCEAN**
the briny deep	**SEA**
the bull (2 wds., Span.)	**EL TORO**
the devil	**SATAN**
the e in est	**EASTERN**
the end	**OMEGA, FINIS**
the 400	**ELITE**
theft	**ROBBERY, BURGLARY**
the good book	**BIBLE**
the inevitable	**DESTINY, FATE**
the intellect	**MIND**
the last	**OMEGA**
the last frontier	**ALASKA, SPACE**
theme	**ESSAY, TOPIC, SUBJECT**
the merchant of Venice	**ANTONIO**
the m in USMC	**MARINE**
the night club set (2 wds.)	**CAFE SOCIETY**
theological school	**SEMINARY**
the one here	**THIS**
the ones here	**THESE**
the one there	**THESE**
the ones there	**THOSE**
theorbo	**LUTE**
the Orient	**EAST**
theorize	**SPECULATE**
theory	**CONJECTURE, HYPOTHESIS**
the p in mph	**PER**
the planet earth	**TERRA**
the populace	**PEOPLE**
the present	**NOW**
the present age	**TODAY**
therapeutic	**CURATIVE**
therapeutic draught	**DOSAGE**
there	**YONDER**
therefore	**ERGO, HENCE, SO**
the r in HRH	**ROYAL**
the r in IRS	**REVENUE**
therm	**CALORIE**
Therma	**SALONIKA**
thermal	**WARM**
thermos	**BOTTLE, JUG**
the same (Lat.)	**IDEM**
thesaurus creator	**ROGET**
these (Fr.)	**CES, CETTES**
thesis	**ESSAY**
the smallest bit	**IOTA**
thespian	**ACTOR**
thespian's signal	**CUE**
Thessaly mountain	**IDA, OSSA**
the sun	**SOL**
the sun (prefix)	**HELIO**
"the terrible"	**IVAN**
the thing	**IT**
"The Thinker" sculptor	**RODIN**
the three wise men	**MAGI**
the tube	**TELEVISION**
the two of us	**WE**
the two together	**BOTH**
thew	**SINEW, MUSCLE**
the way out	**EXIT**
the whole amount	**ALL**
thick	**DENSE**
thick and short	**SQUAT**
thick black liquid	**TAR**

thick board	PLANK	thinly scattered	SPARSE
thick cluster	CLUMP	thin metal disk	PATEN
thick cord	ROPE	thin nail	BRAD
thicken	CLOT	thinner	TURPENTINE
thicket	COPSE, GROVE	thin out	PETER
thicket fence	HEDGE	thin pasteboard	CARD
thick mist	FOG	thin plate of metal	LEAF
thickness	DIAMETER, PLY	thin screen	VEIL
thick piece	CHUNK	thin shelled nut	PECAN
thick porridge	MUSH	thin silk fabric	PONGEE
thick set	STOCKY	thin-skinned	SENSITIVE
thick skinned	CALLOUS	third in number	TERTIARY
thick skulled	STUPID,	third largest planet	URANUS
	OBTUSE	third person	HE, SHE, THEY
thick slice	SLAB	third power	CUBE
thick soup	PUREE	third-rate	INFERIOR
thick string	CORD, TWINE,	thirst quencher	WATER,
	ROPE		DRINK
thick sweet liquid	SYRUP	thirsty	DRY
thick wire ropes	CABLE	thirteen (2 wds.)	
thighbone	FEMUR		BAKER'S DOZEN
thimblerig	CHEAT,	thirty (Fr.)	TRENTE
	SWINDLE	this (Lat.)	HOC
thin	LEAN, SLIM,	this (Sp.)	ESTA, ESTE
	SLENDER, SKINNY	this way	HERE
thin and haggard	GAUNT	thole	PIN, OARPIN
thin and limp	LANK	thong	STRAP
thin and vibrant	REEDY	Thonga	BANTU
thin and withered	WIZENED	thorn	BRIAR, SPINE
thin as air	RARE	thorny, as a plant	SPINY
thin board	SLAT	thorny shrub	ROSE
thin cookie	WAFER	thorough	COMPLETE
thin cord	STRING	thoroughfare	AVENUE,
thin fog	MIST		STREET, ROAD,
thing	OBJECT, ARTICLE		BOULEVARD, HIGHWAY
thing (Lat.)	RES	those in office	INS
thing abandoned by		those summoned for	
its owner	DERELICT	jury duty	TALESMEN
thingamajig	GADGET	thought	IDEA, NOTION,
thing done	DEED, FEAT,		COGITATION
	FACT	thoughtful	PENSIVE,
thing in law	RES		KIND, GENEROUS
thing of small value	TRIFLE	thoughtless	CARELESS,
thing of value	ASSET		STUPID
thing owed	DEBT	thousandth	MIL
things for sale	MERCHANDISE	thrash soundly	DRUB, TAN,
things given	DATA		BEAT
things to be done	AGENDA	thread	FIBER, FILAMENT
think	REASON, DEEM,	threaded nail	SCREW, BOLT
	OPINE, SUPPOSE	threaded steel pin	BOLT
think ahead	PLAN	thread of smoke	WISP
think hard	CONCENTRATE	thread-winding machine	
think logically	REASON		REELER
think over	PONDER	threaten	MENACE
think the world of	IDOLIZE	threatening	OMINOUS
think twice	RECONSIDER	three (Ger.)	DREI
thin layer	FILM	three (prefix)	TRI, TRE,
thinly metallic	TINNY		TER

three-banded armadillo	**APAR**	thug	**HOODLUM**
three-base hit	**TRIPLE**	thumb	**POLLEX**
three-dimensional	**CUBIC**	thumbnail	**BRIEF, CONCISE**
three feet	**YARD**	thump	**POUND, KNOCK**
three-fifths of the earth's		thunder	**RUMBLE**
surface	**OCEAN**	thunder peal	**CLAP**
threefold	**TRINE**	thurible	**CENSER**
three-legged stand	**TRIPOD**	thus	**SO**
three lines of verse	**TRIPLET**	thus (Lat.)	**SIC**
three-masted vessel	**SCHOONER**	thus far	**YET**
three musicians	**TRIO**	thwart	**FOIL, SPITE**
threescore	**SIXTY**	thyme	**HERB**
three-sided figure	**TRIANGLE**	thymus	**GLAND**
threesome	**TRIO**	tiara	**CORONET**
three-spot card	**TREY**	Tibetan capital	**LHASA**
three-toed sloth	**AI**	Tibetan chief	**POMBO**
three-wheeler	**TRICYCLE**	Tibetan gazelle	**GOA**
threnody	**DIRGE, ELEGY**	Tibetan grand lama	**DALAI**
thresh	**BEAT**	Tibetan guide	**SHERPA**
threshing tool	**FLAIL**	Tibetan monk	**LAMA**
threshold	**SILL**	Tibetan ox	**ANOA, YAK**
thrice (mus.)	**TER**	Tibet's neighbor	**BURMA**
thrift	**FRUGALITY**	tibia	**SHIN**
thriftless	**LAVISH**	Tibur	**TIVOLI**
thrifty	**ECONOMICAL**	tic	**SPASM**
thrill	**SHIVER**	tical	**MONEY**
thrill-seeking parachutist		tick	**OPERATE, WORK**
(2 wds.)	**SKY DIVER**	ticker	**WATCH, HEART**
thrive	**PROSPER**	ticket	**CARD**
throat-clearing word	**AHEM**	ticket (sl.)	**DUCAT**
throat sound	**RALE**	ticket half	**STUB**
throaty	**HUSKY, HOARSE**	tickle	**TITILLATE**
throb	**PULSE, PULSATE,**	tidal wave	**EAGRE**
	DRUM, BEAT	tidbit	**GOODY**
throbbing sound	**PITAPAT**	tide	**CURRENT**
throes	**PANGS**	tidings	**NEWS**
throng	**HORDE, HOST,**	tidy	**NEAT, TRIM**
	CROWD	tie	**ASCOT, CRAVAT,**
throttle	**CHOKE**		**BIND, FASTEN,**
through	**PER**		**TETHER**
throw	**CAST, PITCH, LOB,**	tie clasp	**TACK**
	HEAVE, TOSS,	tie off	**BELAY**
	SLING, HURL	tier	**LAYER, ROW**
throw away	**DISCARD**	tie the knot	**WED, MARRY**
throw cold water on		tie up	**BIND, TRUSS**
	DISCOURAGE	tie-up	**JAM**
throwing rope	**LASSO, REATA**	tiff	**SPAT**
throw lightly	**TOSS**	tiffin	**LUNCH**
throw light upon	**ILLUMINE**	tiger	**CAT**
throw off	**EMIT**	tiger cat	**OCELOT, MARGAY**
throw off the track	**DERAIL**	tight	**TENSE, TAUT**
throw out	**EJECT, EVICT**	tightfisted	**STINGY**
throw slowly	**LOB**	tight-lipped	**TACITURN**
thrum	**FRINGE**	tightrope	**WIRE**
thrush	**MAVIS, ORIOLE**	tights	**LEOTARD**
thrust	**PROD, STAB**	til	**SESAME**
thrusting weapon	**SPEAR**	tile	**SLATE**
thud	**BLOW**	tillable	**ARABLE**

tiller	**HELM**	tint	**DYE, HUE, COLOR,**
till the soil	**FARM,**		**SHADE, TINGE**
	CULTIVATE	tiny	**LILLIPUTIAN,**
tilt	**LEAN, CANT, TIP,**		**SMALL, WEE**
	INCLINE	tiny branch	**SPRIG**
tilt, as a ship	**LIST**	tiny distance	**HAIR, NOSE**
tilted	**ALIST**	tiny morsel	**CRUMB**
tilting match	**JOUST**	tiny parasite	**MITE**
tilting over	**ALOP**	tiny particle	**ATOM, MOTE,**
timber	**LOG, WOOD**		**IOTA**
timber hitch	**KNOT**	tiny speck	**DOT, MOTE**
timber tree	**ASH, OAK, ELM**	tip	**END, GRATUITY,**
timber wolf	**LOBO**		**TILT, LEAN, ADVICE**
timbre	**TONE**	tippet	**SCARF**
time	**DURATION, HOUR**	tipping	**ATILT**
time being	**NONCE**	tipple	**BIB**
time division	**YEAR, DAY,**	tiptoe	**CREEP**
	HOUR, MINUTE,	tirade	**PHILIPPIC,**
	MONTH, WEEK,		**HARANGUE**
	SECOND	tire	**FATIGUE, WEARY**
time gone by	**PAST**	tired	**WEARY, SLEEPY**
time limit	**DEADLINE**	tiresome	**WEARY, TEDIOUS**
timely	**OPPORTUNE**	tire support	**RIM**
time of life	**AGE**	tissue	**TELA**
time of year	**FALL,**	Tisza tributary	**SOMES**
	WINTER, SPRING,	titan	**GIANT**
	SUMMER, SEASON	tithe	**TENTH**
timeout	**REST**	titian	**AUBURN**
timepiece	**CLOCK, WATCH**	titillate	**TICKLE**
timer	**STOPWATCH**	title	**NAME, SIR, MADAM**
timetable	**SCHEDULE**	title role	**LEAD**
time-tested literary work		titter	**GIGGLE, TEEHEE**
	CLASSIC	tittle	**IOTA, JOT**
time waster	**IDLER**	tizzy	**FRENZY**
timeworn	**TRITE**	to	**TOWARD**
timid	**SHY**	toad	**FROG**
timid creature	**MOUSE**	toadstool	**MUSHROOM**
timid person	**FAINTHEART**	toady	**PARASITE,**
timing	**PACING**		**SYCOPHANT**
timing device	**METER**	to a great extent	**LARGELY**
timor	**DREAD, FEAR**	toast	**BROWN, SKOAL**
timorous	**FEARFUL**	toasty	**WARM**
timothy	**HAY**	tobacco chew	**QUID**
timpany	**DRUMS**	tobacco container	**HUMIDOR**
tin	**CAN, METAL**	tobacco disease	**WALLOON**
tin alloy	**PEWTER**	tobacco kiln	**OAST**
tincal	**BORAX**	tobacco pipe	**CORNCOB**
tincture	**MYRRH**	tobacco roll	**CIGAR**
tine	**PRONG**	to be (Fr.)	**ETRE**
tinge	**TINT, HUE**	to be (Lat.)	**ESSE**
tinge deeply	**IMBUE**	to be of use	**AVAIL**
tingle	**PRICKLE**	to be sure	**INDEED**
tingling reaction	**THRILL**	toboggan	**SLED**
tiniest bit	**IOTA**	toby	**JUG**
tinkle	**CLINK**	tocsin	**ALARM**
tinkling sound	**PLINK**	today	**NOW, PRESENT**
tinsel	**GLITTER**	toddler	**TOT**

to-do	**COMMOTION, FUSS**
toe ailment	**GOUT**
toe hold	**FOOTING**
toenail beauty treatment	**PEDICURE**
toe the line	**OBEY**
toff	**DANDY**
toffee	**CANDY**
toga	**ROBE**
togetherness	**UNITY**
toggle	**PIN, BOLT**
togs	**CLOTHES**
toil	**LABOR, WORK**
toilet case	**ETUI**
tokay	**WINE**
token	**SYMBOL**
token move	**GESTURE**
token of affection	**CARESS, KISS**
token of regard	**TESTIMONIAL**
token of right	**TICKET**
token of victory	**PALM**
Tokyo's former name	**EDO**
tolerant	**LENIENT, ENDURING**
tolerate	**ENDURE, BEAR, STAND**
toll	**RING, TAX**
tollhouse	**COOKIE**
toll road	**PIKE**
tomahawk	**HATCHET**
to make fun of	**DERIDE**
to make love	**WOO**
tomato (2 wds.)	**LOVE APPLE**
tomato relish	**CATSUP, KETCHUP**
tomb	**CRYPT, VAULT**
tomboy	**HOYDEN**
tomcat	**GIB**
tome	**VOLUME**
tommyrot	**RUBBISH**
tomorrow (Sp.)	**MANANA**
tom-tom	**DRUM**
tone	**SOUND**
tone color	**TIMBRE**
tongue	**LANGUAGE**
tonic	**BRACER**
to no purpose (2 wds.)	**IN VAIN**
too	**ALSO, AND**
tool	**AUGER, PLANE, AWL, HAMMER, SAW, IMPLEMENT**
tool for writing	**PENCIL, PEN**
too much (Fr.)	**TROP**
toon	**MAHOGANY**
to one side	**APART**

toot	**BLAST, WHISTLE**
tooth	**MOLAR, CANINE, INCISOR, FANG**
tooth covering	**ENAMEL**
tooth decay	**CARIES**
tooth doctor	**DENTIST**
toothed wheel	**GEAR, RATCHET**
tooth of a gear wheel	**DENT**
toothpaste container	**TUBE**
toothsome	**TASTY**
top	**SUMMIT, APEX, ACME, PEAK**
topaz	**YELLOW**
top banana	**HEADLINER**
topee	**HELMET, HAT**
toper	**SOT**
topic	**THEME, SUBJECT**
top military officers	**BRASS**
top-notch	**BEST**
top of altar	**MENSA**
top of an apron	**BIB**
top of a wave	**CREST**
top of the head	**PATE**
topper	**HAT**
topple	**TUMBLE, COLLAPSE**
topside	**DECK**
topsy-turvy (2 wds.)	**UPSIDE DOWN**
toque	**HAT, CAP**
Torah	**PENTATEUCH**
torch	**FLARE**
torero	**MATADOR**
torment	**PESTER, TEASE, TAUNT**
tornado	**TWISTER, CYCLONE**
torpid	**INERT, NUMB**
torpor	**APATHY, LETHARGY**
torrent	**DOWNPOUR**
torrid	**HOT**
torso	**BODY**
torte	**CAKE**
torture	**PAIN, ANGUISH**
to set in type	**PRINT**
to some extent (2 wds.)	**IN PART**
toss	**THROW, HEAVE, CAST, HURL, FLING**
toss carelessly	**FLIP**
tossed greens	**SALAD**
tot	**TODDLER**
total	**ADD, ALL, SUM, ENTIRE**
totally	**QUITE**
tote	**CARRY**
to that time	**UNTIL**
to the larboard	**APORT**

to the left	HAW	trace of color	TINGE
to the point	TERSE	tracer	INQUIRY, BULLET
to the rear	ASTERN	trachea	WINDPIPE
to the sheltered side	ALEE	tracing	COPY
to this place	HERE, HITHER	track	TRAIL, SPOOR
toucan	ARACARI	track circuit	LAP
touch	FEEL, ABUT	track down	TRACE
touch down	LAND	track event	SELLING RACE,
touchdown	GOAL		RELAY RACE
touch gently	DAB, PAT	track race	RELAY
touching	MOVING	track runner	MILER
touch up	FINISH	tract	AREA
touch with color	PAINT	tract	DISSERTATION
touchy	TESTY	tractable	DOCILE, PLIANT
tough, as meat	STRINGY	tractate	TREATISE
toughen	HARDEN, TEMPER	traction	PULL, FRICTION
toughen by exercise	INURE,	tract of wasteland	MOOR
	ENURE	trade	SWAP, BARTER,
tough question	POSER		EXCHANGE, COMMERCE
toupee	WIG	trade center	MART,
tourist attraction	RUINS		MARKET
tourist lodging	MOTEL,	trade combination	MERGER
	HOTEL, RESORT	trade for money	SELL
tournament	CONTEST	trademark	BRAND, LABEL
tournament bridge award		trade name	BRAND
(2 wds.)	MASTER POINT	trade on	EXPLOIT
tow	PULL	tradesman	MERCHANT
toward	TO	trading station	POST
toward shelter	ALEE	tradition	LEGEND, CUSTOM
toward the center	INTO	traditional knowledge	LORE
toward the front	ANTERIOR	traditional restriction	TABOO
toward the interior	INLAND	traditional tale	SAGA
toward the left side (naut.)		traduce	DEFAME, MALIGN
	APORT	traffic	COMMERCE, TRADE
toward the stern	AFT	traffic light color	AMBER,
towel	DRY, RUB		RED, GREEN
towel fabric	TERRY	traffic route	LANE
towel word	HERS, HIS	traffic violation	SPEEDING
tower	FORTRESS, SPIRE,	traffic violation charge	FINE
	STEEPLE, BELFRY	tragedy	DISASTER, DRAMA
towering	TALL	tragic	DIRE
tower of ice	SERAC	trail	TRACE, TRACK,
towhead	BLOND		SPOOR
town (colloq.)	BURG	trail blazer	PIONEER
town in New Guinea	LAE	trailing plant	VINE
town map	PLAT	train	TEACH, EDUCATE
townsman	CIT	train (Sp.)	TREN
town's position	SITE	train berth (2 wds.)	BUNK BED
town's principal street		trainer of wild animals	TAMER
(2 wds.)	MAIN STEM	train terminal	DEPOT,
tow rope	HAWSER		STATION
toxic	POISON	train track	RAIL
toy	PLAYTHING	train whistle	TOOT
toy baby	DOLL	traipse	TRAMP, WANDER
trace	VESTIGE	trait	MARK
trace of an ancient		traitor (sl.)	RAT
animal	FOSSIL	traitorous	PERFIDIOUS

tram	**TROLLEY**	travel across snow	**MUSH**
trammel	**ENTANGLE**	traveler	**FARER**
tramp	**BUM, HOBO,**	traveler's choice	**TOUR,**
	VAGABOND		**TRAIN, BUS, PLANE,**
tramp vessel	**STEAMER**		**SHIP, CAR, JET**
trample	**TREAD**	traveler's concern (2 wds.)	
tranquil	**CALM, PEACEFUL,**		**DEPARTURE DATE**
	SERENE	traveler's home	**HOTEL,**
tranquility	**PEACE,**		**MOTEL**
	SERENITY, QUIET	travel fast (2 wds.)	**MAKE TIME**
transaction	**SALE**	traveling bag	**VALISE,**
transcend	**SURPASS**		**SUITCASE**
transcendental	**OBSCURE**	traveling salesman	**DRUMMER**
transcribe	**COPY**	travel on foot	**WALK,**
transcribe shorthand	**TYPE**		**HIKE, MARCH**
transect	**DIVIDE**	travel on horseback	**RIDE**
transfer	**SHIFT, MOVE**	traverse	**CROSS**
transfer sticker	**DECAL**	travesty	**PARODY, SATIRE**
transfix	**PIERCE**	tray	**SALVER, SERVER**
transform	**CONVERT,**	treacherous	**FALSE**
	CHANGE	tread	**STEP, TRAMPLE**
transgress	**SIN**	treasure box	**CHEST**
transient	**BRIEF,**	Treasure State	**MONTANA**
	TEMPORARY	treat	**AMUSE, ENTERTAIN**
transistor set	**RADIO**	treaty	**PACT**
transit	**PASSAGE**	treble	**SOPRANO, TRIPLE**
transit coach	**BUS**	treble clef	**GEE**
transition	**CHANGE,**	tree	**ASH, CEDAR,**
	CONVERSION		**CHESTNUT, FIR, LARCH,**
transitory	**TEMPORAL,**		**OAK, POPLAR,**
	FLEETING		**SAPLING, ELM,**
translate	**INTERPRET**		**PINE, MAPLE,**
translation	**TROT, PONY**		**LINDEN, WALNUT**
translucent	**LIMPID,**	tree (Ger.)	**BAUM**
	CLEAR	tree branch	**LIMB**
transmit	**SEND**	tree covering	**BARK**
transmit in succession		tree dwelling	**NEST**
	HAND DOWN	tree exudation	**LAC, RESIN**
transom	**WINDOW**	tree fluid	**SAP**
transparent	**CLEAR, SHEER**	tree groups	**GROVE**
transparent liquid	**WATER**	treeless	**UNWOODED,**
transpire	**HAPPEN, OCCUR**		**BARE**
transplant	**GRAFT**	treeless Arctic plain	**TUNDRA**
transport	**CARRY**	tree-snake	**LORA**
transportation charge	**FARE**	tree stump	**STUB**
transportation to the		treetop chatter (2 wds.)	
top floor	**ELEVATOR**		**BIRD TALK**
transpose	**REVERSE**	treetop home	**NEST**
transverse	**BEAM, AXIS**	tree trunk	**BOLE**
trap	**SNARE, CAPTURE**	trek	**TRAVEL, TOUR**
trap door	**DROP**	trellis	**ARBOR, LATTICE**
trapeze artist	**ACROBAT**	tremble	**QUAKE, SHAKE,**
trappings	**GEAR**		**SHIVER, QUIVER,**
trash	**WASTE, RUBBISH**		**VIBRATE**
trauma	**SHOCK**	trembling tree	**ASPEN**
travail	**LABOR, WORK**	tremendous	**HUGE**
travel	**TOUR, RIDE,**	tremor	**VIBRATION**
	JOURNEY, VISIT		

trench	**DITCH**
trenchant	**KEEN, CUTTING**
trencherman	**EATER**
trend	**DIRECTION, TURN**
trepidation	**FEAR**
trespass	**INTRUDE**
tresses	**HAIR, CURLS**
trestle	**BRIDGE**
triad	**THREE**
trial	**TEST**
trial package	**SAMPLE**
triangle side	**LEG**
triangular piece in skirts	**GORE**
tribal emblem	**TOTEM**
tribe	**CLAN, FAMILY, BAND**
tribulation	**WOE**
tribunal	**COURT**
tributary	**ARM**
tribute	**PRAISE**
trice	**INSTANT**
trick	**RUSE, HOAX, SHAM, WILE, DUPE**
trickle	**SEEP**
trifle	**FIG, JOT**
trifle fault	**PECCADILLO**
trifling	**PETTY, TRIVIAL**
trig	**SPRUCE, TRIM**
trigonometric function	**SINE, COSINE**
trill	**QUAVER, WARBLE**
trim	**DECORATE, NEAT**
trimming	**RUCHE, FRINGE**
trim off branches	**LOP, PRUNE**
trim the hair	**CLIP**
trim trees	**PRUNE**
Trinacria	**SICILY**
trine	**THREEFOLD**
trinity	**TRIAD**
trinket	**BEAD**
trip	**JOURNEY, STUMBLE, TREK, FALL, VOYAGE, TOUR**
triple	**THREE**
tripod	**EASEL, TRIVET**
trireme	**GALLEY**
Tristan's beloved	**ISOLDE**
trite	**BANAL, HACKNEYED, CORNY**
triton	**EFT, NEWT**
triumph	**WIN, VICTORY**
triumphant exclamation	**AHA, EUREKA**
trivial	**PETTY**
troche	**LOZENGE**
Trojan hero	**PARIS, AENEAS**

Trojan king	**PRIAM**
Trojan mountain	**IDA**
trolley	**TRAM**
trophy	**AWARD, PRIZE**
tropical	**HOT, TORRID**
tropical arum plant	**TARO**
tropical basket fiber	**ISTLE**
tropical cuckoo	**ANI**
tropical fruit	**BANANA, DATE, FIG, MANGO, PAPAW, PINEAPPLE**
tropical grouper	**MERO**
tropical lizard	**AGAMA**
tropical nut	**KOLA**
tropical plant	**ALOE**
tropical tree	**EBOE, PALM**
tropical vine	**LIANA**
tropical water lily	**LOTUS**
trot	**CANTER, JOG, LOPE**
troth	**LOYALTY, PROMISE**
trottoir	**SIDEWALK**
troubador	**MINSTREL**
trouble	**AIL, WOE, ANNOY, ADO, ILL**
trouble (Scot.)	**FASH**
troublesome plant	**RAGWEED, WEED**
troublesome weed	**TARE**
trough	**CONDUIT, CHUTE**
trough to hold hay	**MANGER**
trounce	**DEFEAT**
trousers	**PANTS**
trousers' fabric	**TWILL**
trousers' pocket	**FOB**
trove	**TREASURE**
Troy	**ILIUM**
truce	**ARMISTICE**
trucker	**HAULER, TEAMSTER**
truculent	**SAVAGE, FIERCE**
trudge	**PLOD**
true	**LOYAL, REAL, GENUINE, CORRECT**
true to fact	**LITERAL**
truffle	**TUBER**
truism	**AXIOM**
truly	**YEA, VERILY**
Truman's opponent	**DEWEY**
trump	**RUFF**
trumpet	**HORN**
trumpet fanfare	**TANTARA**
trumpet sound	**BLARE**
trunk of a body	**TORSO**
trust	**BELIEVE, CREDIT**
trustworthy	**RELIANT**
truth	**FACT, HONESTY**
truthful	**HONEST**

try	TEST, ATTEMPT	turn on axis	ROTATE
trying age	TEENS	turn on pivot	SWIVEL
try to secure (2 wds.)	GO FOR	turn outward	EVERT
tub activity	BATH	turn over	OVERSET,
tube	CYLINDER, PIPE		REVERSE, FLOP
tuberous vegetable	POTATO	turn over a new leaf	REFORM
tug	HAUL, DRAG	turnpike	ROAD, HIGHWAY
tumble	FALL	turnpike charge	TOLL
tumbledown dwelling	SHACK,	turnpike exit	RAMP
	SHANTY	turn sharply	VEER
tumbler	GLASS	turpentine distillate	RESIN
tumid	POMPOUS	turret	TOWER
tumult	RIOT, STIR	turtle shell	CARAPACE
tumultuous	TURBULENT,	tusk	FANG, TOOTH
	VIOLENT	tusk material	IVORY
tune	AIR, MELODY, SONG	tussle	STRUGGLE, WRESTLE
tune in secretly	WIRETAP	tuxedo (2 wds.)	DINNER COAT
Tunisian ruler	BEY, DEY	TV emcee Linkletter	ART
turbid	MUDDY	TV emcee Mack	TED
turbine power	STEAM	TV emcee Parks	BERT
turbulent	DISTURBED,	TV in England	TELLY
	RESTLESS	TV outlet	CHANNEL
turf	PEAT, SOD, SWARD	TV part	TUBE
turgid	SWOLLEN, BLOATED	TV program	NEWS, SERIES,
Turk	OTTOMAN		SOAP OPERA,
turkey gobbler	TOM		WESTERN, SPECIAL
Turkish caliph	ALI	TV repeat show	RERUN
Turkish cap	FEZ	TV sponsor's concern	RATINGS
Turkish capital	ANKARA	TV statuette	EMMY
Turkish cavalryman	SPAHI	TV's Uncle Miltie	BERLE
Turkish decree	IRADE	twang	NASALITY
Turkish governor	PASHA	tweak	PINCH
Turkish gulf	COS	tweedle	CAJOLE, WHINE
Turkish hat	FEZ	tweet	CHIRP
Turkish inn	IMARET	tweezers	PINCERS
Turkish judge	CADI	twelfth of a year	MONTH
Turkish money	LIRA, PARA	twelve inches	FOOT
Turkish mountain	ARARAT	twelvemonth	YEAR
Turkish name	ALI	twenty four hours	DAY
Turkish standard	ALEM	twice	BIS
Turkish title	AGA, AMIR,	twig	SHOOT, SPRIG
	EMIR	twilight	EVENING
Turkish tobacco	LATAKIA	twilled woolen fabric	SERGE
Turkish vessel	SAIC	twin	DOUBLE
turmoil	ADO, MELEE	twine	CORD
turn	REVOLVE, ROTATE,	twine about	ENLACE
	SPIN, WHIRL	twinge	PANG, QUALM
turn about	SLUE	twining shoot	BINE
turn aside	AVERT, DETER	twining stem	VINE
turn away	REPEL	twinkle	WINK
turn back	REVERSE	twirl	SPIN
turn down	VETO	twirlers wand	BATON
turn for help	RESORT	twist	WIND
turning part of a dynamo		twist about	SLEW, SLUE
	ROTOR	twisted	WRY
turn in trading stamps	REDEEM	twister	TORNADO,
turn of duty	SPELL		CYCLONE

twist out of shape	**WARP**	type of magazine	
twist to one side	**SLUE**		**PERIODICAL, GLOSSY,**
twist together	**ENTWINE**		**MONTHLY, WEEKLY,**
twit	**TEASE, TAUNT**		**ANNUAL**
twitch	**JERK**	type of ode	**PINDARIC**
twitter	**CHATTER, GIGGLE**	type of painting	**OIL COLOR,**
two	**DUET, DUO, PAIR,**		**PORTRAIT,**
			WATER COLOR,
two below par, in golf	**EAGLE**		**LANDSCAPE, STILL LIFE**
two bit gambler (sl.)	**PIKER**	type of pay	**DAY RATE,**
two cups	**PINT**		**PIECE WORK**
two door auto	**COUPE**	type of perfection	**PARAGON**
two family quarrel	**FEUD**	type of piano	**GRAND,**
twofold	**DOUBLE,**		**UPRIGHT,**
	DUAL, TWIN, TWICE		**BABY GRAND**
two-footed animal	**BIPED**	type of poem	**ODE, SONNET**
two-masted vessel	**YAWL,**	type of puzzle	**JIGSAW**
	KETCH	type of race	**RELAY**
two pints	**QUART**	type of race track	**SPEEDWAY**
two (poetic)	**TWAIN**	type of record player	**STEREO**
two (quartets)	**OCTET**	type of rock	**SANDSTONE,**
			SHALE
two singers	**DUO, DUET**	type of rubber	**LATEX**
twosome	**DUO, PAIR**	type of ruby	**SPINEL**
two spot	**DEUCE**	type of skylight	**LUNETTE**
two times	**TWICE, BIS,**	type of waistcoat	**JERKIN**
	DOUBLE	type of word game	**FILL-IN,**
two-toed sloth	**UNAU**		**CROSSWORD, LOTTO**
two-wheeled vehicle	**CART,**	type of wrench	**SPANNER**
	SCOOTER, BIKE	type row	**LINE**
tycoon	**SHOGUN**	type size	**ELITE, PICA**
tyke	**SHAVER**	typewriter bar	**SPACER,**
type	**SORT, KIND, CLASS,**		**PLATEN**
	ILK, GENRE	typhoon	**CYCLONE**
type collection	**FONT**	typical	**REGULAR, NORMAL**
type measure	**EM, EN**	typographer	**PRINTER**
type of agent	**UNDERCOVER**	tyrant	**DESPOT, DICTATOR**
type of beer	**LAGER,**	Tyre king	**HIRAM**
	PILSNER	Tyrian	**PURPLE**
type of cabbage	**KALE**	tyro	**NOVICE**
type of canoe	**PIROGUE,**	tzigane	**GYPSY**
	PROA, DUGOUT		
type of car	**SEDAN, COUPE**	**U**	
type of cross	**TAU**		
type of drapery	**VALANCE**	u-boat	**SUBMARINE,**
type of employment			**SUB**
(comp. wd.)	**PART-TIME,**	ugly	**HOMELY, HIDEOUS**
	FULL-TIME	ugly old woman	**HAG, CRONE**
type of fabric	**LENO**	uh-huh	**YES**
type of fastener	**HASP**	uh-uh	**NO**
type of fuel	**COAL, GAS,**	ukase	**EDICT, DECREE**
	OIL. PEAT	ulna	**BONE**
type of glazed paper	**GLASSINE**	ulster	**COAT**
type of jacket	**ETON,**	ultimate	**EVENTUAL**
	EISENHOWER, IKE	ultimate end	**GOAL**
type of joke	**PUN**	ultimately (2 wds.)	**IN FINE**
		ultra	**EXTREME**

ululate HOWL, WAIL
umber PIGMENT
umbrage HATRED, CONTEMPT, OFFENSE
umpire REFEREE, ARBITER
unable CANNOT
unabridged COMPLETE, UNCUT
unaccompanied ALONE
unadorned BARE, PLAIN
unadulterated PURE
unaffected SINCERE
unanimity ACCORD, UNITY
unanimously SOLIDLY
unapt DULL, SLOW
unaroused ASLEEP, DORMANT
unaspirated LENE
unassisted ALONE
unassumed NATURAL
unattached SINGLE
unbalanced ALIST, ALOP
unbelievable INCREDIBLE
unbeliever INFIDEL, HERETIC
unbend RELAX
unbroken INTACT
unburden EASE, RELIEVE
unburnt and dried brick ADOBE
unbusy IDLE
uncanny EERIE
unceremonious ABRUPT, INFORMAL
uncertain DOUBTFUL
unchecked FREE, RAMPANT
uncivil RUDE, IMPOLITE, CRUSTY
unclaimed ground (comp. wd.) NO-MAN'S-LAND
uncle (Scot.) EME
uncle (Sp.) TIO
unclean DIRTY
unclose (poetic) OPE
unclosed OPEN
unclothed NUDE, NAKED, BARE
uncommon ODD, RARE
uncomplaining STOICAL
uncomplicated EASY
uncompromising RIGID
unconcealed BARE, OPEN
unconcerned DETACHED
unconcerned, ethically AMORAL
unconditional ABSOLUTE
unconfined LOOSE

unconfirmed gossip RUMOR
unconfused CALM, CLEAR
unconventional (Fr.) OUTRE
uncooked RAW
uncopied ORIGINAL
uncouth CRASS, RUDE
uncovered BARE, OPEN
unctuous OILY, GUSHY
uncultivated FALLOW, WILD
uncultivated plant WEED
uncultured CRUDE
undaunted BOLD, BRAVE
undecided (4 wds.) UP IN THE AIR
undecorated BARE
undeniable TRUE
under BENEATH
under an assumed name INCOGNITO
undercover SECRET
undercover man SPY, AGENT
underground hollow CAVE
underground plant part ROOT
underground worker MINER
underhand SECRETLY
underling MENIAL, INFERIOR
underlying reason RATIONALE
undermine SAP
undershirt VEST
undersized TINY, SMALL, WEE
undersized animal RUNT
understand SEE, REALIZE, KNOW
understanding KEN
understood TACIT
understood by a select few ESOTERIC
undertake ASSUME, ENGAGE
undertaker MORTICIAN
undertaking TASK
under tension (sl.) UPTIGHT
under the weather ILL
undertone ASIDE
underwater AWASH
underworld HADES, SHEOL
underworld god DIS
underworld of myth HADES
undetermined VAGUE
undeveloped stem BUD
undiluted, as liquor NEAT
undisguised NAKED
undistinguished multitude RUCK

undivided	**ENTIRE, ONE, UNITED**	uniform	**MEASURED**
		uniform ornament	**EPAULET**
undo knitting	**RAVEL**	unilateral	**ONE-WAY**
undoing	**RUIN, DOWNFALL**	unimaginative	**DULL, PROSAIC**
undomesticated	**WILD, FERAL**		
undue hurry	**HASTE**	unimportant	**ONE-HORSE, PETTY**
undulate	**SWAY, RIPPLE**	uninformed	**IGNORANT**
unearned cash (2 wds.)	**EASY MONEY**	union weapon	**STRIKE**
		unique	**RARE, CHOICE**
unearth	**UNCOVER, EXHUME**	unique person	**ONER**
unearthly	**EERIE**	unison	**HARMONY, CONCORD**
uneasy	**RESTIVE, RESTLESS**	unit	**ONE**
unemotional	**STOIC**	unite	**WELD, WED, JOIN, ALLY, MARRY, SPLICE, MERGE**
unemployed	**OUT OF WORK, IDLE**		
unencumbered	**FREE**	united	**ONE, WED**
unequal	**UNEVEN, DIFFERENT**	unit of cavalry	**TROOP**
		unit of energy	**ERG, DYNE**
unequal things	**ODDS**	unit of heat	**THERM, CALORY, CALORIE**
unequivocal	**PLAIN, SINCERE**		
		unit of heredity	**GENE**
unerring	**SURE, TRUE**	unit of illumination	**LUX, PHOT**
unescorted male	**STAG**		
uneven	**ROUGH, EROSE**	unit of length	**METER, FOOT, YARD, INCH, MILE**
unexpected difficulty	**SNAG**		
unexpected stroke of luck	**WINDFALL**	unit of light	**LUX, PYR**
		unit of weight (India)	**SER**
unexpected win	**UPSET**	unit of work	**ERG**
unexplored region	**FRONTIER**	unity	**ONE**
unfamiliar	**STRANGE**	universal	**GENERAL, TOTAL**
unfasten	**UNDO**		
unfavorable	**ADVERSE, BAD**	universal language	**IDO**
unfeeling	**STONY, COLD**	universal remedy	**PANACEA**
unfettered	**LOOSE**	universe	**COSMOS**
unfit	**INEPT, INCOMPETENT**	university post	**PROFESSORSHIP**
unfold	**OPEN**		
unfortunate	**ILL**	unkempt	**SHAGGY, TOUSLED**
unfounded report	**RUMOR**	unkind	**CRUEL, MEAN**
unfreeze	**THAW, MELT**	unkind remark	**SLUR**
unfrequented	**LONE**	unlawful	**ILLEGAL**
unfriendly	**COOL, HOSTILE**	unlawful act	**CRIME**
unfruitful	**BARREN**	unleavened corn cake	**TORTILLA**
unfulfilled desire	**WISH**		
unfurl	**SPREAD, UNROLL**	unlighted	**DARK, DIM**
ungainly	**CLUMSY, AWKWARD**	unlock	**OPEN**
		unlucky	**UNTOWARD**
ungentlemanly man	**CAD, LOUT, BOOR**	unmarried	**SINGLE**
		unmarried woman	**MAIDEN**
unhappy	**SAD**	unmetered writing	**PROSE**
unhappy expression	**FROWN**	unmixed	**PURE**
unharmed	**INTACT**	unmounted	**AFOOT**
unhealthy color	**SALLOW**	unmoved	**FIRM**
unhealthily pallid	**PASTY**	unnamed person	**SOMEONE**
unheard of	**STRANGE**	unnecessary	**NEEDLESS**
unheeding	**DEAF**	unnerve	**UPSET**
unheralded	**UNSUNG**		

unobtrusive	**MODEST, RETIRING**	untidy person	**SLOVEN**
		untidy pile	**HEAP**
unoccupied	**EMPTY, IDLE**	untidy woman	**SLATTERN**
unpaved road edges		untie	**LOOSEN**
	SHOULDER, BERM	until now (2 wds.)	**SO FAR**
unpleasant	**NASTY**	untoward	**UNLUCKY**
unpretentious	**MODEST**	untrammeled	**FREE**
unreasoning fear	**PANIC**	untried	**NEW, GREEN**
unrefined	**CRUDE**	untrue	**FALSE**
unrefined metal	**ORE**	untutored	**ILLITERATE**
unresisting	**PASSIVE**	untwist	**RAVEL**
unrestrained pleasure	**FLING, SPREE**	unused	**NEW**
		unusual	**NOVEL, RARE, ODD,**
unrestricted	**OPEN**		**UNCOMMON, ODD,**
unrhymed poetry (2 wds.)			**OUTLANDISH, STRANGE**
	BLANK VERSE	unusually good	**EXCELLENT**
unripe	**GREEN**	unusually sensitive	**ALLERGIC**
unroll	**OPEN**	unusual person (sl.)	**ONER**
unruffled	**CALM**	unveil	**REVEAL**
unruly	**RESTIVE**	unverified report	**RUMOR**
unruly child	**BRAT**	unwanted plant	**WEED**
unruly crowd	**MOB, HORDE**	unwarranted	**UNDUE**
unsatisfactory, as		unwavering	**RESOLUTE**
an excuse	**LAME**	unwearied	**TIRELESS**
unsavory	**TASTELESS**	unwelcome person	**INTRUDER**
unseal	**OPEN**	unwieldy	**BULKY**
unseam	**RIP**	unwieldy object	**HULK**
unseat a monarch	**DEPOSE**	unwilling	**AVERSE**
unseemly	**INAPT, IMPROPER**	unwooded	**TREELESS**
		unwrap	**OPEN**
unseen	**HIDDEN**	unyielding	**FIRM, RIGID**
unselfish	**ALTRUISTIC**	up	**ALOFT, ABOVE, OVER**
unsightly	**UGLY**	up and around	**ACTIVE**
unskilled worker (2 wds.)		upbraid	**SCOLD**
	DAY LABORER	upheave	**LIFT, REAR**
unskillful	**INEPT**	uphold	**BACK, ABET**
unsoiled	**CLEAN**	uplift	**RAISE**
unsophisticated	**NAIVE, CORNY**	uplift spirits	**ELATE**
		upon	**ATOP, ON, ONTO**
unsound	**INSECURE**	upper	**HIGHER, BERTH**
unsparing	**PROFUSE**	upper air	**ETHER**
unspecified amount	**SOME, ANY**	upper Canada	**ONTARIO**
		upper-case letter	**CAPITAL**
unspecified person	**ONES**	upperclassman	**JUNIOR, SENIOR**
unspecified time	**WHENEVER**		**SENIOR**
unspoiled	**FRESH**	uppercut	**PUNCH, BLOW**
unspoken	**TACIT**	upper end	**TOP**
unstable	**ERRATIC**	upper house of the	
unsteady glaring light	**FLARE**	legislature	**SENATE**
unsuitable	**INEPT, UNFIT**	upper limb	**ARM**
unsung	**UNHERALDED**	uppermost	**TOP**
unswerving in allegiance	**LOYAL**	upper Nile native	**NILOT**
untamed	**FERAL, WILD**	upper part	**TOP**
untanned hide	**PELT**	upper story	**ATTIC**
unthankful person	**INGRATE**	uppish person	**SNOB**
untidy	**MESSY**	uppity	**SNOOTY**
untidy heap	**MESS**	upright	**ERECT**

uprightly	**RECTLY**
uprising	**RIOT, REVOLT, MUTINY**
uproar	**CLAMOR, DIN, HURLY-BURLY, RIOT**
uproarious	**RIOTOUS**
uproot	**ERADICATE**
upset	**OVERTURN**
upshot	**RESULT, OUTCOME**
upside down	**INVERTED**
upstanding	**UPRIGHT, HONORABLE**
upstart	**PARVENU**
up to	**UNTIL**
up-to-date	**MODERN**
up to now (2 wds.)	**SO FAR**
up to the time of	**UNTIL**
up to this point	**AS YET, SO FAR**
urban area	**CITY**
urbane	**SUAVE, POLISHED**
urban eyesore	**SKID ROW, SLUM**
urban need (2 wds.)	**RAPID TRANSIT**
urchin	**TAD, GAMIN**
urd	**BEAN**
urge	**COAX, IMPEL, PROD, SPUR, EGG ON, PERSUADE**
urgent	**PRESSING**
urgent wireless signal	**SOS**
urn	**VASE**
ursa	**BEAR**
urticate	**STING**
Uruguay river	**PLATA**
us	**WE**
usable	**FIT**
usage	**HABIT, CUSTOM**
use	**EMPLOY, UTILIZE**
use a broom	**SWEEP**
use a chair	**SIT**
use a crayon	**DRAW**
use a gun	**SHOOT**
use a hammer	**NAIL**
use a knife	**SLICE, CARVE, STAB**
use a lever	**PRY**
use a loom	**WEAVE**
use a needle	**SEW**
use an oven	**BAKE, ROAST**
use a pencil	**WRITE**
use a phone	**CALL, DIAL**
use a razor	**SHAVE**
use a shovel	**DIG**
use a sieve	**SIFT**
use a spade	**DIG**

use bad posture	**SLOUCH**
use boat oars	**ROW**
used	**SECONDHAND**
used up (2 wds.)	**PLAYED OUT**
use dynamite	**BLAST**
use experimentally	**TRY**
useful	**HELPFUL, UTILE**
useful quality	**ASSET**
useless plant	**WEED**
use hindsight (comp. wd.)	**SECOND-GUESS**
use logic	**REASON**
use money	**SPEND, BUY**
use needlessly	**WASTE**
use oars	**ROW**
use pressure	**EXERT**
use scissors	**SNIP, CUT**
use sparingly	**STINT, RATION**
use subterfuge	**CHICANE**
use the brain	**THINK**
use up	**CONSUME, EAT**
U.S. flag	**OLD GLORY, STARS AND STRIPES**
U.S. frigate Constitution (2 wds.)	**OLD IRONSIDES**
usher	**SEATER, ESCORT**
using speech	**ORAL**
U.S. president's home (2 wds.)	**WHITE HOUSE**
U.S. service branch	**NAVY, ARMY, AIR FORCE, MARINES**
U.S. symbol	**EAGLE**
usual	**NORMAL, FAMILIAR**
usually	**GENERALLY**
usurp	**SEIZE, CLAIM**
Utah's flower	**SEGO**
Ute	**INDIAN**
utensil	**TOOL, IMPLEMENT**
utilitarian	**ECONOMIC, PRACTICAL**
utility	**USE**
utmost	**SUPREME**
utopian	**IDEAL**
utopian region	**EDEN**
utter	**SAY, SPEAK, SHEER**
utter affectedly	**MINCE**
utter a shrill cry	**YELP**
utter brokenly	**GASP**
utter confusion	**CHAOS**
utter in a low tone	**MUTTER**
utterly	**TOTALLY, FULLY**
utterly perplexed and confounded (4 wds.)	**AT ONE'S WITS' END**

utter musical tones	**SING**
uxorial	**WIFELIKE**

V

v-shaped cut	**NOTCH**
vacancy	**GAP, BLANK, OPENING**
vacant	**EMPTY, UNRENTED**
vacate	**EVACUATE, LEAVE**
vacation	**HOLIDAY, RECESS**
vacation specialist (2 wds.)	**TRAVEL AGENT**
vacation spot	**RESORT, SPA**
vacillate	**WAVER**
vagabond	**TRAMP, HOBO, GYPSY**
vagrant	**HOBO, TRAMP, BUM, ROVER**
vague	**OBSCURE, DIM**
vain	**IDLE, TRIVIAL**
vain bird's mate	**PEAHEN**
valentine's day archer	**CUPID**
valentine symbol	**HEART**
valet	**MANSERVANT**
valiant	**BRAVE, DARING**
valid	**COGENT, SOUND**
valise	**GRIP, SUITCASE**
valley	**DALE, VALE, DELL**
valley of Argolis	**NEMEA**
valley on the moon	**RILLE**
valor	**PROWESS, COURAGE**
valorous person	**HERO**
valuable	**DEAR, PRECIOUS**
valuable card	**TRUMP, ACE**
valuable fur	**ERMINE, MINK, SABLE**
valuable moth larva	**SILKWORM**
valuable possession	**ASSET**
valuable violin	**AMATI, STRAD**
value	**WORTH**
value highly	**TREASURE**
vamoose	**SCRAM**
vampire	**LAMIA**
van	**TRUCK, FRONT**
vandal	**HUN**
Van Druten character	**MAMA**
vane	**COCK**
Van Gogh	**ARTIST**
vanish	**DISAPPEAR**
vanity	**CONCEIT, PRIDE**
vanity box	**ETUI**
van man	**MOVER**
vanquish	**CONQUER**
vapid	**INSIPID, BLAND**
vapor	**GAS, STEAM, FUME, SMOKE**

vaporizing easily	**VOLATILE**
vaquero	**COWBOY**
vaquero's rope	**RIATA**
vaquero's weapon	**BOLA**
variable	**PROTEAN**
variable star in Cetus	**MIRA**
variation	**DEVIATION**
variegated	**PIED**
variety	**DIVERSITY, MEDLEY**
variety of agate	**ONYX**
variety of apple	**WINESAP, DELICIOUS, McINTOSH**
variety of beet	**CHARD**
variety of cabbage	**CAULIFLOWER, KALE**
variety of cheese	**EDAM, BRIE, GOUDA, CHEDDAR**
variety of grape	**MALAGA**
variety of moth	**LUNA**
variety of wheat	**SPELT**
various	**SEVERAL, SUNDRY, ASSORTED**
varlet	**SCOUNDREL, KNAVE**
varmint	**PEST**
varna	**CASTE**
varnish	**ELEMI, LAC, RESIN**
vary	**DIFFER, ALTER**
varying weight of India	**SER, SEER**
vase	**JAR, URN**
vase-shaped jug	**EWER**
vase with a pedestal	**URN**
vassal	**SLAVE**
vast	**HUGE, ENORMOUS**
vast desert	**SAHARA**
vast expanse	**OCEAN, SEA**
vast number	**MYRIAD**
vast period of time	**EON, AEON**
vat	**CALDRON, TUB**
vault	**LEAP, SAFE**
vaulter's shaft	**POLE**
vaunt	**BOAST, BRAG**
veal	**MEAT**
veal steak	**CHOP**
veer	**SWERVE**
vega	**STAR**
vegetable	**BEET, KALE, LEEK, PEA, BEAN, POTATO, CARROT, RADISH, CORN, LETTUCE, CABBAGE, TOMATO, OKRA, SQUASH, LEGUME**
vegetable box	**BIN**

vegetable ferment	YEAST
vegetable oyster	SALSIFY
vegetable punk	AMADOU
vegetable silk	KAPOK
vehemence	FURY, RAGE
vehicle	AUTO, BUS, TRAIN, TRUCK
vehicle dispatch man	STARTER
vehicle for hauling	TRUCK
vehicle on runners	SLED, SLEIGH
veil	SCREEN, VELUM
veiling material	TULLE
veil of gauze	VOLET
vein	LODE, STREAK, VESSEL
vein of a leaf	RIB
vellum	PARCHMENT
velocity	SPEED
velvet-like fabric	PANNE, VELURE
venal	MERCENARY
vend	SELL, RETAIL
vendetta	FEUD
vendue	AUCTION
veneer	SURFACE
venerable	OLD, WISE, AUGUST
venerate	REVERE
veneration	AWE, RESPECT
Venetian blind part	SLAT
Venetian boat	GONDOLA
Venetian painter	TITIAN
Venetian red	SIENA
Venetian resort	LIDO
Venetian ruler	DOGE
Venetian water taxi	GONDOLA
vengeful Greek goddess	ERIS
venom	POISON
venomous ill-will	SPITE
venomous snake	ADDER, ASP, COBRA
venomous spider	TARANTULA
vent	OPENING, OUTLET
ventilate	AIR
ventilator	AIR SHAFT
venture	DARE, RISK
venturesome	BOLD
Venus' son	CUPID
Venus' sweetheart	ADONIS
veracity	TRUTH, REALITY
veranda	PORCH, STOOP, TERRACE, PATIO
verb form	TENSE
verbatim	WORD FOR WORD
verbose	WORDY

verboten	FORBIDDEN
verdant	LUSH, GREEN
verdict	FINDING, DECISION
Verdi opera	AIDA
verge	BRINK
verglas	GLAZE
verify	AVER, CONFIRM
verily	AMEN, TRULY
veritable	ACTUAL, REAL
vermilion	RED
Vermont tree	MAPLE
vernacular	NATIVE
vernal	SPRING
Verne hero	NEMO
versatile	ADAPTABLE
verse	POEM, ODE, SONNET
verse maker	POET, BARD
version	RENDITION
versus	AGAINST
vertical	ERECT
vertigo	DIZZINESS
verve	ELAN
very	EXTREMELY, EXCEEDINGLY
very (Fr.)	TRES
very cold	ICY
very dry	ARID
very eager	AVID
very fat	OBESE
very good	FINE
very heavy	LEADEN
very hot	TROPICAL
very important persons (abbr.)	VIPS
very impressive	AWESOME
very large	HUGE
very large nail	SPIKE
very nervous (4 wds.)	ON PINS AND NEEDLES
very pale	ASHY
very powerful	POTENT
Very signal	FLARE
very skillful	EXPERT
very small	TEENY, TINY, WEE
very small (prefix)	MICRO
very small paintings	MINIATURE
very small quantity	IOTA
very thin	SHEER, SKINNY, LEAN, GAUNT
very unpleasant	NASTY
very warm	HOT
very wealthy person	MILLIONAIRE
very wet	SOPPY
vesicate	BLISTER
vesicle	SAC, CAVITY

vespers (2 wds.)	EVENING PRAYER
vespid	WASP, HORNET
vessel	CRAFT, BOAT, VEIN, BOWL
vessel for preserves	JAR
vessel in Genesis	ARK
vessel's bow	PROW
vessel's frame	HULL
vest	WAISTCOAT
vestal	CHASTE, PURE
vestibule	ENTRY, HALLWAY, FOYER
vestige	TRACE
vestment	STOLE, ALB, COPE
vestry	SACRISTY
vetch	ERS, TARE
veteran sailor	TAR
veto	DENY, NYET, PROHIBIT
vex	IRK, RILE, PESTER, ANNOY, NETTLE
vexed	SORE, ANNOYED
via	WAY, ROUTE
viable	LIKELY, WORKABLE
viaduct	TRESTLE, BRIDGE
vial	BOTTLE, PHIAL
vibrant	ALIVE, VITAL
vibrate	SWING, QUIVER
vibration	TREMOR
vicar	PARSON
vice	CRIME, EVIL
vicinity	AREA
vicious	MEAN
victim	PREY, SLAVE
victor	WINNER
victory	WIN, TRIUMPH, CONQUEST
victory symbol	LAUREL, VEE
victrola	PHONOGRAPH
victuals	FOOD
video's predecessor	RADIO
vie	CONTEND
view	LOOK, VISTA, SCENE
vigil	WAKE, WATCH
vigilant	ALERT, AWAKE
vignette	PICTURE
vigor	ENERGY, PEP, VIM
vigorous	ENERGETIC, HARDY
vigorous colloquial language	SLANG
vigorous scuffle	TUSSLE
viking	NORSEMAN
vile	BASE, FOUL
vilify	ABUSE, DEFAME
village	HAMLET
village in Ireland	TARA

village in South Africa	STAD
village square in ancient Greece	AGORA
villain in "Othello"	IAGO
villainous	VICIOUS
villain's exclamation	AHA
villain's nemesis	HERO
vim	ENERGY
vindicate	AVENGE
vindictive	MALICIOUS, VENGEFUL
vine	IVY, LIANE, LIANA
vine fruit	BERRY
vinegar	ACETUM
vinous	WINY
vintage	YEAR
vinyl square	TILE
viola	ALTO
violate	DESECRATE
violation of law	CRIME
violence	FEROCITY, RAGE, FORCE
violent	FURIOUS, RAGING
violent anger	RAGE
violent downpour	TORRENT
violent outbreak	ERUPTION
violent pain	PANG, THROE
violent storm	TEMPEST
violent wind	SIMOON(M), TYPHOON, HURRICANE, TORNADO, TWISTER, CYCLONE, MONSOON
violet	MAUVE
violin	FIDDLE
violin bar	FRET
violin maker	AMATI
viper	ADDER, ASP, SNAKE
Virgil's poem	AENEID
Virginia willow	ITEA
virile	MANLY
virtue	EXCELLENCE, PURITY
virtuous	PURE, CHASTE, MORAL
virulent	DEADLY
visage	FACE
viscid	STICKY, WAXY
viscid liquid	TAR
viscous	THICK, VISCID
visible	SEEN
visible outline	SILHOUETTE
visible vapor	STEAM
Visigoth king	ALARIC
vision	DREAM
visit	CALL, SEE
visit a pawnbroker	HOCK
visit frequently	HAUNT
visitor	CALLER

vison	**MINK**	vouch	**ATTEST**
vista	**SCENE, VIEW**	vouchsafe	**GRANT, GIVE**
visual	**SEEN**	vow	**OATH, SWEAR, PROMISE**
visualize	**SEE**	vowel combination	**DIPHTHONG**
vital	**ALIVE**	Vulcan's creation	**TALOS**
vital organ	**HEART, LIVER,**	vulgar	**COMMON, RUDE**
	KIDNEY	vulgarity	**OBSCENITY**
vitality	**VIGOR**	vulnerable	**WEAK**
vitamin B₁	**THIAMIN**	vying	**COMPETING,**
vitamin B₂	**RIBOFLAVIN**		**STRUGGLING**
vitriolic	**CAUSTIC, SCATHING**		
vivid	**LIVELY, BRIGHT,**		
	INTENSE, BRILLIANT,	**W**	
	ACTIVE, STRONG,		
	DARING, CLEAR	wad	**LUMP, BALL, MASS,**
vixen	**SCOLD, SHREW**		**PLUG, STUFF**
vocal	**ORAL**	wading bird	**CRANE, CURLEW,**
vocalize	**SING**		**HERON, IBIS, RAIL,**
vocation	**PROFESSION, CAREER**		**STILT, STORK**
vociferous	**BLATANT, LOUD**	wafer	**BISCUIT, CAKE**
vogue	**STYLE, MODE**	waff	**PUFF, GUST**
voice	**SPEECH**	waft	**BLOW, BREEZE, BECKON**
voice box	**LARYNX**	wag	**HUMORIST**
voice inflection	**TONE**	wage	**SALARY**
voice of the people		wager	**BET**
(Lat., 2 wds.)	**VOX POPULI**	wages	**SALARY, PAY**
void	**EMPTY**	wagon	**CART**
void court proceeding		wagon journey	**TREK**
	MISTRIAL	wagon track	**RUT**
volatile	**LIGHT, AIRY,**	wagtail	**LARK**
	UNSTABLE	wahoo	**PETO**
volcanic ash	**LAVA**	waif	**STRAY, ORPHAN**
volcanic cavity	**CRATER**	wail	**HOWL, BAWL**
volcanic rock column	**BASALT**	wainscot	**PANELING**
volcanic scoria	**SLAG**	waist	**BLOUSE**
volcano in Italy	**ETNA**	waist band	**BELT, SASH**
volcano mouth	**CRATER**	waistcoat	**VEST**
volcano of Martinique	**PELEE**	wait	**LINGER, TARRY, BIDE**
vole	**RODENT**	wait close by	**HOVER**
Volga tributary	**KAMA, OKA,**	waiter	**SERVANT, GARCON**
	SAMARA	waiter at a drive-in	**CARHOP**
volition	**WILL**	waiter's item	**TRAY**
volley	**BARRAGE**	waiter's reward	**TIP**
voluble	**GLIB, CHATTY**	waiting	**EXPECTANT**
volume	**TOME, BOOK**	wait on tables	**SERVE**
volume of maps	**ATLAS**	waive	**RELINQUISH**
voluntary	**INTENTIONAL**	wake	**ROUSE**
volunteer	**ENLIST**	wale	**WELT, WEAL, RIDGE**
Volunteer State	**TENNESSEE**	walk	**PACE, TRED, STEP,**
voluptuous	**SENSUAL**		**STRIDE**
voracious	**GREEDY, HUNGRY**	walk back and forth	**PACE**
voracious eel	**MORAY**	walk clumsily	**LUMBER**
vortex	**EDDY**	walk drunkenly	**STAGGER**
vote against	**CON**	walk fast	**RUN**
vote down	**DEFEAT**	walk for pleasure	**HIKE,**
vote into office	**ELECT**		**STROLL, AMBLE**
voting place	**POLLS**	walk heavily	**TRAMP, TREAD,**
			LUMBER

walking shorts	BERMUDAS	warble	SING, TRILL
walking stick	CANE	war club	MACE
walk in water	WADE	ward	DISTRICT, DIVISION
walk lamely	LIMP	ward off	AVERT
walk leisurely	AMBLE, STROLL	wardrobe	CLOSET
walk like a duck	WADDLE	warehouse	DEPOT, STORAGE,
walk off with	STEAL		ETAPE
walk on	TREAD	wares	MERCHANDISE,
walkout	STRIKE		GOODS, PRODUCTS
walk out on	ABANDON	war fleet	ARMADA
walk over	TRAMPLE	war hero	ACE, AVIATOR
walk pompously	STRUT	war horse	STEED
walk softly	TIPTOE	warlike	HOSTILE
walk the floor	PACE	warlock	SORCERER, WIZARD
walk uncertainly	TOTTER	warm	TEPID, HOT, HEAT
walk wearily	TRUDGE	war machine	TANK
walk with an easy gait	LOPE	warmhearted	TENDER
wall	BASTION, RAMPART	warm season	SUMMER
wallaba tree	APA	warmth	HEAT
wall border	DADO	warmth of color	GLOW
wall bracket	SCONCE	warm up a motor	REV
wall covering	PLASTER, VINYL,	warm up an oven	PREHEAT
	MURAL	warm wind	SOUTHERLY
wall end	GABLE	warn	ALARM, ALERT
wallet	PURSE, BILLFOLD	warning	CAUTION
walleye	FISH, HORSE	warning device	HORN, SIREN,
wall hanging	TAPESTRY		ALARM
wall lining	WAINSCOT	warning sound at sea	FOGHORN
wall ornament	PLAQUE	warp	DISTORT, PERVERT,
wallow	FLOUNDER		CORRUPT
wall painting	MURAL	warrant	PERMIT, WRIT,
wall recess	NICHE		GUARANTEE
Walt Disney elephant	DUMBO	warrior	SOLDIER
waltz	DANCE	Warsaw citizen	POLE
wampum	BEADS	wary	LEERY, CAUTIOUS
wan	PALE, ASHEN	wash	LAVE, LAUNDER,
wand	BATON, ROD		CLEANSE
wander	ERR, ROAM, ROVE,	wash away	ERODE, RINSE
	GAD, MEANDER, STRAY	wash basin	LAVABO, SINK
wander aimlessly	MEANDER	washbowl	SINK, BASIN
wanderer	NOMAD, ROVER,	wash by draining	LEACH
	VAGRANT, VAGABOND	washday	MONDAY
wanderer from duty	TRUANT	wash for gold	PAN
wander from subject	DIGRESS	washing bar	SOAP
wandering	ERRANT, ERRATIC	Washington ballplayer	
wandering laborer	MIGRANT		SENATOR
wane	DECREASE, DECLINE	Washington city	SEATTLE
wangle	MANIPULATE	Washington sound	PUGET
want	DESIRE, LACK, NEED,	wash lightly	RINSE
	CRAVE, WISH	wash the hair	SHAMPOO
want and expect	HOPE	wash vigorously	SCRUB,
wanting	ABSENT, LACKING		SCOUR
wanting in color	PALE	washy	PALE, DILUTED
wanton	LOOSE, OBSCENE	wasp	HORNET
wanton look	LEER	waspish	TESTY
wapiti	DEER, ELK	waste	LOSS, SQUANDER
war	BATTLE, HOSTILITY	waste allowance	TRET

waste away	MOLDER, DECAY, CRUMBLE
waste cloth	RAG
wasteful	EXTRAVAGANT
wasteland	DESERT
waste matter	DROSS, SLAG
wastepaper receptacle	BASKET
waste time	DALLY, LOAF, IDLE
watch	OBSERVE, REGARD, VIGIL
watch chain	FOB
watch closely	EYE
watch face cover	CRYSTAL
watch for	AWAIT
watchful	ALERT, AWAKE, VIGILANT
watchman	GUARD
watch over	TEND
watch pocket	FOB
watch secretly	SPY
watch sound	TICK, TOCK
watchtower	BEACON
watchword	CRY
water	WET, IRRIGATE, SPRINKLE
water (Fr.)	EAU
water after liquor (colloq.)	CHASER
water barrier	DAM
water bird	PELICAN, ERNE, TERN, GULL, DUCK, SWAN
water bottle	CARAFE
water channel	FLUME
water cow	MANATEE
water craft	SHIP, BOAT
water down	WEAKEN
water drain	SEWER, SUMP
water eagle	OSPREY
watered silk	MOIRE
water enthusiast (2 wds.)	SKIN DIVER
waterfall	CATARACT
waterfall (Scot.)	LINN
water flask	CANTEEN
waterfront	HARBOR, DOCK
water grass	REED
water hole	WELL
watering place	SPA
watering tube	HOSE
water jug	OLLA
water lily	LOTOS, LOTUS
waterless	ARID, BONE-DRY
waterlogged	SOAKED
water main	PIPE
water moccasin	COTTONMOUTH

water monster's home (2 wds.)	LOCH NESS
water nymph	NAIAD
water passage	CANAL
water (pharm.)	AQUA
water pipe	MAIN, SPOUT
water pitcher	EWER
water plant	LOTUS
water rat	MUSKRAT
water sound	SPLASH
water sprite	NIX, NIXIE
water vapor	MIST, STEAM
waterway	CANAL
waterway under a road	CULVERT
water willow	OSIER
water witch	DOWSER
watery	AQUEOUS
watusi or frug	DANCE
wave	FLUTTER, FLICKER, BREAKER
wave (Fr.)	ONDE
waver	TEETER, VACILLATE, REEL, FALTER
wave (Sp.)	OLA
wave to and fro	FLAP
wavy	CURLY
wax	CERE
wax (Lat.)	CERA
waxy ointment	CERATE
waxy substance in cork	CERIN
way	METHOD, ROUTE, SYSTEM
way of behaving	MANNER
waylay	AMBUSH
way out	EXIT
wayside hotel	INN, TAVERN, MOTEL
way train	LOCAL
wayward	ERRATIC
weak	NERVELESS, VULNERABLE
weaken	ENERVATE, SAP
weakness	DEBILITY
weak point	FOIBLE
weal	WALE, WELT
wealth	RICHES, ABUNDANCE
wealthy	OPULENT, RICH, AFFLUENT, ABUNDANT
weapon	GUN, RIFLE, ARROW, DART, ARM, SWORD
weapons	ARMS
wear and tear	DAMAGE
wear at edge	FRAY
wear away	ERODE
wear down	EXHAUST
weariness	FATIGUE

wearing apparel	**SUITS, CLOTHES, DRESSES, ATTIRE, CLOTHING**
wearing boots	**SHOD**
wearing clothes	**CLAD**
wearisome	**TEDIOUS, FATIGUING**
wear out	**TIRE**
weary	**TIRED, BORED**
weasel	**STOAT, ERMINE**
weathercock	**VANE**
weather condition	**CLIMATE**
weather forecast	**FAIR, SUNNY, RAIN, CLOUDY, HOT, COLD, MILD, SLEET, SNOW, WARM, HUMID, CLEAR**
weave	**INTERLACE**
weaving device	**LOOM**
webbing	**MEMBRANE**
web-footed bird	**GOOSE, DUCK**
web spinner	**SPIDER**
wed	**MARRY**
wedding	**MARRIAGE, NUPTIALS, UNION**
wedding attendant	**USHER, BRIDESMAID**
wedding band	**RING**
wedding grain	**RICE**
wedding party member	**BEST MAN, BRIDESMAID, MAID OF HONOR**
wedding proclamation	**BANNS, BANS**
wedding ring	**BAND**
wedge in	**JAM**
wedlock	**MATRIMONY**
wed secretly	**ELOPE**
wee	**SMALL, TINY**
weed	**TARE**
weeding implement	**HOE**
wee drink	**NIP**
weep	**CRY**
weep aloud	**SOB**
weeping daughter of Tantalus	**NIOBE**
weevil	**BOLL, RICE, PEA, SEED**
weft	**WOOF, FILLING, WEB**
weigh	**SCALE**
weigh down	**BURDEN**
weighing device	**SCALE**
weigh in mind	**PONDER**
weight	**OUNCE, POUND, TON**
weight allowance	**TARE**
weight for gems	**CARAT**
weight of India	**SER**
weight system	**METRIC**
weighty	**MASSIVE, BULKY**
weir	**DAM, FENCE**
weird	**EERIE, EERY, MACABRE, STRANGE**
weird sisters	**FATES**
welcome	**GREET**
weld	**UNITE**
welfare	**PROSPERITY**
well	**HEALTHY**
well-being	**WELFARE, PROSPERITY**
well-bred	**GENTEEL**
well done!	**BRAVO**
well-heeled	**RICH**
well-informed	**LEARNED**
well-known	**FAMOUS**
well-liked	**POPULAR**
well-skilled	**ADEPT, ABLE**
well-to-do	**RICH**
well-ventilated	**AIRY**
well-worn course	**PATH, TRAIL**
Welsh dog	**CORGI**
welt	**SLASH, STRIP**
wench	**MAIDEN**
went back over	**RETRACED**
went before	**LED**
went beyond the mark	**OVERSHOT**
went by car	**RODE**
went by ship	**SAILED**
went past one's bedtime (2 wds.)	**SAT UP**
went quickly	**SPED**
went to bed (2 wds., colloq.)	**TURNED IN**
went to the bottom	**SANK**
weskit	**VEST**
west	**OCCIDENT**
western	**OMELET, MOVIE, FILM**
Western farm	**RANCH**
Western halter	**HACKAMORE**
Western lily	**SEGO**
Western marsh plant	**TULE**
Western mountains	**SIERRAS**
Western resort	**TAHOE, ASPEN**
Western rope	**LASSO, REATA, RIATA, LARIAT**
Western show	**RODEO**
Western shrub	**SAGE**
Western song (4 wds.)	**HOME ON THE RANGE**
Western weed	**LOCO**
West German capital	**BONN**
West Indian magic	**OBE(AH)**
West Indian product	**RUM**
West Indian volcano	**PELEE**
West Indies rodent	**AGOUTI**

West Point freshman	PLEBE	whir	BUZZ, VIBRATE
West Point student	CADET	whirl	ROTATE, SPIN, SWIRL,
wet	MOIST, DAMP, WATER		TURN, EDDY, REEL,
wet behind the ears	YOUNG		GYRATE, REVOLVE
wet earth	MUD	whirligig	PINWHEEL
wet falling sound	PLOP	whirlwind	CYCLONE, TORNADO
wet ground	BOG, MIRE,	whirlybird	HELICOPTER,
	SWAMP		COPTER, CHOPPER
wet sludge	MIRE	whisk	TUFT, WISP
wet smack	SPLAT	whiskers	BEARD
wet thoroughly	DRENCH	whisper	MURMUR
whack	SLAP	whistle sound	TOOT
whale	CETE, SPERM	whit	BIT, IOTA
whale school	GAM, POD	white	PALE, WAN
whale secretion	AMBERGRIS	white admiral	BUTTERFLY
whale's passenger	JONAH	white and shining	PEARLY
whammy	JINX	white ant	TERMITE
wharf	DOCK, PIER	whitebait	SMELT
whatever the meal is	POTLUCK	white bear	POLAR
what for	WHY	white beet	CHARD
what person	WHO	whitecap	WAVE
wheat	GRAIN	white coal	WATER
wheat chaff	BRAN	whitefish	BELUGA
wheedle	COAX, CAJOLE	white flower	GARDENIA
wheel animalcule	ROTIFER	white frost	RIME, HOAR
wheel covering	TIRE	white jade	ALABASTER
wheel edge	RIM	white lie	FIB
wheel hoop	TIRE	white merganser	SMEW
wheel hub	NAVE	whiten	BLEACH, PALE
wheelman	HELMSMAN	white-plumed heron	EGRET
wheel projection	CAM	white poplar	ABELE
wheel rut	TRACK	white sheep	MERINO
wheel shaft	AXLE	white vestment	ALB
wheel stopper	TRIG	whitewall	TIRE
wheel track	RUT	white walnut	BUTTERNUT
wheeze	GASP	white water	RAPIDS
whelk	SNAIL	white whale	BELUGA
when	AS, UNTIL	white with age	HOARY
wherewithal	MEANS	whiting	CHALK
whet	HONE, SHARPEN	whitlow	FELON
which	THAT	whittle	CUT
which thing	WHAT	whizz	EXPERT
whiff	GUST, PUFF, SNIFF	whoa	STOP
Whig's opponent	TORY	whole	ALL, ENTIRE, TOTAL,
while	AS		INTACT
whilom	FORMER	wholehearted	SINCERE,
whim	CAPRICE		EARNEST
whimper	PULE, WHINE	whole number	INTEGER
whimsical	FANCIFUL	wholesome	HEALTHY,
whin	FURZE, GORSE		VIGOROUS
whine	SNIVEL, WHIMPER	wholly engrossed	RAPT
whining complainer		whoop	HOOT, CHEER
(arch.)	PULER	whoop-de-do	HOOPLA,
whinny	NEIGH		BALLYHOO
whip	CANE, BEAT	whooping cough	PERTUSSIS
whip handle	CROP	whopper	LIE
whipping boy	SCAPEGOAT	whorl	SPIRE

wick	FUSE	wild iris	FLAG
wicked	BAD, EVIL	wild mustard	CHARLOCK
wickedness	EVIL	wild ox	YAK, ANOA
wicker basket	HAMPER,	wild party	ORGY
	PANNIER	wild pig	BOAR
wicker container	BASKET	wild plum	SLOE
wicker cradle	BASSINET	wild rabbit	HARE
wicket	WINDOW, GATE	wild rose	SWEETBRIER
wide	BROAD	wild sheep	ARGAL
wide-awake	ALERT	wild talk	RAVING
wide-brimmed hat	SOMBRERO	wild turnip	RUTABAGA
wide extent	EXPANSE	wild west show	RODEO
wide inlet	BAY	wile	STRATEGEM, TRICK
widely accepted	PREVALENT	will	VOLITION, MIND
widemouthed jug	EWER	willful	INTENTIONAL
widen	DILATE, ENLARGE,	willing	AGREEABLE
	BROADEN	willow	OSIER
wide smile	GRIN	Wilson's thrush	VEERY
widespread	GENERAL	wilt	DROOP, SAG
wide stream	RIVER	wily	ARTFUL, SHREWD,
wide street	AVENUE,		CRAFTY, SLY
	BOULEVARD	win	TRIUMPH, PREVAIL
widgeon	SMEE, DUCK	wince	CRINGE, FLINCH
widget	GADGET	winch	HOIST, HAUL
width	GIRTH, DIAMETER	wind	BREEZE, AIR
width of a circle	DIAMETER	wind (prefix)	ANEM(O)
wield	BRANDISH, PLY	wind about	COIL
wiener	HOT DOG, FRANK	windbreaker	JACKET
wife	SPOUSE, MATE	windflower	ANEMONE
wife of Abraham	SARAH	wind gauge	VANE
wife of Chuchulain	EMER	windhover	KESTREL
wife of Hiawatha	MINNEHAHA	wind indicator	VANE
wife of Jason	MEDEA	winding sheet	SHROUD
wife of Zeus	HERA	wind instrument	BUGLE, OBOE,
wig	PERUKE, TOUPEE		TUBA, FLUTE, HORN,
Wight	ISLE		SAX, CLARINET
wigwam	TEPEE, TENT	windlass	WINCH
wild	FERAL, SAVAGE,	windmill sail	AWN
	UNTAMED	window compartment	PANE
wild allspice	SPICEBUSH	window covering	BLIND,
wild animal	BEAST		SHADE, DRAPE,
wild arum	CUCKOOPINT		SHUTTER, AWNING
wild banana	PAWPAW	window curtain material	SCRIM,
wild beast's covert	LAIR, DEN		LACE
wild buffalo of India	ARNA	window part	SASH, SILL, PANE
wild disorder	RIOT	windpipe	TRACHEA
wild dog of Australia	DINGO	windshield gadget	WIPER
wild donkey	ONAGER	wind spirally	COIL
wildebeest	GNU	windstorm	GALE
wilderness	DESERT	windy	STORMY
wild fancy	VAGARY	Windy City	CHICAGO
wild goat	IBEX	windy month	MARCH
wild grape vine	LIANA	wine barrel	CASK, TUN
wild headlong flight	STAMPEDE	wine bottle	DECANTER
wild hog	BOAR	wine cask deposit	TARTAR
wild horse	MUSTANG	wine colored	PURPLE
wild indigo	BAPTISIA	wine cup	CHALICE

winesap	**APPLE**
wing	**ALA**
winged	**ALAR, ALATE**
winged god	**EROS**
winged horse	**PEGASUS**
winged insect	**BEE, FLY,**
	BUTTERFLY, WASP
winged monster	**HARPY**
winglet	**ALULA**
winglike	**ALAR**
winglike part	**ALA**
wing movement	**FLUTTER**
wing-shaped	**ALARY, ALATE,**
	ALAR
wing tip	**SHOE**
wink	**BLINK**
winner	**CHAMPION, VICTOR**
winnow	**SEPARATE, SIFT**
winsome	**CHARMING,**
	ATTRACTIVE
winter apple	**WINESAP**
winter bird food	**SUET**
wintergreen	**SHINLEAF**
winter hand warmer	**MUFF,**
	MITTEN, GLOVE
winter jacket	**PARKA**
winter melon	**CASABA**
winter moisture	**SNOW**
winter sport	**SLEDDING,**
	SKATING, SKIING
winter vehicle	**SLED, SLEIGH,**
	SNOWMOBILE, TOBOGGAN
winter weapon	**SNOWBALL**
winter white stuff	**SNOW, ICE**
win the regatta	**OUTSAIL**
wintry	**HIEMAL**
wintry glaze	**ICE**
wipe	**DRY, RUB, CLEAN**
wipe out	**ERASE**
wipe the dishes	**DRY**
wire	**CABLE, TELEGRAM**
wire fastener	**NAIL**
wirehair	**TERRIER**
wireless communication	**RADIO**
wire measure	**MIL**
wire nail	**BRAD**
wire rope	**CABLE**
wire-stitching machine	
	STAPLER
wiretap device	**DETECTAPHONE**
wireless signal	**SOS**
wiry	**RANGY, SINEWY**
Wisconsin city	**OSHKOSH,**
	MADISON
wisdom	**SAGACITY**
wise	**SAGACIOUS, SAPIENT,**
	SENSIBLE, SHREWD

wise bird	**OWL**
wise counselor	**NESTOR**
wisecrack	**GIBE, RETORT**
wise king of Pylos	**NESTOR**
wise lawgiver	**SOLON,**
	SOLOMON
wisely cautious	**PRUDENT**
wise man	**SAGE, SEER**
wisent	**BISON**
wise saying	**ADAGE**
wisest Greek in the	
Trojan War	**NESTOR**
wise to	**AWARE**
wish	**DESIRE, HOPE, WANT**
wish undone	**RUE**
wish well	**BLESS**
wishy-washy (comp. wd.)	
	NAMBY-PAMBY
wisp	**STRAND**
wist	**KNOW, GAME**
wistful	**LONGING**
wit	**CLEVERNESS, HUMOR,**
	HUMORIST
witchcraft	**SORCERY**
witch trial city	**SALEM**
with (Fr.)	**AVEC**
withdraw	**RETRACT, RETREAT,**
	SECEDE
withdraw a statement	**RECANT**
withdraw from	
association	**SECEDE**
withdraw from business	**RETIRE**
with force	**AMAIN**
withhold	**DENY**
wither	**SEAR, WILT**
with ice cream, as pie	
(3 wds.)	**A LA MODE**
within	**IN**
within the time of	**DURING**
with less hair	**BALDER**
with one	**ALONG**
without (Fr.)	**SANS**
without (Lat.)	**SINE**
without charge	**FREE, GRATIS**
without company	**ALONE**
without emotion	**DULLY**
without end	**ETERNAL**
without energy	**LANGUID**
without equal	**PEERLESS**
without face value	
(comp. wd.)	**NO-PAR**
without fat	**LEAN**
without knowledge	**IGNORANT**
without much meat	**BONY**
without purpose	**AIMLESS, IDLY**
without reason	**NEEDLESS**
without vigor	**SPIRITLESS**

without warning	**SUDDENLY**
without work	**IDLE**
withstand	**RESIST, OPPOSE, HOLD OFF**
with the mouth wide open	**AGAPE**
with unlimited power	**PLENIPOTENTIARY**
witless	**FOOLISH, STUPID**
witness	**SEE**
witticism	**MOT**
witty	**CLEVER**
witty answer	**REPARTEE**
witty person	**WAG**
wizard	**SORCERER, MAGICIAN**
wizen	**DRY UP, WITHER, SHRIVEL**
wobble	**SHAKE**
woe	**GRIEF, SORROW**
woeful	**SAD, WRETCHED**
woe is me	**ALAS**
wolf	**LOBO**
wolfhound	**BORZOI**
wolfish	**LUPINE**
wolfram	**TUNGSTEN**
wolfsbane	**ACONITE**
Wolverine State	**MICHIGAN**
woman	**LADY, FEMALE**
woman entertainer	**HOSTESS**
woman hater	**MYSOGYNIST**
woman in the U.S. Army	**WAC**
womanish	**FEMALE**
womanless party	**STAG, SMOKER**
womanly	**FEMININE**
woman of breeding	**LADY**
woman of rank	**DAME**
woman's crowning glory	**HAIR**
woman's dress	**GOWN**
woman's dressing gown	**NEGLIGEE**
woman's dressing jacket	**CAMISOLE**
woman's fur garment	**STOLE, WRAP**
woman's garment	**SLIP, BRA, SKIRT, BLOUSE, DRESS, COAT**
woman singer (Fr.)	**CHANTEUSE**
woman's secret	**AGE**
women's patriotic society (abbr.)	**D.A.R.**
womera (2 wds.)	**SPEAR THROWER**
wonder	**MARVEL**
wonderful	**AMAZING, MARVELOUS**

wonderful thing	**MIRACLE**
wonderland girl	**ALICE**
wondrous	**MARVELOUS**
wont	**HABIT, CUSTOM**
woo	**COURT**
wood	**LUMBER, OAK, TEAK, EBONY, WALNUT, CHERRY, BIRCH**
wood alcohol	**METHANOL**
wood bundle	**FAGOT**
wood carver	**HEWER**
woodchopper	**LOGGER, AXEMAN**
wood chopping tool	**AXE, AX**
wood clearing	**GLADE**
woodchuck	**MARMOT**
wood coal	**CHARCOAL, LIGNITE**
wood deities	**FAUNS, SATYRS**
wood-eating ant	**TERMITE**
wooded valley	**GLEN**
wooden box	**CRATE**
wooden container	**BARREL, CASE**
wooden joint part	**TENON**
wooden match	**FUSEE, FUZEE**
wooden nail	**PEG**
wooden shoe	**SABOT, CLOG**
wooden tub	**SOE**
wood knot	**GNARL, KNUR**
woodland	**FOREST**
woodland animal	**DEER**
woodland deity	**FAUN, SATYR**
wood plant	**TREE**
wood sorrel	**OCA**
wood strip	**LATH, SLAT**
woodwind instrument	**FLUTE, OBOE, REED, CLARINET, BASSOON**
woodwork	**MOLDING**
woodworking tool	**ADZE**
woody plant	**TREE**
wooer	**SUITOR**
woof	**FILLING, WEFT**
wool	**FLEECE**
wool blemish	**MOTE**
woolen cap	**TAM**
woolen dress fabric	**DELAINE**
wool fat	**LANOLIN**
wool fiber	**NEP**
woolly	**LANATE**
woozy	**DIZZY, FAINT**
wordbook	**DICTIONARY, LEXICON**
word for opening doors	**SESAME**
word for word	**LITERAL, VERBATIM**

word game	LOTTO, SCRABBLE	work out	SOLVE
wordiness	VERBIAGE	workplace for students	
wording	DICTION	(2 wds.)	DAY SCHOOL
word in Japanese ship		work soil	TILL
names	MARU	work too hard	OVERDO
word inventor	COINER	work unit	ERG
wordless actor	MIME	work with	COOPERATE
word of action	VERB	work with a needle	SEW, KNIT
word of approval	BRAVO	work with oils	PAINT
word of assent	YES	world	UNIVERSE, EARTH
word of disgust	BAH	world goal	PEACE
word of division	INTO	worldly	MUNDANE, EARTHLY
word of farewell	ADIEU, ADIOS	world of canines	DOGDOM
word of gratitude	THANKS	world of illusions	DREAMLAND
word of greeting	HELLO, HI	world's highest mountain	
word of honor	PAROLE, OATH		EVEREST
word of negation	NOT	world-wide	UNIVERSAL
word of regret	ALAS	world-wide complex of	
word of reproof	TUT	statutes	
word on a towel	HIS, HERS		INTERNATIONAL LAW
word on the wall	MENE, TEKEL	worm	ERIA
word puzzle	REBUS,	worn and gaunt	HAGGARD
	CROSSWORD, ACROSTIC	worn away	EROSE
words of understanding		worn out	EFFETE, TIRED,
(2 wds.)	I SEE		JADED
word to call attention	HEY	worn trail	PATH
word with silver or glass	WARE	worrisome offspring	
wordy	PROLIX, VERBOSE	(2 wds.)	
work	LABOR, TOIL		PROBLEM CHILDREN,
workaday	COMMON,		ENFANT TERRIBLE
	ORDINARY	worry	FRET, FUSS, TEASE
	PLY	worry at persistently	NAG
work cattle	OXEN	worsen	DETERIORATE
work crew	GANG	worship	ADORE, LOVE,
work diligently	DRILL, PEG		REVERE, IDOLIZE,
work dough	KNEAD		VENERATE
worker with rattan	CANER	worsted suit fabric	SERGE
worker's concern (2 wds.)		worth	MERIT
	LIVING WAGE	worthless	TRIVIAL, PALTRY
worker's cooperative	ARTEL	worthless bit	ORT
worker's meal (2 wds.)		worthless plant	WEED
	BOX LUNCH	worthy	RELIABLE, VIRTUOUS
work for	SERVE	worthy of belief	CREDIBLE
work for a candidate		would-be socialite	
	ELECTIONEER, CAMPAIGN	(comp. wd.)	NAME-DROPPER
working class	PROLETARIAT	would-be-smoker's tobacco	
working space (2 wds.)		(2 wds.)	CORN SILK
	ELBOW ROOM	wound	INJURY, HARM
work into a mass	KNEAD	wound covering	BANDAGE,
workman	ARTISAN, LABORER		SCAB
work of art	ETCHING, OPUS	wound mark	SCAR, SCAB
work of charity (3 wds.)		woven container	BASKET
	ACT OF LOVE	wrack	TORTURE, CONVULSE
work of fiction	NOVEL	wraith	GHOST, SPECTRE
work of sculpture	FOUNTAIN,	wrangle	SPAR
	STATUE, BUST	wrangler	COWBOY
workout	EXERCISE	wrap	CAPE, SWADDLE, COAT

wraparound **SKIRT**
wrap in bandage **SWATHE**
wrapper **ENVELOPE**
wrap up **FOLD, PACKAGE, END**
wrath **IRE, ANGER**
wreak **INFLICT, CAUSE**
wreath **GARLAND, LEI**
wreathe **ENTWINE, COIL**
wreath of honor **LAUREL**
wreck **SMASHUP**
wrecker (2 wds.) **TOW CAR**
wren **BIRD**
wrench **TWIST, TEAR**
wrest **EXTORT**
wrestle **GRAPPLE**
wrestling pad **MAT**
wretched hut **HOVEL**
wretched (sl.) **RATTY**
wriggle **SQUIRM, WRITHE**
wriggly fish **EEL**
wrinkle **CREASE**
wrist **CARPUS**
wristwatch feature
  (2 wds.) **RADIUM DIAL**
write **INSCRIBE, PEN**
write by machine **TYPE**
write carelessly **SCRAWL,**
SCRIBBLE
write down **PEN**
write hastily **SCRAWL, JOT,**
SCRIBBLE
write music **COMPOSE**
write off **CANCEL, AMORTIZE**
writer of drama **PLAYWRIGHT**
writer of fiction **NOVELIST,**
AUTHOR
writer of plays **DRAMATIST**
writer of travesty **PARODIST**
writer of verse **POET**
writing **DOCUMENT,**
MANUSCRIPT
writing desk **SECRETARY**
writing fluid **INK**
writing implement **PEN, NIB,**
PENCIL, BALL-POINT
writing master **STYLIST,**
CALLIGRAPHER, PENMAN,
ENGROSSER
writing material **PAPER,**
PARCHMENT
writings **LITERATURE**
writing sheet **PAPER**
writing table **DESK**
written acknowledgment
  of a debt **IOU**
written agreement **CARTEL**
written characters **SCRIPT**

written communication **NOTE,**
EPISTLE, LETTER, MEMO
written in verse **POETIC**
wrong **AMISS, INCORRECT**
wrong (prefix) **MIS**
wongdoing **EVIL**
wrong name **MISNOMER**
wry **TWISTED, ASKEW**
wurst **SAUSAGE**
WW II area **ETO**
Wyandotte abode **NEST**
Wyoming city **LARAMIE,**
CASPER
Wyoming mountain range
TETON

X

xanthic **YELLOWISH**
Xanthippe **SHREW**
xebec **BOAT**
xeres **SHERRY**
xylograph **WOODCUT**
xyloid **WOODY**

Y

yabber **TALK, JABBER**
yacht basin **MARINA**
yachting affair **REGATTA**
Yale man **ELI**
yam (2 wds.) **SWEET POTATO**
yank **JERK, PULL**
Yannigan **ROOKIE, RECRUIT**
yard (2 wds.) **THREE FEET**
yard entrance **GATE**
yardstick **RULER**
yarn **TALE, STORY**
yarn fluff **LINT**
yawn **GAPE**
yawning fissure **CHASM**
yea **TRULY**
year **TWELVEMONTH**
yearbook **ALMANAC, ANNUAL**
yearling **COLT**
yearn **PINE, LONG, ACHE**
years of life **AGE**
years thirteen to nineteen
TEENS
yeast **FERMENT, LEAVEN**
yell **CRY, SHOUT, HOLLER**
yellow **GOLDEN, SAFFRON**
yellow-belly **COWARD**
yellow bugle **IVA**

yellow condiment	MUSTARD
yellow fever mosquito	AEDES
yellow gem	TOPAZ
Yellowhammer State	ALABAMA
yellowish-green pear	BOSC
yellowjacket	WASP, HORNET
yellow metal	BRASS, GOLD
yellow of an egg	YOLK
yellow pigment	OCHER, OCHRE
yellow poplar	TULIPWOOD
yellow root	CARROT
yellow shade	AMBER
Yellowstone attraction	GEYSER
yelp	ULULATE, YIP
Yemenite	ARAB
yen	DESIRE, URGE, HANKERING
yeoman	EXON
yes	AYE
yes (Sp.)	SI
yesterday (Fr.)	HIER
yet	HOWEVER, STILL
yield	CEDE
yield a result (2 wds.)	PAN OUT
yield control (2 wds.)	HAND OVER
yielding	SUBMISSIVE
yield under pressure	SAG
yock	YAK, LAUGH
yoke	HARNESS, BIND
yokel	RUSTIC
yonder	THERE
yore	PAST
Yorkshire river	AIRE, URE
you and I	WE, US
you don't say (2 wds.)	DO TELL
young	JUVENILE, FRESH
young animal	PUP, CUB
yound bear	CUB
young bird	NESTLING
young blood	YOUTH, VIGOR
young boy	LAD
young chicken	FRYER
young child	TOT, TODDLER
young conger	ELVER
young cow	CALF
young deer	FAWN
young dog	PUP, PUPPY
young fellow	CHAP
young flower	BUD
young girl	LASS
young goat	KID
young hog	SHOAT, SHOTE
young horse	COLT, FOAL
young lady	GIRL, LASS, DAMSEL, MAID

young man	BOY, LAD
young pig	SHOAT, PIGLET, SHOTE
young salmon	GRILSE, PARR, SMOLT
young seal	PUP
young sheep	LAMB
young socialite, for short	DEB
youngster	CHILD, TOT
young tough	PUNK
young tree	SEEDLING
young woman	GIRL, LASS, MAID, MAIDEN
yours and mine	OURS
youth	BOY, LAD
youthful years	TEENS
yowl	HOWL, CRY
Yugoslav city	BELGRADE, ZAGREB
Yugoslav commune	STIP
Yugoslav leader	TITO
Yugoslav money	DINAR
Yugoslav region	BOSNIA, SLAVONIA
Yugoslav river	DANUBE, SAVA, MORAVA, DRAVA
yukata	KIMONO
Yule	CHRISTMAS, NOEL
yummy	TASTY, DELICIOUS

Z

zany	CLOWN, BUFFOON, SIMPLETON, COMICAL, FOOLISH, CRAZY
zeal	ARDOR
zealot	FANATIC
zealous	EARNEST
zenith	APEX
zephyr	BREEZE
Zeppelin	DIRIGIBLE
zero	NAUGHT, NIL, NOTHING, CIPHER
zest	PEP
zesty flavor	TANG
zibeline	SABLE
zigzag	OBLIQUE, AWRY
zilch	NOTHING, ZERO
zing	SPIRIT, VIM
zip	PEP, FLY
zodiac sign	ARIES, LEO, LIBRA, PISCES, VIRGO, CANCER, AQUARIUS, TAURUS, SAGITTARIUS, GEMINI, CAPRICORN, SCORPIO
Zohar	CABALA

Zola heroine	NANA	zoo resident	ANIMAL
zombie	CORPSE	Zoroastrian	PARSEE, PARSI
zone	REGION, SECTOR	zounds	EGAD
zoo	MENAGERIE	zowie	WOW
zoo animal	LION, TIGER, APE,	Zsa Zsa's sister	EVA
	PANDA, BEAR, SEAL	zucchini	SQUASH
zoo enclosure	CAGE	zwieback	RUSK, BISCUIT
zoology	FAUNA		